T0183907

Lecture Notes in Computer Science 11733

More information about this series at http://www.springer.com/series/7407

Dionisios N. Pnevmatikatos ·
Maxime Pelcat · Matthias Jung (Eds.)

Embedded Computer Systems: Architectures, Modeling, and Simulation

19th International Conference, SAMOS 2019
Samos, Greece, July 7–11, 2019
Proceedings

Editors
Dionisios N. Pnevmatikatos
Technical University of Crete
and ICS - FORTH
Chania, Greece

Maxime Pelcat
INSA Rennes
Rennes Cedex 7, France

Matthias Jung
Fraunhofer IESE
Kaiserslautern, Germany

ISSN 0302-9743 ISSN 1611-3349 (electronic)
Lecture Notes in Computer Science
ISBN 978-3-030-27561-7 ISBN 978-3-030-27562-4 (eBook)
https://doi.org/10.1007/978-3-030-27562-4

LNCS Sublibrary: SL1 – Theoretical Computer Science and General Issues

This Springer imprint is published by the registered company Springer Nature Switzerland AG
The registered company address is: Gewerbestrasse 11, 6330 Cham, Switzerland

Preface

The SAMOS XIX Conference was held in Pythagorion, Greece, in July 2019. SAMOS is a conference with a unique format. Every year, it brings together researchers working on the topic of embedded systems from both academia and industry in the perfect setting of the island of Samos. The SAMOS XIX keynotes covered a wide range of embedded systems design aspects, including computer architectures by Prof. Soner Onder, Michigan Technological University, virtual platforms by Dr. Jacob Engblom, Intel, computing by Prof. Onur Mutlu, ETH Zurich, and education by Prof. Yale Patt, The University of Texas at Austin. A specific focus was also placed on memory systems and quantum computing through tutorials by Prof. Onur Mutlu, ETH Zurich and Dr. Carmen G. Almudéver, Delft University of Technology.

The SAMOS XIX proceedings comprise a selection of 34 publications targeting either systems themselves—through their applications, architectures, and underlying processors—or methods created to automate their design. Three special sessions were introduced in the program to report recent results of European projects, gather novel work on machine learning implementation, and focus on the lessons learnt from meaningful negative experimental results.

The SAMOS XIX Committee would like to acknowledge the generous support of the many reviewers who contributed to the quality of these proceedings. We hope that you enjoy reading them!

July 2019

Dionisios N. Pnevmatikatos
Maxime Pelcat
Matthias Jung

SAMOS 2019 Organization

General Chair

Dionisios Pnevmatikatos — FORTH-ICS and University of Crete, Greece

Program Chairs

Matthias Jung — Fraunhofer IESE, Germany
Maxime Pelcat — European University of Brittany, France

Special Session Chairs

Transprecision Architectures and Memories

Dionysios Diamantopoulos — IBM, Switzerland
Christian Weis — University of Kaiserslautern, Germany

Machine Learning Implementations

Wonyong Sung — Seoul National University, South Korea

Insights from Negative Results

Karol Desnos — IETR, France
Shuvra Bhattacharyya — University of Maryland, College Park, USA and IETR, France

European Projects

Dimitrios Soudris — NTUA, Greece

Tutorial Chairs

Carmen G. Almudéver — Delft University of Technology, The Netherlands
Onur Mutlu — ETH Zurich, Switzerland

Panel Chairs

Trevor Mudge — University of Michigan - Ann Arbor, USA
Yale Patt — University of Texas - Austin, USA

Submission Chair

Andy D. Pimentel — University of Amsterdam, The Netherlands

Web Chair

Jasmin Jahic	University of Kaiserslautern, Germany

Proceedings Chair

Carlo Galuzzi	Swinburne University of Technology, Australia

Publicity Chairs

Farhad Merchant	RWTH Aachen University, Germany
Dimitris Theodoropoulos	FORTH, Greece

Finance Chair

Carlo Galuzzi	Swinburne University of Technology, Australia

Steering Committee

Shuvra Bhattacharyya	University of Maryland, College Park, USA and IETR, France
Holger Blume	Leibniz Universität Hannover, Germany
Ed F. Deprettere	Leiden University, The Netherlands
Nikitas Dimopoulos	University of Victoria, Canada
Carlo Galuzzi	Swinburne University of Technology, Australia
Georgi N. Gaydadjiev	Maxeler Technologies, UK
John Glossner	Optimum Semiconductor Technologies, USA
Walid Najjar	University of California Riverside, USA
Andy D. Pimentel	University of Amsterdam, The Netherlands
Olli Silvén	University of Oulu, Finland
Dimitrios Soudris	National Technical University of Athens, Greece
Jarmo Takala	Tampere University of Technology, Finland
Stephan Wong	TU Delft, The Netherlands

Program Committee

Giovanni Agosta	Politecnico di Milano, Italy
Shuvra Bhattacharyya	University of Maryland, USA
Holger Blume	Leibniz Universität Hannover, Germany
Martin Botteck	Fachhochschule Sudwestfahlen, Germany
Christos-Savvas Bouganis	Imperial College, UK
Jani Boutellier	Tampere University of Technology, Finland
Ulrich Bruening	Heidelberg University, Germany
Ramon Canal	UPC, Spain
Joao M. P. Cardoso	Universidade do Porto/FEUP, Portugal
Luigi Carro	UFRGS, Brazil

Jeronimo Castrillon	TU Dresden, Germany
Henri-Pierre Charles	CEA, France
Ricardo Chaves	INESC-ID, Portugal
Francesco Conti	UniBo, Italy
Mickaël Dardaillon	INSA Rennes, France
Karol Desnos	INSA Rennes, France
Dionysios Diamantopoulos	IBM, Switzerland
Vassilios V. Dimakopoulos	University of Ioannina, Greece
Giorgos Dimitrakopoulos	Democritus University of Thrace, Greece
Nikitas Dimopoulos	University of Victoria, Canada
Pedro Diniz	INESC-ID, Portugal
Lide Duan	University of Texas at San Antonio, USA
Xin Fang	Northeastern University, USA
Tiziana Fanni	UniCa, Italy
Holger Flatt	Fraunhofer-Institute, Germany
Carlo Galuzzi	Swinburne University of Technology, Australia
Georgi N. Gaydadjiev	Maxeler Technologies, UK
Andreas Gerstlauer	The University of Texas at Austin, USA
Michael Glaβ	University of Erlangen-Nuremberg, Germany
John Glossner	Optimum Semiconductor Technologies Inc., USA
Diana Goehringer	Ruhr Bochum, Germany
Ann Gordon-Ross	University of Florida, USA
Xinfei Guo	University of Virginia, USA
Rajiv Gupta	University of California at Riverside, USA
Soonhoi Ha	Seoul National University, South Korea
Frank Hannig	University of Erlangen-Nuremberg, Germany
Christian Haubelt	University of Rostock, Germany
Timo D. Hämäläinen	Tampere University, Finland
Pekka Jääskeläinen	Tampere University of Technology, Finland
Matthias Jung	Fraunhofer IESE, Germany
Christoforos Kachris	Athens Information Technology (AIT), Greece
Georgios Keramidas	TEI of Western Greece, Greece
Angeliki Kritikakou	Inria - Irisa, France
Kevin Martin	Université Bretagne Sud, France
John McAllister	Queen's University Belfast, UK
Paolo Meloni	UniCa, Italy
Nele Mentens	KU Leuven, Belgium
Alexandre Mercat	Tampere University of Technology, Finland
Andreas Moshovos	University of Toronto, Canada
Daniel Mueller-Gritschneder	Technical University of Munich, Germany
Walid Najjar	University of California at Riverside, USA
Chrysostomos Nicopoulos	University of Cyprus, Cyprus
Dimitrios Nikolopoulos	Queen's University Belfast, UK
Alex Orailoglu	UC San Diego, USA
Andrés Otero	Universidad Politécnica de Madrid, Spain

Gianluca Palermo	Politecnico di Milano, Italy
Francesca Palumbo	UniCa, Italy
Anuj Pathania	National University of Singapore, Singapore
Maxime Pelcat	Universite Europeenne de Bretagne, France
Andy Pimentel	University of Amsterdam, The Netherlands
Oscar Plata	University of Malaga, Spain
Dionisios Pnevmatikatos	FORTH-ICS and University of Crete, Greece
Enrique S. Quintana Orti	Jaume I University, Spain
Francesco Regazzoni	Alari, Switzerland
Marc Reichenbach	Friedrich-Alexander-Universität, Germany
Ruben Salvador	Universidad Politécnica de Madrid, Spain
Marco Santambrogio	Politecnico di Milano, Italy
Carlo Sau	UniCa, Italy
Muhammad Shafique	Karlsruhe Institute of Technology, Germany
Magnus Själander	Uppsala University, Norway
Olli Silven	University of Oulu, Finland
Dimitrios Soudris	NTUA, Greece
Ioannis Sourdis	Chalmers University of Technology, Sweden
Leonel Sousa	UT Lisbon, Portugal
Todor Stefanov	Leiden University, The Netherlands
Christos Strydis	Erasmus MS, The Netherlands
Sander Stuijk	Technology University of Eindhoven, The Netherlands
Wonyong Sung	Seoul National University, South Korea
Jarmo Takala	Tampere University of Technology, Finland
Jean-Pierre Talpin	Inria - Irisa, France
George Theodoridis	University of Patras, Greece
Stavros Tripakis	University of California, Berkeley, USA
Theo Ungerer	University of Augsburg, Germany
Norbert Wehn	University of Kaiserslautern, Germany
Christian Weis	University of Kaiserslautern, Germany
Stephan Wong	TU Delft, The Netherlands
Roger Woods	Queen's University Belfast, UK
Sotirios Xydis	National Technical University of Athens, Greece
Hoeseok Yang	Ajou University, South Korea
Tong Zhang	Rensselaer Polytechnic Institute, USA

Additional Reviewers

Akgn, Gkhan
Beichler, Benjamin
Betting, Jan-Harm
Chatzikonstantis, Georgios
Dolz, Manuel F.
Eck, Darren
Ejaz, Ahsen
Friesen, Andrej
Gis, Daniel
Hautala, Ilkka
Hesham, Salma
Igual, Francisco D.
Khan, Mir
Kultala, Heikki

Kumar, Venkatesh
Liang, Terrance
Lopez, Miguel Bordallo
Marques, Diogo
Multanen, Joonas
Neubauer, Kai
Ozen, Elbruz
Rad, Pedram Amini
Rautakoura, Antti
Resende, Joo
Safarpour, Mehdi
Santos, Paulo Cesar
Schneider, Daniel
Smaragdos, Georgios
Snchez, Erica
Tervo, Kati
Toms, Andrs
Vasilakis, Evangelos
Wu, Jiahao

Contents

Multi/Many-core Scheduling

System Energy and Heat Management

Many-core Communication

Electronic System-Level Design and Verification

Special Session: European Projects

System Design Space Exploration

Evaluation of Different Processor Architecture Organizations for On-site Electronics in Harsh Environments

Sven Gesper[1(✉)], Moritz Weißbrich[1], Stephan Nolting[1], Tobias Stuckenberg[1], Pekka Jääskeläinen[2], Holger Blume[1], and Guillermo Payá-Vayá[1]

[1] Institute of Microelectronic Systems, Leibniz Universität Hannover, Appelstr. 4, 30167 Hannover, Germany
gesper@ims.uni-hannover.de

[2] Customized Parallel Computing group, Tampere University, Tampere, Finland

Abstract. Microcontroller units used in harsh environmental conditions are manufactured using large semiconductor technology nodes in order to provide reliable operation, even at high temperatures or increased radiation exposition. These large technology nodes imply high gate propagation delays, drastically reducing the system's performance. When reducing area costs and power consumption, the actual processor architecture becomes a major design point. Depending on the application characteristics (i.e., inherent data parallelisms, type of arithmetic, ...), several parameters like data path width, instruction execution paradigm, or other architectural design mechanisms have to be considered. This paper presents a design space exploration of five different architectures implemented for a 0.18 µm SOI CMOS technology for high temperature using an exemplary case study from the fields of communication, i.e., Reed-Solomon encoder. For this algorithm, an application-specific configuration of a transport-triggered architecture has 37.70x of the performance of a standard 8-bit microcontroller while the silicon area is increased by 4.10x.

Keywords: ASIC · Application Specific Processors · Design Tradeoff Analysis · Harsh environment · MIPS · Processor architecture organization · Transport-triggered architecture · VLIW

1 Introduction

Automotive and aerospace applications with on-site microcontroller-like systems, which provide continuous maintainability and thus, flexibility, are an emerging field of control engineering. Exemplary systems are motor control units for cars, full authority digital engine controls for piston engines, or satellite arbitration systems. The electronic components have to ensure reliable operation even in

D. N. Pnevmatikatos et al. (Eds.): SAMOS 2019, LNCS 11733, pp. 3–17, 2019.
https://doi.org/10.1007/978-3-030-27562-4_1

harsh environmental situations, such as high temperature or increased radiation. Hence, the integrated circuits are manufactured using very large technology nodes and silicon on insulator (SOI) stacks to reduce leakage current and latch-up effect probability [1]. As a drawback, these large technology nodes only provide a moderate operating frequency, reducing the overall system performance. Due to the large silicon structure, the number of transistors and consequently the circuit complexity on a die is limited. Furthermore, the power consumption is restricted for embedded applications. Because of these limitations, the according system's processor architecture organization has a high impact on the overall efficiency. The design space of those architectures includes numerous parameters. Some of the most significant parameters are data path width and microarchitecture organization. The predominant microcontroller data path widths can be classified into 8-, 16-, or 32-bit architectures. The most common instruction execution paradigms are single-cycle, multi-cycle or pipelined execution, which are also directly connected to the architectural design organization, i.e., RISC- or CISC-like design concept. A completely different design concept is presented by the transport-triggered architecture [3]. This architecture performs instructions as side effects to move operations. All of these parameters highly influence the processor's performance as well as silicon area and energy requirements.

In this paper, five different processor architecture organizations were implemented in VHDL and optimized for an exemplary 0.18 µm high-temperature CMOS technology. The resulting implementations, including an application-optimized transport-triggered architecture, were compared in terms of processing performance, silicon area and power consumption using an exemplary case study, i.e., Reed-Solomon encoder. This paper is organized as follows: In Sect. 2, exemplary commercial architectures for harsh environment are compared. Section 3 describes the features of the implemented architectures. The evaluation of these architectures using the aforementioned case study is given in Sect. 4. Finally, a conclusion is drawn in Sect. 5.

2 Related Work

Table 1 shows exemplary commercial microcontrollers specialized for harsh environments. They differ regarding their maximum operating temperature, which ranges from 150 °C up to 225 °C, and clock frequency due to their semiconductor technology and the underlying processor architecture organization. For many architectures, the execution is pipelined in 2 to 8 stages or done by a multi-cycle structure. Deeper pipelined architectures have a higher operating frequency which is not a direct increase in performance, due to data and control hazards in the pipelined execution. Most cores follow the RISC-like design paradigm and include a multiplication unit. The core in [20] also offers a floating-point unit. However, the dynamic range and resolution of floating-point operations is rarely required in embedded applications. The available space for programs in the instruction memory ranges from 2 kB up to 4 MB when using external Flash memory. This exemplary portfolio shows 8-, 16- and 32-bit architectures, allowing a wide spectrum of applications being efficiently implemented.

Table 1. Commercial architectures for digital signal processing in high temperature environment (T = Temperature, MUL = Multiplier, DIV = Divider, FPU = Floating-Point Unit).

Company	Model	Features	T_{max} [°C]	f_{max} [MHz]	Instruction memory
TI	[20]	32-bit, RISC, 8-stage pipeline, MAC, FPU	125/210 °C	150/100	Flash 512 kB
TI	[19]	32-bit, RISC, 8-stage pipeline, MAC	220 °C	150	128 kB (ext. Flash 4 MB)
TI	[21]	16-/32-bit, RISC, 3-stage pipeline, MUL	220 °C	60	64 kB (ext. Flash 1 MB)
Tekmos	[17]	8-bit, RISC, 2 to 3-stage pipeline, DIV & MUL	210 °C	16	2 kB (ext. 64 kB)
Honeywell	[8]	8-bit, RISC, 2 to 3-stage pipeline	225 °C	16	64 kB
VORAGO	[22]	32-bit, RISC, 3-stage pipeline, MUL	200 °C	50	128 kB
Microchip	[11]	16-bit, CISC, 2-stage pipeline, DIV & MUL	150 °C	80	16 kB/32 kB
Freescale	[4]	16-bit, RISC, multi-cycle, DIV & MUL	150 °C	25	16 kB

Table 2. Distinctive architectural features of the presented cores (Regs/R = Register(s), M = Memory, FU = Functional Unit).

CORE	Data word size, Design	Regs.	Type	Instruction execution	Multiplier/Divider unit (Latency)
AVR8	8-bit, RISC	32	R ⇔ R	pipelined (2 stages)	No (-)
NEO430	16-bit, CISC	16	R/M ⇔ R/M	multi-cycle (4..11 cycles)	Yes (16 cycles)
MIPS32	32-bit, RISC	32	R ⇔ R	pipelined (5 stages)	Yes (1..32 cycles)
VLIW-MIPS	32-bit, RISC	32	R ⇔ R	pipelined (4 stages)	Yes (1..32 cycles)
TTA	32-bit (variable)	var.	R/FU ⇔ R/FU	transport-triggered	Yes (1..32 cycles)

3 Processor Architecture Organizations

In this paper, five different processor architectures were implemented in VHDL and evaluated for the purpose of representing a wide variety of different design concepts. These are an AVR8-compatible processor, the NEO430, a MIPS32-compatible processor, a VLIW-MIPS processor with two issue slots. Moreover, different configurations of a transport-triggered architecture (TTA) [10] were also evaluated. The main features of these five cores are summarized in Table 2. The architecture organizations vary in their data width (8/16/32-bit), instruction set architecture (ISA) principles (RISC/CISC), instruction execution paradigm (pipeline/multi-cycle), number of registers and presence of a dedicated hardware accelerator for integer division and multiplication. Each processor is programmable in C language and comes with an according LLVM or GCC based toolchain for compiling and assembling.

3.1 2-Stage Pipeline AVR8 (8-Bit) Processor

The implemented AVR8 processor features a 8-bit architecture with an ISA compatible to the AT90S8515 [12]. The small amount of different instructions

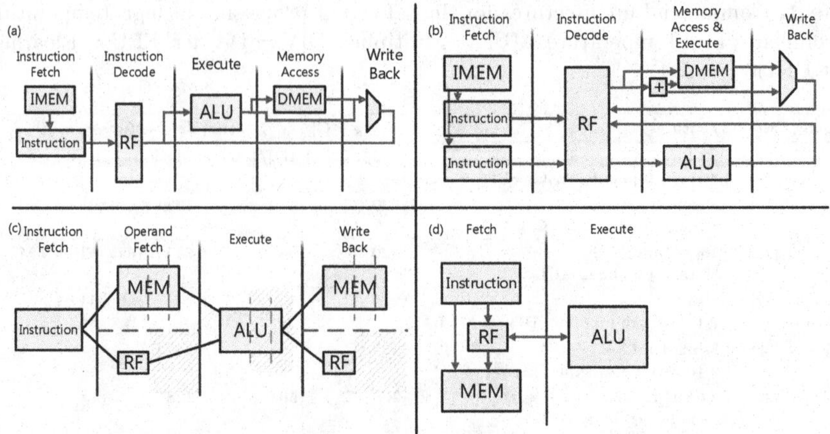

Fig. 1. Simplified architecture overview: (a) MIPS32, (b) VLIW-MIPS, (c) NEO430, and (d) AVR8.

defines a RISC architecture with 16-bit instruction words. These are executed in a two-stage pipeline (see Fig. 1d). Each instruction allows up to two operands, making the AVR a two operand machine. The first operand is always one of 32 registers and serves as data source and destination for the actual operation (e.g., R1 + R2 $\rightarrow$ R1: `ADD R1, R2`). The second operand may also be an immediate (e.g., R1 + Imm $\rightarrow$ R1: `ADIW R1, 0xF`). Complex operations like division or multiplication have to be emulated in software due to the lack of dedicated hardware. The processor implements a Harvard architecture, so the memories for storing data and instructions use separated buses, memories and address spaces. Data and instruction memory can be up to 16 kB and 8 kB, respectively.

3.2 Multi-Cycle NEO430 (16-Bit) Processor

The MSP430 [18] compatible NEO430 [14] implements a 16-bit data path. The 27 instructions of the processor can directly operate on data from the data memory as well as data from the internal register file (16 entries). Just like the AVR8, the NEO430 is a two operand machine (e.g., M[R1] + R2 $\rightarrow$ R2, R1 = R1 + 1: `ADD @R1+, R2`). The instruction encoding is variable as one instruction is built of one to three 16-bit words. Due to the multi-cycle architecture, instruction execution is split into 4 to 11 cycles (see Fig. 1c). The complex operand addressing modes and the variable instruction encoding and execution cycles make the processor a CISC-like architecture. The processor includes a serial multiplier and divider unit which takes 16 cycles per operation. Because of its Von-Neumann architecture organization, the processor has a shared bus for data and instruction memory using a unified address space. However, data is stored in separated memory instances, e.g, ROM for I-Mem and RAM for D-Mem. Data and instruction memory can be up to 28 kB and 32 kB, respectively.

3.3 5-Stage Pipeline MIPS32 (32-Bit) Processor

The implemented MIPS32, based on [13], is a 32-bit architecture and has 5 pipeline stages which support hazard resolution (see Fig. 1a). The 32-bit wide instructions of the ISA form a RISC architecture and support register-to-register operations using a register file with 32 entries. Each instruction can have up to three operands, defining two sources and one destination, making the MIPS32 a three operand machine (e.g., R1 + R2 $\rightarrow$ R3: `ADD R3, R1, R2`). A multiply and accumulate unit as well as a divider unit are available in the execution stage. Those hardware units are implemented using a configurable processing latency of 1 to 32 cycles at design time (see Sect. 3.6). Data and instruction memory use independent 32-bit address spaces with byte-wise alignment.

3.4 4-Stage Pipeline VLIW-MIPS (32-Bit) Processor

The VLIW-MIPS processor is derived from the aforementioned MIPS32 [6]. In contrast to the MIPS32, the VLIW-MIPS uses two parallel issue-slots (see Fig. 1b). Thus, the 64-bit instruction word contains two separate instructions based on the ISA of the MIPS32. Instructions allocated in the first issue-slot are capable of performing memory accesses, while the other one is designated for arithmetic and logic operations. However, the first issue-slot is still able to perform `add` or `sub` instructions by using the adder which was initially only implemented for calculation of base-offset memory addresses. The Execute stage and Memory-Access stage of the MIPS32 are combined in the first issue-slot, while the Memory-Access stages is omitted in the second issue-slot. With this reduction down to 4 pipeline stages, the complexity of forwarding is reduced. The parallel execution of memory accesses along with arithmetic or logic instructions allows the use of instruction-level parallelism in applications due to the high amount of load/store instructions in contrast to pure computational instructions. A typical amount of parallelize-able memory instructions is about 35% (based on SPEC CPU2006 benchmark [7]). Because of data dependencies within an application, the two issues cannot always be fully utilized.

3.5 Transport-Triggered Architecture (32-Bit) Processor

The transport-triggered architecture (TTA) can be described as an exposed data path processor. Functional units are connected through a programmable interconnect, which creates a programmable data path [3,10]. In contrast to describing specific computational operations, the instruction words contain configurations for the interconnections between the functional units. Operands are transferred to a functional unit through programmable sockets, which are basically switches to connect a unit to a set of buses. A unit's operation is triggered as a side-effect of writing data to it. Due to the programmer-visible interconnection network, data can be directed from one unit to another without the need to store intermediate data back to a register file. Thus, the register file is optional but can be attached to the system to store data temporarily. The overall program

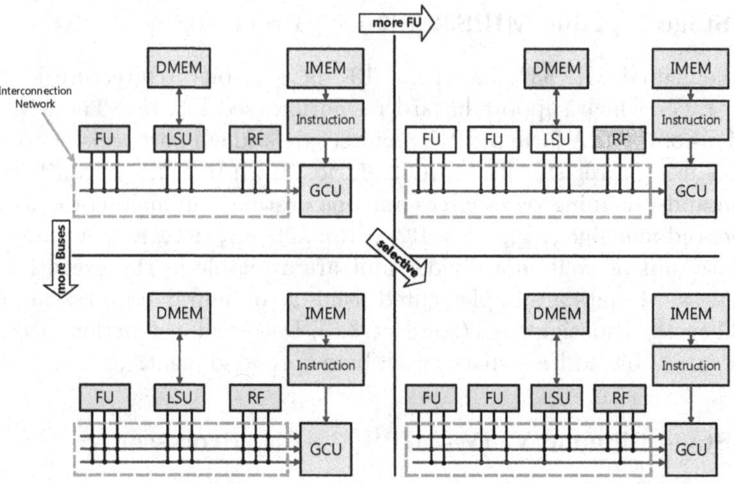

Fig. 2. Different configurations of the transport-triggered architecture (TTA).

flow is controlled by the global control unit (GCU), which performs jumps and function calls. A basic setup of the TTA is shown in Fig. 2. The design allows to add functional units (FU) with custom function units, buses and the selective configuration of sockets in order to have a trade-off between flexibility and complexity, taking profit of the processing characteristics of the target application.

3.6 Fully Configurable Divider Co-processor

When processing divisions or multiplications purely in software, the actual operation is performed by several compare, add/subtract and shift instructions. Obviously, this increases the processing time. As a design parameter for application specific microcontrollers, a dedicated co-processor for integer multiplication or division can massively speed up the calculation of these operations. Since both operations are based on iterative shift-and-add algorithms, a systolic array is suitable for an efficient hardware implementation [15]. This array can be directly implemented on a pipeline structure (Fig. 3a) or can be folded in order to reduce the silicon area requirements (see Table 3 and Fig. 3b,c). However, the resulting folded array unit can not start a new operation every clock cycle and its latency constraints the maximum number of parallel divider units that can be used by a single issue-slot pipeline architecture.

Figure 3 shows the projection of a 4×4-bit non-restoring divider array to a folded structure [15]. In Fig. 3a, the division is performed by a fully pipelined array. This implementation has the shortest critical path and is able to process a new operation every cycle. However, due to the pipelined structure, the silicon area for this implementation is the largest. The folded configurations use an iterative processing scheme, e.g., by using two or one array levels (Fig. 3b/c). This leads to increased latency cycles and short critical paths as well. The silicon area

Table 3. Trade-off between divider configurations for 32-bit division.

Latency	Frequency	Structure	Levels	Area	A single Issue-slot can fully utilize up to
32 cycles	101.5 MHz	folded	1 level	$0.055\,\text{mm}^2$	32 divider units
32 cycles	101.5 MHz	pipelined	1 level	$0.570\,\text{mm}^2$	1 divider units
16 cycles	73.0 MHz	folded	2 levels	$0.063\,\text{mm}^2$	16 divider units
16 cycles	73.0 MHz	pipelined	2 levels	$0.473\,\text{mm}^2$	1 divider units
8 cycles	46.1 MHz	folded	4 levels	$0.086\,\text{mm}^2$	8 divider units
8 cycles	46.1 MHz	pipelined	4 levels	$0.424\,\text{mm}^2$	1 divider units
4 cycles	26.6 MHz	folded	8 levels	$0.130\,\text{mm}^2$	4 divider units
4 cycles	26.6 MHz	pipelined	8 levels	$0.400\,\text{mm}^2$	1 divider units
2 cycles	14.2 MHz	folded	16 levels	$0.212\,\text{mm}^2$	2 divider units
2 cycles	14.2 MHz	pipelined	16 levels	$0.387\,\text{mm}^2$	1 divider units

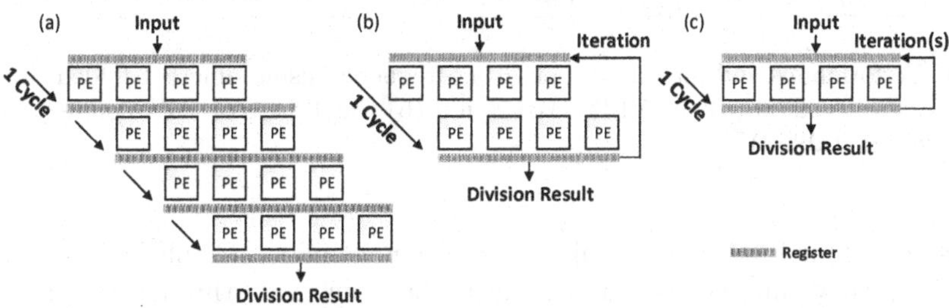

Fig. 3. Different configurations of the 4×4-bit non-restoring divider array. (a) Fully pipelined structure, (b) Two-level folded structure and (c) One-level folded structure.

is significantly reduced (see Table 3) but the folded structure does not allow overlapped execution of multiple divisions. In real applications, the use of a pipelined or folded architecture depends on the application code characteristic. The number of division operations in the code as well as data dependencies influences the maximum number of parallel utilizable divider units. In the VLIW-MIPS and MIPS32, the divide array unit is included in the ALU and can therefore only be used by the first issue-slot. The second issue-slot of the VLIW-MIPS works in parallel but only processes `load-/store` and simple `add-/sub` instructions. Generally, the TTA allows more divider units to work in parallel due to exploited parallelism by several buses, but for an area efficient processor architecture, the implemented number of divider units should agree to the application code characteristics. The NEO430 already includes an optimized divider unit which is folded due to its multi-cycle execution paradigm, while the AVR8 uses software emulation for division (which results in an significant increase of the number of executed instructions on this processor).

To illustrate the performance impact on the target application (see Sect. 4.1) when varying the divider level configuration, an evaluation of a VLIW-MIPS and TTA with different folded divider array configurations is presented in Fig. 4. As shown in Fig. 4a, the maximum throughput for the VLIW-MIPS is achieved by

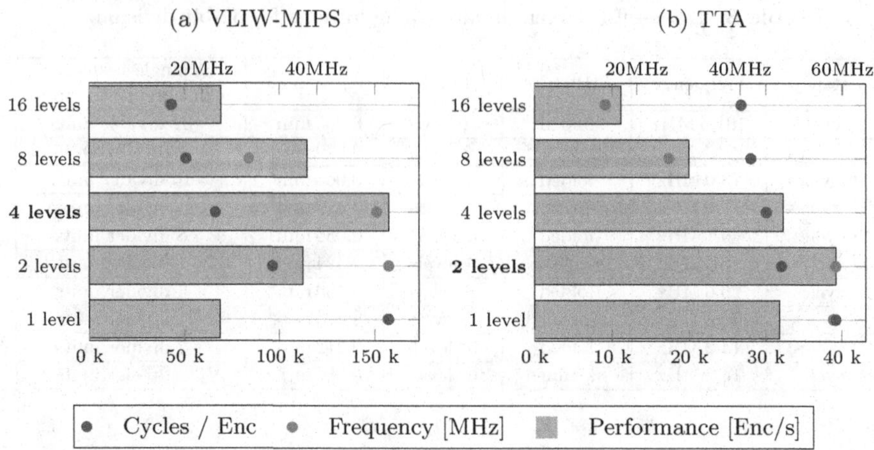

Fig. 4. Performance and maximum operating frequency using different folded divider unit configurations in (a) the VLIW-MIPS and (b) the TTA (see TTA configurations #05 to #09 in Table 4).

the use of a four-level divider unit. This is the optimal trade-off between operating frequency (limited by long timing paths which pass through the divider) and processing latency (required clock cycles for the division operation). For the TTA, the optimum number of levels in the divider is two, as the performance reaches its maximum there, as seen in Fig. 4b. In the TTA, the decrease of the critical path from the four-level divider to the two-level divider unit, which directly increases the maximum operating frequency, has a high positive impact on the total processing performance. In contrast, the increase of the cycles on the VLIW-MIPS processor is higher than the frequency gain, so the processing performance is reduced by a two-level divider. In this paper, only one divider unit with a throughput optimized number of levels is implemented in the MIPS32 and the first issue-slot of the VLIW-MIPS. Multiple divider units can not be efficiently used due to other arithmetic operations scheduled in the same issue-slot. In the TTA, more dividers can be used in parallel by increasing the number of buses. However, the utilization efficiency also depends on the exploitable application code parallelism.

4 Evaluation

In this section, the different processor architectures described in Sect. 3 are compared in terms of silicon area, power consumption and processing performance. For the VHDL synthesis, Cadence Encounter RTL Compiler (RC14.28) was used to create a gate-level netlist. A SOI CMOS technology, capable of high temperature usage and based on transistors with a gate length of 0.18 µm, was used at a corner case of 175 °C at 1.62 V to determine the silicon area requirements and the critical path of the synthesized circuit. The processing performance is measured in simulation for a specific algorithm, i.e., Reed-Solomon encoder, by multiplying the number of executing cycles with the maximum achieved frequency of the synthesized netlist. The switching activity, obtained from gate-level simulation, using Questa Sim (10.6a), running the target application, was used to estimate the power consumption using Synopsys PrimeTime (2017.06) for execution of the application.

4.1 Target Application

The Reed-Solomon algorithm is a forward error correction (FEC) encoder/ decoder for correction of transmission errors in communication applications. It calculates redundancy symbols to be appended to the transmitted data. The configuration of the algorithm used for this paper calculates 16 parity symbols from 239 information symbols which results in 255 codeword symbols in each block [2]. Each symbol has 8-bit, i.e., represents one byte of data. The code is able to correct 8 corrupted symbols per codeword. Configurations with higher redundancy are used for more defective channels, e.g., for the Voyager mission of the NASA [23].

An analysis of the C implementation [16] of the Reed-Solomon algorithm shows the use of 3943 modulo operations in one encode block. These are part of the Galois-Field's arithmetic and could be processed by dedicated Galois functional units (e.g., see ASIP implementation in [5]). In order to offer a flexible implementation of the algorithm for a non-specialized processor, just modulo operations are used as basic operations in the c code for this paper. The modulo operation itself uses the division function.

4.2 TTA Configurations

Due to the large design space of TTA configurations, a minimum configuration was used as a starting point and it was iteratively extended with more functionality in order to increase the performance (i.e., decrease the amount of clock cycles per encode-block run). The set of selected configurations for further evaluation is shown in Table 4. Configuration `#00` shows the minimal C compiler supported hardware setup consisting of one bus, one ALU supporting basic instructions (`add`, `sub`, `and`, `or`, `shift`,... [10]) and a small register file. Based on the utilization of certain parts of the hardware, bottlenecks were found and removed with the TTA toolchain from [10] (e.g., 4 buses in contrast to 1 in configuration `#02`). To avoid the excessive increase of instruction word length, immediate values are shortened to 8-bit. A long immediate unit combines multiple short immediates from several buses to form a longer 32-bit immediate (LImm) [9]. From configuration `#00` to `#04` on, the number of buses, register files or functional units is increased which results in a reduced number of cycles but also in an increase of the instruction word width.

From configuration `#05` to `#09` the number of divider units and their configurations regarding the implemented array-levels (see Sect. 3.6) were varied to reduce the number of cycles, which increases the applications performance. With increased number of divider units, the number of cycles drops due to exploited parallelism in the application. The number of divider units for evaluation in Sect. 4.3 is selected by the configuration's silicon area efficiency, e.g., the silicon area efficiency of the 2-level configuration with 6 instances is higher (normed to performance) than by use of 7 instances.

As mentioned in Sect. 3.6, the configuration with two divider levels provides highest performance for the TTA, as the higher frequency compensates increased number of execution cycles in comparison to divider units with cycle-based faster execution.

4.3 Trade-off Analysis

The instruction memory (I-Mem) and the data memory (D-Mem) of the processors are implemented using multiple single-port RAM macro blocks from the technology library. The bit width of the I-Mem is defined by the architecture's instruction word width while the D-Mem bit width is equal to the actual data path width.

In most of the evaluated architectures, the memory defines the majority of the required silicon area (more than 50%), which is shown in Fig. 5 separated for both, the memories and the core. Due to the wide instruction words (42- to 89-bit), the TTA configurations need large instruction memory sizes.

To achieve higher performance, higher frequency is not necessarily the major design point. The NEO430 operates at about 90 MHz but provides lower performance than the MIPS32, due to the multi-cycle (NEO430) versus the pipelined (MIPS32) instruction execution paradigm (see Fig. 6). Among the configurations of the TTA, there is a variance of up to 17x in performance, which is caused by the major differences in number and type of functional units, size of the register file and interconnection complexity. The differences regarding the resulting silicon area of the TTA configurations are up to 1.84x as shown in Fig. 5.

In Fig. 7, the power requirements of the evaluated architectures are shown. The AVR8 has the lowest requirement, while the TTA #05 demands up to 6.4x the amount of power. This is related to silicon area requirements and operating frequency of the architectures. When comparing processing performance and silicon area (see top of Fig. 8) of the different processor architectures, three clusters can be defined. The smallest architectures (AVR8 and NEO430) also provide the lowest performance. The MIPS32 and VLIW-MIPS provide higher performance with a linear increase in silicon area requirements. The largest architectures with the most variation in performance are presented by the TTA configurations. Not every TTA processor outperforms the MIPS32-based architectures or even the small 8- and 16-bit microcontrollers. The highest performance is provided by the TTA #06 using 6 two-level divider units, which is clocked at approximately 60 MHz. The processing performance is 37.70x the performance of the AVR8 with only an increase in silicon area of 4.10x.

The efficiency of the implementations is calculated by normalizing the silicon area requirement to the reached throughput (Reed-Solomon encodes per second)

Table 4. Different Configurations of the TTA. Colored rows show those configurations selected for later analysis. All divider units use a folded structure. Bus configuration reads as follows: No. of Buses (Immediate Width, No. of Long Immediate Units).

No	Instr. Width	Instr. Count (Mem. Size)	Bus Config.	Divider Conf.	ALU - FU	Register File (32-bit)	Cycles
00	42-bit	3 780(4k)	1 (32-bit, -)	-	1 ALU	1x5	825 577
01	42-bit	3 672(4k)	1 (32-bit, -)	**1x2level**	1 ALU	1x5	249 911
02	58-bit	1 024(1k)	**4** (8-bit, 1x)	**2x**2level	1 ALU+**1 Add**	**3x8**	64 698
03	68-bit	861(1k)	**5** (8-bit, 1x)	2x2level	1 ALU+**2 Add**	**3x16**	53 053
04	89-bit	831(1k)	**6** (8-bit, 1x)	2x2level	1 ALU+2 Add	**2x16+1x32**	50 664
-	89-bit	-	6 (8-bit, 1x)	**6x1level**	1 ALU+2 Add	2x16+1x32	45 443
-	89-bit	-	6 (8-bit, 1x)	**8x**1level	1 ALU+2 Add	2x16+1x32	40 445
05	89-bit	877(1k)	6 (8-bit, 1x)	**10x**1level	1 ALU+2 Add	2x16+1x32	39 201
-	90-bit	-	6 (8-bit, 1x)	**12x**1level	1 ALU+2 Add	2x16+1x32	39 058
-	89-bit	-	6 (8-bit, 1x)	**3x2level**	1 ALU+2 Add	2x16+1x32	42 038
-	89-bit	-	6 (8-bit, 1x)	**4x**2level	1 ALU+2 Add	2x16+1x32	35 614
-	89-bit	-	6 (8-bit, 1x)	**5x**2level	1 ALU+2 Add	2x16+1x32	33 708
06	89-bit	751(1k)	6 (8-bit, 1x)	**6x**2level	1 ALU+2 Add	2x16+1x32	32 042
-	89-bit	-	6 (8-bit, 1x)	**7x**2level	1 ALU+2 Add	2x16+1x32	31 804
-	89-bit	-	6 (8-bit, 1x)	**1x4level**	1 ALU+2 Add	2x16+1x32	53 334
-	89-bit	-	6 (8-bit, 1x)	**2x**4level	1 ALU+2 Add	2x16+1x32	35 010
07	89-bit	697(1k)	6 (8-bit, 1x)	**3x**4level	1 ALU+2 Add	2x16+1x32	30 010
-	89-bit	-	6 (8-bit, 1x)	**4x**4level	1 ALU+2 Add	2x16+1x32	29 298
-	89-bit	-	6 (8-bit, 1x)	**6x**4level	1 ALU+2 Add	2x16+1x32	29 060
-	89-bit	-	6 (8-bit, 1x)	**1x8level**	1 ALU+2 Add	2x16+1x32	37 842
08	89-bit	670(1k)	6 (8-bit, 1x)	**2x**8level	1 ALU+2 Add	2x16+1x32	28 042
-	89-bit	-	6 (8-bit, 1x)	**3x**8level	1 ALU+2 Add	2x16+1x32	27 328
-	89-bit	-	6 (8-bit, 1x)	**4x**8level	1 ALU+2 Add	2x16+1x32	27 330
-	89-bit	-	6 (8-bit, 1x)	**1x16level**	1 ALU+2 Add	2x16+1x32	30 341
09	89-bit	647(1k)	6 (8-bit, 1x)	**2x**16level	1 ALU+2 Add	2x16+1x32	26 773
-	89-bit	-	6 (8-bit, 1x)	**3x**16level	1 ALU+2 Add	2x16+1x32	26 820

for the different processor architectures. Results are shown at the bottom of Fig. 8. The optimum is in the bottom left corner. The TTA configurations #06 and #07 yield the highest efficiency. This is due to the exposed parallelism of the evaluated application. For the VLIW-MIPS, a single issue-slot constrains further possible parallelism of the applications code. More issue-slots would allow more parallelism and divider units but excessively increase the instruction memory size and therefore the silicon area requirements. For the TTA, the units are controlled by short encodings for the corresponding sockets and the total instruction length increase is small for multiple divider units.

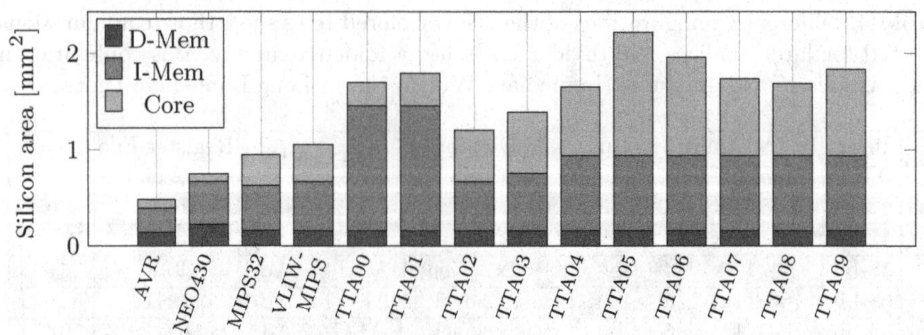

Fig. 5. Silicon area of instruction memory, data memory and core.

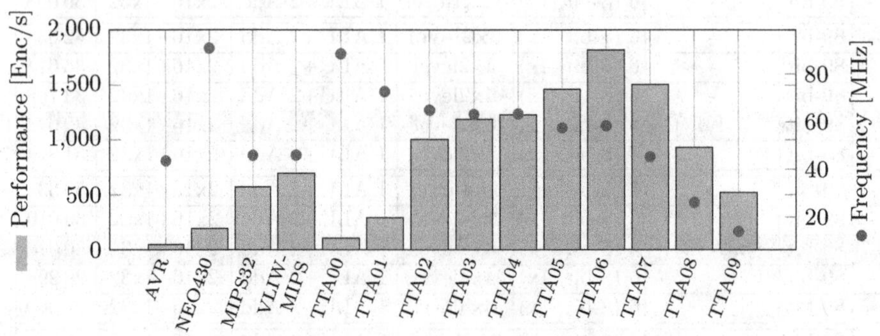

Fig. 6. Performance and frequency of the evaluated architectures.

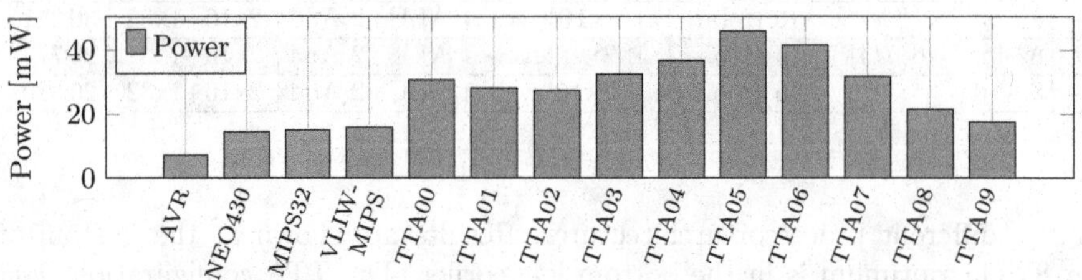

Fig. 7. Power requirements of the processors architectures for executing the Reed-Solomon encoder.

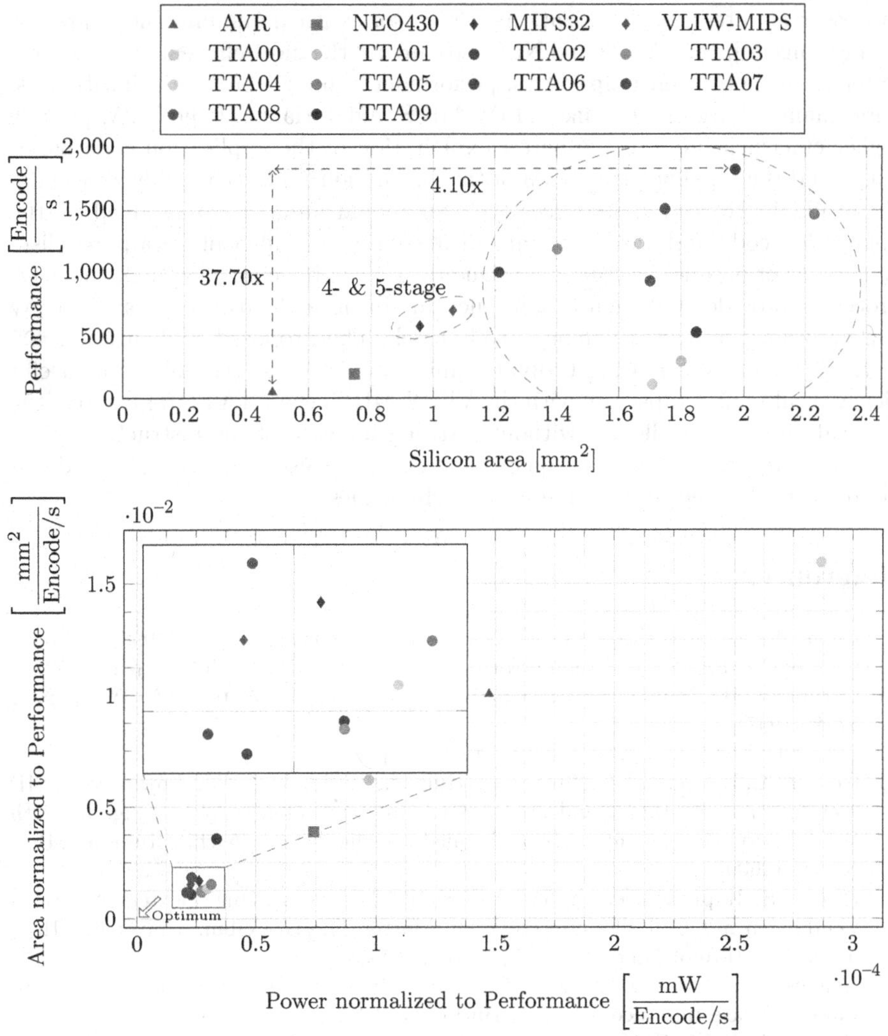

Fig. 8. Top: Silicon area and processing performance of the evaluated architectures. Bottom: Efficiency: Silicon area and power normalized to performance. Zoom of red box in top left of diagram. (Color figure online)

5 Conclusion

In harsh environments, the design space for microcontrollers is large and allows to achieve different goals like minimum silicon area, minimal energy consumption or high processing performance. Different processors architecture organizations differ regarding the efficient use of silicon area and power. However, the efficient use of the processor's resources highly depends on the target application. In this paper, a Reed-Solomon encoder algorithm was used to evaluate different processor architecture organizations. Processors with minimum silicon area or energy consumption (AVR8 and NEO430) are not the most efficient architectures in terms of energy consumption vs. performance and silicon area utilization vs. performance. Larger cores, like VLIW-MIPS and variants of the TTA, provide higher efficiencies due to the better exploitation of the application code parallelism and the pipelined execution of the instructions. The parallel utilization of the available processing resources (i.e., functional units) is constrained by the application code and hardware implementation (i.e., sufficient data parallelism or number of parallel instructions). Due to the flexible customization, the TTA processor provides the highest efficiency in silicon area utilization and energy consumption per Reed-Solomon encode block. The proposed configuration #06 of the TTA processor using 6 divider units provides the best silicon area efficiency results. In comparison with the VLIW-MIPS, the TTA better exploits the application code parallelism without a strong increase of the instruction memory requirement. This makes it an efficient choice for use in area-constrained and performance-limited high-temperature technologies.

References

1. Chen, W., Sadana, D.K., Taur, Y.: SOI CMOS structure, patent (1998)
2. Clarke, C.K.P.: Reed-solomon error correction. BBC R&D White Paper (2002)
3. Corporaal, H.: Microprocessor Architectures: From VLIW to TTA. Wiley, New York (1997)
4. Freescale: MC9S12G (2017). https://www.nxp.com
5. Genser, A., Bachmann, C., Steger, C., Hulzink, J., Berekovic, M.: Low-power ASIP architecture exploration and optimization for reed-solomon processing. In: 20th IEEE International Conference on Applied-specific System, Architectures and Processors (2009)
6. Gesper, S.: Implementierung eines VLIW-MIPS-Prozessors für Hochtemperaturanwendungen mit Compilerunterstützung, Master Thesis, Leibniz Universität Hannover, Institute of Microelectronic Systems (2018)
7. Hennessy, J.L., Patterson, D.A.: Computer Organization and Design: The Hardware/Software Interface. Elsevier, Burlington (2014)
8. Honeywell: HT 83C51 (2011). https://aerospace.honeywell.com
9. Jääskeläinen, P., Kultala, H., Viitanen, T., Takala, J.: Code density and energy efficiency of exposed datapath architectures. J. Sig. Process. Syst. **80**, 49–64 (2015)
10. Jääskeläinen, P., Viitanen, T., Takala, J., Berg, H.: HW/SW Co-design toolset for customization of exposed datapath processors. In: Hussain, W., Nurmi, J., Isoaho, J., Garzia, F. (eds.) Computing Platforms for Software-Defined Radio, pp. 147–164. Springer, Cham (2017). https://doi.org/10.1007/978-3-319-49679-5_8
11. Microchip: PIC24HJ32GP202/204 and PIC24HJ16GP304 (2011). https://www.microchip.com
12. Microchip (former Atmel): AVR AT90S8515. https://microchip.com
13. MIPS Technologies: Programmers Volume II-A: The MIPS32 Instruction Set
14. Nolting, S.: The NEO430 Processor (2019). https://github.com/stnolting/neo430
15. Pirsch, P.: Architekturen der digitalen Signalverarbeitung. Springer, Wiesbaden (2013). https://doi.org/10.1007/978-3-322-96723-7
16. Rockliff, S.: Reed-Solomon (RS) codes (1989). http://eccpage.com/

17. Tekmos Inc.: TK89h51 Microcontroller (2018). https://www.tekmos.com
18. Texas Instruments: MSP430. http://www.ti.com/microcontrollers/msp430-ultra-low-power-mcus/overview.html
19. Texas Instruments: TI SM320F2812-HT (2011). https://www.ti.com
20. Texas Instruments: TI SM320f28335-HT (2014). https://www.ti.com
21. Texas Instruments: TI SM470r1b1m-HT (2015). https://www.ti.com
22. Vorago: VA10800 (2018). https://www.voragotech.com
23. Wicker, S.B., Bhargava, V.K.: Reed-Solomon Codes and Their Applications. Wiley, Hoboken (1999)

CoD: Coherence-on-Demand – Runtime Adaptable Working Set Coherence for DSM-Based Manycore Architectures

Akshay Srivatsa(✉), Sven Rheindt, Dirk Gabriel, Thomas Wild, and Andreas Herkersdorf

Technical University of Munich, Munich, Germany
{srivatsa.akshay,sven.rheindt,dirk.gabriel,
thomas.wild,herkersdorf}@tum.de

Abstract. Embedded system applications, with their inherently limited parallelism, rarely exploit all available processing resources in large DSM-based manycore architectures. In addition, global coherence spanning across all tiles does not scale well. Therefore, we have proposed a region-based cache coherence (RBCC) approach that enables coherence among a selectable cluster of tiles in accordance with application requirements. In this paper, we present a novel RBCC-malloc() extension that transparently tailors coherence to actually shared application working sets at runtime. Further, the design and hardware implementation of a flexibly configurable coherency region manager (CRM) supporting RBCC-malloc() are introduced. We synthesized the CRM on an FPGA for a 64-core system and observed a 57% reduction in BRAM-utilization compared to a global coherence directory for regions with up to 16 cores. Experiments reveal an application acceleration of up to 42% compared to a message passing based implementation. We also demonstrate the advantage of RBCC-malloc() compared to standalone RBCC.

Keywords: Scalable coherence · On-demand coherence · DSM systems

1 Introduction

The introduction of physically distributed memories is one approach to increase the performance of modern manycore architectures. However, to fully exploit the expected benefits is a challenging research topic, especially in terms of programmability, scalability and efficiency. In HPC, explicit message passing communication techniques using standard libraries are used to program such architectures. But this requires modifications to classical shared memory programs to be usable on distributed memory systems. An alternative is to provide a shared memory view of the underlying architecture, i.e. a distributed shared memory (DSM). This requires efficient handling of the actual data transfers as well as the associated control overheads, such as for cache coherence either by software [1–3] or hardware [4–6]. We believe that for large manycore systems with distributed shared memories, coherence efficiency and scalability are crucial factors

D. N. Pnevmatikatos et al. (Eds.): SAMOS 2019, LNCS 11733, pp. 18–33, 2019.
https://doi.org/10.1007/978-3-030-27562-4_2

for application performance. Therefore, we favor our *region-based cache coherence* (RBCC) [7] concept among a limited cluster of tiles, over global coherence. The motivation for RBCC stems from limited degrees of parallelism exhibited by many embedded computing applications [8] that constrain the number of tiles sharing associated data structures. RBCC employs a divide-and-conquer methodology to provide hardware coherence support for a selectable cluster(s) of tiles, improving directory scalability. These, so-called coherency regions are dynamically configured at runtime based on application requirements and comprise arbitrary (adjacent or non-adjacent) tiles interconnected via NoC channels. A coherency region manager (CRM) module is responsible for ensuring and enforcing inter-tile coherence using the concept of RBCC. In our previous work [7], we have introduced and evaluated the RBCC concept using a SystemC simulator platform. We also illustrated the theoretical reduction in directory overheads when using RBCC over global coherence schemes. The major contributions of this paper deal with:

- A novel *RBCC-malloc()* extension that optimizes RBCC by not only confining coherence to regions, but transparently tailoring it to actually shared application working sets within the regions at runtime
- The architectural design, implementation and FPGA evaluation of a flexibly configurable CRM module that supports *RBCC-malloc()*
- The evaluation of *RBCC-malloc()* using a real-world video streaming application.

We synthesize the CRM module as part of a 16-tile 64-core system onto a multi-FPGA platform and analyze the resource utilization and timing numbers. As a use case, we run the feature extraction task of a video streaming application that is executed both in shared memory (using *RBCC-malloc()*) and message passing modes. We analyze the results for varying region shapes, background traffic and impact of *RBCC-malloc()* over RBCC.

2 Related Work

In manycore systems, the underlying architecture tends to bias the programming model. Shared memory programming is preferred when all processing elements have uniform memory access latencies to memory which is kept coherent by snoop-based coherence schemes [9]. For scalability, the trend shifts towards physically distributed memory systems that require either software (programming effort) [1–3] or hardware (scalability, complexity) [4–6] support to enable a coherent shared memory view. Industrial hardware-based cache coherent solutions among others include *Tilera's Tile64*^{TM} [5] and *Cavium Octeon* [6]. These hardware assisted DSM systems provide global coherence, which has scalability issues. Authors of *Stanford DASH* [10] summarize the challenges of hardware-based cache coherent systems underlining the importance of directory scalability. We believe that global coherence for large tiled-manycores is unnecessary, especially as applications tend to saturate for high degrees of parallelism (32 to 48 threads), as exhibited by PARSEC benchmarks [8]. Our RBCC concept [7] presents a scalable yet flexible solution by enabling hardware coherence support to a selectable cluster of tiles. This cluster/region can be dynamically configured at runtime in accordance to application requirements. Majority of research on directory optimization focuses on reducing the number of directory entries (height) using *sparse directories* [11]. The *Select* [12] and *Cuckoo* [13] directories optimize *sparse directories* for size and replacement policies respectively. *LimitLess* [14] optimizes directory scalability using software-assisted directories when the hardware directory reaches its limit. Our RBCC concept is orthogonal to all sparse directory schemes as we focus on reducing the number of sharers (directory width) instead of reducing the number of entries. We additionally introduce *RBCC-malloc()*, which transparently tailors coherence support to actually shared application working sets at runtime. Together, this facilitates a *Coherence-on-Demand* environment for programmers to dynamically create coherent regions with flexible memory ranges in large MPSoCs. The Intel® Xeon Phi [15] can also be configured to only enable coherence for a certain NUMA domain. However, this is a boot time decision and limited to fixed quadrants of the chip which may not be favorable for all applications. *Coherence domain restriction (CDR)* [16] restricts coherence for large MPSoCs similar to RBCC. While CDR is applied to a unified shared memory architecture, RBCC is tailored to DSM systems. Therefore, we have designed the directories for RBCC without the necessity of a home-node, which is required for CDR. Thus, any look-up time or multi-hop accesses to find the home-node are avoided.

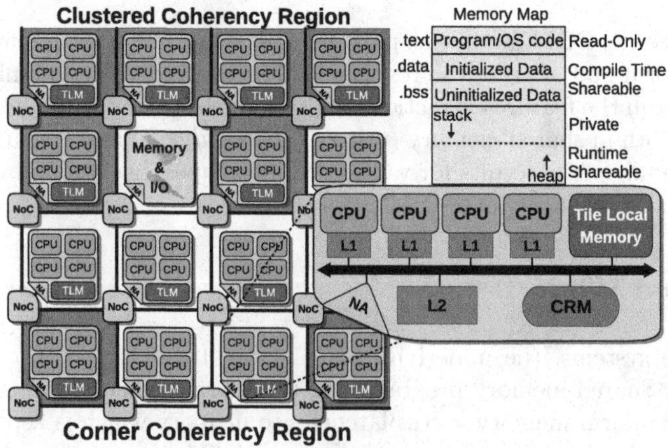

Fig. 1. The invasive computing architecture with multiple coherency regions (Color figure online)

3 Target Architecture and Coherency Region Manager

Figure 1 illustrates our tile-based manycore architecture with region-based cache coherence (RBCC) [7] consisting of an SRAM as distributed tile local memory (TLM) and non-distributed DRAM as global memory. This architecture is also adopted in our DFG SFB/TR 89 Invasive Computing project [17]. Every compute tile consists of four LEON cores coupled with private L1 caches for faster

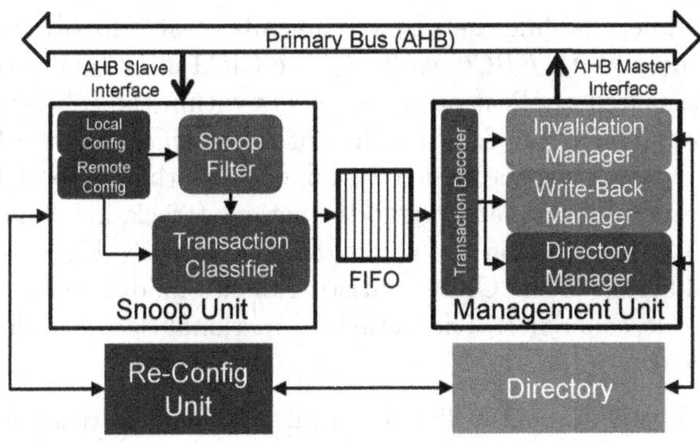

Fig. 2. The internal block diagram of the CRM

local accesses to the TLM. A shared L2 cache reduces remote TLM and global memory access latencies. All sub-modules are connected to the central AHB bus for intra-tile communication. The network adapter provides a gateway to the NoC for inter-tile communication. The architecture has an input/output (IO) tile to access off-chip DRAM and Ethernet. Intra-tile coherence is ensured by a simple snooping-based protocol. The L1 caches operate with a write-through policy and snoop on the central AHB bus to invalidate each other (MI protocol). The L2 caches operate with a write-back policy and support the MSI protocol. Traditional directory-based schemes ensure inter-tile coherence, but offer global coherence spanning all tiles that does not scale. We adopt a coherency region manager (CRM) that enables scalable and efficient inter-tile coherence using our RBCC concept. Although beneficial for area optimization, static regions do not cater to a wide range of individual and/or a mixture of applications. Therefore, our CRM module supports the idea of flexibility by allowing applications to configure coherency regions at runtime based on its requirements. A novel extension, *RBCC-malloc()* further optimizes RBCC by transparently tailoring coherence support within the regions to actually shared application working sets that are only known at runtime (Sect. 3.2). This fits perfectly into the concept of Invasive Computing [17] which is a resource-aware programming paradigm to dynamically schedule multiple applications on manycore architectures. Though RBCC is developed for the Invasive Computing concept, it can be applied to any manycore architecture.

3.1 CRM: Architectural Design and Functionality

The CRM is an IP macro present in every compute tile of our manycore architecture. Unlike traditional directory modules that require load/store miss operations to explicitly pass through them, the CRM is designed as a non-intrusive module that works in parallel by observing bus operations. This design modularity allows for easy integration into most manycore systems. The CRM is a configurable module, enabling users to dynamically create/dissolve variable-sized coherency region(s). With *RBCC-malloc()*, the CRM additionally tailors coherence to actually shared application working sets within the coherency region at runtime. To comprehend the functionality of *RBCC-malloc()*, we first provide functional details regarding the basic CRM operations that support RBCC, such as observing bus transactions and triggering actions (track, invalidate and write-back). Section 3.2 then goes on to explain *RBCC-malloc()*. Figure 2 depicts the internal block diagram of the CRM consisting of sub-modules that are designed to ensure inter-tile coherence. The detailed functionalities of each sub-module are described below.

Snoop Unit. This sub-module listens to all ongoing bus transactions via an AHB slave interface. It is also reachable via a pre-defined memory-mapped address range for coherency region (re)configurations and CRM-to-CRM communication. The *Snoop Unit* detects and classifies relevant bus transactions using the *local* and *remote configuration* tables and sends it to the *Management Unit* via a *FIFO*. The tables contain region configuration information (written by application), which enables every CRM to be aware of its current region and associated address ranges of local and remote shared memory. The *local configuration* table informs the CRM about which remote tiles are allowed a coherent view over its local address range. A single entry in the *local configuration* table consists of:

- Region ID: ID of the current configuration
- Start Address (SA): Begin of shared local address
- End Address (EA): End of shared local address
- Sharers (SHR): Remote tiles allowed to share local address range

The *remote configuration* table informs the CRM about which remote address ranges the local processing cores are allowed to have a coherent view on. A single entry in the *remote configuration* table consists of:

- Region ID: ID of the current configuration
- Start Address (SA): Begin of shared remote address
- End Address (EA): End of shared remote address

The design of *local* and *remote configuration* tables per CRM allows creating flexible and fine granular coherency regions with unidirectional sharing (one tile shares its data, but the other does not) and overlapping regions (a tile is part of two regions), as required by the application. For example, lets assume an application requests for three coherent tiles with bidirectional sharing. This information is handled by the OS which writes into the memory-mapped registers of the CRM on all requested tiles using the RBCC drivers. The fields in the *local configuration* table of Tile A are configured to share the local address range with Tile B and Tile C. The fields in the *remote configuration* tables of Tile B and Tile C are written with the same information to make them aware of this shared remote address range. At this point Tile A unidirectionally shares its local address range with Tile B and Tile C. The same process is repeated on the other two tiles which enables bidirectional sharing of all three TLMs.

Management Unit. This sub-module reacts on incoming *FIFO* transactions sent from the *Snoop Unit.* The *transaction decoder* interprets the transaction and triggers the responsible *Manager* to perform coherence actions. The *Management Unit* is equipped with an AHB master interface to send coherence messages via the bus. To guarantee inter-tile coherence, we devised four transaction categories that are described below.

Directory Update: Upon a read operation from a remote tile on the bus, the *transaction classifier* triggers a directory update request to the *Management Unit.* The *transaction decoder* in-turn triggers the *directory manager* to update the sharer bits for the corresponding address in the *Directory.* Local read accesses are ignored as local caches are kept coherent by the bus snooping protocol.

Invalidation Generation: Upon a write operation on the bus, the *transaction classifier* triggers an invalidation generation request irrespective of its origin (local or remote tile). The *transaction decoder* triggers the *invalidation manager* which looks-up the sharer bits for the written address in the *Directory.* Based on the set sharer bits, invalidation messages are sent out to the corresponding remote CRMs (except the tile which triggered the write) using the AHB master interface. The invalidation message is essentially a write operation addressed to the remote CRM with data being the address to be invalidated.

Invalidation Execution: Upon reception of an incoming invalidation message (from a remote CRM) the *transaction classifier* filters the address to be invalidated and passes it over to the *Management Unit.* The *transaction decoder* triggers the *invalidation manager* which invalidates the corresponding address in the L2 cache. This is done by writing into the control registers of the L2 cache via the AHB master interface. A second dummy write operation is performed on the AHB bus to invalidate the L1 caches through their bus snooping protocol. This dummy write is done with AHB IDLE_TRANS to not modify actual data.

Force Write-back: Upon a write operation to a remote shared memory, the *transaction classifier* triggers a force write-back request to the *Management Unit.* The *transaction decoder* triggers the *write-back manager* to perform an explicit write-back of the corresponding remote address in L2 cache. This is done by writing into the control register of the L2 cache via the AHB master interface.

FIFO Interface. The CRM module operates in parallel to load/store accesses. A mismatch in production rate of the *Snoop Unit* (snooped bus operations) and consumption rate of the *Management Unit* (coherence actions) can lead to transaction loss. Except *Directory Update*, all *Management Unit* operations exhibit non-deterministic completion times depending on bus penalties, number of sharers, etc. This lowers the consumption rate of the *Management Unit* requiring a *FIFO* buffer. If the *FIFO* reaches a predefined *critical_level*, it selectively locks the bus only granting bus access to the CRM and network adapter masters until it reaches a predefined *safe_level*. This solution is deadlock-free and allows the *FIFO* to be emptied, ensuring lossless transactions.

Directory. This sub-module holds book-keeping information for cache coherence. The number of entries is scalable as we use a sparse directory design similar to [11]. The storage for sharer information is further reduced using the RBCC concept by only tracking tiles within a region, making it substantially smaller and scalable compared to global coherence directories [7]. The maximum number of tiles in a region is a design time decision that should be made based on the type of application(s) expected to run on the system. Currently, creating a region that exceeds the maximum number of tiles in a region activates an overflow flag which can be used to trigger an OS interrupt. The *Directory* is implemented as block RAM (BRAM), and we analyze the hardware utilization in Sect. 4.

Re-Configuration Unit. This sub-module is used for runtime coherency region reconfigurations to grow/shrink and/or migrate regions based on available resources. It is connected to the *Directory* to reset book-keeping information upon reconfiguration. Investigations regarding reconfiguration procedure, context switching time and overheads is planned as future work.

3.2 RBCC-malloc(): Runtime Working Set Adaptability

In our previous work [7], we showed how a coherent cluster of tiles is created based on application requirements using RBCC. However, the shareable address range within these tiles covers the entire memory (TLM) range which may not completely contain actually shared data. For example, tile local OS data, processor instructions, processor stacks, etc. are tile private. This results in unnecessary tracking and triggers futile CRM actions, increasing latency and power consumption. Statically allocated shared data are known at compile-time, so the CRM can be configured to only track these address ranges before the application starts. *RBCC-malloc()* extends this to dynamically allocated application data by introducing runtime working set adaptability. We designed a software wrapper around *malloc()* through which an application can specify if data being allocated should be cache coherent. This can also be abstracted by the underlying OS, as it is aware of the regions, making it transparent to the application. Referring to Fig. 3, lets assume an application initially requests 4 tiles (16 cores) from the OS that are cache coherent ❶. Assuming resources are available, the OS sets up a coherency region by writing to the CRM configuration tables of the corresponding tiles via the CRM driver code ❷. The *SA* and *EA* fields are set to track compile-time known statically allocated shared data. Upon confirmation from the CRM, the OS grants the corresponding processing and memory

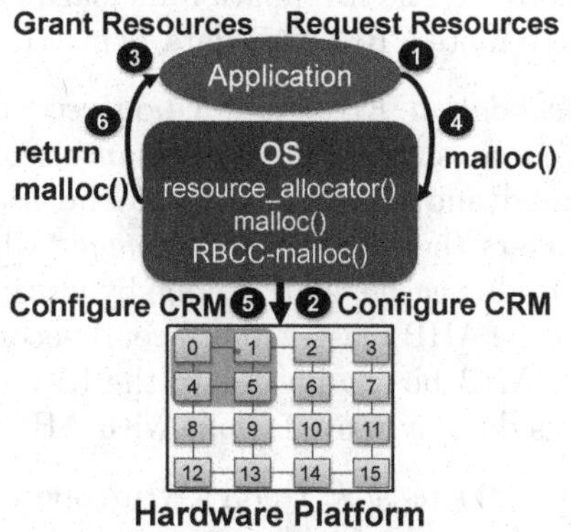

Fig. 3. RBCC-malloc(): an example of runtime working set adaptation

resources to the application ❸. During execution, all dynamic data allocation requests to the OS are handled either by a regular *malloc()* or *RBCC-malloc()* ❹. If the data allocation request originates from within a coherency region, the OS can automatically choose *RBCC-malloc()* over *malloc()*. In this case, the OS first forwards the range of this 'to-be-allocated' working set to the CRM ❺, whose configuration tables are adapted at runtime to additionally track this specific memory range. Upon a successful update, the OS returns a pointer to the newly allocated coherent working set ❻. Conversely, the *free()* is replaced by *RBCC-free()* to clean-up the CRM configuration tables followed by data de-allocation. The CRM configuration penalty/overheads are listed in Table 2. This hardware-software codesign mechanism is triggered by data allocation requests throughout application execution. With *RBCC-malloc()*, the CRM transparently accommodates and tracks actually shared application working set(s) at runtime.

4 Hardware Implementation

We implemented our tile-based manycore design on a multi-FPGA platform consisting of four interconnected Xilinx Virtex-7 (XC7V2000T) FPGAs. We synthesize a 2×2 design on each FPGA that gives us a 4×4 (16 tiles, 64 cores) multi-FPGA system (Fig. 1). Each compute tile contains four LEON3 cores with private 2Way, 4 kB/Way write-through L1 caches and a shared 4Way, 16 kB/Way write-back L2 cache. The caches are non-inclusive non-exclusive (NINE) of each other. We connect each of the four FPGAs with a 32 MB SRAM extension board. Each SRAM memory board is divided among four tiles to serve as 8 MB TLMs. We have synthesized the IO Tile on Tile 5 residing in FPGA 1 to which we additionally connect an Ethernet and DDR extension board.

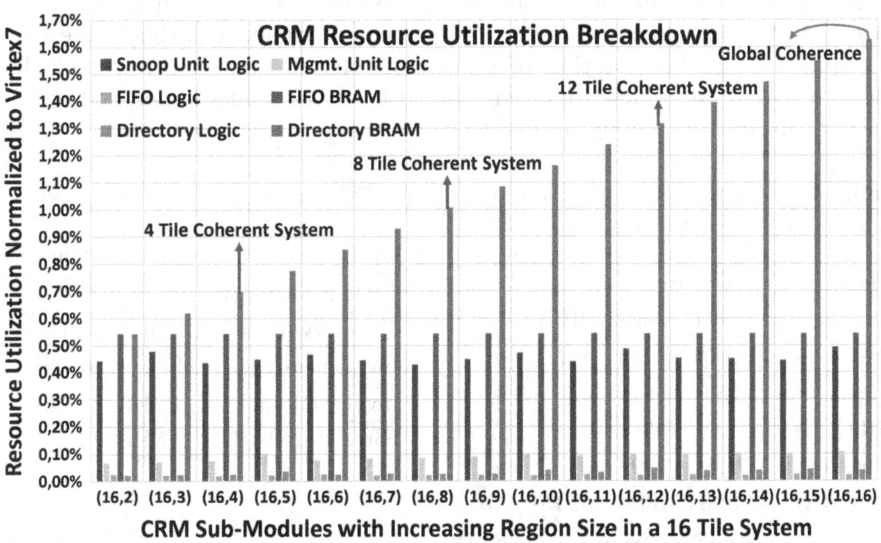

Fig. 4. Resource utilization breakdown into logic and BRAM for all CRM modules

Resource Utilization Analysis. We use the Vivado resource utilization tool to breakdown the CRM's hardware footprint on a sub-module granularity. Table 1 lists the CRM's absolute and relative resource utilization for a 16 tile system with a region size of 4 tiles. The *Snoop Unit* consumes a major part of the overall CRM's logic resources for its snooping, filtering and classification operations. The *Management Unit* does not consume much resources as it only decodes and triggers coherence actions. The *FIFO* and *Directory* are the only sub-modules using BRAMs (in addition to logic resources) for buffering and book-keeping respectively. The FIFO is dimensioned to buffer 4 K transactions and the *Directory* has a sparsity-8 compared to the 8 MB TLM. The CRM's area footprint relative to a single tile (zoomed in Fig. 1) as well as an empty Virtex-7 FPGA are also provided. Next, we analyze the CRM's hardware footprint by varying the region sizes in our 16 tile design from 2 tiles in a region up to all 16 tiles in a region (global coherence). The maximum number of tiles in a region is a design time decision that should be made based on the type of applications expected to run on the system. Figure 4 illustrates the logic (FPGA slices) and BRAM utilization per CRM sub-module for increasing region sizes. The numbers are normalized to the total available resources of a Xilinx Virtex-7 FPGA. The logic resources of the *Snoop Unit* and *FIFO* are independent of the region size. Slight variations of <4.4% and <1% for *Snoop Unit* and *FIFO* respectively are induced by Vivado's place and route algorithm. The logic resources for *Management Unit* and *Directory* increase (very small slope) with increasing region size. This is because additional logic is required to address a larger BRAM via the *Directory Manager*. Figure 4 also illustrates the BRAM utilization for *FIFO* and *Directory* sub-modules. The *FIFO* dimensions are constant for all syntheses and translates to 7 BRAM resources. We can see that this is independent of the region size. The *Directory* BRAM utilization increases linearly with increase in region size. For example, in our 16 tile system with 4 tiles in a region, we save 57% BRAMs compared to global coherence. Designers can choose the best configuration based on the class of applications that are expected to run on the platform. We observe that these synthesized hardware values closely follow the theoretical directory saving results we claimed in our previous work [7]. Slight

Table 1. CRM resource utilization for a 16 tile system with a region size of 4 tiles

Module	Resource			
	LUT	REG	MUX	BRAM
Snoop unit	2904	3133	427	0
Mgmt. unit	530	362	0	0
FIFO	159	43	0	7
Directory	208	129	0	9
$\sum$ **CRM**	**3801**	**3667**	**427**	**16**
w.r.t Tile	3.35%	6.54%	13.44%	8.81%
w.r.t Virtex-7	0.32%	0.15%	0.08%	1.24%

Table 2. CRM operations' latency

Operations	Snoop	Mgmt.
CRM configuration	26 clks	4 clks
Directory update	7 clks	4 clks
Inv. generation	4 clks	10 clks
Inv. execution	2 clks	24 clks
Force write-back	2 clks	9 clks

deviations from the theoretical numbers are due to granularity of usable BRAM blocks by Vivado. This means, BRAM savings will further increase with larger system tile counts.

Operation Numbers and Timing Analysis. Table 2 lists the number of clock cycles taken for every CRM transaction executed by the *Snoop* and *Management Units* (Sect. 3.1). The numbers are taken from cycle accurate ModelSim simulations in a traffic-free system. The clock cycles reported are measured from when the load/store operation is seen by the *Snoop Unit* on the bus. The CRM transactions are then triggered in parallel to the load/store operation. These numbers do not affect coherence in itself, but rather the consistency model. We keep these numbers as low as possible in order to minimize the overheads required for synchronization such as barriers. We use the Vivado timing analysis tool to obtain the maximum achievable frequency. For a standalone CRM design, the maximum delay reported is 8.029 ns (3.008 ns logic delay + 5.021 ns net delay) that allows the CRM to run at ≈ 125 MHz on an FPGA platform.

5 Experimental Evaluation

Video Streaming Application. As a use case, we use the feature extraction task of a video streaming application that can be executed in both shared memory (*rbcc*) and explicit message passing based (*mp*) modes. The feature extraction uses the Harris Corner Detection algorithm to extract feature points from an image. From the hardware perspective, the application exhibits a recursive pattern as illustrated in Fig. 5.

The video input is sent from a host PC frame-by-frame via an Ethernet interface and is received by our platform on the IO Tile. The input frame is transfered to the TLM of a compute tile where the main thread is executed. The main thread prepares a configuration packet which can be controlled from the host PC on a per-frame granularity. This packet contains information such as number-of and/or which-specific cores and tiles to be used, which memory model to use: *mp* or *rbcc* and other image processing specific parameters. The main thread distributes this configuration packet to the selected cores. If *mp* mode is enabled, the remote cores obtain their share of the input image via explicit software messages which does not require cache coherence. If *rbcc* mode is enabled, the remote cores read their share of the input image via remote read accesses assuming a coherent shared memory. The CRM enforces coherence by tracking,

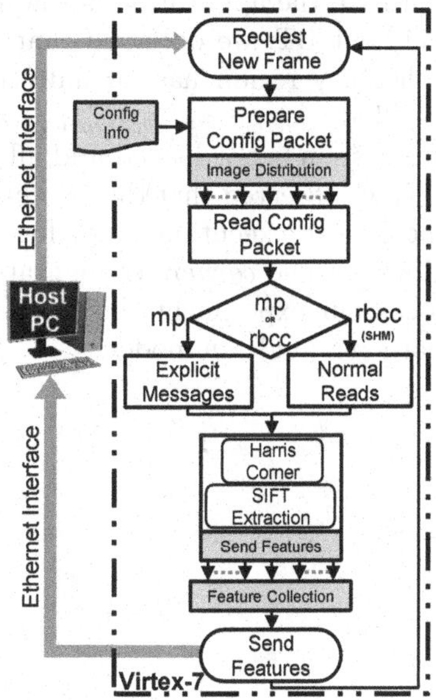

Fig. 5. Main thread execution of the feature extraction task

invalidating and writing-back image data. After processing, all cores transmit feature points extracted from their share of the image back to the main thread. The consolidated feature points along with other statistics are sent to the host PC via Ethernet and visualized as image overlay.

Experimental Setup. We use a 16 tile (64 core) design with 4 tiles (16 cores) in a region as described in Sect. 4. The tiled-manycore system is set to run at 50 MHz due to timing limitations of other sub-modules. We execute the feature extraction phase of the video streaming application in both shared memory (*rbcc*) and message passing (*mp*) modes for a *clustered* coherency region configuration (blue in Fig. 1). Next, we spatially separate the tiles by switching to a *corner* coherency region configuration (green in Fig. 1). Finally, we investigate the impact of background traffic (BT) on both modes and configurations. BT is generated by a separate application that continuously sends synthetic DMAs in parallel to the video streaming application on all tiles excluding the coherency region tiles. We control the BT system load by varying DMA transfer sizes: 50K, 100K, 250K and 500K. For *rbcc* mode runs, the coherency region is configured before the application begins. The CRMs also transparently adapt to application working sets at runtime using *RBCC-malloc()*. For *mp* mode, the CRM is disabled. As input, we provide video streams that vary the number of detected feature points, in-turn varying total execution time. We use popular retro gameplay clips (donkeykong, spaceinvaders, pacman) to limit the video size as we are on an FPGA prototype. We run approximately 600–700 frames of each clip and compare the execution time per-frame for both *mp* and *rbcc* modes. We performed some initial experiments (not shown) to get an impression of how sensitive the application is towards the spatial configuration and BT presence. Without BT, we observed that the spatial locality of the tiles making up the coherency region has virtually no impact on execution time for both modes, i.e. $T_{rbcc\text{-}cluster} = T_{rbcc\text{-}corners}$ and $T_{mp\text{-}cluster} = T_{mp\text{-}corners}$. This is because the system is not loaded and all inter-tile communication are unimpeded. With BT, we observed that the *cluster* configuration is still virtually unaffected (<5% increase in execution time) for both modes, owing to tightly coupled regions. However, the *corners* configuration proved to be sensitive to BT. Therefore we focus our experiments on the *corners* configuration with and without BT for both *rbcc* and *mp* modes.

Application Analysis. Figure 8 illustrates the per-frame execution time for both *mp* and *rbcc* mode executed for the *corners* configuration for all video clips. The second halves of the graphs show results with 50K BT, for easy comparison. The spikes in the first half (without BT) for *rbcc* mode are due to L2 cache misses. The *donkeykong* clip has a constant background with moving objects, resulting in a relatively constant execution time for both modes. We observe a significant gap between the execution time of *rbcc* mode that finishes 42% faster than *mp* mode without BT. With BT, we see delay spikes for both modes due to impeded inter-tile communication. Still, *rbcc* finishes 35% faster than *mp*. The *spaceinvaders* clip has a varying execution time that resembles a fading wave pattern caused by periodic removal of objects (aliens killed), replaced by new ones (aliens re-spawned). Without BT, *rbcc* mode finishes 31% faster than *mp* mode. Both modes are affected by BT, but *rbcc* finishes 29% faster than *mp*. In the *pacman* clip, there is a continuous decrease in execution time for both modes as the detected feature points are diminishing (eaten by pacman). *rbcc* mode finishes 37% and 31% faster than *mp* mode with and without BT respectively.

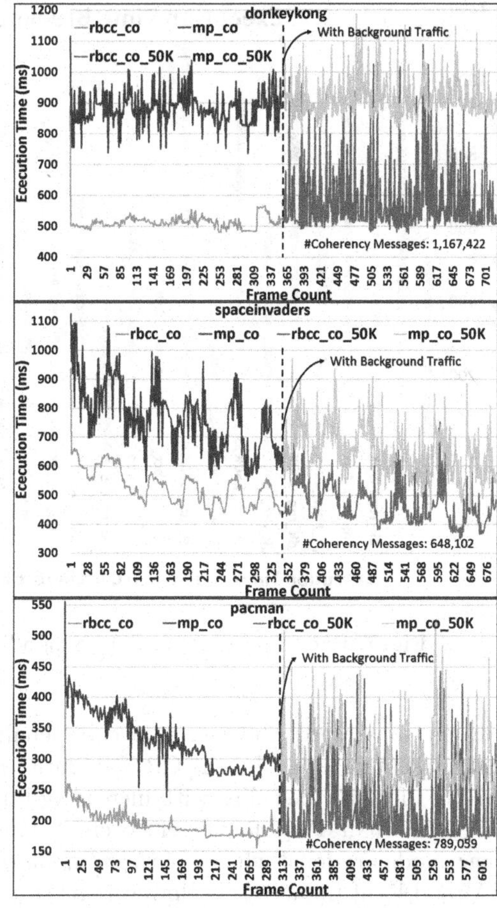

Fig. 6. Per-Frame execution time: *rbcc* & *mp*

Execution Time Breakdown. To comprehend the execution times of *mp* and *rbcc* modes, we break down the numbers to investigate their fundamental differences. From Fig. 5, the major difference lies in the image distribution methodology. For *mp* mode, we split the total execution time (T_{mp}) into image distribution time (IDT) and image processing time (IPT). IDT_{mp} consists of the time to distribute the image using explicit software messages (DMA assisted) and IPT_{mp} is the time taken to process the image. Note that all memory accesses during IPT_{mp} are local as the data has been copied by explicit software messages. For *rbcc* mode, IDT and IPT phases overlap, i.e. the overall execution time (T_{rbcc}) is a mixture of on-demand remote TLM accesses and local processing that cannot

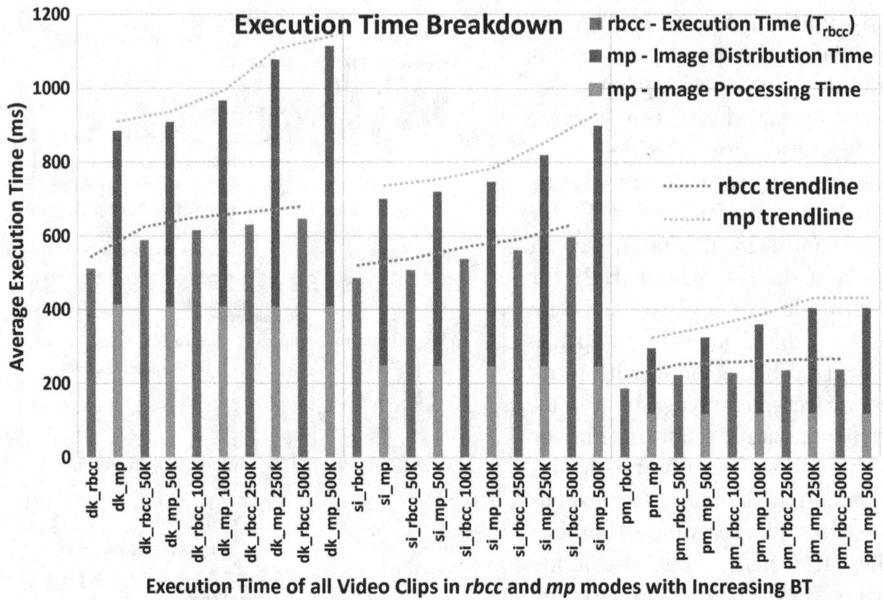

Fig. 7. Execution time breakdown of all clips with and without BT

be easily separated. The remote access penalties are reduced by the L2 cache which is kept coherent by the CRM. Figure 7 illustrates T_{mp} ($IDT_{mp} + IPT_{mp}$) and T_{rbcc} for all video clips with increasing BT. We observe that IPT_{mp} is actually better than T_{rbcc} for all video clips. This is because all memory accesses in *mp* mode are local whereas in *rbcc* mode they result in a mixture of remote TLM and local L2 accesses. However, IDT_{mp} adds a major chunk, thereby significantly increasing the total execution time of *mp* mode. This is due to the software overheads of explicit message passing required for image distribution to all remote tiles. For *rbcc* mode runs, we record high L2 hit rates (>90%) for all video clips, reducing remote TLM access penalties, in-turn processing time. Regarding BT, all inter-tile operations are affected due to the added network load, which is clearly seen in Fig. 7. IDT_{mp} increases with increased BT for all video clips as it consists of remote DMAs that are impeded by BT. Note that increased BT does not impact IPT_{mp} as all memory accesses during processing is local. However, T_{rbcc} increases with BT owing to remote TLM accesses that are now slower due to network load. But, *rbcc* maintains an overall lower execution time and saturates faster than *mp* with increasing BT as seen by the trendlines in Fig. 7. This is because, in *rbcc* mode, inter-tile communication consists of quick load/store accesses which have an overall lower latency with BT than large DMA packets in *mp* mode.

RBCC-malloc() Analysis. With *RBCC-malloc()* we tailor coherence support to actually shared application working sets that are known only at runtime. The *Snoop Unit* uses the address ranges of the application's dynamically allocated data (*malloc()*) as an additional filter to discard irrelevant transaction messages, thereby reducing unnecessary load on the *FIFO* and *Management Unit*. Using hardware counters, we compute the amount of *FIFO* transactions with RBCC (coherence for complete address range within the region) and with *RBCC-malloc()* (tailored coherence for actually shared address ranges within the region). Figure 8 illustrates the average number of *FIFO* transactions for all three video clips executed in the *corners* configuration with standalone RBCC and *RBCC-malloc()*. We can see that *RBCC-malloc()* reduces *FIFO* load by approximately 40% for the feature extraction task. This is because, *RBCC-malloc()* filters-out unnecessary transactions to private data structures such as tile local OS data, core instructions, core stacks, etc., which would otherwise trigger futile coherence actions. Dimensioning the *FIFO* requires knowledge about the class of applications that are expected to run on the system which would prevent frequent application throttling without over-provisioning.

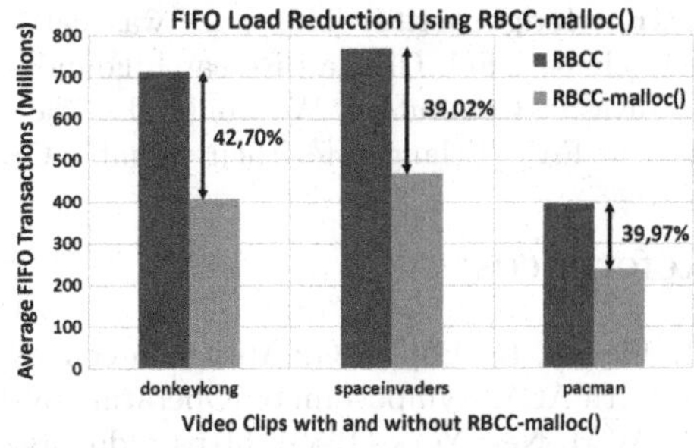

Fig. 8. RBCC-malloc() lowering FIFO Load

6 Conclusion and Future Work

This paper presented a novel *RBCC-malloc()* extension to RBCC that transparently tailors coherence to actually shared application working sets at runtime. We provided design and hardware implementation of a flexibly configurable CRM supporting *RBCC-malloc()* and evaluated real video processing tasks on an operational FPGA prototype. We showed BRAM resource reduction (57%) for a 16 tile system with 4 tiles per region compared to global coherence. We showed that a sub-function of a video streaming application is accelerated by up to 42% using shared memory compared to a message passing based version. We showed that *RBCC-malloc()* reduces *FIFO* load by 40% compared to RBCC. For future work, we are designing smart replacement policies for our sparse *Directory* design. We are developing Pthread support for our architecture to execute a variety of standard shared memory benchmarks that will help us with design decisions like selecting the region size, *FIFO* dimensions and *Directory* sparsity.

Acknowledgements. This work was partly funded by the Deutsche Forschungsgemeinschaft (DFG, German Research Foundation) - Project Number 146371743 - TRR 89: Invasive Computing. We would also like to thank the Computer Science 4 department at FAU, Erlangen for their valuable OS support.

References

1. Fleisch, B., Popek, G.: Mirage: a coherent distributed shared memory design. In: 12th ACM Symposium on Operating Systems Principles SOSP 1989, pp. 211–223. ACM, New York (1989). https://doi.org/10.1145/74850.74871
2. Bennett, J.K., Carter, J.B., Zwaenepoel, W.: Munin: distributed shared memory based on type-specific memory coherence. In: 2nd ACM SIGPLAN Symposium on Principles &Amp; Practice of Parallel Programming. ACM, New York (1990). https://doi.org/10.1145/99163.99182
3. de Dinechin, B.D.: Kalray MPPA®: massively parallel processor array: Revisiting DSP acceleration with the kalray MPPA manycore processor. In: 2015 IEEE Hot Chips 27 Symposium, pp. 1–27, August 2015. https://doi.org/10.1109/HOTCHIPS.2015.7477332
4. Lenoski, D., et al.: The stanford dash multiprocessor. Computer **25**(3), 63–79 (1992). https://doi.org/10.1109/2.121510
5. Wentzlaff, D., et al.: On-chip interconnection architecture of the tile processor. IEEE Micro **27**(5), 15–31 (2007). https://doi.org/10.1109/MM.2007.4378780
6. Kessler, R.E.: The cavium 32 core octeon ii 68xx. In: 2011 IEEE Hot Chips 23 Symposium (HCS), pp. 1–33, August 2011. https://doi.org/10.1109/HOTCHIPS.2011.7477487
7. Srivatsa, A., et al.: Region based cache coherence for tiled MPSoCs. In: 30th IEEE International System-on-Chip Conference (2017). https://doi.org/10.1109/SOCC.2017.8226059
8. Southern, G., Renau, J.: Analysis of PARSEC workload scalability. In: IEEE International Symposium on Performance Analysis of Systems and Software (ISPASS), pp. 133–142, April 2016. https://doi.org/10.1109/ISPASS.2016.7482081
9. Eggers, S.J., Katz, R.H.: Evaluating the performance of four snooping cache coherency protocols. In: 16th Annual International Symposium on Computer Architecture ISCA 1989, pp. 2–15. ACM, New York (1989). https://doi.org/10.1145/74925.74927
10. Hennessy, J., Heinrich, M., Gupta, A.: Cache-coherent distributed shared memory: perspectives on its development and future challenges. Proc. IEEE **87**(3), 418–429 (1999). https://doi.org/10.1109/5.747863
11. Gupta, A., Weber, W.D., Mowry, T.: Reducing memory and traffic requirements for scalable directory-based cache coherence schemes. In: International Conference on Parallel Processing, pp. 312–321 (1990)
12. Yao, Y., et al.: Selectdirectory: a selective directory for cache coherence in many-core architectures. In: Design, Automation Test in Europe Conference Exhibition (DATE), pp. 175–180, March 2015
13. Ferdman, M., et al.: Cuckoo directory: a scalable directory for many-core systems. In: IEEE 17th International Symposium on High Performance Computer Architecture, pp. 169–180, February 2011. https://doi.org/10.1109/HPCA.2011.5749726
14. Chaiken, D., Kubiatowicz, J., Agarwal, A.: Limitless directories: a scalable cache coherence scheme. In: ASPLOS IV, pp. 224–234. ACM, New York (1991). https://doi.org/10.1145/106972.106995

15. Sodani, A., et al.: Knights landing: second-generation intel xeon phi product. IEEE Micro **36**(2), 34–46 (2016). https://doi.org/10.1109/MM.2016.25
16. Fu, Y., Nguyen, T.M., Wentzlaff, D.: Coherence domain restriction on large scale systems. In: 48th International Symposium on Microarchitecture MICRO-48, pp. 686–698. ACM, New York (2015). https://doi.org/10.1145/2830772.2830832
17. Teich, J., et al.: Invasive computing: an overview. In: Multiprocessor System-on-Chip (2011)

RRAMSpec: A Design Space Exploration Framework for High Density Resistive RAM

Deepak M. Mathew[1(✉)], André Lucas Chinazzo[1], Christian Weis[1], Matthias Jung[2], Bastien Giraud[3], Pascal Vivet[3], Alexandre Levisse[4], and Norbert Wehn[1]

[1] Technische Universität Kaiserslautern, Kaiserslautern, Germany
{deepak,chinazzo,weis,wehn}@eit.uni-kl.de
[2] Fraunhofer Institute for Experimental Software Engineering (IESE), Kaiserslautern, Germany
matthias.jung@iese.fraunhofer.de
[3] Univ. Grenoble Alpes, CEA-LETI, MINATEC Campus, Grenoble, France
{bastien.giraud,pascal.vivet}@cea.fr
[4] Embedded System Laboratory (ESL), EPFL, Lausanne, Switzerland
alexandre.levisse@epfl.ch

Abstract. Resistive RAM (RRAM) is a promising emerging Non-Volatile Memory candidate due to its scalability and CMOS compatibility, which enables the fabrication of high density RRAM crossbar arrays in Back-End-Of-Line CMOS processes. Fast and accurate architectural models of RRAM crossbar devices are required to perform system level design space explorations of new Storage Class Memory (SCM) architectures using RRAM e.g. Non-Volatile-DIMM-P (NVDIMM-P). The major challenge in architectural modeling is the trade-off between accuracy and computing intensity. In this paper we present RRAMSpec, an architecture design space exploration framework, which enables fast exploration of various architectural trade-offs in designing high density RRAM devices, at accuracy levels close to circuit level simulators. The framework estimates silicon area, timings, and energy for RRAM devices. It outperforms state-of-the-art RRAM modeling tools by conducting architectural explorations at very high accuracy levels within few seconds of execution time. Our evaluations show various trade-offs in designing RRAM crossbar arrays with respect to array sizes, write time and write energy. Finally we present the influence of technology scaling on different RRAM design trade-offs.

Keywords: RRAM · ReRAM · Crossbar · NVM

1 Introduction

In present day off-chip memory hierarchy, there exists a large gap in bandwidth between main memory (DRAM) and storage memory (NAND Flash/HDD). Some of the new emerging *Non-Volatile Memory* (NVMs), such as *Resistive RAM* (RRAM), *Spin-Transfer Torque Magnetic RAM* (STT-MRAM) and *Phase Change Memory* (PCM), exhibit the potential to bridge this gap since they have

D. N. Pnevmatikatos et al. (Eds.): SAMOS 2019, LNCS 11733, pp. 34–47, 2019.
https://doi.org/10.1007/978-3-030-27562-4_3

the performance and cost per bit in between DRAM and Flash [1–3]. Therefore, in recent years, an additional layer of memory hierarchy called *Storage-Class Memory* (SCM) [4,5] is under discussion in order to integrate these emerging NVMs into the existing memory hierarchy.

Metal oxide based RRAM is a promising emerging NVM candidate for SCM due to its properties such as fast switching (∼100 ns for writes), good scalability, and CMOS compatibility. The integration of RRAM in the CMOS process is done in the *Back-End-Of-Line* (BEOL). Despite the above mentioned advantages, adoption of RRAM as an SCM in embedded and high performance computer architectures is still facing challenges due to variability issues [6–8] and sneak currents [9,10] in high density crossbar arrays. RRAM crossbar memories will have shorter read and write latencies than flash, with lower leakage and higher density than DRAM, making it an ideal candidate for SCM [1]. Therefore, researchers and industry consortia are exploring novel hybrid memory architectures such as NVDIMM-P [11], where RRAM and DRAM share the main memory address space. In order to conduct early design space explorations for such novel memory architectures using RRAM, fast and accurate architectural models of high density RRAM crossbar memories are required. Such a model has to provide timings, energy, and area of the high density RRAM from low level parameters of the RRAM device at high accuracy and fast execution speed.

A RRAM cell model with a voltage dependent write time, and an array model with an accurate voltage drop analysis are the essential components required for developing such an architectural modeling framework. The existing RRAM modelling frameworks [12–14] are either less accurate due to the approximate array voltage drop analysis or very slow since they depend on SPICE simulations [9]. This paper makes the following new contributions:

1. We present an architectural modeling approach to evaluate timings, energy consumption, and silicon area of high density RRAM crossbar memories.
2. We prove that the conventional modelling approach (assuming constant sneak currents) fails at lower technology nodes due to increased voltage drop in the crossbar array, and due to the non-linearity of the selector.
3. We show the trends in RRAM read/write times and energies with the increase in crossbar array size. Contrary to the popular belief, we show that the write time can decrease with the increase in array size.
4. Finally, we compare the output of our framework with a state-of-the-art NVM modelling framework [12].

RRAMSpec gets a technology input file and an architectural input file. The technology input file includes RRAM cell, selector, and CMOS technology related parameters. The architectural input file contains the required density, the optimization target (fixed, performance, energy) etc.

This paper is organized as follows. RRAM technology, operation, and the sneak current problem with crossbar arrays are discussed in Sect. 2. In Sect. 3, we summarize the previous works in RRAM crossbar array modeling. Our modeling approach is detailed in Sect. 4. The results are discussed in Sect. 5. Finally, Sect. 6 concludes this paper.

2 RRAM Background

A basic metal-oxide RRAM cell has a *Metal-Insulator-Metal* (MIM) structure with the insulator layer composed of a binary or ternary transition metal oxide (e.g. HfO2, TaO2, SrTiO3) [15]. The resistance state of the cell, either a *High Resistance State* (HRS) or a *Low Resistance State* (LRS), is used to store logic 0 and logic 1 respectively. When writing a 1 to RRAM, known as SET operation, it switches from HRS to LRS. When writing a 0 to RRAM, known as RESET operation, the device switches from LRS to HRS. For bipolar RRAMs, the switching process (SET or RESET) depends on the polarity of the applied voltage, while for unipolar RRAMs the switching happens irrespectively of the polarity of the applied voltage. In this paper, we focus mainly on bipolar metal-oxide RRAMs, although it is easily extendable for unipolar RRAMs. Further details of the switching mechanism of RRAMs is explained in [15].

The simple MIM structure of RRAM device permits building high density crossbar arrays with minimum cell size ($4F^2$), where F is the minimum feature size of the technology node, which corresponds to half of the minimum metal pitch. Figure 1 shows the schematic of an $m \times n$ crossbar array with m *Wordlines* (WLs) and n *Bitlines* (BLs). RRAM cells are placed at the intersection of each WL and BL. *Analog Multiplexer* (AMUXes), which are connected to the edge of WLs and BLs connect the selected lines to a voltage V_{SEL} and unselected lines to the voltage V_{USEL}.

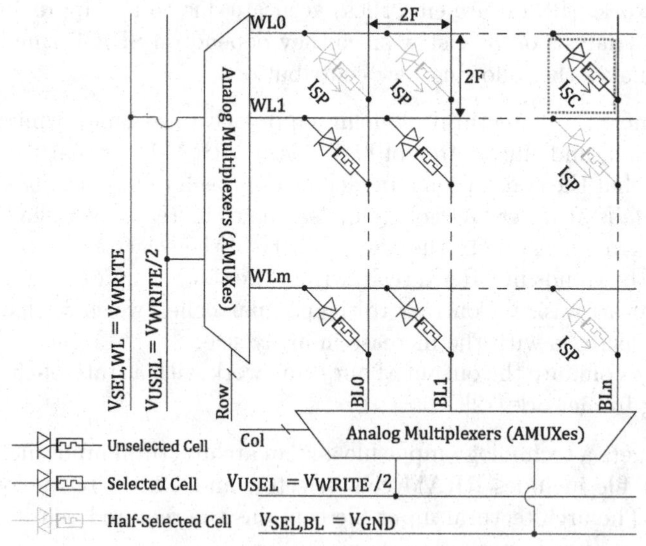

Fig. 1. Basic biasing scheme to perform a SET operation.

Figure 1 shows the array voltages for performing a write (SET in this case) operation on the cell farthest from AMUXes. A voltage V_{WRITE} is applied to the selected WL. The selected BL is grounded. This will ensure that the full write voltage is applied to the selected cell. All unselected WLs and BLs are supplied by a voltage $V_{WRITE}/2$ such that the effective voltage across the unselected cells is zero, preventing any unwanted current flowing through these cells. This biasing scheme, known as *Half-Bias Scheme* [10], is commonly used for biasing RRAM crossbar arrays. All cells, which share the WL or BL with the selected cell, known as *Half-Selected Cells*(HSCs), experience sneak path currents (I_{SP}) due to the voltage $V_{WRITE}/2$ across them. These sneak currents cause additional voltage degradation in the selected WL/BL, thereby reducing the effective voltage across the selected cell. Since the time for RRAM SET or RESET operation exponentially increases with the decrease in write voltage [9,16], the voltage degradation due to sneak currents largely increases the write time, and may even cause write failures.

To mitigate the sneak current problem, a selector device (eg. a bipolar diode) is integrated to the RRAM cell as shown in Fig. 1. The selector device has a non-linear switching characteristic similar to a diode, resulting the device significantly reducing current flow at low voltages. This limits the sneak currents flowing through HSCs. However, even using selectors with a non-linearity factor of ~1000, the total sneak current in arrays larger than 1 Mb may be comparable to the selected cell current. Therefore, there exist various sneak current compensation schemes [17–19], which increase the reliability of the read and SET operations by externally emulating the sneak currents. But, these schemes do not reduce the effect of the voltage drop across the crossbar array.

There are two main components of the voltage drop: the drop across the AMUXes, and the drop across the metal lines. Due to the relatively high voltages needed for the resistive state switching, thicker oxide transistors, which have higher resistance for the same area, are necessary for designing AMUXes in advanced technology nodes (≤65 nm). Furthermore, as the metal wire width shrinks with the technology scaling, its sheet resistance increases. Both effects result in higher voltage drop in the crossbar array.

3 Related Work

In this section, we briefly describe state-of-the-art RRAM/NVM modeling frameworks, their drawbacks, and the advantages of RRAMSpec in comparison to the existing modelling frameworks.

NVsim [13] is the first architectural exploration framework for NVMs, which models a variety of NVMs including RRAM crossbar memories. Later, Poremba et al. presented an advanced version of this framework called DESTINY [12], which permits 3D-modelling of NVMs. Both NVSim and DESTINY have two major drawbacks. Firstly, they assume a constant I_{SP} across all HSCs in the crossbar array, which does not hold for RRAM crossbar arrays using selector devices, especially in advanced technology nodes. In Sect. 5, we show that the error using this approach can go even higher than 100% for large arrays in advanced technology nodes. Secondly, they do not consider the voltage drop on the selected WL and BL of the crossbar array, which has a large impact on

RRAM cell write time as explained in Sect. 2. Instead, they use a cell write voltage and write time provided by the designer as an input parameter. In contrast, RRAMSpec calculates the voltages and sneak currents at each HSC. Its RRAM cell model calculates the write time based on the effective write voltage on the selected cell considering the crossbar array size. Recently, Levisse et al. [14] proposed a methodology calculating analytically the voltage drop evolution across the array (assuming constant I_{SP} across all HSCs) while not considering the effect on the programming time. Another RRAM modeling framework proposed by [9] invokes HSPICE to simulate the complete crossbar array. Therefore, it is not suitable for fast design space explorations with multiple array sizes due to its long simulation time.

None of these frameworks consider the fact that periphery circuitries can be partially placed below the crossbar array in high density RRAM crossbar memories [20]. In RRAMSpec, we consider the placement of the periphery below the crossbar array, and model the influence of crossbar array scaling on the voltage drop across the AMUXes and the crossbar array metal lines.

4 Modelling of RRAM

In this section, we present the various models used in the RRAMSpec framework.

4.1 RRAM Cell and Selector

The RRAM cell is modelled as two resistance states: HRS and LRS, provided by the designer. The cell switching time for an applied write voltage on the selected cell (V_{SC}) is calculated based on the following equation [9,16]:

$$t_{SET/RESET} = C_{S/R} \cdot e^{-K_{S/R} \cdot V_{SC,S/R}} \tag{1}$$

The parameters $C_{S/R}$ and $K_{S/R}$ are constants which depends on RRAM cell properties. The selector is modelled as a look-up table with the voltages and respective currents (see Table 1) extracted from measured data of a state-of-the-art selector device [21]. The designer can modify the input file to add another selector.

4.2 Crossbar Array

In the center of our modelling approach is the crossbar array model, which accurately calculates the currents and voltages at each node inside the crossbar array. In a crossbar array as shown in Fig. 1, there is no current flowing through unselected cells due to the half-bias scheme. Therefore, we can neglect the voltage drop on the unselected cells, and use a reduced array as depicted in Fig. 2 for performing steady state analysis. This reduced model largely improves the simulation time without affecting the accuracy[1]. In Fig. 2, R_{AMUX} is the driver resistance of the AMUX. In state-of-the art RRAM chips [20] drivers are

[1] The number of components in simulation are reduced from $\mathcal{O}(\#WLs \times \#BLs)$ to $\mathcal{O}(\#WLs + \#BLs)$.

placed underneath the crossbar array. Therefore, larger array sizes provide more space to fit the drivers below the array. This allows larger driver transistors, and lowers R_{AMUX}. V_{ED} in Fig. 2 is the maximum voltage applied to AMUXes. This voltage is limited by the breakdown voltage of the transistors in AMUX. Therefore, it is a CMOS technology related parameter provided by the designer. The existing modelling approaches [12, 13] assume a constant sneak path current along the HSCs. We calculate the sneak path current (I_{SP}) at each HSC using an iterative approach, since the error in array voltage drop calculation using constant sneakpath current approach is very high in lower technology nodes due to the increased WL/BL resistance. In Sect. 5, we perform a quantitative analysis of the error in array voltage drop calculation using constant sneakpath current approach in comparison to our new approach and SPICE simulations using the reduced array model.

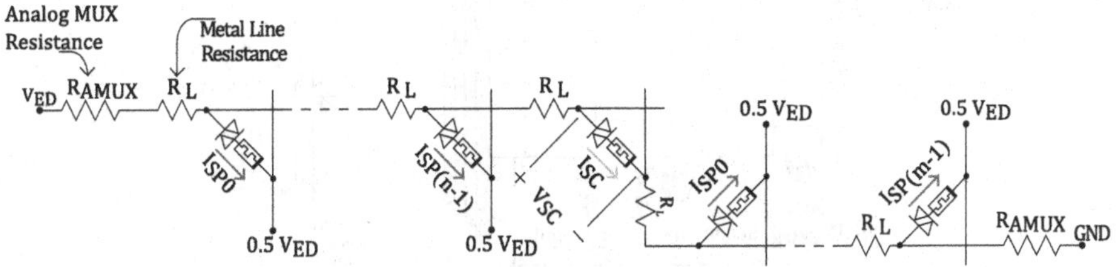

Fig. 2. Reduced array model for steady state analysis of an $m \times n$ array.

Assuming V_{ED} at the AMUX for a write operation, RRAMSpec iterates inwards calculating the voltages and currents at each HSC. Finally, the voltage V_{SC} and current I_{SC} on the worst-case cell in the array (the cell farthest from WL and BL AMUXes) is calculated via multiple iterations. The cell-switching time is computed with Eq. 1 using the calculated V_{SC}. The sum of cell switching time and the RC delay of the WL/BL is used to calculate the internal write time of the crossbar array. This process is repeated for different array sizes. Our modelling approach also checks that the voltage on the cells near to AMUX is not causing unwanted resistance switching due to write disturbance while writing to the farthest cell.

Reading data from the selected RRAM cell is performed by applying a voltage (V_{READ}) on the AMUXes and sensing the current flow. We assume the *Primary Sense Amplifiers* (PSAs) to be placed underneath the array along with AMUXes. For a reliable read operation, it is important that the ratio of the cell currents in LRS and HRS is high enough for the sense-amplifier to sense. Therefore, to find the optimal read voltage, V_{READ}, the designer provides a *Design Current Ratio*, $I_{RATIO} = I_{LRS}/I_{HRS}$ according to the sense-amplifier specifications. RRAMSpec performs a binary search between 0 V and the previously defined V_{WRITE} to find the minimum voltage that provides the required I_{RATIO}. This voltage is selected as the V_{READ}. RRAMSpec also ensures that the selected V_{READ} is low enough to avoid any disturbance on the resistance state of the read cell (read-disturbance). Reading an RRAM cell in a crossbar array typically involves an additional sneak current estimation step before the actual read process itself [17–19]. Therefore, the internal read time is calculated by summing up the individual delays: the sneak current estimation delay, the sensing delay, and the RC delay of WL/BL.

4.3 RRAM Architecture

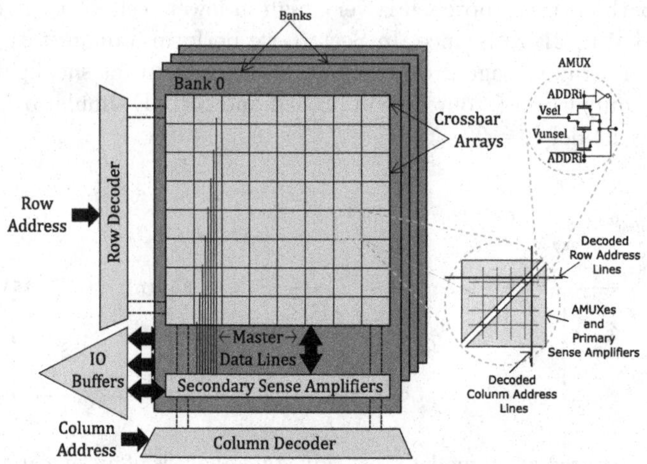

Fig. 3. Architecture of the RRAM.

Figure 3 shows the internal architecture of a complete RRAM memory modelled in RRAMSpec. It consists of several banks. Each bank has its own row/column decoders and secondary sense-amplifiers. The global circuitries such as data IO lines and command lines are shared between multiple banks. A bank is organized as a 2-D matrix of crossbar arrays. AMUXes and PSAs are placed under the crossbar array. Row and column addresses are decoded at the edge of each bank, similar to the decoding scheme in DRAMs. A single bit is accessed from each crossbar array during a read or write operation. The number of activated crossbar arrays at each access depends on the data bus width and the prefetch size. For a x4 chip with a prefetch size of 8, 32 crossbar arrays are activated in parallel, and the 32 bits are transferred to/from secondary sense amplifier. Various decoding delays, command delays and data transfer delays are added to the internal write/read times calculated in Sect. 4.2 to estimate the total write/read times of the RRAM chip.

4.4 Area Model

In a memory chip, the peripheral circuitries such as row and column decoders, sense amplifiers etc. occupy a considerable fraction of the total silicon area. But, the BEOL integration of RRAM enables fabrication of crossbar arrays' internal control circuitries (AMUXes and PSAs) underneath the memory array itself [20].

This improves the area efficiency (bits/area), but limits the total area of the AMUXes and the control circuitries to the area of the crossbar array itself.

The schematic of an AMUX modelled in our framework is shown in Fig. 3. Our area model calculates the maximum width of each transistor in the AMUX such that the complete periphery fits under the memory array, i.e. the total area of AMUXes should not exceed the area of the crossbar array. The resistance of AMUX transistors is then calculated using their width. For square arrays, the number of AMUXes increases linearly with the array size, i.e. number of rows and columns, while the crossbar array area increases quadratically. This provides more space for placing the AMUXes underneath the crossbar array, permitting to increase the width of driver transistors in AMUXes, thereby decreasing their resistances. However, for very small arrays, due to both the constant area occupied by the control circuitry and the minimal width of each transistor, the set of AMUXes might not fit underneath the memory array. In those scenarios, the area occupied by AMUXes and PSAs is used for the total chip area calculation. In addition to the crossbar array area, the total chip area calculation also includes area occupied row/column decoders, secondary sense amplifiers, I/O drivers etc.

4.5 Energy Model

RRAMSpec calculates the operational energy for reads and writes, and the leakage energy when the RRAM crossbar memory is in the idle state. The following sources of operational energy are accounted: crossbar array, global circuitries, and global interconnects. Inside the crossbar array, static current flow during reads and writes (both I_{SC} and I_{SP}), and the capacitive charging currents of metal lines during voltage transitions ($V_{WRITE}/2$ to V_{WRITE}, $V_{WRITE}/2$ to V_{GND}, and $V_{WRITE}/2$ to V_{READ}) are considered. Among these two sources, the power originated from high static currents (~50–150 μA) is dominant. Energy model uses the static currents which are already calculated by the crossbar array model described in Subsect. 4.2. The energy due to capacitive charging of metal lines during read or write operation is calculated using the following equation.

$$E = C \cdot (V_1^2 - V_{HALF} \cdot V_1) \tag{2}$$

In this equation, C represents the line capacitance, and V_1 indicates the operational voltage, which is either V_{WRITE} or V_{READ}. V_{HALF} is the half-bias voltage, which is fixed to $V_{WRITE}/2$. In global circuitries and interconnects, majority of the energy is consumed during voltage transitions due to the capacitances of metal lines. Global wires are usually wider and thicker than the local wires. Moreover, they are also much longer, resulting in an appreciable amount of energy spent in each transition. The idle state leakage currents are negligible inside crossbar arrays and their periphery circuitries due to the half-bias scheme. Therefore, the major sources of leakage energy are the voltage level translators [22] used in global address decoder circuitries. RRAMSpec calculates the leakage in those voltage level translators based on the number of address lines of the device.

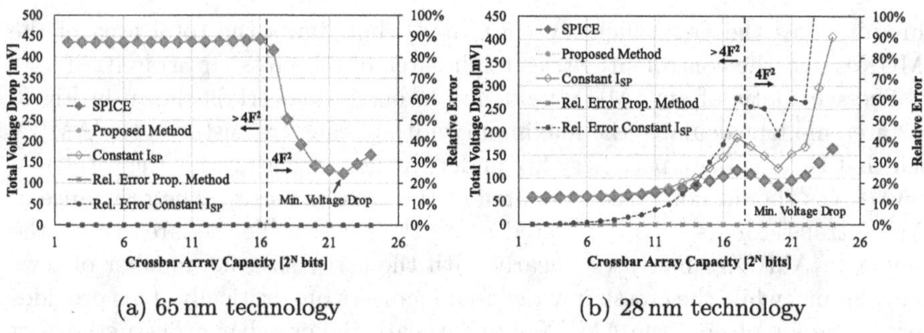

Fig. 4. Comparison of the accuracy of proposed method with SPICE and constant sneakpath approach for different crossbar array sizes (e.g. $2^{20} = 1K$ x $1K$, $2^{21} = 1K$ x $2K$, $2^{22} = 2K$ x $2K$, and so on).

5 Results and Discussion

In this section, we first compare the results of the array voltage drop calculations using our new method to the constant sneak path current (I_{SP}) approach and to SPICE simulations. Our SPICE simulations are based on the RRAM memory device and selector models from [16] and [21], respectively. Table 1 lists the CMOS and RRAM technology parameters used for our analysis. Figure 4 depicts the comparison results of voltage drop calculations using different methods for crossbar arrays at 65 nm and 28 nm CMOS technology nodes. The periphery is designed using thick oxide transistors that support high voltages (5 V for the 65 nm and 3.3 V for the 28 nm) needed for performing writes. The total voltage drop in Fig. 4 is the sum of voltage drops in crossbar array metal lines and the AMUX while performing a SET operation. We consider a single bit access per crossbar array. For crossbar arrays at 65 nm (Fig. 4a), both, the total voltage drop calculated using our approach and the drop calculated using constant I_{SP} approach matches with the voltage drop calculation using SPICE simulations. Therefore, the relative error in our modelling approach and in the constant I_{SP} approach compared to SPICE simulations is very low. But, for crossbar arrays at 28 nm (Fig. 4b), the total voltage drop calculated using the constant I_{SP} approach deviates much from the voltage drop calculated using SPICE. The relative error is very high (>100%) for high density crossbar arrays. The huge error in voltage drop calculation using the constant I_{SP} approach is due to the increased metal line resistance at 28 nm compared to 65 nm. The high metal line resistance ($R_{\square}$ in Table 1) results in a large difference in the voltages at the first cell and the last cell of the selected WL and BL, resulting in large difference in the sneak currents. The constant I_{SP} approach fails here because it assumes the same sneak current across all HSCs. On the other hand, as demonstrated in Fig. 4, our approach calculates the array voltage drop at negligible relative error in comparison with SPICE even for larger arrays. This is because it calculates the voltages and currents at each node in an iterative way as explained in Sect. 4.2. This clearly shows a major drawback of the existing modelling approach in state-of-the-art RRAM modelling frameworks [12,13]. Besides that, our new methodology provides a very good speed versus accuracy trade-off. On an Intel Xenon CPU (X5680) it performs the exploration for 2 × 2 to 8K × 8K array sizes in less than two seconds, while SPICE takes around four minutes to complete using the reduced array.

Table 1. CMOS and RRAM technology parameters.

	65 nm	28 nm
R_{HRS} [KΩ]	30	300
R_{LRS} [KΩ]	4	7
I_{CC}[a] [μA]	150	50
V_{PP} [V]	5	3.3
I_{SP} [nA]	69	21
$R_{\square}$[b] [mΩ]	150	450

Selector I-V Table						
V [V]	0	1.5	1.7	1.9	2.1	2.3
$I_{65\,nm}$ [A]	0	462 p	523 p	585 p	647 p	708 p
$I_{28\,nm}$ [A]	0	24 n	538 n	8.1 μ	63 μ	205 μ
V [V]	2.5	2.55	2.6	2.65	2.7	2.75
$I_{65\,nm}$ [A]	4.2 n	699 n	26 μ	121 μ	240 μ	368 μ
$I_{28\,nm}$ [A]	406 μ	462 μ	518 μ	576 μ	635 μ	695 μ

[a] Compliance current: the limiting current for *SET* operation.
[b] $R_{\square}$ is the sheet resistance of metal lines.

Another interesting trend in Fig. 4 is the decrease in total voltage drop with the increase in crossbar array capacity, especially for 65 nm technology, which is explained as follows. The AMUXes and other periphery circuitry are constructed underneath the crossbar array [20]. For any crossbar array capacity, there is a lower limit on the minimum area occupied by the complete periphery due to the required minimum dimensions (forced by the design rules of CMOS technology) of the thick oxide transistors (minimum width, minimum length etc.) used in designing the AMUXes. If the area of a crossbar array is smaller than the minimum required area by the periphery, then the spacing between cells in the crossbar array is increased (i.e $>2F$ in Fig. 1) such that it occupies the same area as the periphery. Those crossbar array capacities that do not permit a $4F^2$ RRAM cell size are indicated in Fig. 4 as the $>4F^2$ region. In this region, the periphery and AMUXes are designed using minimum size transistors, resulting in a huge voltage drop in them. Thus, the total voltage drop, which is the sum of voltage drops in crossbar array metal lines and the AMUX is also very high, ~425 mV for 65 nm technology. The small value of the total voltage drop (~50 mV) for 28 nm in Fig. 4b is attributed higher HRS of the 28 nm cell compared to the 65 nm cell, resulting in a (~10×) lower SET current. Expanding the array capacity in the $>4F^2$ region slightly increases the total voltage drop due to the increase in the length of metal lines, and the increase in sneak currents due to the rise in number of cells. This is more prominent in Fig. 4b due to the higher metal line resistance in 28 nm.

If the area of a crossbar array is larger than the minimum required area by the periphery (indicated as $4F^2$ region), then the periphery can be expanded such that its area is matched with the area of the crossbar array. This permits to increase the width of transistors (i.e. decreasing their resistance) used in

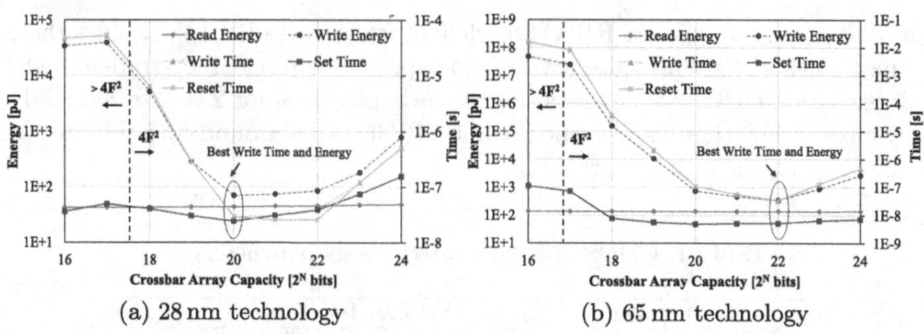

(a) 28 nm technology (b) 65 nm technology

Fig. 5. Comparison of energies and write times for different crossbar array sizes during the architectural exploration of a 1 Gb RRAM bank.

designing AMUXes, resulting in a decrease in the voltage drop in AMUXes. This explains the sudden decrease in the total voltage drop in Fig. 4 with the increase in crossbar array capacity at the starting of $4F^2$ region. Even a small decrease in AMUX resistance will result in a large change in the total voltage drop for 65 nm due to the high current flow in the crossbar array. Further increasing the array capacity will result in a point where the voltage drop in the metal lines exceeds the voltage drop in the AMUXes. The total voltage drop increases beyond this point with increasing array size since the metal line resistance is dominant in this region. This transition point in Fig. 4 corresponds to an array capacity of 2^{22} bits and 2^{20} bits for 65 nm and 28 nm technology nodes respectively.

Next, we show the influence of the total voltage drop on the read and write timings (SET and RESET), and energies of various crossbar array capacities. Figure 5 plots the results obtained during the architectural exploration of a complete 1 Gb RRAM bank at 65 nm and 28 nm technology nodes using RRAMSpec. Figure 5a plots the variation of SET and RESET times for different crossbar array capacities in 28 nm technology node. There is a direct correlation between the voltage drop in Fig. 4b and the SET time in Fig. 5a due to the exponential voltage-time dependency of RRAM cell, which is modelled using Eq. 1. Therefore, the crossbar array capacity, which results in the minimum SET time in Fig. 5a is also the one with minimum voltage drop in Fig. 4b. This results in an optimal array capacity of 2^{20} bits for SET. For RESET operation, the minimum RESET time is achieved for an array capacity of 2^{22}. Therefore, the optimal array size with respect to write time (the maximum of SET and RESET times) is 2^{20}. When RESET starts, the selected cell is in LRS. Therefore, it withdraws high current from the driver, resulting in a large voltage drop in the AMUX, and consequently very high RESET times. Thus, allowing wider AMUX transistors ($4F^2$ region) will result in a large decrease in the RESET time as shown in Fig. 5a. On the other hand, SET time is not much reduced by the increase in AMUX transistor width. The reason for this is the small current flow through the device under SET due to its HRS, causing less voltage drop in AMUX. A similar behavior can be observed in Fig. 5b for the 65 nm technology node.

In both Figs. 5a and b, the write energy follows the same trend of write time. It is worth to note that increasing the array size can reduce the total energy spend during a write operation, even though more cells are leaking (HSCs). This is because larger arrays allow wider AMUXes, which drastically reduces the voltage drop in the AMUX due to lower resistance. This results in a larger voltage across the selected cell, decreasing write time and write energy. However, the read energy remains nearly constant while increasing the array size due to very low sneak currents at read voltages. Read voltages are usually much lower than the write voltages, thus, the non-linear selector blocks the sneak currents.

Table 2. Comparison of RRAMSpec with DESTINY

1 Gb bank	DESTINY	RRAMSpec
Area (mm^2)	17.97	10.30
Crossbar array size	2K by 512	1K by 1K
Read latency (ns)	1.37	20.93
Write latency (ns)	53.35	41.38
Read energy (pJ)	42.95	43.64
Write energy (pJ)	72.33	69.76
Leakage power (mW)	7278	0.68

The validation of our modelling approach against the manufactured prototype testchip of high density RRAM crossbar [20] is not possible since the manufacturer does not disclose their proprietary RRAM cell/selector technology details. Instead, we compare the results of RRAMSpec with a state-of-the-art NVM modeling framework, DESTINY [12]. We performed the architectural exploration of a 1 Gb RRAM bank with 4 bits per access using RRAMSpec and DESTINY, targeting a write latency optimized solution. It is important to note that DESTINY does not compute the write latency of the RRAM cell, instead, this value has to be provided by the designer. RRAMSpec calculates the cell write latency based on the available voltage at the selected cell, which is accurately computed considering the crossbar array size, and sneak currents through each HSC as explained in Sect. 4.2. Therefore, in order to ensure a fair comparison, DESTINY is provided with the RRAM cell write latency, which is already calculated by RRAMSpec. Table 2 shows the comparison results. The chip area estimated by DESTINY is 74% larger than the value computed by RRAMSpec. This is possibly due to the fact that DESTINY does not consider the placement of peripheries underneath the crossbar array. The higher read latency in RRAMSpec compared to DESTINY is mainly originated from the current sensing delay, and the additional sneak current compensation delay. DESTINY outputs a very high leakage power of 7.2 W. We assume this overestimation of the leakage power is due to the assumption that row decoders are present in each cross-point array, and the absence of *Phase* signals [22] that can be activated only during operation.

6 Conclusion and Future Work

In this paper, we presented RRAMSpec: an architectural modeling approach, and a design space exploration framework to evaluate timings, silicon area, and energy consumption of high density RRAM devices. We validated the modeling against SPICE simulations using physics based RRAM models. Sample explorations using RRAMSpec showed optimum array sizes in terms of write/read energies and timings for different technology nodes. Finally, we compared the obtained evaluation results with a state-of-the-art NVM modelling framework. We mainly focused here on bipolar metal-oxide RRAMs, however our framework and modeling approach is extendable to crossbar arrays in general. More advanced features such as multi-bit access per subarray, multi-level cells, and modelling of 3D vertical RRAMs will be included in the future version of the framework. We are not considering the influence of programming voltage on the endurance and retention time of RRAM devices. This will be modelled in the future version of our exploration framework. Later, the tool will be published as open source.

Acknowledgment. This work was funded by the Carl-Zeiss Stiftung under the Nachwuchsförderprogram 2015 and the EU OPRECOMP project (http://oprecomp.eu) under grant agreement No. 732631. This work was also supported by the the Fraunhofer High Performance Center for Simulation- and Software-based Innovation and ERC Consolidator Grant COMPUSAPIEN (Grant No. 725657). The authors thank the Electronic Materials Research Lab (EMRL) at the RWTH Aachen for their great support.

References

1. Chen, Y., Petti, C.: ReRAM technology evolution for storage class memory application. In: 46th European Solid-State Device Research Conference (ESSDERC), pp. 432–435 (2016)
2. Fong, S.W., Neumann, C.M., Wong, H.S.P.: Phase-change memory towards a storage-class memory. IEEE Trans. Electron Devices **64**(11), 4374–4385 (2017)
3. Cappelletti, P.: Non volatile memory evolution and revolution. In: 2015 IEEE International Electron Devices Meeting (IEDM), pp. 10.1.1–10.1.4 (2015)
4. Freitas, R.F., Wilcke, W.W.: Storage-class memory: the next storage system technology. IBM J. Res. Dev. **52**(4/5), 439–447 (2008)
5. Lam, C.H.: Storage class memory. In: 10th IEEE International Conference on Solid-State and Integrated Circuit Technology, pp. 1080–1083 (2010)
6. Chen, A., Lin, M.: Variability of resistive switching memories and its impact on crossbar array performance. In: 2011 International Reliability Physics Symposium, pp. MY.7.1–MY.7.4 (2011)
7. Fantini, A., et al.: Intrinsic switching variability in HfO2RRAM. In: 5th IEEE International Memory Workshop, pp. 30–33 (2013)
8. Kao, Y.-F., et al.: A study of the variability in contact resistive random access memory by stochastic vacancy model. Nanoscale Res. Lett. **13**(1), 213 (2018)

9. Xu, C., et al.: Overcoming the challenges of crossbar resistive memory architectures. In: IEEE 21st International Symposium on High Performance Computer Architecture (HPCA), pp. 476–488 (2015)
10. Ghofrani, A., Lastras-Montao, M.A., Cheng, K.: Toward large-scale access-transistor-free memristive crossbars. In: The 20th Asia and South Pacific Design Automation Conference, pp. 563–568 (2015)
11. JEDEC: DDR5 & NVDIMM-P Standards Under Development. https://www.jedec.org/news/pressreleases/jedec-ddr5-nvdimm-p-standards-under-development
12. Poremba, M., et al.: DESTINY: a tool for modeling emerging 3D NVM and eDRAM caches. In: Design, Automation Test in Europe Conference Exhibition (DATE), pp. 1543–1546 (2015)
13. Dong, X., et al.: NVSim: a circuit-level performance, energy, and area model for emerging nonvolatile memory. IEEE Trans. Comput.-Aided Des. Integr. Circ. Syst. **31**(7), 994–1007 (2012)
14. Levisse, A., et al.: Architecture, design and technology guidelines for crosspoint memories. In: IEEE/ACM International Symposium on Nanoscale Architectures (NANOARCH), pp. 55–60 (2017)
15. Wong, H.S.P., et al.: MetalOxide RRAM. Proc. IEEE **100**(6), 1951–1970 (2012)
16. Fleck, K., et al.: Uniting gradual and abrupt set processes in resistive switching oxides. Phys. Rev. Appl. **6**, 064015 (2016)
17. Levisse, A., et al.: Capacitor based SneakPath compensation circuit for transistor-less ReRAM architectures. In: IEEE/ACM International Symposium on Nanoscale Architectures (NANOARCH), pp. 7–12 (2016)
18. Levisse, A., et al.: SneakPath compensation circuit for programming and read operations in RRAM-based CrossPoint architectures. In: 15th Non-Volatile Memory Technology Symposium (NVMTS), pp. 1–4 (2015)
19. Baek, J., et al.: A reliable cross-point MLC ReRAM with sneak current compensation. In: 2015 IEEE International Memory Workshop (IMW), pp. 1–4 (2015)
20. Liu, T., et al.: A 130.7 mm^2 2-layer 32 Gb ReRAM memory device in 24 nm technology. In: 2013 IEEE International Solid-State Circuits Conference Digest of Technical Papers, pp. 210–211 (2013)
21. Kim, S., Lee, W., Hwang, H.: Selector devices for cross-point ReRAM. In: 2012 13th International Workshop on Cellular Nanoscale Networks and their Applications, pp. 1–2 (2012)
22. Keeth, B., et al.: DRAM Circuit Design: Fundamental and High-Speed Topics, 2nd. Wiley-IEEE Press, Hoboken (2007)

Deep Learning Optimization

Efficient Dynamic Device Placement for Deep Neural Network Training on Heterogeneous Systems

Zi Xuan Huang, Shen Yu Fu([✉]), and Wei Chung Hsu

Department of Computer Science and Information Engineering, National Taiwan University, Taipei, Taiwan
{r06922100,d03922013,hsuwc}@csie.ntu.edu.tw

Abstract. Deep Neural Networks (DNNs) based learning methods have brought revolutionary advances in computer vision and machine learning. However, training a DNN model often requires very intensive computational resources. For edge incremental learning, more energy efficient learning solutions are called for. Heterogeneous computing is more power efficient, and has been increasingly popular for embedded platforms. Therefore, how to deploy training models on heterogeneous platforms to support edge learning is a critical issue.

Due to the increasing size of DNNs, it is rather difficult to determine how to dispatch a large number of operations to proper devices. One state-of-art approach uses reinforcement learning to address this device placement issue, but is too costly to apply in an embedded setting. In this paper, our approach leverages the information available from the computational graph of the model, and the dynamic profiles of run time and communication time of each device, to more efficiently deploy operations on heterogeneous systems. We use Critical Earliest Finish Time (CEFT) algorithm together with the Partitioned Boolean Quadratic Assignment Problem (PBQP) solver to find a cost-effective placement, and dynamically adjust assignments during the training process, which makes our method more adaptive and effective for different computational environments. On AlexNet, VGG, Inception, ResNet, RNNLM and other well-known models, our approach significantly outperforms traditional algorithms and reinforcement learning based methods.

1 Introduction

Over the past few years, DNNs have brought revolutionary advances to many areas. Consider high-end cell phones, for example, embedded systems equipped with edge learning capabilities are increasingly popular. More and more devices need to support continuous training. Hence, a fast training process can not only improve the performance of the devices but also encourage more developers to target edge incremental learning.

The models of DNNs have become more complex. Furthermore, the training time and computation resource requirements have also kept increasing. With a heterogeneous environment of CPU/GPU/DSP/AI-accelerator on many embedded devices, it is important to specify how each operation in a neural network to deploy to those heterogeneous devices, referred to as the device placement problem.

D. N. Pnevmatikatos et al. (Eds.): SAMOS 2019, LNCS 11733, pp. 51–64, 2019.
https://doi.org/10.1007/978-3-030-27562-4_4

Unfortunately, device placement in heterogeneous systems is not trivial, and often handled by experts with domain knowledge. Nevertheless, this traditional method is inefficient and often fails to find the best placement. So in recent years, Mirhoseini et al. [1] proposed to solve the device placement problem on heterogeneous system using a reinforcement learning approach, based on the policy gradient method. According to their experiments, the reinforcement learning approach indeed identified some more time-saving device placements compared to human solutions, but more practical approaches are called for. For example, using the reinforcement learning approach to find device placement for each model needs to run between 12 to 27 h under 80 to 160 GPUs. For general machine learning developers, such a burden is not affordable. Furthermore, reinforcement learning tends to find local optimal solutions since it is based on the policy gradient method. Therefore, the reinforcement learning approach has not been widely accepted.

In this paper, we propose a more practical method through a mapping of the device placement problem to general graph theory based approach. Based on the device placement for learning models, we combined the CEFT algorithm, which aims for reduced execution time for parallel computation, with the PBQP solver, which can effectively minimize the cost of computation placement of devices with different communication cost. The proposed approach is illustrated in Fig. 1. Note that, statically determined assignments for a heterogeneous system would not work since the environment with different amount of computation resources have different effects on the computation graph under different placements. Besides, different types of heterogeneous devices would also affect the result of placement, statically determined assignments might be inaccurate if we cannot obtain the specifications of target machine in advance. Hence, we run both CEFT and PBQP algorithms to determine which algorithm could be better than the other in the current environment during the training process. This adaptive, dynamic approach incurs very low overhead. Compared with past methods which usually rely on static placement, our method can automatically adjust assignments according to different environments. This proposed approach is more suitable for embedded systems because most of machine learning developers do not know what type of devices will actually run their models in practice. In addition, our method does not require expensive searching of effective device placement for each different learning model.

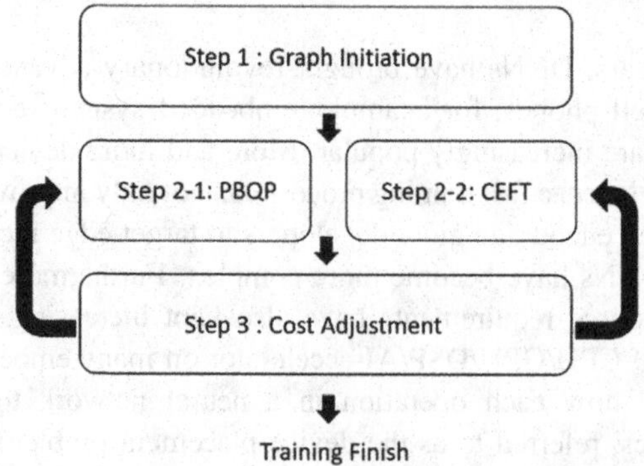

Fig. 1. An overview of the dynamic device placement model.

2 Definition

A deep neural network consists of a directed graph of layers that receive, process, and output data. Input data enters the graph through an input layer. Starting from the input layer(s), each layer of the graph is scheduled to execute in a topological order. Data flow through layers along directed edges, similar to data dependences of instructions in a basic block.

The layers within a DNN consist of standard mathematical operations such as convolution, activation, pooling, and full-connected layer. For each standard mathematical operation, a basic unit is assigned to a device every time. Therefore, we can consider each operation as a node in a graph, and the edges represent the interdependencies of operations as illustrated in Fig. 2. The main task of this work is to find a device placement solution that minimizes the total execution time.

2.1 Co-location Operations

Due to the increasing size of DNNs, if we dismantle the entire model into basic standard mathematical operations to construct a graph, it will be very large and complicated. Hence, a common practice is to put several operations into a group, and using groups as basic units in assignment. Although this method can effectively reduce the complexity and computation time of finding a device placement, it could miss the opportunity to locate the best placement. In this paper, our approach can maximize the full potential of device placement without co-locating operations.

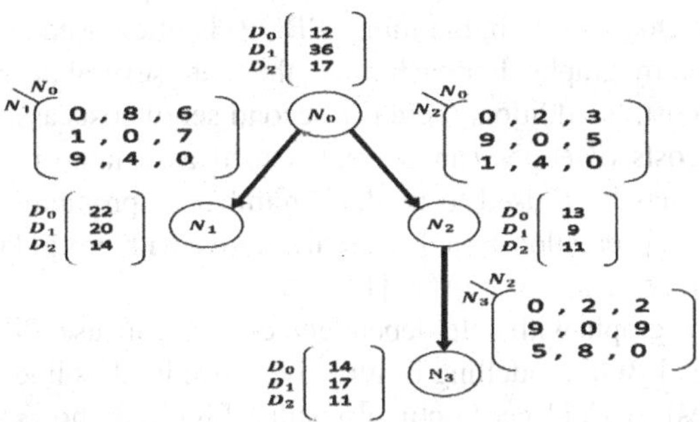

Fig. 2. Example of a simple DNN device placement problem mapping to the graph theory problem. $N_0 \sim N_3$ represent operations in DNN and $D_0 \sim D_2$ represent available devices in a heterogeneous system. Our purpose is to find an assignment in order to minimize training time.

2.2 Operations Cost

In the problem of device placement, the following two costs are the main considerations:

- **Computation Cost.** It represents the execution time for one basic operation running on a specific device. For example, for a tensor with size 128 × 128, the cost of the add operation is 0.2 ns, we use a cost vector to record the time for every basic operation executed on each device as illustrated in Fig. 2.

- **Communication Cost.** It represents the time for data transfer between different devices. As shown in Fig. 2, we use a cost matrix to record data transfer time between various pairs of devices.

2.3 The Optimization Problem

Given a DNN graph G, we record the computation cost for all operations N ∈ G under every available heterogeneous devices $D_0 \ldots D_n$ to form the product space N × D. Since the cost of each edge is determined by the pair of device assignment, we must compute the cost of all path P in the graph implied by each assignment, I, of the nodes of G, drawn from points in this space. The task before us is to find the point in the product space N × D × P of instantiations of G, which minimizes the total cost.

With the above representation, we can map the problem of device placement to a graph theory problem, and in the next section, we introduce the algorithms we used in order to find the most efficient device placement.

3 Algorithms

In Sect. 2, we show that how to create a graph which can represent the device placement problem. We can also map the graph to the well-known existing optimization problem—PBQP.

3.1 Partitioned Boolean Quadratic Programming

Partitioned Boolean Quadratic Programming (PBQP) is often used to solve assignment problems represented by graphs. For each node, there are several possible assignments, each with a known cost. In addition, there is a second set of costs associated with edges in the graph. The costs of edges can be represented as a table indexed by pairs of assignments. PBQP has been used to model a number of problems in compiler optimizations such as register allocation for architectures with irregular instruction sets [15], and instruction selection on DAGs [14].

Once we have a graph with interdependencies, we can use PBQP to search for optimal assignments. PBQP modelling is attractive since it takes linear time (relative to the number of edges) to yield near optimal results. Figure 3 shows the example why PBQP solver is needed for device placement problem which is also the same graph as Fig. 2. As we see, if we just simply choose the lowest cost for each operation as in Fig. 3a, the solution would not be optimal as the outcome of Fig. 3b.

In general, when an operation has multiple direct successors and/or predecessors, the placement of same operation may not be optimal for all. Choosing one placement over another may limit the choice of devices that can be used in successor/predecessor operations, or may require the insertion of expensive data communication primitives. PBQP allows us to model these complicated device placement costs at the abstraction level and to find solutions with an off-the-shelf PBQP solver. In this work, we used the PBQP solver of Scholz et al. [2], which finds the minimum cost solution for the entire DNN graph. In other words, the goal here is to minimize the total execution time of a

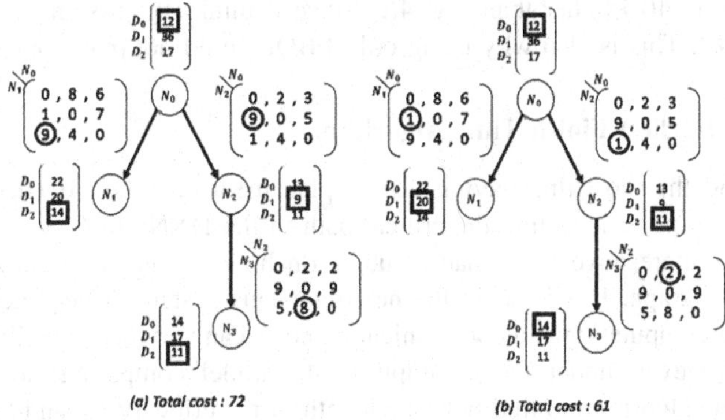

Fig. 3. Example of simple PBQP problem. (a) use a greedy algorithm to find the minimum cost solution (b) gives the optimal solution.

DNN graph. However, with the common parallel computing platforms, the total cost for the entire graph does not necessary represent the total of execution time. Figure 4 shows why the PBQP solver fails to minimize execution time under common multi-core parallel computing. In Fig. 4(a), it is a simple graph which is constructed by 6 nodes and assign all of them to GPU kernel. It is worth noting that node 4 does not have GPU kernel implementation, so it will be assigned to CPU that cost 12 time units which is longer than others. Since the path 1-2-4-6 and path 1-3-5-6 can execute in parallel, the critical path cost is 23 rather than 25. As we change the placement policy to our PBQP solver as illustrated in Fig. 4(b), we will find that if we assign node 2 to CPU instead of GPU, it can minimize the cost since no communication between node 2 and node 4 is required. The execution time of node 4 can reduce from 12 to 8 time units, which is more than the amount of time node 2 increases.

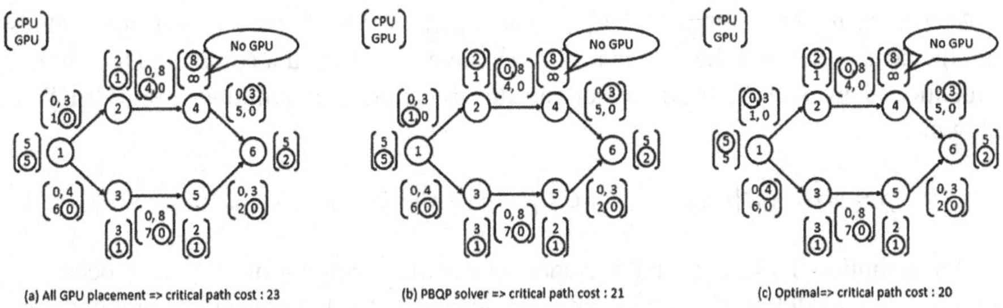

Fig. 4. A simple example shows why total cost is not appropriate for execution under parallel computing architectures.

In Fig. 4(c), we can see that if we assign CPU to node 1 instead of node 2, it can further reduce the cost of critical path since the communication is not needed between node 1 and node 2. Although node 3 has a significant increase in cost, it has no impact since it is not on the critical path. However, the PBQP solver would select the placement in Fig. 4(b) rather than Fig. 4(c) since it thinks the assignment yields the lowest total cost. This is also why using only PBQP could not reach our goal.

3.2 Critical Earliest Finish Time Algorithm

In order to find the most time-saving device placement on a heterogeneous parallel machine, the key point is to find the critical path in the DNN graph.

In the past, there have been many studies on how to find the critical path in a directed acyclic graph. However, in the heterogeneous system, it becomes a difficult problem where computation and communication costs can vary between different types of devices. However, under the assumption of parallel computing, we can use a polynomial time algorithm to find both the length of the critical path and an allocation of operations to devices on that path. Figure 5 gives a list of notations and their descriptions that we will be used for the rest of this paper.

Notation	Description
CEFT	The dynamic programming array
P	Number of devices
T	Number of operations
E	Number of edges
$P(t_i)$	Parents of the task t_i
$C_{comp}(t_i, p_j)$	Execution time of operation t_i on processor p_j
$C_{comm}\{(t_i, p_j), (t_k, p_l)\}$	Communication time between t_i on device p_j and t_k on device p_l

Fig. 5. List of notations

According to the definition of C_{comp} and C_{comm} in Fig. 5, we can get both values from the cost vector and the cost matrix if we have constructed a complete DNN graph as mentioned in Sect. 2. Next, we define the dynamic programming array CEFT as following:

$$\mathrm{CEFT}(t_i, p_j) = max_{T_k \in \mathrm{P}(t_i)} \{ min_{p_l \in (0,\cdots,p-1)} \{ C_{comp}(t_i, p_j) + \mathrm{CEFT}(T_k, p_l) + C_{comm}\{ (t_i, p_j), (T_k, p_l) \quad (1)$$

Our definition 1 of the CEFT includes an optimal mapping of tasks to processors, and allows us to define a more accurate critical path for heterogeneous architectures than past approaches. However, there are an exponential number of possible allocations of tasks to processors, so any algorithm that considers all mappings individually will require exponential time [2]. Here we adopt a dynamic programming approach [3] that computes the length of a path in the dependence graph using our CEFT-based definition of dependence length. Nevertheless, we should not use dynamic programing approach directly to find the critical path, since we assume that the length of two different paths can be computed independently. In practice, the length of a path depends on the device allocation of the operations in the path. If a single operation appears on multiple different paths, each path may require a different allocation to minimize the path length. In this paper, we use task duplication and favor lowest cost allocation [3] to solve this problem:

However, in a heterogeneous system, we would expect to have unlimited computation resources for each kind of device in order to guarantee we can exploit the maximum parallelism in applications. If there are insufficient computation resources to support full parallelization, CEFT algorithm does not necessarily run better than using the PBQP solver alone.

4 Design Methodology

In this section, we describe a hybrid solution, which combines CEFT with PBQP. We divide our approach into three steps as illustrated in Fig. 1.

4.1 Graph Initialization

At the beginning of the training process, we measure the execution time of each operation running on different devices in order to fill in its cost vector. If one operation is not suitable or there is no kernel implementation to a specific device, we will fill ∞ in its corresponding cost vector entry which represents infinite cost and our algorithm will certainly avoid to choose it in order to minimize the cost.

As for cost matrices, according to experiment results, we learned that the communication time mainly affected by data size and the kind of devices. Since we can get the size of data for each operation at the beginning, we can measure the time for each size of data communicating between different devices and fill in the corresponding cost matrix entries.

Both the computation and the communication cost are measured according to the actual run of the devices, our method can be adapted to a variety of different environments. The initialization cost may increase as the model becomes more complex. However, since it is one-off action and the training time of DNN is often very long, the time spent on graph initialization is relatively insignificant.

4.2 Device Placement

After graph initialization, we decide the device placement for each operation according to the cost we measured in step 1. In Sect. 3, we have introduced two algorithms that could solve the device placement problem, and one is more suitable to the other under different environments. The PBQP solver can find a placement near optimal through minimizing the total execution and communication cost in the graph. However, on a heterogeneous and parallel machine, minimizing the total cost may not yield the shortest runtime since we should consider about the critical path issue for parallel execution. The performance of the two algorithms vary depending on the number of resources the actual machine has.

In our approach, we first determine whether computation resources are sufficient to support fully parallel execution. If resources are enough, we will simply select PBQP as our algorithm. Otherwise, we run both PBQP and CEFT at the beginning, and test which one delivers better performance on the underlying heterogeneous system. It is hard to define how many resources can CEFT outperforms PBQP, and it also depends on the waiting cost during runtime which we will discuss at Sect. 4.3. It is not expensive to run both algorithms for DNN applications since both can run in linear time.

4.3 Dynamic Cost Adjustment

However, if our method ends up dispatching too many operations to a specific device so that the resource is oversubscribed, some operations may have to wait for the device becoming available. In order to address this issue, we implement a runtime feedback, error correction mechanism to reduce such device waiting time.

We record the time for each operation enters and exits the wait queue to measure waiting time. The reason why we need to measure waiting time is that both CEFT and PBQP algorithms assume that once an operation is dispatched, the operation will start executing immediately. However, computation resources are limited, we should measure this cost which is ignored by our algorithm. In other words, the actual cost for an operation execute on a specific device should include the time waiting for computation resources.

After a few epochs, we will have the actual average execution time measured for each operation. So we could update the corresponding cost vector entries and go back to step 2 to run PBQP and CEFT again in order to find a new device placement according to the actual cost. If there is an operation, which has too large wait cost, PBQP and CEFT will try to avoid this assignment in order to minimize the total cost next time. Our approach is dynamic and a lot more adaptable than traditional static approach.

5 Evaluation

We apply our proposed method to assign operations to devices using five popular neural networks in deep learning literature: AlexNet, VGG, Inception-V3, ResNet, Recurrent Neural Network Language Model. We compare our method against existing baselines described in Sect. 5.2.

In our experiments, the available devices are 1 Intel I7-7700 CPU with four cores and two GeForce GTX 1060 GPUs.

5.1 Experiment Setup

We evaluate our approach on five established deep learning models:

- ***AlexNet*** [4] is a convolutional neural network. It contains eight layers, the first five are convolutional layers, some of them followed by max-pooling layers(https://en.wikipedia.org/wiki/Convolutional_neural_network#Pooling_layer), and the last three are fully connected layers. It used the non-saturating ReLU activation function, which showed improved training performance over tanh and sigmoid.

- ***VGG*** [5] is a convolutional neural network of increasing depth using an architecture with very small (3 × 3) convolution filters, which shows that a significant improvement on the prior-art configurations can be achieved by pushing the depth to 16–19 weight layers.
- ***Inception-V3*** [6] is a widely-used architecture for visual feature extraction. The Inception network has multiple blocks. Each block has several branches of convolutional and pooling layers, which are then concatenated to make the inputs for the next block.
- ***ResNet*** [7] is a residual learning framework to ease the training of networks that are substantially deeper than those used previously. Authors explicitly reformulate the layers as learning residual functions with reference to the layer inputs, instead of learning unreferenced functions.
- ***Recurrent Neural Network Language Model*** (RNNLM) with multiple LSTM layers [8, 9]. The main feature of this model is that it has large potential for parallel executions since once inputs and parent operations are available, each LSTM layer can all begin to execute.

5.2 Baselines

- ***ALL-CPU***: In this placement, we dispatch all operations in the model to one CPU.
- ***ALL-GPU***: In this placement, we dispatch all operations which have GPU kernel implementation to one GPU. If there are some operations cannot dispatch to GPU, we will put them on CPU.
- ***MinCut*: A** traditional algorithmic for graph theory problem. In this placement, we split the graph to different group according to specific rule [10] and dispatch to each device.
- ***RL-Based***: Reinforcement learning based approach for device placement problem [1] is a state-of-the-art method now for device placement.
- ***Optimal Solution***: In order to compare the upper-bound with each placement policy, we use exhaustive search to find the optimal placement for some simple DNNs.

5.3 Algorithm Analysis

As we mentioned above, CEFT and PBQP have their pros and cons. In Fig. 6(a), we allow only one operation to be executed at the same time on CPU and GPU respectively. Obviously, using PBQP can run better than using CEFT for all cases. However, as we increase our computation resources which can let four operations to be executed on CPU and two operations to be executed on GPUs at the same time, CEFT now outperforms PBQP for most cases as shown in Fig. 6(b). We also believe that if we increase a few more computation resources, CEFT can find a near-optimal placement.

According to the experiments results, if we do not have enough computation resources, choosing PBQP would be more favorable. On the contrary, if the computation resources are sufficient to support a certain degree of parallelization, CEFT would be the better choice. The trade-off between the two algorithms depends on the actual environment.

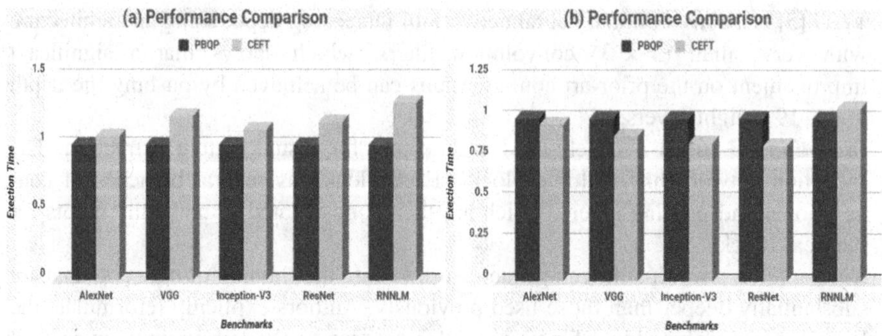

Fig. 6. The comparison between PBQP and CEFT. In Fig. 6(a), there is only one computation resources for both CPU and GPU. In Fig. 6(b), the amount of computation resources is 4 and 2 for CPU and GPU respectively.

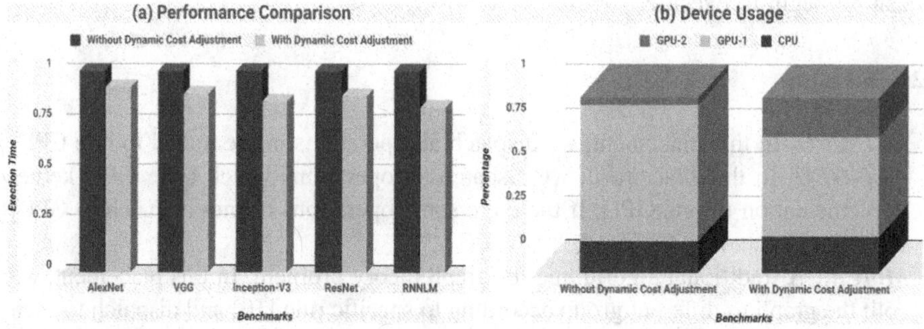

Fig. 7. Compare our method with and without dynamic cost adjustment in terms of time-saving and device usage.

5.4 Performance Comparison

We first investigate whether dynamic cost adjustment works or not. In Fig. 7(a), our method with dynamic cost adjustment improves performance, since it enables our algorithm to consider the impact of operation wait time. In Fig. 7(b), we can see that devices have indeed more evenly executed, which can enable more operations to run in parallel.

We now present the per-step execution time of the placements found by each baseline and by the optimal solution. The benchmarks that use the exhaustive search to find the optimal solution need to group their operations in order to reduce the complexity and are limited to smaller models. They are used only as a reference for evaluating our CEFT + PBQP approach.

In Fig. 8(a), all of the benchmarks are simplified. We can observe the times each approach take that run on different models in a single step. Our method can find a more efficient placement in every benchmark than the All-GPU policy. The reason why there is still an obvious gap between our approach and the optimal solution is that we do not have unlimited resources to execute all operations in parallel and our dynamic cost adjustment mechanism cannot play a role in a single-step measurement. Hence, sometimes it cannot find a placement that is very close to the optimal placement.

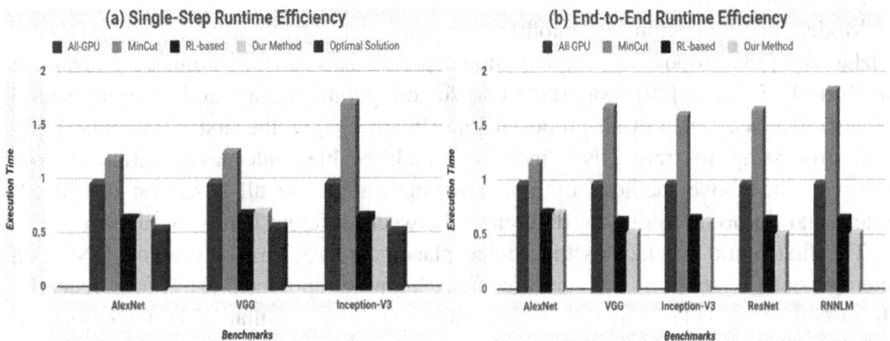

Fig. 8. Compare our method with each baseline in single-step and end-to-end runtime respectively.

In Fig. 8(b), we present the end-to-end run times of the placements found by our method and by the baselines. In this case, since our dynamic cost adjustment mechanism works, our method is 40% better than All-GPU policy, and 20% better than RL-based methods. Besides time-saving issue, our method has multiple advantages over the RL-based method. For instance, the RL-based method needs a much higher cost for training a reinforcement learning for one placement. Moreover, since our method finds the device placement during runtime, it is more adaptable for different environments. In contrast, the RL-based methods must use the same machine, which plans to train the model and select device placements.

6 Related Work

As DNN applications become increasingly more important, optimization for these models has attracted much attention. For instance, Tensorflow XLA [17], which is a domain-specific compiler for optimizing DNN models. Amazon NNVM/TVM [29], Facebook Glow [30], UIUC DLVM [31] and Intel nGraph are virtual machines to support multiple DNN domain specific languages and multiple target hardware platforms. These compiler-based approaches are all using the computational graph generated from various DNN frontends as the Intermediate Representation (IR) for common machine independent optimizations. With machine independent optimizations and target specific backend optimizations, DNN training and influencing could enjoy improved speed and memory usage.

Many optimizations for DNN focus on parallel processing on distributed systems. They can be roughly divided into data parallelization and model parallelization. Data parallelism exploitation is the most commonly used parallelization scheme such as [25]. Seide proposed 1-bit Stochastic Gradient Descent (SGD), which quantizes the gradients by one bit per value to reduce the communication for data parallelism. Zhou et al. [26] also speeds up convolutional neural networks by low-bit-width weights, activations and gradients. Strom [27] proposed to send gradients only when it is larger than a threshold.

Model parallelization is another approach of DNN training optimization. Krizhevsky [28] proposed to exploit model parallelism on fully-connected layers of AlexNet [4]. Li et al. [29] proposed a two-stage pipeline on training Recurrent Neural Network (RNN). Halep et al. proposed PipeDream [30] as the first work using pipelined processing to train DNN models, which enables inter-layer parallelization. However, the above methods of model parallelization are all based on distributed system and do not consider the differences between different hardware platforms.

The first work that tackles the device placement problem for training DNNs on heterogeneous system is the reinforcement learning approach [1]. More recently, Mirhoseini et al. [11] proposed a hierarchical architecture that adds a feedforward neural network to automatically classify operations into groups. Gao et al. [12] proposed Spotlight based on the development of a customized proximal policy optimization theory, designed to find optimal device placements for training deep neural networks. The device placement problem is modeled as a Markov Decision Process (MDP), which is the first MDP model for addressing this issue. However, these methods still rely on the policy gradient algorithm and need too large training cost.

7 Conclusion

We have proposed a new and highly efficient approach to find the most time-saving placement of devices during the training process. We map the device placement problem as graph theory related problem. Efficient algorithms like CEFT and PBQP are adopted to find a most time-saving placement depending on the available computing resources available on the target platform. The assignment considers both the execution time and the required communication cost for various heterogeneous devices. We also incorporate with dynamic cost adjustments to avoid the impact of incorrect time estimation due to unexpected device wait time. Our approach is adaptive and flexible to deploy onto different hardware platforms since the cost of operations and communications are set at runtime and our dynamic cost adjustments deal with estimation errors due to unexpected device wait time. We have implemented our approach and tested on the five popular DNN benchmarks. On these benchmarks, and a few different heterogeneous computing platforms, our approach is 20% better than the state-of-the-art device placement, and also significantly outperforms other traditional works.

References

1. Mirhoseini, A., et al.: Device Placement Optimization with Reinforcement Learning (2017)
2. Scholz, B., Eckstein, E.: Register Allocation for Irregular Architectures (2002)
3. Vasudevan, A., Gregg, D.: Mutual Inclusivity of the Critical Path and its Partial Schedule on Heterogeneous Systems (2017)

4. Krizhevsky, A., Sutskever, I., Hinton, G.E.: ImageNet Classification with Deep Convolutional Neural Networks (2012)
5. Simonyan, K., Zisserman, A.: Very Deep Convolution Networks for Large-Scale Image Recognition (2014)
6. Szegedy, C., Vanhoucke, V., Ioffe, S., Shlens, J.: Rethinking the Inception Architecture for Computer Vision (2016)
7. He, K., Zhang, X.: Deep Residual Learning for Image Recognition. (2016)
8. Zaremba, W., Sutskever, I., Vinyals, O.: Recurrent neural network regularization (2014)
9. Jozefowicz, R., Vinyals, O., Schuster, M., Shazeer, N., Wu, Y.: Exploring the limits of language modeling (2016)
10. Chevalier, C., Pellegrini, F.: Improvement of the efficiency of genetic algorithms for scalable parallel graph partitioning in a multi-level framework. In: Nagel, W.E., Walter, W.V., Lehner, W. (eds.) Euro-Par 2006. LNCS, vol. 4128, pp. 243–252. Springer, Heidelberg (2006). https://doi.org/10.1007/11823285_25
11. Mirhoseini, A., Goldie, A., Pham, H., Steiner, B., Le, Q.V., Dean, J.: A hierarchical model for device placement (2018)
12. Gao, Y., Li, C., Li, B.: Spotlight: Optimizing Device Placement for Training Deep Neural Networks (2018)
13. Tjalling, C.: Assignment problems and the location of economic activities. Econometrica **25**, 53–76 (1957)
14. Eckstein, E., König, O., Scholz, B.: Code instruction selection based on SSA-graphs. In: Krall, A. (ed.) SCOPES 2003. LNCS, vol. 2826, pp. 49–65. Springer, Heidelberg (2003). https://doi.org/10.1007/978-3-540-39920-9_5
15. Scholz, B., Eckstein, E.: Register Allocation for Irregular Architectures (2002)
16. Anderson, A., Gregg, D.: Optimal DNN Primitive Selection with Partitioned Boolean Quadratic Programming (2018)
17. Dean, J.: TensorFlow (2016). https://autodiff-workshop.github.io/
18. Karypis, G., Kumar, V.: Metis: Software package for partitioning unstructured graphs, partitioning meshes, and computing fill-reducing orderings of sparse matrices (1998)
19. Shulman, J.: Optimizing Expectations: From Deep Reinforcement Learning to Stochastic Computation Graphs (2016)
20. Pham, H., Guan, M.Y., Zoph, B., Le, Q.V., Dean, J.: Efficient neural architecture search with parameter sharing (2018)
21. Karypis, G.: Metis–unstructured graph partitioning and sparse matrix ordering system (1995)
22. Kohler, W.H.: A preliminary evaluation of the critical path method for scheduling tasks on multiprocessor systems. IEEE Trans. Comput. **100**(12), 1235–1238 (1975)
23. Topcuoglu, H., Hariri, S., Wu, M.-Y.: Performance-effective and low-complexity task scheduling for heterogeneous computing. IEEE Trans. Parallel Distrib. Syst. **13**(3), 260–274 (2002)
24. Kwok, Y.-K., Ahmad, I.: Dynamic critical-path scheduling: an effective technique for allocating task graphs to multiprocessors. IEEE Trans. Parallel Distrib. Syst. **7**(5), 506–521 (1996)
25. Seide, F., Fu, H., Droppo, J., Li, G., Yu, D.: 1-bit stochastic gradient descent and its application to data-parallel distributed training of speech DNNs (2014)
26. Zhou, S., Ni, Z., Zhou, X., Wen, H., Wu, Y., Zou, Y.: Dorefa-net: Training low bitwidth convolutional neural networks with low bitwidth gradients (2016)
27. Strom, N.: Scalable distributed DNN training using commodity GPU cloud computing
28. Krizhevsky, A.: One weird trick for parallelizing convolutional neural network (2014)

29. Paul, G.: Allen School of Computer Science & Engineering. University of Washington, Amazon AI team (2017). https://tvm.ai/2017/10/06/nnvm-compiler-announcement.html
30. Rotem, N., Fix, J., Abdulrasool, S., et al.: Glow: Graph Lowering Compiler Techniques for Neural Networks (2018)
31. Wei, R., Schwartz, L., Adve, V.: DLVM: A Modern Compiler Infrastructure for Deep Learning Systems (2018)

Skipping CNN Convolutions Through Efficient Memoization

Rafael Fão de Moura[1(✉)], Paulo C. Santos[1], João Paulo C. de Lima[1], Marco A. Z. Alves[2], Antonio C. S. Beck[1], and Luigi Carro[1]

[1] Informatics Institute, Federal University of Rio Grande do Sul, Porto Alegre, Brazil
rfmoura@inf.ufrgs.br

[2] Department of Informatics, Federal University of Paraná, Curitiba, Brazil

Abstract. Convolutional Neural Networks (CNNs) have become a *de-facto* standard for image and video recognition. However, current software and hardware implementations targeting convolutional operations still lack embracing energy budget constraints due to the CNN intensive data processing behavior. This paper proposes a software-based memoization technique to skip entire convolution calculations. We demonstrate that, by grouping output values within proximity-based clusters, it is possible to reduce by hundreds of times the amount of memory necessary to store all the tables. Also, we present a table mapping scheme to index the input set of each convolutional layer to its output value. Our experimental results show that for a YOLOv3-tiny CNN, it is possible to achieve a speedup up to 3.5× while reducing the energy consumption to 22% of the baseline with an accuracy loss of 7.4%.

Keywords: Convolutional Neural Networks · Computation reuse · Memoization

1 Introduction

Supported by advancements in machine learning algorithms, Convolutional Neural Networks (CNNs) have been broadly used in modern applications, such as image classification [16], speech recognition [6], and natural language processing [3] tasks. In addition to the algorithmic advances, efforts in architectural research have also contributed to make feasible the employment of CNNs, ranging from General Purpose Processors (GPPs) and Graphics Processing Units (GPUs) to custom accelerator designs [2,18,19]. Meanwhile, an increasing interest in migrating the execution of CNNs to embedded systems is leveraged by the Internet of Things (IoT) era, as already seen in self-driving vehicles, audio, and image recognition software running into mobile devices. However, current hardware designs used to accelerate CNNs execution still have concerns related to energy consumption and do not entirely fulfill the energy constraints of embedded systems [9].

A significant part of the execution time of a CNN, as well as its energy consumption, is spent performing convolution operations [10]. At their core, a

D. N. Pnevmatikatos et al. (Eds.): SAMOS 2019, LNCS 11733, pp. 65–76, 2019.
https://doi.org/10.1007/978-3-030-27562-4_5

convolution is composed fundamentally by multidimensional dot product operations on a data streaming. Thereby, the most costly operations involved in a convolution are the data movements and the floating-point multiplications and additions [9]. Therefore, such convolutional kernels must be accelerated, either by reducing the time of such operations or by skipping them, to improve the overall CNNs execution time.

Meanwhile, CNNs present characteristics of data compression along with their convolutional layers. For instance, to perform inference over one input image in *YoloV3-tiny* CNN [16], nearly 10 GB of temporary data is generated and processed between different layers. However, one can observe that, for a universe of N input images, the classifier vector output will be represented into 320 Bytes. Since the amount of data generated and processed is thousands of times higher than the output size, it is expected that there would be high levels of redundancy in the intermediate data. Thereby, the data redundancy can be exploited to improve performance and energy efficiency. Such behavior makes CNNs suitable for applying memoization techniques.

Memoization is an old technique, which has been used to shorten the runtime of applications [20]. This technique works by keeping in storage results of previous execution for future reuse, thus saving time and energy if the algorithmic way demands more than a lookup search. In the past years, memoization approaches have been proposed at different levels of implementation and abstraction, varying from function-level in software to Functional Unit (FU)-level in hardware [5,20]. Employing the memoization technique can be suitable for accelerating CNNs since there are many opportunities for computing reuse. Moreover, by using memoization, both energy and performance improvements can be achieved as already presented in recent literature [5,9]. Nevertheless, memoization-based approaches have a trade-off between performance savings and data storage size. The memoization overheads come due to storing previous results in a table and looking up that table at every next execution. Since the cost per lookup table access is proportional to its size, identifying the most suitable memoization technique is essential to achieve the best relation between performance and table access time.

To overcome the limitations mentioned above, we propose a software-based memoization technique to replace the entire convolution computations by a single lookup table search implemented as a hash table. Although there are reuse opportunities in the kernel of CNNs, we demonstrate that measuring the table sizes necessary to keep all the different output values for each convolutional layer in a *YOLOv3-tiny* CNN [16] reveals a costly amount of memory. Further, we present a methodology to reduce the output table sizes by grouping the output values into range-based clusters according to their proximity values, which drastically reduces the amount of memory necessary to keep the convolution values.

To ensure the effectiveness and correctness of computing reuse and memoization, we propose an indexing table scheme to map each set of inputs in each convolutional layer to its corresponding output value. By implementing these techniques in the open-source *Darknet* framework [15], it is possible to achieve a performance speedup up to 3.5×, while reducing the energy consumption by a factor of 4.5× by allowing an accuracy loss of 7.4% due to output values clustering.

The main contributions of this paper are listed as follows:

1. We explore computation reuse and memoization as a software-based technique to improve CNNs execution.
2. We propose a technique to reduce the amount of memory necessary to store the lookup tables by grouping output values into range-based clusters making memoization feasible for the CNNs realm.
3. In contrast to previous works, we replace entire convolution computations by lookup table search with low accuracy loss.

The rest of this paper is organized as follows: Sect. 2 presents a general overview of CNNs layout and processing and also discusses the state-of-art hardware and software techniques to accelerate CNNs execution. The proposed technique and their implications are presented in Sect. 3. Section 4 introduces the methodology, experimental setups, and results used to evaluate this work. Finally, a brief conclusion and future works are drawn in Sect. 5.

2 Background and Related Work

In this section, the basics of CNNs are presented. After, a review of the state-of-art researches regarding CNNs acceleration is done.

2.1 CNN Basics

A CNN performs feature extraction using series of *convolutional layers* and then it is followed by *classification layers* that analyze features and classify input images. Figure 1 shows an example of a convolutional layer. Each layer takes as input RxC values distributed along N *channels* (or *input feature maps*) and *convolves* it with M sets of $NxKxK$ filters generating M output feature maps with $R'xC'$ values each. The filters represent the weights that are previously obtained in the training phase using a learning algorithm such as back-propagation. For each filter of the M sets, the convolution is performed by sliding the filter across the input feature map according to a stride value. At each overlapping of the filter over the input feature map, the values are multiplied and accumulated together, giving one value to the output feature map. Generally, after a convolution, an activation function is applied on the output feature maps, and, occasionally, it is also followed by a subsampling operation [1].

In general, the layout of a CNNs is composed of many layers in which the output of the previous layer is the input of the subsequent layer. As the depth of the network increases, higher recognition accuracy can be achieved. For instance, state-of-the-art CNNs, such as GoogLeNet [21] and YOLOv3 [16], have 20 and 75 convolutional layers, respectively.

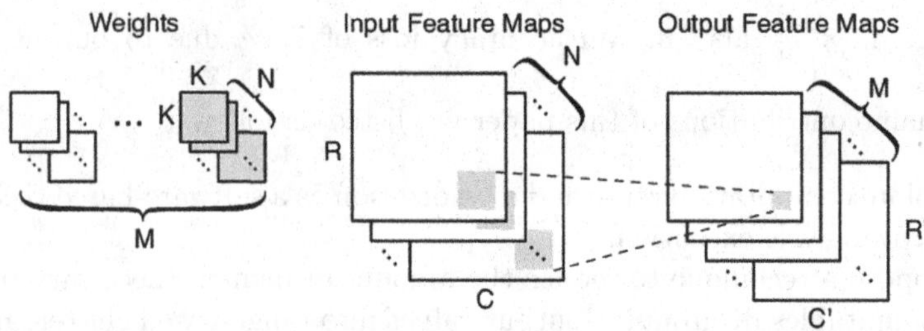

Fig. 1. Parts of a convolutional layer. Adapted from [1]

2.2 Software-Based Techniques for Efficient CNN Execution

Past works have shown different approaches for obtaining small networks by shrinking, factorizing, or compressing pre-trained networks [4], as well as for reducing the number of computation or memory access by pruning, quantizing, or decreasing the precision of a network [8]. Although novel CNN architectures have been proposed to provide smaller and faster models for mobile and embedded vision applications, such as MobileNet [7], we focus on the optimization of existing CNN architectures to further improve performance under the same hardware.

Recently, [22] has proposed an unified framework to compress and accelerate CNN inference through product quantization. This technique exploits opportunities of replacing inner product computation by addition operation if inner products between the input and quantized weights have been computed in advance. In another study, [12] proposes modifications to Winograd-based CNN architecture to reduce the number of multiplications by combining two methods: Winograd's minimal filtering algorithm and network pruning. The authors have moved *ReLU* operation into Winograd domain to increase weight sparsity, and then pruned the weights in the Winograd domain to exploit weight sparsity.

Afterward, previous works indicate that reuse opportunities can deliver efficient CNN models by exploiting data redundancy and similarity if we allow a little accuracy loss [12,22]. Though, most of the past works have a common drawback since they require retraining or modifying the network topology. Also, most of these characteristics related to data redundancy and operation reuse have been explored in hardware accelerators, as described in the next section.

2.3 Computation Reuse-Based Accelerators

In the past years, several accelerators were proposed to explore data redundancy, weight/input similarity, and reuse opportunities in convolutional neural networks. The study presented by [17] reuses computation from one execution of the CNN to the next and applies the reuse taking into account the similarity found in the inputs of each layer. The authors have applied linear quantization of inputs to increase the redundancy, which favors the efficiency of the proposed mechanism, with a minimal impact on accuracy. [5] exploits weight repetition to reuse CNN sub-computations (dot product results), to reduce off-chip memory reads and also to compress network model size. They propose the Unique Weight CNN Accelerator, which unifies two opportunities to eliminate multiplication and memory reads: by factorizing dot products as sum-of-products-of-sum expression, and later by reusing the partial product when the filters slide.

In another proposal, [14] introduces a methodology to replace CNN multiplication with lookup searches in an associative memory. The authors provide a theoretical analysis of the additive error and present an algorithm to minimize it. However, the gains depend on the associative memory blocks to reduce the power and execution time of floating point units. Instead, our proposal to reuse a coarse-grained computation (a full convolution) can leverage the use of GPPs.

Following the same idea of [9,14] explores computation reuse through a reconfigurable Bloom filter unit that supports approximate set membership queries with a tunable rate of errors to store frequent computation patterns and return the products without executing the operands on energy-intensive Floating-Point Units (FPUs). The authors implemented the Bloom filter unit with resistive memory elements to provide energy efficient storage of common multiplication patterns in each layer of a Neural Network (NN).

All these approaches that employ memoization for convolution products depend on custom hardware, and the improvement provided may not justify the costs to produce them. The main drawback of multiplication reuse resides on increased energy consumption, since a 16-bit fixed-point multiplication in 32 nm is 0.4 pJ, whereas the corresponding table lookup costs 2.5 pJ, considering a 32K-entry 16-bit SRAM [5,13]. Instead, our proposal to reuse a coarse-grained computation can provide energy savings by reducing the amount of table lookups even on GPPs. Therefore, when we master the technique of reusing convolutional operations, the benefits come virtually for free, and it is a much easier way than try to brute force optimize the hardware.

3 Proposed Approach

In this section, we explore computation reuse opportunities in CNNs by replacing the execution of entire convolution calculations by memory lookups. Based on this idea, we propose a hash table scheme to associate an arbitrary input with its corresponding output value for each layer's filter. Further, we measure the amount of memory necessary to store all the tables, and we develop a proximity range-based clustering mechanism to reduce the table sizes making feasible the employment of memoization in the CNN realm.

3.1 Replacing CNN Calculations with Memory Accesses

Since data redundancy and data similarity are found in the inputs, weights and feature maps for inferring a batch of images, the memoization technique can be considered as an alternative for the convolutional execution model. To avoid costly multiplications and additions, we associate every pair of input (I_i) and weight (W_k) producing a single output (O_{ik}) of a feature map in lookup tables. The implementation of a CNN with a reduced number of convolution operations relies on an offline memoization mechanism that generates these tables to be used at running time.

Figure 2 illustrates both the offline analysis and online execution mechanisms. The flowchart of the memoization *Offline analysis flow* described in Fig. 2 comprises two main execution blocks: the *CNN execution*, and the *Memoization profiler*. First, we run all the memoization training set of images, and we store the inputs and their corresponding outputs for all convolutional layer's filters.

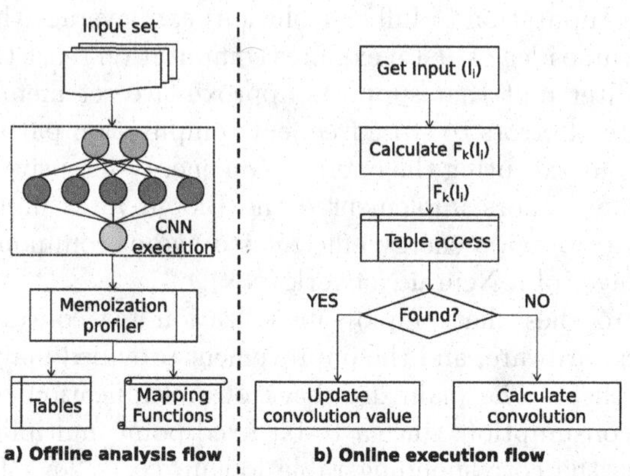

Fig. 2. The proposed approach depicted in two flowcharts: (a) offline analysis and online execution flow.

As soon as we have gathered all the convolutional values $\{I_i, W_k, O_{ik}\}$ from the execution of a memoization set, the *Memoization profiler* processes the collected data and generates two output files: the output *Tables* and the *Mapping Functions* files. The output *Tables* are hash tables that enclose all the convolutional values generated during the *CNN execution*. The *Mapping Functions* are indexing functions in charge of coordinating the appropriate mapping for any input to its corresponding output. From the set theory perspective, the convolution operation regarding each weight set and input can be seen as a bijective function $F(I_i, W_k)$ that convolves an input I_i over the filter weight W_k. To ensure the correct index mapping for any input to its corresponding output, we create a function that reflects the same bijective function behavior in the convolution operation.

Now that we have the hash tables with convolution values in memory, the execution flow of each convolutional layer follows the *Online execution flow* described in Fig. 2. First, the input is read, and we apply a Mapping Function to calculate a table index. As soon as we have a table index associated with the input value, we try to retrieve the entry for a convolution output from the hash table. If an entry is found in the table, the corresponding position of the feature map is updated with the value retrieved. Otherwise, we must calculate the convolution value associated with the current input.

Though, it is only viable to memoize a subset of a large dataset like MSCOCO, which provides a representative part of the convolutional operations. Even using a memoization set of 500 random images, the offline mechanism generates huge tables, which requires up 12 GB of storage memory.

3.2 Redundant Data on CNNs

Storing all the outputs for any memoization set as presented in the previous section can be a limiting factor for this implementation since it is a one-to-one relationship of $(I_{\mathrm{i}}, W_{\mathrm{k}})$ and O_{ik}, which may introduce repeated entries in the lookup table. However, inputs tend to present redundancy within a single picture and even among different images that generate repeated convolution results. The goal of exploiting this inherent redundancy is not only to reduce the table size but also to improve spatial and temporal locality, thus benefiting the execution on CPUs.

To illustrate the above-mentioned data redundancy, Table 1 shows the computation reuse percentage to run different numbers of images from MSCOCO dataset [11] along YOLOv3-tiny [16] convolutional layers. For instance, by analyzing a single image (second column), the first convolutional layer presents up to 26% of the convolutions that can be reused from previous convolutions. That is, the same pattern of input I_{i} and weight W_{k} are repeatedly found in the first layer producing the output pattern of O_{ik}, which can be replaced by a single table search. Table 1 also indicates that, as the number of images in the batch increases, the reuse ratio for each convolutional layer grows too. Such behavior is essential to provide scalability to this CNN implementation. Thus, by eliminating the redundant entries in the offline analysis, we found that the 3 GB of storage memory is needed instead of the former 12 GB.

Table 1. Computation reuse percentage running different numbers of images in YOLOv3-tiny CNN.

Convolutional Layer	Number of Images: 1	10	100	1k
	Compute Reuse (%)			
#1	26	34	68	94
#2	23	29	52	88
#3	21	25	44	83
#4	15	19	32	71
#5	6	11	20	56
#6	0	1	6	35
#7	0	1	9	53
#8	0	0	3	22
#9	0	1	6	40
#10	0	1	11	57
#11	0	0	2	15
#12	0	1	10	54
#13	1	5	36	81

3.3 Range-Based Clustering to Reduce Lookup Tables

As described in the previous section, we measured the amount of memory required to store all the unique pairs $\{I_{\mathrm{i}}, W_{\mathrm{k}}\}$ and the corresponding output O_{ik} to create the relationship $\{I_{\mathrm{i}}, W_{\mathrm{k}}\} \rightarrow O_{\mathrm{ik}}$ in the table. However, the amount of memory to store different entries remains prohibitive to CPUs, indicating that we have to find a way to reduce even more the table size. To make the proposed memoization technique feasible, we introduce a range-based clustering mechanism that groups entries by its proximity and provides smaller lookup tables.

Our technique groups convolution values within ranges in a four-step procedure, which requires modification to the *Memoization profiler* presented in Fig. 2. Firstly, all the output values for each layer in the CNN are sorted in ascending order. Then, we create clusters that minimize the distance among the entries. Each number in a cluster is enclosed within an interval defined by a bottom value and a top value. The top values are determined by multiplying the bottom values by a pre-defined range (typically a percentage). Thirdly, we replace all the convolution values inside each cluster by their average value. Finally, as a result of the clustering, both the *Tables* and the *Mapping Functions* in Fig. 2 are updated to generate the correct output values.

As a result of the mechanism proposed to reduce the table sizes, Fig. 3 presents a tunable accuracy correlation among the table sizes, and proximity values, and their respective accuracy levels. For the four range distances (0.1% to 1%) illustrated in Fig. 3, the table sizes vary from 220 MB to 4.35 MB in contrast to 12 GB, when none table reduction technique is employed, and 3 GB, when repeated entries are removed. As we have approximated the convolution results by reducing the *Output set* size, one can observe an accuracy drop over the original CNN detection. The normalized accuracy over the original CNN execution varies from 98.9% to 92.5% when the range distance is increased from 0.1% to 1%.

4 Methodology and Evaluation

To evaluate the proposed mechanism, we implemented the algorithm flow described in Fig. 2 in Darknet framework [15]. We used a random subset of the MSCOCO dataset [11] as input for the offline memoization technique of the YOLOv3-tiny model [16]. Then, another random subset of MSCOCO dataset was used in the execution, which runs the modified Darknet coupled with our memoization technique and YOLOv3-tiny.

Further, we ran all experimental scenarios in the system described in Table 2 to measure the execution time. We estimated the accuracy of our implementation by analyzing the *confusion matrix* of YOLOv3-tiny's predicted classes. To compare our experiments, we took the original Yolov3-tiny implementation and predictions accuracy as the baseline.

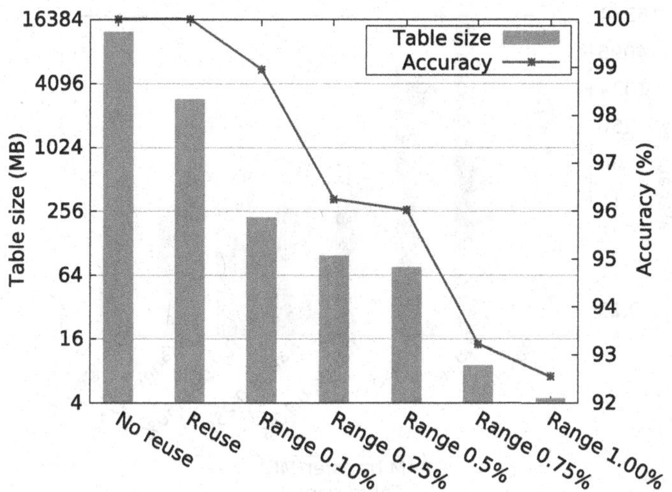

Fig. 3. Table sizes and accuracy loss.

4.1 Performance and Energy Consumption Evaluation

To obtain a significant performance on traditional CPUs, we have to find a sweet spot between CPU's memory performance and table size, as well as considering the trade-off between table size and accuracy previously illustrated in Fig. 3. As our proposal of using memoization aims to replace multiplications and additions by lookup searches, it is expected an increase of main memory accesses when compared to the original CNN execution.

Figure 4 shows the absolute values for the amount of stored data and main memory access for each experiment. By storing all generated data, the ***No reuse*** experiment demands nearly 12 GB of memory space, while it requires 3.2 GB of data moved from main memory to the Last-Level Cache (LLC). On the other hand, by applying the proposed technique, the demand for memory space and data transferring decreases. By removing the redundant entries (***Reuse*** in Fig. 4) we can reduce the amount of data placed in memory from 12 GB to 3 GB, though this approach still needs 2.8 GB of data transferring.

Table 2. System configuration.

CPU processor
Intel(R) Core(TM) i5-7500 CPU; 4 cores; 3.40GHz;
AVX2 Instruction Set Capable;
32KB IL1 cache; 32KB DL1 cache;
1MB L2 cache;
6MB L3 cache;
Total Power - 65W;
DRAM
DDR4 2133MHz;
Total DRAM Size 16GB;
Total Power - 6.4W;

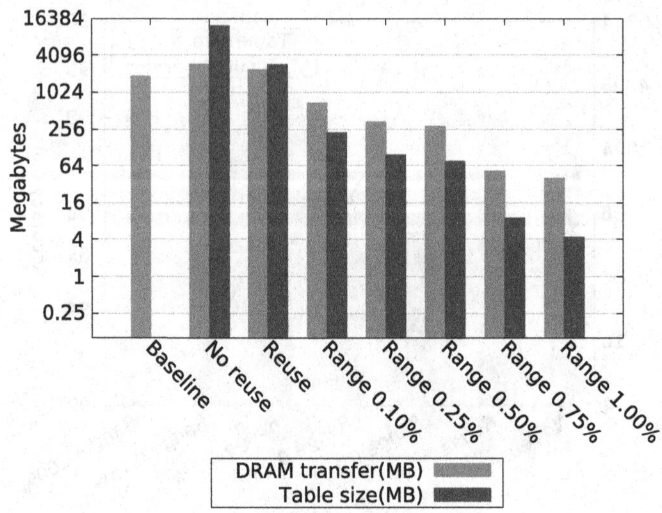

Fig. 4. Table sizes and DRAM transfers.

Further, by applying the proposed technique and clustering the values within the range of 1% (***Range 1.00%*** in Fig. 4), the demanded amount of data drops to 4.2 MB. This aggressive reduction on the memory footprint allows more efficient exploration of the cache memories, which directly reflects on the data movement behavior, thus reducing DRAM transfer from 3.5 GB to 52 MB.

Influenced by the table size and the amount of data moved from the main memory, the performance and energy consumption are presented in Fig. 5. Orthogonally, the accuracy of the experimented CNN is dependent on the representativeness of data in lookup tables.

In comparison to the baseline, the ***No Reuse*** experiment presents a negative impact due to the increasing data access, as presented in Fig. 5. This impact leads to a performance reduction of 23%, although energy consumption has barely decreased. Considering the ***Reuse*** experiment, due to the elimination of repeated entries, the performance is improved by 2.3×. In both cases, ***No Reuse*** and ***Reuse*** achieves 100% of original CNN accuracy, which is possible due to the maintenance of all original values. However, the amount of memory demanded by this configuration becomes a significant drawback.

The experiments presented by ***Range 0.10%***, ***Range 0.25%***, ***Range 0.50%***, ***Range 0.75%***, ***Range 1.00%*** show a performance improvement of 2.3×, 2.8×, 3.1×, 3.4×, and 3.5×, respectively. Similarly, the energy consumption is reduced in 72%, 74%, 75%, 77%, and 78%, respectively. Despite the positive impact on performance and energy, the accuracy is reduced due to the lack of data representativeness in the tables. Thus, in Fig. 5 it is possible to observe the impact of different *Ranges* on accuracy, which varies from 98.9% to 92.5% over the original YOLOv3-tiny accuracy.

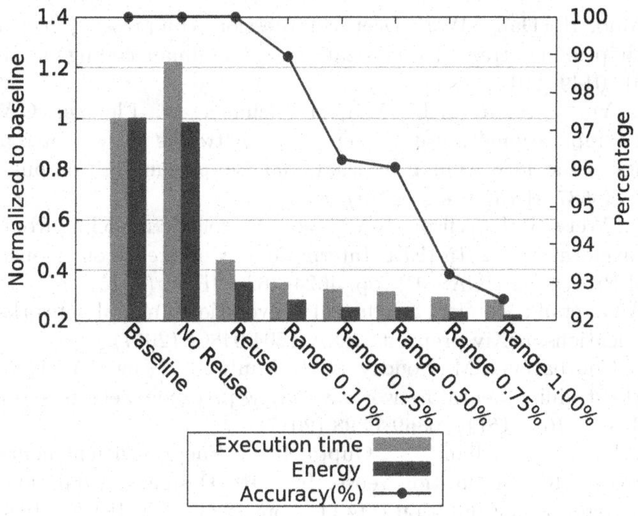

Fig. 5. Speedup and energy consumption normalized to baseline.

5 Conclusion and Future Work

In this work, we exploit data redundancy and proximity in neural networks leveraged by a software-based memoization technique to skip entire convolution operations. We designed a workflow that analyzes a training set and generates hash tables for future reuse in the running time. By using a range-based clustering, we make the size of the lookup tables smaller, at a cost to the accuracy of prediction. Our experimental results show that our implementation can improve the execution time by 3.5× over the baseline CNN running a YOLOv3-tiny model. We have shown how the performance improvement provided by our technique is strictly dependent on a tunable accuracy loss. Thus, the energy savings can be improved by a factor of 4.5×, at the cost of 7.4% of accuracy loss over the original CNN execution. In future works, we intend to investigate the proposed technique on larger CNN models, and also investigate whether the variances of data set and CNN models influence the opportunities for memoization.

Acknowledgements. This work was supported by CAPES, CNPQ and FAPERGS.

References

1. Alwani, M., Chen, H., Ferdman, M., Milder, P.: Fused-layer CNN accelerators. In: The 49th Annual IEEE/ACM International Symposium on Microarchitecture, p. 22. IEEE Press (2016)
2. Choquette, J., Giroux, O., Foley, D.: Volta: performance and programmability. IEEE Micro **38**(2), 42–52 (2018)
3. Dauphin, Y.N., Fan, A., Auli, M., Grangier, D.: Language modeling with gated convolutional networks. In: Proceedings of the 34th International Conference on Machine Learning, vol. 70, pp. 933–941. JMLR.org (2017)

4. Han, S., Mao, H., Dally, W.J.: Deep compression: compressing deep neural networks with pruning, trained quantization and huffman coding. arXiv preprint. arXiv:1510.00149 (2015)
5. Hegde, K., Yu, J., Agrawal, R., Yan, M., Pellauer, M., Fletcher, C.W.: UCNN: exploiting computational reuse in deep neural networks via weight repetition. In: Proceedings of the 45th Annual International Symposium on Computer Architecture, pp. 674–687. IEEE Press (2018)
6. Hoshen, Y., Weiss, R.J., Wilson, K.W.: Speech acoustic modeling from raw multichannel waveforms. In: 2015 IEEE International Conference on Acoustics, Speech and Signal Processing (ICASSP), pp. 4624–4628. IEEE (2015)
7. Howard, A.G., et al.: Mobilenets: efficient convolutional neural networks for mobile vision applications. arXiv preprint. arXiv:1704.04861 (2017)
8. Hubara, I., Courbariaux, M., Soudry, D., El-Yaniv, R., Bengio, Y.: Quantized neural networks: training neural networks with low precision weights and activations. J. Mach. Learn. Res. **18**(1), 6869–6898 (2017)
9. Jiao, X., Akhlaghi, V., Jiang, Y., Gupta, R.K.: Energy-efficient neural networks using approximate computation reuse. In: 2018 Design, Automation & Test in Europe Conference & Exhibition (DATE), pp. 1223–1228. IEEE (2018)
10. Jouppi, N.P., et al.: In-datacenter performance analysis of a tensor processing unit. In: 2017 ACM/IEEE 44th Annual International Symposium on Computer Architecture (ISCA), pp. 1–12. IEEE (2017)
11. Lin, T.-Y., et al.: Microsoft COCO: common objects in context. In: Fleet, D., Pajdla, T., Schiele, B., Tuytelaars, T. (eds.) ECCV 2014. LNCS, vol. 8693, pp. 740–755. Springer, Cham (2014). https://doi.org/10.1007/978-3-319-10602-1_48
12. Liu, X., Pool, J., Han, S., Dally, W.J.: Efficient sparse-winograd convolutional neural networks. In: International Conference on Learning Representations (ICLR) (2018)
13. Muralimanohar, N., Balasubramonian, R., Jouppi, N.P.: Cacti 6.0: a tool to model large caches. HP laboratories, pp. 22–31 (2009)
14. Razlighi, M.S., Imani, M., Koushanfar, F., Rosing, T.: LookNN: Neural network with no multiplication. In: Proceedings of the Conference on Design, Automation & Test in Europe, pp. 1779–1784. European Design and Automation Association (2017)
15. Redmon, J.: Darknet: open source neural networks in C (2013–2016). http://pjreddie.com/darknet/
16. Redmon, J., Farhadi, A.: Yolov3: an incremental improvement. arXiv preprint. arXiv:1804.02767 (2018)
17. Riera, M., Arnau, J.M., González, A.: Computation reuse in DNNs by exploiting input similarity. In: Proceedings of the 45th Annual International Symposium on Computer Architecture, pp. 57–68. IEEE Press (2018)
18. Shafiee, A., et al.: ISAAC: a convolutional neural network accelerator with in-situ analog arithmetic in crossbars. ACM SIGARCH Comput. Archit. News **44**(3), 14–26 (2016)
19. Sodani, A.: Knights landing (KNL): 2nd generation Intel® xeon phi processor. In: 2015 IEEE Hot Chips 27 Symposium (HCS), pp. 1–24. IEEE (2015)
20. Suresh, A., Rohou, E., Seznec, A.: Compile-time function memoization. In: Proceedings of the 26th International Conference on Compiler Construction, pp. 45–54. ACM (2017)
21. Szegedy, C., et al.: Going deeper with convolutions. In: Proceedings of the IEEE Conference on Computer Vision and Pattern Recognition, pp. 1–9 (2015)
22. Wu, J., Leng, C., Wang, Y., Hu, Q., Cheng, J.: Quantized convolutional neural networks for mobile devices. In: Proceedings of the IEEE Conference on Computer Vision and Pattern Recognition, pp. 4820–4828 (2016)

Fully Distributed Deep Learning Inference on Resource-Constrained Edge Devices

Rafael Stahl[1(✉)], Zhuoran Zhao[2], Daniel Mueller-Gritschneder[1], Andreas Gerstlauer[2], and Ulf Schlichtmann[1]

[1] Technical University of Munich, Munich, Germany
{r.stahl,daniel.mueller,ulf.schlichtmann}@tum.de
[2] University of Texas at Austin, Austin, USA
zhuoran@utexas.edu, gerstl@ece.utexas.edu

Abstract. Performing inference tasks of deep learning applications on IoT edge devices ensures privacy of input data and can result in shorter latency when compared to a cloud solution. As most edge devices are memory- and compute-constrained, they cannot store and execute a complete Deep Neural Network (DNN). One possible solution is to distribute the DNN across multiple edge devices. For a complete distribution, both fully-connected and feature- and weight-intensive convolutional layers need to be partitioned to reduce the amount of computation and data on each resource-constrained edge device. At the same time, resulting communication overheads need to be considered. Existing work on distributed DNN execution can not support all types of networks and layers or does not account for layer fusion opportunities to reduce communication. In this paper, we jointly optimize memory, computation and communication demands for distributed execution of complete neural networks covering all layers. This is achieved through techniques that combine both feature and weight partitioning with a communication-aware layer fusion approach to enable holistic optimization across layers. For a given number of edge devices, the schemes are applied jointly such that the amount of data to be exchanged between devices is minimized to optimize run time.

Experimental results for a simulation of six edge devices on 100 Mbit connections running the YOLOv2 DNN model show that the schemes evenly balance the memory footprint between devices. The integration of layer fusion additionally leads to a reduction of communication demands by 14.8%. This results in run time speed-up of the inference task by 1.15x compared to partitioning without fusing.

Keywords: Deep learning · Distributed computing · IoT

This work is partly funded by National Science Foundation (NSF) grant NSF CNS-1421642 in the USA and the German ministry of education and research (BMBF) under grant number 01IS17028F as part of the ITEA3 project COMPACT with reference number 16018.

D. N. Pnevmatikatos et al. (Eds.): SAMOS 2019, LNCS 11733, pp. 77–90, 2019.
https://doi.org/10.1007/978-3-030-27562-4_6

1 Introduction

In the context of the Internet of Things (IoT), deep learning has emerged as a valuable tool to process complex or noisy sensory input at high quality. A Deep Neural Network (DNN) is trained upfront with high computational effort with a large input data set. After training is completed, the DNN can be given previously unseen input data and will, e.g., return a classification result. The latter task is called inference and is the focus of this paper. Inference is also a resource-intensive operation since a large amount of input or intermediate data and trained weights have to be stored and many computational operations are required. Therefore, it is not possible to perform this task on a single small edge device. While this could be solved by deploying more powerful edge devices, the cost of such a solution is prohibitive. Another possible solution is off-loading of the inference to powerful servers in the cloud. However, this approach introduces privacy issues concerning the input data and requires high bandwidth to the cloud [3]. Other approaches shrink and prune the total size of the DNN, but this reduces the model's accuracy and might make it no longer viable for a given problem [2,7].

An orthogonal solution is the utilization of multiple edge devices to cooperate on executing the inference task. In many IoT applications, a large number of edge devices is available and connected with each other via some local network. When inputs arrive rarely, most devices are idle. A device receiving an input can use the idle time of the other edge devices to solve the inference task offering a low-cost but efficient solution. Existing approaches for distributed execution of DNN inference tasks across clusters of edge devices, however, often only consider a subset of DNN layers and still require a powerful gateway device to execute other parts of a network [11]. Other approaches [6] are able to distribute an entire network, but have limitations in the type and size of layers that can be fitted, and they do not consider opportunities to improve communication demands further.

In this paper, we investigate methods for distributed execution of complete DNNs covering all types of layers while jointly optimizing for computation, memory and communication demands. We build on our prior work [11] that introduced an approach for memory- and communication-aware partitioning and fusing of feature-dominated early convolutional layers. We extend this approach with novel methods to partition convolutional and fully-connected layers whose weight data size dominates their input and output data size. This allows partitions for all layers to be executed in a parallel fashion on several small edge devices to enable a fully distributed inference. The computation and memory footprint of processing and storing feature and weight data is evenly distributed over all devices, such that the DNN inference task can be scaled down for any size of IoT edge device. A major problem with partitioning is that the inputs and outputs of these layers need to be communicated from one edge device to the other. We further present a new scheme to minimize this communication overhead by enabling fusing across all types of layers. In detail, the contributions of this paper are:

(1) A memory- and communication-aware partitioning scheme for fully-connected and weight-intensive convolutional layers that, when combined with prior schemes on feature-intensive convolutional layer partitioning, enables complete distribution of arbitrary state-of-the-art DNNs.
(2) A new method that can fuse fully-connected or convolutional layers such that each fused layer partition can be processed on a single device without the need to communicate intermediate data between layers with other edge devices.
(3) An integer linear programming (ILP) formulation to identify the best partitioning and fusing scheme for a given DNN. The scheme minimizes the communication demand of exchanging input and output data between devices. This leads to a significant reduction in inference run time, which strongly depends on communication time.

Experimental results show that the memory footprint is scaled down evenly with the number of available edge devices. Optimizing the partitioning schemes with layer fusion leads to 14.8% reduced communication demand, while executing the inference task for the YOLOv2 DNN on six edge devices with 100 Mbit connections. This results in a run time speed-up by 1.15x compared to only partitioning the outputs.

2 Related Work

Fully distributed inference is tackled by MoDNN [6]. MoDNN distributes a DNN across multiple mobile phones connected via a wireless network. The approach also targets the distribution of both the layer input and output data as well as the weight data across devices. While they are able to partition weights, they use an approach that focuses heavily on sparse fully-connected layers (i.e., fully-connected structures, where some weights are zero). It is not optimized for communication in dense layers, and weight-intensive convolutional layers are not addressed. Furthermore, they process networks in a layer-by-layer fashion, which requires all devices to synchronize and exchange data after each layer. Their method could be combined with the layer fusion proposed in this work to minimze communication overhead after adding additional constraints.

Other works approach the execution of an inference task on edge devices from a different angle by pruning and quantizing the model [2,7]. Yet another line of work has focused on distributing different parts of a model to different tiers of processing power with the possibility of early exits that would make them edge-only [10]. Both of these are orthogonal methods to the one proposed here.

The distribution of the model was also tackled in a different context for hardware acceleration of DNNs in [1]. The central idea of that work is to fuse the first few layers of the network in order to reduce total data transfer to and from the chip. In that work, the memory-constrained device is the accelerator instead of an IoT edge device. Fusing optimizations for the accelerator are only investigated for the first layers. By contrast, the fusing approach presented in this paper targets the later network layers, for which the weight data dominates. Both techniques can possibly be combined.

The work in this paper builds on our prior work on adaptive distributed deep learning inference in clusters with dynamic availability of edge nodes [11]. This prior work presented a fusing approach for multiple layers with focus on data partitioning in the first layers. However, it does not consider weight partitioning. At some depth in the DNN, it is no longer possible for that approach to store the large weight data on a single device. This requires later layers to be evaluated on a central powerful gateway edge device that has sufficient memory. These constraints are removed by the approach presented in this work, enabling a fully distributed inference on a set of memory-constrained edge devices.

3 Background on DNNs

The basic DNN inference structure for image recognition can be described as follows: The input of the DNN is an image with each pixel of each color channel being represented by a neuron. It is processed by a number of convolutional layers that apply multiple learned filter functions to their layer input to produce a set of feature maps with each feature map corresponding to a learned filter. These feature maps should capture different characteristics of the image. With a high number of filters in each layer, the number of feature maps typically grows with each convolutional layer. Therefore, aside from convolutional layers there are also pooling layers, which shrink the width and height of feature maps in order to allow a higher number of features to be extracted. The number of intermediate feature maps increases while they loose resolution. As a result, the input and output data dominate the memory usage for the first layers of a DNN, and in the later layers the weights dominate. These later layers are in the focus of this work. Distribution strategies for early layers are described in our prior work [11].

If the DNN has just the task of classifying what it sees, the last few layers typically consist of fully-connected layers as seen in AlexNet [4] and VGGNet [9]. Another possible task is object localization in the image along with classification of multiple objects. In that case the last few layers will also be convolutional and the network is called a Fully Convolutional Network (FCN) [5]. YOLOv2 [8] is used to evaluate our proposed layer fusion method. YOLOv2 is a FCN that follows the typical data size distribution described above.

3.1 Fully-Connected Layers

A fully-connected layer has the distinctive property that all input neurons are connected to all output neurons. Its operation can be expressed as:

$$b_{k,l} = f\Big(\sum_{m=1}^{M_l} a_{m,l} \cdot w_{m,k,l}\Big), \quad k \in \{1, \ldots, K_l\} \tag{1}$$

where for the l-th layer, $a_{m,l}$ is the m-th element of the vector of input neurons $\mathbf{a}_l \in \mathbb{R}^{M_l}$, $b_{k,l}$ is the k-th element of the vector of output neurons $\mathbf{b}_l \in \mathbb{R}^{K_l}$, $w_{m,k,l}$ is the m,k-th element of the weight matrix $\mathbf{W}_l \in \mathbb{R}^{M_l \times K_l}$ and f is the nonlinear activation function.

For fully-connected layers, the number of weights Q_l that have to be stored determines mainly the memory demand of the inference task. Biases can also be considered weights, but since they are comparably negligible in size, they are not considered for distribution in this work. The computation time is dominated by the number of multiplication operations R_l. For a fully-connected layer, we obtain:

$$Q_l = R_l = K_l \cdot M_l \tag{2}$$

3.2 Convolutional Layers

The input to a convolutional layer are multiple two-dimensional feature maps. For example, an input image is represented as three feature maps, one map for each color channel. Multiple image filters are applied that take all input feature maps into consideration by applying classical image filtering to each of them with a two-dimensional kernel. The resulting images of a single filter are all added up to a single output feature map. Since there are usually multiple filters, the output of convolutional layers are multiple feature maps. The layer's operation can be expressed as:

$$\mathbf{B}_{o,l} = f\Big(\sum_{c=1}^{C_l} \text{corr}(\mathbf{A}_{c,l}, \mathbf{W}_{c,o,l})\Big), \quad o \in \{1, \ldots, O_l\} \tag{3}$$

where the matrix $\mathbf{A}_{c,l}$ is the c-th input feature map of the input tensor $\mathbf{A}_l \in \mathbb{R}^{X_l \times Y_l \times C_l}$, the matrix $\mathbf{B}_{o,l}$ is the o-th input feature map of the output tensor $\mathbf{B}_l \in \mathbb{R}^{X_l \times Y_l \times O_l}$ and the matrix $\mathbf{W}_{c,o,l}$ is the kernel connecting the c-th input feature map with the o-th output feature map. The kernels are elements of the four-dimensional weight tensor $\mathbf{W}_l \in \mathbb{R}^{U_l \times V_l \times C_l \times O_l}$. The activation function is again f. The function $\text{corr}(\mathbf{A}, \mathbf{W})$ computes the two-dimensional cross-correlation, for which the x, y-th element is computed with:

$$\text{corr}(\mathbf{A}, \mathbf{W})_{x,y} = \sum_{(u=-\lfloor \frac{U}{2} \rfloor)}^{\lfloor \frac{U}{2} \rfloor} \sum_{(v=-\lfloor \frac{V}{2} \rfloor)}^{\lfloor \frac{V}{2} \rfloor} a_{x+u,y+v} w_{u,v} \tag{4}$$

The size of the input tensor $\mathbf{A}_l$ is $M_l = X_l \cdot Y_l \cdot C_l$, the size of the output tensor is $K_l = X_l \cdot Y_l \cdot O_l$. The number of weights Q_l to be stored and the number of multiplication operations R_l for a convolutional layer, can be given as:

$$Q_l = U_l \cdot V_l \cdot C_l \cdot O_l, \quad R_l = X_l \cdot Y_l \cdot U_l \cdot V_l \cdot C_l \cdot O_l \tag{5}$$

Convolutional layers of DNNs are very heavy on computational and memory resources, requiring to distribute these layers, if only constrained edge devices are available.

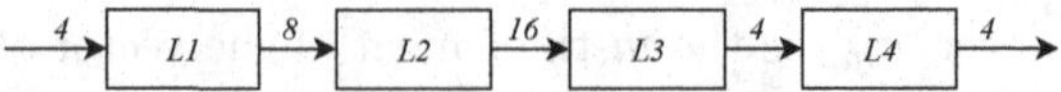

Fig. 1. 4-Layer example on a single device

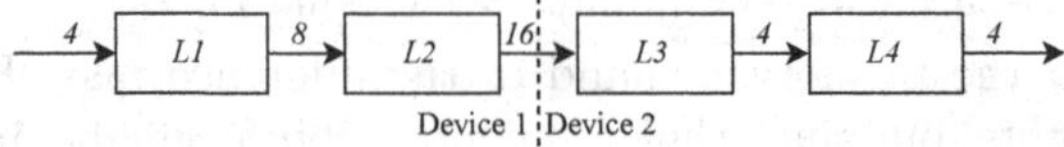

Fig. 2. 4-Layer example with Sequential Layer Mapping

3.3 Distributed Inference

As was already pointed out, for fully-connected layers and later convolutional layers, the number of weights stored in the weight matrix and weight tensor dominate the memory demand. Hence, we approximate the memory footprint F_n with the number of weights stored on the device n. The computational effort is dominated by the multiplications with the weights. Computation on the devices can be parallelized for distributed inference, where T denotes the number of sequential multiplications on the longest path when executing the layers in parallel. As the devices are bandwidth-constrained, the overall run time of the inference task also depends strongly on the communication load C to exchange input or output data between the devices. Overall, larger number of devices leads to lower memory footprint F_n per device, more communication demand C and more parallelism (lower T), where changes in C and T impact run time in opposing ways. Considering that we map a network with L layers to a single device we obtain:

$$F_n^{(N)} = \sum_{l=1}^{L} Q_l, \quad T^{(N)} = \sum_{l=1}^{L} R_l, \quad C^{(N)} = 0 \tag{6}$$

This is illustrated for a fully-connected 4-layer example in Fig. 1, where the edges are annotated with the input/output sizes of the layer. For this example, we obtain: $F_1^{(N)} = 4 \cdot 8 + 8 \cdot 16 + 16 \cdot 4 + 4 \cdot 4 = 240$, $T^{(N)} = 240$ and $C^{(N)} = 0$.

A straight-forward solution for reducing F_n is to distribute different layers to different devices also known as layer pipelining. Using again the above example for two available devices, we can map layers 1 and 2 to device 1 as well as layers 3 and 4 to device 2 as shown in Fig. 2. Here we obtain intuitively: $F_1^{(DL)} = 4 \cdot 8 + 8 \cdot 16 = 160$, $F_2^{(DL)} = 16 \cdot 4 + 4 \cdot 4 = 80$, $T^{(DL)} = 240$ and $C^{(DL)} = 16$. The memory footprint is determined by the larger set of layers as $F_1^{(DL)}$, because the weights are not distributed evenly across the two devices. Moreover, this method does not utilize any parallelism for a single input, leading to the same high run time as for running on a single device. This mapping can be improved by using layer partitioning as proposed in this paper in the following.

4 Layer Partitioning Methods

The central idea of our approach is to apply layer partitioning on the DNN with the objective to evenly distribute the weight data and computational load across

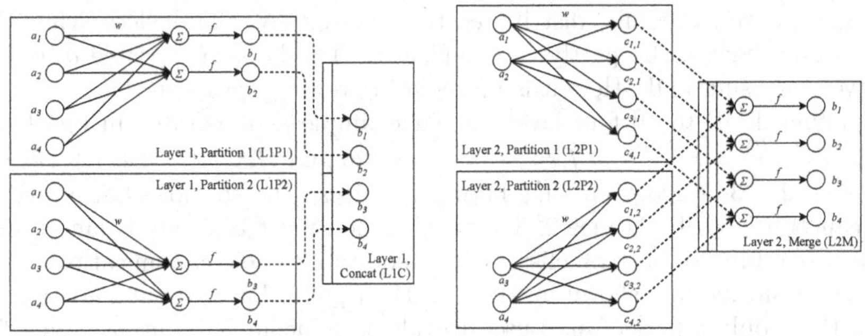

Fig. 3. LOP (left) and LIP (right)

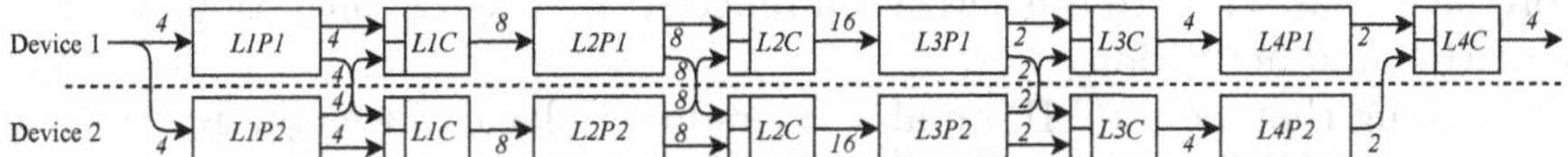

Fig. 4. 4-Layer example with Layer Output Partitioning

all available devices while minimizing the inference latency. A partitioning can be achieved by splitting either the inputs or the outputs of the layers and mapping one partition of each layer to each device. Input and output partitioning is simple and very effective to distribute the weight data while minimizing communication. In the following, we first discuss these partitioning schemes for the case of fully-connected layers, for which, to the best of our knowledge, such communication-aware solutions were not described yet. As new contributions, we show how partitioning schemes for fully-connected layers can be further improved in terms of communication demand by applying a newly proposed layer fusing scheme. Additionally, we extend all partitioning and fusing schemes to weight-intensive convolutional layers, which were not addressed by existing work before.

4.1 Layer Output and Input Partitioning (LOP and LIP)

In Layer Output Partitioning (LOP) as illustrated in Fig. 3 on the left, we use all of the input $\mathbf{a}_l$ and a part of $\mathbf{W}_l$ to calculate only a subset of output neurons $\mathbf{b}_l$. These outputs can then be fully finalized by applying the activation function f. The final output values then only have to be concatenated (*Concat*) to obtain the full output vector $\mathbf{b}_l$.

Assuming that we use LOP on all L layers for N devices, we obtain the memory footprint $F_n^{(LOP)}$, the execution time $T^{(LOP)}$ and the communication demand $C^{(LOP)}$ as follows:

$$F_n^{(LOP)} = \sum_{l=1}^{L} Q_l \cdot \frac{1}{N}, \quad T^{(LOP)} = \sum_{l=1}^{L} R_l \cdot \frac{1}{N}, \tag{7}$$

$$C^{(LOP)} = \sum_{l=1}^{L} C_l^{(LOP)} = \sum_{l=1}^{L} \Big((M_l - o_{l-1}\frac{M_l}{N}) \cdot (N-1) + K_l \cdot \frac{N-1}{N} \Big)$$

The inputs have to be fully distributed to the other $(N-1)$ devices, while the outputs only have to be partly communicated. The boolean variable o_l is 1 if the layer l is using LOP. Here it is representing reuse of previous data.

Applying LOP to all four layers of our example as illustrated in Fig. 4, we obtain: $F_1^{(LOP)} = F_2^{(LOP)} = T^{(LOP)} = \frac{240}{2} = 120$ and $C^{(LOP)} = 4+4+4+8+8+2+2+2 = 34$ (arrows crossing between devices). It also shows how previous data can be reused by Device 2. The memory footprint is evenly balanced and we can make full use of parallelism, while requiring some communication.

The second method shown in Fig. 3 on the right is Layer Input Partitioning (LIP). Here, only a part of $\mathbf{a}_l$ is used to calculate incomplete output values for $\mathbf{b}_l$. The number of weights required per device remains unchanged compared to LOP. Because these output values are incomplete, they have to be summed up, before being passed on to the activation function f. A merge operation does the summation and activation.

Assuming that we use LIP on all l layers for N devices, we obtain the same memory footprint $F_n^{(LIP)} = F_n^{(LOP)}$, and the same execution time $T^{(LIP)} = T^{(LOP)}$ as for LOP. The communication demand is:

$$C^{(LIP)} = \sum_{l=1}^{L} C_l^{(LIP)} = \sum_{l=1}^{L} \left(M_l \cdot \frac{N-1}{N} + K_l \cdot (N-1) \right) \tag{8}$$

Here, the outputs have to be fully distributed to the device performing the merging, while the inputs only have to be partly communicated and there is no opportunity for data reuse. This results in large communication overhead when LIP is used by itself. Applying LIP to the example would result in $C^{(LIP)} = 48$.

It is possible to partition the weights in other ways, but this will necessarily increase the required input or output size compared to strict LOP or LIP. For sparse weight data, only the non-zero weight data has to be distributed evenly.

4.2 Fused Layer Partitioning (FUSE)

Every *Concat* or *Merge* operation uses data from all partitions and is therefore a synchronization point preventing parallelism. When combining both LOP and LIP, we achieve layer fusion that eliminates one such synchronization point. The combined operation is shown in Fig. 5. The operation uses LOP on the first layer, but instead of applying the concatenation operation on the partial outputs $\mathbf{b}_l$, LIP is now performed on its following layer. Since the intermediate values c are partial outputs and cannot be passed to the activation function before being summed up, there can be only exactly two consecutive layers that are fused by this method.

Not all layers of the network need to be fused and for an uneven number of consecutive layers this is not even possible. Layers that cannot be fused, can still fall back to LOP or LIP to fulfill memory constraints. Considering this, we obtain the same memory footprint $F_n^{(FUSE)} = F_n^{(LOP)}$, and the same execution time $T^{(FUSE)} = T^{(LOP)}$. Given a certain network of L layers, we define $o_l = 1$

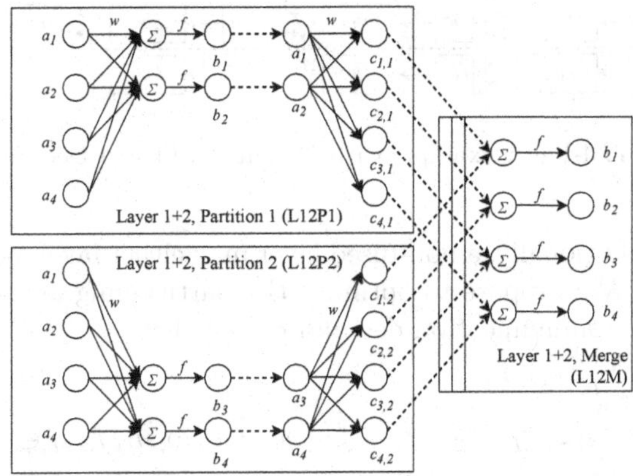

Fig. 5. Fused Layer Partitioning

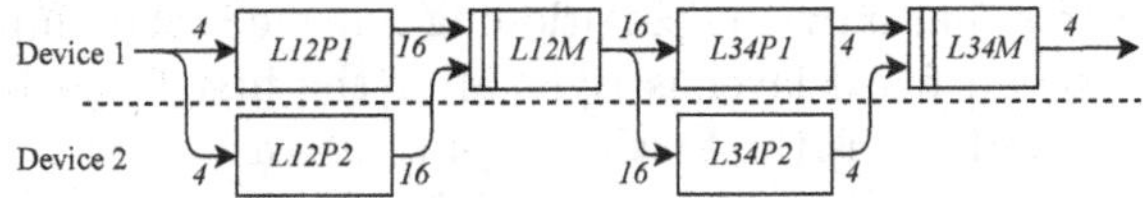

Fig. 6. 4-Layer example with Fused Layer Partitioning

if layer l is using LOP, $i_l = 1$ if it is using LIP, $f_l = 1$ if it is the first layer of a fused layer and $s_l = 1$ if it is the second layer of a fused layer, otherwise all variables are zero. With this we can formulate the communication demand C as:

$$C_l^{(FUSE1)} = M_l \cdot (N-1), \quad C_l^{(FUSE2)} = K_l \cdot (N-1) \tag{9}$$

$$C^{(FUSE)} = \sum_{l=1}^{L} \left(o_l C_l^{(LOP)} + i_l C_l^{(LIP)} + f_l C_l^{(FUSE1)} + s_l C_l^{(FUSE2)} \right) \tag{10}$$

Here, the outputs of the first layer and the inputs of the second layer do not need to be communicated.

When applying Fused Layer Partitioning with two fusions to our example as shown in Fig. 6, we get: $C^{(FUSE)} = 4 + 16 + 16 + 4 = 40$ while F and T remain unchanged compared to LOP. This is a worse result than LOP, but this is because two fusions are not a good solution for the given example.

4.3 ILP for Partitioning and Fusing Decision

Fusing at every possible opportunity as done in Fig. 6 can possibly be an inferior solution to carefully selecting which layers to fuse. The saved communication is dependent on the output and input layer sizes, which can vary greatly between layers. Furthermore, layers can only be fused pairwise. If a layer's output or input is fused, its input or output can in turn no longer be fused and has to be

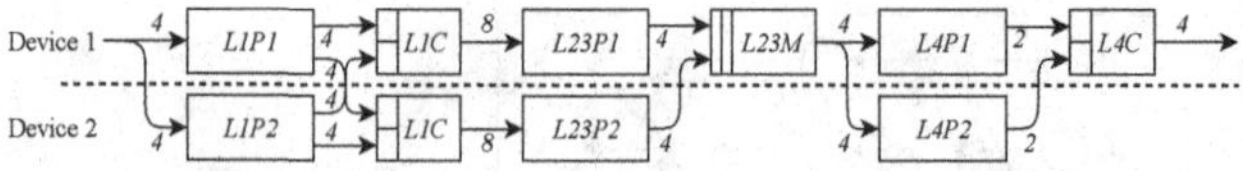

Fig. 7. 4-Layer example with Optimized Fusion Decision

communicated. Additionally, a non-fused layer may either favor LOP or LIP partitioning schemes. We propose to optimize the partitioning and fusing decision by minimizing the communication demand C as follows:

$$
\begin{aligned}
&min_{\mathbf{o},\mathbf{i},\mathbf{f},\mathbf{s}} \; C^{(FUSE)} && \\
&\quad s.t. \; \forall_{l=1\ldots L} \quad o_l + i_l + f_l + s_l = 1 \quad o_l, i_l, f_l, s_l \in \{0,1\} && (11)\\
&\quad \forall_{l=1\ldots L-1} \quad s_{l+1} = f_l && (12)\\
&\quad f_L = 0 && (13)
\end{aligned}
$$

for which (11) assures that only one partitioning scheme is chosen per layer, (12) assures that the second fused layer is right after the first fused layer and (13) prohibits that the last layer is the first layer of a fusion.

Optimizing the partitioning and fusing decision for our running example leads to the solution shown in Fig. 7. LOP is used for layer 1 and 4 and layer 2 and 3 are fused. A significant reduction is achieved with $C^{(FUSE)} = 22$. This is because the largest communication demand is between layers 2 and 3, which is removed by the fusing decision. Hence, the ILP considers the input and output sizes of all layers to decide on the best partitioning scheme of each layer. The value of C of course is only a rough indicator for the communication impact on a real DNN inference implementation, but our experimental results show that C correlates very well with the run time of the inference task.

4.4 Partitioning of Convolutional Layers

The proposed layer partitioning schemes can also be applied to two consecutive convolutional layers as illustrated in Fig. 8. The figure assumes that three of the feature maps are inside one partition and the data required for one single partition is highlighted. Here, the output feature maps of the first layer are partitioned instead of the output neurons. The first layer only applies a subset of the filters and produces, hence, only parts of the intermediate feature maps. Mathematically it is equivalent to implementing Eq. 3 only for a subset of the o indices assigned to this device. The device only needs to store its own filter weights.

In the second layer, all of the filters are applied to each of the input feature maps. However, only the filter channels corresponding to those partial inputs are required. The partially known input feature maps are correlated and summed up, resulting in partial outputs for all output feature maps. This implements Eq. 3, but now only for a subset of the c indices.

The nonlinear activation function cannot be applied on these partial outputs, because the total sum over c is incomplete. Hence again a merge step is required

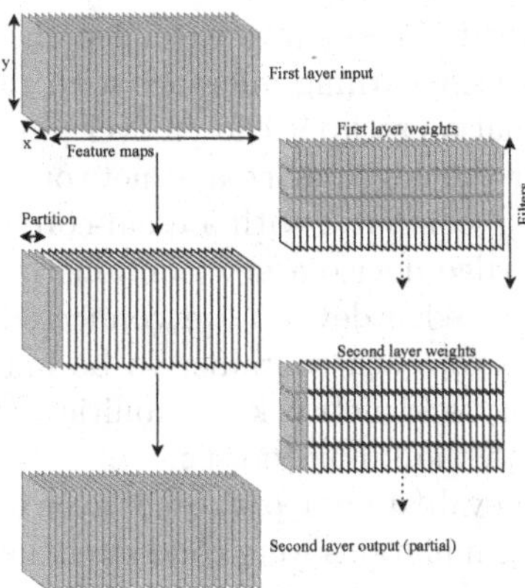

Fig. 8. Convolution weight partitioning

to sum up the partial results and evaluate the activation function. The equations derived for F_n, T and C for the fully-connected layers are also valid for the convolutional layers as we used the same symbols M_l, K_l, Q_l and R_l to denote the important parameters for both layers. As for fully-connected layers, the number of weights per device F_n and the number of multiplications T can be divided evenly by the number of devices. This is especially useful because the memory footprint to store the weight tensors is often very high for later convolutional layers of the DNN.

5 Experimental Results

We implemented a fully distributed inference approach using the layer partitioning methods on a set of edge devices on top of the framework from [11]. Edge devices fulfill two different roles during the inference process. Either they provide the input data as the source device, or they assist with the inference as worker devices. The work in [11] delegates all processing of the weight-dominated later layers of the DNN to a single powerful central gateway device. We adapt the framework such that the source device collects the initial results from the early DNN layers for further distribution. The prior existing communication pattern did not require long-running connections between devices. However, with layer fusion, all output data has to be synchronized at least every two layers between worker devices. This causes a large number of messages to be exchanged between source and worker devices. For the overall run time, it is essential that the connections between the source device and all worker devices remain open, which is enabled in our extended framework. The two partial convolution operations that implement LOP and LIP were implemented with the same linear algebra functions as the baseline convolution. To implement layer fusion, these operations were combined into a single operation, for which all communication and memory copies were stripped. These steps extended the existing framework to enable a fully distributed deep learning inference with support for layer fusion.

For evaluation, an emulation setup is chosen over physical devices in order to have accurate control over the edge device and network properties. The emulation host is a Linux desktop computer with a quad-core processor and 16 GB of RAM. For each emulated edge device a new containerized Docker environment is created and all emulated edge devices are connected via a bridged virtual network. This setup allows for each container to be individually configured in terms of processor, memory and network capabilities. Incoming and outgoing bandwidth was limited with the Linux tool `tc`.

YOLOv2 [8] is used to evaluate our proposed layer fusion method. For each measurement result, three simulations were conducted and the results were averaged to take run time variability into account.

5.1 Evaluation of LOP vs. Layer Fusion

Table 1. Run time and memory footprint F_n comparison for YOLOv2

Bandwidth			Number of devices					Run time [s]			Mem. F_n [MB]
10 Mbit	100 Mbit	1 Gbit	1	3	5	6	7	LOP	FUSE	Speed-up of FUSE vs. LOP	
✓						✓		74.2	64.2	1.16x	34
	✓					✓		11.6	10.1	1.15x	34
		✓				✓		5.92	5.59	1.06x	34
	✓		✓					13.1	13.3	0.99x	204
	✓			✓				8.64	8.26	1.05x	68
	✓				✓			10.5	9.35	1.12x	41
	✓						✓	12.1	11.0	1.10x	29

Table 1 shows the total inference time and memory footprint for different edge device and network parameters for LOP alone vs. Layer Fusion (FUSE). As expected, when increasing the number of devices we observe a proportional decrease of F_n, which allows to scale the inference task for the available memory resources of the edge devices equally for LOP and FUSE.

Existing work is not able to partition weight-dominated convolutional layers. Hence, we can only compare to a baseline that executes on a single node. Here, some reduction in run time can be seen when using other idle nodes for the inference task. There are several effects that influence the final run time of the inference task compared to the theoretical values of T and C when using different numbers of edge devices. First, there is some latency that has to be added for every message between devices. Also, the early layers of the YOLOv2 network are included to see the full run time. Hence, the run time varies when increasing the number of devices. Communication and parallelism have opposing impacts on run time, so that no clear trend is observed when going from three to seven devices.

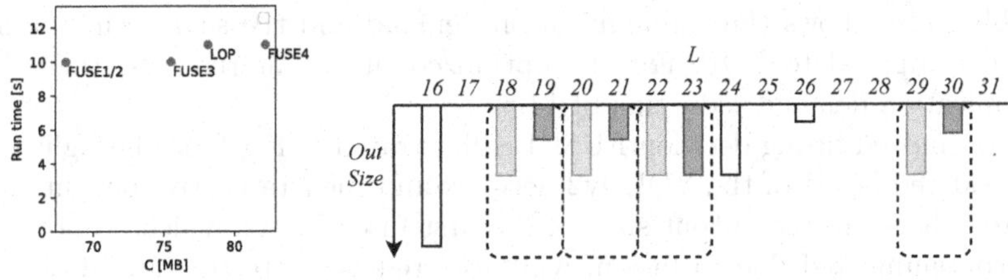

Fig. 9. Fusion decisions for YOLOv2 (left) and decision FUSE1 (right)

When comparing layer fusion to applying LOP only, a clear benefit can be seen in terms of run time. The benefit is lower, when the available bandwidth is very high (1 Gbit) as the Fusing only improves communication demand. The speed-up of FUSE is generally higher, the more number of devices are involved, because there is more communication happening which can be positively affected by layer fusion. Yet, also here some variance is observed. But clearly, it can be seen that layer fusion achieves a significant speed-up without imposing additional costs.

MoDNN [6] does not strictly adhere to the LOP or LIP schemes, so their layers cannot be directly fused. However, fusing can be supported by adjusting the first layer to follow LOP and the second layer to follow LIP. This will not be a restrictive constraint on their method, because they focus on sparse networks. So to cluster complete LOP or LIP nodes, only few connections need to be moved.

5.2 Optimization of Partitioning and Fusing Decisions

To evaluate the ILP optimization for finding an optimal partitioning and fusing decisions, several alternatives in the YOLOv2 model were simulated for 100 Mbit bandwidth and six devices. Table 2 shows which layers were fused for all possible variants. Solving the ILP results in the optimized solutions FUSE1 and FUSE2. Figure 9 on the left shows the communication size C and the measured run time. As can be seen, there is a good correlation between C and the run time, indicating that the solution of the ILP can give a good fusing decision for DNNs. Yet, the ILP needs to be evaluated for more networks to strengthen these results.

Table 2. Communication demand for fusion decisions for YOLOv2

Variant	Fused layers	C [MB]	C saving [%]
LOP	None	78.1	0.00
FUSE4	19 + 20, 21 + 22, 23 + 24, 29 + 30	82.2	−5.00
FUSE3	18 + 19, 21 + 22, 23 + 24, 29 + 30	75.5	3.60
FUSE2	18 + 19, 20 + 21, 23 + 24, 29 + 30	68.1	14.8
FUSE1	18 + 19, 20 + 21, 22 + 23, 29 + 30	68.1	14.8

Table 2 also shows the communication demand and the savings in communication compared to LOP. For the optimized fusing alternatives, there is a communication demand reduction of 14.8%.

An optimized fusing decision FUSE1 is illustrated in Fig. 9 on the right with the considered layers of the YOLOv2 network and their respective output sizes. The green bars are the output sizes of the first fused layers, which do not need to be communicated due to fusion, while the red ones are the output sizes of the second layers, for which all partial outputs need to be communicated, hence increasing communication size compared to LOP. As can be seen layers with large output size are selected as first layers.

6 Summary and Conclusions

In this paper, an approach for partitioning and fusing consecutive weight-intensive fully-connected or convolutional DNN layers targeting memory-constrained edge devices was presented. This method allows a complete DNN application to be executed in a fully distributed manner on resource-constrained edge clusters. In the process, it reduces communication overhead and therefore improves inference run time. Additionally, an ILP optimization is given, so that optimal fusing decisions can be made.

References

1. Alwani, M., Chen, H., Ferdman, M., Milder, P.: Fused-layer CNN accelerators. In: MICRO (2016)
2. Bhattacharya, S., Lane, N.D.: Sparsification and separation of deep learning layers for constrained resource inference on wearables. In: SenSys (2016)
3. Kang, Y., et al.: Neurosurgeon: collaborative intelligence between the cloud and mobile edge. In: ASPLOS, pp. 615–629 (2017)
4. Krizhevsky, A., Sutskever, I., Hinton, G.E.: Imagenet classification with deep convolutional neural networks. In: NIPS (2012)
5. Long, J., Shelhamer, E., Darrell, T.: Fully convolutional networks for semantic segmentation. In: CVPR (2015)
6. Mao, J., et al.: MoDnn: local distributed mobile computing system for deep neural network. In: DATE (2017)
7. Motamedi, M., Fong, D., Ghiasi, S.: Fast and energy-efficient CNN inference on IoT devices. arXiv preprint arXiv:1611.07151 (2016)
8. Redmon, J., Farhadi, A.: Yolo9000: better, faster, stronger. arXiv preprint arXiv:1612.08242 (2016)
9. Simonyan, K., Zisserman, A.: Very deep convolutional networks for large-scale image recognition. arXiv preprint arXiv:1409.1556 (2014)
10. Teerapittayanon, S., McDanel, B., Kung, H.: Distributed deep neural networks over the cloud, the edge and end devices. In: ICDCS (2017)
11. Zhao, Z., Barijough, K.M., Gerstlauer, A.: DeepThings: distributed adaptive deep learning inference on resource-constrained IoT edge clusters. IEEE TCAD **37**, 2348–2359 (2018)

System Security

A Latency-Optimized Hash-Based Digital Signature Accelerator for the Tactile Internet

Friedrich Pauls[1,2(✉)], Robert Wittig[2], and Gerhard Fettweis[1,2]

[1] Barkhausen Institut, 01062 Dresden, Germany
friedrich.pauls@barkhauseninstitut.org
[2] Vodafone Chair Mobile Communications Systems,
Technische Universität Dresden, 01062 Dresden, Germany
{robert.wittig,gerhard.fettweis}@tu-dresden.de
https://barkhauseninstitut.org, http://www.vodafone-chair.org

Abstract. Tactile Internet as evolution of the Internet of Things will enable real-time interactive applications in industry and society. It requires low latency and security. Security comprises encryption and data authentication. Digital signatures enable the latter. With the rise of quantum computers, most currently employed digital signature schemes will become unsecure. One promising post-quantum secure algorithm is the eXtended Merkle Signature Scheme (XMSS). It is computationally expensive and thus contradicts low latency requirements. This paper proposes a latency-optimized accelerator for hash-based digital signature processing for the XMSS algorithm. Our architecture improves the latency of signing and verification into the sub-millisecond range.

Keywords: Tactile Internet · Post-quantum cryptography · Hash-based signatures · Hardware accelerator · XMSS · Keccak · SHAKE128

1 Introduction

The paradigm of the Tactile Internet as evolution of the Internet of Things (IoT) will enable real-time interactive systems in a variety of different areas such as automation, transportation, gaming, education, and healthcare. Key requirements of the Tactile Internet are ultra-low latency, extremely high availability, reliability and security [1,10]. It has been shown, that a round-trip latency of

This research was co-financed by public funding of the state of Saxony/Germany and by the European Social Fund in the framework of the Young Investigators Group “Communication Infrastructures for Attonets in 3D-Chip-Stacks (Atto3D)” under grant number 100339530. This publication contains results of the fast semantics project which is a member of the fast2020 research cluster. It is being financed by the ‘Zwanzig20 - Partnerschaft für Innovation’ initiative of the Federal Ministry for Education and Research of Germany under the grant number FKZ03ZZ0521D.

D. N. Pnevmatikatos et al. (Eds.): SAMOS 2019, LNCS 11733, pp. 93–106, 2019.
https://doi.org/10.1007/978-3-030-27562-4_7

under 1 ms is a requirement for applications in, e.g., autonomous driving, vehicle-to-infrastructure communication, control communications, or in other forms of human-to-machine and machine-to-machine communications [16].

Another key requirement is security. It encompasses both encryption and data authentication. In this work, we focus on the latter. Digital signatures provide data authentication. They enable the receiver of a message to make sure that it comes from a trustworthy source (authenticity), and that it has not been modified in between (integrity). This becomes especially important in safety-relevant use-cases, e.g., in autonomous driving, or for emergency braking messages.

In recent years, there have been advancements in the field of quantum computing. If quantum computers scale as expected, most currently used digital signature schemes like the Rivest-Shamir-Adleman (RSA) cryptosystem or the Elliptic Curve Digital Signature Algorithm (ECDSA) will be broken [5]. Quantum computing seems to be far away. However, proposed use cases like fully autonomous driving will also still need several years until deployed in large scale. Because of the stringent latency requirements, most security primitives need to be implemented with hardware support. This makes it infeasible to update the deployed infrastructure and devices to post-quantum secure algorithms on a software basis.

The authors in [5] show three different classes of post-quantum-secure signatures: lattice-based, multivariate-quadratic-equation, and hash-based signatures. In this work, we focus on hash-based signatures, and in particular on the eXtended Merkle Signature Scheme (XMSS) proposed in [8]. The scheme is provably-secure under minimal security assumptions and is in the final steps of adoption for internet protocols by the Internet Research Task Force (IRTF) [5,11]. Design of hash-based signature schemes and its security parameters have been studied in [7]. Several variants of hash-based signatures have been proposed. Among XMSS [8], a variant of the Lamport-Diffie-Winternitz-Merkle (LMS) scheme has been proposed [14]. XMSS relies on weaker security properties of the underlying hash function than LMS. For XMSS a second-preimage resistant hash function is sufficient, whereas LMS requires collision resistance. XMSS also has slightly smaller signatures as compared to LMS. A stateless hash-based signature scheme called SPHINCS has been proposed in [4] and its variant SPHINCS+ is considered in the second round of the NIST Post-Quantum Cryptography Standardization Process [3]. Both schemes have signatures sizes many times larger than those of XMSS, which increases end-to-end latency significantly due to data transfer time.

Disadvantages of hash-based signatures are the relatively large signature size and the processing requirements. The high processing demand of XMSS and the ultra low-latency requirements contradict each other, especially in constrained embedded environments. To summarize, the Tactile Internet requires low-latency and data security in order to enable promising future use-cases. Currently used digital signature schemes provide data authentication, but are susceptible to quantum computer attacks. Hash-based signatures, and in particular XMSS, are promising candidates to solve that problem at the drawback of large signatures and high processing requirements.

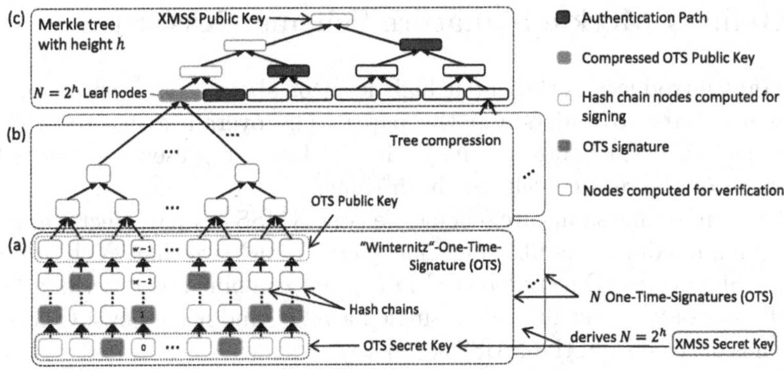

Fig. 1. Overview of the XMSS scheme (Color figure online)

Related Work. The authors in [15] present an optimized XMSS software implementation called *MultiBuffer* on Intel Haswell and Skylake architectures with the AVX2 vector instruction set. They compare their results to the reference implementation [12].

As XMSS, and hash-based digital signatures in general, rely heavily on hash computations, general hardware accelerators, e.g., for the Secure Hash Algorithm 3 (SHA-3) family [2] and in particular for SHAKE128 can be considered as related to this work. In [13,19] dedicated accelerators are presented. In [9,18] application specific processors are developed to process SHA-3 hashes. These implementations do not take the specifics of XMSS into account.

The work in [17] presents SHA-256-specific software optimizations, a general SHA-256 hardware accelerator, and an XMSS-specific accelerator architecture using SHA-256.

Our Contribution. This paper investigates whether XMSS is compatible with the low-latency requirements of the Tactile Internet. Similar to [17], we present an XMSS-specific accelerator using a hardware-software co-design. In contrast to [17] we use the SHAKE128 hash function of the SHA-3 family. Our architecture employs instruction set extensions in a Cadence Tensilica LX6 RISC processor with a tailored buffer architecture. Further, we present an optimal area-time-energy trade-off for the round function computation of SHAKE128. In addition, we identify which operations do not depend on a specific message and thus can be computed in advance without adding to overall latency.

Organization. The remainder of the paper is organized as follows. Section 2 provides a birds-eye view on XMSS. In Sect. 3 we describe our implemented architecture followed by a performance evaluation in Sect. 4. Section 5 concludes the paper.

2 eXtended Merkle Signature Scheme (XMSS)

This section introduces XMSS at a high level of abstraction with a focus on concepts necessary to understand the paper. The overall structure of XMSS is shown in Fig. 1. Each box (or node) in the figure represents either a hash computation or the result itself, the hash value.

XMSS is an N-time signature scheme, i.e., one XMSS key pair (secret and public) can sign a maximum number of N messages. To achieve that, N *Winternitz-*One-Time Signatures (OTS), depicted in (a), are combined as described below. Each OTS can only be used to sign a single message, and has its own OTS secret key which is derived from the XMSS secret key.

The upper ends of the hash chains in (a) form the OTS public key. A binary hash tree (b) compresses it into a single hash value to form a compressed OTS public key. A Merkle hash tree (c) with height h combines all $N = 2^h$ compressed OTS public keys into a single XMSS public key at its root.

To generate a XMSS public key, all hash chains of all N OTSs need to be fully computed, their public keys need to be compressed, and finally they are combined in the Merkle hash tree.

To sign a message, it is linked to an OTS by positional encoding. Each column in (a) forms a hash chain with a defined length w. By selecting a hash value at a particular position within a hash chain, $log_2(w)$ bits of the message can be encoded. All selected hash values (blue nodes) form the OTS of the message. In addition to that, the signature contains all complementary values of the Merkle tree, which are necessary for the receiver to compute the root node, i.e. the XMSS public key. These values are called authentication path (brown nodes).

For verification, the positions of the OTS nodes are reconstructed from the received message. The OTS values from the signature are used as the starting point to compute the hash chains up until the top node (position $w - 1$). The hash values of the OTS public key candidate will match if and only if both message and signature are unaltered. The OTS key candidate is then compressed (b), and the root node of the Merkle tree (c) is computed with the help of the provided authentication path. The message is authentic, if the computed root node matches the XMSS public key.

2.1 SHAKE128 as Hash Function for XMSS

A hash function maps a bit string of arbitrary length to a bit string of a fixed length. The input is called message, the output is the hash value. The XMSS standard leaves several options for hash functions. We use SHAKE128 as defined in the SHA-3 standard [2]. It is an instance of the Keccak [6] algorithm and provides a security level of 128-bit. With a block size of 168 byte, it has the capability to process the XMSS hash functions in a single iteration. This is beneficial in our low-latency focus.

It follows a simplified description of the SHAKE128 operation, which is sufficient to follow the paper. A detailed overview can be found in [2,6].

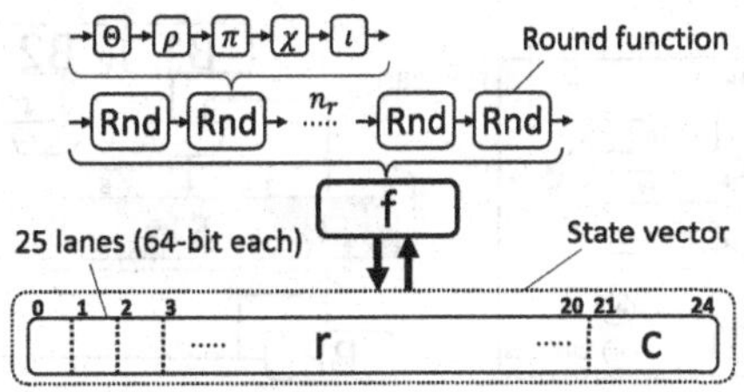

Fig. 2. Keccak-p permutation

SHAKE128 can be considered as mode of operation of the Keccak-p $[b = 1600, n_r = 24]$ permutation. A permutation operates on a $b = 1600$ bit vector called state. Figure 2 provides an illustration. Initially the state is set to the input values. The function f modifies the state by applying a round function *Rnd* $n_r = 24$ times to the state. The *Rnd* function itself comprises five transformations $\theta, \rho, \pi, \chi,$ and ι. From an implementation point of view those are mostly XOR operations. The interested reader may refer to [2] for more details.

The state vector comprises 25 lanes each 64-bit wide. It defines two regions, the rate with a width of $r = 1344$ bit (lane 0 to 20), and the capacity with a width of $c = 256$ bit (lane 21 to 24).

To compute a hash for a message with length l_{msg}, first a specific bit pattern, called padding, with length l_{pad} is added. l_{pad} is chosen in such a way to make sure $l_{\text{msg}} + l_{\text{pad}}$ is an integer multiple of the rate r. Then, the first r-bit block of the padded message is loaded into the state vector and the permutation function f is invoked. This process repeats for the following r-bit blocks until the whole padded message is absorbed. Loading in this context means to bit-wise XOR the current state with the input data. The hash value (in our case 32 byte), is obtained by reading lane 0 to 3.

3 System Design for Low-Latency XMSS Processing

Our objective is to achieve an end-to-end latency of about 1 ms as seen from the application. This budget includes time for sensor input and application processing, data transmission, and, in our case, time for data authentication. We assume the time budget for data authentication to be around 100 µs for both sign and verification procedures. This chapter summarizes relevant architecture details and design decisions.

As shown in [15] even a state-of-the-art desktop processor needs several milliseconds to process XMSS sign and verify operations. In a constrained embedded environment a software-only approach will not succeed to reach a design goal of under 100 µs, thus a hardware-software co-design is necessary.

The developed solution will be integrated into a System-on-Chip (SoC). We use the Cadence Tensilica LX6 RISC processor and extend its pipeline with specialized instructions. Compared to a dedicated hardware solution, this process

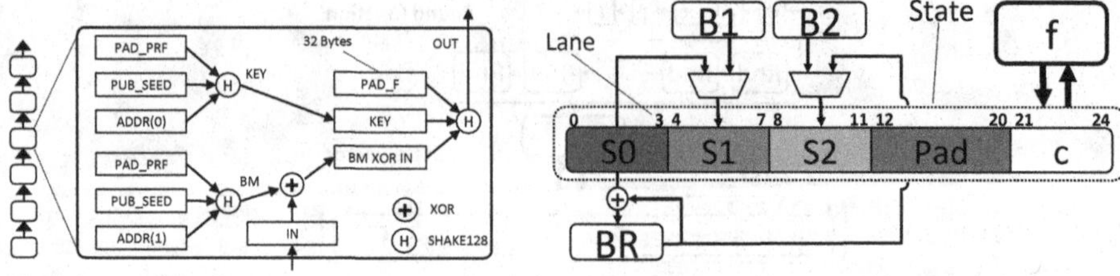

Fig. 3. WOTS+ hash chain computation

Fig. 4. XMSS accelerator design

provides fast development, well integrated test and verification capabilities, and a flexible HW/SW integration.

First, we identified the most critical parts using software profiling. It shows that over 96% of the time is needed for hash processing. In particular, the authentication path and the Winternitz One-Time-Signature (WOTS+) computation consume the most processing time.

Figure 3 shows the necessary steps to compute a single node in the hash chain. The hash function H (here SHAKE128) is computed three times. In each invocation, three 32-byte input arguments are loaded and one 32-byte output is produced. These arguments are:

PAD_PRF. A padding used for domain separation of different functions. Here for the pseudo-random-function (PRF) as defined in the XMSS scheme.
PAD_F. The same as PAD_PRF, but for the XMSS function F.
PUB_SEED. A public seed associated with the public key.
ADDR(x). An address, specifying the exact position of the current node in the XMSS scheme and in the current hash chain.

To compute a single node, a total of 288 bytes must be loaded into the state and 96 bytes need to be extracted. We created a tailored buffer architecture to minimize the load on the memory interface and thus to maximize performance. We show this in the following section.

3.1 Keccak State Vector Register and Optimized Buffer Structure

As explained in Sect. 2.1 and shown in Fig. 2, a bit vector with 25 lanes, each 64-bit wide, holds the state. For maximum performance, we match that with 25 64-bit hardware registers which are able to hold the entire state. In addition, hardware to compute the permutation function f is added. At this stage the architecture can be considered as general Keccak hardware accelerator without buffers and it needs 257 cycles for a single WOTS+ node computation. Table 1 shows how many cycles are consumed for load and store instructions and for the permutation function f. As next step, we added a hardware padding generator (PG) and a result shift mechanism which is used to feed results from one iteration back into the state register. Both measures reduce the cycle count to 201. Now, load and store instructions account for 42% of the total cycles.

Our buffer architecture as shown in Fig. 4 aims to reduce the load and store operations. It has two buffers B1 and B2, which serve Slot S1 (lane 4–7), and Slot S2 (lane 8–11) respectively. A result buffer (BR) can store the output hash value of the permutation. BR also serves S2. In addition, S0 can be directly fed back to S1, we call this result shift. The PG (not shown) generates the values for PAD_PRF, and PAD_F, as well es the padding for the SHAKE128 in lane 12 to 20, as described in Sect. 2.1. An example schedule for the hash chain computation is shown in Fig. 5. It shows pseudo code for one iteration. In step (0), B1 is loaded with PUB_SEED. In (1), B2 is loaded with the address ADDR(n,1) of the current iteration n. In (2), the kec_init() instruction initializes the state vector with the specified contents. Immediate operands of this instruction control the data path of all buffers and the results shift. S0, S1, S2 are loaded with padding PAD_PRF (from PG), and the contents of B1, and B2 respectively. In (3), the permutation function is invoked and the result from S0 is XORed with the contents of BR which holds the input IN(n-1) of the previous iteration. The result is written to BR. To compute the KEY, in (4), S0, S1, and S2 are initialized with PG(PRF), B1, and B2. The kec_wr_state() instruction can modify arbitrary bytes in the state. This is used in (5) to change ADDR(n,1) to ADDR(n,0) directly, instead of loading it. Step (6) permutes the state and the result, KEY, resides in S0. In (7) the results shift mechanism is used to load S0 into S1. S2 is loaded with (BM XOR IN(n-1)) from BR. (8) clears BR. (9) permutes the state to obtain the output which is stored to BR. It serves as the input IN(n) for the next iteration. With the tailored buffers, the time for one node computation can be reduced to 92 clock cycles. Only eight of the initially 85 cycles remain for memory operations. Now, 73 of the 92 cycles (79%) are needed for the permutation. We will show how to reduce this further in the next section.

3.2 Improving the Round Function Computation

In the previous chapter we observed that the time for the permutation now dominates the computation time with 79%. Each permutation f needs $n_{\mathrm{r}} = 24$

	Instruction	Description	B1	B2	BR
	0) load_buf()	B1←PUB_SEED	PUB_SEED	-	IN(n-1)
loop(n)	1) load_buf()	B2←ADDR(n,1)	-	ADDR(n,1)	-
	2) kec_init()	S0←PG(PRF), S1←B1, S2←B2	-	-	-
	3) permute24()	BR←BR + S0	-	-	BM+IN(n-1)
	4) kec_init()	S0←PG(PRF), S1←B1, S2←B2	-	-	-
	5) kec_wr_state()	ADDR(n,1) ← ADDR (n,0)	-	-	-
	6) permute24()	S0←KEY	-	-	-
	7) kec_init()	S0←PG(F), S1←S0, S2←BR	-	-	-
	8) clear_rbuf()	BR←0	-	-	-
	9) permute24()	BR←OUT(n) = IN(n)	-	-	IN(n)

Fig. 5. Schedule for the hash chain computation

Table 1. Total cycle counts for one WOTS+ node computation for different optimization steps. Each value is broken down into cycles that are needed by instructions for load, store, and for the permutation function f.

Architecture	Number of Cycles (% of Total)				
	Total	Load	Store	f	Other
Keccak HW	257	90 (35%)	40 (16%)	73 (28%)	54 (21%)
+ Padding Gen./Result Shift	201	63 (31%)	22 (11%)	73 (36%)	42 (21%)
+ Tailored Buffers (FB-EL1)	92	6 (7%)	2 (2%)	73 (79%)	11 (12%)
+ Round Function (FB-EL3)	43	6 (14%)	2 (4%)	24 (56%)	11 (26%)

iterations of the round function *Rnd*. See also Fig. 2. Currently, in each clock cycle, one iteration is performed. The idea is to divide the 24 iterations into epochs in which L_e iterations are processed in a single clock cycle. We call L_e the epoch length. The number of clock cycles for each permutation then reduces from 24 to $24/L_e$.

This offers a trade-off between the area, energy and time. The higher L_e, the higher the area and the power, but the lower the maximum clock frequency of the design. To find an optimal solution we implemented hardware versions for $L_e \in \{1, 2, 3, 4, 6, 8, 12, 24\}$. The LX6 processor has a 7-stage pipeline and we use 128 KB of tightly coupled memory for instructions and 2 × 128 KB for its two 64-bit wide data memory ports. The designs were synthesized in a Globalfoundries 22 nm FD-SOI technology in a 0.6 V process (typical corner, 25 °C).

To select the optimal solution, we calculated area × time (AT) and area × time × energy (ATE) products for all designs. For the area A, only our accelerated processor core w/o memory was considered. For the energy, the memory was considered as well. The sum of the sign and verification times is used as performance reference for T. Figure 6 shows the AT and ATE products normalized to the respective optimal solution, which is $L_e = 4$ for the AT, and $L_e = 3$ for the ATE product. Figure 7 shows the maximum attainable clock frequency $f_{\text{clk,max}}$ and the core area over the epoch length. For $L_e > 4$ the critical path of the accelerator starts to dominate the critical path of the processor. We choose the architecture with minimal ATE product for further consideration and refer to it as FB-EL3 (*Fully-Buffered, Epoch Length* $L_e = 3$). As reference, we use design FB-EL1 (*Fully-Buffered,* $L_e = 1$). FB-EL3 reduces the cycle count to 43 and has a 36% lower AT and a 58% lower ATE product compared to FB-EL1.

4 Performance Evaluation

This sections shows selected performance measures of the previously introduced architecture *FB-EL3*. The design minimizes ATE product within our parameter space. We compare the results to the Cadence Tensilica LX6 processor *CT-LX6*

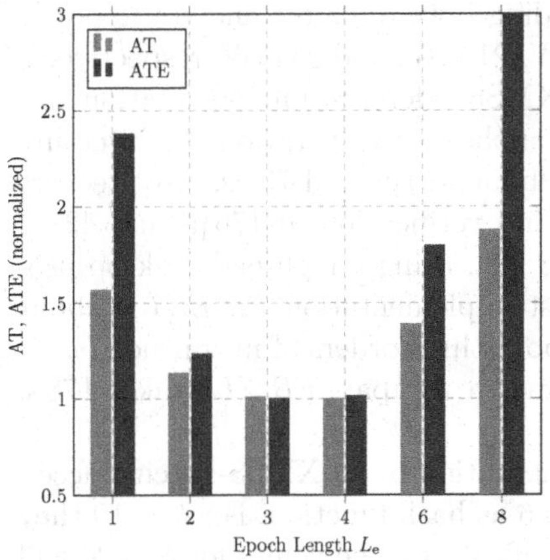

Fig. 6. Normalized AT and ATE product over epoch lengths $1 \leq L_e \leq 8$

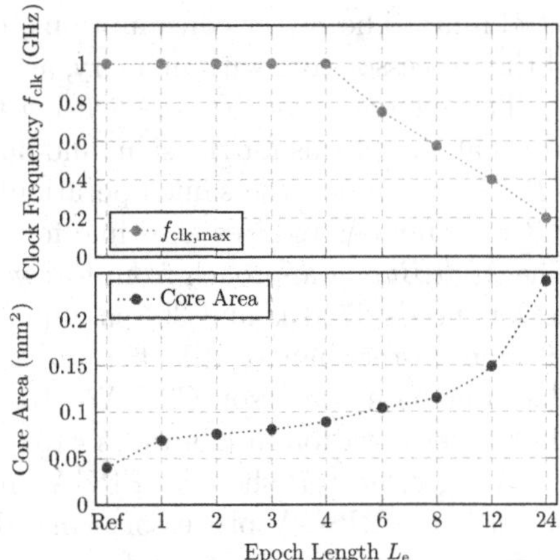

Fig. 7. Maximum clock frequency $f_{\text{clk,max}}$ and core area over epoch lengths $1 \leq L_e \leq 24$. *Ref* is our reference architecture CT-LX6

without instruction extensions, as well as to *FB-EL1*. Furthermore, we compare the performance of the sign, verify and key generation operations to a state-of-the-art software implementation from Oliveira et al. called *Multi Buffer* [15] and to the XMSS-specific hardware accelerator from Wang et al. [17].

All our designs use the maximum attainable frequency of $f_{\text{clk}} = 1\,\text{GHz}$. For this first evaluation, synthesis, pre-layout simulation, and verification was performed. Further synthesis parameters and the used memory subsystem are as described in Sect. 3.2. This evaluation does not include place-and-route or following steps. Thus, realistically achievable clock frequencies in a manufactured silicon chip will be lower, area and power values may be higher. This has to be considered when interpreting the results shown here.

The execution times were obtained from a cycle-accurate hardware/software simulator. All results have been obtained using the hash operation SHAKE128. We assumed a small message size of 128 B. Performance results are averaged over 32 samples.

4.1 Implementation Results

Table 2 summarizes synthesis results and performance of sign and verify operations for a tree height $h = 20$ and $w = 16$. Architecture *FB-EL1* has 143.8×10^3 cells from which 54.9×10^3 can be accounted to our added instruction extensions. This is an increase of about 62% compared to *CT-LX6* which has 88.8×10^3 cells. Architecture *FB-EL3* has 173.1×10^3 cells from which 84.2×10^3 account for the accelerator. This version increases the number of cells by 95% compared to the base core *CT-LX6*. mmmThe estimated processor core areas (w/o memory) of the architectures *CT-LX6*, *FB-EL1*, and *FB-EL3* are $0.040\,\text{mm}^2$, $0.069\,\text{mm}^2$, and

0.081 mm^2. The power consumptions, including both dynamic and static power of the processor core with memory, are 9 mW, 21 mW, and 25 mW, respectively.

The reference core *CT-LX6* using the XMSS reference implementation [12] needs about 149 ms for the sign, and 36 ms for the verify operation. Architecture *FB-EL1* processes the same operations in about 330 µs and 79 µs. Architecture *FB-EL3* further reduces the time for sign and verification to 176 µs and 42 µs. The *MultiBuffer* approach from the work in [15], using a high-end desktop processor, needs 3740 µs and 300 µs. Our fastest implementation *FB-EL3* is about 19 times faster than MultiBuffer [15] and about three orders of magnitude faster than our base processor *CT-LX6*. To generate a key pair *FB-EL3* takes 178 s, the implementation in [15] takes 410 s.

Wang *et al.* [17] show an FPGA implementation of an XMSS-specific accelerator and a RISC-V processor using SHA256 as hash function. For $h = 10$ they achieve 23.5 ms for signing and 6.5 ms for verification. The values for $h = 20$ will be higher. *FB-EL3* is about two orders of magnitude faster, a direct comparison is however nonproductive. We compare cycle counts to better account for differences in clock frequencies of their FPGA implementation and our design which is intended for silicon implementation, but this neglects differences in maximally attainable clock frequencies due to different architectures. For signing, *FB-EL3* needs about 176×10^3 cycles and is still about 10 times faster than the approach in [17] which needs 1.99×10^3 cycles. One reason might be that SHA256 needs at least two iterations to process all input data of an XMSS hash computation whereas SHAKE128 only needs one iteration. Another factor is probably that our overall architecture makes more aggressive use of area in favor of latency.

Table 3 gives an overview of the energy consumption of sign and verification operations as well as AT and ATE product for both operations combined. *CT-LX6* consumes 1357 µJ for the sign and 328 µJ for the verify operation. *FB-EL1* consumes 7.0 µJ and 1.7 µJ, *FB-EL3* lowers the consumption further down to 4.4 µJ and 1.1 µJ. The AT and ATE products were calculated using the added

Table 2. Overview of area, power, and processing times.

We compare our best design *FB-EL3*, against our reference cores *CT-LX6*, *FB-EL1* ($f_{clk} = 1$ GHz). The sign, verify and key generation times ($h = 20$, $w = 16$) are also compared against the state-of-the-art software implementation from Oliveira et al. called *MultiBuffer* [15] ($f_{clk} = 4$ GHz).

	Cells (10^3)	ΔCells (10^3)	(rel.)	Area (mm^2)	Power (mW)	Sign (µs)	Verify (µs)	KeyGen (s)
CT-LX6	88.8	0	(+ 0%)	0.040	9	149k	35.9k	-
FB-EL1	143.8	54.9	(+62%)	0.069	21	330	79	-
FB-EL3	173.1	84.2	(+95%)	0.081	25	176	42	178
MultiBuffer [15]						3740	300	410
Wang *et al.* [17]						(23.5k)[a]	(6.5k)[a]	-[a]

[a] In [17] $h = 10$ is used. Comparison of key generation times would be nonproductive.

Table 3. Energy consumption of sign and verify operations, AT, and ATE product, both normalized to architecture for FB-EL3 ($h = 20$, $w = 16$).

	Energy (µJ)		AT (norm)	ATE (norm)
	Sign	Verify	(Sign + Verify)	
CT-LX6	1357	328	424	387
FB-EL1	7.0	1.7	1.60	1.59
FB-EL3	4.4	1.1	1	1

times for sign and verify operations, and the area from Table 2. The values shown have been normalized to the fastest architecture *FB-EL3*. The AT (ATE) products of *CT-LX6*, *FB-EL1*, and *FB-EL3* are 424 (387), 1.60 (1.59), and 1 (1). In terms of area-time and area-time-energy product *FB-EL3* is 63% better than *FB-EL1* and over two orders of magnitude better than *CT-LX6*.

4.2 Performance of Sign and Verify Operations

This section analyzes the performance of the sign and verify operations in more detail. For this study, we divide the time measurements for the sign operation into the following four sub-operations:

Msg Hash. Digital signature algorithms can often only sign a fixed-length bit string. To be able to handle messages of arbitrary lengths, a fixed-length hash or fingerprint of the message is created. This fingerprint is signed with the actual sign algorithm. For our studies, we assumed a short message length of 128 Byte.

Auth path. Computation of the authentication path.

WOTS+ sign. Computation of WOTS+ sign operation.

Other. Summarizes remaining computations which are not one of the above. E.g. message copying, or secret key de-/serialization.

Table 4 shows how much processing time is needed for each sub-operation of the sign operation. In addition the verify operation and the total sum of both sign and verification is given. All values are shown for four different tree heights $h \in \{5, 10, 16, 20\}$. With rising h, the total sign time increases from 124 µs ($h = 5$) to 176 µs ($h = 20$) by about 42%. The time for verification increases from 39 µs ($h = 5$) to 42 µs ($h = 20$) by about 8%. The total sign time increases from 163 µs ($h = 5$) to 218 µs ($h = 20$) by about 34%. The *Msg hash* operation is constant over h and takes only 0.6 µs. The processing of *Other* takes only between 5 µs and 10 µs. The *Auth path* calculation takes from 91 µs ($h = 5$) to 137 µs ($h = 20$). The *WOTS+ sign* operation is constant over h and takes about 28 µs. The bottom part of Table 4 shows the relative processing times of the sign sub-operations. The two most time-intensive operations are the *Auth path* computation and the *WOTS+ sign* procedure, which consume more than 74% and 16% of the total sign time.

Table 4. Processing Times of XMSS Operations (top) and relative times of sign sub-operations (bottom) for architecture FB-EL3

	Sign (S) (µs)					Verify (V) (µs)	Sign + Verify (µs)
h	Msg hash	Auth path	WOTS+ sign	Other	Total	Total	Total
5	0.6	91.1	27.8	4.6	124.0	38.6	162.6
10	0.6	127.4	28.5	6.4	162.8	39.3	202.1
16	0.6	133.0	28.4	8.5	170.5	40.9	211.5
20	0.6	136.8	28.4	10.0	175.7	42.0	217.7
	Relative times sign operations (%)						
5	0.5	73.5	22.4	3.7	100		
10	0.4	78.2	17.5	3.9	100		
16	0.3	78.0	16.7	5.0	100		
20	0.3	77.8	16.2	5.7	100		

4.3 Latency Considerations

This section summarizes the shown results with respect to our initial goal to minimize the latency for the sign and verification procedures. XMSS, and hash-based signature schemes in general, have large signatures, i.e., 2820 B in our example. Thus, an additional requirement to achieve a low latency are transmission links with high data rates.

Unless otherwise noted, we use architecture *FB-EL3* with XMSS tree height parameter of $h = 20$ when referring to processing times. The observed processing times are $t_{\text{sign}} = 175.7\,\mu\text{s}$ for the sign and $42.0\,\mu\text{s}$ for the verify operation. In Table 4 we observe that about 78% of the sign operation is used for the *Auth path* operation. The computation of the authentication path is, however, independent of the data (or message) of a specific sign operation. Thus, the *Auth path* operation can be processed in advance of the event of a signature request from an application. In general, *Msg hash*, *WOTS+ sign*, and *Other* depend on the message data. Following this observation we assume:

1. The rate with which the application requests signatures, denoted as α_{sign}, is well below $1/t_{\text{sign}}$, or $\alpha_{\text{sign}} \ll 1/t_{\text{sign}}$. E.g., with $t_{\text{sign}} = 176\,\mu\text{s}$, this gives $1/t_{\text{sign}} \approx 5680/\text{s}$. In short, we are not throughput constrained.
2. Two consecutive sign request have a minimum distance of the maximum observed time for a sign operation $t_{\text{sign,max}}$.

Under those assumptions, the *Auth path* computation will not have an influence on the signing latency observed by an application. Let t_{AuthPath} be the time for processing the *Auth path* operation. Then, the optimized latency, denoted as t'_{sign}, can be expressed as $t'_{\text{sign}} = t_{\text{sign}} - t_{\text{AuthPath}}$. For our example case, this would result in a sign latency of $t'_{\text{sign}} = 176\,\mu\text{s} - 137\,\mu\text{s} = 39\,\mu\text{s}$, a further reduction of 78%. In total, the overall latency for the sign and verify operations is reduced from 218 µs to 81 µs by 63%.

5 Conclusion

The Tactile Internet requires ultra-low latency and security. Digital signatures play a key role for data authentication and thus for security in general. Currently used signature schemes will become insecure once quantum computers arise. One promising post-quantum secure signature algorithm is XMSS. Its high processing demand makes it challenging to meet the proposed end-to-end latency of 1 ms, especially in embedded environments.

In this study, we focused on a low-latency implementation of XMSS by means of an application-specific integrated processor. We identified the hash chain computation of XMSS and its interaction with the used hash function, SHAKE128, as key spot to reduce memory accesses during the hash chain computation.

Our design implements the Keccak-p[1600] permutation by using a 1600-bit state register complemented with a buffer architecture specifically tailored to the hash chain computation. Two buffers, a special result buffer, a result shift mechanism, and a padding generator minimized the load on the memory interface by reducing the cycles for load/store operations from 130 to only eight.

The computational time was further reduced by combining several iterations of *Rnd* into epochs of length L_e. We found out that the design with $L_e = 3$ was optimal in terms of the ATE product which was about 58% lower than the design without combined iterations. With this final design, we achieved a sign and verification time of 176 µs and 42 µs. This is about three orders of magnitude faster then our embedded reference core and about 19 times faster than the software solution on a high-end desktop PC [15]. Our solution is about 10 times faster than the XMSS-specific accelerator presented in [17].

The estimated energy consumption for a sign (verify) operation was 4.4 µJ (1.1 µJ). The core area was $0.081\,\text{mm}^2$ in a 22 nm FDSoI technology.

We argued that, if the application request signatures well below the throughput limit of the accelerator, the latency could be reduced even further. From a latency perspective, the authentication path computation can be done in advance of a sign request. This further reduces the sign time from 176 µs to 39 µs by about 78%. The total time for sign and verification reduces from 218 µs to 81 µs by about 63%. Our results show that ultra-low latency operation of XMSS is feasible and that our objective to stay below 100 µs for both signing and verification could be achieved under the stated assumptions.

References

1. The Tactile Internet, August 2014. https://www.itu.int/oth/T2301000023/en
2. SHA-3 Standard: Permutation-Based Hash and Extendable-Output Functions, August 2014. https://doi.org/10.6028/NIST.FIPS.202

3. Status Report on the First Round of the NIST PQC Standardization Process, January 2019. https://doi.org/10.6028/NIST.IR.8240
4. Bernstein, D.J., et al.: SPHINCS: practical stateless hash-based signatures. In: Oswald, E., Fischlin, M. (eds.) EUROCRYPT 2015. LNCS, vol. 9056, pp. 368–397. Springer, Heidelberg (2015). https://doi.org/10.1007/978-3-662-46800-5_15
5. Bernstein, D.J., Lange, T.: Post-quantum cryptography. Nature **549**, 188–194 (2017)
6. Bertoni, G., Daemen, J., Peeters, M., Van Assche, G.: The KECCAK reference, Version 3.0., January 2011. http://keccak.noekeon.org/Keccak-reference-3.0.pdf
7. Buchmann, J., Dahmen, E., Szydlo, M.: Hash-based digital signature schemes. In: Bernstein, D.J., Buchmann, J., Dahmen, E. (eds.) Post-Quantum Cryptography. Springer, Heidelberg (2009). https://doi.org/10.1007/978-3-540-88702-7_3
8. Buchmann, J., Dahmen, E., Hülsing, A.: XMSS - a practical forward secure signature scheme based on minimal security assumptions. In: Yang, B.-Y. (ed.) PQCrypto 2011. LNCS, vol. 7071, pp. 117–129. Springer, Heidelberg (2011). https://doi.org/10.1007/978-3-642-25405-5_8
9. Elmohr, M.A., Saleh, M.A., Eissa, A.S., Ahmed, K.E., Farag, M.M.: Hardware implementation of a SHA-3 application-specific instruction set processor. In: 2016 28th International Conference on Microelectronics (ICM), pp. 109–112, December 2016
10. Fettweis, G.P.: The tactile internet: applications and challenges. IEEE Veh. Technol. Mag. **9**(1), 64–70 (2014)
11. Huelsing, A., Butin, D., Gazdag, S., Rijneveld, J., Mohaisen, A.: XMSS: extended Merkle signature scheme. RFC 8391, May 2018. https://tools.ietf.org/html/rfc8391
12. Huelsing, A., Rijneveld, J.: Implementation of XMSS and XMSSMT as specified in draft-itrf-cfrg-xmss-hash-based-signatures-12. Technical report, January 2018. https://huelsing.net
13. Knezevic, M., et al.: Fair and consistent hardware evaluation of fourteen round two SHA-3 candidates. IEEE Trans. Very Large Scale Integr. (VLSI) Syst. **20**(5), 827–840 (2012)
14. McGrew, D., Curcio, M., Fluhrer, S.: Hash-Based Signatures. Internet-Draft draft-mcgrew-hash-sigs-13, Internet Engineering Task Force, September 2018. https://datatracker.ietf.org/doc/html/draft-mcgrew-hash-sigs-13. work in Progress
15. de Oliveira, A.K.D.S., Lopez, J., Cabral, R.: High performance of hash-based signature schemes. Int. J. Adv. Comput. Sci. Appl. **8**(3), 421–432 (2017)
16. Simsek, M., Aijaz, A., Dohler, M., Sachs, J., Fettweis, G.: 5G-enabled tactile internet. IEEE J. Sel. Areas Commun. **34**(3), 460–473 (2016)
17. Wang, W., et al.: XMSS and embedded systems - XMSS hardware accelerators for RISC-V. IACR Cryptology ePrint Archive 2018, p. 1225 (2018)
18. Wang, Y., Shi, Y., Wang, C., Ha, Y.: FPGA-based SHA-3 acceleration on a 32-bit processor via instruction set extension. In: 2015 IEEE International Conference on Electron Devices and Solid-State Circuits (EDSSC), pp. 305–308, June 2015
19. Wong, M.M., Haj-Yahya, J., Sau, S., Chattopadhyay, A.: A new high throughput and area efficient SHA-3 implementation. In: 2018 IEEE International Symposium on Circuits and Systems (ISCAS), pp. 1–5, May 2018

Fault Sensitivity Analysis of Lattice-Based Post-Quantum Cryptographic Components

Felipe Valencia[1(✉)], Ilia Polian[2], and Francesco Regazzoni[1]

[1] ALARI, Università della Svizzera Italiana (USI), Lugano, Switzerland
valena@usi.ch, regazzoni@alari.ch

[2] ITI, University of Stuttgart, Stuttgart, Germany
ilia.polian@informatik.uni-stuttgart.de

Abstract. Post-Quantum Cryptography (PQC) is currently receiving significant interest, as the construction of a practical quantum computer capable of executing Shor's algorithm is expected in the near-to-medium future. Lattice-based PQC algorithms are among the most promising candidates discussed today, due to their performance and versatility. In this paper, we demonstrate fault sensitivity analysis (FSA) of circuit blocks used in lattice-based cryptographic implementations and a representative complete post-quantum algorithm. FSA correlates the sensitivity of the algorithm's circuit implementation to faults with the processed data and recovers parts of the used secret key. In contrast to other types of fault attacks, FSA makes limited assumptions about the precision of fault injections and is therefore accessible even to poorly-equipped adversaries. We investigate traditional FSA based on simple models as well as its more advanced variants using templates with different construction procedures and aggregation functions, and systematically explore the conditions under which the analysis is successful. To the best of our knowledge, this is the most complex cryptographic implementation so far broken by FSA, and the first such PQC implementation.

1 Introduction

Peter Shor developed in 1994 a quantum algorithm able to solve the integer factorization and discrete logarithm problems in polynomial time [36]. The hardness of these two algorithms is the foundation for current public key cryptography, implying that our public key infrastructure will not be secure any more once a quantum computer able to run this algorithm will be available. The improvements of quantum technologies in last years increase the probability to have such a quantum computer in the next decades. Therefore, the research community is studying and developing cryptographic algorithms robust against quantum attacks. Such algorithms, known as *Post-Quantum Cryptography* (PQC), are currently going under the evaluation and scrutiny of the academic community

D. N. Pnevmatikatos et al. (Eds.): SAMOS 2019, LNCS 11733, pp. 107–123, 2019.
https://doi.org/10.1007/978-3-030-27562-4_8

and standardization bodies. The most notable example is the National Institute of Standards and Technology (NIST), which is currently running a contest for standardization of quantum resistant primitives.

Quantum resistant algorithms are usually classified based on the underlying hard problem, the most common being code-based [10], hash-based [32] and lattice-based [14]. *Lattice-Based Cryptography* (LBC) uses lattice problems such as Closest-Vector Problem (CVP) and Shortest Vector Problem (SVP). The distinguishing features of LBC over the other families are its versatility and performance. Because of this, a large number of algorithms submitted to the NIST competition and admitted to the second round are based on lattices.

Mathematical robustness is however not sufficient any more to guarantee security. Once an algorithm is implemented in a physical device (i.e. processor, microcontroller, etc.) an adversary can also exploit the weaknesses of the implementation to gain information about the secret key. These attacks, called *physical attacks*, use the relation between the processed data and a physical observable to extract secrets. Example of physical attacks are power analysis [18], timing attacks [17], attacks [8], and electromagnetic attacks [1].

The basic idea of fault attacks, the focus of this paper, consists in inducing the device into an anomalous behavior and exploit it in different ways. *Differential Fault Analysis* (DFA), for instance, consists in inserting a fault and analyzing the correct and the faulty output to recover the secret key [31]. Another popular fault attack was presented by Li *et al.* [21], and it is called Fault Sensitivity Analysis. Their attack does not require knowledge of faulty ciphertexts, but just the knowledge that the fault happened. To recover the secret key, this attack exploits the correlation between the critical fault level, e.g., the timing information where the system starts to fail, and, similar to power analysis, the data to construct the hypothesis on the secret key.

In this paper, firstly we evaluate the robustness of arithmetic operators used in hardware implementations of lattice-based algorithms against FSA. Then, to verify the possibility of successfully attacking using FSA these components when instantiated within a whole circuit, we attacked a complete implementation of a post-quantum algorithm: Lotus, which follows the public key encryption proposed by Lindner-Peikert [22] and is robust against chosen-plaintext attacks (CPA).[1]

The paper is organized as following, Sect. 2 introduces the background of LBC and physical attacks, and Sect. 3 summarizes the state of the art. Section 4 presents the experimental setup, the procedure to perform FSA and components we attacked.

[1] Despite recently not being included among the second round of the NIST standardization process, we selected Lotus as example of complete algorithm, because it uses (although with different parameters) all the basic blocks (vector/matrix operation, threshold as decoding function, hash functions and the Fujisaki-Okamoto transform) that constitute the foundation of several lattice-based schemes, thus it is representative of several submission still in the competition.

2 Background

Lattice-Based Cryptography: Lattice-Based Cryptography are cryptographic primitives that based their security on the hardness of lattices problems [2]. A *lattice* L is defined as discrete set of points in the space $\mathbb{R}^N$. Every element in L can be described as a linear combination of N linearly independent vectors $b_1, b_2, ..., b_N$, called the lattice's *basis.* The two fundamental problems used in lattice-based cryptography are *Shortest Vector Problem* (SVP) and *Closest Vector Problem* (CVP). Knowing the lattice basis, CVP consists in finding the vector in a lattice that is the closest to a given vector (this vector is not necessarily in the lattice). CVP is equivalent to SVP if the given vector is the zero vector. These problems have different variants [24,25,28]. The *Learning With Errors* (LWE), which is equivalent to CVP, has been used to build several cryptosystems. LWE consists of finding $x \in \mathbb{Z}^M$, given $(A, b = A * x + e \bmod Q)$, where N and Q are fixed parameters, $N \geq 1$, $Q \geq 2$. A is a matrix in $\mathbb{Z}_Q^{M \times N}$ and e is an error vector taken from a random probability distribution χ in $\mathbb{Z}_Q$, where $\mathbb{Z}_Q^N$ is a set of n-dimensional vectors modulus Q [34]. LWE can be also defined in a ring, which helps to reduce the memory footprint because the matrix A can be converted into a vector of length N. In that case one of the most time consuming operation is the vector/polynomial multiplication, which can be accelerated using the Number Theoretic Transform (NTT). NTT is a Fast Fourier Transform defined in a ring and its usage constrains the possible values of Q and N. Moreover, other important block is the discrete sampler. The random probability distribution can be uniform, Gaussian or binomial. In general, most of the algorithm submitted to NIST contest use lattice theory to build a system with CPA security that is then converted to CCA secured through any variant of Fujisaki-Okamoto transform.

Physical Attacks: Physical attacks are attacks during which the adversary tries to gain information about the secret key by observing and/or manipulating their physical implementation of a cryptographic algorithm. These attacks can be passive, such as side-channel attacks, or active (such as fault-injection attacks). *Side-channel attacks* observe parameters like the power consumed by the circuit [16] or the time needed to compute certain operation [17] and relate this information with the secret data processed by the device. *Fault-injection attacks* induce a physical disturbance during the circuit's operation via, e.g., manipulating the circuit's power-supply or clock connections or applying electromagnetic or laser pulses [6]. Fault injections can corrupt the control flow (e.g., jump over a password check) or induce small differentials in cryptographic computations which can be used for cryptanalysis (called *differential fault analysis* or DFA) of the algorithm under attack [38].

Fault-Sensitivity Analysis: Fault-sensitivity analysis (FSA), another type of fault attack, uses the correlation between the data processed by a device and the sensitivity of this device to faults. The attack consists in repeating the cryptographic operation while gracefully degradating an operational parameter of the device, for instance duration d of a specific clock cycle, until the circuit starts failing. The sensitivity is defined as the first (maximal) d which lead to circuit failure. FSA analyzes the correlation between d and the portion of the secret key processed by the module under attack. For instance, if the circuit has a critical path of 10ns, firstly an attacker supplies input $Input_1$, decreases the clock period to 9.99ns and checks the correctness of the output. If the output is incorrect, the attackers notes 9.99ns as the d parameter associated to $Input_1$. If the output is correct, the clock period is reduced of another 0.01ns and the correctness of the output is checked again until a failure is found. Once a fault is identified, the attacker restart the procedure, this time using $Input_2$, $Input_3$, till $Input_n$. A more detailed description on how to perform the attack is presented in Sect. 4.2.

Contrary to DFA, FSA does not need precise knowledge of the faulty ciphertexts. To perform the attack two conditions are needed: (1) the attacker should understand how the fault sensitivity (d) depends on processed data (secret key portion) and (2) it must be possible to divide the key in small portions and attack each component independently [21]. If the circuit is too complex to attack directly, its sensitivity can be modeled using *templates* [27]. We will explain this technique further below.

3 State of the Art

Prior Work on Fault Attacks on Lattice Algorithms: Security analysis against fault attacks on lattice algorithms has been already performed on NTRUsign assuming a model where attacker can insert faults in some coefficients but he does not control the position. It was shown that a larger security parameter for NTRUsign does not necessary protect the system against fault analysis attack [15]. Also, attacks that use skipping fault in the random sampler, for reducing the rank of the random vectors, were analyzed in signature schemes, specially those ones with Fiat-Shamir and Hash-and-Sign construction [12]. Further, the effects of randomization, skipping and zeroing faults were systematically analyzed to identify the vulnerabilities of signature schemes [7] and Ring-LWE encryption [39].

Prior Work on Fault-Sensitivity Analysis: When FSA was first introduced by Li *et al.* [21], it was applied to two types of AES S-Boxes, recovering all 16 key components of the low-power PPRM1-AES [30] using 50 ciphertexts and 3 out of 16 components of WDDL-AES protected against differential power analysis [37] using 1200 ciphertexts. The attack on the second S-Box was revisited using a template built using 180 plaintexts, recovering 7 bits of one byte using 400 plaintexts [20]. The effectiveness of FSA can be improved by combining it with collision side-channels attacks, as it was presented by Moradi *et al.* [29]. Also, Melzani *et al.* [27] presented how to enhance FSA using templates. From a set of keys and plaintexts, they obtained the intermediate values of AES at specific position and the fault sensitivity, and then created a correspondence between them. When doing this, the same intermediate value could be generated multiple times, each time with a different sensitivity; the authors used an aggregation function (minimum, mean or maximum) to collapse multiple observed sensitivities into one value.

Prior Work on Countermeasures Against FSA: To counteract FSA, Endo *et al.* [11] proposed to generate an enable signal that keeps the values of the combinational logic under attack separated from the last register. If enable signal is set the register input is the real result, otherwise a random value. The enable signal is generated from the clock using delay blocks, which can be configured using a one-time-memory. This countermeasure has a cost of 10% in the chip area. Another countermeasure that uses delay blocks to make uniform the arrival time of the signals and the depth of networks with sensitive gates, was proposed by Ghalaty *et al.* [13]. This implementation was associated with an overhead of 20% of gates. A further countermeasure uses four types of masked S-Boxes randomly assigned to key components, thus preventing collision FSA [19]. Finally, Arribas et al. prove practically and theoretically that countermeasures which achieve glitch resistance are also effective against FSA [4]. Investigations of physical attacks on latice-based cryptography focused on analyzing the schemes against power analysis and differential fault attacks, but none of them have tackled the vulnerability against FSA. In this paper, we will fill this gap.

4 FSA on PQC Components

We implemented the arithmetic operators of lattice-based cryptography and simulated them to apply fault sensitivity analysis. The faults that we induce are timing violations faults. We carried out experiments with and without template, and identify their vulnerabilities. The attack is focused on attacking the operations between vector components. In the following we detail the tool chains we used, the modules we attack, and the procedure we followed for the evaluation.

4.1 Experimental Setup

For every evaluated component we used the classical ASIC design process. We described the circuit using VHDL, we synthesized and we placed and route, and we extract the timing information needed for the simulation. In the synthesis step, we let the design tool select the adder and multiplier most suitable for our designs. Our evaluation setup allows to obtain the best possible timing information that can be obtained in simulation, since it includes the delay of the gate as well as the ones of the interconnection extracted from the layout. The tool chain comprised the following version of the tools: *ModelSim 10.4d*, *Synopsys K-2015.06-SP5* and *Encounter 14.26.* To allow reproducibility of our results, we selected as target library the *FreePDK 45 nm.* To allow comparison with previous design, we report the area occupation computed as gate equivalent after the synthesis.

To calculate the fault sensitivity, we perform several simulations, using different clock period, of the post layout circuit with annotated delay, also obtained after place and route. We started the simulation with a period equal to the critical path, and we gracefully degradate it till all the outputs are incorrect. The actual fault sensitivity analysis has been carried out using a dedicated routine developed in *Matlab 2016a.*

4.2 Detailed Description of FSA Process

FSA uses a model to estimate the sensitivity for every possible key, and then correlate the result with the sensitivity measure. Similar to power analysis attacks, it is expected that the correlation of the correct key will be the highest. In the case of FSA template, the model is replaced with a template built profiling the device.

As described in Fig. 1a the attack consists in few steps. The first one is measuring the fault sensitivity of the circuit while it is computing with a set of known inputs (pt) and the correct key (Kc). As many similar attacks, the know portion of data can be in the input or output. In addition, the attacker needs a target intermediate value that is linked with the secret key.

In the second step, the attacker attempts to recover a portion of the secret key, all possible intermediate values are calculated using the known data and all possible values of key portion, then the sensitivity is estimated from the intermediate values. Finally, the sensitivity measured (or simulated in our case) from the real device is correlated with the estimated sensitivity of possible keys. The key with higher correlation is expected to be the correct one.

An improvement of the attack exploits templates instead of models. Figure 1b depicts the process to create a template. First, an input vector is generated, this vector should contain the largest amount of possible combination of inputs (ideally all the possible combination for the target portion of the key). When the bit length of the inputs and the number of inputs do not allow the attacker to evaluate all possible input combination, the attacker evaluates a randomly selected subset of inputs. This would make the attack practical but it also reduces its effectiveness. Then, the sensitivity is measured on a device similar (ideally, identical) to the one which will be attacked. Several different inputs could produce the same intermediate value while having different sensitivity. In this case, it is necessary to reduce all sensitivity values having the same intermediate value through an aggregation function. The most common aggregation functions are minimum, mean and maximum [27].

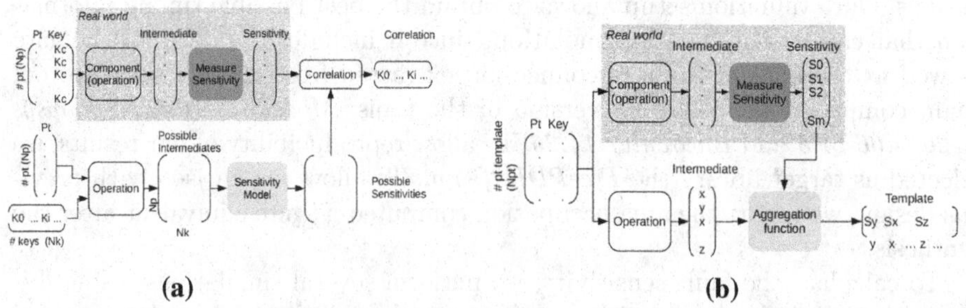

Fig. 1. (a) Pictorial description of FSA. (b) Template creation for FSA

In this work we use the Hamming Weight (HW) model to estimate the sensitivity[2]. Hamming weight model assumes that the sensitivity depends on the number of 1's of the intermediate values. When performing the template FSA, we evaluate the attack using as aggregation functions the minimum, maximum and mean, since they have been successfully used in the past [27]. We refer to the models obtained using templates with the name of the aggregation function.

4.3 Components Under Attack

To evaluate the impact of fault sensitivity, we carried out the attack on basic modules and on a complete lattice based schema. Lattice-based cryptography performs modular operations, commonly the modulus is a prime or a power of 2 (In such case the modular operation can be seen as a truncation). Therefore, we evaluate the multiplication and addition using modulus 12289, 32768 (2^{15}) and 8192 (2^{13}). We refer to these modules with the operation name (*add*, *mult*), in case of modular operation we use the suffix *mod* followed by the modulus, otherwise we place the number of bits. For instance addMod12289 means adder with modulus 12289 and add15 means adder of 15 bits input. Modular operations base on these modulus are used in NewHope [3], Hila5 [35], Compact-LWE [23], Round2 [5], Frodo [9], Lotus [33] among others. Also, we analyzed the addition and multiplication of 15 bits without modulus.

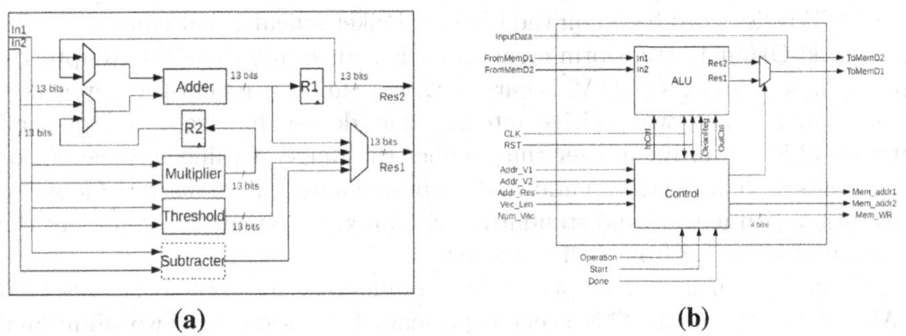

Fig. 2. (a) Block diagram of ALU used in Lotus implementation. (b) Block diagram matrix processing unit vector

To evaluate the feasibility of the attack on a complete schema, we implemented Lotus decryption with CPA security. This correspond to a decryption of a general Public Key Encryption (PKE) proposed by Lindner-Peikert with the Lotus parameters. Lotus is representative of lattice-based schemes, including the ones still considering in the second round of the NIST Competition. In fact, contrary to other cryptographic suites that are either Public key Encryption (PKE)

---

2 We also used the Zero-model and a model where sensitivity depends on the magnitude of the key but we did not obtained successful results.

robust against Plain-Text Attacks or Key Encryption Mechanism robust against Cipher-Chosen Attacks (CCA), Lotus also includes a CCA-PKE, thus covering a wider range of primitives. Several algorithms like NewHope, Kyber, Lizard, among others, are based on the arithmetic blocks used in Lotus. As a result, the procedure of FSA we explored here can be directly mapped to other lattice based algorithms.

Figure 2a depicts a block diagram of the ALU of our circuit, which is composed of adder, multiplier, threshold, subtractor (For key generation) and two registers. Figure 2b presents the core for matrix/vector operations.

Algorithm 1 Key generation

Input: Public parameter N, Q , L, s

1: $A \leftarrow U \ (\in \mathbb{Z}_Q^{N\times N})$
2: $R \leftarrow G_{(0,s)} \ (\in \mathbb{Z}_Q^{N\times L})$
3: $S \leftarrow G_{(0,s)} \ (\in \mathbb{Z}_Q^{N\times L})$
4: $P = R - AS \ (\in \mathbb{Z}_Q^{N\times L})$
5: **return** (S_k, P_k)= (S,P)

Algorithm 2 Encryption Enc_{cpa}

Input: $M \in \{0,1\}^L$,randomness

1: $e_1 \leftarrow G_{(0,s)} \ (\in \mathbb{Z}_Q^{1\times N})$
2: $e_2 \leftarrow G_{(0,s)} \ (\in \mathbb{Z}_Q^{1\times N})$
3: $e_3 \leftarrow G_{(0,s)} \ (\in \mathbb{Z}_Q^{1\times L})$
4: $c_1 = e_1 A + e_2 \ (\in \mathbb{Z}_Q^{1\times N})$
5: $c_2 = e_1 P + e_3 + Encode(M) \ (\in \mathbb{Z}_Q^{1\times L})$
6: **return** (c_1, c_2)

More in details, Lotus is a lattice-based cryptosystem, that contains a PKE scheme and a Key Exchange Mecahnism (KEM) scheme. In this work we only considered Lotus-PKE. The security is based on the hardness of LWE problem. Lotus-PKE is designed based on the Lindner-Peiker scheme, that combined with the Fujisaki-Okamoto transform create a PKE with security against Adaptative Cipher-Chosen Attacks (CCA2 security). Algorithm 1 presents the key generation, N and L are two positive integers that define the size of vectors and matrices, Q is a positive integer that defines the range of values for the vector components. U represents an uniform distribution and $G_{(0,s)}$ a discrete Gaussian distribution with mean 0 and standard deviation s. The symbol $\leftarrow$ represent the operation of sampling from a distribution.

The encryption and decryption for a Lindner-Peiker scheme is presented in Algorithms 2 and 3. This scheme presents CPA security. Two additional functions are defined: Encode, which multiplies every bit of a bit-stream times $\lfloor Q/2 \rfloor$, and Decode, which returns a bit in 1 for every vector component in $[\lfloor Q/4 \rfloor, \lfloor 3 \cdot Q/4 \rfloor)$ and 0 otherwise.

To apply the Fujisaki-Okamoto transform it is necessary to define two hash functions G and H, and symmetric encryption/decryption algorithms SE_{ksym}/SD_{ksym}, with key $ksym$. The modified encryption and decryption are presented in Algorithms 4 and 5 respectively. The bit concatenation is notated as $||$

Algorithm 3 Decryption Dec_{cpa}

Input: c_1, c_2

$\bar{M} = c_1 S + c_2$ $(\in \mathbb{Z}_Q^{1 \times L})$

return ($M = Decode(\bar{M})$ $(\in \{0,1\}^L)$)

Algorithm 4 Encryption Enc_{cca}

Input: $M \in \{0,1\}^L$

$\sigma \leftarrow U$ $(\in \{0,1\}^L)$

$c_{sym} = SE_{G(\sigma)}(M)$

$h = H(\sigma || c_{sym})$

$(c_1, c_2) = Enc_{cpa}(\sigma, h)$

return (c_1, c_2,c_{sym})

Algorithm 5 Decryption Dec_{cca}

Input: c_1, c_2,c_{sym}

$\sigma' = Dec_{cpa}(c_1, c_2)$

$h' = H(\sigma' || c_{sym})$

$(c_1', c_2') = Enc_{cpa}(\sigma', h')$

if $(c_1', c_2') \neg (c_1, c_2)$ **return** *Failure*

else return ($M' = SD_{G(\sigma')}(c_{sym})$)

In the experiments with single components we were controlling directly the inputs of each module, attempting to recovery the secret one. This approach is however hardly applicable to a complete implementation, since often it is not possible to directly control the inputs of single modules within a whole circuit. However, they can be controlled indirectly. For instance, Lotus decryption (Algorithm 3 uses as input two cipher-texts vector c_1, c_2) and matrix key S. It is thus possible to know that at a given cycle, the first component of c_1 and of S are multiplied. We can thus attack that cycles to obtained the first component of S. The attacker repeats the procedure component by component to recover the whole S.

5 Results

In this section we first present the results for single components (adders and multipliers), namely for 4 versions of these components used in different lattice-based algorithms. Then we present results for Lotus decryption, which uses both an adder and a multiplier; our attack targets the multiplication operation.

5.1 Multiplier

The first component that we analyzed is the multiplier with 4 different versions: a normal multiplier of 15 bits, and three modular multipliers. The analysis has been performed using 50k plain-texts for the attack and 200k plain-text for building the template. Table 1 presents a summary of the area and critical path delay of the multipliers, adders and the complete Lotus decryption circuit used in this analysis. Note that the Lotus decryption uses AddMod8192 and MultMod8192 as submodules.

For the modular version of the multiplier the correct key is recovered when using mean and maximum templates, for the case of the general 15 bits multiplier, the attack is successful only with hamming weight model. Figures 3a, b, c and d present the evolution of correlation of the correct key using mean template for modular multiplication and HW model for normal multiplier. The x-axis is the number of plaintexts used in the attack and the y-axis is the absolute correlation, every line represents the correlation of a key and the correct one is marked in red.

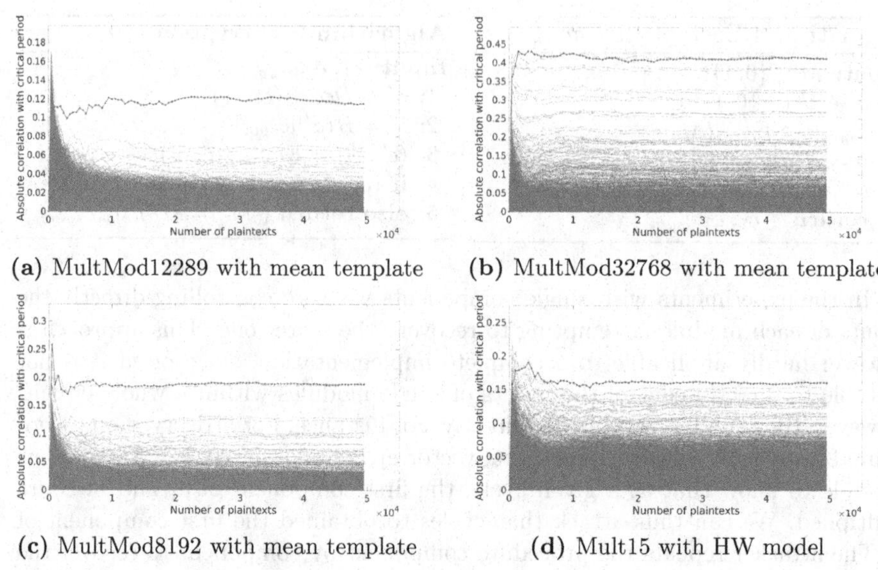

(a) MultMod12289 with mean template (b) MultMod32768 with mean template

(c) MultMod8192 with mean template (d) Mult15 with HW model

Fig. 3. Evolution correct key correlation in multiplier (Color figure online)

MultMod12289 is the component that presents higher leakage, specially with the mean template, where the correct key is recovered using 1500 plaintexts and the difference with the second key is very visible. Maximum template has a similar result but in this case 14k plaintexts are needed. With the minimum template the correct key is also recovered when using 50k plaintexts but the second key is very close.

The results of multMod32768 using templates present 2 keys with higher correlation that are very close to each other, in the case of maximum and mean the correct key is slightly higher. With the hamming weight model the correct key is in the third position. In the module multMod8192 the correct key is recovered with mean and maximum template but the second key is very close. In the module mult15 the correct key is recovered using 7500 plaintext and the hamming weight model. With templates it is not possible to obtained the correct key. It is caused by the fact that in this case the template has 2^{30} entries, therefore the number of ciphertexts needed to get a relevant profile of the circuit behavior is much higher than in previous cases.

Previously, we evaluated multipliers with parameters for different algorithms, but every multiplier can have many implementations. Hence, we analyzed different implementations of multmod12289. This module has two main components, a multiplier and a divider. There are two multiplier architectures in DesignWare library, *pparch* (delay-optimized) and apparch (area-optimized). Also, there are three divider architectures cla, cla2, cla3 (restoring carry-look-ahead, {1, 2, 3}-way overlapped synthesis model). Thus, we evaluate the attack with the 6 possible combinations. Results show that different implementations change the effectiveness and confidence of the attack but all considered changes are not significant and all implementations are vulnerable, therefore countermeasures need to be applied to prevent the attack. Still, we can highlight that the attack fails with HW model in all the cases, with max template it fails with the architectures (apparch, cla) and succeeds with very low confidence with (pparch, cla3), and the most vulnerable configuration to the attack is (apparch, cla3) using mean template.

5.2 Adder

We performed the analysis of the adder with the same parameters than for the multiplier. In the case of addMod12289 the correct key is recovered with around 20k plaintexts when using the mean template. It is also recovered with the maximum template but the second more probable key is very close. For addMod32768 the correct key is recovered with HW model, mean and maximum template. In all the three cases, the second key is very close to the first one, and both keys are differentiated only for 1 bit. For the modules addMod8192 and add15 the key can not be recovered with any model. Figures 4a and b present the evolution of the correlation when increasing the plaintexts using mean template in the modules addMod12289 and addMod32768, respectively.

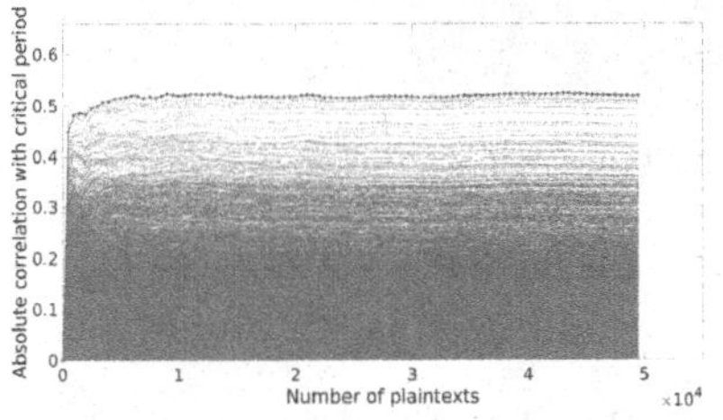

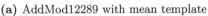

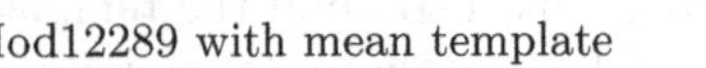
(a) AddMod12289 with mean template

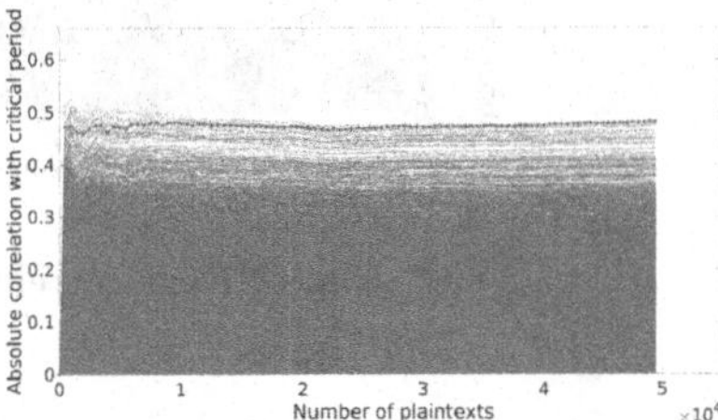

(b) AddMod32768 with mean template

Fig. 4. Evolution correct key correlation in adder

5.3 Lotus

FSA and FSA Template. In the Lotus module we attack a cycle that perform the multiplication because this is more vulnerable that the addition. Figure 5 shows how the attack is performed in a multicycle architecture. In the Algorithm 3, we are attacking the first line, when the second component of A multiplies the second component of c_1. Note that the same point can be attacked in the first line of Algorithm 5. In the experiments of Lotus we use 50k plain-texts for performing the attack and 100k for building the template. The HW model can successfully recover the key with around 5k plain-texts. Figures 6 presents how the correct key correlation changes over the numbers of plaintexts used in the attack. The results show that attempts to recover the key using templates are not successful. Also in this case, we believe that the number of plaintexts and data needed to build a working template is significantly higher because the circuit is more complex and it has more key independent signals that difficult the profiling.

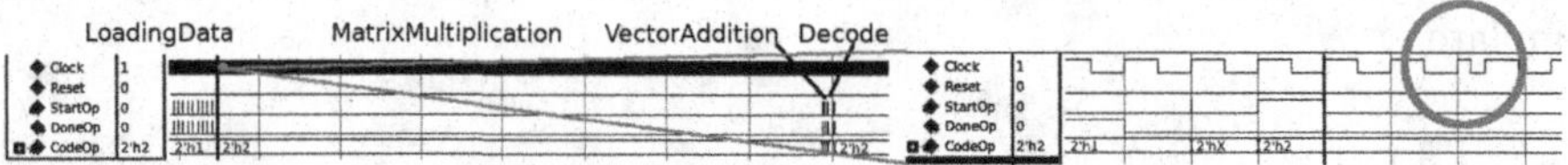

Fig. 5. Waveform for FSA attack on Lotus. Attacking the multiplication between 1st key component and 1st ciphertext component performed in the 3th cycle of matrix multiplication.

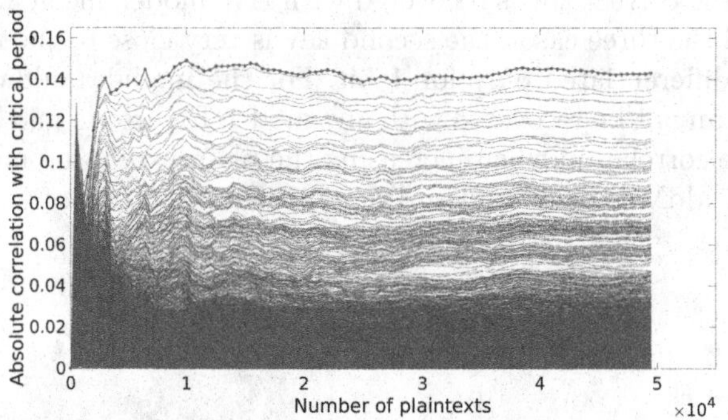

Fig. 6. Keys correlation for Lotus module

To explore how the number of plaintexts used to build the template affects the success of key recovery attack, we carried out experiments on individual bits. Firstly, we create a template considering only a specific bit. Then we perform the attack assuming that we know all bits of the target sub-key but the chosen one. We perform this experiment for every bit. This experiment was carried out using different amount of plaintexts for building the template. Then, we sort the bits according to the difference between the correlation of the correct key and the maximum correlation of any incorrect key; the resulting order is 8-11-7-10-12-9-6-13-3-1-4-5-2. This parameter shows how easy is to recover the correct key. Finally, we increase the amount of bits which we try to recover based on the obtained order.

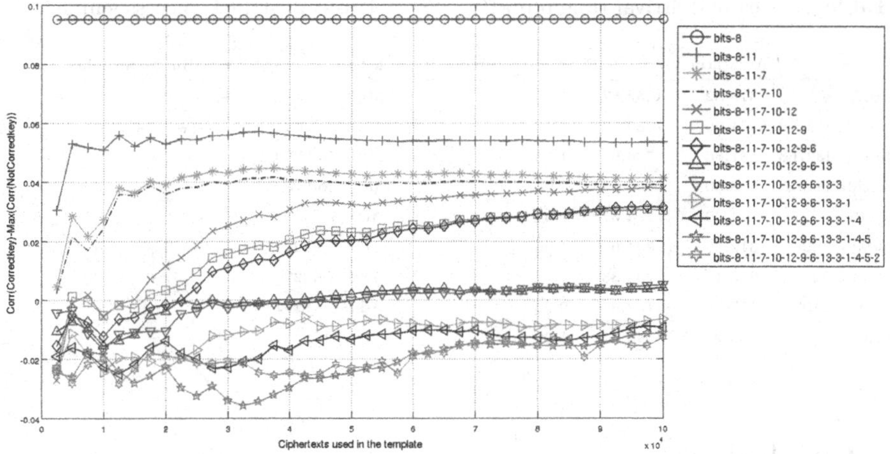

Fig. 7. Recovered bits vs plaintexts used in the template

Figure 7 shows in the x-axis the number of plaintexts used for building the template, and y-axis shows the correlation of the correct key minus the maximum correlation of an incorrect key. When the curve is positive, the correct key has the highest correlation. Figure 7 shows that generally the amount of bits recovered is directly proportional to the amount of plaintexts used for building the template. If FSA is given 4 (or more) correct key bits, it is capable of recovering the remaining 9 bits, but it can not, in this particular case, recover all 13 bits with no prior knowledge.

Another promising technique to build the template is to use the Hamming weight. This technique was used to build practical templates to attack ECDSA algorithms on a 32-bits platform [26], where the conventional template would have needed 2^{32} entries. We applied this technique for Lotus. Analyzing the generated template we see that the relation between the sensitivity and the HW is almost linear. Furthermore, if we modify the template through a linear regression, we obtain a template which allow us to recover the correct bit.

AddMod8192 and MultMod8192 with Gaussian Distribution. When building the template for single modules we assume that the key can take any possible value between 0 to $modulus - 1$ (8191 in this case). However in Lotus, and in other lattice-based algorithm, the key is generated with a Gaussian distribution. Therefore, we run the same experiments with addMod8192 and multMod8192, which are the modules used in Lotus, but constraining the possible values of the key to a Gaussian distribution. In this case the correct key can not been recovered in multMod8192 but, on the other hand, it can be recovered in addMod8192 using mean template. The difference with following keys is very small in terms of correlation.

Table 1. Area and arrival time report

Module	Area [μm^2]	Area [GE]	Arrival time [ns]
Mul15	1318.82	1652.67	1.96
MultMod12289	5931.00	7432.33	7.80
MultMod32768	587.86	736.67	1.53
MultMod8192	558.60	699.99	0.96
Add15	171.30	214.67	0.94
AddMod12289	312.55	391.67	1.96
AddMod32768	226.10	283.33	0.94
AddMod8192	155.34	194.67	0.96
LotusDec	2909.24	3645.67	1.00

Table 2. Attack success summary

Module	HW	Min	Mean	Max
Mult15	++	–	–	–
MultMod12289	–	++	++	+
MultMod32768	-	-	+	+
MultMod8192	–	–	+	+
Add15	–	-	–	–
AddMod12289	–	–	+	+
AddMod32768	–	-	+	+
AddMod8192	–	–	-	-
LotusDec	++	–	–	–

6 Conclusions

Post-quantum cryptographic implementations must be protected against physical attacks. We investigated the vulnerability of hardware blocks found in lattice-based post-quantum algorithms to fault-sensitivity analysis (FSA) and showed that most of these blocks can be broken for at least one parameter setting (which the adversary is free to choose). We also studied the cases when FSA techniques that were successful for other attack targets previously reported in the literature (e.g., templates) were not effective in the considered scenario, with the objective to identify the root causes for FSA failure. For the first time, we applied FSA to a complete post-quantum algorithm, Lotus, and showed that a successful attack on its component (here: multiplier) compromises the security of the entire algorithm. It is somewhat unexpected that the algorithm's high complexity, which prevents classical attacks, is essentially useless against FSA because the attacker can focus on one specific operation. Our future research will focus on countermeasures against FSA, leveraging our newly established understanding of conditions under which FSA failed in our experiments. Table 1 summarizes the area and arrival time of the modules. Table 2 present a summary of successful attacks using Hamming Weight model (HW) and templates with Min, Mean and Max aggregation functions: ++ = Correlation of correct key K_corr is clearly higher compared with other keys; + = Correlation of K_corr is slightly higher compared with a different (incorrect)key; - = correct key is not in the first position but it is close to it, – = correct key is not identifiable.

Acknowlegments. This work has been partly funded by European Union Horizon 2020 research and innovation programme under SAFEcrypto project (grant agreement No 644729) and by the Swiss National Science Foundation (project No P1TIP2_181305).

References

1. Agrawal, D., Archambeault, B., Rao, J.R., Rohatgi, P.: The em side-channel(s). In: CHES 2002, pp. 29–45 (2003)
2. Ajtai, M.: Generating hard instances of lattice problems (extended abstract). In Proceedings of the twenty-eighth annual ACM symposium on Theory of computing - STOC 1996, Association for Computing Machinery (ACM) (1996)
3. Alkim, E., et al.: Newhope - algorithm specifications and supporting documentation (2018)
4. Arribas, V., De Cnudde, T., Sijacic, D.: Glitch-resistant masking schemes as countermeasure against fault sensitivity Analysis. In: FDTC (2018)
5. Baan, H., et al.: Round2: KEM and PKE based on GLWR. Cryptology ePrint Archive, Report 2017/1183 (2017)
6. Bar-El, H., Choukri, H., Naccache, D., Tunstall, M., Whelan, C.: The sorcerer's apprentice guide to fault attacks. Proc. IEEE **94**(2), 370–382 (2006)
7. Bindel, N., Buchmann, J., Krämer, J.: Lattice-based signature schemes and their sensitivity to fault attacks. Cryptology ePrint Archive, Report 2016/415 (2016)
8. Boneh, D., DeMillo, R.A., Lipton, R.J.: On the importance of eliminating errors in cryptographic computations. J. Cryptol. **14**(2), 101–119 (2001)
9. Bos, J., et al.: Frodo: take off the ring! practical, quantum-secure key exchange from LWE. Cryptology ePrint Archive, Report 2016/659
10. Cayrel, P.-L., El Yousfi Alaoui, S.M., Hoffmann, G., Meziani, M., Niebuhr, R.: Recent progress in code-based cryptography. In: Kim, T., Adeli, H., Robles, R.J., Balitanas, M. (eds.) ISA 2011. CCIS, vol. 200, pp. 21–32. Springer, Heidelberg (2011). https://doi.org/10.1007/978-3-642-23141-4_3
11. Endo, S., Li, Y., Homma, N., Sakiyama, K., Ohta, K., Aoki, T.: An efficient countermeasure against fault sensitivity analysis using configurable delay blocks. In: 2012 DFTC. IEEE, September 2012
12. Espitau, T., Fouque, P.-A., Gérard, B., Tibouchi, M.: Loop-abort faults on lattice-based fiat-shamir and hash-and-sign signatures. Cryptology ePrint Archive, Report 2016/449 (2016)
13. Ghalaty, N.F., Aysu, A., Schaumont, P.: Analyzing and eliminating the causes of fault sensitivity analysis. In: Proceedings of the Conference on Design, Automation & Test in Europe, DATE 2014, European Design and Automation Association, Leuven, Belgium, pp. 204:1–204:6 (2014)
14. Howe, J., Pöppelmann, T., O'neill, M., O'sullivan, E., Güneysu, T.: Practical lattice-based digital signature schemes. ACM Trans. Embed. Comput. Syst. **14**(3), 1–24 (2015)
15. Kamal, A.A., Youssef, A.M.: Fault analysis of the NTRUSign digital signature scheme. Crypt. Commun. **4**(2), 131–144 (2012)
16. Kocher, P., Jaffe, J., Jun, B.: Differential power analysis. In: CRYPTO, pp. 388–397 (1999)
17. Kocher, P.C.: Timing attacks on implementations of Diffie-Hellman, RSA, DSS, and other systems. In: CRYPTO, pp. 104–113 (1996)
18. Kocher, P., Jaffe, J., Jun, B.: Differential power analysis. In: Wiener, M. (ed.) CRYPTO 1999. LNCS, vol. 1666, pp. 388–397. Springer, Heidelberg (1999). https://doi.org/10.1007/3-540-48405-1_25
19. Li, Q., Zhou, F., Wu, N., Yasir: An efficient countermeasure against fault sensitivity analysis using hybrid parallel s-boxes. In: Proceedings of The World Congress on Engineering and Computer Science 2017, Lecture Notes in Engineering and Computer Science, Newswood Limited, October 2017

20. Li, Y., Ohta, K., Sakiyama, K.: Revisit fault sensitivity analysis on WDDL-AES. In: 2011 IEEE HOST. IEEE, June 2011
21. Li, Y., Sakiyama, K., Gomisawa, S., Fukunaga, T., Takahashi, J., Ohta, K.: Fault sensitivity analysis. In: Mangard, S., Standaert, F.-X. (eds.) CHES 2010. LNCS, vol. 6225, pp. 320–334. Springer, Heidelberg (2010). https://doi.org/10.1007/978-3-642-15031-9_22
22. Lindner, R., Peikert, C.: Better key sizes (and attacks) for LWE-based encryption. In: Kiayias, A. (ed.) CT-RSA 2011. LNCS, vol. 6558, pp. 319–339. Springer, Heidelberg (2011). https://doi.org/10.1007/978-3-642-19074-2_21
23. Liu, D., Li, N., Kim, J., Nepal, S.: Compact-LWE: enabling practically lightweight public key encryption for leveled IoT device authentication. Cryptology ePrint Archive, Report 2017/685 (2017)
24. Liu, Y.-K., Lyubashevsky, V., Micciancio, D.: On bounded distance decoding for general lattices. In: Approximation, Randomization, and Combinatorial Optimization. Algorithms and Techniques, pp. 450–461 (2006)
25. Lyubashevsky, V.: Lattice-based identification schemes secure under active attacks. In: Cramer, R. (ed.) PKC 2008. LNCS, vol. 4939, pp. 162–179. Springer, Heidelberg (2008). https://doi.org/10.1007/978-3-540-78440-1_10
26. Medwed, M., Oswald, E.: Template attacks on ECDSA. In: Chung, K.-I., Sohn, K., Yung, M. (eds.) WISA 2008. LNCS, vol. 5379, pp. 14–27. Springer, Heidelberg (2009). https://doi.org/10.1007/978-3-642-00306-6_2
27. Melzani, F., Palomba, A.: Enhancing fault sensitivity analysis through templates. In: HOST 2013, Austin, TX, USA, 2–3 June 2013, pp. 25–28 (2013)
28. Daniele, M., Oded, R.: Lattice-based cryptography. In: Bernstein, D.J., Buchmann, J., Dahmen, E. (eds.) Post-Quantum Cryptography, pp. 147–191. Springer, Heidelberg (2009). https://doi.org/10.1007/978-3-540-88702-7_5
29. Moradi, A., Mischke, O., Paar, C., Li, Y., Ohta, K., Sakiyama, K.: On the power of fault sensitivity analysis and collision side-channel attacks in a combined setting. In: Preneel, B., Takagi, T. (eds.) CHES 2011. LNCS, vol. 6917, pp. 292–311. Springer, Heidelberg (2011). https://doi.org/10.1007/978-3-642-23951-9_20
30. Morioka, S., Satoh, A.: An optimized s-box circuit architecture for low power AES design. In: Kaliski, B.S., Koç, K., Paar, C. (eds.) CHES 2002. LNCS, vol. 2523, pp. 172–186. Springer, Heidelberg (2003). https://doi.org/10.1007/3-540-36400-5_14
31. Paillier, P.: Evaluating differential fault analysis of unknown cryptosystems. In: Imai, H., Zheng, Y. (eds.) PKC 1999. LNCS, vol. 1560, pp. 235–244. Springer, Heidelberg (1999). https://doi.org/10.1007/3-540-49162-7_19
32. Pereira, C.C.F., Puodzius, C., Barreto, P.S.L.M.: Shorter hash-based signatures. J. Syst. Softw. **116**, 95–100 (2016)
33. Phong, L.T., Hayashi, T., Aono, Y., Moriai, S.: LOTUS: algorithm specifications and supporting documentation (2018)
34. Regev, O.: The learning with errors problem. In: Proceedings of 25th IEEE Annual Conference on Computational Complexity (CCC) (2010)
35. Saarinen, M.-J.O.: Hila5: on reliability, reconciliation, and error correction for ring-LWE encryption. Cryptology ePrint Archive, Report 2017/424 (2017)
36. Shor, P.W.: Algorithms for quantum computation: discrete logarithms and factoring. In: Proceedings 35th Annual Symposium on Foundations of Computer Science. Institute of Electrical & Electronics Engineers (IEEE) (1994)
37. Tiri, K., Verbauwhede, I.: A logic level design methodology for a secure DPA resistant ASIC or FPGA implementation. In: DATE (2004)

38. Tunstall, M., Mukhopadhyay, D., Ali, S.: Differential fault analysis of the Advanced Encryption Standard using a single fault. In: Workshop in Information Security Theory and Practice, pp. 224–233 (2011)
39. Valencia, F., Oder, T., Guneysu, T., Regazzoni, F.: Exploring the vulnerability of R-LWE encryption to fault attacks. In: CS2 Workshop at HiPEAC2018 Conference, Manchester, United Kingdom, 22–24 January 2018 (2018)

Multi/Many-core Scheduling

Scalable Optimal Greedy Scheduler for Asymmetric Multi-/Many-Core Processors

Vanchinathan Venkataramani(✉), Anuj Pathania, and Tulika Mitra

National University of Singapore, Singapore, Singapore
{vvanchi,pathania,tulika}@comp.nus.edu.sg

Abstract. Ubiquitous asymmetric multi-core processors such as *ARM big.LITTLE* combine together cores with different power-performance characteristics on a single chip. Upcoming asymmetric many-core processors are expected to combine hundreds of cores belonging to different types. However, the accompanying task-to-core mapping schedules are the key to achieving the full potential of such processors. Run-time scheduling on asymmetric processors is a much harder problem to solve optimally than scheduling on symmetric processors with equivalent cores. We present the first-ever greedy scheduler to be proven theoretically optimal (under certain constraints) for asymmetric processors. The proposed scheduler, called *A-Greedy*, improves throughput by 26% and reduces average response time by up to 45% when compared to the default *Linux* scheduler on *ARM big.LITTLE* asymmetric multi-core.

Keywords: Multi-/many-cores · Asymmetric processors · Scheduling · Optimal greedy · *ARM big.LITTLE*

1 Introduction

Upcoming asymmetric many-core processors are expected to house together hundreds of heterogeneous cores grouped into homogeneous tiles connected using an interconnect on a single chip as shown in Fig. 1 [10]. They are an evolution of current asymmetric multi-core processors such as *ARM big.LITTLE* that are now commonplace. Asymmetric many-cores are designed to execute tens of multi-threaded applications on its hundreds of cores using one-thread-per-core model in order to reduce context switching overheads [12]. An Operating System (OS) sub-routine called scheduler determines the allocation of the cores among the applications. The discrete scheduling problem of allocating multiple cores to multiple applications optimally on asymmetric processors is in general NP-Hard and is commonly solved using heuristics [21].

Authors in [9] showed that the scheduling problem can be solved optimally using dynamic programming in polynomial time for symmetric processors containing cores with equivalent performance although with high scheduling overheads. Presence of a large number of cores in many-cores puts greater emphasis

D. N. Pnevmatikatos et al. (Eds.): SAMOS 2019, LNCS 11733, pp. 127–141, 2019.
https://doi.org/10.1007/978-3-030-27562-4_9

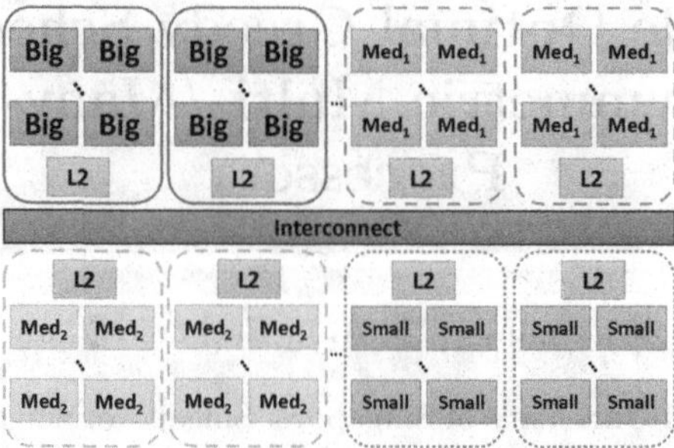

Fig. 1. An abstract block diagram of an asymmetric many-core processor containing clusters of cores with different power-performance characteristics.

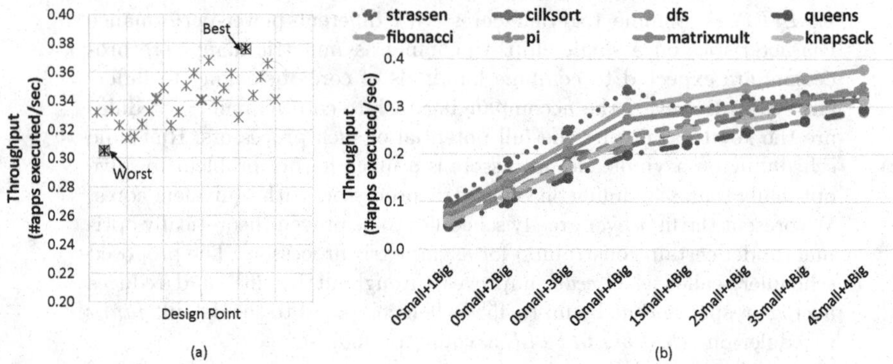

Fig. 2. (a) Throughput with two applications (*MatrixMult* and *Pi*) when executed with different asymmetric core allocations on *Kirin 960* (b) Throughput of different applications when executed in isolation with different asymmetric core allocations on *Kirin 960*.

on scheduler scalability than multi-cores especially for use at run-time [17,23]. Authors of [18] showed that the scheduling problem for symmetric processors can also be solved optimally using a greedy scheduler for applications with concave speedups but with several magnitudes lower scheduling overheads. Thus, the greedy scheduler can be used for run-time scheduling on symmetric many-cores.

The problem of scheduling on asymmetric processors is, however, more difficult to solve optimally than equivalent scheduling on symmetric processors as the scheduler needs to determine not just the number of cores allocated to each application but also the type of each of those allocated cores [8]. Thus, the involved design space that needs to be explored is further enlarged. For example, consider the case wherein we need to schedule two applications on *Huawei Kirin 960 octa-core ARM big.LITTLE* asymmetric multi-core with a cluster of four *Big* cores and a cluster of four *Small* cores. There will be twenty five design points on *Kirin 960* (0 to 4 cores in each cluster allocated to one application and remaining cores allocated to the other application). While on an equivalent octa-core symmetric multi-core, we will have only nine design points (0 to 8 cores for one application and remaining to the other application).

Motivational Example: A scheduler's efficacy can be measured using the throughput it can sustain on its underlying processor. **Throughput** is defined as the number of applications finishing per unit time. Figure 2(a) shows the throughput for all possible core allocations between the two applications (*Matrix-Mult* and *Pi*) on *Kirin 960*. Results show that the throughput in the best-case is 1.23x higher than the worst-case, necessitating a sophisticated scheduler.

The performance improvement with increasing core allocation for a multi-threaded application is dependent on the parallel portion of the application as governed by the Amdahl's Law [1]. Parallelization may incur overheads arising from coherence, inter-thread communication, etc. in processors. Thus, every subsequent core allocation brings in lower or equal improvement than the antecedent allocation resulting in multi-threaded applications to exhibit concave throughput increase. Fortunately, we observe that several of the multi-threaded applications that exhibit concave throughput behavior on symmetric processors also exhibit near-concave throughput behavior on asymmetric processors. Figure 2(b) shows the concavity in throughput increase for different applications when executed with different asymmetric allocations on *Kirin 960*. This concavity observation can be utilized to design an optimal greedy scheduler for asymmetric processors. In practice, the proposed scheduler can also accommodate minor non-concavity using concave approximations [22] without deviating significantly from the optimal. Though uncommon, applications that do not exhibit concave speedup exist [20] and this work is not applicable to them.

Our Novel Contributions: We make the following novel contributions within the scope of this work.

- We are the first to present a greedy scheduler that can optimally schedule multi-threaded applications with concave throughput increase on asymmetric processors. We present the proofs to theoretically support our claim.
- We implement our proposed greedy scheduler on a commercial-grade *Kirin 960* asymmetric multi-core and show its performance to be near-equivalent to an optimal ILP-based scheduler. The performance is also shown to be higher than the default *Linux* scheduler and state-of-the-art heuristic scheduler [13].

2 A-GREEDY: Greedy Scheduler for Asymmetric Multi-/Many-Cores

We describe *A-Greedy*, a greedy scheduler that exploits concave throughput behavior in multi-threaded applications to make efficient use of the underlying asymmetric processor. For brevity, we assume that the asymmetric processor contains cores of only two types - *Big* and *Small*. However, *A-Greedy* can be generalized to asymmetric processors with any number of core types.

2.1 Model

Let B and S denote the total number of cores of type *Big* and *Small*, respectively in the processor. Let T denote the total number of independent applications executing on the processor indexed using i. We assume that all applications derive higher performance on n *Big* cores than n *Small* cores, where $n \geq 1$. Furthermore, we also assume that the performance of an individual application i remains unaffected by other applications executing in parallel. Note that this assumption is needed only for designing a theoretically optimal algorithm. Our experimental evaluation includes interferences among the applications.

Let B_i and S_i be the number of cores of type *Big* and *Small* respectively that are allocated to application i. Let P_{B_i,S_i} represent the throughput (performance) of application i when simultaneously executed on B_i *Big* and S_i *Small* cores. Let THD_i denote the maximum multi-threading factor of application i, which determines the maximum number of cores, i.e., $B_i + S_i$ that can be assigned to application i. Let $P_{B_i,S_i} = 0$, if $B_i + S_i > THD_i$.

The problem of throughput maximization on asymmetric processors can then be described as:

$$\text{Maximize:} \sum_{i=1}^{T} P_{B_i,S_i}$$

subject to the following constraints:

$$\sum_{i=1}^{T} B_i \leq B \,, \sum_{i=1}^{T} S_i \leq S \text{ and } \forall i \in \{1, 2, \ldots, T\}(B_i + S_i) \leq THD_i$$

We use profiling to obtain P_{B_i,S_i} for all possible core allocations. We observe that the applications exhibit concave throughput behavior, i.e., the increase in throughput when a core is allocated is less than or equal to the increase in throughput experienced in the previous core allocation when adding cores belonging to a particular type. The concavity observed on asymmetric processors as shown in Fig. 2(b) needs to be mathematically represented. Concavity due to the allocations of additional n *Big* (or *Small*) cores while starting with having different number of *Big* (or *Small*) cores but the same number of *Small* (or *Big*) cores, i.e., $B_i \to B_i + n$ versus $B_i' \to B_i' + n$ (or $S_i \to S_i + n$ versus $S_i' \to S_i' + n$) can be described using the equations below.

$$\forall n \geq 0,\ P_{B_i'+n,S_i} - P_{B_i',S_i} \geq P_{B_i+n,S_i} - P_{B_i,S_i} \text{ if } B_i' \leq B_i \tag{1}$$

$$\forall n \geq 0,\ P_{B_i,S_i'+n} - P_{B_i,S_i'} \geq P_{B_i,S_i+n} - P_{B_i,S_i} \text{ if } S_i' \leq S_i \tag{2}$$

We also assume that the allocation of n *Big* (or *Small*) cores while having the same number of *Big* (or *Small*) cores is independent of the number of *Small* (or *Big*) cores allocated already.

$$\forall n \geq 0,\ P_{B_i+n,S_i'} - P_{B_i,S_i'} = P_{B_i+n,S_i} - P_{B_i,S_i} \ \ \forall S_i', S_i \in [0, S] \tag{3}$$

$$\forall n \geq 0,\ P_{B_i',S_i+n} - P_{B_i',S_i} = P_{B_i,S_i+n} - P_{B_i,S_i},\ \ \forall B_i', B_i \in [0, B] \tag{4}$$

2.2 Algorithm

The greedy algorithm proposed in *A-Greedy* scheduler consists of the following steps performed sequentially at every invocation.

1. Start with an empty allocation for all applications, i.e., $\forall i \in \{1, 2, \ldots, T\}$, $B_i = 0$ and $S_i = 0$.
2. Sort all applications $i \in \{1, 2, \ldots, T\}$ that has been allocated with less than THD_i cores in descending order of highest possible throughput gain by allocating one more free core of any type and add them to a queue.
3. Allocate a core of that type to application i in front of the queue from which it derives the maximum throughput.
4. Update the throughput value and reposition the entry associated with application i in the queue according to its revised throughput only if $(B_i + S_i) < THD_i$. As the queue is sorted, we can use binary search to perform fast insertions. Otherwise, pop the element from the queue.
5. Repeat Steps 3 and 4 if there are applications left in the queue and if any core is left unallocated.
6. Execute the applications with the greedy allocation.

The above greedy algorithm is straightforward to implement. Nevertheless, the algorithm results in a schedule that provides optimal allocations that maximizes total throughput on asymmetric many-cores under the throughput concavity assumption. We provide the proof for its theoretical optimality next.

2.3 Optimality Proof

Theorem 1. *The A-Greedy scheduler optimally maximizes the aggregate throughput on an asymmetric processor.*

Proof. We prove this theorem using the induction method. There are two possible scenarios that need to be inductively proven sub-optimal – unidirectional moving of cores between two applications and swapping of heterogeneous cores between two applications. Let $[\{B_1, S_1\}, \{B_2, S_2\}, ..., \{B_T, S_T\}]$ be the greedy core allocation chosen by our proposed *A-Greedy* scheduler.

Moving Cores Unidirectionally Between Applications

Base Case: We do not start with moving one *Big* (or *Small*) core between applications as it reduces to the allocation problem in symmetric processors. Authors in [18] have proven this move to be sub-optimal. Thus, we only show detailed proof for the case where one *Big* core and one *Small* core is removed from Application x and given to Application y. Without loss of generality, the proof below will also hold for other possible combinations if (i) one *Big* and one *Small* core is removed from Application x and given one each to Application y and Application z, respectively, (ii) one *Big* and one *Small* core is removed respectively from Application x and y, and then given to Application z, (iii) one *Big* and one *Small* core is removed respectively from Application v and x, and then given to Application y and z. Due to the space constraint all the cases cannot be shown here in detail.

Let us begin with the assumption that $[\{B_1, S_1\}, ..., \{B_x - 1, S_x - 1\}, ..., \{B_y + 1, S_y + 1\}, ..., \{B_T, S_T\}]$ is instead the optimal allocation where one *Big* core and one *Small* core is removed from Application x and given to Application y. For the assumed optimal allocation to be better than the greedy core allocation, gain in throughput of Application y with allocation of more cores must outweigh the loss in throughput of Application x due to the removal of those cores and thereby the following inequality must hold.

$$P_{B_x-1,S_x-1} + P_{B_y+1,S_y+1} > P_{B_x,S_x} + P_{B_y,S_y} \tag{5}$$

As *A-Greedy* chose to allocate the additional *Big* core to Application x instead of Application y, then the following inequality must be true.

$$P_{B_x,S_x} - P_{B_x-1,S_x} \geq P_{B_y+1,S_y} - P_{B_y,S_y} \tag{6}$$

As *A-Greedy* chose to allocate the additional *Small* core to Application x instead of Application y then the following inequality must be true.

$$P_{B_x,S_x} - P_{B_x,S_x-1} \geq P_{B_y,S_y+1} - P_{B_y,S_y} \tag{7}$$

Using Eq. (4), we know that the following equations are true.

$$P_{B_x-1,S_x} - P_{B_x-1,S_x-1} = P_{B_x,S_x} - P_{B_x,S_x-1} \tag{8}$$

$$P_{B_y,S_y+1} - P_{B_y,S_y} = P_{B_y+1,S_y+1} - P_{B_y+1,S_y} \tag{9}$$

Adding Eqs. (6) and (9) we get:

$$\begin{aligned} P_{B_x,S_x} - P_{B_x-1,S_x} + P_{B_y,S_y+1} - P_{B_y,S_y} \geq P_{B_y+1,S_y} - P_{B_y,S_y} \\ + P_{B_y+1,S_y+1} - P_{B_y+1,S_y} \end{aligned} \tag{10}$$

Using the inequality in Eq. (7) in Eq. (10) we get:

$$P_{B_x,S_x} - P_{B_x-1,S_x} + P_{B_x,S_x} - P_{B_x,S_x-1} \geq P_{B_y+1,S_y+1} - P_{B_y,S_y} \tag{11}$$

Using Eq. (8) in Eq. (11) we get:

$$P_{B_x,S_x} - P_{B_x-1,S_x} + P_{B_x-1,S_x} - P_{B_x-1,S_x-1} \geq P_{B_y+1,S_y+1} - P_{B_y,S_y} \tag{12}$$

By solving and rearranging Eq. (12) we get:

$$P_{B_x,S_x} + P_{B_y,S_y} \geq P_{B_x-1,S_x-1} + P_{B_y+1,S_y+1} \tag{13}$$

Equation (13) is in contradiction to Eq. (5). Hence, we prove that the allocation chosen by the greedy scheduler is optimal.

Inductive Assumption: We assume that the greedy allocation is optimal and of higher or equal performance than any allocation where n cores are removed from Application x and distributed among all the other tasks in any combination. Mathematically, we assume that the following inequality is true.

$$P_{B_x,S_x} - P_{B_x-n,S_x-n} \geq P_{B_1+\alpha_1,S_1+\beta_1} - P_{B_1,S_1} + .. + P_{B_T+\alpha_T,S_T+\beta_T} - P_{B_T,S_T} \quad (14)$$

where $\alpha_1 + ... + \alpha_T = \beta_1 + ... + \beta_T = n$

Inductive Step: Now we assume optimal allocation, which is different from the greedy allocation. In this optimal allocation, n cores are removed from Application x and distributed among all the other applications in the same combination as in the inductive assumption in Eq. (14). In addition, $n + 1^{th}$ *Big* and *Small* cores are removed from Application x and are given to Application y without loss of generality. For assumed optimal allocation to be better than greedy allocation, the following inequality must hold.

$$\begin{aligned} P_{B_1+\alpha_1,S_1+\beta_1} - P_{B_1,S_1} + ... + P_{B_y+\alpha_y+1,S_y+\beta_y+1} - P_{B_y,S_y} + ... + \\ P_{B_T+\alpha_T,S_T+\beta_T} - P_{B_T,S_T} > P_{B_x,S_x} - P_{B_x-n-1,S_x-n-1} \end{aligned} \quad (15)$$

As *A-Greedy* allocated a *Big* and *Small* core to Application x with B_{x-n-1} *Big* and S_{x-n-1} *Small* cores already allocated to it instead of Application y, by the greedy design of *A-Greedy*, the following inequality must be true.

$$P_{B_x-n,S_x-n} - P_{B_x-n-1,S_x-n-1} \geq P_{B_y+\alpha_y+1,S_y+\beta_y+1} - P_{B_y+\alpha_y,S_y+\beta_y} \quad (16)$$

By adding Eq. (16) with Eq. (14) we get:

$$\begin{aligned} P_{B_x,S_x} - P_{B_x-n-1,S_x-n-1} \geq P_{B_1+\alpha_1,S_1+\beta_1} - P_{B_1,S_1} \\ +... + P_{B_y+\alpha_y+1,S_y+\beta_y+1} - P_{B_y,S_y} + ... + P_{B_T+\alpha_T,S_T+\beta_T} - P_{B_T,S_T} \end{aligned} \quad (17)$$

Equation (17) is in contradiction to Eq. (15) proving that the greedy allocation under *A-Greedy* is optimal instead of the assumed optimal allocation in the inductive step. Thus, unidirectional movement of cores between applications is a sub-optimal scenario.

Swapping Asymmetric Cores Between Applications

Base Case: As in the previous scenario, we only show the detailed proof for the case where one *Small* core is removed from Application x and given to Application y and one *Big* core is removed from Application y and given to Application x. Without loss of generality, the proof below will also hold for other possible combinations. Let us begin with the assumption that $[\{B_1, S_1\}, ..., \{B_x + 1, S_x - 1\}, ..., \{B_y - 1, S_y + 1\}, ..., \{B_T, S_T\}]$ is instead the optimal allocation. For this to be true, throughput in this assumed optimal allocation has to be better than the greedy core allocation as stated in the following inequality.

$$P_{B_x+1,S_x-1} + P_{B_y-1,S_y+1} > P_{B_x,S_x} + P_{B_y,S_y} \quad (18)$$

Since *A-Greedy* adds one core at a time, let us start from an intermediate allocation $[\{B_1, S_1\}, ..., \{B_x, S_x - 1\}, \{B_y - 1, S_y\}, ..., \{B_T, S_T\}]$ which is the predecessor allocation to both greedy and optimal allocation. In the greedy algorithm, one *Big* core is added to Application y followed by one *Small* core to

Application x from the intermediate allocation. For the assumed optimal allocation, one *Big* core is added to Application x and one *Small* core is added to Application y from the same intermediate allocation. Since *A-Greedy* chose to allocate the additional *Big* core to Application y instead of Application x, followed by additional *Small* core to Application x instead of Application y, the following inequalities must hold.

$$P_{B_y,S_y} - P_{B_y-1,S_y} \geq P_{B_x+1,S_x-1} - P_{B_x,S_x-1} \tag{19}$$

$$P_{B_x,S_x} - P_{B_x,S_x-1} \geq P_{B_y,S_y+1} - P_{B_y,S_y} \tag{20}$$

Using Eq. (4), we know that the following equation is true.

$$P_{B_y,S_y+1} - P_{B_y,S_y} = P_{B_y-1,S_y+1} - P_{B_y-1,S_y} \tag{21}$$

Replacing R.H.S in Eq. (20) using Eq. (21) and adding Eqs. (19) and (20) we get:

$$\begin{aligned} P_{B_y,S_y} - P_{B_y-1,S_y} + P_{B_x,S_x} - P_{B_x,S_x-1} \geq \\ P_{B_x+1,S_x-1} - P_{B_x,S_x-1} + P_{B_y-1,S_y+1} - P_{B_y-1,S_y} \end{aligned} \tag{22}$$

By rearranging Eq. (22) we get:

$$P_{B_x,S_x} + P_{B_y,S_y} \geq P_{B_x+1,S_x-1} + P_{B_y-1,S_y+1} \tag{23}$$

Equation (23) is in contradiction to Eq. (18). Hence, we prove that the allocation chosen by the greedy scheduler is optimal.

Inductive Assumption: We assume that the greedy allocation is optimal with equal or higher performance than any allocation where n *Small* cores from Application x is swapped with n *Big* cores from other applications in any combination. Mathematically, we assume that the following inequality is true.

$$P_{B_x,S_x} - P_{B_x+n,S_x-n} \geq P_{B_1-\alpha_1,S_1+\beta_1} - P_{B_1,S_1} + ... + P_{B_T-\alpha_T,S_T+\beta_T} - P_{B_T,S_T} \tag{24}$$

where $\alpha_1 + ... + \alpha_T = \beta_1 + ... + \beta_T = n$

Inductive Step: Now we assume that the optimal allocation is different from the greedy allocation. In this assumed optimal allocation, n *Small* cores from Application x are swapped with n *Big* cores from other applications in the same combination as in the inductive assumption (Eq. (24)). In addition, $n+1^{th}$ *Small* core from Application x is swapped with *Big* core in Application y without loss of generality. For the assumed optimal allocation to be better than the greedy allocation, the following inequality must hold.

$$\begin{aligned} P_{B_1-\alpha_1,S_1+\beta_1} - P_{B_1,S_1} + ... + P_{B_y-\alpha_y-1,S_y+\beta_y+1} - P_{B_y,S_y} + ... + \\ P_{B_T-\alpha_T,S_T+\beta_T} - P_{B_T,S_T} > P_{B_x,S_x} - P_{B_x+n+1,S_x-(n+1)} \end{aligned} \tag{25}$$

As *A-Greedy* allocated a *Big* core to Application y, followed by a *Small* core to Application x, by greedy design following inequality must be true.

$$P_{B_x+n,S_x-n} - P_{B_x+n+1,S_x-(n+1)} \geq P_{B_y-\alpha_y-1,S_y+\beta_y+1} - P_{B_y-\alpha_y,S_y+\beta_y} \tag{26}$$

By adding Eq. (26) with Eq. (24) we get:

$$\begin{aligned} P_{B_x,S_x} - P_{B_x+n+1,S_x-(n+1)} \geq P_{B_1-\alpha_1,S_1+\beta_1} - P_{B_1,S_1} + ...+ \\ P_{B_y-\alpha_y-1,S_y+\beta_y+1} - P_{B_y,S_y} + ... + P_{B_T-\alpha_T,S_T+\beta_T} - P_{B_T,S_T} \end{aligned} \quad (27)$$

Equation (27) is in contradiction to Eq. (25) proving greedy allocation under *A-Greedy* is optimal instead of the assumed optimal allocation in the inductive step. Thus, swapping of asymmetric cores between applications is a sub-optimal scenario. *A-Greedy* is therefore proven to be optimal using induction.

2.4 Complexity

The *A-Greedy* scheduler requires sorting of the tasks according to their throughput, which introduces a worst-case overhead of $O(T \lg T)$. It also requires repositioning of the applications in the queue using binary search after every core allocation introducing a worst-case overhead of $O((B + S) \lg T)$. Therefore, the total worst-case computational-overhead of our *A-Greedy* scheduler is $O(\max\{B{+}S, T\} \lg T)$. The need for the sorted applications queue data structure introduces a worst-case space-overhead of $O(T)$ for *A-Greedy*.

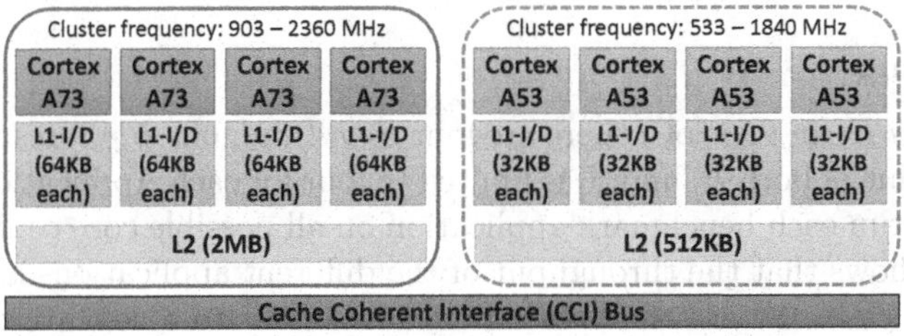

Fig. 3. *Huawei Kirin 960 octa-core ARM big.LITTLE* platform block diagram

3 Experimental Evaluations

In this section, we show the efficacy of our proposed *A-Greedy* scheduler on a commercial state-of-the-art asymmetric multi-core.

3.1 Benchmarks and Multi-threading Model

In this evaluation, we utilize eight multi-threaded benchmarks: *CilkSort, DFS, Fibonacci, Knapsack, MatrixMult, Pi, Queens, Strassen*, from *LACE* benchmark suite [5]. These applications are representative of a real-world asymmetric processor workload and are implemented using a work-stealing framework in which slave threads grab work from a centralized queue managed by a master thread. We suitably modify these applications to make them *malleable* [6], i.e., it is possible for the scheduler to change the number of cores allocated to them during their execution. Malleability is shown to enable efficient utilization of the underlying processing resources [6]. Though multi-threaded benchmark suites like *Parsec* [2] are also compatible with our proposed algorithm, it is not possible for us to change the number of cores allocated to them at run-time making them non-malleable. Hence, we do not utilize them in this work.

3.2 Evaluation Setup

We use state-of-the-art *HiKey 960* embedded platform with *Huawei Kirin 960 octa-core ARM big.LITTLE* asymmetric multi-core processor (Fig. 3) as a proof-of-concept testbed for our evaluation on existing silicon. Figure 3 also summarizes the system specifications of this architecture. There are two clusters: a low-performance cluster consisting of four *ARM Cortex-A53* (*Small*) cores and a high-performance cluster containing four *ARM Cortex-A73* (*Big*) cores. The clusters are connected by a cache-coherent bus interface. We ideally want to run the applications at the maximum system frequency on all eight cores as the primary objective in this work is to improve the performance. However, the system gets automatically throttled due to thermal constraints. Hence, in order to make use of all available cores without throttling affecting our evaluations, we run the small cores at 533 MHz and big cores at 903 MHz. The experimental evaluations implicitly reflect the impact of inherent shared-resource contention.

3.3 Profiling

In the *Huawei Kirin 960* SoC, there are four *Small* and four *Big* cores. Hence, the maximum value of both B_i and S_i is limited to four for each Application i. Therefore, we first run each benchmark application on all possible core configurations. Figure 2(b) shows that the throughput of the different applications is concave in almost every case. We use the profiled data and fit it to a concave curve using regression. The fitted values are then utilized in *A-Greedy* to make scheduling decisions. The comparative baselines use the original unmodified values as they do not require concave smoothing to operate.

3.4 Evaluation Systems and Metrics

A-Greedy scheduler can be utilized in both closed and open systems. We describe these systems alongside their preferred optimization metric.

Closed System. In a closed system, applications executing in the system restart execution immediately after their completion. System *throughput* is often used as the performance metric [7] in these systems.

Open System. In an open system: (i) applications enter and leave the system at any time and (ii) run-time scheduling overhead needs to be minimal. *Response time*, i.e., the time elapsed between an application's arrival and exit is a common metric optimized in open systems [7] as it captures both waiting and execution time. Thus, we use *average response time* as the performance metric for our open system evaluations. Applications arrive in the open system using a uniform distribution and permanently leave once they complete execution.

3.5 Comparative Baselines

We evaluate our proposed *A-Greedy* scheduler against three baselines:

ILP. An *ILP*-based scheduler implemented using *Gurobi* [16] that utilizes the measured throughput values as input to obtain the optimal scheduling decision. Though the *ILP* scheduler is guaranteed to present optimal results even in the absence of concavity, it cannot scale beyond dozen cores due to its exponential computational complexity and is therefore infeasible in-practice for use as a run-time scheduler in asymmetric many-cores.

Linux. Our platform's default *Linux* scheduler (4.14.0-rc7-linaro-hikey960) that is based on a load-balancing algorithm described in [4].

MTS-Like. Existing scheduler called *MTS* [13] first maximizes performance by allocating cores to the application thread that has the highest Instruction per Second (IPS). In this step, cores are considered in decreasing order of their performance. Next, it swaps cores allocated to different application threads to improve the system power-efficiency. As we focus on performance, we only utilize the first step of *MTS*. The original performance metric (IPS) used in *MTS* is changed to throughput for a fair comparison with the *A-Greedy* scheduler. *MTS* treats each application thread independently. Thus, it is unable to utilize the throughput concavity (observed when considering the allocation dependency among the application threads) and thereby compute the optimal schedule. Major difference between *MTS* and *A-Greedy* is theoretical as former is proposed purely as a heuristic. Since we modify the design parameters of original *MTS* algorithm extensively to be within the purview of this work, we rename the version we implement and compare against as *MTS-Like*.

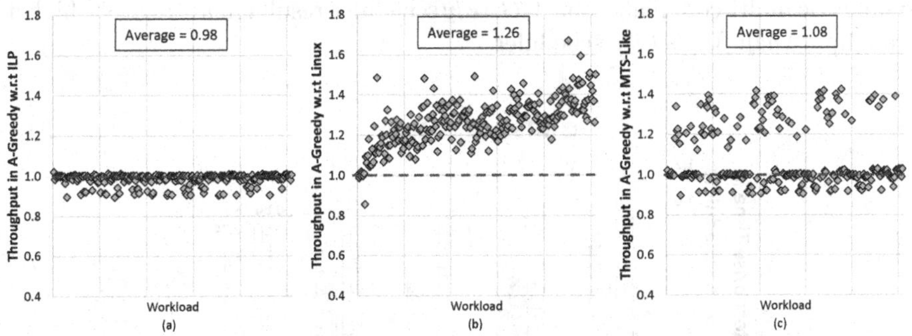

Fig. 4. Throughput obtained under proposed *A-Greedy* scheduler normalized to (a) exhaustive *ILP* scheduler (note that the slight drop in performance is due to concave approximation) (b) default *Linux* scheduler and (c) *MTS-Like* heuristic scheduler on *Kirin 960* asymmetric multi-core.

Invocation. In closed-system, *MTS-Like* and *A-Greedy* schedulers are invoked only once as the application mix does not change over time. For open-systems, scheduling decisions in *MTS-Like* and *A-Greedy* are re-calculated when applications enter or leave the system. Note that the *Linux* scheduler is invoked at the default 10 ms period in both these systems as we make no changes to it.

3.6 Asymmetric Multi-Core Evaluations

Closed System Results. A workload is defined as the set of applications that execute in the multi-core. We restrict the number of applications from 1–8 (eight cores in the system) and generate 255 workloads by exploring all possible application combinations. Figure 4(a) reports the throughput obtained using *A-Greedy* scheduler with respect to the *ILP* scheduler in the closed system for these workloads. This figure shows that the throughput under *A-Greedy* scheduler is on average 0.98x of the throughput achievable under *ILP* scheduler. Even though both *A-Greedy* and *ILP* are theoretically optimal, the drop in performance for some workloads can be explained due to the use of regression-based convex approximations for fitting the throughput in *A-Greedy* (*ILP* utilizes real throughput values) for making scheduling decisions.

We also compare our proposed *A-Greedy* scheduler with the default *Linux* scheduler [4] that performs Completely Fair Scheduling on our asymmetric multi-core in Fig. 4(b). For this experiment, we launch each application with eight threads. Current *Linux* scheduler uses priority of applications in the system to allocate time slices for executing them on different types of cores. Thus, it does not have any mechanism to use application information to take efficient decisions at run-time. Figure 4(b) shows that the proposed *A-Greedy* scheduler provides on average 26% higher throughput than the default *Linux* scheduler.

Finally, we compare the proposed *A-Greedy* scheduler with the *MTS-Like* heuristic scheduler on our asymmetric multi-core in Fig. 4(c). On the small size asymmetric multi-core platform, *A-Greedy* scheduler results in average 8% higher throughput than *MTS-Like* scheduler.

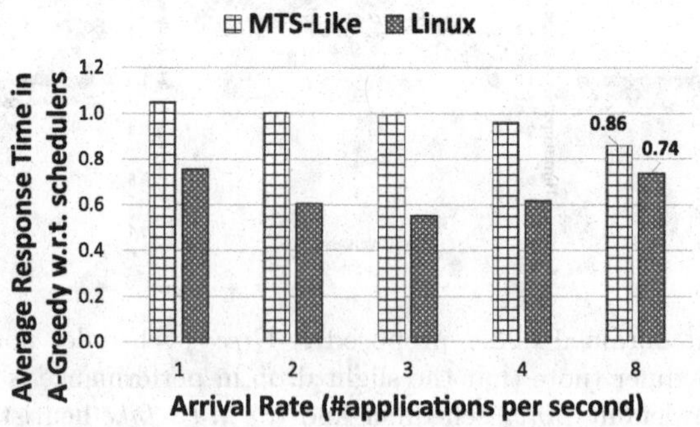

Fig. 5. Average response time under *MTS-Like* and *Linux* normalized to *A-Greedy* on *Kirin 960* asymmetric multi-core modeling an open system.

Open System Results. We compare the performance of *A-Greedy*, *Linux* and *MTS-Like* schedulers under different open system loads in Fig. 5. The number of applications arriving in the open system (per second) is varied from one to eight, i.e. low to high load. The maximum number of applications arriving in the system is fixed to eight as there are only eight cores in the system. From Fig. 5, we see that the *A-Greedy* scheduler reduces the average response time by up to 14% and 45% when compared to the *MTS-Like* and *Linux* schedulers.

3.7 Scalability Analysis

We report the run-time of *ILP* and *A-Greedy* schedulers on the *Big* core for representative scheduling problems with different number of cores and workload sizes in Table 1. We fix the number of cores in a cluster to four for the scalability experiments as the hardware platform that was used to collect profiling data had only four cores per cluster. The load is varied from 12.5% to 100% many-core utilization i.e., the number of applications in the many-core ranges from (*#cores*/8) to (*#cores*). Though the problem-solving time of *ILP*-based scheduler is in the order of milliseconds for an 8-core asymmetric multi-core with two clusters, the problem-solving time increases exponentially for a higher number of cores (or clusters). For instance, a 64-core asymmetric many-core scheduling problem in *ILP* does not terminate even after hours. However, *A-Greedy* proposed in this work only takes 47 ms to schedule 512 applications on a 512-core processor.

4 Related Work

Scheduling for asymmetric multi-/many-cores has been an active subject of research since their inception [11]. A number of works looked into maximizing performance under power-constrains for asymmetric processors [3,13,19,24]. For instance, authors in [13] first map application tasks to achieve high throughput but swap tasks in the second phase to meet the power constraints. However, these works do not determine the number of cores (spanning multiple asymmetric core types) allocated to multi-threaded applications at run-time and do

Table 1. Problem-solving time (in ms) for *ILP* and *A-Greedy* scheduler on varisized representative scheduling problems. ILP-scheduler does not terminate (N.T.) for #cores ≥64.

Load \ #cores	ILP				A-Greedy						
	8	**16**	**32**	**≥ 64**	**8**	**16**	**32**	**64**	**128**	**256**	**512**
12.5%	16	266	26,190	N.T.	0.03	0.03	0.09	0.23	0.60	2	6
25%	30	506	52,086	N.T.	0.02	0.05	0.13	0.34	1	3	12
50%	45	823	110,849	N.T.	0.03	0.06	0.21	0.54	2	6	24
100%	56	1,603	209,830	N.T.	0.03	0.09	0.27	0.91	3	12	47

not perform evaluations on real-world platforms. Authors of [14,15] proposed controller/economic theory based mechanisms on *ARM big.LITTLE* asymmetric multi-core platforms for meeting the quality of service requirements under power-constraints. However, threads belonging to same/different applications are considered independently. Additionally, it is very hard to provide any guarantees on scheduling decisions taken by these mechanisms. To the best of our knowledge, none of the aforementioned work has proposed a low-overhead scheduling algorithm that can be proven to obtain an optimal schedule (under certain constraints) with a proof-of-concept implemented and evaluated on a real-world hardware platform.

5 Conclusion

In this work, we present *A-Greedy*, the first-ever scheduler to be proven theoretically optimal (under certain constraints) for asymmetric multi-/many-core processors. Experimental evaluation on *Kirin 960* asymmetric multi-core shows that the throughput in *A-Greedy* is on average 0.98x the throughput of an optimal ILP-based scheduler but with minimal scheduling overheads. *A-Greedy* provides 26% higher throughput and up to 45% lower average response time than the default Linux Scheduler on *Kirin 960*. *A-Greedy* also provides up to 8% higher throughput and up to 14% lower average response time than state-of-the-art *MTS-Like* heuristic scheduler. Scalability analysis show that *A-Greedy* is fast enough to perform run-time scheduling for large-size asymmetric many-cores.

Acknowledgment. This work was supported by the National Research Foundation, Prime Minister's Office, Singapore under its Industry-IHL Partnership Grant NRF2015-IIP003. We thank the anonymous reviewers for their valuable feedback and insights.

References

1. Amdahl, G.M.: Validity of the single processor approach to achieving large scale computing capabilities. In: AFIPS (1967)
2. Bienia, C., et al.: Parsec 2.0: a new benchmark suite for chip-multiprocessors. In: PMBS (2009)
3. Cong, J., et al.: Energy-efficient scheduling on heterogeneous multi-core architectures. In: ISLPED (2012)
4. Corrêa, M., et al.: Operating system multilevel load balancing. In: SAC (2006)
5. van Dijk, T., et al.: Lace: non-bocking split deque for work-stealing. In: Euro-Par (2014)
6. Feitelson, D.G., et al.: Toward convergence in job schedulers for parallel supercomputers. In: JSSPP (1996)
7. Feitelson, D.G., et al.: Metrics and benchmarking for parallel job scheduling. In: JSSPP (1998)
8. Goens, A., et al.: Analysis of process traces for mapping dynamic KPN applications to MPSoCs. In: IESS (2015)

9. Gulati, D.P., et al.: multitasking workload scheduling on flexible-core chip multiprocessors. In: PACT (2008)
10. Henkel, J., et al.: Invasive manycore architectures. In: ASP-DAC (2012)
11. Kumar, R., et al.: Single-ISA heterogeneous multi-core architectures: the potential for processor power reduction. In: MICRO (2003)
12. Libutti, S., et al.: Co-scheduling tasks on multi-core heterogeneous systems: an energy-aware perspective. Comput. Digit. Tech. **10**, 77–84 (2016)
13. Liu, G., et al.: Dynamic thread mapping for high-performance, power-efficient heterogeneous many-core systems. In: ICCD (2013)
14. Muthukaruppan, T.S., et al.: Hierarchical power management for asymmetric multi-core in dark silicon era. In: DAC (2013)
15. Muthukaruppan, T.S., et al.: Price theory based power management for heterogeneous multi-cores. In: ASPLOS (2014)
16. Optimization, G.: Gurobi optimizer 8.0. Gurobi (2018). http://www.gurobi.com
17. Pathania, A.: Scalable Task Schedulers for Many-Core Architectures. Ph.D. thesis, Karlsruhe Institute of Technology, Germany (2018)
18. Pathania, A., et al.: Optimal greedy algorithm for many-core scheduling. IEEE Trans. Comput. Aided Des. Integr. Circuits Syst. **36**, 1054–1058 (2017)
19. Pd, S.M., et al.: 3D many-core microprocessor power management by space-time multiplexing based demand-supply matching. IEEE Trans. Comput. **64**, 3022–3036 (2015)
20. Ristov, S., et al.: Superlinear speedup in HPC systems: why and when? In: FedCSIS (2016)
21. Singh, A.K., et al.: Mapping on multi/many-core systems: survey of current and emerging trends. In: DAC (2013)
22. Stuber, M.D., et al.: Convex and concave relaxations of implicit functions. Optim. Methods Softw. **30**, 424–460 (2015)
23. Venkataramani, V., et al.: Scalable dynamic task scheduling on adaptive many-core. In: MCSoC (2018)
24. Winter, J.A., et al.: Scalable thread scheduling and global power management for heterogeneous many-core architectures. In: PACT (2010)

Platform-Agnostic Learning-Based Scheduling

Andreas Prodromou[1(✉)], Ashish Venkat[2], and Dean M. Tullsen[1]

[1] University of California, San Diego, USA
{aprodrom,tullsen}@ucsd.edu
[2] University of Virginia, Charlottesville, USA
venkat@virginia.edu

Abstract. Heterogeneous architectures have become increasingly common. From co-packaging small and large cores, to GPUs alongside CPUs, to general-purpose heterogeneous-ISA architectures with cores implementing different ISAs. As diversity of execution cores grows, predictive models become of paramount importance for scheduling and resource allocation. In this paper, we investigate the capabilities of performance predictors in a heterogeneous-ISA setting, as well as the predictors' effects on scheduler quality. We follow an unbiased feature selection methodology to identify the optimal set of features for this task, instead of pre-selecting features before training. Finally, we incorporate our findings in ML-based schedulers and evaluate their sensitivity to the underlying system's level of heterogeneity. We show our schedulers to perform within 2–11% of an oracular scheduler across a variety of underlying heterogeneous-ISA multicore systems without modification.

1 Introduction

Modern multicore architectures employ cores that are increasingly heterogeneous in terms of their microarchitectural characteristics. These architectures, dubbed single-ISA (Instruction Set Architecture) heterogeneous multicores [7,8], improve the throughput and efficiency of mixed workloads, by catering to their diverse execution characteristics, such as variability in instruction-level parallelism, cache access patterns, branch behavior, etc. Heterogeneous-ISA multicore architectures [1,2,4,10,15–17] further exploit an additional degree of freedom by allowing multiple co-packaged ISAs. These architectures benefit from a phenomenon called *ISA affinity* – the inherent preference of an application code region to efficiently execute on a particular ISA [4,17]. By synergistically exploiting ISA affinity and microarchitectural heterogeneity, these architectures provide significant (>30%) additional gains in performance and energy efficiency.

This increasing trend in on-chip heterogeneity has only further highlighted the critical need for intelligent workload scheduling, since the potential performance and power benefits of these architectures arrive from smart job-to-core assignment. State-of-the-art scheduling mechanisms rely on predictive

D. N. Pnevmatikatos et al. (Eds.): SAMOS 2019, LNCS 11733, pp. 142–154, 2019.
https://doi.org/10.1007/978-3-030-27562-4_10

models to make active performance predictions for any code region in execution, and further leverage such predictions to make appropriate job allocation decisions [3,13,18]. This work advances state-of-the-art scheduling mechanisms by developing learning-based schedulers that are flexible enough to operate efficiently, regardless of the degree of heterogeneity that the underlying hardware exhibits – including both microarchitectural heterogeneity and ISA-heterogeneity.

On a single-ISA heterogeneous multicore, the performance difference of a code region can be vastly different across different cores depending upon their microarchitectural diversity. ISA heterogeneity further exacerbates the difficulty of performance prediction due to the more complex set of parameters that potentially affect performance. This paper deals with the challenging problem of scheduling mixed workloads on general-purpose heterogeneous-ISA architectures that employ fully disjoint ISAs (ARM's Thumb, x86-64, and Alpha) as proposed by Venkat and Tullsen [17].

This paper examines a variety of machine learning techniques to perform cross-core and cross-platform performance prediction, where the target core potentially differs in terms of its CPU microarchitectural traits, cache organizations, ISA, inorder/out-of-order execution semantics, vector support, and floating point support. These ML-based predictors are trained on an extensive simulation-based dataset [17] to capture the interaction between an application's execution characteristics and the architectural and microarchitectural traits of the underlying hardware, and further project the execution of any given code region on arbitrary processor hardware. The dataset includes 72 SPEC simpoint workloads, each simulated on 600 different cores executing multiple ISAs. To the best of our knowledge, this is the most extensive heterogeneous-ISA, cycle-accurate, simulation-based dataset in the literature.

The contributions of this work are:

1. Design of accurate ML-based cross-core and cross-platform performance predictors, which are to the best of our knowledge, the first predictors to effectively cross general-purpose ISA boundaries.
2. In-depth characterization of ML-based performance predictors.
3. Demonstration of an effective ML-based heterogeneous-ISA job scheduler.

2 Motivation

Cross-Platform Performance Prediction. Job schedulers benefit from accurate performance predictions. On a complex system, trial and error scheduling on a complex system (many threads, diverse cores) is (1) unlikely to find the optimal schedule, and (2) likely to sample many poor schedules (sacrificing performance) before finding good ones. A scheduler that can predict the performance of any given application on any core can intelligently distribute jobs for maximal throughput without the overhead of sampling all possible permutations.

Intuitively, we expect that a system's level of heterogeneity can affect the difficulty of the scheduling problem. In other words, it should be easier to create good schedulers for systems with lower diversity. For predictive schedulers, the prediction error should have a smaller impact on realizing efficient schedules on less diverse systems. This paper proposes and formalizes techniques to quantitatively estimate the **Ease-of-Scheduling** (EoS) on any given heterogeneous multicore, and further showcase it as an objective function that represents an unbiased way of selecting heterogeneous-ISA multicore benchmark systems.

We find that a system's scheduling difficulty level (EoS), a performance predictor's accuracy, and a scheduler's efficiency (one that internally uses said predictor) are intertwined in often unpredictable ways. For example, less accurate predictors do not guarantee worse schedulers, and more accurate predictors do not guarantee better ones. We address this ambiguity by first identifying multicore systems that cover a wide spectrum of heterogeneity, and then focusing on training accurate per-core performance predictors. We finally aggregate our arsenal of tools (diverse systems, a variety of predictors, and schedulers) to measure the efficiency, overheads, and performance of our learning-based schedulers.

Limitations in Prior Work. This paper also identifies and addresses some common limitations in prior prediction-based scheduling proposals. First, multicore systems under test are often predefined and do not change throughout each proposal, resulting in inflexible solutions with low potential adaptability. Second, a closely related and frequently-observed drawback is the use of small datasets on which predictors are trained and evaluated. Note that large datasets are difficult to construct, particularly if the data is accumulated via simulations (slow). In studies where profiling is used, the hardware cannot be significantly varied, so a large dataset would require tens of thousands of benchmarks.

Several prior studies select one machine learning algorithm, often a linear model, which according to our findings is not necessarily the best option for most cases. Discussion of other available algorithms and how well they perform in the presented use cases is often omitted. Aside from the limited exploration of available algorithms, researchers often pre-select the input features of their models. This selection tends to reflect the collective knowledge of this field and includes variables that have been identified in the past to track dynamic characteristics. However, with modern execution environments we are able to collect significantly more measurements, especially if simulations are used. Furthermore, even though feature selection often requires significant skill and time investment, some ML algorithms are particularly good at filtering features and internally discarding those that have no impact on the final prediction.

In this work, we address these drawbacks. First, our EoS-based system selection allows us to demonstrate the adaptability of our schedulers. Second, we use the largest available dataset that fits our needs. Third, we use three different machine learning algorithms as predictors. Fourth, we never hand-select features for training – instead, we allow our machine learning models to (brute-force) explore the dataset during training and decide which features they should be using to optimize their prediction accuracy. We show that our methodology results in predictive models that generalize and adapt to a variety of underlying systems without modification.

3 Related Work

Single-ISA heterogeneous architectures are proposed by Kumar, et al. [7], with processor manufacturers currently offering heterogeneous products [5,6,14]. Scheduling and resource management for these architectures has been extensively studied, as well (examples include [3,12,13] and more).

The primary focus of this work, *general-purpose* heterogeneous-ISA multi-core architectures [4,15,17], include microarchitecturally heterogeneous cores that implement different ISAs and have been demonstrated to result in significant added benefits compared to its single-ISA counterpart. The ISAs we use in this study are Thumb, Alpha, and x86-64. Recently, the composite-ISA architecture [15] has demonstrated how a heterogeneous-ISA CMP can be based on feature-diverse variations of a single ISA, significantly alleviating concerns regarding their commercial viability. This research would apply to composite-ISA architectures as well. Beyond performance and energy benefits, exploiting heterogeneous-ISA architectures has been shown to improve security against code-based attacks, such as Return-Oriented Programming, by frequently switching ISAs [16]. Systems combining CPUs and GPUs (or accelerators) in the same package are also examples of heterogeneous-ISA architectures [11], however they are beyond the scope of this work.

Barabalace et al. [1,2] propose Popcorn Linux, an OS that facilitates running and migrating applications on general-purpose heterogeneous-ISA systems. Our work assumes similar support. Popcorn Linux includes a basic scheduler that relies on application instrumentation to generate a mapping of functions to cores. LACross [18] is a cross-platform scheduler that uses the LASSO linear regression algorithm to predict a phase's performance and power. LACross is shown to provide efficient resource management on two heterogeneous machines.

4 Dataset Overview

We use a Gem5 and McPAT simulation-based dataset of 43200 samples, consisting of 72 workloads simulated on 600 cores (200 microarchitecturally-diverse cores for each ISA - Thumb, Alpha and x86-64) [17]. Participating features can be separated into two main categories: (1) workload profiling features, and (2) core microarchitectural specifications. In this section we provide more details regarding the dataset we use.

4.1 Workloads and Core Configurations

Each workload in our dataset is a Simpoint phase of 100 million (Alpha) instructions. Table 1 presents a description of the 600 cores in this dataset. Further details on how configuration points were chosen by the creators of this dataset can be found in [17].

Table 1. Description of core configuration points. Adapted from the design space exploration presented in [17].

Design Parameter	Design choices
ISA	Thumb, Alpha, x86-64
Execution Semantics	In-order, Out-of-Order
Branch Predictor	Local, Tournament
Reorder Buffer - Register File (ROB - Int. regs - FP regs)	64-96-64, 128-160-96
Issue Width - Functional Units (Width - Int. ALUs - Int. mult - FP ALUs - FP mult - SIMD)	1-1-1-1-1-1 1-3-2-2-2-2 2-3-2-2-2-2 4-3-2-2-2-2 4-6-2-4-2-4
Load Store Queue Sizes	16, 32 entries
Cache Hierarchy (L1 - L2 - L3) 32K/4 → 32KB, 4-way	32K/4 - 32K/4 - 4M/4 32K/4 - 32K/4 - 8M/8 64K/4 - 64K/4 - 4M/4 64K/4 - 64K/4 - 8M/8

4.2 Dataset Partitions

Dynamic workload features can vary according to the core they execute on; for example, instruction count will be constant within an ISA, but different across ISAs, while cache misses will vary by core features and ISA. This section of the dataset contains profiling measurements obtained via simulations. Specifically, each workload is characterized by 30 features, which are presented in Table 2a.

In addition to dynamic workload features, cores in our dataset are also characterized by 18 static features that describe their microarchitecture. These features are typically available from the manufacturer. Table 2b presents more details.

Table 2. Dataset features: Workload profiling features (a) are collected from all 600 cores. CPU-microarchitectural features (b) describe each core.

Feature Names (grouped)	Description
APPID	Unique workload identifier. Never used for testing or training
INT_R, FP_SIMD_R, BR_R, LOAD_R, STORE_R	Dynamic count of five instruction types: Int, fp or simd, branch, load, store
INT_N, FP_SIMD_N, BR_N, LOAD_N, STORE_N	Normalized dynamic instruction count
OPS	Total number of operations. Varies across ISAs
<TYPE>_HITS_R, <TYPE>_MISS_R, <TYPE>_MISS_N	Raw count of hits and misses, and miss ratio. TYPE=$I (I-cache), $D (D-cache), L1 ($I & $D), L2. Total of 12 features in this group.
FETCH, ISSUE	Dynamic fetch and issue rates
REF_IPC	Performance measurement (in aIPC)
MISSPRED	Branch missprediction rate
D_PROC_PWR, D_CORE_PWR	Dynamic processor and core power consumption (McPat)

(a) Dynamically-collected features

Feature Names	Description
CPUID	Unique core identifier. Never used for testing or training.
ISA (THUMB, ALPHA, X86)	Core's ISA. Categorical feature.
SEMANTICS (IO, OOO)	In-order or Out-of-Order. Categorical feature.
BR_PRED (LOCAL, TMNT)	Core's branch predictor, local or tournament. Categorical feature.
WIDTH	Core's width
ROBSIZE	Reorder buffer size
INTREGS, FPREGS	Number of int and fp registers
LSQSIZE	Load-Store Queue size
L1SIZE, L2SIZE	Cache sizes for L1 (kB) and L2 (LLC, MB)
INTALUS, FPALUS	Number of int and fp ALUs
INTMULTDIV, FPMULTDIV	Number of int and fp multiply-divide units
SIMD	Number of SIMD units
AREA	Core's area (McPat)
PEAKPOWER	Core's peak power (McPat)

(b) Statically-collected features

4.3 Data Splitting into Training and Test Sets

Due to the properties of this dataset, splitting it into a training and test set is a challenge. If not careful, we can leak information between the two sets, often resulting in unrealistically accurate predictors. We find that if a workload A runs on CPUs 1 and 2, both samples must reside in the same set. Otherwise, the trained predictor has full information about workload A when making predictions. Similarly, workload A and workload B, on any pair of CPUs, where A and B are different phases of the same benchmark, should also not be split across training and test, since phases may share code and certainly share the dataset.

We address these issues by employing a Leave-One-Group-Out (LOGO) cross-validation methodology. Following the LOGO strategy, one group is assigned as the test set, while all other groups form the training set. Training and testing are performed in a loop, with each group assigned as the test set at least once. We define each benchmark, with all its phases and including runs on all cores as a LOGO group.

5 Experimental Methodology

The scope of this work is twofold. First, we seek to explore a variety of ML-based predictors, each under numerous combinations based on their internal configuration parameters. Second, we want to study the efficacy of these predictors in the context of job scheduling.

5.1 Predictor Evaluation Methodology

In this work, we study three ML-based performance predictors:

- **Ridge Regression (RR)**, a variant of Linear Regression that penalizes large coefficients, providing increased protection against overfitting.
- **Decision Trees (DT)** algorithms that generate a binary decision tree during training, with each decision node predicated on exactly one input feature.
- **Random Forests (RF)** that generate a collection of decision trees during training. When queried for a prediction, an average of the decision tree responses is returned.

Table 3. Configuration flags description (ML Suite)

Flag	Description
Scale	Performs data scaling
Whiten	Performs data whitening
RefCore	Reference core selection (1-600)
KeepRAW	Keeps features with raw values (e.g. INT_R)
KeepPower	Keeps profiled dynamic power features
KeepL1	Keeps L1 cache features
KeepL2	Keeps L2 cache features
Target	Sets the prediction target (typically, aIPC)
KeepRefTarget	Keeps the profiled target (aIPC) value
KeepFI	Keeps Fetch/Issue rate measurements
TreeDepth	Used with tree-based algorithms

Our trained models accept two inputs: (a) application-specific features (obtained via profiling on a "reference" core), and (b) target core-specific features. They output a performance prediction for the given application-core pair measured in *Alpha Instructions-Per-Cycle* (αIPC). When dealing with multiple ISAs, IPC is not a fair metric since the number of dynamically executed instructions can vary drastically across ISAs. We use Alpha as our base for comparison, allowing us to fairly track execution progress. Due to the use of a reference core, our predictors operate in a one-to-many fashion and are capable of extrapolating runtime performance, from the reference core to any target core in our dataset.

Workloads are characterized using 30 features in our dataset. It is possible that not all these features are necessary for accurate predictions. Furthermore, highly-correlated features or features at different scales can also have a negative impact, requiring appropriate data whitening and data scaling, respectively. Our predictor configuration methodology defines 10 boolean flags (Table 3). Each flag controls the amount of information available during training. For example, the "keepL1" flag defines whether the input to the ML model will include L1 cache information (size, number of misses, etc.). The "RefCore" flag defines which of our 600 cores will be used as the reference (profiling) core. To reduce the number of experiments, we allow the RefCore flag to take two values: It can either use a mid-range Alpha core (core #300), or a mid-range x84-64 core (#500).

We perform a brute force exploration over the space generated from our flags. Consequently, we explore 1024 different configurations of the RR model, and 5120 versions of the DT and RF models (×5 since we also explore 5 different values of tree depth). Finally, we identify the most accurate predictor of each algorithm. Throughout our methodology, we avoid pre-selecting and hardcoding the features of our exploration. Instead, our ML models explore all possible configurations and "decide" which features lead to the most accurate predictions.

5.2 Scheduler Evaluation Methodology

Workload Execution Protocol. We enforce a workload execution protocol to ensure fairness during our experiments. For each system-scheduler combination we study, we execute 200 randomly chosen workloads from our dataset. A new workload appears as soon as a previous workload completes its execution, such that at any given time, the number of in-flight workloads equals the number of cores in the underlying system. For larger experiments (e.g. Ease-of-Scheduling), we draw a list of 200 workloads before the experiment begins and we use the same list for every sub-experiment. This way we can ensure fairness in comparing systems and schedulers.

Choosing Benchmark CMP Systems. To train robust performance predictors that can adapt to varying hardware heterogeneity, it is important to choose diverse benchmark multicore systems; not only in terms of microarchitecture, but also with respect to the resulting scheduling difficulty. We can expect that systems with similar cores will be easier to schedule than one with more diverse cores. For this work, we select three 4-core, three 8-core and three 16-core heterogeneous-ISA CMP benchmark systems. Specifically, we select an easy, a medium, and a hard system, that exhibit varying degrees of scheduling difficulty.

We devise an experiment, called "Ease of Scheduling", to rate systems in terms of their scheduling difficulty. EoS relies on the fact that a random scheduler will perform closer to an optimal scheduler (that provides the best performance) on easier systems (e.g., a homogeneous multicore system). As the system's diversity grows, a random scheduler's efficiency will reduce compared to that of the optimal scheduler.

Using our dataset, we randomly draw heterogeneous-ISA multicore systems. Specifically, we draw 2500 4-, 8- and 16-core systems for a total of 7500 systems. On each system, we apply our workload execution protocol and we use a random scheduler. We repeat the experiment 300 times to minimize noise from random decisions. Finally, we compare the average performance against that of the optimal scheduler. Figure 1 shows our results. Each system is characterized by its EoS rating (Y-axis) and its per-core performance in αIPC (X-axis).

Ease-of-Scheduling is an unbiased selection mechanism, since we cannot influence the ranking of systems. With benchmark systems ranging from the easiest 4-core to the most difficult 16-core system, we (1) efficiently cover a wide range of underlying systems, and (2) can demonstrate that our predictive schedulers adapt well to a variety of underlying systems.

Our results also verify our intuition: Easier systems tend to have more balanced cores in terms of performance, while more difficult systems typically have a small number of high-performance cores and a large number of low-performance cores. We omit presenting the microarchitectural configuration of each

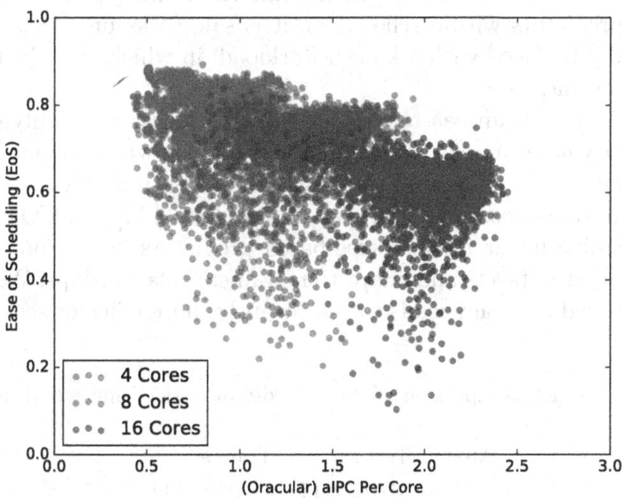

Fig. 1. Randomly-drawn heterogeneous-ISA systems rated in terms of scheduling difficulty. From each cluster, the highest (easiest), median, and lowest (hardest) points are chosen as benchmark systems.

multicore benchmark system (total of 84 cores), due to space restrictions. However, we note that some of the microarchitectural traits of each system can be inferred from their EoS rating.

6 Results

This section presents the results of our study. We first evaluate our ML-based performance predictors as standalone modules. We then examine schedulers that incorporate these schedulers.

6.1 Performance Predictors

ML Space Exploration: Training Accurate Performance Predictors. We present the results of our exploration over the three Machine Learning (ML) algorithms we use and over the design space generated by our configuration flags, as described in Sect. 5.1. After running all possible configurations, we identify the most accurate trained model from each algorithm.

Table 4 presents the prediction accuracy comparison between the three winners. Since we want our performance predictors to be as close to ground truth as possible, we chose to focus on two metrics – *Mean Absolute Error (MAE)*, the average distance of predictions from reality, measured in αIPC, and *Standard Deviation (STD)*, the distribution of prediction errors from each predictor. Using MAE and STD we are essentially describing a bell curve that characterizes prediction error for each predictor. Finally, we report accuracy on both the previously unseen test set, as well as the known training set. Since we intend to use these predictors within schedulers, it is safe to assume that a scheduler will occasionally be faced with a known workload, in which case the training set accuracy is relevant.

When dealing with unseen test set queries, we measure roughly equal accuracy across our winner models. When queried with known data, our linear (RR) model's accuracy remains around the same level as with its test set queries. On the other hand, tree-based predictors report very low MAE and STD for training set queries. Unlike linear models, tree-based predictors have more capacity to characterize larger datasets and adapt to non-linear relationships. We later show how this improved accuracy leads to significantly more efficient scheduling.

Table 4. Accuracy comparison of three predictors (MAE measured in αIPC)

Model	Test set		Train set	
	MAE	STD	MAE	STD
RR	0.23	0.3	0.21	0.26
DT	0.22	0.35	0.07	0.04
RF	0.19	0.31	0.03	0.04

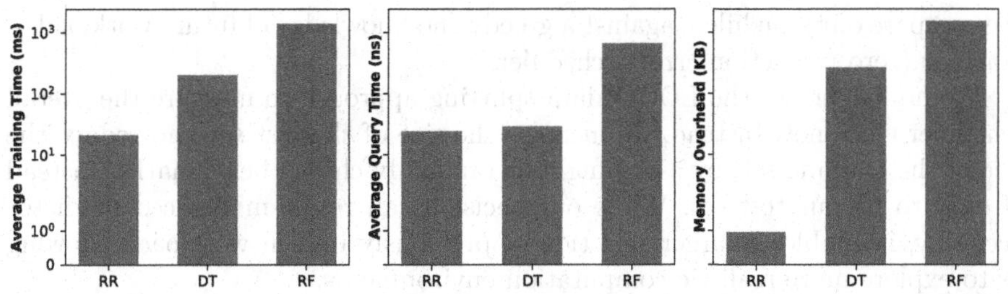

Fig. 2. Predictor algorithm overhead comparison: Training time (left), Query time (middle), Memory overhead (right). Y axes shared and in log scale.

Predictor Overhead Evaluation. This section presents an overhead comparison for our three models. We perform the following experiments on a system with an i7-3770K processor running at 2.9 GHz and 16 GB of memory. We use the algorithm implementations from sklearn [9].

First, we vary the dataset size and train each model 100 times to report average training overhead. Training times for a dataset of 30k entries are 21 ms, 203 ms, and 1.4 s for RR, DT, and RF respectively (Fig. 2 – left). Training overhead has little significance in choosing a model, since it happens infrequently. For extremely large datasets however, RF's overhead might become prohibitive.

We measure query overhead (Fig. 2 – middle), by asking each trained model for 55 k predictions and report the average time per prediction. Overhead per query for RR, DT, and RF is 24 ns, 29 ns, and 667 ns respectively. Query overhead is an important metric, since predictions can be part of the critical path, especially in the context of job scheduling. RR and DT are comparable, however RF is significantly slower.

Finally, we measure the memory overhead of each model (Fig. 2 – right). Linear models only need to store their coefficients' values. Tree-based models must store a condition value and a feature identifier for each node. We assume that all condition and coefficient values require 64 bits and the number of features defines the number of bits necessary to represent them. The RR model needs 960 bits, the DT model 276 kB, and the RF model 1.5 MB. Overall, RF is expensive compared to the others. Although it does provide high accuracy, the predictions do not necessarily translate to a significant gain in scheduler efficiency, as observed later.

6.2 ML-Based Schedulers

Performance Comparison of ML-Based Schedulers. This section presents insights derived in the exploratory part of this work. Specifically, we link each of our three predictive models to a scheduler and report its efficiency. Each scheduler receives an $N \times N$ prediction matrix from its predictor and then decides on the appropriate schedule such that it maximizes the system's overall performance (sum of αIPC from all N core-workload pairs in the chosen schedule).

We compare our schedulers against a greedy (no knowledge of future workloads), oracular (zero prediction error) scheduler.

We no longer use the LOGO data splitting approach to measure the overall scheduler efficiency. Instead, we increase the size of the test set and reduce the size of the training set, by assigning four randomly chosen benchmarks (instead of one) to be our test set. While our decision can result in reduced predictor accuracy, it enables a larger selection of previously unseen workloads allowing us to explore more realistic computation environments.

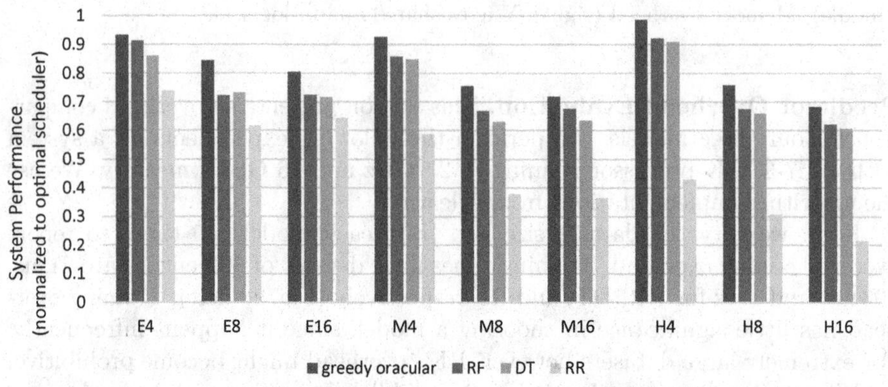

Fig. 3. Scheduler performance comparison on Heterogeneous-ISA systems.

For this experiment, we randomly select input workloads that create a mix of 50% unseen and 50% previously seen workloads, resembling a typical IaaS (Infrastructure-as-a-Service) environment (e.g., Amazon's EC2) – some users use EC2 instances to run the same application every time (such as a web server), while others execute a more diverse mix of workloads (software development).

Figure 3 presents our results, normalized to the optimal schedule (maximum-achievable overall throughput). We first observe that the RF-based scheduler has an advantage compared to the other ML-based schedulers. However, the much cheaper DT-based scheduler scores very close, across all systems. Compared to RF, DT reports a 2.8% average performance reduction (6.2% max reduction), while it outperforms RF on the easy 8-core (E8) system by 1.2%. We further observe that our RF scheduler is within 2.2–11.2% (7.5% on average) from an oracular scheduler, and DT within 1.6–16.8% (10% average).

Our RR-based scheduler shows significantly reduced performance due to the reduced training set size. While the (test set) accuracy of all our models drops due to the reduced training data set, RR is affected the most, with its MAE doubling and STD increasing by almost 3x. For comparison, tree-based models only experience 6% MAE and STD degradation from the reduced training dataset. Furthermore, tree-based prediction accuracy on the training set is excellent, which provides a significant advantage over RR in this experiment.

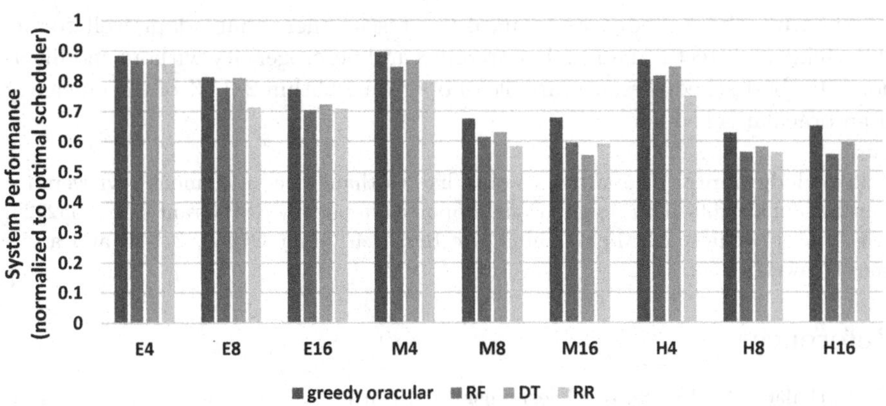

Fig. 4. Scheduler performance comparison on Single-ISA heterogeneous systems.

Performance Comparison on Single-ISA Heterogeneous Systems. To demonstrate the adaptability of our schedulers to less complex systems, we also examine single-ISA heterogeneous systems. We repeat the EoS-based system selection presented in Sect. 5.2. However, this time we enforce our systems to only use Alpha cores. We must note that our predictors have not been re-trained between the two experiments. Figure 4 presents our results.

We first observe that, unlike with heterogeneous-ISA systems, the DT scheduler has an advantage over RF. The added complexity of the RF predictor does not appear to be as beneficial in the single-ISA case. We can also observe that our linear predictor now reports comparable efficiency as RF and DT (1.5–4.8%). This happens due to the reduced scheduling difficulty on single-ISA systems (higher EoS values). Our best scheduler (DT) performs within 0.2–12.5% across all systems compared to the oracular scheduler (4% on average).

Scheduler Sensitivity to Underlying System. From Fig. 3, we observe that our tree-based (DT, RF) schedulers are affected by the transition from 4 to 8 cores, but their performance remains almost intact when we move from 8 to 16 cores. In comparison, the oracular scheduler is affected by both transitions ($4 \rightarrow 8$, $4 \rightarrow 16$), albeit with a smaller impact. These trends are also observed when our schedulers accompany single-ISA systems (Fig. 4). Our results show that tree-based schedulers were able to mostly overcome (1) the increase in scheduling difficulty between 8 and 16-core systems, and (2) the variety of underlying ISAs.

7 Conclusions

With the increased adoption of heterogeneity in modern systems, predictive models invariably enjoy attention from the scientific community for applications in scheduling, power management, resource management, and resource allocation. In this work, we first present an exhaustive exploration and analysis of the abilities of ML models to act as cross-core cross-platform performance predictors.

We then use these predictors to implement schedulers that adapt well to the underlying architectural and microarchitectural heterogeneity without modification. Our best schedulers are capable of operating within 2–11% of the efficiency of an oracular scheduler.

Acknowledgments. The authors would like to thank the anonymous reviewers for their helpful insights. This research was supported in part by NSF Grant CNS-1652925, NSF/Intel Foundational Microarchitecture Research Grant CCF-1823444, and a gift from Huawei.

References

1. Barbalace, A., Lyerly, R., Jelesnianski, C., Carno, A., Chuang, H.R., Ravindran, B.: Breaking the boundaries in heterogeneous-ISA datacenters. In: ASPLOS (2017)
2. Barbalace, A., et al.: Popcorn: bridging the programmability gap in heterogeneous-ISA platforms. In: ECCS, p. 29. ACM (2015)
3. Craeynest, K.V., Jaleel, A., Eeckhout, L., Narvaez, P., Emer, J.: Scheduling heterogeneous multi-cores through performance impact estimation (PIE). In: ISCA, pp. 213–224, June 2012. https://doi.org/10.1109/ISCA.2012.6237019
4. DeVuyst, M., Venkat, A., Tullsen, D.M.: Execution migration in a heterogeneous-ISA chip multiprocessor. In: ASPLOS XVII (2012)
5. Greenhalgh, P.: Big. LITTLE processing with arm cortex-A15 & cortex-A7. In: ARM White Paper, pp. 1–8 (2011)
6. Kahle, J.: The cell processor architecture. In: MICRO, p. 3. IEEE Computer Society (2005)
7. Kumar, R., Farkas, K.I., Jouppi, N.P., Ranganathan, P., Tullsen, D.M.: Single-ISA heterogeneous multi-core architectures: the potential for processor power reduction. In: MICRO (2003)
8. Kumar, R., Tullsen, D.M., Ranganathan, P., Jouppi, N.P., Farkas, K.I.: Single-ISA heterogeneous multi-core architectures for multithreaded workload performance. In: ISCA (2004)
9. scikit learn: Scikit-learn python library. http://scikit-learn.org/stable/
10. Lim, K., Balkind, J., Wentzlaff, D.: Juxtapiton: enabling heterogeneous-ISA research with RISC-V and SPARC FPGA soft-cores. arXiv preprint arXiv:1811.08091 (2018)
11. Mittal, S., Vetter, J.S.: A survey of CPU-GPU heterogeneous computing techniques. ACM Comput. Surv. (CSUR) **47**(4), 69 (2015)
12. Somu Muthukaruppan, T., Pathania, A., Mitra, T.: Price theory based power management for heterogeneous multi-cores. In: ASPLOS 2014. ACM (2014)
13. Torng, C., Wang, M., Batten, C.: Asymmetry-aware work-stealing runtimes. In: ISCA 2016 (2016). https://doi.org/10.1109/ISCA.2016.14
14. Variable, S.: A Multi-Core CPU Architecture for Low Power and High Performance. Whitepaper (2011). http://www.nvidia.com
15. Venkat, A., Basavaraj, H., Tullsen, D.M.: Composite-ISA cores: enabling multi-ISA heterogeneity using a single ISA. In: HPCA 2019 (2019)
16. Venkat, A., Shamasunder, S., Shacham, H., Tullsen, D.M.: HIPStR: heterogeneous-ISA program state relocation. In: ASLPOS (2016)
17. Venkat, A., Tullsen, D.M.: Harnessing ISA diversity: design of a heterogeneous-ISA chip multiprocessor. In: ISCA (2014)
18. Zheng, X., John, L.K., Gerstlauer, A.: Accurate phase-level cross-platform power and performance estimation. In: DAC (2016)

System Energy and Heat Management

Using Frame Similarity for Low Energy Software-Only IoT Video Recognition

Larissa Rozales Gonçalves(✉), Lucas Klein Draghetti, Paolo Rech, and Luigi Carro

Universidade Federal do Rio Grande do Sul, Porto Alegre, Brazil
{lrgoncalves,lucas.kleindraghetti,prech,carro}@inf.ufrgs.br

Abstract. Embedded video-processing applications are everywhere, and need to be low-energy in order to extend battery life. Convolutional Neural Networks (CNNs), frequently used for this task, fail to explore the intrinsic redundancy present in videos: similarity between sequential frames means that analyzing all frames can be avoided. On top of that, while several hardware solutions for low-energy execution have been proposed, they require extra or dedicated hardware, which makes them non attractive for low cost applications. In this work we propose a technique that uses frame similarity to identify and process only areas that have a significant difference when comparing two subsequent frames. Our technique reduces energy consumption by discarding unneeded operations, and can also be used in low-cost hardware readily available for IoT applications. We obtain up to 12-80x speedup of CNN execution with software-only modifications that require no network retraining while impacting little on accuracy.

Keywords: Convolutional Neural Networks · IoT · Security cameras

1 Introduction

Interpreting the content of a video is relevant in several applications, ranging from autonomous cars to security systems. Using Convolutional Neural Networks (CNNs) for video recognition has become common, as they are able to not only detect object positions, but also to categorize them. Currently, CNNs work by processing each image independently, and do not take into account that two consecutive frames in a video might be highly similar.

State-of-the-art CNNs for video processing can run at over 40 fps when executed on GPUs [9]. The needed frame rate, however, is dependent on the application, meaning that such a high rate might not be necessary. Video processing, for example, usually takes at least 24 fps, while hand gesture recognition uses only 10 fps [15]. Moreover, in a study from 2011, more than 70% of video surveillance recording was reported to be done at 10 fps or less [3].

For battery dependent devices that perform video processing, it is important to keep frame rate as low as possible, while still high enough for the target

D. N. Pnevmatikatos et al. (Eds.): SAMOS 2019, LNCS 11733, pp. 157–168, 2019.
https://doi.org/10.1007/978-3-030-27562-4_11

application, as more frames being processed per second imply higher battery consumption. Thus, in the context of IoT, where several devices can be bounded by battery life and where video processing is relevant for tasks such as monitoring, it is essential to keep energy consumption low.

GPUs can process CNNs faster than CPUs, as convolutions, an essential operation for the network, are commonly represented using matrix operations, a task the former excels at due to their highly parallel nature. However, in general, GPUs consume much more energy than CPUs, which is not ideal under battery constraints. As discussed before, it might not be necessary to use the high frame rates GPU execution can provide; furthermore, CPUs have the advantage of being low-cost when compared to GPUs, hence closer to IoT requirements.

In this work we explore the intrinsic redundancy presentend in video frames. We propose a technique that locates differences between the next image to be evaluated by the network by comparing it against the previous one, and then processes only parts where changes have been identified. This strategy means that high power GPUs can be avoided, as the necessary sub set of the image being processed can be handled by common low energy CPUs. We target security cameras as our application of interest since they can have a fixed camera standpoint, have high stability between frames and, as reported before, low framerate requirements, making processing only limited areas where there had been changes a natural idea. Our results show that one can achieve reductions in execution time and energy by a factor of up to 80x.

It is important to notice that all our modifications are software-only, and so no additional specific hardware is required. There is also no need to retrain the network, since we do not modify execution parameters. Furthermore, as long as predicted areas are consistent, accuracy impacts are minimal.

This work is organized as follows. Section 2 describes related work. Section 3 explains our method of partial window processing and how the required frame comparison was done, and Sect. 4 details why frame skipping is possible. Section 5 presents our results, and Sect. 6 our conclusions and future work.

2 Related Work

As Neural Networks (NNs) have become the state-of-the-art solution for a wide range of applications, several works that target their acceleration, energy reduction, or both have been proposed. A survey on the topic can be found in [14]. GPUs are also commonly used for processing CNNs, but their high energy consumption makes them inadequate for IoT applications that have tight energy constraints.

When accelerating CNNs with specific hardware, both energy and execution time can be reduced, as the hardware accelerators are obviously specialized for the task. While several such accelerators have been proposed, for example Eyeriss [2] and DianNao [1], their downside is that adding required additional hardware can be expensive, and reusing current hardware is impossible.

Works that, like ours, consider inherent similarity between frames to accelerate CNN execution have been proposed. In [10] the authors take advantage of input similarity and use linear quantization to analyze two consecutive inputs, then store and reuse results for inputs that have not changed. In [18], they explore motion information in videos by using the block-matching algorithm to estimate object motion between frames. Both of these techniques, however, rely on specific hardware.

Software techniques that require no additional hardware, like our work, are limited, and often rely on GPUs. Video classification techniques [6,17], for example, aim to analyze and classify videos as a whole into categories. While this differs from our work, which evaluates frames separately, for certain applications it might be more interesting to do the analysis as a whole. The downside, however, is that this cannot be done in real time, as it needs the entire video beforehand. Software acceleration techniques for other kind of networks, such as LSTMs [12], have also been proposed, but can not be applied directly to CNNs, as they rely on LSTM structure.

3D CNNs [4] that consider both spatial and temporal features have also been proposed. While our work is based on the temporal locality of videos as well, we use regular 2D CNNs for the task, and consider temporal locality only when comparing frames. Since a new model is proposed in their work, retraining is also needed.

Fast YOLO [13] pairs the use of YOLO for video processing in embedded systems with motion inference to propose a new architecture. However, not only this approach implies training the new architecture from scratch, it cannot be applied to existing architectures. [16] proposes a new architecture focusing on object tracking, which is relevant for our work; however, like Fast YOLO, it also needs to be trained again.

NoScope [5] accelerates video inference by training small NNs as a specialized models of a large, reference NN, for target objects and target videos; it also uses difference detectors that, similar to our work, compare whether frame contents have changed or not based on the high temporal locality of videos. This technique requires new training to be done in order to obtain the specialized models, and also relies on GPUs. Our work, in comparison, can be applied to already-trained models without needing to perform any modifications, and can be run on a low cost, low energy CPU. In summary, in this work we present a strategy that is software based, does not require retraining nor changing topology, and can be adapted to any CNN architecture.

3 Partial Window Processing

As already mentioned, this work uses the insight that between different frames there is a lot of temporal redundancy, which in turn can be used to save computations. By comparing frames, our work is able to determine which sections of an image have changed or not. Due to temporal locality, changes that can occur between two frames are limited, meaning we can either discard a whole frame, keeping the computation results from the previous one (in case nothing is determined to have changed), or process only a fraction of the image, reducing the total number of computations performed.

With less frames needing to be analyzed, total energy spent is lowered, as the number frames per watt rises. On top of that, unless the whole frame content changes, there is no need to perform all operations, so energy consumption is reduced even more.

Our work focuses on the convolutional layers of CNNs, as they are its most costly part. We aim to perform only needed convolutions and reuse as many results from previous runs as possible. As our target application concerns fixed security cameras, it is very unlikely that a total frame change will happen, unless considerable time has passed, supporting our reason to apply it in this context, as it will be demonstrated in the experimental section.

3.1 Frame Comparison

Previous frame

Current frame

Predicted area

Fig. 1. Differences predicted between two frames

Frame comparison is necessary to evaluate the amount of differences between two images. This detection needs to be efficient in order to not jeopardize the object detection framework performances. When a frame is computed, we compare it with the subsequent frames using Sum of Squared Differences. This comparison outputs the coordinates of a frame portion that is significantly different from the previous frame. It is worth noting that, on a parallel architecture, the comparison of pixels is a dot operation performed in constant time.

The highest overhead of this technique would be the load of images from memory. However, both frames are already available, as they must be loaded to be processed by the neural network. The only high overhead for the comparison could come from the number of possible rectangles that bound the area that has changed, which could be very high. To avoid excessive overhead, we have simplified the algorithm so that it only evaluates squares with sizes that are multiples of a given variable. The value used for our evaluation was 26, as it is a multiple of the used image size of 416 × 416, and other sizes were too big or too small. As the computation was around 1 or 2 orders of magnitude faster, the accuracy was maintained.

The output of our code is the rectangle that has the biggest size and a normalized sum of squared differences higher than a predefined threshold. This threshold was calibrated empirically so that the algorithm finds all important image differences in the chosen camera, but also does not get mistaken by small pixel variations in the background. If other cameras were to be used, or if the camera placement was different, other thresholds might prove to be better, as number of pixels and camera focus can change.

After the comparison is done, the second frame will be executed, but only the layer outputs affected by the rectangle area will be recalculated.

An example on the impact of partial window processing can be seen in Fig. 1. As a person moves from left to right, all the background information is the same. Moreover, the only part of the image that must be recomputed is the one concerning the new space the person is occupying, and the space they were occupying before, since a different object that could be suffering occlusion could now be detected.

3.2 Partial Execution

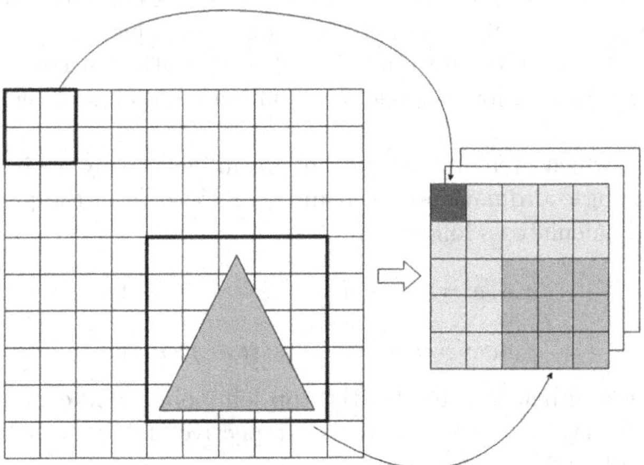

Fig. 2. Input image example and corresponding influence on output feature map (Color figure online)

In order for our partial processing technique to work, the prediction for the first image needs to be calculated on its entirety. After that, the stored values for each convolutional layer are those of this first run. Before starting the execution for the next image, we can use a frame comparison method, as already explained in Sect. 3.1, and detect changes between the two frames.

Since we stored all values of the previous frame, this means that there would be no need to rerun the network if one wanted to predict the same image again - the values would have already been stored, and the same applies for the output result. Furthermore, we apply this strategy not only to identical images, but also to images that are very similar - in our case, frames in a video next to each other that have been evaluated as having no relevant differences.

As explained above, partial windows are identified when a differences exist but, at the same time, the frames present significant similarity. In this case, the network receives from the Frame Comparison routine the coordinates of a partial window, represented by its top left and lower right coordinate points, which marks the area of an image that has changed and needs to be recalculated. This window highlights only part of the input, which, in turn, only affects a section of the output.

Figure 2 illustrates the described effect. We exemplify this with an input image of size 10×10, as shown in the left side of the figure; we then assume the first layer has filters of size 2×2, and a stride of 2, which would result in the feature map shown in the right side of Fig. 2. In this case, the 2×2 square highlighted on the top left of the input would influence only the dark blue square of the output, as pointed by the top arrow.

Accordingly, if we were to compare frames, and the detected Partial Window were to be the area showcasing the red triangle, we would only need to compute the corresponding red squares shown in the output to the right of Fig. 2. This means we could reuse all values in blue squares, which correspond to 64% of the total area. Furthermore, each filter of a layer generates one feature map. As it is common to have several filters per layer, our technique would scale to all of them, further decreasing the total number of computations needed; the network used in our experiments, for example, has 16 filters in its first layer, and savings are applied to all of them.

To discover which areas of the output are influenced by a given input, we take the bounding coordinate points x and y received from the partial window algorithm, and calculate as follows:

$$x\_new = x/stride - (size - stride) \tag{1}$$

$$y\_new = y/stride - (size - stride) \tag{2}$$

where x_new is the new x value for the top left point, $size$ correspond to the filter size of the layer, and $stride$ to its respective stride. New bottom right coordinates are found accordingly:

$$x\_new = x/stride + (size - stride) \tag{3}$$

$$y\_new = y/stride + (size - stride) \tag{4}$$

We have demonstrated how our technique works for one layer; extending it to further layers is trivial: we recalculate the influence window for each layer based on the previous one, exactly as it would be done if it was the first. As we get deeper into the network, however, our gains diminish, until execution is exactly the same as the regular network. This happens because the influence window gets larger, while the feature map size gets smaller, and, at some point, they become the same.

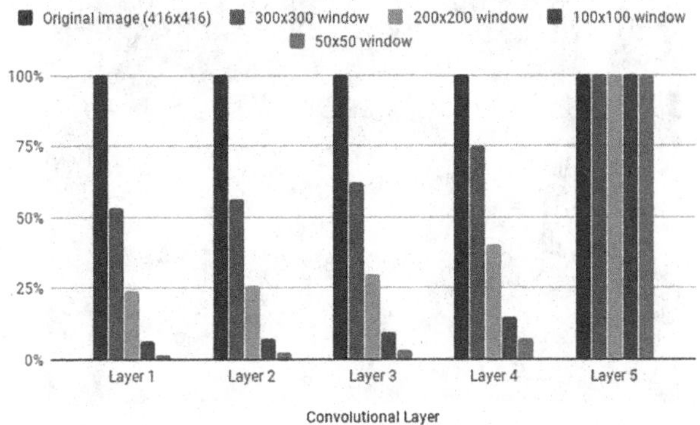

Fig. 3. Multiplications per convolutional layer for Tiny YOLO

Figure 3 demonstrates the diminishing gains effect of applying the proposed technique to Tiny YOLO [9]. The percentage of multiplications we need to do in each layer increases as the layers get deeper; at layer 5, the benefits of Partial Processing saturate, and the network is computed the same way as it would if our technique had not been used. Each network architecture has its own saturation point, as the window size is dependent on both stride and filter size.

Also relevant is how window size impacts on the number of total operations. The bigger the window, the bigger the area of influence which is discovered, and so more multiplications will be needed. Figure 3 shows this effect. The amount of differences between images directly impacts how much time and energy our technique is able to save, so a video where very little moves between frames would present higher savings than a video with constant changes.

Overall, our additions to the original framework code are the Frame Comparison routine, explained before, and the modifications to the original convolutional layer algorithm. The latter consists of calculating the new window size and setting the multiplication range for convolutions accordingly. Since values for all the network need to be stored, our technique also implies in a memory overhead. The total memory needed is equivalent to the number of outputs in each layer where our technique will be applied. As seen in Fig. 3, not all layers can benefit from it, so each network configuration will have its equivalent memory overhead.

4 Frame Skipping

As our technique is made to work at low frame rates, and we skip frames aiming at energy efficiency, information loss could become a problem. However, we can analyze videos to determine the minimum speed an object or person would have to move, at a determined frame rate, for their presence to be completely lost.

Fig. 4. Corridor size

If we take Fig. 4, we can infer the corridor size by assigning a height to the person walking through it, if this information is not present. Table 1 shows the approximate size the corridor would have compared to assigned heights. We can then use this number to discover the movement speed needed for something to not show in any of the sampled frames.

For example, if we assume the person has 1.60 m, and we were sampling the video at 1 fps, then the speed needed for a complete loss would be around 18.54 km/h, as shown in Table 1. If we sampled the video at 2 fps, that speed would go up to around 37.08 km/h. When considering average human running speed is around 13 km/h [7], even a reduced frame rate of 1 fps should still capture all important events.

5 Results

We have modified the Darknet neural network framework [8] in order to implement both the comparison between frames and the actual processing of only a partial area of the image, subsequently meaning that only a section of the network is calculated. We have chosen Darknet as it offers support for several CNN configurations, including YOLO [9], more specifically Tiny YOLO, our target network model due to its high frame rate capabilities. The videos we use are from the CAVIAR Test Case Scenarios [11], and they show hallways in a shopping centre. All videos are originally 25 fps, but, as already explained, we sample them at lower rates.

Table 2 shows our results in relation to an already sampled video. We take as the baseline the original CNN run on a video sampled in either 10 or 25 frames; our technique, on top of doing that, also provides frame skipping and partial processing. The Total Frames column refers to how many frames are processed in the baseline version, which are the same frames our method recieves as input; we, however, skip a percentage of these frames when they are deemed too similar, as shown in the Skipped Frames column and as already discussed in Sect. 4. The threshold we use for frame comparison is different for each video, chosen mainly considering its effect on accuracy; unlike the rest of our technique, that is automatized and requires no user input, the threshold needs to be set offline and by the user before the CNN can run. Both accuracy and speedup are based on the sampled baseline, meaning our gains in relation to the original, complete video, are even bigger, as will be shown next. Accuracy is measured in simple terms: if our technique detected the exact same objects as the original, then we consider no errors were present. Otherwise, if we detect an object the original network did not, or if we fail to detect one it did, it is considered an error.

Table 1. Corridor size and speed comparison

Person height	Corridor length	fps	Speed needed
1.60 m	5.15 m	1	18.54 km/h
1.60 m	5.15 m	2	37.08 km/h
1.70 m	5.48 m	1	19.7 km/h
1.70 m	5.48 m	2	39.4 km/h
1.80 m	5.8 m	1	20.88 km/h
1.80 m	5.8 m	2	41.76 km/h

As the comparison method explained in Sect. 3.1 is used, it inevitably adds an overhead to the CNN. However, when compared to the time it takes to process one frame in the original network, our overhead is less than 1% : 0.9% per frame. Our technique can reduce the time taken per frame execution by up to 20%, meaning the overhead is minimal comparing to our gains. Furthermore, when we skip a frame, we completely eliminate frame processing time, and only comparison time is taken into account. All our speedup results reported in this section include the comparison overhead.

We show that our technique can achieve up to 4.42x speedup when comparing to an already sampled video, while keeping accuracy losses lower than 10%. Video contents affect our maximum speedup - if the entire video frame is always changing, then our results will not offer a big speedup. On the other side, if either the video does not present many changes, or if they occur in limited areas, we will greatly reduce the needed processing time.

The video WalkByShop1front, for example, presents several frames where nothing happens, meaning we can skip several of them; furthermore, when changes are present, they are restricted to limited areas of the image, meaning our detected partial window is relatively small, and we can save several more

Table 2. Results

Video	Sampling	Total frames	Skipped frames	Accuracy	Speedup
WalkByShop1front	10	236	71.18%	95.33%	4.42x
WalkByShop1front	25	95	66.31%	92.63%	3.41x
WalkByShop1cor	10	236	30.50%	94.06%	1.91x
WalkByShop1cor	25	95	2.1%	94.73%	1.20x
TwoLeaveShop1cor	10	135	31.85%	96.29%	1.95x
TwoLeaveShop1cor	25	54	5.55%	98.14%	1.31x
OneShopOneWait1cor	10	138	14.49%	92.02%	1.49x
OneShopOneWait1cor	25	56	7.14%	91.07%	1.26x
ThreePastShop1cor	10	165	1.81%	92.72%	1.20x
ThreePastShop1cor	25	66	1.51%	96.96%	1.11x

computations. The other analyzed videos are of scenes where not only more activities are happening, but also frames change constantly, so our gains are limited; however, even in that case we still outperform the sampled baseline. It is worth noting that Partial Processing can provide significant speedups even when not many frames can be discarded. The video ThreePastShop1cor at a sampling of 25 only has 1.51% of its frames skipped, and still presents gains of 10% over the baseline.

Table 3 shows how much speedup our technique can achieve in relation to the whole processing of the original video instead of an already sampled version. The speedup of applying sampling only is limited - when we sample at 10 frames, our maximum speedup will be around 10x. Our technique, however, is able to achieve even more gains over it. Table 3 also shows how our technique depends on the application's behaviour - since frames in the video ThreePastShop1cor keep changing a lot, our speedup is limited. On the other side, WalkByShop1front, with its limited local changes, can be processed much faster, up to almost 80x the original speed.

Our energy gains are directly proportional to the speedup, as power in a CPU has approximately a fixed value, and we reduce the time it takes to complete the task. This means that we can achieve up to 4.42 times energy reduction in comparison to the same video using only a sampling technique. Furthermore, if we compare to the original CNN execution, sampling only is able to reduce energy by 23.2 times, and our method can bring that number up to 79.4 times.

Table 3. Speedup in relation to original unsampled video

Video	Sampling	Sampling speedup	Total speedup
WalkByShop1front	10	9.4x	39.6x
WalkByShop1front	25	23.2x	79.4x
ThreePastShop1cor	10	9.8x	11.8x
ThreePastShop1cor	25	25.3x	28.2x

6 Conclusion and Future Work

In this work, we have shown a technique that requires no extra hardware, network retraining or CNN architecture modification, and is still able to achieve great execution speedup and energy reduction, while keeping accuracy losses low.

We have demonstrated our results using Tiny YOLO, focusing on its potential high framerate. Despite that, our technique can work with any CNN architecture that needs to identify bounding boxes in an image. As long as the images the network needs to analyze in sequence present high temporal locality, our method should obtain gains. In the worst case, where the whole image always changes, we keep the regular CNN execution results and do not impact accuracy, adding only image comparison overhead.

In the future, we plan to extend our technique to work on GPU execution as well, as they are commonly used for running CNNs. We will also explore more advanced methods of comparing frames, so that object movement can be tracked with more accuracy.

Acknowledgements. This work was supported by CAPES, CNPQ and FAPERGS.

References

1. Chen, T., et al.: DianNao: a small-footprint high-throughput accelerator for ubiquitous machine-learning. SIGARCH Comput. Archit. News **42**(1), 269–284 (2014). https://doi.org/10.1145/2654822.2541967
2. Chen, Y.H., Krishna, T., Emer, J.S., Sze, V.: Eyeriss: an energy-efficient reconfigurable accelerator for deep convolutional neural networks. IEEE J. Solid-State Circ. **52**(1), 127–138 (2017). https://doi.org/10.1109/JSSC.2016.2616357
3. Honovich, J.: Average frame rate video surveillance 2011 (2011). https://ipvm.com/reports/recording-frame-rate-whats-actually-being-used
4. Ji, S., Xu, W., Yang, M., Yu, K.: 3D convolutional neural networks for human action recognition. IEEE Trans. Pattern Anal. Mach. Intell. **35**(1), 221–231 (2013). https://doi.org/10.1109/TPAMI.2012.59
5. Kang, D., Emmons, J., Abuzaid, F., Bailis, P., Zaharia, M.: Optimizing deep CNN-based queries over video streams at scale. CoRR abs/1703.02529 (2017). http://arxiv.org/abs/1703.02529
6. Karpathy, A., Toderici, G., Shetty, S., Leung, T., Sukthankar, R., Fei-Fei, L.: Large-scale video classification with convolutional neural networks. In: The IEEE Conference on Computer Vision and Pattern Recognition (CVPR), June 2014
7. Livingit: average human running speed: broken down age-wise (2018). https://www.iamlivingit.com/running/average-human-running-speed
8. Redmon, J.: Darknet: open source neural networks in c (2016). http://pjreddie.com/darknet/
9. Redmon, J., Divvala, S., Girshick, R., Farhadi, A.: You only look once: unified, real-time object detection. In: 2016 IEEE Conference on Computer Vision and Pattern Recognition (CVPR), pp. 779–788, June 2016. https://doi.org/10.1109/CVPR.2016.91

10. Riera, M., Arnau, J., Gonzalez, A.: Computation reuse in DNNs by exploiting input similarity. In: 2018 ACM/IEEE 45th Annual International Symposium on Computer Architecture (ISCA), pp. 57–68, June 2018. https://doi.org/10.1109/ISCA.2018.00016
11. Robert, F., Santos-Victor, J.C.: CAVIAR: context aware vision using image-based active recognition (2006). http://homepages.inf.ed.ac.uk/rbf/CAVIAR/
12. Sen, S., Raghunathan, A.: Approximate computing for long short term memory (LSTM) neural networks. IEEE Trans. Comput.-Aided Design Integr. Circ. Syst. **37**(11), 2266–2276 (2018). https://doi.org/10.1109/TCAD.2018.2858362
13. Shafiee, M.J., Chywl, B., Li, F., Wong, A.: Fast YOLO: a fast you only look once system for real-time embedded object detection in video. CoRR abs/1709.05943 (2017). http://arxiv.org/abs/1709.05943
14. Sze, V., Chen, Y.H., Yang, T.J., Emer, J.S.: Efficient processing of deep neural networks: a tutorial and survey. Proc. IEEE **105**(12), 2295–2329 (2017). https://doi.org/10.1109/JPROC.2017.2761740
15. Tan, C., Kulkarni, A., Venkataramani, V., Karunaratne, M., Mitra, T., Peh, L.S.: LOCUS: low-power customizable many-core architecture for wearables. ACM Trans. Embed. Comput. Syst. **17**(1), 16:1–16:26 (2017). https://doi.org/10.1145/3122786
16. Teng, Z., Xing, J., Wang, Q., Lang, C., Feng, S., Jin, Y.: Robust object tracking based on temporal and spatial deep networks. In: 2017 IEEE International Conference on Computer Vision (ICCV), pp. 1153–1162, October 2017. https://doi.org/10.1109/ICCV.2017.130
17. Yue-Hei Ng, J., Hausknecht, M., Vijayanarasimhan, S., Vinyals, O., Monga, R., Toderici, G.: Beyond short snippets: deep networks for video classification. In: The IEEE Conference on Computer Vision and Pattern Recognition (CVPR), June 2015
18. Zhu, Y., Samajdar, A., Mattina, M., Whatmough, P.N.: Euphrates: algorithm-SoC co-design for low-power mobile continuous vision. CoRR abs/1803.11232 (2018). http://arxiv.org/abs/1803.11232

Design and Optimization of an ARM Cortex-M Based SoC for TCP/IP Communication in High Temperature Applications

T. Stuckenberg(✉), M. Gottschlich, S. Nolting, and H. Blume

Institute of Microelectronic Systems, Leibniz Universität Hannover, Appelstr. 4, 30167 Hanover, Germany
{stuckenberg,gottschlich,nolting,blume}@ims.uni-hannover.de

Abstract. TCP/IP protocol stacks are usually complex protocols which require a high amount of computational power for the benefit of reliable communication. Therefore, a powerful and energy demanding processing core with an operating system is needed to achieve high data rates. In communication systems that are placed in a high temperature environment, e.g. electronics close to car engines or in aerospace applications, installation space is limited, temperatures of up to 175 °C occur and a high energy consumption leads to further self-heating. Thus, a robust high temperature ASIC is mandatory in order to provide an energy efficient and small processing platform.

Special forms of the TCP/IP stack like Lightweight IP (lwIP) or Micro IP (uIP) are built for small or even embedded processors without the need of an operating system. In this work we implemented the lwIP and uIP stacks on the ARM Cortex-M0 and ARM Cortex-M3 processors and measured the throughput of the resulting System on Chips (SoC) designed for high temperature applications. The results show a relatively poor throughput of maximum 20.29 MBit/s even for the more powerful Cortex-M3 processor using the lwIP stack. Software and hardware improvements like a Direct Memory Access (DMA) mechanism and extended checksum hardware could increase the performance by 1250% resulting in 228 MBit/s.

As an exemplary target application, powerline communication in high temperature environment is chosen and a Design Space Exploration (DSE) was performed on the available physical parameters of a 180 nm SOI technology, capable of operating at 175 °C. Results show that the best performing processor-software-combination is the Cortex-M0 which has a size of only 0.374 mm^2 and a power consumption of less than 1 mW at 10 MBit/s targeted throughput for the powerline application running the uIP stack. The increase in silicon area is only 9.7% and still this SoC is 2.57 times smaller and has 18.1 times less energy consumption compared to the Cortex-M3 baseline implementation.

Keywords: ASIC · ARM · High temperature · lwIP · Powerline communication · TCP/IP · uIP

D. N. Pnevmatikatos et al. (Eds.): SAMOS 2019, LNCS 11733, pp. 169–183, 2019.
https://doi.org/10.1007/978-3-030-27562-4_12

1 Introduction

The Internet of Things (IoT) currently gains increasing attention in all areas of communication systems. One of these is the powerline communication, which is considered as one promising approach to connect all kinds of devices [7]. In this technology the existing power distribution network is used to transmit data on unused frequency bands by modulating it on the power signal. Throughout the years different powerline standards have emerged where the most common ones in Europe and America are presented by the HomePlug Alliance standards and based on the IEEE 1901 standard [20]. The data rates of these standards increased from 10 MBit/s in the HomePlug 1.0 standard [13] in 2001 to more than 1 GBit/s in today's HomePlug AV2 [14]. The latest powerline standards are designed for in-house multimedia streaming and provide very high throughput which is usually not required in industrial applications (e.g. sensor data streaming or controlling actuators). Additionally, this high throughput comes with an overhead in silicon area, energy consumption and functionality. Therefore, the HomePlug Alliance created a less powerful but more robust standard named HomePlug GreenPHY for the use in IoT applications [15]. This standard only supports a so-called ROBO mode, that provides a robust communication over an OFDM-based communication system. By redundantly spreading the information in frequency and time a more reliable packet transmission is achieved, which also needs smaller hardware compared to the other standards. The drawback of this robust communication is a maximum throughput of 10 MBit/s.

HomePlug GreenPHY provides a lot of benefits, but it is designed for commercial use under regular environmental conditions like operational temperatures of up to 85 °C or the use of a regular power socket. In harsh environmental industrial applications e.g. electronic parts in vehicles, space missions or planes non of these conditions apply. High temperatures of up to 180 °C are affecting electronic part which are located close to car engines or turbines of planes. With the increased need of communication, especially in modern cars, which are heading towards autonomous driving or aerospace applications, powerline communication capable of operating under harsh environmental conditions are a promising technology [11,18,22].

In this work we focus on controlling the data transmission via powerline by TCP/IP communication to create an interface for applications that work on IP-based communication in high temperature conditions. A significant advantage of using TCP/IP together with powerline communication is that electronic parts can be replaced, added or removed without re-configuring every single component of the network. For this protocol stack a processor core is required which is as small as possible, consumes a minimum of energy and is still powerful enough to process the TCP/IP stack.

A platform series that is able to provide processor with the above listed features, is the ARM Cortex-M series providing a powerful 32 Bit instruction set architecture (ISA) [1,23,28]. As the processors of choice we use the ARM Cortex-M3 and the ARM Cortex-M0 which are two of the smallest processors from the Cortex-M series and are made available by ARM Limited in their own

DesignStart Eval program [3,4]. Using this DesignStart platform we explore software and hardware parameters to optimize the throughput, silicon area, latency and energy consumption in order to find an optimal implementation for the use of TCP/IP communication in a high temperature, low power environment.

This paper is organized as follows: Sect. 2 shows the related work of ARM cores in ASIC technologies and state-of-the-art TCP/IP implementations in software and hardware. In Sect. 3 the evaluation platform is introduced and first throughput measurements are performed. In Sect. 4 hardware and software optimizations are realized to increase the throughput of the SoC. Section 5 shows the results of ASIC synthesis in a high temperature 180 nm SOI technology. In Sect. 6 results from ASIC synthesis and throughput measurements are evaluated together in a Design Space Exploration (DSE) and an algorithm is chosen that is optimal for the target application. A conclusion is given in Sect. 7.

2 Related Work

Various ASIC implementations have been developed for the ARM Cortex-M series for commercial use. Table 1 shows an exemplary comparison of state-of-the-art consumer chips using ARM Cortex-M processors. They all target small ASIC designs which have a very low dynamic power consumption but only one of these cores is built to operate in a high temperature environment. The product offered by VARAGO is capable to operate in harsh environmental conditions of up to 200 °C and has an ARM Cortex-M0 core as processing unit. As we will see later in this work a market-available ARM Cortex-M0 ASIC-SoC without hardware extensions is not ideal for the target of this work.

Table 1. Comparison of commercially available ARM Cortex-M based products and their temperature ranges.

	Core	Technology	max. Temp °C
STM [2]	M0	40 nm-LP	125
STM [2]	M3	40 nm-LP	125
Freescale [2]	M4	180 nm-ULL	125
STM [2]	M7	28 nm-HPM	125
VORAGO [6]	M0	130 nm HARDSIL	200

Many TCP/IP implementations can be found in literature. A lot of the implementations target a throughput rate of more than 1 GBit/s to keep up with the increasing amount data transfers needed in multimedia streaming or data center applications [19,24,25]. Several different approaches are made regarding the portion of hardware used in these implementations. They range from CPUs with operating systems [21] to fully custom hardware designs [19]. One promising approach is a protocol offload engine as described in [17]. This approach benefits from the use of a small general purpose processing unit as well as the speed of a custom hardware accelerator for computation intensive tasks. The idea of offloading the TCP checksum calculation has been described in [16] and an adapted version will be used in this work to calculate the TCP and IP checksum simultaneously. Two of the smallest implementations that do not need an operating system but still providing the full TCP/IP functionality are the Lightweight IP (lwIP) and Micro IP (uIP) stacks [9,10]. Both of these stacks will be evaluated in this work.

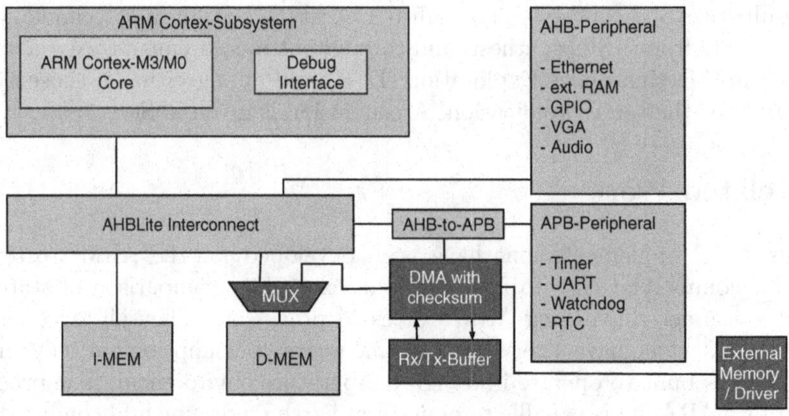

Fig. 1. The ARM DesignStart system with custom DMA hardware extension with access to the DMEM and external memory (highlighted in darker color).

3 System Design

The framework used in this work is the ARM DesignStart Eval platform [26]. It is dedicated for developing System-on-Chip (SoC) architectures, which are based on ARM-Cortex processors. Figure 1 shows the basic structure of the hardware components of the DesignStart system. Components highlighted in darker color are hardware extensions designed in this work to increase the performance of the system. The interconnection bus of this SoC is an advanced high-performance bus lite (AHBLite) that connects instruction memory (IMEM), data memory (DMEM) and external peripherals, such as Ethernet interfaces or GPIO to the Cortex-Subsystem. Peripherals, which need lower bandwidth, e.g. timer modules, are mapped via an additional advanced peripheral bus (APB) extension [3,4].

The ARM Cortex Subsystem in Fig. 1 consists of a Cortex-M processor where the actual model can be chosen from the whole Cortex-M processor family. Here we use the Cortex-M0 and Cortex-M3 processors which are two of the smallest processors in this series. Table 2 shows a comparison of the hardware structure of these two processors. The main difference is the memory architecture where the Cortex-M0 is a von-Neumann architecture and the Cortex-M3 is a Harvard architecture. Additionally, the Cortex-M3 has a hardware divider and multiply-and-accumulate (MAC) unit. The Cortex-M0 has neither of these meaning that divisions and MAC operations have to be calculated in software using the Arithmetic Logic Unit (ALU). This results in a trade-off between long computation times versus less silicon area [28].

In this work we use the ARM MPS2+ development kit with an integrated Cyclone V FPGA (5CEBA9F31C8N) to emulate the DesignStart system with either of the Cortex-M processors. This development board also allows to profile the code of the lwIP and uIP stacks and measure the throughput using the built-in Ethernet port. For the latter, an Iperf2-Server application is implemented on top of the lwIP or uIP stack, which is also running on the Cortex-M processor [8]. Table 3 shows the throughput rates measured for different combinations of processor and TCP/IP stack using an FPGA clock frequency of 25 MHz for all designs. Since the target platform is an ASIC-SoC the operational frequency of the FPGA design will be fix for the rest of this work and is not increased by e.g. pipelining, due to comparison reasons. It can be seen that the Cortex-M3 processor has a higher throughput compared to the Cortex-M0 independent of the TCP/IP stack implementation. This is due to the more powerful ISA of the Cortex-M3 processor, which results in a reduced number of assembly instructions. The other insight that can be drawn from Table 3 is that the lwIP stack is faster than the uIP stack.

4 Hard- and Software Optimization

As shown in the previous section the lwIP stack achieves higher throughput rates than the uIP stack. Since both stacks implement the same basic functions of TCP/IP and additionally uIP is built to be the more reduced stack, it is not intuitive why lwIP is faster. A profiling of the code execution has been performed for both stacks running on the Cortex-M3 processor. Figure 2 shows the results of that profiling. In Fig. 2(a) the processing of a TCP/IP data packet is shown. First, it is transferred from the Ethernet driver to the DMEM of the system. Then the packet is processed as shown in Fig. 2(b). Here, the IP part of the packet is extracted, processed and then the TCP checksum is evaluated. At last, the TCP header is extracted, the Iperf2 application is executed and an answer is generated. The latter is then transferred back to the external memory or device. In Fig. 2(a) and (b) we can see a large difference in the processing time between lwIP and uIP, which is due to the different calculation algorithms of the TCP checksum. The lwIP's checksum calculation is more efficient and does not use specialized hardware on the Cortex-M3 e.g. a divider. Therefore, we ported the checksum calculation of lwIP to uIP, which results in the processing time shown in Fig. 2(c). With this improvement the total processing time of the uIP stack can be reduced to 195 µs, which is faster then the lwIP's processing time.

Table 2. Comparison of ARM Cortex-M0 and ARM Cortex-M3 regarding their hardware structure and functional units.

	Cortex-M0	Cortex-M3
ARM architecture	ARMv6-M	ARMv7-M
Pipeline stages	3	3
Architecture	von-Neumann	Harvard
MAC unit	No	Yes
Hardware divider	No	Yes
Cache support	No	No

Table 3. Comparing the throughput rate and speedup of lwIP and uIPm against uIP. The FPGA operating frequency is 25 MHz.

	Cortex-M0		Cortex-M3	
	[MBit/s]	Speedup	[MBit/s]	Speedup
uIP	12.76	1.0	16.96	1.0
lwIP	14.00	1.1	20.29	1.2
uIPm	16.60	1.3	25.31	1.5

The resulting throughput of that modification can be seen in the third row of Table 3 referred as uIPm. The speedup of lwIP and uIPm is calculated against the basic uIP implementation. It can be seen that uIPm has a higher throughput than the original uIP and is even though higher than the lwIP implementation. It reaches a maximum speedup of up to 1.5 compared to the standard uIP implementation.

With these implementations we are already able to provide the necessary throughput for the HomePlug GreenPHY standard with both the lwIP and uIPm implementation, but the cores will not be able to process a more complex application than the fairly simple Iperf2 server or keep up with upcoming standards that will require a higher throughput rate. This would also be the case for the ARM Cortex-M0 integration by VORAGO (refer Sect. 2), which is able to operate at 200 °C but is already fixed in its ASIC design. Therefore, it is useful to further investigate mechanisms to increase the throughput of the system to either be able to run applications in parallel or in case no other application is needed, to reduce the operating frequency as far as possible, which also reduces the energy consumption of the system. Furthermore, the ARM Cortex-M series supports a deep sleep mode and wake-up interrupt controller (WIC) that are able to reduce the power consumption to a minimum [23,27]. Hence, it might be useful to keep the computation time for one package as short as possible and send the core system to deep sleep mode for saving energy.

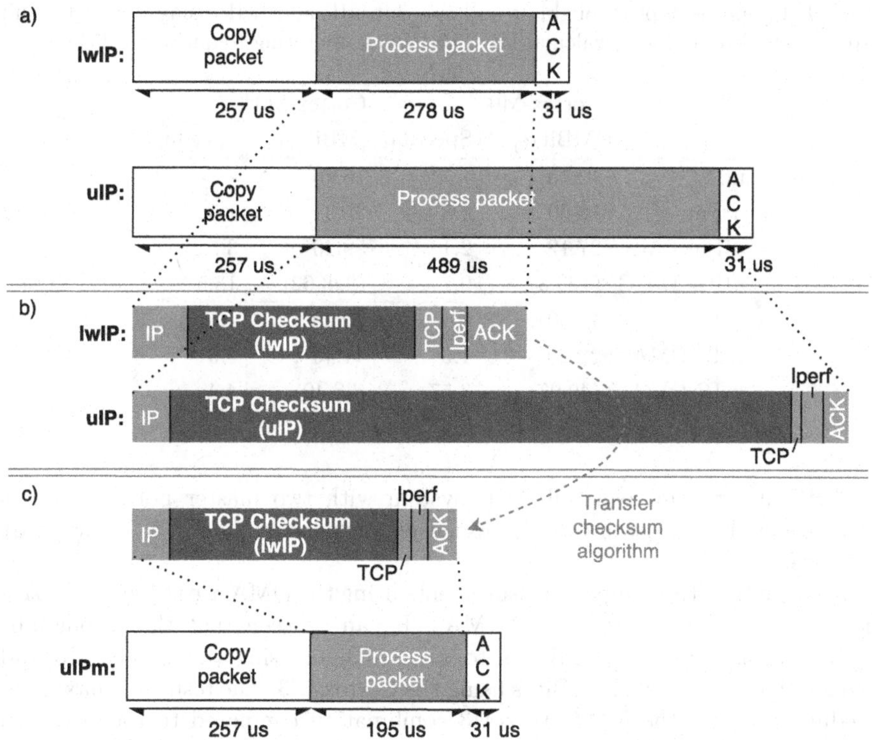

Fig. 2. Profiling results for uIP and lwIP running on the Cortex-M3 divided in (a) total processing time of one TCP/IP packet, (b) detailed comparison of processing times on the processor cores and (c) improvement of uIP processing time by using the lwIP checksum calculation.

One mechanism to increase the throughput of the system is a direct memory access (DMA), which is able to run mostly independent of the Cortex-M processor. Thus, it is possible to process one data packet while transferring the subsequent one using the double buffering principle. The integration of this DMA mechanism is shown in Fig. 1 in darker colors. The DMA has direct access to the DMEM of the processor, the Ethernet interface or external memory (depending on the application) and is integrated into the APB system to send interrupts to the processor core.

As soon as the DMA detects an incoming or outgoing data packet it sends an interrupt to the processor to avoid simultaneous access to the DMEM[1]. The DMA then transfers the packet from/to the DMEM into/from the external data interface and clears the interrupt. The maximum stall time of the processor is 15.78 µs, which is defined by to the maximum size of one Ethernet packet that is 1500 Byte. The stalling of the processor could only be avoided by changing

[1] The ASIC technology does not provide a dual-port memory capable of operating in a high temperature environment of up to 175 °C.

Table 4. Comparison of throughput and speedup uIP and lwIP using the DMA and hardware checksum (D&C) calculation. The FPGA operating frequency is 25 MHz.

	Cortex-M0		Cortex-M3	
	[MBit/s]	Speedup	[MBit/s]	Speedup
uIP	12.76	-	16.96	-
uIPm	16.60	1.3	25.31	1.5
uIPm DMA	27.12	2.1	59.40	3.5
uIPm D& C	(123.3)	9.7	(228.62)	13.5
lwIP	14.00	-	20.29	-
lwIP DMA	22.20	1.6	41.46	2.0
lwIP D&C	(49.97)	3.57	(88.40)	4.4

the AHBLite system to a full AHB system with two master ports, which is not considered in this work due to extensive changes in the ARM DesignStart structure.

The results of throughput measurements using the DMA are shown in Table 4 and are marked with the suffix "DMA". It can be seen that the throughput of uIP increases from 16.6 MBit/s to 27.12 MBit/s using the Cortex-M0 and from 25.31 MBit/s to 59.40 MBit/s using the Cortex-M3. The resulting maximum speedup is 3.5 for the uIP-Cortex-M3 combination compared to the standard uIP implementation. The throughput of lwIP is increased from 14.00 MBit/s to 22.20 MBit/s for the Cortex-M0 and from 20.29 MBit/s to 41.46 MBit/s using the Cortex-M3. The resulting maximum speedup for lwIP is 2.

As of now, the most time consuming operation that limits the throughput are the TCP and IP checksum calculations as depicted in Fig. 2. Both of these checksum are calculated on 16 Bit words and overlap in parts of the required input data necessary to calculate them. Therefore, the checksums can be calculated iteratively while transfering the data between the external memory and internal memory. This idea has been shown to significantly increase the performance of TCP/IP-based communication [12,16].

The structure of our checksum calculator is shown in Fig. 3 based on the idea of Hsiao et al. [16] and is adapted to work with our DMA system. The 32 Bit word of one DMA transfer is split into two sub-words of 16 Bit, which are summed using the ones complement in the first full adder (FA1). The sum and carry are passed to the second full adder (FA2), where they are summed with the current accumulator value (ACCU). The carry bit of this summation is stored in a register and will be added up during the consecutive DMA transfer. After the last DMA transfer the result is stored in a register, which is accessible from the Cortex-M processor core in case of receiving a packet. In case of transmitting the packet, the TCP checksum is inserted into the outgoing header directly. Therefore, a control unit for resetting the registers and storing the results at the required locations is needed.

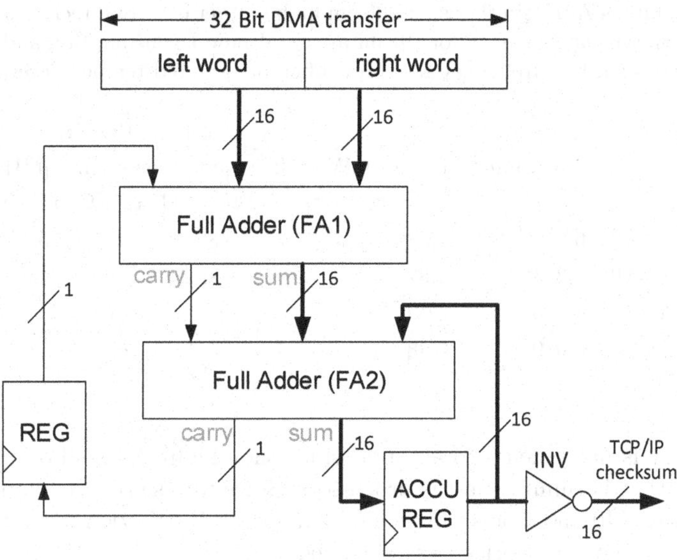

Fig. 3. Structure of hardware extension to the DMA calculating the checksum of both TCP and IP. An extra controller is needed to read TCP and IP checksum when finished calculation.

The increased throughput rates of this hardware checksum extension combined with the DMA transfers is shown in Table 4 with the suffix "D&C". The throughput rates shown in brackets are interpolated rates calculated with Eq. 1, because these can not be run on the evaluation board MPS2+. The Ethernet port is only capable of transfering data at a rate of 100 MBit/s. The values of the latest lwIP improvements could be tested, but are interpolated too for comparison reason.

$$R_{D\&C} = \frac{t_{trans,old} + t_{proc,old}}{t_{trans,new} + t_{proc,new}} * R_{DMA} \quad (1)$$

In Eq. 1 $R_{D\&C}$ is the data rates using both checksum and DMA hardware calculation and R_{DMA} uses the DMA extension only. t_{trans} and t_{proc} are the transmission and processing times for a single packet measured with the profiler.

The hardware extension calculating the checksums could speed-up the uIP stack to 228.62 MBit/s and the lwIP stack to 88.4 MBit/s, which is up to 13.5 times faster than the original uIP stack implementation.

5 ASIC Synthesis

To evaluate the size of the processor cores and the additional modules that have increased the system performance significantly (as described in the previous section), an ASIC synthesis is done for the SoC system. Here, the instruction and

Table 5. Results of ASIC synthesis for 180 nm high temperature SOI technology targeting 25 MHz operating frequency for silicon area and power consumption and 125 MHz the maximum operating frequency for three different targeted temperatures.

Module	Target: 25 MHz		Target: 125 MHz		
	Area [mm^2]	Power [mW MHz^{-1}]	max. Frequency [MHz]		
			25 °C	125 °C	175 °C
Cortex-M3	0.913	25.32	82.0	51.7	50.4
Cortex-M0	0.315	9.37	102.5	63.6	61.4
DMA	0.040	0.49		n/a	
CKSM	0.019	0.48		n/a	

data memory is not taken into account, since they highly depend on the target application that is running on the processors. Since we use the same application for the Cortex-M0 and Cortex-M3, the difference in instruction memory is only 6.5%[2] and the data memories have about equal sizes.

The technology used for this synthesis is a 180 nm silicon-on-insulator (SOI) technology which is capable of performing in temperatures of up to 175 °C and supply voltages as low as 1.62 V.

The results of area and power consumption estimation are given in Table 5 for a targeted operating frequency of 25 MHz. Since we are using an SOI technology, about 99% of the power loss is caused by the dynamic part, independent of the surrounding temperature. This means that the power consumption of the system scales linearly with its operating frequency [5]. The results for the max. operating frequency are generated by setting the targeted frequency to 125 MHz and target temperature of 25 °C, 125 °C and 175 °C. It can be seen that the maximum operating frequency decreases with temperature. Table 5 shows that the Cortex-M3 core is the largest and most power consuming part. When using the Cortex-M0 instead, the area is reduced by 65% and the power consumption by 63%. The DMA hardware unit only has 4% of the size of a Cortex-M3 processor or 13% of the size of a Cortex-M0 processor and its energy consumption scales similarly. The checksum hardware unit is even smaller and only needs 6% of the size and 5.1% of the energy compared to a Cortex-M0. The maximum operating frequency of the Cortex-M0 is 61.4 MHz and for the Cortex-M3 it is 47.9 MHz. Therefore, the throughput of the system could be further increased in the ASIC technology, since the operating frequency of the FPGA was fixed at 25 MHz.

With these results we are now able to compare the throughput, the size and energy consumption of the different configurations and tune them for our targeted application.

[2] Measured using the binary code of the GCC cross compiler with optimization -O3.

6 Design Space Exploration

The results of ASIC synthesis and throughput measurements are evaluated in a design space exploration (DSE) to find an optimal implementation for the target application of powerline communication in a high temperature environment. Figure 4 shows the area of the M0-SoC system and M3-SoC system from Sect. 5 compared to the logarithmically scaled throughput measured in Sect. 4. The theoretical optimum can be found in the bottom right corner, where the area is minimal and the throughput is maximized. The M0-SoC and the M3-SoC can be distinguished mainly by their silicon area. It can be seen that the M0-SoC and the M3-SoC running the uIPm D&C are the closest to the theoretical optimum, where the M0-SoC unit is closer and therefore referred as the most efficient implementation in this work.

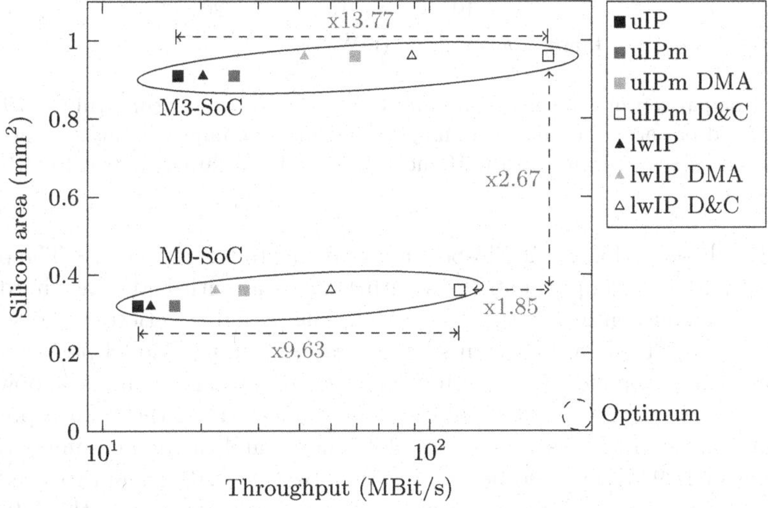

Fig. 4. Comparison of the Cortex-M0 and Cortex-M3 SoC concerning their silicon area and throughput rate running either the uIP or lwIP stack.

If we take a close look at the power consumption and area of the best performing algorithm, which is the uIPm implementation it can be seen that the throughput of the SoC systems is higher than needed for all implementations in this work. Therefore, we are interested in the minimum operating frequency that provides just enough throughput for the HomePlug GreenPHY system reducing the energy consumption of the system significantly. Figure 5 shows the area of the SoC designs compared to their energy consumption. The optimum of is located the bottom left corner where silicon area and energy consumption are minimal. The operating frequencies of the different SoC systems are reduced to match a throughput of 10 MBit/s. Since the power consumption scales linearly with the frequency in SOI technology, we extrapolate the dynamic power consumption part of the ASIC synthesis results from Sect. 5 [5]. It can be seen that the

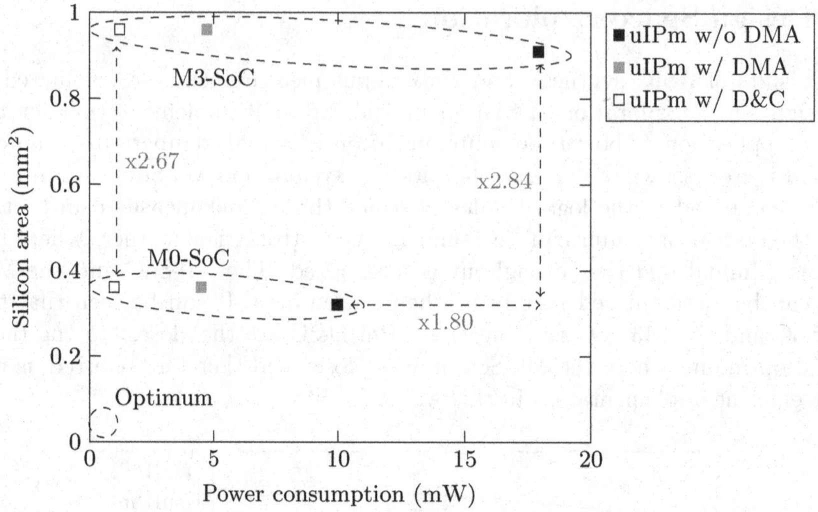

Fig. 5. Comparison of the Cortex-M0 and Cortex-M3 processor concerning their silicon area and power consumption running the uIPm stack implementation. Operating frequencies are scaled to match the HomePlug GreenPHY throughput of 10 MBit/s.

M0-SoC still outperforms the M3-SoC but only due to its smaller size. The power consumption of the implementations with DMA and with DMA and hardware checksum calculation are close to identical. The actual selection of the system now results in a trade-off between silicon area and computational performance.

If the target application running on the SoC system requires a powerful instruction set (e.g. hardware divider) or should perform at the highest possible throughput, the M3-SoC systems should be chosen and the maximum operating frequency of 47.9 MHz should be set. The drawback of that configuration is, that the M3-SoC is about 2.7 times larger in silicon area compared to the M0-SoC. In case the available space and energy consumption are very limited the M0-SoC system should be chosen as the most area and energy efficient implementation in this work.

7 Conclusion

The goal of this work was to find an optimized SoC system that is able to run in a high temperature environment with limited available area and power consumption for automotive or aerospace powerline applications. We started with running and profiling the lwIP and uIP stacks on the ARM-Cortex-M0 and ARM-Cortex-M3 processors, which resulted in a maximum throughput rate of 20.29 MBit/s for the lwIP on the Cortex-M3 processor.

Transferring the checksum calculation code from lwIP to uIP increased the uIP performance to 25.31 MBit/s running on the more powerful Cortex-M3 processor.

Further improving the data transfer with a dedicated DMA and calculating the checksum for the TCP and IP protocol in hardware on the fly further increased the performance to 228.62 MBit/s for the uIP and 88.4 MBit/s for the lwIP on the Cortex-M3 processor. The maximum gained speedup is 13.5 for the uIP implementation with DMA and hardware checksum calculation unit.

Results from ASIC synthesis targeting a high temperature technology were then used to compare the processors in silicon area and power consumption. Here, the Cortex-M3 processor is about 2.67 times larger than the Cortex-M0. Equally, the power consumption scales linear with area and operating frequency in SOI technology. It was shown that the DMA and checksum calculation hardware is small compared to the size of the processor cores and only minorly increase the total silicon area of the SoC.

An analysis of throughput, silicon area and power consumption showed that the uIP stack running on the Cortex-M0 processor is the optimal combination of processor and TCP/IP regarding thorughput rate, energy consumption and area, which can provide a maximum throughput of 123.3 MBit/s. A reduction of the operating frequency can further decrease the power consumption to less that 1 mW matching the throughput requirements of the HomePlug 1.0 and HomePlug GreenPHY standards of 10 MBit/s.

The processor stack combination providing the highest throughput rate is the Cortex-M3 with the uIP stack including the DMA and checksum calculation. Here, a maximum throughput of 228.6 MBit/s is reached with a size of less than 1 mm^2 and a power consumption of 28 mW.

References

1. Arm Limited: Arm 180 nm Ultra-Low-Power Platform. https://static.docs.arm.com/pfl0307/10/PIPD_Platform_TSMC_180ULL_BR_NC.pdf. Accessed 15 Jan 2019
2. Arm Limited: Arm Cortex-M Series Processors. https://developer.arm.com/products/processors/cortex-m. Accessed 23 Feb 2019
3. Arm Limited: Arm Cortex-M0 DesignStart Eval User Guide (2017)
4. Arm Limited: Arm Cortex-M3 DesignStart Eval RTL and FPGA Quick Start Guide (2017)
5. Vandana, B.: A theoretical study of low power Soi technology. IOSR J. VLSI Signal Process. **2**, 30–37 (2013). https://doi.org/10.9790/4200-0253037
6. Bannatyne, R., Gifford, D., Klein, K., McCarville, K., Merritt, C., Neddermeyer, S.: Creation of an ARM® Cortex®-M0 microcontroller for high temperature embedded systems. In: Additional Conferences (Device Packaging, HiTEC, HiTEN, & CICMT), pp. 31–35 (2017). https://doi.org/10.4071/2380-4491.2017.HiTEN.31
7. Chauvenet, C., Etheve, G., Sedjai, M., Sharma, M.: G3-PLC based IoT sensor networks for SmartGrid. In: 2017 IEEE International Symposium on Power Line Communications and its Applications (ISPLC), pp. 1–6, April 2017. https://doi.org/10.1109/ISPLC.2017.7897113
8. Dugan, J., Elliott, S., Mah, B.A., Poskanzer, J., Prabhu, K.: iPerf - the ultimate speed test tool for TCP, UDP and SCTP. https://iperf.fr/. Accessed 21 Feb 2019

9. Dunkels, A.: Design and implementation of the LwIP TCP/IP stack. Technical report, Swedish Institute of Computer Science, February 2001. https://doi.org/10.1145/1066116.1066118
10. Dunkels, A.: The uIP embedded TCP/IP stack - reference manual. Technical report, Swedish Institute of Computer Science, June 2006
11. Gouret, W., Nouvel, F., El-Zein, G.: Powerline communication on automotive network. In: 2007 IEEE 65th Vehicular Technology Conference - VTC2007-Spring, pp. 2545–2549, April 2007. https://doi.org/10.1109/VETECS.2007.524
12. Henriksson, T., Persson, N., Liu, D.: VLSI implementation of internet checksum calculation for 10 gigabit Ethernet. In: Proceedings of Design and Diganostics of Electronics, Cricuits and Systems, pp. 114–121 (2002)
13. HomePlug Powerline Alliance: HomePlug 1.0 Specification. Standard, HomePlug Power Alliance, CA, USA, December 2001
14. HomePlug Powerline Alliance: HomePlug AV2 Technology. Standard, HomePlug Power Alliance, CA, USA, Deember 2010
15. HomePlug Powerline Alliance: HomePlug Green PHY. Standard, HomePlug Power Alliance, CA, USA, July 2013
16. Hsiao, Y., Chen, M., Huang, K., Chu, Y., Yeh, C.: High speed UDP/IP ASIC design. In: 2009 International Symposium on Intelligent Signal Processing and Communication Systems (ISPACS), pp. 405–408, January 2009. https://doi.org/10.1109/ISPACS.2009.5383815
17. Jang, H., Chung, S.H., Yoo, D.H.: Design and implementation of a protocol offload engine for TCP/IP and remote direct memory access based onhardware/software coprocessing. Microprocess. Microsyst. **33**(5–6), 333–342 (2009). https://doi.org/10.1016/j.micpro.2009.03.001
18. Jones, C.H.: Communications over aircraft power lines. In: 2006 IEEE International Symposium on Power Line Communications and Its Applications, pp. 149–154, March 2006. https://doi.org/10.1109/ISPLC.2006.247452
19. Langenbach, U., Berthe, A., Traskov, B., Weide, S., Hofmann, K., Gregorius, P.: A 10 GbE TCP/IP hardware stack as part of a protocol acceleration platform. In: 2013 IEEE Third International Conference on Consumer Electronics Berlin (ICCE-Berlin), pp. 381–384, September 2013. https://doi.org/10.1109/ICCE-Berlin.2013.6697997
20. Latchman, H.A., Katar, S., Yonge, L., Gavette, S.: Homeplug AV and IEEE 1901: A Handbook for PLC Designers and Users, 1st edn. Wiley-IEEE Press, Hoboken (2013)
21. Mahbub, H., Raj, J.: High Performance TCP/IP Networking. Pearson Prentice Hall, New Jersey (2004)
22. Mumtaz, S., Alsohaily, A., Pang, Z., Rayes, A., Tsang, K.F., Rodriguez, J.: Massive internet of things for industrial applications: addressing wireless iot connectivity challenges and ecosystem fragmentation. IEEE Ind. Electron. Mag. **11**(1), 28–33 (2017). https://doi.org/10.1109/MIE.2016.2618724
23. Saunders, M.: Minimizing ARM Cortex CPU power by carefully considering and implementing combinations of these techniques, developers can realize substantial advantages. SILICON LABS, p. 1, September 2014
24. Sidler, D., István, Z., Alonso, G.: Low-latency TCP/IP stack for datacenter applications. In: 2016 26th International Conference on Field Programmable Logic and Applications (FPL), pp. 1–4, August 2016. https://doi.org/10.1109/FPL.2016.7577319

25. Sutter, G., Ruiz, M., López-Buedo, S., Alonso, G.: FPGA-based TCP/IP checksum offloading engine for 100 Gbps networks. 2018 International Conference on ReConFigurable Computing and FPGAs (ReConFig), pp. 1–6 (2018)
26. Trevor, M.: The Designer's Guide to the Cortex-M Processor Family - A Tutorial Approach. Elsevier, Oxford (2013)
27. Yiu, J.: The Definitive Guide to ARM Cortex-M0 and Cortex-M0+ Processors, 2nd edn. Newnes, Newton (2015)
28. Yiu, J.: ARM Cortex-M for beginners - an overview of the arm Cortex-M processor family and comparison. ARM White Paper, March 2017

An Open-Hardware Platform for MPSoC Thermal Modeling

Federico Terraneo(✉), Alberto Leva, and William Fornaciari

DEIB, Politecnico di Milano, Milan, Italy
{federico.terraneo,alberto.leva,william.fornaciari}@polimi.it

Abstract. Current integrated circuits exhibit an impressive and increasing power density. In this *scenario*, thermal modelling plays a key role in the design of next generation cooling and thermal management solutions. However, extending existing thermal models, or designing new ones to account for new cooling solutions, requires parameter identification as well as a validation phase to ensure correctness of the results. In this paper, we propose a flexible solution to the validation issue, in the form of a hardware platform based on a Thermal Test Chip (TTC). The proposed platform allows to test a heat dissipation solution under realistic conditions, including fast spatial and temporal power gradients as well as hot spots, while collecting a temperature map of the active silicon layer. The combined power/temperature map is the key input to validate a thermal model, in both the steady state and transient case. This paper presents the current development of the platform, and provides a first validation dataset for the case of a commercial heat sink.

Keywords: MPSoC · Thermal modeling · Dark silicon

1 Introduction

In the history of thermal management for multi/many-core CPUs/GPUs and MPSoCs, two "revolutions" can be observed. The first one dates back to the release of the Pentium, and consisted in the need for a heat sink and a fan. The second one, corresponding to the introduction of computational sprinting techniques like the Intel Turbo Boost, consisted in thermal management becoming vital for the operation itself of a chip.

Before the first revolution, CPUs resembled ordinary integrated circuits. After, their packaging had to be specifically designed to take thermal dissipation into account. Before the second revolution, with reasonable dissipation conditions, CPUs could operate at their maximum performance state indefinitely. After, they had become so power-dense to not allow such an operation anymore, at least with market-affordable dissipation systems, and thus to require a mechanism that permits maximum power only within a certain thermal budget.

As such, modern chips require dynamic thermal management, as not reacting promptly enough to highly variable and hardly predictable power bursts would

D. N. Pnevmatikatos et al. (Eds.): SAMOS 2019, LNCS 11733, pp. 184–196, 2019.
https://doi.org/10.1007/978-3-030-27562-4_13

cause unacceptable reliability issues, or even thermal runaway. And looking at the future, high-performance CPUs and MPSoCs – for consumer, datacenter, supercomputing and exascale applications – strongly need improvements in cooling solutions and thermal management, as such improvements could immediately entail increases in performance and profitability.

The importance of thermal modeling in the development of next generation solutions to the thermal wall issue cannot be overstated. Fast, accurate, steady state and transient thermal models are needed to cost-effectively explore the design space of thermal management [9] and cooling solutions. Doing so however requires thermal models with a significant degree of flexibility, such as the ability to quickly and accurately introduce models for evaporative cooling, peltier cooling, liquid cooling, as well as a library of off-the-shelf heat sinks. All those models would also need to accurately support transient simulations for them to be useful in the development of dynamic thermal management policies.

Existing thermal models would need significant redesign to reach the level of flexibility required for future integrated circuits thermal design space exploration. Improvement of existing thermal models as well as the design of new ones is however hindered by one major issue: the difficulty of validating them.

Thermal models are either obtained from first principle equations describing the thermal phenomenon or through empirical correlations when detailed modeling would be too compute intensive [4,12]. Thermal conduction in solids is an example where first principle modeling is employed, while natural and forced convection in fluids is an example where empirical correlations are commonplace. In both cases, a thermal model critically depends upon a number of parameters, such as material properties, geometric dimensions and empirical coefficients. A precise identification and validation of such parameters requires experiments. Since the main purpose of an MPSoC thermal model is the faithful reproduction of an integrated circuit temperature map under operating conditions, the main experiment requirement is to subject an integrated circuit not just to a known power, but also a known power spatial distribution across the silicon die, and to be able to measure a temperature map of the active silicon layer. Such requirements are incompatible with ordinary MPSoCs, due to the uncertainty in the power distributions as well as the general lack of temperature sensors, and instead call for custom hardware dedicated to thermal model validation.

In this paper we present a platform for MPSoC thermal modeling conceived to fulfill the needs just evidenced. This platform is based on a Thermal Test Chip (TTC), an integrated circuit containing an array of power dissipating elements and an array of temperature sensors. Our thermal platform is capable of applying a generic power dissipation pattern to the thermal test chip and measuring the corresponding temperature map, at a rate up to 1 kHz. This capability allows to measure the temperature map of an integrated circuit subject to reference power dissipation maps, and thus to design and validate thermal models.

A first dataset is provided with this paper, consisting in the result of thermal experiments performed on a commercial heat sink. Plans are to offer the community a variety of data sets, so as to allow validating models under heterogeneous operating conditions, possibly also off-design. Although the presented platform is complete, we are currently developing support tools to interface the platform to a PC and integrate it in MPSoC simulation tools to support hardware-in-the-loop simulations, as well as finalizing the documentation. When this is done, we plan to release the design files of the platform as open hardware together with the microcontrollers firmware and support tools, to allow researchers to build their own apparatus.

2 Related Work

Numerous thermal simulators specifically designed for CPUs/MPSoCs were proposed in the literature. Among the most successful ones are HotSpot [5] and 3D-ICE [13]. HotSpot supports the simulation of both 2D and 3D integrated circuits, can simulate thermal dissipation through a simple model for an heat sink, air flow and fan, as well as a secondary heat transfer path through the printed-circuit board. 3D-ICE supports 2D and 3D integrated circuits as well, but in addition it can simulate heat dissipation through liquid flow in microchannels etched in the silicon and passively cooled embedded MPSoCs [7]. Although both simulators have been validated, extending them to support other cooling solutions in order to explore different heat dissipation solutions, or just to keep up with the diversity of modern technologies, e.g. the ubiquitous heat pipes used in laptop computers, would require additional validation. Other simulators exist, such as Therminator [20] – targeted to smartphone thermal simulation but limited to steady state only – and an MPSoC simulation workflow [21] including a thermal model. Despite the numerous thermal simulators available, the range of heat dissipation solutions that can be represented by state-of-the-art thermal simulators is somewhat limited, as simulators are inflexible in nature, tightly coupled with a few cooling solutions, and not easy to extend. We argue that one of the main reasons that hindered the rise of more generic thermal simulators lies in the corresponding validation and parameter identification difficulty.

Validation and parameter identification of a thermal model can be performed in a number of ways. A first possibility would be to take an off-the-shelf processor, connect it to the desired thermal dissipation solution, run benchmarks that cause well-defined power dissipation patterns, and measure the chip temperature with its internal temperature sensors. This solution has unfortunately a large number of drawbacks that make it impractical. First, although the total power being fed to a chip can be measured, there is no easy way to measure the power *spatial distribution* across the silicon die. Moreover, the chip floorplan and the placement of temperature sensors is only known by the manufacturer, making parameter identification extremely difficult. Finally, although high accuracy on-chip temperature sensors can be made [3], those commonly found in off-the-shelf processors are low-resolution, affected by significant noise, and few in number.

Another validation solution could be to decap an off-the-shelf MPSoC and collect a thermal map using a thermal camera [1,11]. This solution allows to achieve high resolution thermal maps, but prevents the chip under test from being connected to an arbitrary heat dissipation solution, and the thermal maps obtained in this way can be significantly different than the ones in real-world operating conditions [6]. Moreover, this validating solution does not solve the issue of the lack of knowledge on the spatial distribution of power dissipation, as the obtained map is of temperature and not power.

Thermal test chips are integrated circuits containing a number of resistive heaters, to dissipate power in a controlled way, and a number of temperature sensors, to probe the active silicon temperature when connected to an arbitrary cooling solution. Such chips represent the perfect solution to thermal model parameter identification and validation. Thermal test chips are however a niche product, manufactured by a small number of companies [14,18], and although available for a number of years, to date they have not seen widespread use in academia for thermal model validation. One of the reasons for this fact is that thermal test chips are either sold as bare die requiring bonding, individual components, or with very basic breakout boards [19]. The time and effort required to design an entire thermal validation platform is thus a major stopgap.

This paper means to provide an answer to this important necessity; in detail, we present a general-purpose, flexible thermal platform as a "turnkey" solution to perform accurate and repeatable experiments on heat dissipation. We believe this to be a real step forward because to the best of our knowledge, no other such solution is to date available, not even as a commercial product.

3 The Platform

The proposed thermal platform is built around a TTV-1202 [17] thermal test chip. The chip has a silicon die area of 10.23×10.23 mm, mounted in a flip-chip configuration onto a BGA substrate. The chip is organised as a 4×4 array of individual cells, each capable of temperature sensing and power generation through a resistive element. The heating element in each cell is capable of dissipating up to 12 W, for a total chip power dissipation of 192 W. However, the actual maximum power dissipation depends upon the cooling solution provided, as the chip temperature has an absolute maximum rating of 150 °C.

An analysis of the requirements of thermal experiments has been performed, resulting for the platform in the following design requirements.

- It should be possible to produce arbitrary patterns of power dissipation across the TTC, thus requiring an array of voltage sources to drive the resistive elements inside the TTC. This solution allows to test realistic spatial power dissipation patterns of CPUs and MPSoCs, as well as hot spots.
- The aforementioned array of voltage sources need to be software controllable, and adequate support software is needed to perform a "playback" of a given power waveform to each heating element, thus allowing to test realistic temporal power dissipation patterns that are produced as a result of code execution in CPUs and MPSoCs.

- A readback of the power value being applied to the chip is desired to compensate for physically generated inaccuracies, including e.g. power loss in the wires connecting the driving subsystem to the TTC.
- A temperature sensing period as low as 1ms should be possible, to capture the fast thermal transients that occur in the active silicon layer [16].
- A temperature resolution of 0.1 °C is desired to see the detail of thermal transients, and to capture accurate steady state thermal maps.

The proposed thermal test platform fulfils all those requirements; its hardware design and firmware is detailed in the following.

3.1 Hardware Infrastructure

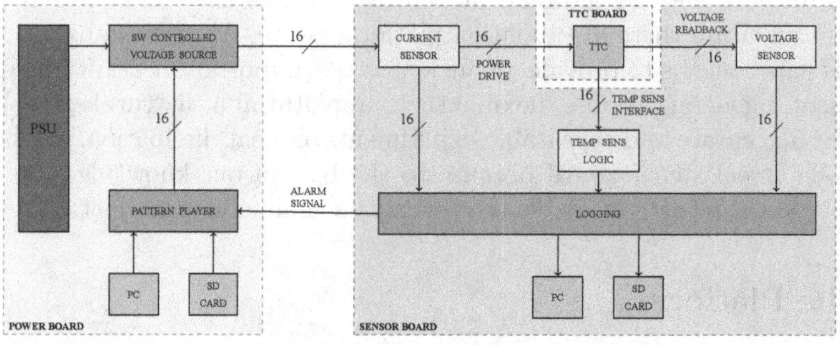

Fig. 1. Block diagram of the platform hardware.

Figure 1 shows a block diagram of the hardware infrastructure. The hardware architecture is composed of three distinct boards: a carrier for the TTC, a sensing board for measurements and a power board for the generation of power profiles.

The TTC carrier board holds the thermal test chip and provides mechanical support for the heat dissipation solutions to be tested. It was designed to not have any electrical component besides the TTC, to provide maximum flexibility in thermally connecting the TTC to different kind of heat dissipation solutions. A metal backing plate is fixed to the bottom of the board to provide the required mechanical rigidity in case heavy heat sinks are used. Moreover, this backing plate provides binding posts for standard LGA 1150 PC heat sinking solutions.

The sensor board holds the circuitry required for sensing the thermal map of the TTC and for the power map readback. The TTV1202 temperature sensing capability is based on silicon diodes, whose forward voltage linearly depends on the junction temperature. Diodes in various cells are connected in a multiplexed 4×4 matrix arrangement matching the cell layout. Each row and column signal is duplicated allowing a four wire measurement arrangement, eliminating measurement errors due to resistive losses. Four 4-way analog multiplexers are used to switch the current source and ADC inputs to any of the 16 diodes, and a software driver cycles through all sensors. The temperature resolution is 0.1 °C.

In order to be able to know exactly the power being fed to each element, a voltage and current sensor are added to each of the 16 lines coming from the power board. Current sensors are implemented using 20 m Ohm current sense resistors and high-side amplifiers. Voltage sensing is performed using a 4 wire measurement approach. Voltage resolution is 6 mV, current resolution 0.5 mA. Voltage, current and temperature are measured at up to 1 kHz.

An STM32 ARM Cortex M4 microcontroller completes this board, performing measurements, providing an overtemperature alarm to the power board and logging the measured data. Logging can either be performed to a PC through an USB port, or through an SD card resulting in standalone operation.

The sensor board voltage and current sensors have been calibrated against a 0.8% accuracy multimeter. Temperature measurements have been calibrated using a class A RTD temperature sensor as a reference. A soft calibration feature of the firmware allows easy calibration by editing calibration parameters in a configuration file on the SD card. The processing of the raw readings using the calibration parameters is performed on-line by the microcontroller.

The last board is the power board. This is composed of a backplane where eight power supply blades are connected. Each blade is a software controllable dual output power supply providing power to two TTC heating elements. The backplane contains a similar microcontroller than the one in the sensor board (Fig. 2).

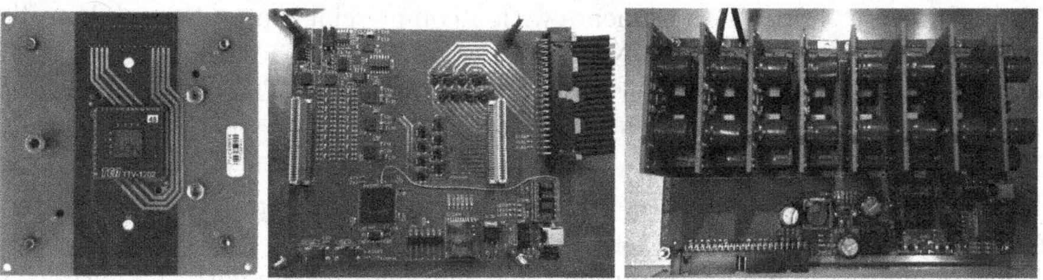

Fig. 2. Thermal test platform boards: carrier (left), sensor (middle), power (right).

3.2 Firmware Architecture

The firmware for the sensor and power board is structured as in Fig. 3. Both firmwares are written in C++ and use the Miosix [15] operating system.

The sensor board has drivers for the temperature, voltage and current sensors, which are operated by a sampling thread operating at 1 kHz. The sampling thread collects the raw measurements, computes the values using the calibration parameters made available by the configuration loader, and checks that the temperatures are still within the safe limit, signaling an alarm to the power board if

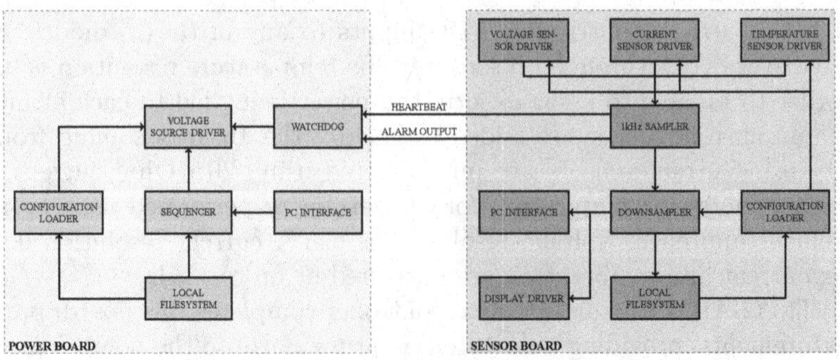

Fig. 3. Block diagram of the platform software.

required. A heartbeat signal is also provided to protect the system. The power board cuts off power to the TTC should the alarm be raised, or in the case of irregularities in the heartbeat signal. Sensor data is always sampled at 1 kHz, downsampled to the requested rate, and logged to the PC or local filesystem. The power board has a driver for the software controllable power supply and a sequencer thread that produces the desired power waveform either from the local filesystem or PC.

4 Experimental Evaluation

We performed a series of experiments with a commercial copper heat sink available at Digikey, of type HS483-ND, attached to the TTC, both under natural convection and forced convection using a P14752-ND fan. The collected dataset can be used to integrate a model of that heat sink in any thermal simulator. This dataset, consisting of 39 experiments, for a total of 78 individual figures showing power and temperature, is too large to fit in the paper, so only selected figures are reported. The full dataset is available[1] in the form of raw `csv` files that can be directly used to compare the experiment results with the output of a thermal simulator for validation and parameter identification.

Additionally, to show how the proposed thermal experimentation platform can be integrated with an architectural simulator, we performed an experiment with a power trace coming from the simulation of an MPSoC executing a subset of the MiBench benchmarks.

4.1 A First Dataset

To accurately model a heat sink both in transient and steady state, we designed a campaign composed of three groups of experiments using 13 different power maps each, for a total of 39 experiments. The 13 power maps are constructed using different patterns of activation of the heating elements, providing a 3 W power

[1] https://doi.org/10.5281/zenodo.2871796.

to active heating elements, and 0.2 W to inactive ones. The last four patterns are dedicated to hotspots, where only one heating element is given 7 W, leaving all the other at 0.2 W.

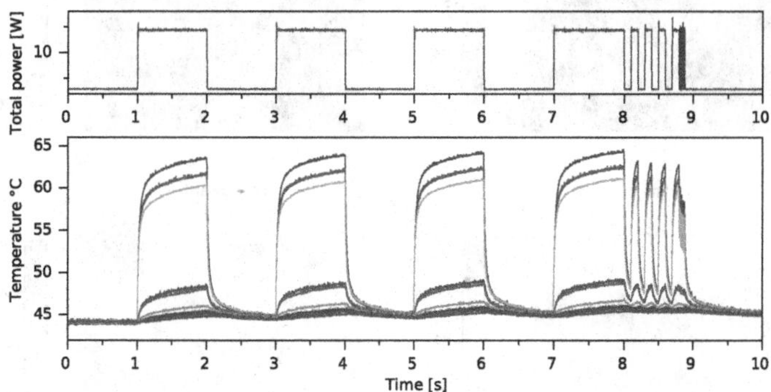

Fig. 4. Temperature profile produced by a step response of four heating elements with period 2 s, 200 ms 20 ms.

Of the three group of experiments, the first uses the 13 patterns to identify the fast thermal dynamics occurring near the silicon active layer. To this end, a sequence of step responses is used alternating between the given pattern and a blank pattern where all heating elements provide 0.2 W. The step responses is repeated with a 2 s, 200 ms and 20 ms period. Figure 4 shows one of the 13 patterns which consists in turning on the four heating elements in the northwest side of the chip. The top part shows the readback of the total power provided to the heating elements, while the bottom part shows the corresponding temperature of each of the 16 heating elements (each shown in a different color), sampled at 1 kHz. The heating element reaching the highest temperature is the one in the corner of the chip, as it can dissipate heat laterally only to two of its sides. The two elements with only one side at the corner of the chip reach the second highest temperature (both reach the same temperature and thus the traces overlap), followed by the fourth activated element. The other heating elements, even though they are kept at a constant power, exhibit a temperature increase due to thermal coupling. As can be seen, the proposed thermal platform allows to capture high resolution temperature transients of the TTC attached to the desired thermal dissipation solution, providing validation and identification information for transient thermal simulations.

The second and third group of experiments is instead dedicated to the identification of the slow thermal dynamics, caused by the heat sink heating up. One set of experiments was performed under natural convection the other with the fan active at full power. Each experiment group consists in applying each of the 13 patterns as a single 30 min long step response. Although the experiment dataset includes full thermal transients used for heat sink transient modelling, we will here present them in the form of a steady state temperature map with

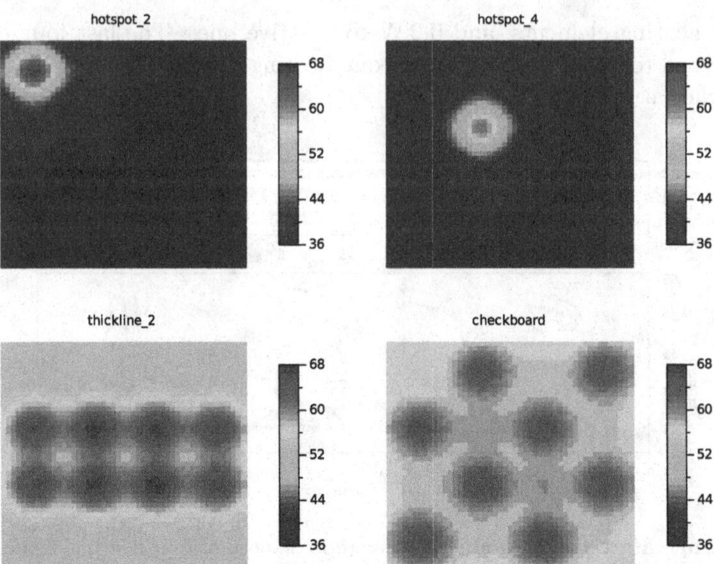

Fig. 5. Steady state temperature map interpolated from the TTC sensors, for four different conditions taken from the dataset.

the temperature at the end of the 30 min step response. Figure 5 shows four of the 13 experiments with the fan active. The top two experiments are hot spot experiments, where a single heating element is dissipating 7 W, while all the other 0.2 W. In the left case, where the hotspot is in the corner, a temperature of 68.3 °C is reached, and the maximum thermal gradient is 32.5 °C. In the right case, the hotspot can better conduct heat laterally, thus its temperature is lowered to 61.9 °C, and the maximum thermal gradient has been reduced too, to 24.9 °C. The bottom experiments instead explore the case where 8 heating elements are active at 3W, and the other at 0.2W. The left case shows a maximum temperature of 68.2 °C, while the right one shows that spreading heating elements reduces the maximum temperature to 66.6 °C and the gradient to 10.5 °C.

4.2 Simulation Flow Integration Example

The proposed thermal platform is not limited to producing step responses or steady-state studies, but is also very useful for showing the behaviour of a dissipation setup in the face of a thermal load coming from real software execution. To show this, the proposed platform, with the same heat sink as in the previous experiments, was connected to the simulation flow [21], which uses GEM5 [2], McPAT [10] and Orion [8] to simulate an MPSoC power consumption. The example configuration of the simulation flow was used, which simulates a 12 core architecture with four tiles of 3 cores interconnected by NoC routers. Each core is an Alpha out-of-order processor executing Mibench benchmarks. Table 1 reports

Table 1. Microarchitectural parameters.

Processor core	2 GHz, out-of-order Alpha core
Functinal Units	4 Int-ALU, 2 Int-Mult/Div, 2 FP-Mult/Div
L1 cache	64 kB 2-way set assoc. split I/D, 2 cycles latency
L2 cache	512 KB per bank, 8-way associative
Coherence Prot.	MESI
Router	3-stage wormhole switched with 64b link width, 4vcs per vnet
Topology	2D-mesh 4 tiles 2×2 (3 CPU per tile)
Technology	32 nm at 1.1 V

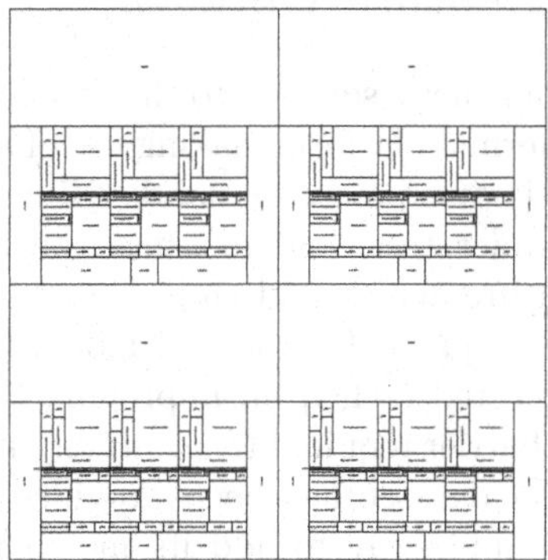

Fig. 6. Floorplan of the simulated MPSoC.

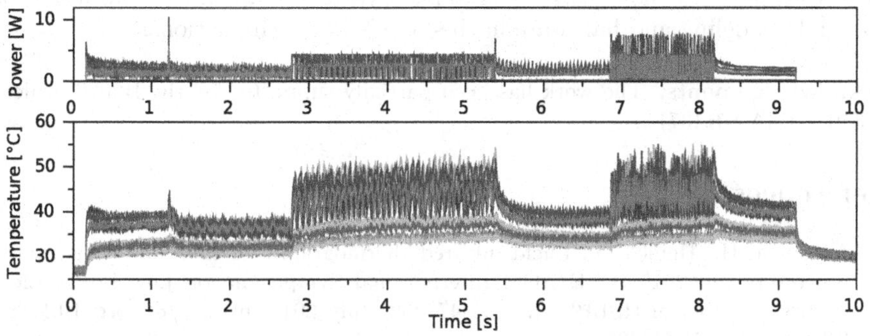

Fig. 7. Temperature profile produced by the TTC sensors when subject to the power computed by simulating the execution of seven mibench benchmarks.

the main architectural parameters. The simulation flow includes a floorplan to grid mapper that can produce power values for a uniform grid. We configured the grid as 4×4, thus matching the heating elements of the thermal test chip (Fig. 6).

The top part of Fig. 7 shows the power applied to each of the 16 heating elements (each shown using a different color), while the bottom part shows the temperature trace of each of the TTC heating elements (again each shown with a different color). The experiment was performed with the heat sink under natural convection while executing a sequence of Mibench benchmarks, namely basicmath, bitcount, crc, fft, sha1, stringsearch.

As can be seen, the proposed thermal platform can be integrated in an MPSoC simulation workflow instead of a simulated thermal model. Although the number of heating elements is fixed to 16, interpolation can be used to map an arbitrarily complex floorplan into the available elements.

5 Conclusions and Future Work

This paper has presented a generic solution to the problem of validating thermal models, in the form of a thermal platform making use of a thermal test chip. This solution allows to apply a known power spatial distribution to a TTC connected to the cooling solution under test, and measure the corresponding transient and steady state temperature across said chip. This platform allows to collect the critical measurements required for thermal model parameter identification and validation, and is expected to help in improving the flexibility of thermal simulator by lowering the barrier required to accurately model innovative cooling solution. A first validation dataset has been provided for a commercial heat sink, and work is already underway to add its model to the 3D-ICE thermal simulator, as well as to characterise other heat dissipation solutions. When the PC-side software support tools are complete, we plan to publish its design as Open Hardware, to allow researchers to build their own apparatus and use it for heat sink modeling and hardware-in-the-loop MPSoC simulations.

Acknowledgements. The work has been partially supported by the H2020 project RECIPE (GA 801137).

References

1. Amrouch, H., Henkel, J.: Lucid infrared thermography of thermally-constrained processors. In: 2015 IEEE/ACM International Symposium on Low Power Electronics and Design (ISLPED), pp. 347–352, July 2015. https://doi.org/10.1109/ISLPED.2015.7273538
2. Binkert, N., et al.: The gem5 simulator. SIGARCH Comput. Archit. News **39**(2), 1–7 (2011). https://doi.org/10.1145/2024716.2024718
3. Choi, W., et al.: A compact resistor-based CMOS temperature sensor with an inaccuracy of 0.12 $^{\circ}C$ (3σ) and a resolution FoM of $0.43pJK^2$ in 65-nm CMOS. IEEE J. Solid-State Circ. **53**, 3356–3367 (2018). https://doi.org/10.1109/JSSC.2018.2871622
4. Li, D., Tan, S.X., Tirumala, M.: Architecture-level thermal behavioral characterization for multi-core microprocessors. In: 2008 Asia and South Pacific Design Automation Conference, pp. 456–461, March 2008. https://doi.org/10.1109/ASPDAC.2008.4483994

5. Huang, W., Ghosh, S., Velusamy, S., Sankaranarayanan, K., Skadron, K., Stan, M.: HotSpot: a compact thermal modeling methodology for early-stage VLSI design. IEEE Trans. Very Large Scale Integr. (VLSI) Syst. **14**(5), 501–513 (2006). https://doi.org/10.1109/TVLSI.2006.876103
6. Huang, W., Skadron, K., Gurumurthi, S., Ribando, R.J., Stan, M.R.: Differentiating the roles of IR measurement and simulation for power and temperature-aware design. In: 2009 IEEE International Symposium on Performance Analysis of Systems and Software, pp. 1–10, April 2009. https://doi.org/10.1109/ISPASS.2009.4919633
7. Iranfar, A., et al.: Thermal characterization of next-generation workloads on heterogeneous MPSoCs, pp. 286–291, July 2017. https://doi.org/10.1109/SAMOS.2017.8344642
8. Kahng, A., Li, B., Peh, L.S., Samadi, K.: Orion 2.0: a fast and accurate NoC power and area model for early-stage design space exploration. In: Design, Automation Test in Europe Conference Exhibition, DATE 2009, pp. 423–428, April 2009. https://doi.org/10.1109/DATE.2009.5090700
9. Leva, A., Terraneo, F., Giacomello, I., Fornaciari, W.: Event-based power/performance-aware thermal management for high-density microprocessors. IEEE Trans. Control Syst. Technol. **26**(2), 535–550 (2018). https://doi.org/10.1109/TCST.2017.2675841
10. Li, S., Ahn, J.H., Strong, R.D., Brockman, J.B., Tullsen, D.M., Jouppi, N.P.: The McPAT framework for multicore and manycore architectures: simultaneously modeling power, area, and timing. ACM Trans. Archit. Code Optim. **10**(1), 5:1–5:29 (2013). https://doi.org/10.1145/2445572.2445577
11. Mesa-Martinez, F.J., Nayfach-Battilana, J., Renau, J.: Power model validation through thermal measurements. In: Proceedings of the 34th Annual International Symposium on Computer Architecture, ISCA 2007, pp. 302–311. ACM, New York (2007). https://doi.org/10.1145/1250662.1250700
12. Rai, D., Yang, H., Bacivarov, I., Thiele, L.: Power agnostic technique for efficient temperature estimation of multicore embedded systems. In: Proceedings of the 2012 International Conference on Compilers, Architectures and Synthesis for Embedded Systems, CASES 2012, pp. 61–70. ACM, New York (2012). https://doi.org/10.1145/2380403.2380421
13. Sridhar, A., Vincenzi, A., Atienza, D., Brunschwiler, T.: 3D-ICE: a compact thermal model for early-stage design of liquid-cooled ICs. IEEE Trans. Comput. **63**(10), 2576–2589 (2014). https://doi.org/10.1109/TC.2013.127
14. Tarter, T.: Tools for thermal analysis: thermal test chips. IEEE CPMT (2014)
15. Terraneo, F.: Miosix embedded OS. http://miosix.org
16. Terraneo, F., Leva, A., Fornaciari, W.: Event-based thermal control for high power density microprocessors. In: Fornaciari, W., Soudris, D. (eds.) Harnessing Performance Variability in Embedded and High-performance Many/Multi-core Platforms, pp. 107–127. Springer, Cham (2019). https://doi.org/10.1007/978-3-319-91962-1_5
17. Thermal Test Vehicles. http://thermengr.com/html/thermal_test_vehicles.html
18. Thermotest Chip. https://nanotest.eu/en/ttc
19. TTB-6101 Socketed Thermal Test Board. http://www.thermengr.com/html/ttb-6101.html

20. Xie, Q., Dousti, M.J., Pedram, M.: Therminator: a thermal simulator for smartphones producing accurate chip and skin temperature maps. In: 2014 IEEE/ACM International Symposium on Low Power Electronics and Design (ISLPED), pp. 117–122, August 2014. https://doi.org/10.1145/2627369.2627641
21. Zoni, D., Terraneo, F., Fornaciari, W.: A DVFS cycle accurate simulation framework with asynchronous NoC design for power-performance optimizations. J. Signal Process. Syst. **83**(3), 357–371 (2016). https://doi.org/10.1007/s11265-015-0989-1

Many-core Communication

PIMP My Many-Core: Pipeline-Integrated Message Passing

Jörg Mische(✉), Martin Frieb, Alexander Stegmeier, and Theo Ungerer

Institute of Computer Science, University of Augsburg, 86159 Augsburg, Germany
joerg.mische@gmail.com,
{martin.frieb,alexander.stegmeier,ungerer}@informatik.uni-augsburg.de

Abstract. To improve the scalability, several many-core architectures use message passing instead of shared memory accesses for communication. Unfortunately, Direct Memory Access (DMA) transfers in a shared address space are usually used to emulate message passing, which entails a lot of overhead and thwarts the advantages of message passing.

Recently proposed register-level message passing alternatives use special instructions to send the contents of a single register to another core. The reduced communication overhead and architectural simplicity lead to good many-core scalability. After investigating several other approaches in terms of hardware complexity and throughput overhead, we recommend a small instruction set extension to enable register-level message passing at minimal hardware costs and describe its integration into a classical five stage RISC-V pipeline.

1 Introduction

Message passing is a promising technique to achieve better scalability of multi- and many-cores [7]. Although there are several approaches to use message passing in many-core architectures [3,6,9,13], none of them endangered the dominance of shared memory multi-cores. We believe that message passing is not integrated with sufficient rigour into the microarchitecture for its advantages to come to light. In fact, there are many architectures where a Network on Chip (NoC) is used to connect the cores, but mostly it is only used to connect the processing cores with a shared memory controller [12]. If message passing is supported by hardware, memory accesses to a shared address space are usually used to transmit messages.

For example, one of the first message passing many-cores, the Intel Single-chip Cloud Computer (SCC) [9], provides so-called Message Passing Buffers (MPBs), small scratchpad memories tightly coupled to each core, that can be accessed by all other cores via the NoC. To send a message, the sender writes the message to the MPB of the receiver and notifies the receiver via a separate mechanism that a message has arrived. Subsequently, the receiver reads the message from its MPB. The distant read and write accesses to the MPB are translated to messages for the NoC, thus the original messages are actually transmitted via the NoC.

D. N. Pnevmatikatos et al. (Eds.): SAMOS 2019, LNCS 11733, pp. 199–211, 2019.
https://doi.org/10.1007/978-3-030-27562-4_14

However, the intermediate translation to memory accesses creates overhead and finally the MPBs form a kind of shared memory, which – depending on the implementation – may cause a bottleneck.

To reduce the vast overhead of shared buffer based message passing, customized instructions to send and receive messages at register level can be used. Such a technique is used by the Sunway SW26010 processor [17], building block of the Sunway TaihuLight, as of November 2018 the third fastest supercomputer in the world [1]. We adopt this idea but use different instructions for minimal hardware costs. Our contributions are:

- *Pipeline Integrated Message Passing (PIMP)*, a set of instructions to enable message passing at register level.
- The cheap integration of these instructions into a classical processor pipeline.
- An FPGA prototype and cycle-accurate simulator.
- A comparison with other message passing many-cores.

2 Architectural Support for Message Passing

2.1 Shared Memory Interface

Any multi-core with shared memory can support message passing when the sender writes the message to a shared memory location and the receiver reads it. However, two memory accesses require two expensive transmissions over the interconnect that connects the cores with the shared memory. Therefore, current many-cores with message passing support have tightly coupled scratchpad memories for every core that are designated to store messages. They are called Message Passing Buffers (MPBs) and since either the sender's (pull) or the receiver's (push) MPB is used, only one transmission via the interconnect is necessary.

Three factors complicate message passing via MPBs:

1. Every potential communication channel requires its distinct fraction of the MPB memory. If the messages are too long, they must be split into multiple shorter messages to not exceed the maximum size of the MPB.
2. MPB memory can only be reused, when the message was completely copied by the receiver.
3. The receiver must be notified, when a message has arrived.

Consequently, MPB memory must be managed and reading and writing the MPB must be synchronized by additional signaling: the sender must not write to the MPB before the receiver has read the previous message and the receiver must not read the MPB before the sender has written the message to it. Notifying the receiver when a message has arrived is a big problem, when only shared memory is available for inter-core communication. The receiver has to poll a memory location. Either separate flags [9] or a flag that is appended to the message [13] can be used to monitor if the message transmission is completed. Either way, the notification costs at least one additional transmission and a lot of unnecessary memory reads at the receiver.

To further speed up the message passing, Direct Memory Access (DMA) controllers can be used to perform the memory transfer in the background, while the core pipeline can continue with useful computations. The majority of current message passing many-cores use this technique (e.g. Kalray MPPA [4], T-CREST [13], CompSoC [6]).

Although shared-memory-based message-passing architectures are the most common choice, they suffer from limited MPB and message size, additional signaling and complicated notification. PIMP addresses these problems by providing an unlimited sequence of small messages, no additional signaling and a tightly integrated notification mechanism.

2.2 Register-Level Interface for Long Messages

Alternatively, the message passing interface can be directly integrated into the instruction set. The Raw microprocessor [14] uses a register mapped interface that is tailored to the underlying packet switching network protocol. Each core has 4 registers that are dedicated to the 4 independent NoCs of the Raw chip. To send a message, the length and destination of the message are written at once into the register (cf. the head flit of a network packet). By subsequent writes to the register the message payload (cf. body flits) is transfered to the network controller. The target core receives the message payload by reading the dedicated register. One drawback of this interface is that the receiver cannot determine the sender of a message. Therefore the communication channels must be clearly specified and distinct, or the message body must contain an additional sender id. Another drawback is the overhead for the message header. For longer messages it is not a problem, but short messages of only one word require two writes to the network interface.

The Tilera architecture [3] is the commercial successor of the Raw architecture and provides the same message passing interface, but there are multiple registers for receiving a message in order to receive up to 4 messages concurrently. Additionally, two of the Tilera NoCs are used for a cache-coherent shared memory protocol, hence shared memory based message passing is also possible.

The multi-word register-level interfaces are optimized to operate with packet based network routers, but for short messages the overhead in terms of network bandwidth and communication latency is high. With PIMP long messages are simply split in a sequence of short messages.

2.3 Register-Level Interface for Short Messages

Table 1 gives an overview of the various word-size message passing interfaces. In the picoArray architecture [5] the channels between cores are defined at compile time, but there are blocking instructions to send a single data word (32 bits) over a specified channel (*put*) and to receive a single data word from a specified channel (*get*).

A very similar instruction based interface is used by the Sunway SW26010 processor [17], but its topology is a real NoC where any node can communicate

Table 1. Comparison of single word register-level message passing interfaces. Italic operands are registers that are written.

	picoArray	Sunway	RC/MC	PIMP
Blocking send	`put` Word, Port `send` Node, Word	`send` Word, Node	`send` Word, Node	`bns self`
Blocking receive	`get` Port, *Word*	`receive` *Word*, *Node*	`any` *Node* `recv` *Word*, Node	`bnr self` `src` *Node* `recv` *Word*

Non-blocking send	n/a	n/a	`cong t0`
			`bnez t0, NotReady`
			`send` Node, Word
				`bns NotReady`
				`send` Node, Word

Non-blocking receive	n/a	`receive_test` *Word*, *Node* `beq` Word, `NotReady`	`any` *Node* `bltz` Node, `NotReady` `recv` *Word*, Node	`bnr NotReady` `src` *Node* `recv` *Word*

with any other node. The *send* instruction has two operands: the destination and a data word. Consequently, only short messages of the size of one data word (64 bit) are transmitted. When a message has arrived, the *receive* instruction fetches it from the network controller and writes the data word to one register and the sender's node number to another register. Non-blocking receive is provided by the *receive_test* instruction that is similar to the *receive* instruction, but writes a special value into the sender node register instead of blocking the pipeline. Non-blocking sending is not possible. From a user perspective, the interface of Sunway is easy-to-use and cleaner than PIMP. But its implementation is costly (stall mechanism, double register write) and not as flexible (only blocking send) as PIMP.

Writing two registers by one instruction is uncommon in RISC architectures and requires additional data paths in the pipeline. Therefore the RC/MC architecture [11] uses a different *recv* instruction: the register of the sender operand is not written, but read. Thus, a data word from a specific sender is read. If there is none available yet, it blocks. To receive a message from an arbitrary node, the *any* instruction must be executed in advance, to determine the sender of the oldest received message.

The *send* instruction is in fact identical to the Sunway instruction and there are two further instructions for non-blocking communication, because *send*, *any* and *recv* are blocking. *probe* checks if a message from a specific node has arrived and *cong* tests if a message can be sent.

3 Pipeline Integrated Message Passing

The PIMP interface was created to allow very fast message passing of short messages. Non-blocking primitives allow overlapping of waiting times with computation and the hardware costs are very low.

3.1 Instruction Set Extension

The Message Passing Interface (MPI) [10] is the de-facto standard for writing message passing applications. Therefore, we studied implementations of several MPI library functions to find an optimal register-level message passing interface. In the MPI programming model, a function typically waits for messages from specific nodes in a specific order. The messages do not arrive in this order but have to be buffered until the sequential operation of a function requires it.

At first glance, the RC/MC specific receive instruction seems ideal for implementing MPI. The library programmer does not need to care about the message order, he just fetches messages from the network interface controller (NIC) in the order that is best for processing them. The NIC buffers messages that arrived too early and stalls the processor pipeline, if the required message has not yet arrived. However, in our experiments we observed, that the actual message sequence differs significantly from the expected sequence. Thus, many messages have to be buffered, in particular if the number of participating cores increases.

Unfortunately, the costs of the special receive buffer are high and grow quadratically. An alternative would be to have a separate FIFO for every sender, but for 64 or more cores the hardware costs are also much too high. Dynamically assigning a small number of FIFOs is also not possible, because if there are not enough FIFOs, what should be done with messages from further cores? Dropping them is not possible. Either way, there is no alternative to buffering the messages by software. Maybe, some hardware extensions could speed up the buffering, but they will not make a software solution redundant.

Since the specific receive feature of RC/MC cannot replace software-sided message buffering, we discarded this idea and instead use a receive mechanism similar to the Sunway *receive* instruction: a simple FIFO buffer and a *recv* instruction that dequeues sender and payload at once. But to avoid writing two registers with one instruction, the *recv* instruction only returns the payload data word. If the sender of a message should be determined, the *source* instruction must be executed before the *recv* instruction. The *source* instruction reads the sender's id from the front of the FIFO, but does not dequeue this element. Dequeuing is restricted to the *recv* instruction.

The *send* instruction is identical to implementations in Sunway and RC/MC: two operands, one for the target and one for the payload data. But in contrast to the other implementations, all three instructions (*source*, *recv* and *send*) are non-blocking. If the receive buffer is empty or the send buffer is full, the instruction's behavior is undefined. This simplifies the hardware, but to avoid the undefined behavior, the buffer state must be checked in advance.

Instead of transferring the buffer state to a register and then checking the value of the register, we provide branch instructions for checking the buffers. The *brs* (branch if ready to send) instruction branches, if the send buffer is not full and *bar* (branch if any message received) instruction branches, if the receive buffer is not empty. Integrating these instructions into the processor pipeline is very cheap, because the multiplexer in the branch unit is only extended by two signals from the send (buffer full) and the receive buffer (buffer empty) and the decode stage must set the select signal for the multiplexer accordingly.

The inverse branches *bns* (branch if not ready to send) and *bnr* (branch if nothing received) can be used to emulate blocking send and receive instructions. As shown in last column of Table 1, self-referential branches are put directly before the non-blocking instructions. In an energy-optimized implementation, the self-referential *bnr* branch can be detected and used to suspend the core as long as no message arrives.

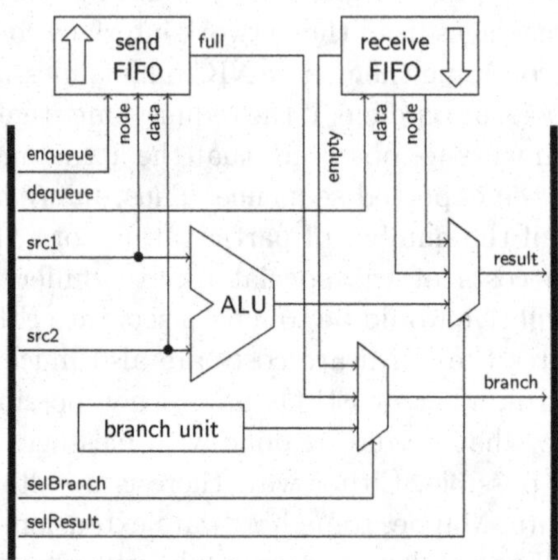

Fig. 1. Integration of the FIFOs into the execute stage of a RISC pipeline.

3.2 Pipeline Integration

Both the Sunway and the RC/MC processor have customized NoCs, optimized for fast single-word transfers. Nevertheless, any NoC that is able to send word-size messages and that guarantees that messages arrive in the same order as they were injected, can be used with PIMP. Preserving the message sequence is required to be able to send data packages that are longer than one word.

Two ordinary FIFOs connect the core pipeline with the NoC router. The send FIFO buffers messages from the pipeline to the router while the receive FIFO buffers messages from the router to the pipeline. Thus, NoC and core are decoupled and can be driven with different clock rates to save energy or cores can be completely power gated.

As shown in Fig. 1, the FIFOs are connected by four signals each. The *full* and *empty* signals are multiplexed with the output of the branch unit, while the *node* and *data* outputs of the receive FIFO are multiplexed with the ALU result. The *node* and *data* inputs of the send FIFO are hardwired to the operand outputs of the register set. If the multiplexers are really inserted after the ALU and after the branch unit, this might prolong the critical path and decrease the

Table 2. FPGA utilization of synthesized cores

	Pipeline			Send buffer			Receive buffer			Router		
	ALM	FF	BR	ALM	FF	BR	ALM	FF	BR	ALM	FF	BR
RC/MC32	2035	1551	4096	8	6	544	2810	2284	0	1029	1326	0
RC/MC	2041	1551	4096	8	6	544	1940	1193	0	1094	1333	0
PIMP	1984	1551	4096	8	6	544	8	8	1088	1120	1324	0
Without NI	1825	1549	4096	0	0	0	0	0	0	0	0	0

clock rate. However, the signals from the FIFOs are stable very early within the cycle and therefore the multiplexers can be integrated into the ALU and the branch unit without affecting the critical path.

All remaining modifications only affect the decode stage, which must be extended to demultiplex the additional instructions. For the branch instructions, additional select signals to the multiplexer after the branch unit are necessary. The send instruction asserts an exception if the *full* signal is high, otherwise it asserts the *enqueue* signal to write to the send FIFO. An exception is also raised when *empty* is high and a src or recv instruction is recognized. Otherwise src selects *node* and recv selects *data* in the multiplexer after the ALU. Only recv asserts the *dequeue* signal to remove the last entry in the receive FIFO.

4 Evaluation

The source code of the FPGA models, simulators and benchmarks is available at https://github.com/unia-sik/rcmc/.

4.1 FPGA Hardware Costs

We implemented a manycore with PIMP interface in VHDL and synthesized a FPGA prototype. The VHDL code is based on the freely available VHDL model of RC/MC [11]. The cores are similar to the RISC-V Rocket core [8]: a classical five stage in-order RISC pipeline that implements the RISC-V RV64I [15] instruction set (only integer arithmetics, no floating point support). Each core has its own private scratchpad memory. The lightweight PaterNoster NoC [11] connects the cores. It supports word-size messages, as well as longer messages consisting of multiple shorter messages that are delivered in order.

To evaluate the hardware costs, a PIMP prototype with 4×4 cores, 64 KiByte scratchpad memory, a send buffer with 8 entries and a receive buffer with 16 entries was built. It is compared to a RC/MC manycore with the same configuration, with a larger receive buffer (32 entries, named RC/MC32) and a single core without network interface. All prototypes were synthesized for an Altera Stratix IV E FPGA and the resource usage of a core was determined by averaging over all 16 cores.

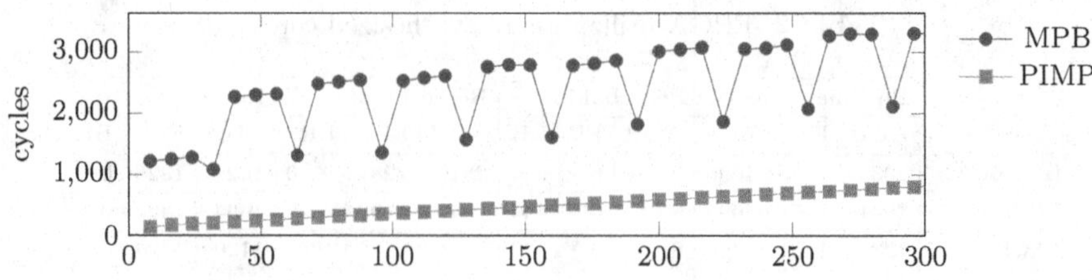

Fig. 2. Round trip time depending on the message length

Table 2 shows the logic utilization in terms of ALMs (the elementary logic blocks of Altera FPGAs), single bit flip-flops (FF) and on-chip block RAM bits (BR). The logic utilization of the pipeline is roughly 10% higher for RC/MC and PIMP, compared to the single core without network interface. The difference between RC/MC and PIMP is so low that typical fluctuations between different synthesis runs may be higher. But the receive buffer makes a big difference: due to the complex organisation in RC/MC, it cannot be mapped to block memory and therefore utilizes many ALMs and flip-flops. Even worse, the utilization grows rapidly when increasing the receive buffer size, which can be seen when RC/MC and RC/MC32 are compared. By contrast, the PIMP receive FIFO can be mapped to block memory and only utilizes a few ALMs to manage the head and tail of the FIFO buffer. Increasing its size only requires more block memory and a few additional ALMs due to the wider index to address the entries.

4.2 Experimental Setup

The FPGA prototype is very limited in the number of cores, available memory per core and lacks floating point support. Therefore we used the simulator of RC/MC [11] to compare the performance of PIMP. Since we are only interested in the message passing communication throughput, we did not model the cache hierarchy but instead assumed that all memory can be accessed within one cycle, just like in the FPGA prototype.

The modifications for PIMP compared to RC/MC are small and so are the differences in the execution time of applications. For blocking send and receive, PIMP requires one more instruction and thus one more cycle even when there is no stall. In the case of a stall, it always waits a multiple of three cycles due to the branch instruction, therefore it takes also one cycle more on average. Otherwise, when the non-blocking capabilities are used, PIMP requires only one branch and no comparison to detect a blocking situation. Altogether, these differences are so small that they vanish in the noise of the network communication. At the scale of the diagrams presented here, the PIMP and RC/MC results are identical, therefore the performance numbers for RC/MC are not presented separately.

To model MPB based message passing, we recreated an architecture similar to the Intel SCC [9], but with RISC-V ISA. Each RISC-V core has 8 KiB MPB scratchpad memory with a latency of one cycle. Remote MPBs are accessed via

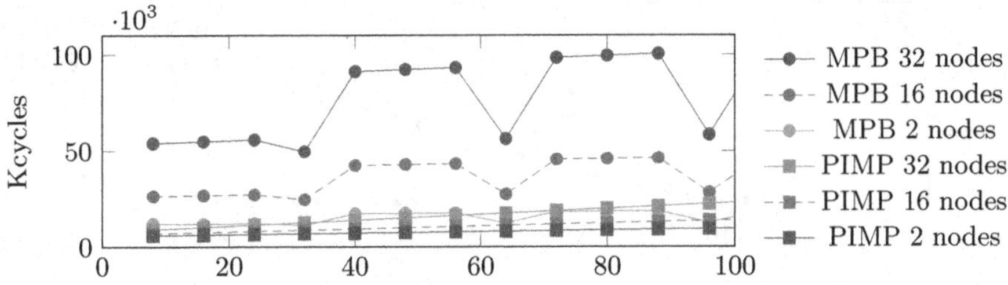

Fig. 3. Broadcast duration depending on message length

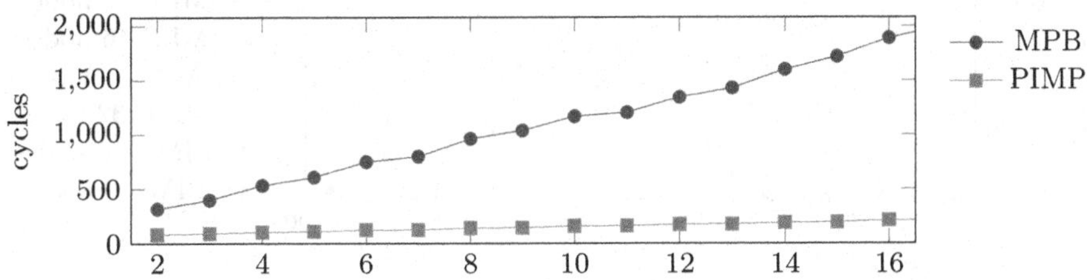

Fig. 4. Barrier duration depending on number of nodes

the NoC at cache line granularity, hence a response message has a payload of 32 bytes or two 128 bit flits. To facilitate comparison, the same PaterNoster NoC as in RC/MC and PIMP is used.

We choose the SCC architecture for comparision, because its architecture is very similar to many recently presented message passing many-cores [4,6,13] and its architectural details are well documented. Furthermore, only small adaptions were necessary to use RCCE [16], the lightweight message passing library of SCC. It is a subset of MPI optimized for on-chip networks. By using a third-party library, we avoid biased results due to less effort on optimizing the competing architecture.

4.3 Microbenchmarks

In the first experiment we measured the time it takes to send a message to another node and back to the original sender. Figure 2 shows this round trip time depending on the length of the message. Although transportation times in the NoC are subtracted, the MPB messages need much more time for a round trip. If the message size is 8 bytes or shorter, PIMP requires 139 cycles, while MPB needs 1218 cycles. Each additional 64-bit word takes 18 cycles for PIMP and 33 cycles with MPB. Furthermore, it takes an extra 1000 cycles with MPB if the message is not a multiple of the cache line size (32 bytes).

The same effect can also be seen when a message is broadcast to all nodes (Fig. 3). Additionally, the number of participating threads has an important influence. The duration of a broadcast operation is directly proportional to the

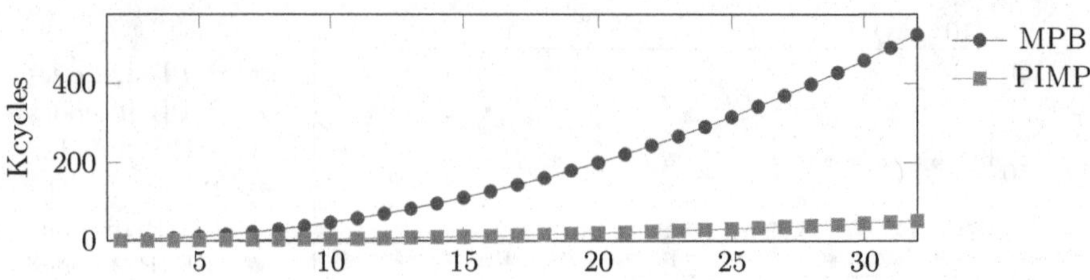

Fig. 5. Alltoall duration dependig on number of nodes

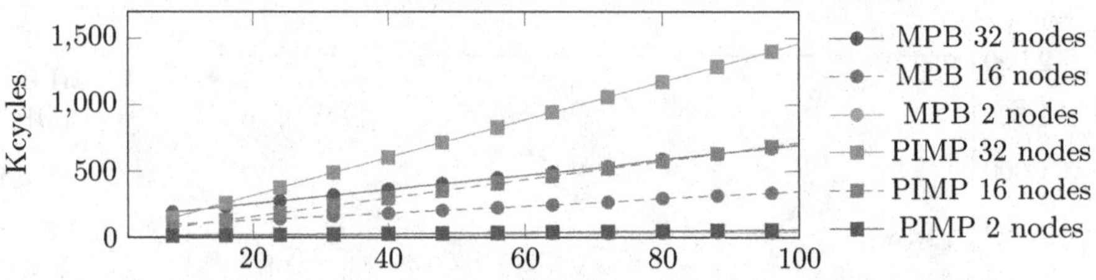

Fig. 6. Reduce duration depending on message length

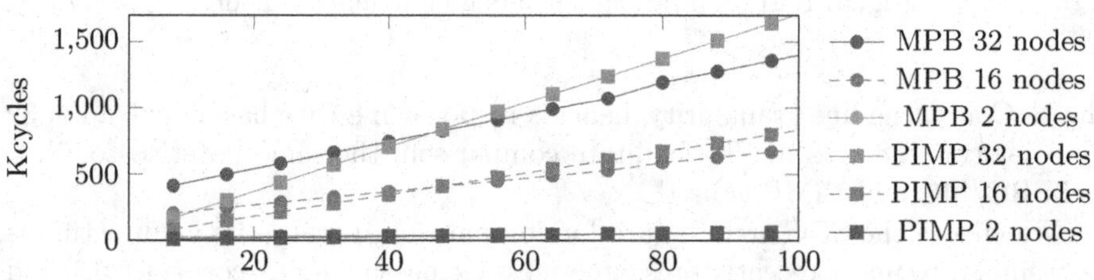

Fig. 7. Allreduce depending on message length

number of nodes, if the number of nodes is doubled, the time for a broadcast doubles, too. As presented in Fig. 4, the time a barrier takes, grows linearly with the number of participating threads. However, the initial overhead with two threads is much higher for MPB (317 against 83 cycles) and it grows faster (120 against 9 cycles/thread).

The alltoall collective communication pattern is not supported by RCCE, but we implemented it using basic send and receive functions of RCCE. Its communication grows quadratically with the number of threads and so does the execution time of the function (Fig. 5). Again, the overhead of MPB is much higher and grows faster than for PIMP.

But PIMP is not always better. Although the reduce operation for single words is faster with PIMP, if more than one word per node is involved, the MPB interface is faster (Fig. 6). The reason for that is the asymmetry of the communication: all nodes send data to one single node that computes the reduce operation. Since the MPB is 40 times larger than the PIMP receive buffer, the

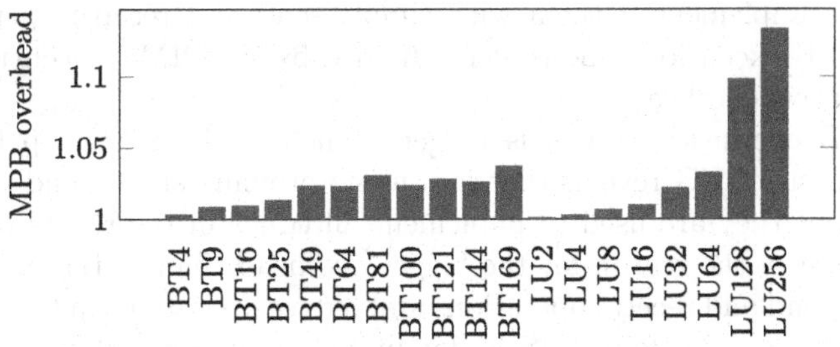

Fig. 8. NPB benchmarks ported for RCCE

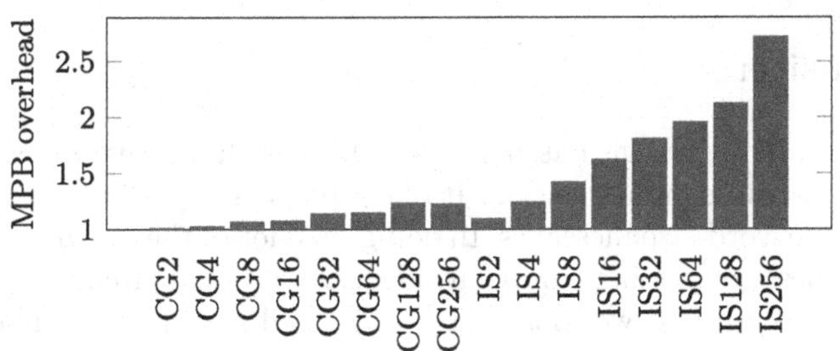

Fig. 9. Recently ported NPB benchmarks

overlapping of communication and computation is better and results in significantly faster execution with MPBs.

The allreduce operation is a reduce operation followed by a broadcast of the result. It is implemented in this way in the RCCE library and hence the good performance of the reduce is diminished by the bad performance of the broadcast (Fig. 7). Nevertheless, MPB is still faster for messages larger than 64 bytes, but the difference is small.

4.4 Real Workloads

The performance of MPB and PIMP was also compared by benchmarks that allow a more realistic evaluation of the performance gain of PIMP. We used some benchmarks from the NAS parallel benchmark suite [2] and problem size A. The benchmarks BT and LU are part of the RCCE source code distribution and we could directly use these ports to RCCE. Figure 8 shows the execution time of MPB relatively to the execution time with PIMP. The number appended to the benchmark name idicates the number of threads. The overhead of MPB grows with growing thread number, but on average it is about 2%.

We ported two additional benchmarks from the NAS parallel benchmark suite. CG had to be translated from FORTRAN to C and then the MPI primitives had to be replaced by their RCCE counterparts. IS is already available in C, but it uses the alltoall MPI primitives, which are not available in RCCE.

Therefore we implemented them with simple send and receive operations. In Fig. 9 the MPB execution time is again divided by the PIMP execution time to show the relative overhead.

The MPB overhead for CG is bigger than for BT or LU, up to 23%. A detailed analysis of CG reveals that it consists of many single send and receive operations, but they are used to implement allreduce in the recursive doubling variation. That is the reason for the bigger overhead than in BT or LU, where only explicit send and receive operations and reduce operations in the centralized implementation can be found. IS is dominated by its alltoall communication, which results in a large MPB overhead that grows with the number of threads at the same time.

5 Conclusion

Pipeline Integrated Message Passing (PIMP) is an alternative message passing interface for on-chip communication. It offers particular instructions to directly send and receive word-size messages. In doing so, a lot of the overhead of memory access based message passing can be avoided. Under most circumstances, PIMP is faster, especially if real workloads are considered and if the number of nodes is high.

Due to its low hardware costs PIMP is suitable for embedded systems, but beyond that its scalability may also be useful in massively parallel computing. An impressive indication for such a high performance application is the very similar architecture inside the Sunway TaihuLight, one of the fastest supercomputer available.

References

1. The TOP500 List November 2018. https://www.top500.org/lists/2018/11/
2. Bailey, D.H., et al.: The NAS parallel benchmarks. Int. J. High Perform. Comput. Appl. **5**(3), 63–73 (1991)
3. Bell, S., et al.: Tile64-processor: a 64-core SoC with mesh interconnect. In: International Solid-State Circuits Conference (ISSC) (2008)
4. de Dinechin, B.D., et al.: A distributed run-time environment for the kalray MPPA-256 integrated manycore. Proc. Comput. Sci. **18**, 1654–1663 (2013)
5. Duller, A., et al.: Picoarray technology: the tool's story. In: DATE (2005)
6. Goossens, K., et al.: Virtual execution platforms for mixed-time-criticality systems: the CompSOC architecture. ACM SIGBED Rev. **10**(3), 23–34 (2013)
7. Kumar, R., et al.: The case for message passing on many-core chips. Technical report UILU-ENG-10-2203 (CRHC 10–01), University of Illinois at Urbana Champaign (2010)
8. Lee, Y., et al.: A 45nm 1.3 GHz 16.7 double-precision GFLOPS/W RISC-V processor with vector accelerators. In: ESSCIRC, pp. 199–202 (2014)
9. Mattson, T.G., et al.: The 48-core SCC processor: the programmer's view. In: High Performance Computing, Networking, Storage and Analysis (SC) (2010)
10. Message Passing Interface Forum: University of Tennessee: Message-Passing Interface Standard, Version 3.0 (Sep 2012)

11. Mische, J., Frieb, M., Stegmeier, A., Ungerer, T.: Reduced complexity many-core: timing predictability due to message-passing. In: Knoop, J., Karl, W., Schulz, M., Inoue, K., Pionteck, T. (eds.) ARCS 2017. LNCS, vol. 10172, pp. 139–151. Springer, Cham (2017). https://doi.org/10.1007/978-3-319-54999-6_11
12. Sodani, A., et al.: Knights landing: second-generation intel xeon phi product. IEEE Micro **36**(2), 34–46 (2016)
13. Sørensen, R.B., et al.: Message passing on a time-predictable multicore processor. In: Symposium on Real-time Distributed Computing, pp. 51–59 (2015)
14. Taylor, M.B., et al.: The raw microprocessor: a computational fabric for software circuits and general-purpose programs. IEEE Micro **22**(2), 25–35 (2002)
15. Waterman, A., Asanović, K.: The RISC-V instruction set manual, volume I: user-level ISA, document version 2.2. RISC-V Foundation, May 2017
16. der Wijngaart, V., et al.: Light-weight communications on Intel's single-chip cloud computer processor. ACM SIGOPS Oper. Syst. Rev. **45**(1), 73–83 (2011)
17. Zheng, F., et al.: Cooperative computing techniques for a deeply fused and heterogeneous many-core processor architecture. J. Comput. Sci. Technol. **30**(1), 145–162 (2015)

SHARQ: Software-Defined Hardware-Managed Queues for Tile-Based Manycore Architectures

Sven Rheindt[1(✉)], Sebastian Maier[2], Florian Schmaus[2], Thomas Wild[1], Wolfgang Schröder-Preikschat[2], and Andreas Herkersdorf[1]

[1] Technical University of Munich (TUM), Arcisstr. 21, 80333 Munich, Germany
sven.rheindt@tum.de

[2] Friedrich-Alexander-Universität Erlangen-Nürnberg (FAU), Schlossplatz 4, 91054 Erlangen, Germany

Abstract. The recent trend towards tile-based manycore architectures has helped to tackle the memory wall by physically distributing memories and processing nodes. Distributed operating systems and applications allow to exploit the increased scalability of such architectures, but still face the data-to-task locality challenge. As inter-tile communication, thread synchronization and data transport often impose significant software overhead on such architectures, many applications would benefit from a more efficient and powerful communication primitive with minimal software involvement.

We propose software-defined hardware-managed queues for distributed computing architectures that enable efficient inter-tile communication by leveraging application-specific queues with arbitrarily sized elements. To ensure (remote) processing of queued elements, SHARQ introduces the concept of an optional handler task, which is scheduled by hardware on demand. Queue and memory management, intra- and inter-tile data transfer, and handler task invocation are entirely handled by hardware. Only the dynamic queue creation at runtime is performed in software.

As an example use-case, we integrated SHARQ into the MPI library. The evaluation with the MPI-based NAS benchmarks shows a reduction in execution time by up to 48% for the communication intense IS kernel in a 4×4 tile design on an FPGA platform with a total of 80 LEON3 cores.

Keywords: Distributed architectures · Hardware accelerator · Inter-tile communication · Hardware/software codesign · MPMC queue · NoC

1 Introduction

Performance scaling of computer architectures is highly dependent on memory access latency and bandwidth. As the memory wall hindered the further scaling of classical multi-core architectures, tile-based manycore architectures have become popular [1]. Although the physically distributed memories and processing nodes reduce access hot-spots and latencies, this approach did not yet solve

D. N. Pnevmatikatos et al. (Eds.): SAMOS 2019, LNCS 11733, pp. 212–225, 2019.
https://doi.org/10.1007/978-3-030-27562-4_15

the data-to-task locality issue. Distributed and parallel operating systems [2] and applications help to exploit the increased scalability of these architectures but are in need of efficient mechanisms for inter-tile communication (ITC), thread synchronization and data transport. Common communication patterns of parallel applications, libraries, and operating systems require the transfer of arbitrary data to remote tiles and its subsequent processing. Use-cases vary from inter-tile task scheduling, message passing in, e.g. the MPI library, or job and data distribution of pipelined applications. In the sketched scenarios, a queue is beneficial and hence often used as data structure to facilitate such communication and therefore requires an efficient implementation to avoid performance bottlenecks.

A significant amount of research has been conducted in the area of improving software queue implementations for shared memory architectures, like the scalable multi-producer multi-consumer MS queue [3]. Research has also been conducted into hardware support and acceleration of both task scheduling [4–9] on various architectures, as well as general-purpose queues in the context of classic shared memory architectures [10,11]. However, little effort has yet been invested into concepts to implement efficient inter-tile queues within highly scalable NoC-based multi-tile systems [12,13]. Those architectures often lack the support for inter-tile cache coherence and remote atomic primitives, and therefore thread synchronization and other inter-tile communication has to be made explicitly. Together with non-uniform memory access properties, this imposes significant software overhead in the form of multiple and costly round-trips, consumed CPU time on both sides, as well as scheduling overhead. We therefore argue for a more efficient and powerful concept with minimal software involvement to conquer the challenges of distributed architectures.

In this work, we propose SHARQ, a software-defined, hardware-managed queue concept that enables efficient, low-latency inter-tile communication by facilitating multi-producer multi-consumer queues with arbitrary sized and structured application-specific queue elements. SHARQ builds upon the previously published idea of remote atomic primitives [13] and couples it with the goal of minimizing software overhead for queue and memory management, data transfers and task invocations. To ensure (remote) processing of queued elements, SHARQ introduces the concept of an optional handler task, which is scheduled by hardware on demand. The SHARQ hardware unit entirely handles the multi-producer multi-consumer (MPMC) first-in first-out (FIFO) queue management, initiates intra- and inter-tile DMA transfers, takes care of memory management and conditionally invokes handler tasks. The flexibility of dynamic queue creation with arbitrary element sizes and queue lengths at runtime is still given, since the software allocates and defines them.

2 Related Work

We classified the related work by using the following two dimensions: 1. whether queues are exclusively used for task scheduling and distribution or if a general purpose usage is possible, and 2. whether the architecture and concept is distributed (e.g. using a NoC and distributed memory) or not. Apart from these main categories, we further compared relevant features in Table 1.

A good amount of research work has been focused on the optimization of task scheduling and distribution. The queues used in those concepts *do not* allow a general purpose usage (e.g. with user-defined elements). This research has been conducted for both classic shared-memory architectures, as well as multi-tile architectures with distributed memory.

Table 1. Related work feature comparison

Related Work		General Purpose	Distr. Arch.	MPMC Queue	Data Trans.	Task Invoc.	Q in reg. Memory	HW Eval.
Petrovic	[4]	✗	✓	✓	✗	?	✗	✓
Sanchez	[5]	✗	✓	✓	✗	✗	✗	✓
IsoNet	[6]	✗	✓	✓	✗	✗	✗	✗
TCU	[7]	✗	✓	✓	✗	✓	✗	✓
Sharma	[8]	✗	✗	?	✓	✓	✗	✓
Carbon	[9]	✗	✗	✓	✗	✓	✗	✗
CAF	[10]	✓	✗	✓	✗	✗	✓	✗
HAQu	[11]	✓	✗	✗	✗	✗	✗	✗
RQ	[12]	✓	✓	✓	✓	✗	✓	✓
CaCAO	[13]	✓	✓	✓	✗	✗	✓	✓
SHARQ		✓	✓	✓	✓	✓	✓	✓

For the latter, Petrović et al. [4] accelerated algorithmically optimized critical section code by leveraging the message buffers of the Mellanox Tile-GX processor, that are a form of hardware-based queue implementation. However, the number of queues and maximum queue size are intrinsically limited due to the hardware limitation in number and size of the message buffers. Sanchez et al. [5] presented a per-core hardware message passing unit that accelerates distribution of task descriptors in large-scale mesh-based multi-core systems. The queue length is hardware limited and the element size restricted to task descriptors. With IsoNet [6], Lee et al. proposed a dedicated mesh network of scheduling and load-balancing nodes that dynamically re-distribute jobs system-wide in case of imbalance. This mechanism uses distributed queues, but is implemented as a separate and fully combinatorial network, hindering performant scalability to big architectures. Pujari et al. [7] presented a thread control unit (TCU). This FIFO queue based hardware scheduler maps lightweight tasks to the job queues of cores of a NoC-based many-core architecture. The TCU operates on fixed size 2 pointer objects and implements its per core queue memory in dedicated hardware resources. Sharma et al. [8] built a hardware-managed work queue and scheduler with program and data prefetch, that also considers the management and distribution of the data that a task requires. This concept targets a classic shared memory architecture as compared to a distributed processing and memory architecture. The high amount of dedicated memory that is added to every processing core further adds significant hardware state to the design. Kumar et al. [9] presented Carbon, a hardware task scheduler using task queues in order to accelerate highly parallel fine-grained task scheduling in manycore systems. Carbon is tailored to the scheduling of fine-grained tasks and the authors admitted that the centralized concept is a drawback. As all these approaches specifically target task scheduling and restrict their queue element size to pointers or task descriptors, no general purpose usage of those queues is possible. Required thread data would have to be transferred across the memory hierarchy.

Besides the focus on task scheduling, a few proposals are actually tackling general-purpose queues. Wang et al. proposed a dedicated hardware unit CAF [10] connected to the chip interconnect that manages a variable number of variably sized queues in general-purpose memory. However, the authors admit that CAF is implemented as a centralized component. Lee et al. [11] added hardware accelerated queue operations in shared memory to individual processing cores in a multi-core architecture. However, they acknowledged, that their HAQu concept only provides advantages for single-producer single-consumer queues, which represent a rather small share of the actual usage of queues and therefore limits the applicability of their idea. HAQu and CAF are as well only concerned with handling queue descriptors and element pointers, while the payload needs to be transferred via the normal memory hierarchy. Brewer et al. [12] built a remote queuing mechanism (RQ) for the Cray T3D platform using DMA transfers and fetch-and-increment operations. Due to the additional software overhead introduced by this separation of the payload transfer from the atomic queue access, this approach is similar to a mixture of our software emulated variant and CaCAO [13] and therefore different from SHARQ. In CaCAO, we previously proposed hardware accelerated inter-tile queue operations for software-managed queues. However, CaCAO was only capable of inserting element pointer into a bounded buffer residing in memory. The actual data had to be transferred via the distributed memory hierarchy, the memory management had to be done in software and no receiver notification was available. Further, no operating system integration was available and only micro benchmarks were used.

The main intention of those papers is to optimize the atomic pointer enqueue and dequeue operations through the introduction of hardware controllers. The transfer of the actual data associated with the managed pointers has mostly been neglected or has not been inherently coupled to the queue management. After all, hardware units that were optimized for a shared-memory architecture are mostly not applicable to a distributed computing architecture due to the potentially missing data-to-task locality and the thereby arising need for costly round-trips and data transfers, as we will show in Sect. 4.

3 SHARQ

Since inter-tile communication (ITC) is crucial for the efficient operation of distributed architectures, these platforms are mostly equipped with the following mechanisms for ITC: 1. *remote procedure calls* (RPCs), allowing procedure execution on remote tiles, 2. *remote task invocation*, allowing task scheduling on remote tiles, and 3. *hardware-based, direct memory access (DMA) data-transfers*. Although the existing ITC mechanisms are already powerful, an efficient implementation of a user-defined multi-producer multi-consumer queue data structure is a precious extension to this portfolio. But even with the advanced task invocation capability of existing DMA mechanisms [14], the

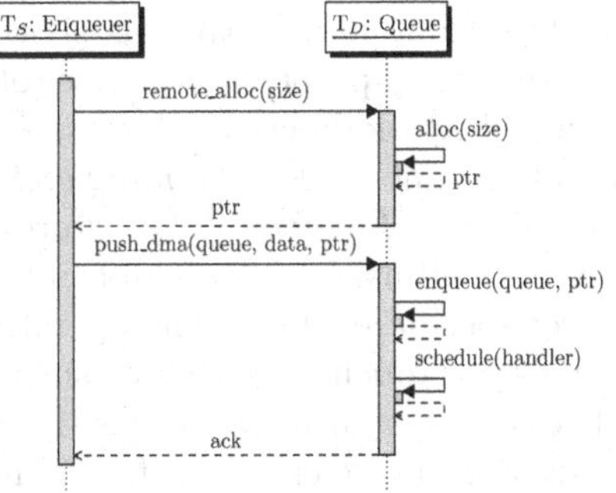

Fig. 1. Sequence diagram illustrating a remote enqueue operation in software

sequence of operations shown in Fig. 1 is necessary to perform a remote enqueue: 1. destination buffer allocation, consuming CPU time on the source (T_S) and destination tile (T_D), 2. DMA data transfer with subsequent handler task invocation on T_D, 3. atomic enqueue operation by a core on T_D, 4. scheduling of a handler task to process the enqueued element before, 5. signaling back the acknowledgement. This – for the time being – software-centric mechanism still has several drawbacks: multiple round trips, the consumption of CPU time on both sides, invocation of several control flows and interaction with the scheduling and dispatching subsystem are required.

SHARQ. Therefore, we propose *software-defined hardware-managed queues* that enable efficient, low-latency inter-tile communication by facilitating multi-producer multi-consumer queues with arbitrary sized and structured application-specific queue elements. SHARQ queues are *software-defined* to achieve flexibility and *hardware-managed* to enable efficiency and performance. Whether a specific operation is performed in hardware or software is influenced by its frequency, complexity and performance requirements. Therefore, rather complex and rare operations like the creation of SHARQ queues is handled in software, while the following performance-critical operations are handled by the SHARQ hardware unit: 1. MPMC FIFO queue management 2. memory management 3. data transfer 4. handler task invocation.

Queue Creation. SHARQ queues reside in memory and no specific hardware resources are consumed to store queue elements or even queue metadata. Arbitrary queues (element size and queue length) can be dynamically allocated and defined in any of the existing (physically distributed) memories. We call the resulting object a *queue descriptor*, which contains all information describing the particular queue instance and does not have to be registered with the SHARQ hardware unit, since its sole existence within the system's memory is sufficient. The user then only holds a queue handle, i.e. a pointer to the queue descriptor, which uniquely identifies each queue in the system. The queue descriptor consists of four major parts as shown in Fig. 3: 1. *Queue Header:* stores the software-defined properties (number of queue elements, maximum queue element size, handler task descriptor & its maximum concurrency) and holds the internal state of the queue; 2. *Allocator Stack:* stores pointers to unused, i.e., free payload buffers; 3. *Bounded Buffer:* stores the actual FIFO queue element order, i.e. pointers to all used payload buffers; 4. *Payload Buffers:* the actual buffers used for user-specific payload. The operating system allocates the required memory for the whole queue descriptor using the standard malloc() API and initializes it. The cost of creating a queue is therefore minimal and allows for quick, flexible and scalable queue creation at runtime.

Software API. Special care is taken to avoid introducing software overhead for queue operations and therefore only a thin API wrapper is used that involves triggering the hardware managed operation (writing specific hardware registers) and reading back a result code. Concurrent access to these registers is handled in hardware so that no locking within the driver is required and operations from different cores can be triggered in parallel. However, any software access to

```
shq_t shqCreate(size_t maxEntries, size_t maxSize);
int shqDestroy(shq_t q);

int shqRegisterHandler(shq_t q, task_t *handlerTask,
 ↪    size_t maxHandlers);

int shqEnqueueSync(shq_t q, void *elem, size_t size);
int shqEnqueueAsync(shq_t q, void *elem, size_t size,
 ↪    task_t *completionTask);

int shqDequeue(shq_t q, void *buffer, size_t size);
int shqDequeueFromHandler(shq_t q, void *buffer,
 ↪    size_t size);
```

Fig. 2. API of SHARQ

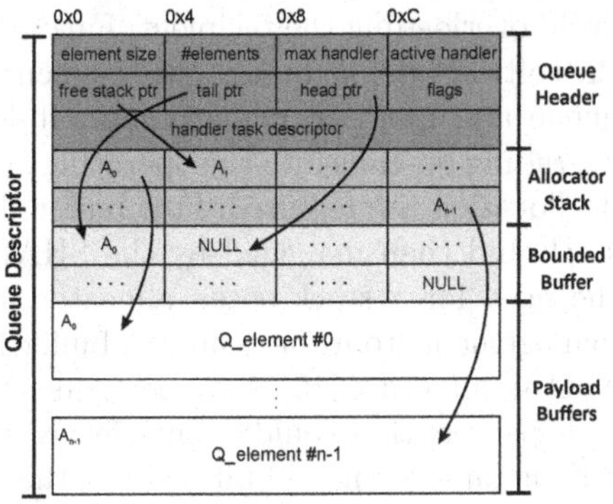

Fig. 3. Queue descriptor

the queue (destroying a queue, modifying properties like the handler tasks and its maximum concurrency or reading the performance counters of the queue) has to be synchronized with the hardware. Special locking/unlocking operations provided by the hardware unit allow temporarily blocking the access to the queue for hardware operations, e.g. locking the enqueue port enables a controlled emptying of the queue before destroying it. Subsequent hardware operations return with a status that indicates the locked queue.

Figure 2 shows the API that is exposed to users of SHARQ queues. All API functions (except `shqCreate()`) require a queue handle to uniquely identify a queue in the system. The current implementation offers several operations: Create/destroy a queue, local enqueue, local dequeue, local dequeue from handler task, register handler task, as well as synchronous and asynchronous remote enqueue.

Handler Task. To ensure processing of queued elements, SHARQ further introduces the concept of an optional handler task which is conditionally scheduled by the SHARQ unit on demand. In the queue initialization stage, this optional handler task and its maximum concurrency can be user-defined. The SHARQ unit invokes the handler task upon a successful enqueue operation if the number of active handler tasks is lower than the specified concurrency level. In order for the hardware to keep track of active handler tasks, a special dequeue operation is used to identify the operation as being performed by a handler task. The contract between hardware and software is that the handler task will always terminate as soon as a dequeue operation returns no element. Thus the hardware will decrease the count of running handler tasks by one after a special dequeue operation returned no element. In our prototype, the handler task invocation utilizes a hardware scheduler [7] that enables interrupt-less scheduling. We however want to highlight that a hardware scheduler is no conceptual requirement.

Queue and Memory Management. SHARQ queues are bounded MPMC FIFO queues, which are suitable as the fundamental abstraction layer for communication since these data structures have desirable properties: It is bounded in size and maintains the order of elements (FIFO ordering). Limiting the queue size creates usually desirable back-pressure in queue-based communication systems to avoid overloading the recipient. Furthermore, this bounded nature together with the software-defined maximum element size per queue enables efficient hardware queue and memory management. It has the advantage that no performance-degrading up-calls into the operating system for dynamic memory allocation and deallocation are required. Free buffer slots are initially provided in the allocator stack and then managed by the SHARQ unit during queue operations. While the need for a stack-based allocator may not be obvious, decoupling memory management from the bounded buffer becomes a requirement in a packet-based NoC architecture [15], since each queue operation can potentially consist of multiple packets that could be interleaved with operations from different tiles. When relying on a bounded buffer alone, the whole queue access – including the transmission of the element – would have to be performed without being interleaved by other queue operations. This decoupling allows the SHARQ unit to handle requests on a packet granularity and to always keep the queue in a consistent state since buffers only become visible after the transmission is completed. E.g. for an enqueue operation, first a free slot is popped from the allocator stack, then the payload is transferred into the appropriate buffer before it becomes visible in the bounded buffer for dequeuers.

SHARQ Operations and Data Transfer. Each tile is equipped with one SHARQ hardware unit – accessible from any CPU in the system – that handles queue operations for every queue residing in this tile's memory. Enqueue and dequeue operations could therefore potentially exist in a local and remote variant. We not only outsourced the atomic queue operations, the memory management and the handler task invocation into dedicated hardware but intrinsically coupled them with the existing DMA engine for data transfer. As CPUs only have to trigger operations, minimal software involvement is achieved.

Since a remote enqueue requires a transfer via the NoC and might take longer to complete, this operation is available in a synchronous and an asynchronous variant. On every enqueue operation the SHARQ unit performs the following steps that are depicted in Fig. 4: 1. receive enqueue operation from a local (1a) or remote (1b) core, 2. read the metadata from the queue header, 3. pop a pointer to a free buffer slot from the allocator stack, 4. copy/receive the element payload to that free buffer slot (4a for local enqueue; 4b for remote synchronous enqueue; asynchronous enqueue is not shown), 5. insert this pointer into the bounded buffer, 6. conditionally invoke a handler task by interacting with the hardware scheduler, 7. send a response code to the initiating core (7a for local; 7b for synchronous remote).

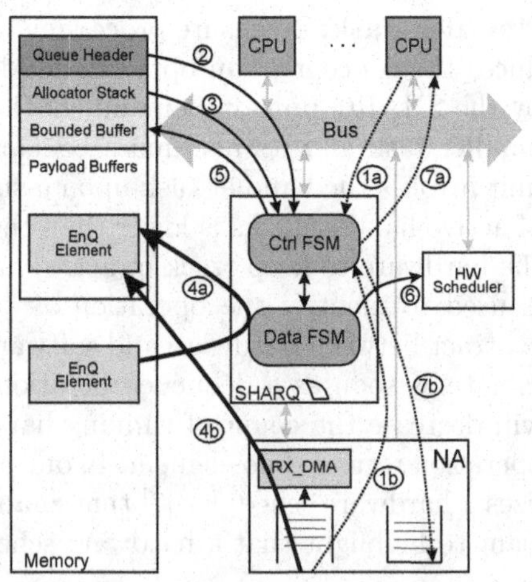

Fig. 4. Enqueue operation sequence

The synchronous remote enqueue directly transfers the element payload along with the request metadata via the remote DMA unit and returns synchronously after the operation including payload transfer is completed (or has failed). Upon reception, the metadata is forwarded to the SHARQ unit that performs steps 2–3. The retrieved pointer is the destination address of the element payload and hence where the remote DMA unit copies the payload to in step 4b. If the queue was full or another error occurred, the element payload has to be dropped upon reception. The advantage of synchronously sending the element payload might degrade performance in the case of an often full queue that leads to frequent payload dropping. For this reason and to enable latency hiding, we also developed an asynchronous remote enqueue where the actual element payload is transferred separately from the enqueue request which only includes a pointer to the element. The operation returns directly after step 2 instead of step 7 and the return code indicates whether the operation failed or will be successful. Upon reception of the request, the SHARQ tries to allocate a slot from the stack. If successful, first the response is sent to the initiator – allowing its resumption of processing – and then SHARQ sets up a concurrent pull-DMA that pulls the actual element payload into the queue. Otherwise, an error response is sent to the initiator without the need for dropping any payload. This variant also allows to specify a task that is scheduled on the initiating tile to signal the completion of the enqueue operation. It should be noted, that this task is different from the handler task described before and is usually used to free the send buffer.

On every dequeue operation, the SHARQ unit accordingly performs the following steps (different from Fig. 4): 1. receive dequeue operation from core, 2. read the metadata from the queue header, 3. get the next dequeue pointer from the bounded buffer, 4. transfer the element payload from that dequeue pointer to the user-specified target, 5. push this pointer onto the allocator stack, 6. send a response code to the initiating core. Local enqueue and dequeue both use a local-DMA engine that is not shown in Fig. 4 due to abstraction. The implementation of the remote dequeue operation remains part of future work.

Emulating SHARQ in Software. To compare SHARQ with a software-based approach, we also implemented a software variant of the queue, that offers the same features and API. The queue descriptor largely consists of the same internal data structures. All queue operations are implemented in software and access to the internal state of the queue is synchronized using mutual exclusion based on locks. Local enqueue and dequeue operations only involve manipulation of the queue state, copying the payload and – for the enqueue operation – conditionally scheduling a handler task. For payloads larger than 32 bytes the local copy operation uses DMAs instead of memcopy. Software-based remote enqueue operations are much more involved and behave similar to the sequence shown in Fig. 1, but instead of returning the destination address to the sender and performing a push DMA, a pull DMA is used to copy the payload into the queue. The powerful RPC mechanisms available on our platform and hardware support for pull DMAs with automatic task invocation on completion, enable us to avoid a second round trip during remote enqueue operations. Nevertheless, additional overhead is introduced by the task scheduler, descriptor locking and by consuming CPU time on both sides. In detail the following steps are performed during a remote enqueue operation: 1. send an RPC with the enqueue request from sender to receiver, 2. handle the request on receiver side and allocate a buffer slot from the allocator stack, 3. trigger a pull DMA on receiver side to copy the actual payload, 4. on completion make the item available by putting it in the bounded buffer, 5. signal the completion of the operation to the sender using remote task invocation, 6. schedule a handler task at receiver side (if required).

4 Evaluation

4.1 Experimental Setup and Hardware Evaluation

We evaluated SHARQ using an existing prototype and added a SHARQ unit to each of its tiles. The prototype implementation features a 4×4 tile design with 5 LEON3 cores per tile and 8 MB of tile-local memory (TLM). L1-DCache and L1-ICache both are 16 kByte large with 2 Sets and 32 Byte Cachelines. The L2-Cache is 64 kByte large with 4 Sets and 32 Byte Cachelines. Branch Prediction and Floating-Point Unit are enabled. Since one core per tile is dedicated to system tasks like interrupt and RPC handling, a total of 64 cores are available for application use. We run a distributed operating system [2] that is able to exploit the described hardware features. The implemented prototype system is synthesized on an FPGA system consisting of four Xilinx Virtex-7 2000T. The whole prototype is operated at a clock frequency of 50 MHz due to bottlenecks in other components.

The hardware resource utilization of each SHARQ unit is by design independent of the queue and element sizes or the number of queues allocated in the system. Further, only a minimal overhead is introduced when scaling the tile count in the system. To maintain concurrent queue operations from several source tiles, less than 80 Bits per additional tile are needed. In a 1×1 design, the synthesized SHARQ unit uses 4774 look-up-tables (LUTs) and 1245 flip-flops (FFs) of the Virtex-7 2000T, whereas in a 4×4 design each per-tile SHARQ unit utilizes 4771 LUTs and 1266 FFs. These are roughly 10% of the resources of the five LEON3 cores (without BRAM and DSPs) instantiated per tile. The resource usage is almost independent of the system size and only the required 80 Bits per additional tile accumulate. Calculations showed that even for a design with 512 tiles (2560 cores) only one and a half 36 kBit block-RAMs are additionally needed. The SHARQ concept is therefore scalable to system sizes that far exceed the current state of the art. Furthermore, the frequency analysis of the SHARQ unit showed that it is able to run at roughly 180 MHz, independent of the system size.

4.2 Microbenchmarks

First, we analyzed the behavior of SHARQ by implementing two microbenchmarks and comparing the results to the software-emulated variant (SWQ) described earlier. In the following, both benchmarks and their results are described.

Local Costs of Queue Operations. Queue operations – whether performed in hardware or software – come with costs (e.g. in form of CPU time or latency). The purpose of this microbenchmark is to determine the local costs of queue operations for the initiating CPU. To reproducibly measure the minimal costs involved with a queue operation, we avoid contention on the queue by performing only one operation at a time. Furthermore, we avoid other system activity that might affect shared system resources like the NoC. Each operation is performed 512 times to receive a reliable result. The average duration of these operations in clock cycles are visualized in Fig. 5a and b for transfer sizes of 4 and 2048 bytes, respectively. The execution order combined with a sufficiently large queue length ensures that none of the enqueue or dequeue operations fails due to a full or empty queue. The operations shown in these figures from left to right are: local dequeue (LD), local enqueue (LE), remote enqueue synchronous (RES), remote enqueue asynchronous until return (REAR) and remote enqueue asynchronous until the execution of the completion task (REAC).

The results for the local operations LD and LE lead to the following two observations: 1. both operations have a certain overhead as depicted in Fig. 5a, which is roughly twice as big for the software-emulated variant compared to SHARQ, and 2. with increased element size the additional duration is equal for both approaches since it purely arises from the larger data transfer, which utilizes the same local DMA engine. Analyzing the synchronous remote enqueue (RES) showed another two key observations: 3. whereas software-emulated remote operations come at an extremely high fixed cost, SHARQ adds negligible overhead, 4. for bigger element sizes, RES performs faster than LE due to the doubled effective memory bandwidth since source and destination buffer are not in the same memory. The asynchronous remote enqueue variants REAR and REAC added the following insights: 5. by design, the duration required until SHARQ answers a remote asynchronous enqueue operation (REAR) is independent of the element size, 6. the total duration of the asynchronous variant (REAC) exceeds the synchronous one due to an additional round-trip in hardware and the scheduling overhead for the completion task. The results further showed that the standard deviation of SHARQ is lower than the corresponding software-emulated variant by a factor between 2.1 (REAC) and 11.3 (RES).

Synthetic End-to-End Performance. In a distributed manycore system, end-to-end performance of ITC primitives – even under heavy load – is crucial for overall system performance. This synthetic benchmark, therefore, aims to evaluate the behavior of SHARQ in the presence of many concurrent enqueuing and dequeuing requests and for different element sizes. Throughout this benchmark, a varying number of tiles perform synchronous remote enqueue operations on the same SHARQ queue with all of their four application cores. Each application core enqueues exactly 8192 elements of a specific size into the queue.

The corresponding SHARQ queue is located on tile zero and is configured with a maximum of four handler tasks that dequeue the elements and dismiss them. Apart from these handler tasks, no additional application tasks are executed on tile zero. The end-to-end communication hence involves a remote enqueue operation including the transfer of the element to the queue on tile zero and a dequeue operation performed by the handler task.

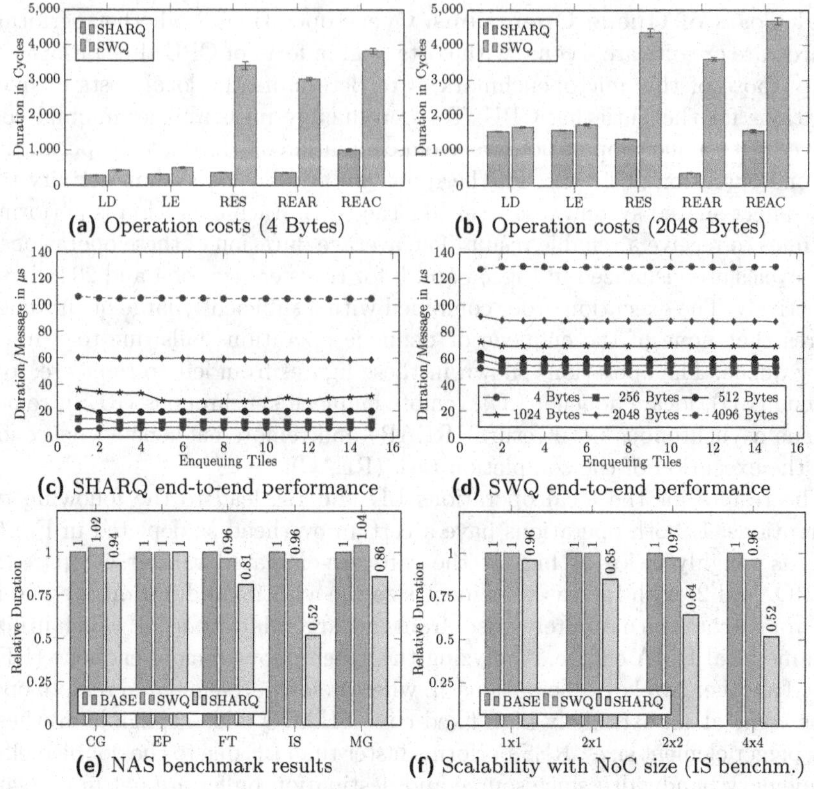

(a) Operation costs (4 Bytes) **(b)** Operation costs (2048 Bytes)

(c) SHARQ end-to-end performance **(d)** SWQ end-to-end performance

(e) NAS benchmark results **(f)** Scalability with NoC size (IS benchm.)

Fig. 5. Benchmark results

Figure 5c and d show the resulting costs for the hardware and software-emulated implementation of SHARQ for different element sizes. These graphs visualize the end-to-end costs in form of average duration per message in microseconds. This metric has been determined by measuring the total time required until all messages from the sending tiles were received by a handler on tile zero and dividing this duration by the total number of transmitted messages. Figure 5c further illustrates the huge overhead of software-emulated remote enqueue operation that was explained above. For large element sizes both variants converge since the costs are dominated by the actual data transfer. Furthermore, the results show no noteworthy performance degradation for an increased amount of concurrent enqueuers. The improved utilization of the NoC bandwidth through higher concurrency explains the minor performance increase since the gaps between data transfers of the same source tile are interleaved with transfers of others tiles. One major take-away is that especially for small element sizes SHARQ outperforms a software-emulated variant by a factor of up to 6.6.

4.3 Macrobenchmarks

To benchmark the performance of SHARQ with real-world applications, we chose the NAS Parallel Benchmarks (NPB). The NPB consist of several applications that are designed to evaluate the performance of parallel (super) computers. It is based on MPI, that already existed in form of a runtime library for our prototype system.

MPI Library and SHARQ Integration. Our implementation of MPI maps the MPI processes in one-to-one correspondence (i.e. exclusive) to cores that may be located on different tiles. Depending on the location of the involved processes the communication might either take place locally or between different tiles. Since inter-process communication is performed in a synchronous fashion, sender and receiver have to be registered as soon as they are ready for a transmission. The existing implementation therefore sends an internal message (68 Bytes) to the receiver in order to register its send request. If the receiver is ready to receive the actual message, the transfer can happen immediately in form of a DMA. Otherwise the transfer is deferred. The internal message has to be transferred by allocating remote memory on the receiver side through a remote task invocation that is followed by a DMA. Finally, a handler task is scheduled on receiver side in order to register the send request with the receiver (by enqueuing it to the queue of pending communication operations).

In order to simplify and speedup this MPI-internal synchronization process, we introduce one SHARQ queue per MPI process. The sole purpose of these SHARQ queues is to receive send requests from other processes and register them with the receiver process. Any remote allocation and the manual transfer of the internal message via DMA is therefore obsolete. Registering a send operation at receiver side boils down to either a local or remote enqueue and the execution of the SHARQ handler task. As many of the more complex MPI operations (e.g. `MPI_broadcast()`) are implemented using synchronous `MPI_send()`/ `MPI_receive()` operations, even those operations profit from this optimization.

NAS Parallel Benchmarks. We configured the benchmark to use all available 64 cores and run them with the problem size class 'S' to fit in the tile-local memory. Due to restrictions of the NPB suite only five benchmarks are able to be run in this configuration: CG (Conjugate Gradient), EP (Embarrassingly Parallel), FT (Fast Fourier-Transform), IS (Integer Sort), and MG (Multigrid). The benchmarks were run with three different MPI runtime implementations: **BASE:** MPI using the existing communication primitives: remote task invocation and DMA transfers; **SWQ:** MPI using the software emulated queue variant with the SHARQ API; and **SHARQ:** MPI enhanced with SHARQ as described in Sect. 4.3.

The evaluation results are shown in Fig. 5e. Many benchmarks profit from our SHARQ-enhanced implementation: especially the most communication intense IS kernel [16] shows a reduction in execution time to 52% compared to the BASE variant. But even benchmarks with fewer communication [16], like CG, FT and MG experience a performance speedup between 6% and 19%. Only the EP benchmark does not profit from SHARQ, since it essentially does not communicate. Figure 5f highlights the scalability of SHARQ and the increasing relative advantage for increased communication in the IS benchmarks, since the same problem size is split between 4, 8, 16 and 64 cores (4 application cores per tile). Whereas a single-tile architecture has a minor profit from SHARQ, multi-tile systems highly benefit.

5 Conclusion and Future Work

In this paper we presented software-defined hardware-managed queues as a hardware support mechanism for efficient inter-tile communication. This approach tackles many of the recurring problems that arise for inter-tile communication in these systems by offloading performance critical features to the SHARQ hardware unit: (remote) memory management, DMA transfers, efficient operation of an MPMC queue and conditionally invoking handler tasks on the receiver side. Unlike software queues it offers a significant performance improvement by offloading transfers and queue operations to hardware while freeing up CPUs to actual computation workload and still keeping the flexibility of a software-based approach (i.e., dynamic creation of an arbitrary number of queues with arbitrary queue lengths, element sizes and handler tasks).

We developed the SHARQ hardware unit, implemented it in an FPGA based prototype system and added an API to our distributed operating system. As one example application we accelerated an existing MPI library implementation with SHARQ. An evaluation with the NAS Parallel Benchmarks has shown significant performance improvements of up to 48% for benchmarks with intense communication. Microbenchmarks compared the SHARQ approach to a software-emulated variant and further demonstrated the efficiency, especially for small and medium object sizes. In addition these benchmarks showed, that our implementation behaves resilient in the contended case with a significant number of concurrent queue operations.

While the current implementation of SHARQ offers FIFO order, future versions might as well offer additional support for data structures like priority queues. SHARQ is a generic and powerful tool to further speedup and simplify other complex and recurring inter-tile communications within applications, library implementations and even the OS. As one example use-case within an operating system, we are currently exploring the advantages of SHARQ for our distributed network stack. In the future, SHARQ queues could also be used as an asynchronous system interface, allowing applications to enqueue system requests across isolation domains, as described in [17]. Traditional system calls could therefore be replaced with lightweight queue operations, while the SHARQ handler mechanism would ensure their processing e.g. on dedicated OS cores.

Acknowledgements. Funded by the Deutsche Forschungsgemeinschaft (DFG, German Research Foundation) – project number 146371743 – TRR 89: Invasive Computing. We also thank G. Drescher, J. Rabenstein and T. Langer from FAU, as well as A. Preißner, O. Lenke and L. Nolte from TUM for their excellent help.

References

1. Teich, J., et al.: Invasive computing: an overview. In: Multiprocessor System-on-Chip, pp. 241–268 (2011). https://doi.org/10.1007/978-1-4419-6460-1_11
2. Oechslein, B., Schedel, J., et al.: OctoPOS: a parallel operating system for invasive computing. In: Proceedings of the International Workshop on Systems for Future Multi-Core Architectures. EuroSys, pp. 9–14 (2011)

3. Michael, M.M., Scott, M.L.: Simple, fast, and practical non-blocking and blocking concurrent queue algorithms. In: ACM Symposium on Principles of Distributed Computing, pp. 267–275 (1996). https://doi.org/10.1145/248052.248106
4. Petrovic, D., et al.: Leveraging hardware message passing for efficient thread synchronization. TOPC **2**(4), 24:1–24:26 (2016). https://doi.org/10.1145/2858652
5. Sánchez, D., et al.: Flexible architectural support for fine-grain scheduling. In: ASPLOS Conference Proceedings, pp. 311–322 (2010). https://doi.org/10.1145/1736020.1736055
6. Lee, J., Nicopoulos, C., Lee, H.G., Panth, S., Lim, S.K., Kim, J.: IsoNet: hardware-based job queue management for many-core architectures. IEEE Trans. VLSI Syst. **21**(6), 1080–1093 (2013). https://doi.org/10.1109/TVLSI.2012.2202699
7. Pujari, R.K., Wild, T., Herkersdorf, A.: TCU: a multi-objective hardware thread mapping unit for HPC clusters. In: Kunkel, J.M., Balaji, P., Dongarra, J. (eds.) ISC High Performance 2016. LNCS, vol. 9697, pp. 39–58. Springer, Cham (2016). https://doi.org/10.1007/978-3-319-41321-1_3
8. Sharma, R.R., et al.: Exploring hardware work queue support for lightweight threads in MPSoCs. In: Conference on Reconfigurable Computing and FPGAs (ReConFig), pp. 1–6 (2012). https://doi.org/10.1109/ReConFig.2012.6416747
9. Kumar, S., Hughes, C.J., Nguyen, A.D.: Carbon: architectural support for fine-grained parallelism on chip multiprocessors. In: Symposium on Computer Architecture (ISCA), pp. 162–173 (2007). https://doi.org/10.1145/1250662.1250683
10. Wang, Y., Wang, R., Herdrich, A., Tsai, J., Solihin, Y.: CAF: core to core communication acceleration framework. In: Conference on Parallel Architectures and Compilation (PACT), pp. 351–362 (2016). https://doi.org/10.1145/2967938.2967954
11. Lee, S., et al.: HAQu: hardware-accelerated queueing for fine-grained threading on a chip multiprocessor. In: Conference on High-Performance Computer Architecture (HPCA), pp. 99–110 (2011). https://doi.org/10.1109/HPCA.2011.5749720
12. Brewer, E.A., et al.: Remote queues: exposing message queues for optimization and atomicity. In: ACM Symposium on Parallel Algorithms and Architectures (SPAA), pp. 42–53 (1995). https://doi.org/10.1145/215399.215416
13. Rheindt, S., Schenk, A., Srivatsa, A., Wild, T., Herkersdorf, A.: CaCAO: complex and compositional atomic operations for NoC-based manycore platforms. In: Berekovic, M., Buchty, R., Hamann, H., Koch, D., Pionteck, T. (eds.) ARCS 2018. LNCS, vol. 10793, pp. 139–152. Springer, Cham (2018). https://doi.org/10.1007/978-3-319-77610-1_11
14. Zaib, A., et al.: Efficient task spawning for shared memory and message passing in many-core architectures. J. Syst. Archit. - Embed. Syst. Design **77**, 72–82 (2017). https://doi.org/10.1016/j.sysarc.2017.03.004
15. Heisswolf, J., et al.: The invasive network on chip - a multi-objective many-core communication infrastructure. In: Conference on Architecture of Computing Systems (ARCS), Workshop Proceedings, pp. 1–8 (2014)
16. Subhlok, J., Venkataramaiah, S., Singh, A.: Characterizing NAS benchmark performance on shared heterogeneous networks. In: Parallel and Distributed Processing Symposium (IPDPS) (2002). https://doi.org/10.1109/IPDPS.2002.1015659
17. Maier, S., Hönig, T., Wägemann, P., Schröder-Preikschat, W.: Asynchronous abstract machines: anti-noise system software for many-core processors. In: Proceedings of the 9th International Workshop on Runtime and Operating Systems for Supercomputers (ROSS) (2019). https://doi.org/10.1145/3322789.3328744

5. [illegible] fast and practical non-blocking concurrent [illegible] algorithms. In: ACM Symposium on Principles of Distributed Computing [illegible] (2004) [illegible]
6. [illegible] memory management of threads [illegible] (2010) [illegible]
[illegible]
6. [illegible] Lee, H. [illegible] based [illegible] management for [illegible] (2017) [illegible]
7. [illegible] A.: [illegible] In: [illegible] (eds.) [illegible] 2016. LNCS, vol. 9837, pp. [illegible] Springer, Cham (2016). https://doi.org/10.1007/978-3-[illegible]
8. [illegible] framework for [illegible] computing [illegible] (2012) [illegible]
9. [illegible] architectural support for [illegible] parallelism [illegible] (2007) [illegible]
10. [illegible] (2011) [illegible]
11. Lee, [illegible] for the [illegible] (2017) [illegible]
12. [illegible] In: ACM Symposium on Parallelism in Algorithms and Architectures (SPAA), pp. [illegible] (2016) [illegible]
13. [illegible] LNCS, vol. [illegible] Springer, Cham (2018). https://doi.org/10.1007/978-3-[illegible]
14. [illegible] (2017) [illegible]
15. [illegible] In: Conference on Architectural Support for Programming Languages and Operating Systems [illegible] (2014)
16. [illegible] In: Parallel and Distributed Processing Symposium [illegible] (2013) [illegible]
17. [illegible] In: Proceedings of the [illegible] Operating Systems [illegible] (2010) [illegible]

Electronic System-Level Design and Verification

Access Interval Prediction for Tightly Coupled Memory Systems

Robert Wittig(✉), Friedrich Pauls(✉), Emil Matus(✉), and Gerhard Fettweis(✉)

Vodafone Chair for Mobile Communications Systems,
Technische Universität Dresden, Dresden, Germany
{robert.wittig,friedrich.pauls,emil.matus,gerhard.fettweis}@tu-dresden.de

Abstract. Today, processing elements of embedded systems usually share some amount of the available on-chip memory in order to maximize the area utilization. However, sharing memory incurs runtime conflicts, which entail performance penalties. To ease this restriction, we introduce a method for memory Access Interval Prediction. It minimizes conflicts by predicting the interval between two consecutive memory accesses. In contrast to contemporary work, we do not rely on compile time information or other a priori knowledge. Standard benchmarks show that we can predict over 80% of all memory access intervals correctly, thereby significantly reducing the number of access conflicts.

Keywords: Memory prediction · Access interval · Shared memory · MPSoC

1 Introduction

The sharing of memory with a multitude of processing elements presents a widely adopted approach to tackle the area and power constraints imposed by the utilization wall [12]. However, with a growing number of master ports accessing a shared memory system, the number of access conflicts rises. Thus, the overall memory latency and the average execution time increase.

Hence, designers introduced predictive memory transactions. This can be described as "if an access happens, how long will it take in the worst case scenario?". Thus, the memory system must process each transaction within a restricted time limit. Possible means are: time division multiplexing (TDM), prioritizing and tree structures. However, these techniques introduce additional delays, confining their application to lower level memory hierarchies (L2, L3 cache, DDR-RAM). With the growing depth of hierarchy, the extra latency can be well hidden.

In contrast, tightly coupled memory (TCM) often has a flat hierarchy with a latency of only one clock cycle. Every additional delay would lead to a significant decrease in system performance. Consequently, the application of the above mentioned techniques is unsuitable. This is why designers mainly focus on optimizing the arbitration logic of the memory system [2]. Conflict avoidance is only

D. N. Pnevmatikatos et al. (Eds.): SAMOS 2019, LNCS 11733, pp. 229–240, 2019.
https://doi.org/10.1007/978-3-030-27562-4_16

addressed by means of interleaved memory bank mapping [3]. However, these solutions fail to acknowledge different run-time priorities for masters accessing the memory. For example, tasks in wireless communication platforms usually have priorities assigned to them [5].

Other approaches for TCM focused on conflict detection during compile time. To avoid conflicts, code and data is placed in optimized memory banks with continuous mapping. Albeit better suited for priority handling and conflict avoidance, only a limited set of application constellations can be taken into account for optimization.

In order to tackle the problem of memory contention, we propose a novel approach for run-time conflict detection. Access Interval Prediction (AIP) is suited for TCM systems, and does not rely on compile time information or any other a priori knowledge. Instead we predict the interval between two subsequent memory accesses. The prediction can then be used to pre-arbitrate masters. This reduces conflicts without adding additional delay to the arbitration logic. Our analysis shows that AIP improves the performance of TCM systems by up to 64%. At the same time, AIP also increases the relative memory utilization by up to 77%.

We also present three different estimators to facilitate AIP: maximum likelihood, counter based and a method coined Access Look-ahead Buffer (ALB). For evaluation and comparison we use the standard SPECCPU benchmark suite and a cycle accurate, commercial CPU model. Specific architectures and implementation results are especially not shown in this paper. Those analyses will be covered in our future work.

The remainder of this paper is organized as follows: Sect. 2 explains necessary background information. Section 3 gives an overview over contemporary work. In Sect. 4, we introduce AIP and the different estimators. Afterwards, we evaluate the performance and discuss the results in Sect. 5. Finally, Sect. 6 gives an outlook into future work.

2 Background

A memory system arbitrates multiple masters to multiple memory banks. A master can be a CPU port, a network interface, or any other entity that needs access to the shared memory system. The memory banks are organized either in interleaved or continuous fashion. The former maps consecutive addresses to different banks, the latter approach only to a single one. The memory access system comprises a control unit and and interconnect (e.g. a bus or switching network). The control unit is dedicated to address translation/decoding, and access arbitration (i.e. conflict detection/resolving; access scheduling, prioritization and memory protection).

It is possible for multiple masters to access the memory system concurrently. However, if the same memory bank is requested, a conflict occurs and the masters are stalled. The control unit resolves the conflict by arbitrating one master at a time. This process entails a conflict penalty of several clock cycles. The reason for this penalty lies in the tightly coupled nature of memory systems in MPSoCs. In these systems, the logic paths from masters to memory banks and vice versa are often the critical path in the system. This prohibits the deployment of priority encoders, which would result in additional delay and diminish the overall system performance.

3 Related Work

Contemporary work offers an abundance of related topics in the area of embedded, shared memory systems. This section describes some of them and highlights the differences to the proposed AIP method.

The T-Crest [9] architecture uses time division multiplexing (TDM) and a tree like structure to arbitrate requests with different priorities. This ensures an upper bound of time spent for a memory transaction. When accessing memory with a high latency, like DDR-RAM, the additional delay for TDM and priority encoders can be well hidden. However, the approach is not applicable to TCM systems with single cycle latency.

Another approach with TDM and a round-robin arbitration scheme is presented in [6]. The MERASA architecture features a two-level arbiter to schedule requests from one core and between multiple cores. However, it also has the same disadvantages like mentioned before.

Other approaches focus on special DRAM controllers to minimize conflicts and limit worst-case access latency for off-chip transactions. PRET [8] and PALLOC [15] are representing two such architectures. They are dividing the available DRAM resource into multiple logical banks for independent use. [11] showed that the banking approach is also applicable to on-chip SRAM. However, a priori information obtained at compile time is required and only a limited set of application constellations can be taken into account.

The design of on-chip memory arbiters for TCM has also received much attention [1,2,4,7,13]. These systems share a certain amount of scratchpad memory between multiple cores. Because of the required low latency, additional logic for prioritizing transactions is omitted, resulting in good average performance at the cost of high priority tasks.

In contrast, our approach of Access Interval Prediction aids on-chip memory arbiters for TCM. This in turn leads to a significant reduction in execution time for high priority tasks without increasing the logical path between master and memory. Additionally, no compile time or other a priori knowledge is required.

4 Access Interval Prediction

4.1 Motivation and System Overview

Consider a high priority master (HPM) access trace to a single memory bank, shown in Fig. 1(a). The transactions appear at different, seemingly arbitrary time intervals, but the memory bank is not fully utilized. Hence, the idle periods can

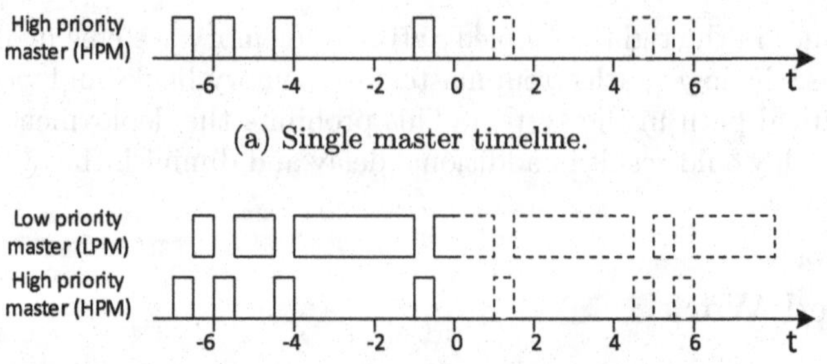

(a) Single master timeline.

(b) Optimal access with two masters without conflicts.

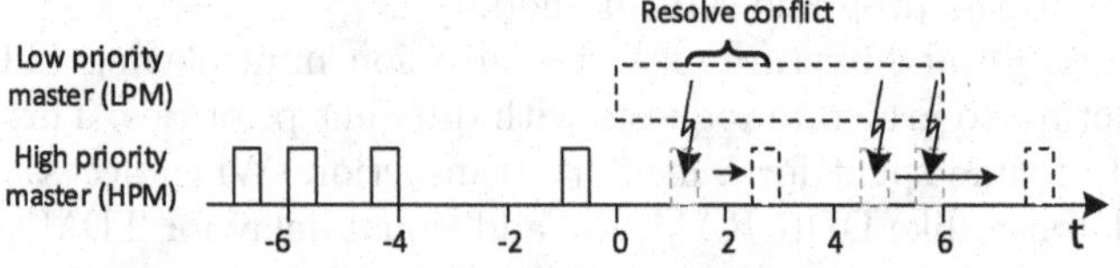

(c) Real scenario with two masters and conflicts.

Fig. 1. Memory access traces.

be exploited by an additional low priority master (LPM). In the optimal case, no interference occurs, Fig. 1(b). Thus, the overall performance of the HPM is not affected, and the memory utilization is increased. Unfortunately, the lack of a priori knowledge may result in the conflicts shown in Fig. 1(c). Consequently, the overall system performance diminishes due to the overhead associated with the conflict resolution. This is even more critical for high priority tasks with real-time restrictions. In this case, either no memory sharing can be performed, or the system has to be designed for worst case scenarios (maximum number of conflicts).

In order to avoid the penalty incurred by conflict detection and resolution, we propose a scheme called Access-Interval-Prediction (AIP). The basic principle relies on the prediction of the time interval between two subsequent memory accesses of the HPM. Within the predicted interval, any other low-priority master can access the same memory bank without interference.

Figure 2 presents an overview of the system assumed throughout the paper. We use the Xtensa LX6 processor as HPM. The configuration has one instruction and data port with 64 bit width each. Furthermore, the processor uses very long instruction words (VLIW), enabling the fetch and execution of multiple instructions at once. As LPM, we use a data movement engine, which accesses the memory every cycle. The shown system can be extended for multiple HPMs and different priority levels. However, the focus in this paper will lie in a system with only one HPM and LPM. For simplicity, we further assume that AIP is performed for the instruction *or* the data port of the HPM, but not for both simultaneously. The HPM port without AIP is assumed to have its private memory bank.

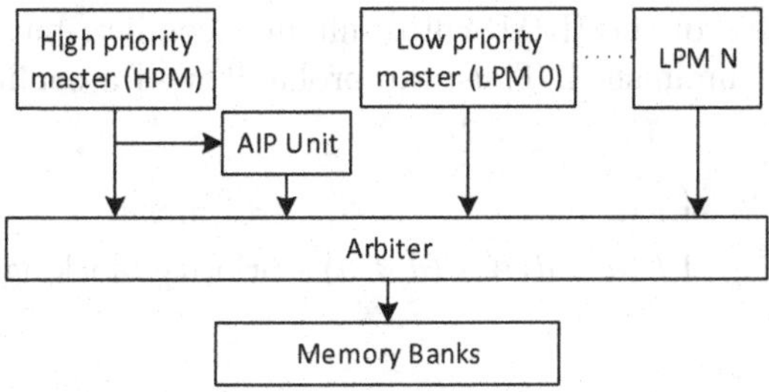

Fig. 2. Memory system with Access Interval Prediction.

The arbiter can be a low latency architecture like [7]. Since the AIP unit generates the control signals for the arbiter in advance, no additional logic has to be inserted into the critical path. In the case of a correct prediction, the HPM can be pre-arbitrated in the estimated cycle, resulting in no additional delay.

Finally, we distinguish between two different memory bank configurations. One is made of only one bank that is shared between HPM and LPM. This configuration is especially useful to focus on the performance of AIP. The second configuration is made of four banks ordered in interleaved fashion. This corresponds to a banking factor of two (two masters access four banks), commonly found in literature [7]. We will refer to these configurations as *banked* and *interleaved* system throughout the paper.

As software, the HPM executes the standard SPECPU 2006[1] [10] integer benchmark suite. All benchmarks were conducted with a cycle accurate SystemC simulator.

4.2 Theory

We define $d = d_i$ as the i-th randomly distributed access interval between two consecutive memory transactions of a single PE. An observation of d can take realizations between 1 and L and is denoted as $d_i \in \{1, ..., L\}$. For every interval i, we want to have an estimator $\hat{d}$ such that the error $\tilde{d} = d - \hat{d}$ becomes zero with high probability: $\max P(\tilde{d} = 0)$.

The probability of a true prediction is given by: $P(\hat{d} = d)$. In this case, we can pre-arbitrate the HPM port with no penalty. If the predicted interval is longer than the true interval $P(\hat{d} > d)$, a conflict penalty is incurred because LPM and HPM want to access the memory at the same time. If, in contrast, the predicted interval is shorter than the true interval $P(\hat{d} < d)$, two different scenarios are possible. (1) We can block the banks exclusively for the HPM port (priority blocking). This entails no conflict, but reduces the throughput of the LPM. (2) The LPM can access the banks after the miss-prediction (free-for-all). In this

[1] Compiler issues prevented the use of the most recent SPECCPU 2017 version.

case, the next access of the HPM will result in a conflict, but the throughput of the LPM is not diminished. Thus, the probability of a conflict free access is given by

$$P_{\text{cfa}} = \begin{cases} P(\hat{d} = d) & \text{free-for-all} \\ P(\hat{d} = d) + P(\hat{d} < d) & \text{priority blocking.} \end{cases} \quad (1)$$

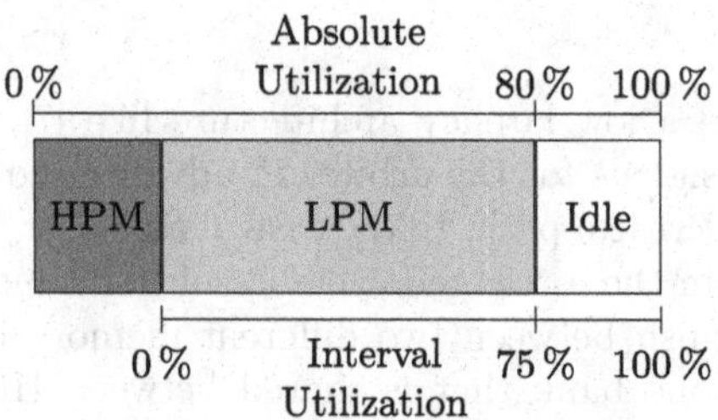

Fig. 3. Difference between *absolute* and *interval* utilization. In this example the absolute utilization sums up to 80%. The interval utilization is only 75%.

The average interval $A = E[d]$ is a measure of the *absolute* memory utilization by the HPM. Additionally, the *interval* utilization U_{I} can be seen as the percentage of idle cycles that can be utilized by the LPM. As such, U_{I} can be seen as the relative throughput of the LPM. It can also be treated as the overall system performance, because the memory utilization is directly related to the system workload. Figure 3 illustrates the difference between absolute and interval utilization.

Furthermore, we calculate the performance impairments of memory sharing. For this, we measure the total execution time with and without AIP for the system introduced in Fig. 2. With increasing A, there are less transactions taking place on average. Thus, conflicts are less likely to occur. On the other hand, a high conflict penalty increases the impairment caused by memory sharing.

4.3 AIP Estimators

In order to facilitate AIP, we introduce three different estimators based on: maximum likelihood (ML), counter and access look-ahead buffer (ALB).

Maximum Likelihood Estimator. The ML estimator uses the probability mass function (PMF) of the random variable d. The estimation is than given by: $\hat{d} = \arg\max_d P(d)$. The underlying assumption is that most transactions from a CPU happen in a regular interval. Hence, the PMF exhibits a peak at a specific interval location. Consequently, the interval value associated with the peak is selected for prediction.

If, for example, over 50% of all intervals had a length of N, the predicted interval would always be N. The required PMF can be constructed a priori for each program or it can be build dynamically during run-time, e.g. with simple counters that count each interval. Of course, it is possible to use more sophisticated statistical estimators [14], but this lies outside of the scope of this paper.

Counter Based Estimator. This approach reflects the fact that large parts of a program, e.g. loop execution, often exhibit a linear access pattern. Hence, the current access interval is a linear function of the previous access intervals. Therefore, the counter method measures the span of past intervals and exploits them for the next interval prediction. In this paper, we only consider the simplest version in which the predicted interval is equal to the last measured interval. This results in a very simple architecture with only a single interval counter. With this simplification, the counter method is a special case of the ALB with a size of one.

Access Look-Ahead Buffer. The ALB estimator is inspired by the principle of a cache. But instead of saving data blocks, the ALB stores access time intervals associated with a memory address. It relies on the fact that a memory address exhibits the same access interval when encountered multiple times. Of course this is not always true because (1) branches, interrupts and other program flows might cause deviations and (2) the size of the ALB may limit the performance. Because of the limited size, correct predictions might be overwritten by other addresses.

5 Simulation Results

5.1 Average Interval

Figure 4 shows some example PMFs of the access intervals for the instruction and the data port. As mentioned previously, we use the integer test suite of the SPECCPU 2006 benchmark. For the instruction port, up to 80% of all transaction have an interval of one cycle, meaning an access is performed every cycle. For the data port, most applications have their peek at an interval of nine cycles, except for the test-case Sjeng, which has its peek at two cycles. This results in a higher absolute utilization of the instruction port compared to the data port. The latter one shows a higher variance with respect to the access interval.

Based on the PMF, it is possible to calculate the average interval A for each test-case. As indicated, there is a significant difference between the instruction and data port of the deployed Xtensa LX6 processor. This was to be expected, since an instruction fetch in current processor architectures can take place almost every cycle. However, the instruction port is only utilized between 50% ($A = 2$) and 70% ($A = 1.36$). The data port utilization is even less, and lies between 5% ($A = 19.68$) and 26% ($A = 3.87$). The results show that the absolute utilization

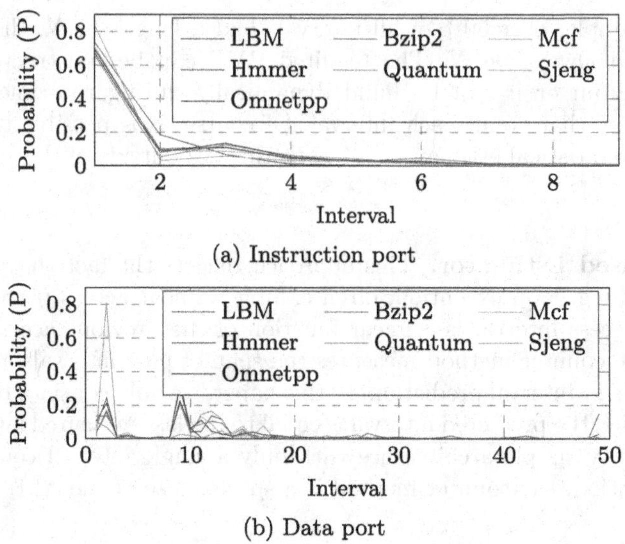

(a) Instruction port

(b) Data port

Fig. 4. Probability mass functions of access interval distribution.

for instruction as well as data port are significantly below 100%. Thus, there are enough free cycles for other masters to operate on the same memory without interference.

5.2 Prediction Accuracy

Next, we compare the accuracy of the different estimators. As described in Sect. 4, we first focus on a memory system with a single, shared memory bank. Figure 5 shows the probability of a conflict free access P_{cfa} in FFA and blocking mode for different sizes of the ALB. The actual prediction accuracy $P(\hat{d} = d)$ equals P_{cfa} in FFA mode, see (1). The overall range of accuracy lies between 30% and 85%. It can be noted that the performance increases due to the size is at most 21%.

Table 1 shows the performance of all three estimators for both memory systems. It can be seen that AIP has a profound impact on the banked system, significantly increasing the percentage of conflict free accesses. The ML estimator even achieves 100% at the instruction port. There, every interval is equal or longer than the predicted interval of one cycle. In this case, the blocking mode effectively reserves the memory for the HPM, leaving no cycles for the LPM to access the memory. In general, all estimators achieve better results at the instruction port. At the data port, access intervals have a higher variance, which makes them less predictable.

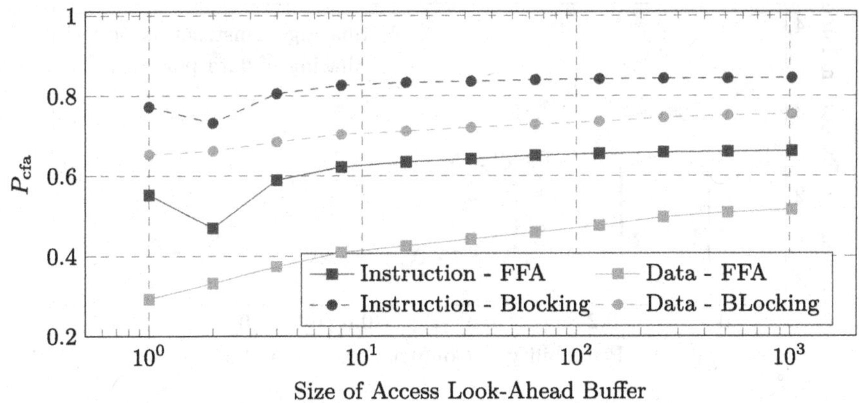

Fig. 5. Prediction accuracy for different sizes of the Access Look-Ahead Buffer. Graphs are given for free-for-all (FFA) and blocking mode.

The interleaved memory system also benefits from AIP. In this case, even if the prediction was wrong, the HPM and LPM might access different memory banks. Thus, P_{cfa} is increased although the prediction accuracy of the estimators remain unchanged. Because of this, even the simple counter estimator achieves 89% conflict free accesses.

In general, Table 1 shows, how AIP significantly improves P_{cfa} for both memory systems. The next subsection shows, how this translates into measurable performance gains.

Table 1. Probability of conflict free access P_{cfa} for the different estimators and memory systems. The shown numbers correspond to FFA / Blocking mode and are given in *percent*.

Memory system	AIP port	Estimator			
		None	ML	Counter	ALB (1024)
Banked	Instruction	0 / -	74 / 100	55 / 77	66 / 84
	Data	0 / -	41 / 79	29 / 65	51 / 75
Interleaved	Instruction	75 / -	94 / 100	89 / 94	92 / 96
	Data	75 / -	85 / 95	82 / 91	88 / 94

5.3 Performance Improvement of AIP

Based on the probability of conflict free accesses, it is possible to evaluate the performance impact of AIP. Figure 6 shows the normalized execution times when memory sharing is used, either for the instruction or data port. The point at $P_{\mathrm{cfa}} = 1$ is the reference point. It equals the performance when no memory sharing is performed.

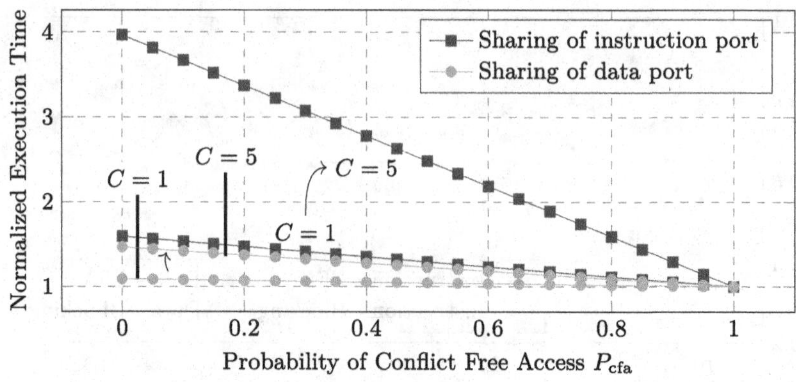

Fig. 6. Performance gain of AIP.

It can be seen that the execution time decreases with P_{cfa}, because less conflicts occur. The execution time also rises with the conflict penalty C, because occurring conflicts entail more penalty cycles. Since the instruction port of the HPM has a higher absolute utilization, the impairment caused by memory sharing is greater than at the data port. Together with Table 1, it is now possible to determine the performance impact of memory sharing, with and without AIP. For example, the interleaved system without AIP achieves $P_{cfa} = 75\%$. If memory sharing is performed at the instruction port, the normalized execution time is given by 1.74 ($C = 5$). When using the ALB estimator, P_{cfa} is increased to 96%. Hence, the execution time is decreased to 1.15 (with blocking mode). This equals a performance gain of 34%. The gain of AIP for the banked system is at most 64%.

These results indicate that AIP can be used to increase the performance of shared TCM systems. This is true for banked as well as interleaved memory systems.

5.4 Interval Utilization and System Performance

Next, we show an evaluation of the interval utilization as introduced in Sect. 4.2. With FFA mode, the LPM can effectively access the memory every cycle. Hence, an U_I of 100% is achieved for all estimators. With blocking mode, U_I is reduced significantly. Without any estimation, U_I equals zero because the memory banks get blocked for the HPM exclusively and no sharing can be performed. The same is true for the ML estimator at the instruction port ($\hat{d}$ equals 1). In general, there is a trade-off between FFA and blocking mode for all estimators. FFA achieves a higher U_I at the cost of a lower P_{cfa} and execution speed. The blocking mode increases P_{cfa} by reserving the memory (partly or completely) (1), which in turn results in smaller utilization values. Table 2 summarizes these results.

Like explained in Sect. 4.2, the interval utilization can also be seen as the overall system throughput. As such it is clear that the blocking mode reduces the system performance in favor of the HPM execution speed. However, in combination with AIP the blocking mode can still achieve up to 77% of interval utilization. In situations where the overall system performance has a higher relevance than the execution speed of the HPM, the FFA mode should be deployed.

Table 2. Interval utilization U_I for the different estimators and memory systems. The shown numbers correspond to FFA / Blocking mode and are given in *percent*.

Memory system	AIP port	Estimator			
		None	ML	Counter	ALB (1024)
Banked	Instruction	100 / 0	100 / 0	100 / 24	100 / 52
	Data	100 / 0	100 / 62	100 / 62	100 / 77
Interleaved	Instruction	100 / 0	100 / 0	100 / 24	100 / 52
	Data	100 / 0	100 / 62	100 / 24	100 / 77

6 Conclusion and Outlook

In this work we introduced a new technique called Access Interval Prediction (AIP). By avoiding conflicts in the memory system, it minimizes the measured execution time. The used benchmarks show a performance gain of up to 66%. At the same time, AIP increases the memory utilization, because multiple masters can access the same memory with less conflicts. We also showed the trade-off between high performance and high memory utilization. Out of the three introduced AIP estimators, the ALB offers the best trade-off between high memory utilization and lowest execution time. In addition, no additional logic has to be inserted into the critical path between processor and memory. This makes AIP suitable to be deployed with tightly coupled memory systems.

In the future, we would like to increase the performance of the AIP estimators by introducing ideas known from cache design like way associativity. In the next paper we will also introduce a VLSI implementation to embed AIP in a common chip design.

Acknowledgment. This publication contains results of the fast semantics project, which is a member of the fast2020 research cluster. It is being financed by the 'Zwanzig20 – Partnerschaft für Innovation' initiative of the Federal Ministry for Education and Research of Germany under the grant number FKZ03ZZ0521D.

References

1. Ax, J., et al.: CoreVA-MPSoC: a many-core architecture with tightly coupled shared and local data memories. IEEE Trans. Parallel Distrib. Syst. **29**(5), 1030–1043 (2018). https://doi.org/10.1109/TPDS.2017.2785799
2. Bates, D., Bradbury, A., Koltes, A., Mullins, R.: Exploiting tightly-coupled cores. In: SAMOS. IEEE (2013). https://doi.org/10.1109/SAMOS.2013.6621138
3. Gautschi, M., Rossi, D., Benini, L.: Customizing an open source processor to fit in an ultra-low power cluster with a shared L1 memory. In: GLSVLSI. ACM Press, New York (2014). https://doi.org/10.1145/2591513.2591569
4. Gelado, I., Cabezas, J., Navarro, N., Stone, J.E., Patel, S., Hwu, W.M.W.: An asymmetric distributed shared memory model for heterogeneous parallel systems. In: ASPLOS. ACM Press, New York (2010). https://doi.org/10.1145/1736020.1736059
5. Haas, S., et al.: A Heterogeneous SDR MPSoC in 28 nm CMOS for low-latency wireless applications. In: DAC. ACM Press, New York (2017). https://doi.org/10.1145/3061639.3062188
6. Paolieri, M., Quiñones, E., Cazorla, F.J., Bernat, G., Valero, M.: Hardware support for WCET analysis of hard real-time multicore systems. In: ISCA. ACM Press, New York (2009). https://doi.org/10.1145/1555754.1555764
7. Rahimi, A., Loi, I., Kakoee, M.R., Benini, L.: A fully-synthesizable single-cycle interconnection network for Shared-L1 processor clusters. In: DATE. IEEE (2011). https://doi.org/10.1109/DATE.2011.5763085
8. Reineke, J., Liu, I., Patel, H.D., Kim, S., Lee, E.A.: PRET DRAM controller: bank privatization for predictability and temporal isolation. In: CODES+ISSS. ACM Press, New York (2011). https://doi.org/10.1145/2039370.2039388
9. Schoeberl, M., et al.: T-CREST: time-predictable multi-core architecture for embedded systems. J. Syst. Architect. **61**(9), 449–471 (2015). https://doi.org/10.1016/j.sysarc.2015.04.002
10. SPEC: SPECCPU 2006 (2006). https://www.spec.org/cpu2006/
11. Tretter, A., Giannopoulou, G., Baer, M., Thiele, L.: Minimising access conflicts on shared multi-bank memory. ACM Trans. Embed. Comput. Syst. **16**(5s), 1–20 (2017). https://doi.org/10.1145/3126535
12. Venkatesh, G., et al.: Conservation cores. In: ASPLOS. ACM Press, New York (2010). https://doi.org/10.1145/1736020.1736044
13. Wittig, R., Hasler, M., Matus, E., Fettweis, G.: Queue based memory management unit for heterogeneous MPSoCs. In: DATE. IEEE, March 2019. https://doi.org/10.23919/DATE.2019.8715129
14. Wittig, R., Hasler, M., Matus, E., Fettweis, G.: Statistical access interval prediction for tightly coupled memory systems. In: Cool Chips 22. IEEE (2019)
15. Yun, H., Mancuso, R., Wu, Z.P., Pellizzoni, R.: PALLOC: DRAM bank-aware memory allocator for performance isolation on multicore platforms. In: RTAS. IEEE (2014). https://doi.org/10.1109/RTAS.2014.6925999

Experimental Evaluation of Probabilistic Execution-Time Modeling and Analysis Methods for SDF Applications on MPSoCs

Ralf Stemmer[1(✉)], Hai-Dang Vu[2], Kim Grüttner[3], Sebastien Le Nours[2], Wolfgang Nebel[1], and Sebastien Pillement[2]

[1] University of Oldenburg, Oldenburg, Germany
{ralf.stemmer,wolfgang.nebel}@uol.de

[2] University of Nantes, IETR, UMR CNRS 6164, Nantes, France
{hai-dang.vu,sebastien.le-nours,sebastien.pillement}@univ-nantes.fr

[3] OFFIS e.V., Oldenburg, Germany
kim.gruettner@offis.de

Abstract. Early validation of software running on multi-processor platforms is fundamental to guarantee that real-time constraints will be fully met. In the domain of timing analysis probabilistic simulation techniques tackle the problem of scalability. However, creation of probabilistic SystemC models remains a difficult task and is not well supported for multi-processors systems. In this paper we present a modeling workflow that will then be used for an experimental evaluation of probabilistic simulation techniques. For the modeling process a measurement-based approach is proposed to favor the creation of trustful models. The evaluated probabilistic simulation techniques demonstrate good potential to deliver fast yet accurate estimations for multi-processor systems.

Keywords: Statistical Model Checking · Probabilistic SystemC model · Multi processor

1 Introduction

Multi-processor systems are increasingly adopted to implement high performance time critical systems. In the design of such systems, early verification that real-time constraints are fully met is fundamental to prevent costly design cycles.

This work has been partially sponsored by the DAAD (PETA-MC project under grant agreement 57445418) with funds from the Federal Ministry of Education and Research (BMBF). This work has also been partially sponsored by CampusFrance (PETA-MC project under grant agreement 42521PK) with funds from the French ministry of Europe and Foreign Affairs (MEAE) and by the French ministry for Higher Education, Research and Innovation (MESRI).

D. N. Pnevmatikatos et al. (Eds.): SAMOS 2019, LNCS 11733, pp. 241–254, 2019.
https://doi.org/10.1007/978-3-030-27562-4_17

Timing analysis of parallel software running on multi-processors is hard, especially because of possible interferences among application tasks due to contention at the shared resources of the processor (*i.e.*, communication bus, shared memory, shared caches). In this context, appropriately capturing and analyzing low-level influences of platform shared resources early in the design process represents a challenging effort. Existing real-time analysis methods, *i.e.*, simulation-based and formal mathematical approaches, show limitations to deliver fast yet accurate estimation of timing properties.

Probabilistic models represent a possible solution to capture variability caused by shared resources on parallel software execution [13]. Quantitative analysis of probabilistic models can then be used to quantify the probability that a given time property is satisfied. Numerical approaches exist that compute the exact measure of the probability at the expense of time-consuming analysis effort. Another approach to evaluate probabilistic models is to simulate the model for many runs and monitor simulations to approximate the probability that time properties are met. This approach, which is also called Statistical Model Checking (SMC), is far less memory and time intensive than probabilistic numerical methods and it has been successfully adopted in different application domains [11]. In the field of embedded system design, executable specifications built with the use of the SystemC language are now widely adopted [1]. SystemC models used for the purpose of timing analysis typically capture workload models of the application mapped on shared computation and communication resources of the considered platform. Timing annotations are commonly expressed as average values or intervals with estimated best case and worst case execution times. The adoption of SMC techniques to analyze SystemC models of multi-processor systems is promising because it could deliver a good compromise between accuracy and analysis time, yet it requires a more sophisticated timing model based on probability density functions, inferred from measurements on a real prototype. Thus, the creation of trustful probabilistic SystemC models is challenging. Since SMC methods have rarely been considered to analyze timing properties of applications mapped on multi-processor systems with complex hierarchy of shared resources, exploring their application on trustful probabilistic SystemC models remains a significant research topic.

In this paper, we present an experimental modeling setup that is used to evaluate the efficiency of SMC methods for multi-processor systems. The contributions of this paper are twofold. The first contribution deals with the modeling process, including a measurement-based approach, to appropriately prepare timing annotations and calibrate SystemC models. The second contribution is about the evaluation of SMC methods efficiency with respect to accuracy and analysis time. Evaluation is done by comparing a real multi-processor implementation with related estimation results. To restrict the scope of our study, we have considered applications modeled as Synchronous Data Flow Graphs (SDFGs). We have evaluated our setup on a Sobel filter case study. Two configurations of the hardware platform with different levels of complexity are considered to analyze the relevance and effectiveness of SMC methods.

This paper is organized as follows. In Sect. 2 we provide an overview and discussion of relevant related work. Section 3 presents the established modeling and analysis approach. The experimental results are described in Sect. 4. Section 5 discuss the benefits and limitations of the presented approach.

2 Related Work

Timing analysis approaches are commonly classified as (1) simulation-based approaches, which partially test system properties based on a limited set of stimuli, (2) formal approaches, which statically check system properties in an exhaustive way, and (3) hybrid approaches, which combine simulation-based and formal approaches.

Simulation-based approaches require extensive architecture analysis under various possible working scenarios. However, due to insufficient corner case coverage, simulation-based approaches are limited to determine guaranteed limits about system properties.

Statistical Model Checking (SMC) has been proposed as an alternative to formal approaches to avoid an exhaustive exploration of the state-space model. SMC refers to a series of techniques that are used to explore a sub-part of the state-space and provides an estimation about the probability that a given property is satisfied. Various probabilistic model-checkers support statistical model-checking, as for example UPPAAL-SMC [5], Prism [9], and Plasma-Lab [7].

We have presented a comparison of formal model checking with SMC in [16]. A multi-processor system was modeled using timed automata and probabilistic timed automata in UPPAAL-SMC. While formal methods use only best and worst case execution times the SMC method allows to model the distribution of execution times between those limits. The possibilities of modeling such a distribution is limited due to UPPAALs modeling language. In contrast to that work, our new SystemC approach allows to not only use a rough model of the distribution but the actual measured execution times. Furthermore we refined the communication model to better cover the computation overhead on the CPUs that accesses the communication infrastructure.

Authors in [3,4] propose a measurement-based approach in combination with hardware and/or software randomization techniques to conduct a probabilistic worst-case execution time (pWCET) through the application of Extreme Value Theory (EVT). In difference to their approach, we apply a Statistical Model Checking (SMC) based analysis capturing the system modus system modus operandi. This enables the obtainment of tighter values compared to the EVT approach. Yet our method could benefit from their measurement methodology.

An iterative probabilistic approach has been presented by Kumar [8] to model the resource contention together with stochastic task execution times to provide estimates for the throughput of SDF applications on multiprocessor systems. Unlike their approach, we apply an SMC based analysis which enables a probabilistic symbolic simulation and the estimation of probabilistic worst-case timing bounds of the target application with estimated confidence values.

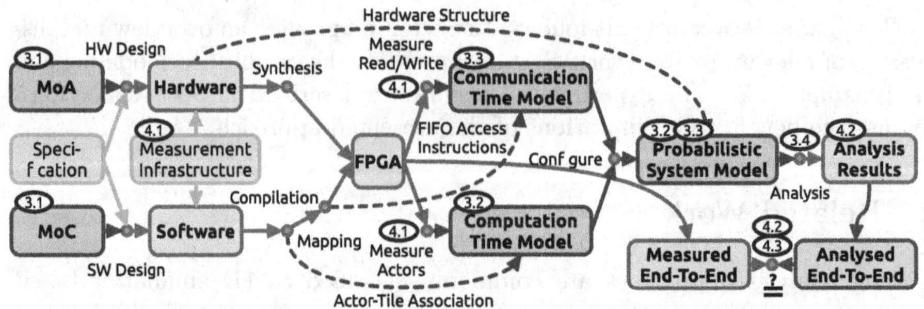

Fig. 1. Overview showing where and how the models introduced in Sect. 3 are used. The circled numbers reference the sections where more details can be found.

In [14] integration of SMC methods in a system-level verification approach is presented. It corresponds to a stochastic extension of the BIP formalism and associated toolset [2]. An SMC engine is presented to sample and control simulation execution in order to decide if the system model satisfies a given property. The preparation process of time annotations in the system model is presented in [13] where a statistical inference process is proposed to capture low-level platform effects on application execution. A many-core platform running an image recognition application is considered and stochastic extension of BIP is then used to evaluate the application execution time.

A solution is presented in [12] to apply SMC analysis methods for systems modeled in SystemC. The execution traces of the analyzed model are monitored and a statistical model checker is used to verify temporal properties. The monitor is automatically generated based on a given set of variables to be observed. The statistical model-checker is implemented as a plugin of the Plasma-Lab. In the scope of our work, we adopt the approach presented in [12] to analyze time properties of multi-core systems modeled with SystemC.

To the best of our knowledge, no other work attempted to systematically evaluate the benefits of using SMC to analyze the timing properties of SDF based applications on multi-processor systems, targeting more tightness of estimated bounds and faster analysis times.

3 Characterization and Modeling Approach

Figure 1 shows a detailed insight in our approach, highlighting the models we use (purple rectangle). The circled number above those rectangles references the section where those models are explained in detail. Other references point to the related experiment Sect. 4. We design our system following the hardware (HW) and software (SW) models in Sect. 3.1. The HW and SW designed following those models get extended by a measurement infrastructure introduced in Sect. 4.1 and described in detail in [15]. The mapped and scheduled software gets mapped and executed on the designed hardware that gets instantiated on an FPGA. This *real system* is used to characterize the timing behavior of the HW

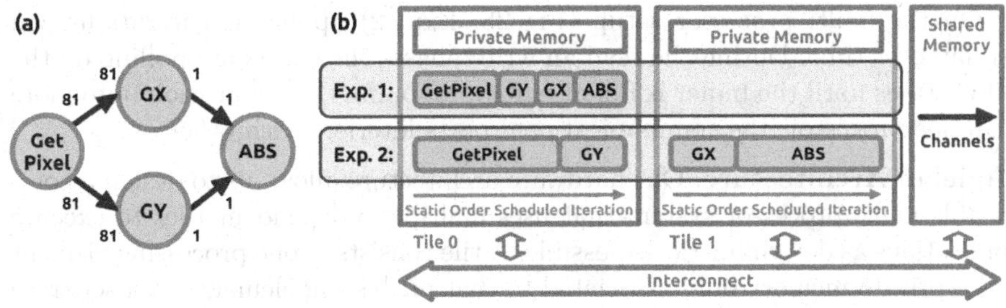

Fig. 2. (a) A Sobel filter modeled as an SDFG. A pixel matrix gets processed in *GX* and *GY* and returned to the *ABS* actor that calculates the resulting pixel. (b) Our platform consisting of two tiles. In the first experiment, all actors are mapped to *Tile 0*, in the second experiment both tiles are used. The order of the mapped actors represents their scheduling.

components as well as the software. The insight in the instantiated system allows modeling the communication in detail, considering the computational overhead by the software (derived from its instructions) that manages the communication between shared resources (See Sect. 3.3). For the computational part of our application, we can model its timing behavior on a specific hardware in detail as described in Sect. 3.2. The modeled communication and computation time then get integrated into a probabilistic SystemC model. This model then gets used for execution time analysis focusing on the distribution of the execution time. Using the architecture and computation model for designing our system allows us to do some assumptions on our performance models (visualized as dotted lines in Fig. 1). We analyze this model using a statistical model checker as explained in Sect. 3.4. In our experiments (Sect. 4) we compare the analysis results with the observed behavior of the system.

3.1 System Model

This section explains our software and hardware model, as well as the mapping and scheduling of the SW on the HW. These models are the input models we use to constraint our HW platform and our SW. This allows us to do assumptions on the resulting system we can later use to model its timing behavior.

Model of Computation (SDF): The Sobel filter (see Fig. 2a), used in our experiments, follows SDF semantics that was proposed by [10]. SDF model of computation offers a strict separation of computation and communication phases of actors. During the computation phase, no interference with any other actor can occur. The actors are statically scheduled and will not be preempted.

The channels used for communication between actors are implemented as FIFO buffers on a shared memory. For the single processor setup (Fig. 2b, Exp. 1), the communication time will be deterministic because the shared memory is actually only used by a single processor. Beside the data dependencies, and so the communication channels, there is no further synchronization.

On the multi processor setup (Fig. 2b, Exp. 2) application iterations can overlap over time. During the read an write phases the actors are polling on the FIFO states until the buffer is full or empty. Mapping the application onto more than one processor, the communicational parts interfere each other.

Model of Architecture: Our hardware architecture allows us to design a composable multi processor system that uses multiple independent tiles to execute applications as deterministic as possible. A tile consists of one processing element and a private memory only associated to that processing element via a separate bus. It can execute software without interfering with other tiles as long as the software only accesses the private memory. For our example we use a MicroBlaze as processing element.

To improve the determinism for our experiments, we start with a single processor. This allows the assumption that accessing the shared memory (see Fig. 2b) will always be exclusive. Later we add a second processor and change the mapping of the application to add communication interference to the system.

The whole execution platform consists of multiple tiles, buses and shared memories. While a tile can be connected to multiple interconnects, we assume that every memory is connected to only one interconnect. Furthermore we assume that tiles can only communicate via a shared memory. In the experiments, without loss of generality, the used interconnects support a first-come first-serve-based communication protocol.

All channels buffers are mapped onto shared memory, while the actors are stored on private memory of the tiles they get executed on (Fig. 2b). This setup is fully composable such that the computation phases of any actor (taking place locally on private memory) can be considered independent from communication phases (taking place via the data bus supporting a single-beat transfer style).

3.2 Computation Model

All computation times are related to the mapped software (i.e. SDF actors and channels) on a specific hardware architecture. For this reason, the annotation of any delays (in cycles) to the models takes place after the mapping process as shown in Fig. 3 top left corner.

The execution of an actor's computation phase for a specific architecture can be represented by a single delay $d \in \boldsymbol{D}_c$ for each execution. To model an actor, its execution time gets measured and the delay vector $\boldsymbol{D}_c$ gets derived from the measured values in a way that the distribution of possible delay in $\boldsymbol{D}_c$ follows the distribution measured delays of the characterizing actor. Each element in $\boldsymbol{D}_c$ of an actor is a sample from the measurement. In the SystemC implementation, those values get selected by a `GetDelay` function as shown in Fig. 3 top left part.

3.3 Communication Model

The communication timing model requires more effort compared to the computation model. To cover interference on the shared resources inside the analysis, there are four things to consider:

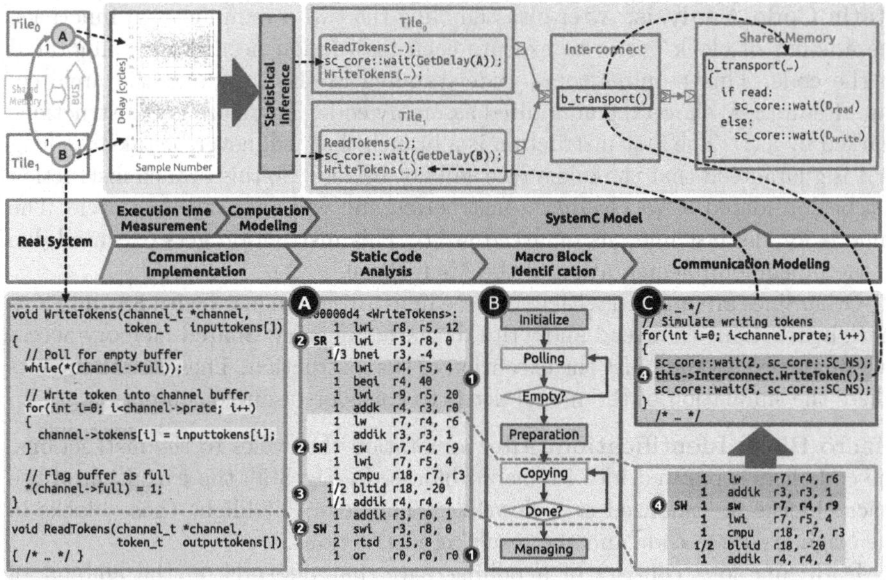

Fig. 3. This figure shows the whole process of creating a SystemC model (purple) from a real system (top left corner). In blue, the approach to model the computation time is showed, in green the process for modeling communication. (Color figure online)

- The communication between actors includes computational parts for accessing the private memory data and calculating addresses.
- The amount of traffic generated on the interconnect depends on the number of tokens that get communicated.
- The communication function needs to wait and check repetitively the state of the channels buffer to have tokens or space available (aka polling).
- To model bus contention as precisely as possible, the moment of shared memory access must be as accurate as possible.

Since the communication model is crucial, the behavior of this part is modeled in detail to come as close as possible to the real system. The process to get this model can be applied for many different architectures, we demonstrate it for a MicroBlaze architecture. The whole process is visualized in Fig. 3 on the bottom half using `WriteTokens` as example. The following paragraphs explain the single steps of this process. The same process has been done for `ReadTokens` as well.

Communication Implementation: Communication is done by two functions used in the implemented software. One function is `WriteTokens` that write tokens onto the shared memory (Used as example in Fig. 3 bottom left) and the other function is `ReadTokens` that reads from shared memory. So only those two functions need to be modeled in detail, while all other parts of the SDF application gets represented by its computation time $d \in \boldsymbol{D}_c$ (Sect. 3.2). The functions were analyzed in detail via static code analysis on instruction set level.

Static Code Analysis: After disassembling the two communication functions, the amount of clock cycles to execute each instruction needs to be annotated to the code. This requires some understanding of the code and the architecture. Figure 3 Ⓐ shows the annotated assembly code. There are two instructions marked by a ①. The first instruction is a branch that will never be taken as long as it is guaranteed that the token rate will not be zero. So this branch instruction can be considered a *No Operation* instruction and will only take one cycle. The same is for the last line, also marked as ①. This instruction gets executed due to the pipeline implementation of the MicroBlaze.

Other lines are marked with ②. These lines are commented with `SR` and `SW` to mark instructions that read and write to shared memory. Shared memory access takes more cycles than just the execution of the instruction. These are the points where the simulation of the model needs to consider resource contention.

Macro Block Identification: After annotation the cycles to the instructions, the code gets separated into its macro blocks. In Fig. 3 Ⓑ the execution of the macro blocks is visualized as a flowchart. The colors highlight those blocks in the original source code and the resulting instructions.

Both functions consists of a polling part that depends on the amount of polling iterations n (Fig. 3 Ⓑ upper loop), and a part where the tokens get copied which depends on the amount t of tokens (Fig. 3 Ⓑ lower loop). The amount n of polling iterations is determined during the analysis of the model and varies between each SDF execution iteration i. For a single processor setup with a valid scheduling, the amount of polling will always be one ($n = 1 \ \forall \ i$). The token transfer rate t equals the consume and produce rate of the actors that access the channel.

There may be some instructions that need to be considered for two macro blocks. For example in the instruction listing Fig. 3 Ⓐ mark ③ shows a situation where not only a branch instruction but also the one after is part of the *Copying* block and the *Managing* block. While for the branching instruction it is obvious since it can be taken or not, the next instruction gets executed in both situations due to the architecture specific pipeline implementation.

Communication Modeling: Next, the SystemC model can be built out of the macro blocks. This is shown in Fig. 3 Ⓒ for the *Copying* block. This block must be split into three parts. The 1st and the 3rd parts are the instructions before and after the shared memory access (③) and can be represented by a SystemC `wait` statement. The 2nd part is the shared memory access. The instruction for the shared memory access gets represented by a function call that will trigger the interconnect module of the SystemC system model. The read and write access to a shared resource gets represented by the delay vectors $\boldsymbol{D_r}$ and $\boldsymbol{D_w}$ that is represented the same way as for computation in Sect. 3.2.

By representing all macro blocks with `wait` statements and interconnect accesses, the communication can be modeled in detail. The interconnect module itself can now represent the behavior of the interconnect and the shared memory that is connected to the interconnect.

3.4 Statistical Model-Checking of Probabilistic SystemC Models

Statistical Model Checking (SMC) refers to a series of simulation-based techniques that can be used to answer two types of question [11]: (i) What is the probability that the system satisfies a property (*quantitative analysis*) and (ii) Is the probability that the system satisfies a property greater or equal to a threshold value (*qualitative analysis*)? The core idea of SMC is to monitor a finite set of simulation traces which are randomly generated by executing the probabilistic system. Then, statistical algorithms can be used to estimate the probability that the system satisfies the property. In the scope of this paper, we consider two algorithms: *Monte Carlo* with *Chernoff-Hoeffding bound* (Monte Carlo) for quantitative analysis and *Sequential Probability Ratio Test (SPRT)* for qualitative analysis (see details in [13]). Although SMC only provides an estimation, the algorithms presented below offer strict guarantees on the precision and the confidence of the test.

The statistical model-checker workflow that we consider takes as inputs a probabilistic model written in SystemC, a set of observed variables, a Bounded Linear Temporal Logic property (BLTL), and a series of confidence parameters needed by the statistical algorithms. First, users create a *configuration file* that especially contains the properties to be verified, the observed variables and the temporal resolution. The configuration file is then used by the *Monitor and aspect-advice generator* (MAG) tool proposed by V.C. Ngo in [12] to generate an aspect-advice file and a monitor model. The aspect-advice file declares the monitor as a *friend* class, so that the monitor can access to the private variables of the observed model. Then, the generated monitor and the probabilistic SystemC model are instrumented and compiled together to build an executable model.

In the simulation phase, Plasma Lab iteratively triggers the executable model to run simulations. The generated monitor observes and delivers the execution traces to Plasma Lab. An execution trace contains the observed variables and their simulation instances. The length of traces depends on the satisfaction of the formula to be verified. This length is finite because the temporal operators in the formulas are bounded. Similarly, the required number of execution traces depends on the statistical algorithms in use supported by Plasma Lab.

In the Sobel filter case study, we create the probabilistic SystemC model by using the distributions provided by GNU Scientific Library (GSL) [6]. These distributions represent the variation of the computation time of four actors of the Sobel filter. In the scope of this paper, we use the uniform and normal distributions. In each iteration of simulation of the probabilistic SystemC model, the computation time is assigned to a value that is randomly chosen following the distributions. In the SystemC model, the communication time is represented by `wait` statements. Wait durations depend on the estimated read/write delays and the number of polling states.

To apply the uniform distribution, the computation time is randomly chosen from a value in the interval of [BCET, WCET] of the measured data. While in the normal distribution, we consider the mean μ and the variance σ of the corresponding measured delays. It is desired to create a probability distribution that accurately reflects the distribution of the measured delays to verify the accuracy of the uniform/normal distributions. This is realized by reading a delay value of every actor from a text file that provides the raw measured computation time of this actor. We refer these raw data to the injected data. The distribution of the randomly selected delay values from the raw measured data file is uniform.

4 Experiments

In this section we describe our experiments and discuss the results. We use a SystemC implementation of our models described in Sect. 3. The timing behavior got characterized as described in Subsects. 3.2 and 3.3.

4.1 Experiment Definition

In our experiment we successively consider a single processor system and a multi processor system as shown in Fig. 2b. For the single processor setup, all actors of the SDF application shown in Fig. 2a are mapped to *Tile 0*. For the multi processor setup, two actors are mapped to *Tile 0* and two to *Tile 1*. This allows us to do an analysis with and without having to consider bus contention. We then compare the analysis results with focus on the communication model.

A shared memory is used for the data exchange between actors for both setups. In a multi processor setup, all processors have access to the shared memory, but not to the private memory of the different processors. The interconnect to the shared memory uses First-Come First-Serve arbitration and a Single-Beat transfer protocol. The channels are organized as FIFO buffers with 4 Bytes for each token and have a fixed buffer size.

The measurement technique we use in the experiments to get the different delay vectors of different components is based on one presented in [15]. An IP-Core which is connected via a dedicated AXI-Stream bus to communicate with each MicroBlaze processor without interfering with the main system buses, is used. The measured cycle-accurate timings were forwarded via an UART interface without influencing the timing behavior of the platform under observation. In order to achieve that, the code of the application is instrumented in a minimal way (for details refer to [15]).

4.2 End-to-end Timing Validation

In this subsection, we evaluate the best-case and worst-case end-to-end latencies, denoted in the following as BC latency and WC latency. We declare the estimated latency as an observed variable *t_latency* in the configuration file used for the SystemC model generation for Plasma Lab. To quantitatively evaluate the latency, the analyzed property is: "*What is the probability that the end-to-end latency stays within an interval* $[d_1, d_2]$?". This property can be expressed in BLTL with the operators F for "eventually": $\varphi = F_{\leq T}((t\_latency \geq d_1) \& (t\_latency < d_2))$.

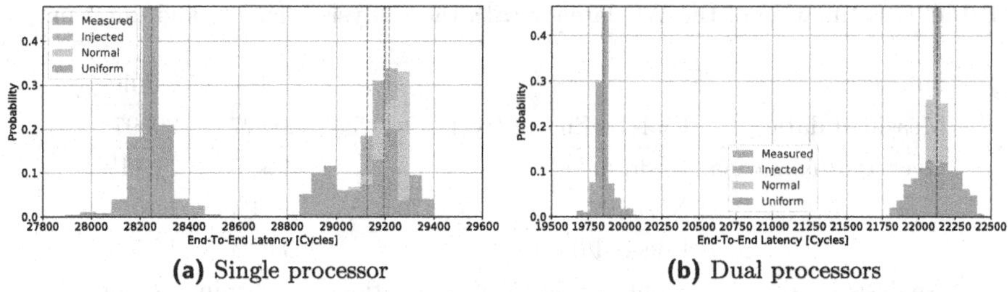

(a) Single processor **(b)** Dual processors

Fig. 4. Analysis results using the different distributions (normal/uniform) or the injected data for the computation time comparing with the measured results in the (a) single processor and (b) dual processors experiments.

This property is then analyzed through a finite set of simulations controlled by Plasma Lab. In each simulation, Plasma Lab observes the end-to-end latency of a particular iteration to determine the probability that the latency stays in the interval $[d_1, d_2]$. Figure 4 presents the probability distribution of the analysis results comparing to the measured results of the single processor and dual processors experiments. We use the Monte Carlo algorithm to analyze this property with the absolute error $\delta = 0.02$ and the confidence 98%.

In the single processor experiment, the normal distribution and the injected data show a similar shape of the distribution to the measured data (Fig. 4a). The uniform distribution shows the same range of variation comparing to the measured data (600 cycles), while a smaller variation (400 cycles) is observed in the case of the normal distribution and the injected data. The uniform data presents the most over-estimation comparing to injected and the normal distributed.

In the dual processors experiment, the analyzed results of the normal distribution and the injected data (Fig. 4b) show the similar range of variation (around 400 cycles) and the shape of the distribution comparing to the measured data. All the analyzed results clearly over-estimate the measured data and the uniform distribution still shows a more pessimistic over-estimation.

The fact that the uniform distribution can show a more pessimistic over-estimation is because in that case the WC computation time of each actor has a higher probability to be taken into account during the analysis process than in the normal distribution and the injected data.

4.3 Evaluation of Statistical Model Checking Methods

We want now to bound the WC latency within a threshold value d for the two experiments. Thus, we analyze the property: *"The cumulative probability that the end-to-end latency (t_latency) stays below time bound d"*. This property can be translated in BLTL with the operator G for "always": $\varphi = G_{\leq T}(t\_latency \leq d)$.

The temporal modal operator G is applied that allows us to check whether all the latencies of several successive iterations during the simulation time T stay below d. To analyze this property, we apply two statistical algorithms: Monte

Table 1. Estimation of the WC latency with the analysis accuracy and duration.

Subject		1 Tile	2 Tiles
Measured data	End-To-End in Cycles	28527	20097
Over-approximation	Uniform	3.55%	11.71%
	Normal	3.11%	11.01%
	Injected data	3.53%	11.51%
Analysis time	Monte Carlo (5757 simulations)	4.25 min	12 min
	SPRT (342 simulations)	11 s	22 s

Carlo (the absolute error $\delta = 0.02$ and the confidence 98%) and SPRT ($\alpha = \beta = 0.001, \delta = 0.01$). Table 1 summarizes the results of the over-approximation of the three cases and the analysis time for the uniform distribution.

In the single processor experiment, the WC latency of the probabilistic SystemC model applying the uniform, normal and injected data is bounded to 29541, 29415 and 29535 cycles, respectively, comparing to 28527 cycles of the WC measured latency. The uniform distribution shows the most pessimistic over-estimated WC latency of 3.55% compared to the measured data. In the dual processors experiment, we also get the over-estimation of the WC latency in all three cases and the over-estimation results is around 11%. The uniform distribution still presents the most pessimistic over-estimated results of 11.71% compared to the measured data.

For each experiment, the statistical algorithms observe the same number of simulation runs (see Table 1). Since SPRT observes a smaller number of simulation than Monte Carlo, it takes less analysis time to analyze one property. In the second experiment, the higher analysis time for each iteration leads to a higher overall analysis time compared to the first experiment. In the case that we only want to bound a probability with a threshold value, SPRT is more efficient than Monte Carlo in terms of analysis time.

4.4 Discussion

In the case of experiment with one processor the difference between the measured and approximated latency is acceptable. In the dual processors experiment the bias between the real-measured latency and the simulated latencies comes from a pessimistic communication model and the lack of consideration of data dependencies between actors.

The different range of variation in the experiments can be explained by the variation of *GX* and *GY*. They have a higher impact on a single processor system because there they sum up. On the dual processors system, their variation are less dominant because of the synchronizing behavior *ABS* that reduce the impact of the variation. So the variation of *GY* execution time does not matter as long as *GX* has not finished and vice versa.

The bias between the measured and the simulated latency comes from a pessimistic shared memory model and the lack of consideration of data dependencies between actors. In the real application, the two actors GX and GY have equal execution time in one iteration due to their symmetry. The ABS actor waits for the slowest dependent actor (GX, GY). In our simulation the delay of GX and GY gets selected independently. Therefore, the measured timings for faster executions get covered by the slower delays.

In the experiments, worst case end-to-end latency was estimated with an approximation close to 3% and 11% compared to real implementations. With our old models used inside UPPAAL SMC we got 15% for 2 tiles [16]. One benefit of our approach lies in the possibility to control the number of simulation runs given a level of confidence. In [16] we showed that a simulation (inside UPPAAL SMC) for low confidence (99.5%) can be several times faster than analyzing the same model using a formal approach. The results showed that the SPRT analysis of the model for the 2-tile configuration took 22 s. The more abstract Timed Automata model from [16], with a less detailed communication model and with the same analysis configuration, took about 10.3 s on the same CPU.

5 Summary and Future Work

In this work, we have presented a modeling setup that is used to evaluate the efficiency of SMC methods to analyze real-time properties of SDF applications running on multi-processor systems. Our approach uses real measured execution times to annotate a probabilistic SystemC model. The viability of our approach was demonstrated on a Sobel filter running on a 2 tile platform implemented on top of a Xilinx Zynq 7020. In contrast to traditional real-time analysis methods the SMC approach requires a more sophisticated model of the execution time distribution and thus can tackle the limitations to deliver fast yet accurate timing estimations. Our experiments showed that the selection of the probabilistic distribution function is crucial for the quality of analysis results. The SPRT simulation method proved significantly reduced analysis time compared to Monte-Carlo. By controlling the number of simulation runs, a trade-off between high confidence and fast analysis time is possible. In future work we will increase the number of tiles to evaluate the scalability of our approach. Additionally we want to improve our model by considering data dependencies since SystemC allows us to also do a functional simulation of our system.

References

1. Association, I.S., et al.: IEEE Standard for Standard Systemc Language Reference Manual. IEEE Computer Society, New York (2012)
2. Basu, A., et al.: Rigorous component-based system design using the bip framework. IEEE Softw. **28**(3), 41–48 (2011). https://doi.org/10.1109/MS.2011.27
3. Cazorla, F.J., et al.: Proxima: improving measurement-based timing analysis through randomisation and probabilistic analysis. In: 2016 Euromicro Conference on Digital System Design (DSD), pp. 276–285. IEEE (2016)

4. Cazorla, F.J., et al.: PROARTIS: probabilistically analyzable real-time systems. ACM Trans. Embed. Comput. Syst. (TECS) **12**(2s), 94 (2013)
5. David, A., et al.: Statistical model checking for networks of priced timed automata. In: Fahrenberg, U., Tripakis, S. (eds.) FORMATS 2011. LNCS, vol. 6919, pp. 80–96. Springer, Heidelberg (2011). https://doi.org/10.1007/978-3-642-24310-3_7
6. GSL. https://www.gnu.org/software/gsl/
7. Jegourel, C., Legay, A., Sedwards, S.: A platform for high performance statistical model checking - plasma. In: Flanagan, C., König, B. (eds.) TACAS 2012. Lecture Notes in Computer Science, vol. 7214, pp. 498–503. Springer, Heidelberg (2012)
8. Kumar, A.: Analysis, design and management of multimedia multi-processor systems. Ph.D. thesis, Eindhoven University of Technology (2009)
9. Kwiatkowska, M., Norman, G., Parker, D.: PRISM 4.0: verification of probabilistic real-time systems. In: Gopalakrishnan, G., Qadeer, S. (eds.) CAV 2011. LNCS, vol. 6806, pp. 585–591. Springer, Heidelberg (2011). https://doi.org/10.1007/978-3-642-22110-1_47
10. Lee, E.A., Messerschmitt, D.G.: Synchronous data flow. Proc. IEEE **75**(9), 1235–1245 (1987)
11. Legay, A., Delahaye, B., Bensalem, S.: Statistical model checking: an overview. In: Barringer, H., et al. (eds.) RV 2010. LNCS, vol. 6418, pp. 122–135. Springer, Heidelberg (2010). https://doi.org/10.1007/978-3-642-16612-9_11
12. Ngo, V.C., Legay, A., Quilbeuf, J.: Statistical model checking for SystemC models. In: 2016 IEEE 17th International Symposium on High Assurance Systems Engineering, pp. 197–204 (2016)
13. Nouri, A., Bozga, M., Moinos, A., Legay, A., Bensalem, S.: Building faithful high-level models and performance evaluation of Manycore embedded systems. In: ACM/IEEE International Conference on Formal Methods and Models for Codesign (2014)
14. Nouri, A., Bensalem, S., Bozga, M., Delahaye, B., Jegourel, C., Legay, A.: Statistical model checking QoS properties of systems with SBIP. Int. J. Softw. Tools Technol. Transfer **17**(2), 171–185 (2014)
15. Schlaak, C., Fakih, M., Stemmer, R.: Power and execution time measurement methodology for SDF applications on FPGA-based MPSoCs. arXiv preprint arXiv:1701.03709 (2017)
16. Stemmer, R., Schlender, H., Fakih, M., Grüttner, K., Nebel, W.: Probabilistic state-based RT-analysis of SDFGs on MPSoCs with shared memory communication. In: 2019 Design, Automation & Test in Europe Conference & Exhibition (DATE), March 2019

Software Passports for Automated Performance Anomaly Detection of Cyber-Physical Systems

Uraz Odyurt[1(✉)], Hugo Meyer[1], Andy D. Pimentel[1], Evangelos Paradas[2], and Ignacio Gonzalez Alonso[2]

[1] Informatics Institute (IvI), University of Amsterdam, Amsterdam, The Netherlands
{u.odyurt,h.d.meyer,a.d.pimentel}@uva.nl
[2] ASML Netherlands B.V., Veldhoven, The Netherlands
{evangelos.paradas,ignacio.alonso}@asml.com

Abstract. Software performance anomaly detection is a major challenge in complex industrial cyber-physical systems. The automated comparison of runtime execution metrics to reference ones provides a potential solution. We introduce the concept of software passports, intended to act as a signature construct for runtime performance behaviour of reference executions. Our software passport design is based on Extra-Functional Behaviour (EFB) metrics. Amongst such metrics, our focus has been especially on CPU time, read and write communication event counts of different processes. The notion of phases for systems with repetitive tasks during their execution and its fundamental role in our software passports has also been elaborated. We employ regression modelling of our collected data for comparative purposes. The comparison reveals inconsistencies between the execution at hand and the software passport, if present. Such inconsistencies are strong indicators for presence of performance anomalies. Our design is capable of detecting synthetically introduced performance anomalies to the real execution tracing data from a semiconductor photolithography machine.

Keywords: Software passports · Performance anomaly detection · Industrial cyber-physical systems · Regression modelling

1 Introduction

There has been an increasing dependence on complex embedded systems within the industry. As every generation of microprocessors becomes more capable and more power-efficient than its predecessor, embedded nodes are deployed more than ever. Capabilities of embedded, i.e., purpose-built, computing power has

This paper is composed as part of the research project 14208, titled *"Interactive DSL for Composable EFB Adaptation using Bi-simulation and Extrinsic Coordination (iDAPT)"*, funded by The Netherlands Organisation for Scientific Research (NWO).

D. N. Pnevmatikatos et al. (Eds.): SAMOS 2019, LNCS 11733, pp. 255–268, 2019.
https://doi.org/10.1007/978-3-030-27562-4_18

allowed companies to develop increasingly complex systems involving heterogeneous elements, such as hardware architectures and operating systems, as well as many connected nodes. One major concern for any computing system is the occurrence of performance anomalies. These anomalies may be short-lived with negligible effects, may be constantly reoccurring and affecting the system, or may lead to an unresponsive state. Whichever the case, for anomalies to be avoided, there is a need for *anomaly detection*.

The analysis of performance behaviour and anomaly detection has become more and more time consuming, considering the sharp increase in the complexity of industrial cyber-physical systems. It is difficult to pin-point the actual anomaly, when it is happening, and where it is happening. This translates to increased number of costly downtimes for the types of systems involved in high-tech industry, e.g., a semiconductor photolithography machine.

It is our intention to tackle this challenge by developing methods and tools, facilitating automated monitoring and management of *Extra Functional Behaviour (EFB)*. In this context, EFB are the collection of behavioural metrics of a system, which are not part of its functional description, i.e., EFB are not encoded in software. However, there is an intimate dependency relationship between functional and non-functional behaviour, such that the non-functional behaviour is a consequence of the combination of functional behaviour, plus applied environmental variables. Input data is considered as an environmental variable as well. Examples of EFB metrics are CPU utilisation, occupied memory size, read and write frequencies, message sizes, delays, and lifetimes, amongst others. Throughout this paper, we will be considering CPU time, number of read events, number of write events, as well as durations of events and process executions as our main metrics to explain methods and demonstrate findings.

It is imperative to have mechanisms for anomalous performance behaviour detection in complex industrial cyber-physical systems, more than conventional computing systems. Any unexpected performance behaviour collected from the software portion of an industrial cyber-physical system is a strong indication of the whole system behaving outside its anticipated boundaries. In other words, the reliability of the whole system, depends on the reliability of its software. This is not an easy task. However, considering the operational specificities of these systems, there are angles to be exploited. Such types of systems are highly repetitive in the tasks they perform by definition. For instance, a semiconductor photolithography machine is designed to perform collections of tasks over and over for a large number of wafers. Another example is a radar system, applying same object detection workflows and algorithms over and over. It would be a generally valid expectation to have similar EFB metric values during the execution of similar tasks, as long as the system is performing correctly. This knowledge will serve us as a precursor to developing reference executions and EFB metric readings, to be compared with future ones. Such repetitive nature will allow us to divide the execution in compartments and consider clear and separate parts.

To be able to detect deviations from the expected performance behaviour, there is a need for comparative analysis of monitored performance behaviour against reference ones. We introduce *software passports* as a representation of these references. Software passports can be considered in two types, static and dynamic. Further analysis will also provide clear insights regarding the process or processes responsible for anomalous behaviour, as well as their contribution, since our software passport design includes separate regression models per every process involved in the execution. This root cause identification may be done in an automated fashion, if the comparison results are fairly clear-cut. We can summarise a high-level view of our approach towards anomaly detection using software passports in Fig. 1, including the optional analysis for identification of the root cause and a possible actuation step to rectify the issue. The whole workflow is to be continuously repeated. Our main focus in this paper has also been highlighted in the figure.

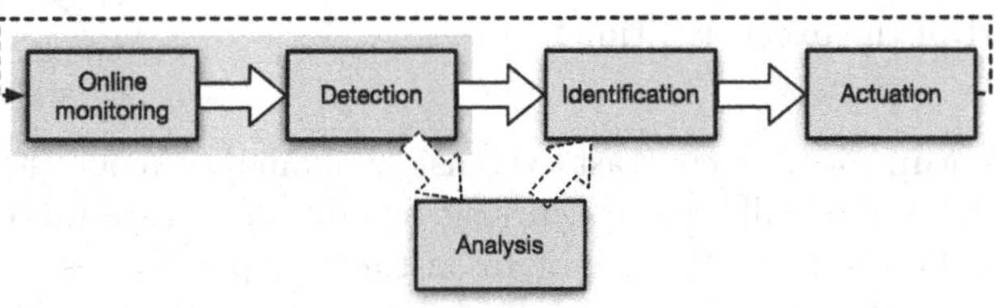

Fig. 1. The high-level view of our anomaly detection workflow, including the optional analysis for identification and this paper's main focus (highlighted in yellow) (Color figure online)

Aside from the software passport's definition and its varieties, we provide the experimental results of our early prototype. We compare software passports generated based on reference runs, against executions involving deliberately injected anomalies. The following section provides background information and our industrial use-case. Section 3 describes our software passport design, continued by a description of our methodology in Sect. 4. After elaborating achieved experimental results in Sect. 5, we provide related work and our conclusions in Sect. 6 and Sect. 7, respectively.

2 Background and Industrial Use-Case

The notion of performance anomaly is especially important for industrial embedded systems, as it is critical for these systems to deliver the functionality when it is being demanded. For instance, a semiconductor photolithography machine is designed to deliver a certain production yield and it has to fulfil such requirements, ideally at all times.

2.1 Performance Anomalies

Before we continue, let us first define what performance anomalies and faults are. A *performance anomaly* is any *readily* detectable deviation in the system's performance behaviour. For instance, if a computational job takes significantly longer than it should to be fulfilled, a performance anomaly has occurred. Detecting the actual *fault* causing the performance anomaly however, requires *insight* and analysis of the internal interactions of the system. As such, a performance anomaly is the result of a fault, but at the same time, not all faults will necessarily lead to a performance anomaly, as performance behaviour also depends on environmental variables. Accordingly, we define two types of anomalies, namely, transient and persistent anomalies.

Transient Anomalies. A transient anomaly is visible for a short period of time, or occurs only a few times. In such cases, either the fault is a short-lived one, or its impact to the overall execution is rather contained. For instance, with regards to timeliness, transient anomalies could be seen as delayed tasks in a contained part of the execution timeline.

Persistent Anomalies. In contrast to transient anomalies, a persistent anomaly is of the type that either will keep reoccurring, or will create cascading delays for all onwards tasks. This could be because of, for instance, dependencies between tasks. The overall cost to the execution is higher for such anomalies. Figure 2 depicts conceptual representations of transient and persistent anomalies alongside the comparison of their effect on the execution time. This is a rather simplified example and intends to convey the definitions of introduced constructs.

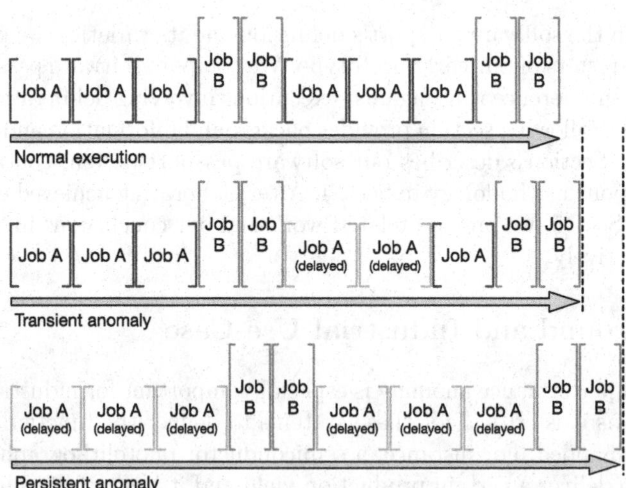

Fig. 2. The impact of transient and persistent performance anomalies in systems with repetitive tasks

2.2 Industrial Use-Case

Our industrial use-case and the primary source of our data is ASML's semiconductor photolithography systems. These systems are typical examples of complex heterogeneous cyber-physical systems. They involve many computing nodes with different hardware architectures, running different operating systems and communicating via different messaging subsystems. Still, there is a close interdependency amongst different computing nodes, making these systems highly sensitive to untimeliness. In short, it is highly important to assure timely behaviour of different cyber elements in these cyber-physical systems, detect performance anomalies, and possibly react to them. We would like to reiterate that the most important criteria to be fulfilled here is the timeliness of different machine tasks, performed by multiple processes.

3 Software Passports

Our software passport design is intended to act as a reference for executed processes to be compared against. Software passports include EFB metric recordings from previous executions. We consider two types of software passports, *static* and *dynamic*.

Static Software Passports. Static software passports are generated from previous reference executions as post-mortem constructs. Any current execution that is supposed to match a reference one can be compared against the latter's software passport. The amount of deviation could potentially reveal performance anomalies. Interactions related to static software passports are depicted in Fig. 3.

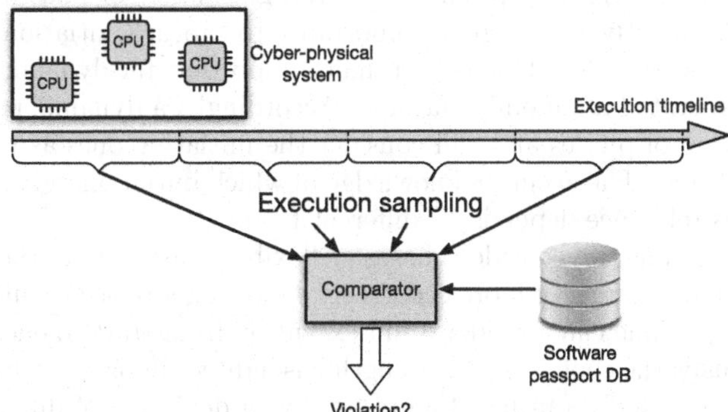

Fig. 3. High-level view of static software passports and their usage

Dynamic Software Passports. Dynamic passports as shown in Fig. 4 and as the name suggests, are created in an online fashion, taking the immediate previous steps as references to the upcoming ones. That is, initial stages of an execution involving repetitive tasks could be used for passport generation and the following ones will be checked against them. This may also be in combination with previously generated static passports.

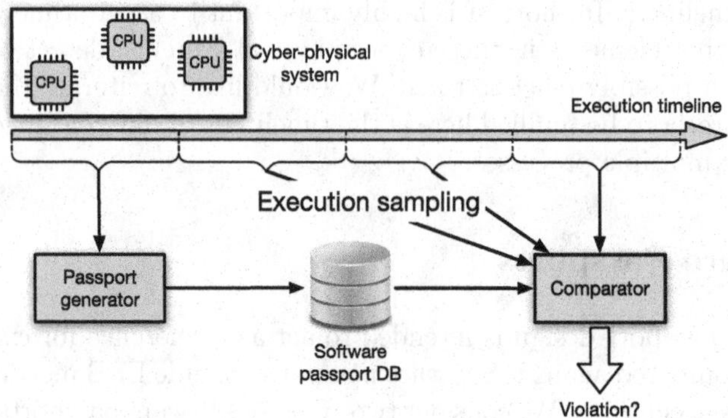

Fig. 4. High-level view of dynamic software passports and their usage

3.1 Execution Phases

With that in mind, let us go through the concept of execution phases. A phase is considered as the duration in which the system is performing a recognisable and contained part of its overall job. Remember that we are dealing with a system that executes repetitive tasks, making the recognisability of phases even more tangible. Consequently, it is of great importance to capture initiation and termination of phases correctly. This is even more important for dynamic passports, as they are generated in an online fashion. Accordingly, a dynamic passport will detect repetition of phases and will consider the initiating ones as reference for the upcoming ones. The accurate knowledge of which initial phase, or phases are to be taken as reference depends on different factors.

At the same time, we consider phases as flexible constructs in the sense that one can decide how large, or more accurately, how long a phase should be. As an extreme example, one can consider a full execution from start to end as a single phase. Obviously, the choice of phase length has a direct impact on the generated software passport and its utility. Figure 5 shows a depiction of different *atomic phases* for different repetitive jobs, as well as larger *combo-phases* composed of a repeated pattern of atomic phases.

To put this into context, consider that a semiconductor photolithography machine's jobs are defined as batches of wafers. Each wafer could employ a different image for die exposure and these batches are all queued up in the

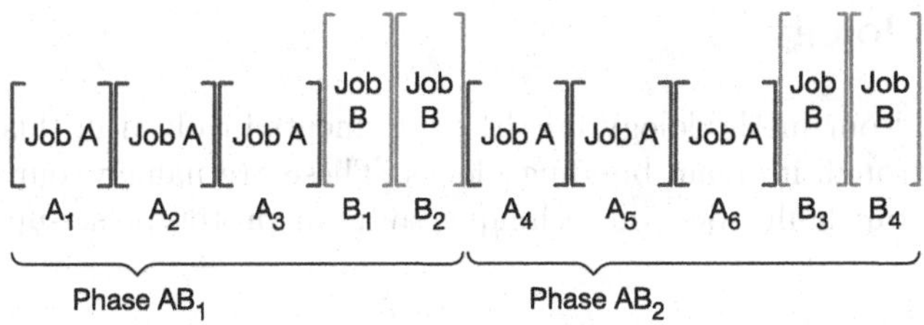

Fig. 5. Atomic and combo-phases

machine's job queue. One can naively consider a whole queue of wafer batches, a single batch, a single wafer, or a single image exposure as phases from large to small, respectively.

A software passport can have different formats. Some of the considerations influencing this choice are types of collected data, i.e., EFB metrics in our case; phase structure, i.e., whether the passport is representing combo-phases or atomic ones; and gaps present in data point sets, i.e., how distant clusters of data points are from one another. We will mention two possible formats here, a passport including average, maximum and minimum values for a phase dataset, and a passport including one or more regression models. The immediate advantage of the latter is its compactness and relative sophistication. For our experiments, we have considered and built passports using the regression format. Depending on the distribution of points one can choose different regression modelling techniques. We have considered linear, multiple linear and polynomial regression models. Regression models can capture the trend of different metrics over time.

3.2 Data Collection

An appropriate way of sampling arbitrary portions of an industrial cyber-physical system's performance behaviour is through EFB metrics. EFB metrics provide extra-functional performance readings of a system's execution, which are influenced by both functional behaviour and environmental conditions. Although EFB metrics provide a complete view over the system, the challenge present here is the sheer amount of available and collected data for this type of monitoring.

An efficient, but still complete, technique in order to track system behaviour is to collect monitoring data through major communication subsystems [10,11]. In this method, i.e., *communication-centric monitoring*, we are planting snippets as probes in the interface library code of the major communication subsystem. This library is used by many processes and thus, such an invasive probing allows us to capture calls from any user of the subsystem and provides us with details on communication and computation events. Though not a full picture of the system's operation, communication-centric monitoring provides sufficient detail on performance behaviour trends [10,11]. After applying necessary transformations on the collected traces, we will end up with traces composed of *read*, *write* and *compute* events, allowing us to perform a *replay simulation*.

4 Methodology

To understand our methodology for the experiments involved in this paper, we have to go through its main building blocks. These are namely, our simulation environment, our fault injection technique, and our prototype set-up.

4.1 Simulation Environment

The aforementioned replay simulation closely resembles the actual system's behavioural trends and is interchangeable with it. Previously, we have shown [10, 11] the power of communication-centric modelling of cyber-physical systems and how its deployment can facilitate the performance behaviour analysis of such systems. This facilitation is mainly about having valid performance trend detection, while reducing the monitoring effort by considering a smaller active portion of the system. As a result, a smaller, but impactful part of the system will be considered for EFB metrics collection, followed by performance trend detection.

Accordingly, collected traces will be used to generate a model of the system, to calibrate this model for conformance with the actual execution conditions, and eventually, to run the calibrated model as a replay simulation. The exact same monitoring performed on the actual system is also present within the replay simulation. This means that one of the outputs of our replay simulation is tracing data with the exact same format of the tracing data used for its calibration. That is how we validated the replay capability of our simulation.

There is also a need for presence of critical states in the system, to be able to demonstrate the potential of software passports in action. The replay simulation of the system will accept manipulated input to create scenarios resembling critical states. In other words, the replay simulation is to be used as a generator of monitoring data for fault injection. Thus, the output of the replay simulation can be considered as tracing data collected from a system with anomalous performance behaviour. The reason we are using the output of such a replay simulator and not the actual system for passport generation is that the fault injection cannot be done on the actual system at this point.

4.2 Fault Injection

Fault injection can turn into a vast topic on its own rather quickly. Within the scope of this paper, we have focused on a specific set of fault injections. As we have explained before [10,11], events involve process idleness and CPU access delay. Duration of an event (t_E), which is the elapsed time from its initialisation (t_{ini_E}) till its end (t_{end_E}), is made up of CPU access delay ($delay_E$), CPU time ($comp_E$) and idleness ($idle_E$), such that

$$t_E = t_{end_E} - t_{ini_E} = delay_E + comp_E + idle_E.$$

We are considering synthetic increases to the duration of the event ($t_{E_{synth}}$), which means that we are increasing the combined duration of CPU access delay ($delay_E$) and idleness ($idle_E$), such that

$$t_{E_{synth}} = comp_E + (delay_E + idle_E + delay_{synth}).$$

Note that CPU access delay and idleness result from different conditions and we are not able to distinguish between them using the deployed tracing mechanism. While CPU access delay is simply a wait before CPU availability, idleness could be a result of I/O waits, or functional and data dependencies to other processes. Nevertheless, our synthetic manipulation of traces does not depend on the distinction of the two, since we will be adding to the overall delay of an event, i.e., anything other than $comp_E$.

4.3 Prototype Set-Up

To assess the detection potential of our software passports, we have designed two experiment workflows, one for generation of software passports, and the other to demonstrate their usage as a reference. An overview of our workflows can be seen in Fig. 6.

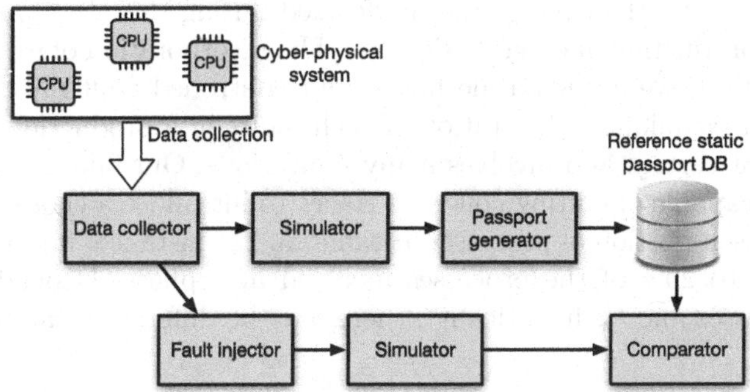

Fig. 6. Software passport generation and fault injection workflows

Passport Generation Workflow. Considering the top flow given in Fig. 6, the data collector includes our communication-centric tracing techniques and tools [10,11]. What has been added here is the phase discovery. Each task of the system involves a number of processes. Considering the repetitive tasks we are dealing with, as explained in Sect. 3, we are able to detect per process start and end times for the set of events involved in processing of, in our case, different wafers. In this case, the detection is based on the dips in the CPU utilisation graph of the execution. For instance, a batch of ten wafers will have eleven distinctly observable dips, roughly representing transitions between wafers. This allows us to clearly separate each wafer's processing duration as a single phase.

After choosing one of the phases, the data representing this phase, which is part of the whole reference execution, is used as an input for our replay simulation. Same metrics are also collected from the simulation as output, which is extremely close to the real execution. The passport generator will consider per process cumulative CPU time, cumulative read events, and cumulative write events to generate regression models for the software passport. Usage of cumulative values in performance monitoring can be desirable, as it provides a monotonically increasing function.

Fault Injection Workflow. As shown in the bottom flow of Fig. 6, fault injection is applied on tracing data before executing a simulation based on it. The output of the simulator and execution times of processes are collected and compared to reference executions. If the execution time is significantly longer, the collection of points for per process CPU time, read events and write events will be checked against relevant software passports. We can check the goodness of fit for a software passport's regression model, given the collection of metrics in time as our observation. There are multiple techniques to check goodness of fit, but within the scope of this paper, we are using *coefficient of determination (R^2)* and *Root-Mean-Square Deviation (RMSD)* tests.

5 Experimental Results

As indicated before, the experiments performed during this study are based on a mixture of production and synthetic data. The incorporation of synthetic data was a necessity as we needed a mechanism for controlled fault injection to test our developed techniques. Generation of such faults in a production system, on demand, is not certain and involves many limitations. Our fault injector implementation is capable of editing collected traces to introduce a chosen amount of delay to a chosen portion of processes at random. For instance, we can introduce 10% of delay to 20% of the processes involved in a phase. Depending on the delayed processes and their criticality, there may be different total phase delays introduced.

5.1 Detection Results

In order to demonstrate our implementation of software passports and anomaly detection in action, we will present one of the processes from the tested phase. The detection includes two steps. First, the *length of the phase*, i.e., the execution duration of the phase, is checked. Note that the length of a phase should not be mistaken with the execution duration of a process in the phase, as the latter could be shorter. A 10% or above increase will be followed by a comparison against the software passport for that phase. The software passport includes three regression models per every process involved in the phase, for cumulative CPU time (depicted in Fig. 7a), for cumulative read events (depicted in Fig. 7b), and for cumulative write events.

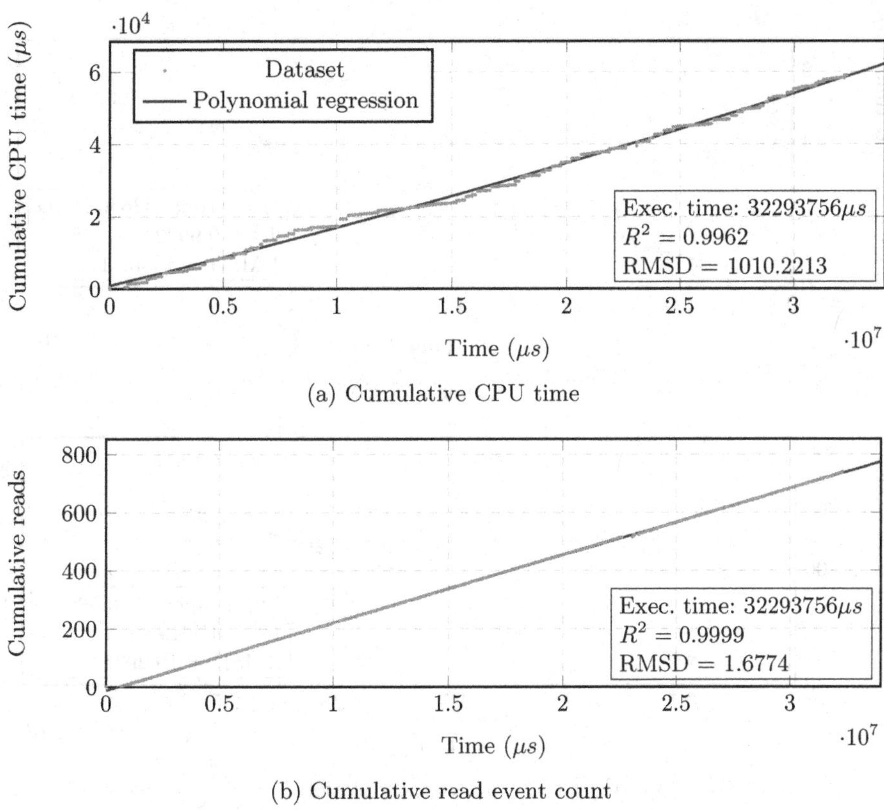

(a) Cumulative CPU time

(b) Cumulative read event count

Fig. 7. Two software passports for an example process involved in the tested phase, with polynomial regressions, $(7.994\text{e}{-12})x^2 + (1.534\text{e}{-3})x + 890.944$ and $(-7.755\text{e}{-15})x^2 + (2.343\text{e}{-5})x - 12.813$, for cases (a) and (b), respectively

These regressions' goodness of fit is checked against the current execution tracing data of the phase, after which a 5% or above difference between R^2 values, or RMSD values, will be interpreted as a violation. Figure 8a and b show the example process' CPU time and read event count violations compared to its passports, respectively. Note that there is no write event count violation, as this process is a consumer of data and does not perform any writes using the communication subsystem. Also, the library we use for regression model generation does support simple linear, multiple linear and curvilinear regressions. The choice will depend on the data, though linear regression models are the most common [6].

A comparison, based on regression models is especially useful for production environments, where the comparison happens in real-time. During online sampling, the comparison does not have to be postponed until reaching the end of the phase under scrutiny. Partial sampling, resulting in data points for a portion of the phase, will already be used for the goodness of fit check. The goodness of

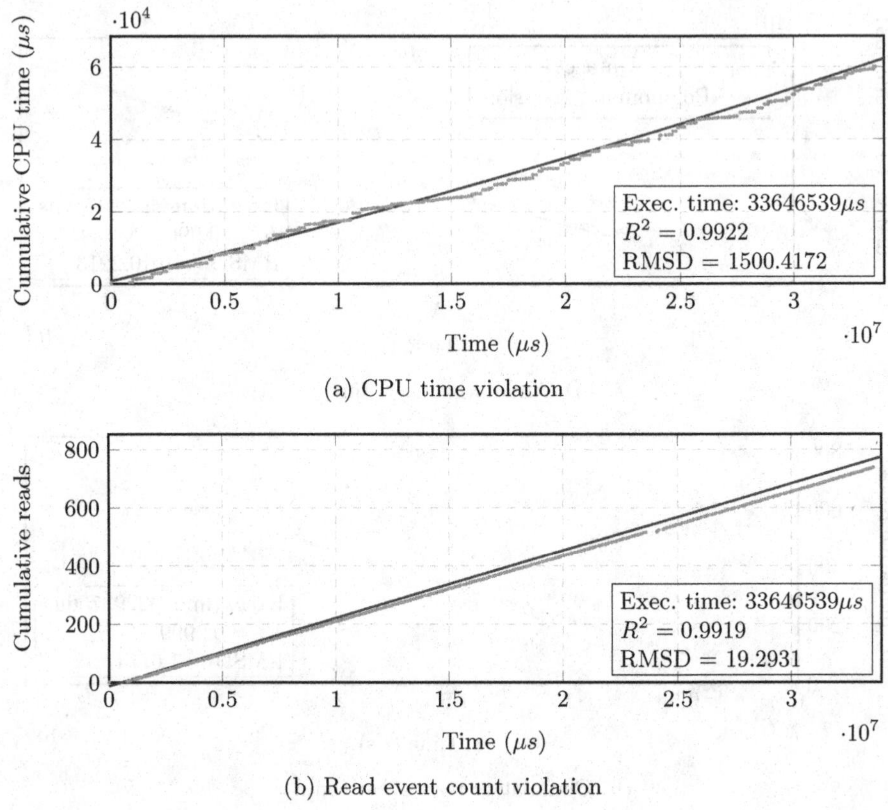

(a) CPU time violation

(b) Read event count violation

Fig. 8. Software passport violations for different metrics of an example process involved in the tested phase

fit check provides us with the analysis capability, revealing the contribution of different processes, which is not detectable solely based on the execution time.

5.2 Towards Identification

As it was shown in Fig. 1, to be able to perform identification, i.e., detect the root cause of the violation at hand, one might have to carry on with extra analysis. As we have separate passports per metric and per process in our design, it would be fairly straight forward to detect the violating processes. If the deviation in these contributing processes happens around the same time, or there is an obvious single initiator process with a large amount of deviation, we will have a clear-cut case. However, as there are usually functional and data dependencies amongst processes, interpreting violations will not be trivial. The link between metric violations and application-level behaviour of the system should be taken into account as well.

As part of our future work, there will be a need for a better understanding of behavioural variations and performing verifications, e.g., visual verification. A complex scenario could be simplified by breaking some of the irregular phases into smaller ones. Generating different non-linear regression models, such as isotonic regression, should also be considered.

6 Related Work

The common use of regression models as a statistical tool for data estimation and inference is well argued in the literature [3,6]. This is especially true for different performance parameters of application processes as Lee and Brooks suggest [8]. Lee et al. also employ the notion of piecewise polynomial regression [9]. We have conducted a comparable strategy by dividing a timeline into meaningful phases, based on drastic changes in the values of CPU utilisation. Though, our division criteria aims at having meaningful and repeatable phases. We are not using all points from an execution, i.e., certain unsuitable parts are being omitted. Regression modelling has also been taken advantage of by Joseph et al. and Barnes et al., for correlating micro-architectural parameters with processor performance [7] and exploring parallel programme scalability [1], respectively. Regression modelling has been the choice of Torr and Murray [12], as well as Chen et al. [4], within the domain of image processing.

When it comes to anomaly detection in general, a comprehensive overview can be grasped by looking at two elaborate surveys by Chandola et al. [2] and Ibidunmoye et al. [5]. Our categorisation of anomalies as transient and permanent certainly fits the categorisation given in [5]. It is worth repeating that our focus for data collection is on EFB, which is arguably rather similar to the notion of Key Performance Indicators (KPI) used in other works. Another characteristic, separating our work, is its applicability to industrial cyber-physical systems, which by default involve repetitive tasks.

7 Conclusion and Future Work

In this work, we have shown that the use of software passports can be advantageous for performance anomaly detection of systems with repetitive tasks. We have argued in favour of a segmenting approach when characterising repetitive tasks and we have elaborated different phase constructs, as well as software passports based on them. We have also described our experiment set-up and detection results achieved using our prototype. We can conclude that though an initial version, software passports display a promising potential as a reference construct for comparative performance anomaly detection.

Our fault injection technique for anomaly introduction was based on manipulating simulations of the real system, also previously developed by us. This can be followed by considering fault injection within the actual system. A more complete software passport design is also part of our future work agenda. For instance, finding the right balance between the phase length, passport's detection capability, and computational effort for passport generation is the key for online deployment of dynamic passports. Additionally, not every change in performance behaviour of a system is an indication of anomalous behaviour. We would like to develop soft and hard limits for violation detection and interpretations based on them, leading to a more elaborate detection of anomalies. Another lead we would like to follow is the categorisation of different types of anomalies, which will facilitate the decision making process when choosing effective actuation mechanisms.

References

1. Barnes, B.J., Rountree, B., Lowenthal, D.K., Reeves, J., de Supinski, B., Schulz, M.: A regression-based approach to scalability prediction. In: Proceedings of the 22nd Annual International Conference on Supercomputing, ICS 2008, pp. 368–377 (2008)
2. Chandola, V., Banerjee, A., Kumar, V.: Anomaly detection: a survey. ACM Comput. Surv. **41**(3), 15:1–15:58 (2009)
3. Chatfield, C.: Model uncertainty, data mining and statistical inference. J. Roy. Stat. Soc. Ser. A (Stat. Soc.) **158**(3), 419–466 (1995)
4. Chen, D., Shao, X., Hu, B., Su, Q.: Simultaneous wavelength selection and outlier detection in multivariate regression of near-infrared spectra. Anal. Sci. **21**(2), 161–166 (2005)
5. Ibidunmoye, O., Hernández-Rodriguez, F., Elmroth, E.: Performance anomaly detection and bottleneck identification. ACM Comput. Surv. **48**(1), 4:1–4:35 (2015)
6. Jain, R.: The Art of Computer Systems Performance Analysis: Techniques for Experimental Design, Measurement, Simulation, and Modeling. Wiley, New York (1990)
7. Joseph, P.J., Thazhuthaveetil, M.J.: Construction and use of linear regression models for processor performance analysis. In: The Twelfth International Symposium on High-Performance Computer Architecture 2006, pp. 99–108 (2006)
8. Lee, B.C., Brooks, D.M.: Accurate and efficient regression modeling for microarchitectural performance and power prediction. In: Proceedings of the 12th International Conference on Architectural Support for Programming Languages and Operating Systems, pp. 185–194. ASPLOS XII (2006)
9. Lee, B.C., Brooks, D.M., de Supinski, B.R., Schulz, M., Singh, K., McKee, S.A.: Methods of inference and learning for performance modeling of parallel applications. In: Proceedings of the 12th ACM SIGPLAN Symposium on Principles and Practice of Parallel Programming, PPoPP 2007, pp. 249–258 (2007)
10. Meyer, H., Odyurt, U., Polstra, S., Paradas, E., Alonso, I.G., Pimentel, A.D.: On the effectiveness of communication-centric modelling of complex embedded systems. In: 2018 IEEE International Conference on Parallel Distributed Processing with Applications (ISPA), pp. 979–986, December 2018
11. Odyurt, U., Meyer, H., Polstra, S., Paradas, E., Alonso, I.G., Pimentel, A.D.: Work-in-progress: communication-centric analysis of complex embedded computing systems. In: 2018 International Conference on Embedded Software (EMSOFT), pp. 1–3, September 2018
12. Philip, H.S., Torr, D.W.M.: Outlier detection and motion segmentation, vol. 2059 (1993)

Modeling Nested for Loops with Explicit Parallelism in Synchronous DataFlow Graphs

Alexandre Honorat[1(✉)], Karol Desnos[1], Maxime Pelcat[1,2], and Jean-François Nezan[1]

[1] Univ Rennes, INSA Rennes, CNRS, IETR - UMR 6164, 35000 Rennes, France
{alexandre.honorat,karol.desnos,maxime.pelcat, jean-francois.nezan}@insa-rennes.fr

[2] Institut Pascal, UCA, SIGMA, CNRS - UMR 6602, Clermont-Ferrand, France

Abstract. A common problem when developing signal processing applications is to expose and exploit parallelism in order to improve both throughput and latency. Many programming paradigms and models have been introduced to serve this purpose, such as the Synchronous DataFlow (SDF) Model of Computation (MoC). SDF is used especially to model signal processing applications. However, the main difficulty when using SDF is to choose an appropriate granularity of the application representation, for example when translating imperative functions into SDF actors. In this paper, we propose a method to model the parallelism of perfectly nested `for` loops with any bounds and explicit parallelism, using SDF. This method makes it possible to easily adapt the granularity of the expressed parallelism, thanks to the introduced concept of SDF *iterators*. The usage of SDF iterators is then demonstrated on the Scale Invariant Feature Transform (SIFT) image processing application.

Keywords: SDF · Parallelism

1 Introduction

Signal processing applications are generally compute intensive and constrained in terms of throughput and latency. For example, the throughput of video displays is constrained in Frame Per Second (FPS). Parallelization of such applications is the key to meet their throughput and latency requirements: when possible, data are processed simultaneously by different Processing Elements (PEs).

Parallelization of `for` loops can be achieved automatically in the code through OpenMP, or directly using threads. However, it is not possible to handle

This project has received funding from the European Union's Horizon 2020 research and innovation programme under grant agreement №732105 (project CERBERO) and from the Région Bretagne (France) under grant ARED 2017 ADAMS. We also thank Antoine Morvan and Florian Arrestier for their valuable comments.

D. N. Pnevmatikatos et al. (Eds.): SAMOS 2019, LNCS 11733, pp. 269–280, 2019.
https://doi.org/10.1007/978-3-030-27562-4_19

all the cases with OpenMP, as distributed memory; moreover threads require to manually add synchronizations and communications in the code. Thus, applications are usually *modeled*, in order to, first, expose their parallelism, and secondly, analyze this available parallelism and synthesize efficient schedules. A common model for signal processing applications is the Synchronous DataFlow (SDF) [10] Model of Computation (MoC), in which applications, e.g. video encoders [16], are modeled by SDF graphs. Vertices of SDF graphs encapsulate the processing code while edges model the data transfers. SDF graphs express parallelism in two ways: by the different paths in the graphs (task parallelism), and by the possible executions of the same process on different chunks of data (data parallelism). Only static applications where all communications are known in advance, and fixed, can be modeled by SDF graphs. Thus, it is possible to derive static schedules from SDF graphs. One can model single `for` loops by SDF graphs, as long as the loop can be divided in sub-parts accessing chunks of data of equal size, to respect the restriction of fixed amount of data communication. However, there is no general technique to model multiple nested `for` loops in the SDF MoC, especially when bounds of the inner loops are varying.

The contribution of this paper is the modeling, by SDF graphs, of multiple perfectly nested loops with explicit parallelism and variable bounds in their inner loops. In loops with explicit parallelism, all iterations are independent. Perfectly nested loops perform computation only in the innermost loop. This contribution is motivated by two facts. First, variable amounts of data can be modeled by the Cyclo-Static Data Flow (CSDF) [2] MoC, an extension of SDF; but previous experiments on modeling using the CSDF MoC have shown that this model is not easy to understand for designers and does not always offer a competitive benefit. This has been stated by the creators of the SDF-based language StreamIt [21], in a review of their own work [20] (see their Sect. 5.2). Another option is to use dynamic dataflow MoCs such as Kahn Process Networks (KPN) [8], but KPNs are hard to analyse and are not statically schedulable. Hence, we focus on SDF graphs instead. Second, we need to model nested loops in SDF graphs in order to finely control the granularity of the application representation. Moreover, the representation should be easily adaptable to the target architecture, especially to its number of PEs, while staying independent from the architecture.

A direct application of this contribution is the modeling of a computer vision feature detection application. Indeed, keypoints detection is performed on images at different resolutions and different blur levels. Thus, nested loops iterate over images of different sizes so the loops have variable bounds.

In this paper, we introduce the notion of SDF *iterators* modeling and optimize multiple nested loops with variable bounds. Iterators are demonstrated on a Scale Invariant Feature Transform (SIFT) keypoints detection [13] application, modeled by an SDF graph. Iterators help modeling and parallelizing SIFT detection, although some nested loops process images of variable sizes. At the same time, iterators help reducing the scheduling complexity since it is possible to adapt the number of parallel executions with regard to the number of PEs.

The paper is organized as follows. SDF graphs are presented in Sect. 2, as well as the SIFT application that will illustrate different examples along the paper. Then the parallelization of single loops with SDF graphs is recalled in Sect. 3. The main contribution, SDF iterators for multiple perfectly nested loops with explicit parallelism and with variable bounds, is detailed in Sect. 4. Results of an evaluation of iterators on SDF are presented in Sect. 5. Related work, in Sect. 6, is followed by a conclusion.

2 Context

Section 2.1 recalls briefly the semantics of SDF graphs, while Sect. 2.2 presents an overview of the SIFT application that is later modeled by SDF graphs.

2.1 SDF Graphs

SDF graphs are directed multi-graphs composed of vertices, called *actors*, and edges, called *buffers*. Actors represent processing operations, while buffers represent the data communication between the different actors. The abstract unit of data is called *token*. Each buffer b is annotated with rates: a production rate $\mathrm{prod}(b) \in \mathbb{N}^*$ at the source of b, and a consumption rate $\mathrm{cons}(b) \in \mathbb{N}^*$ at the target of b. Production and consumption rates may not be equal: this is how data parallelism is expressed in SDF graphs. For example if an actor a_1 sends 6 tokens to an actor a_2 through buffer b, whereas a_2 expects 3 tokens at the other end of the buffer b, it means that a_2 will be executed twice: once on the first 3 tokens and another time on the last 3 tokens on b.

The minimal number of executions of each actor in order to leave all buffers as the same state as initially, is called a *repetition vector* and is derived from the buffers production and consumption rates. The repetition vector does not always exist, for example when rates in graph loops are not consistent and lead to a buffer overflow or underflow.

2.2 SIFT Keypoints Detection Application

Scale Invariant Feature Transform (SIFT) computes keypoints by comparing points in the original image with the same points in blurred images obtained from the original one, and at different resolutions. Figure 1a details the main steps: first the original image is upscaled once, and downscaled several times to build the images at various resolutions. Each resolution is called an *octave*. Then, the image at each octave is blurred several times. A blur level corresponds to a *layer*. All images are stored in a 4-dimensional (4-D) array; the dimensions are, in order: octave, layer, height, width. Difference of Gaussians (DoG), gradient, and rotational metrics are computed from this 4-D array. Each metric computation produces an array of the same size, except the DoG which produces one less layer. At last, keypoints detection is performed on these three 4-D arrays. Then, the extraction step refines the computed keypoints.

Two main problems arise when modeling SIFT detection by an SDF graph. First, the number of keypoints to detect is unknown since it depends on the image content. Second, the images to process stored in the 4-D array have different sizes depending on their octave, whereas the SDF MoC imposes data transfers of fixed size. The problem on number of keypoints is easily fixed by setting a maximum. For the second problem, the naive way to model different octaves is to create a specific actor for each image size, which is not convenient because the model cannot be adapted to different numbers of octaves. Another difficulty is that the computation on the smallest image resolution, i.e. the last octave, is faster than the computation of the first octave by several orders of magnitude. Indeed, for an image of 640×800 pixel, the image is upscaled once and downscaled five times by a factor 2 on each dimension; thus the ratio of the number of pixels in the first octave over the last is $4^6 = 4096$. If several Processing Elements (PEs) are available, an important question is how to parallelize the computation equally among them. Figure 1b illustrates this problem with three layers, three octaves, and four available PEs. One option is to assign each layer to a PE, but then

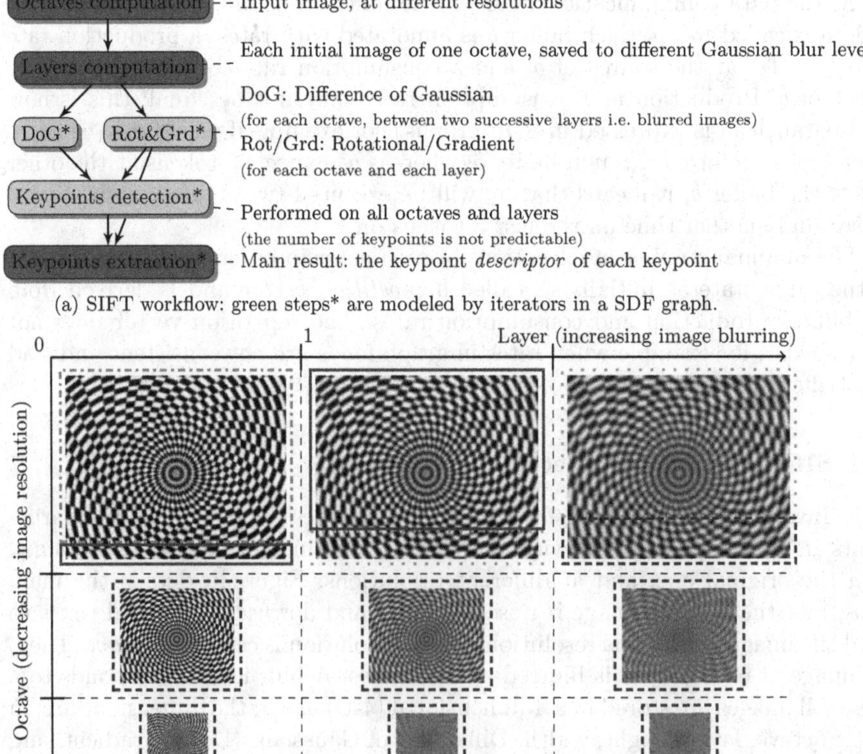

(a) SIFT workflow: green steps* are modeled by iterators in a SDF graph.

(b) Layers and octaves in SIFT with four different region of equal processing amount.

Fig. 1. SIFT image processing application: main steps 1a and data storage 1b

a PE is not used. The opposite option is to assign each octave to a PE, but then a PE is not used, and computations are unbalanced. An example of equal distribution of the computation on the four PEs is shown in the boxes of the four colors red, blue, green and yellow (each with a specific pattern). Each color encloses one quarter of the computation. It is clear on that example that boxes do not match the image bounds.

The iterators introduced in Sect. 4 can handle this computation partitioning while staying in the SDF model. Iterators are used to model and parallelize the green steps in the workflow in Fig. 1a, in our case according to the number of available PEs, and without duplicating any actor for each octave. Before describing the iterators in details, modeling and parallelization of single loops by SDF graphs is recalled in Sect. 3.

3 Modeling of Single Loops with Explicit Parallelism

This section discusses the modeling of single `for` loops using SDF graphs. `for` loops are a basic control structure of any imperative language. The code in Listing 1 illustrates a simple `for` loop. It iterates over an `input` array, processes each element and stores the result in an `output` array; both arrays having the same size `N`, it represents a map operation. The parallelism is explicit: there is no dependency between the iterations of the loop, and `process` is a pure function.

```
for (int i = 0; i < N; ++i) {
  output[i] = process(input[i]);}
```

Listing 1: Simple one dimensional (1-D) `for` loop, with explicit parallelism.

Figure 2a depicts the modeling by a SDF graph of a map operation with a controllable degree of parallelism. p is the degree of expressed data parallelism: the Map actor is executed p times, on chunks of data of size $\frac{N}{p}$. If $p = N$, all data parallelism is expressed, however, it is not always useful to express all the parallelism, especially if the amount of PEs is way smaller than N. The code of the actor `Map` is almost the same as in Listing 1; the only difference lies in the loop index bound that is now `N/p` instead of `N`. p must be a divisor of N.

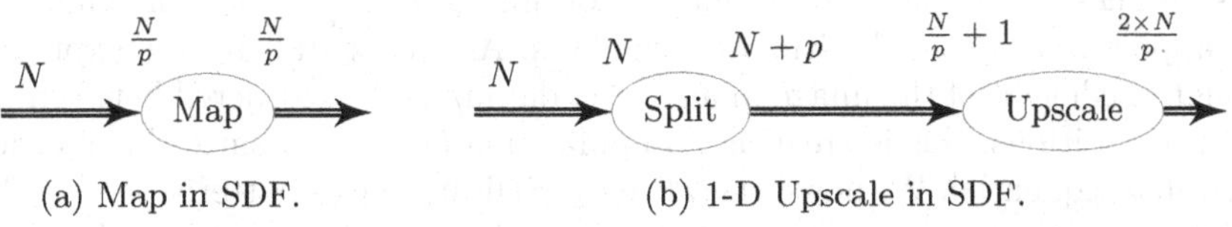

(a) Map in SDF. (b) 1-D Upscale in SDF.

Fig. 2. Map and Upscale at a coarse-grain level.

In image processing, a common operation is to perform an upscale, increasing the resolution of the image with interpolation. This operation is more generic than map since the output array has not the same size as the input, and since several elements of the input array are accessed simultaneously to perform the interpolation. A code example is shown in Listing 2 for the 1-D case.

```
for (int i = 0; i < N; ++i) {
  output[2*i] = input[i];
  if (i < N-1) {
    output[2*i+1] = interpolation(input[i], input[i+1]);
  } else {
    output[2*i+1] = input[i];}}
```

Listing 2: Simple 1-D upscale, by interpolation on the element and its successor.

The modeling of an upscale is similar to a map, but it requires extra data to apply the interpolation on the borders of the chunks of the original array. The last element of a chunk is a copy of the first element of the next chunk. These extra data can be added by a copy actor preceding the upscale actor. The SDF modeling of an upscale operation is depicted in Fig. 2b, where the actor performing the interpolation is called Upscale, and the copy actor is called Split. Split is executed only once, while Upscale is executed p times. The code of the Upscale actor, in Listing 3, is simpler than the original one, in Listing 2, since the border case needs no more to be handled thanks to the copy performed by Split.

```
for (int i = 0; i < N/p; ++i) {
  output[2*i] = input[i];
  output[2*i+1] = interpolation(input[i], input[i+1]);}
```

Listing 3: Upscale SDF actor code.

The upscale modeling pattern presented in Fig. 2b is used to model the computation of the upscale of the input image in the first step of SIFT, as shown in Fig. 1a. An image has two dimensions but the data parallelism is expressed only on the height of the image, divided by the number of PEs. The same pattern is also used for the second step of SIFT: the layers computation. However, the algorithm to compute the different layers consists of two successive 1-D Gaussian blurs on lines of the image, each blur performing a transposition. The Gaussian blur applies a 1-D stencil with two neighbors. As data parallelism is expressed through the height of the image in any case, data must be reordered between the two transpositions; this is creating an application bottleneck since this reordering is fully sequential. We now generalize the SDF modeling patterns seen in this section for single `for` loops to perfectly nested loops with explicit parallelism.

4 Modeling of Nested Loops with Explicit Parallelism

In this section, perfectly nested loops with explicit parallelism are considered. An example is given in Listing 4, with three nested loops. The index bounds of the inner loops may depend on the outer loop indexes, as abstracted by the functions f1 and f2, which can be any mathematical function. The parallelization of nested loops of the same form than in Listing 4 is described in Sect. 4.1, and their modeling by SDF graphs with iterators is discussed in Sect. 4.2.

```
for (int i = 0; i < N1; ++i) {
  for (int j = 0; j < f1(i); ++j) {
    for (int k = 0; k < f2(i, j); ++k) {
      output[i][j][k] = process(input[i][j][k]);}}}
```

Listing 4: Three nested for loops, with explicit parallelism.

4.1 Iteration Space Splitting

An important property of the SDF MoC is that the rates of data exchanges are fixed. Thus, the only solution to model by SDF graphs loops as in Listing 4 is to split the whole iteration space into chunks of equal sizes. These chunks do not always match the loop bounds as depicted in Fig. 1b. In Listing 4, the whole iteration space size $\mathcal{S}_{it}$ is $\sum_{i=0}^{N1}\left(\sum_{j=0}^{f1(i)} f2(i,j)\right)$. In this example, the iteration space size equals the total size of the array to process, it is a map operation.

The most straight forward way to cut the whole iteration space into chunks of equal size is to simulate the execution of the loop. A variable *iter* storing the total number of performed iterations is incremented instead of calling the process function. Each time the *iter* variable reaches a multiple of chunk_size, the loop indexes are recorded and will be used as start/stop indexes for the real execution of the loops. This algorithm is written in Listing 5, with chunk_size being equal to any divisor of $\mathcal{S}_{it}$. The role of a SDF iterator is to send the recorded indexes to split the real execution of the loops.

Note that this simulation can be done offline: the start/stop indexes only need to be saved in order to be used in the real execution of the loop (where the process is performed). Besides, this simulation can be easily adapted to any number d of nested loops: the structure is the same as the original nested loops.

```
int iter = 0;
for (int i = 0; i < N1; ++i) {
  for (int j = 0; j < f1(i); ++j) {
    for (int k = 0; k < f2(i, j); ++k) {
      if (iter++ % chunk_size == 0) {
        record(i,j,k); }}}}
```

Listing 5: Iteration space simulator for three perfectly nested for loops with explicit parallelism. The recorded indexes will be stored in the SDF iterator.

4.2 SDF Iterators

An SDF iterator actor provides the start and stop indexes for each execution of the process actor modeling the nested loops. Thus, if the nested loops iteration space $\mathcal{S}_{it}$ is divided into p chunks, the iterator is executed once and the processing actor is executed p times. The code for the processing actor is similar to its original version in Listing 4, the only difference concerns the indexes that are set by the iterator output. The modeling of the perfectly nested loops in SDF graphs is depicted in Fig. 3. $\mathcal{S}_{it}$ elements are sent to the Process actor, which is processing them by chunks of size $\frac{\mathcal{S}_{it}}{p}$. For each execution of Process, the iterator produced $2 \times d$ indexes: one start index and one stop for each loop of the d nested loops. These indexes correspond to the one recorded during the loop simulation presented in Listing 5, considering that the stop indexes of one execution of the process are the start indexes of its next execution. Hence, the p executions of Process can be performed in parallel. Note that the map and upscale patterns described in Fig. 2b can also be applied to this general case of nested loops.

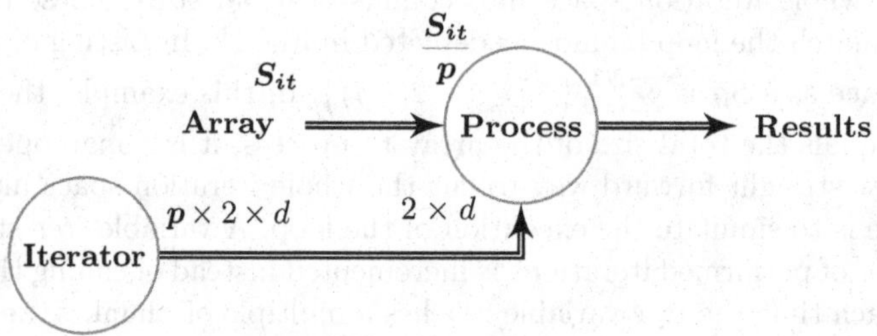

Fig. 3. Modeling of iterators in SDF

Finally, iterators empower the designer to control data parallelism in SDF graphs for any perfectly nested loops with explicit parallelism. Iterators induce two drawbacks which can be overcome. The first drawback occurs when tagging an actor a, parallelized with an iterator, with a measured execution time C_a. Indeed, the execution time is then not only dependant on the actor code, but also on the chunk size. This drawback is easily overcome using symbolic expressions of the execution time: $C_a(p) = \frac{C_a(1)}{p}$; that is, when a is parallelized over p chunks, the execution time of each execution of a is equal to its sequential execution time divided by the number of chunks. The second drawback is the restriction to nested loops with explicit parallelism. However, this restriction can be removed in some cases thanks to prior source-to-source code transformations.

5 Evaluation

SDF iterators are now used to model the SIFT keypoints detection application. In SIFT detection, images from different resolutions and blur levels are processed and this implies to iterate over a 4-D array with four perfectly nested loops. The two innermost loops iterating over the height and width of images have exponential bounds depending on the top loop index. The top loop iterates over the octaves and the second loop iterates over the layers. If octaves are indexed by the variable i, the image height (respectively, width) to be processed is the biggest resolution height (resp. width) divided by 2^i. SDF iterators are used to model such loops, expressing a degree of parallelism $p \in \{1, 2, 4, 5, 10, 20\}$ (this set contains the common divisors of the sizes of all the 4-D arrays).

The SIFT detection code is a slightly modified version of the ezSIFT[1] implementation. The SDF model of SIFT is built under the PREESM [17] framework, which also performs static scheduling and generates the static parallelized code. Another parallel version of SIFT has been implemented using OpenMP, mainly with `parallel for` pragma above the loops iterating over the height of the images. The keypoint detection step requires a critical section to add the detected keypoints into a common list.

The execution times of the PREESM version and the OpenMP version of SIFT have been reported in Table 1. All experiments used an Intel(R) Xeon(R) CPU E5-2650 v4 @ 2.20GHz processor and the GCC compiler version 5.4.0. Both PREESM and OpenMP execution times are similar, the best speedup (in bold) is achieved alternatively by PREESM and OpenMP.

Table 1. Number of scheduled tasks, execution times in ms, and speedup for different number of cores. Execution time is an average on 200 runs.

#Cores	#Tasks	PREESM time (Speedup)	OpenMP time (Speedup)
1	190	669 (0.96x)	645 (**ref.**)
2	293	412 (1.56x)	406 (**1.59x**)
4	355	277 (**2.33x**)	281 (2.29x)
5	386	263 (2.45x)	255 (**2.53x**)
10	541	171 (**3.77x**)	182 (3.54x)

The number of scheduled tasks when unfolding the SDF graph of SIFT is also reported in Table 1. This number is the sum of the repetition vector, i.e. the sum of the minimal number of executions of each actor. As PREESM supports parameterized SDF graphs [5], first introduced in [1], the expressed degree of parallelism p is set according to the number of cores. The number of tasks is not multiplied by a factor equal to the number of cores since not all steps of SIFT are parallelized through iterators, as shown in Fig. 1a.

This evaluation shows that it is possible to model and parallelize an application having perfectly nested `for` loops with variable index bounds thanks to SDF iterators. We achieve competitive performances against OpenMP, that we

[1] See code on: https://sourceforge.net/projects/ezsift/.

could even improve by adding delays in the SDF graph (delays create pipelining). Finally, we are able to control the expressed degree of parallelism, although restricted to be a divisor of the size of the considered iteration space.

6 Related Work

The modeling of nested `for` loops in SDF graphs thanks to iterators is related to two main aspects: specialized dataflow languages, especially for image processing applications where at least two dimensions are considered, and dataflow graph clustering, since iterators impact on the degree of data parallelism.

6.1 On Specialized Dataflow Languages

The most relevant dataflow MoC for image processing is the Multidimensional Synchronous Dataflow (MDSDF) MoC [14], expressing data parallelism across several dimensions. However this MoC does not solve the problem of variable image sizes such as in the SIFT octaves: it needs one specialized actor per size. Moreover, only a few tools [9], such as ArrayOL [3], support the MDSDF MoC.

The Brook stream language [12] supports a subset of MDSDF graphs, expressed directly as `C++` code. Brook only handles kernels with affine bounds, and thus cannot be used for variable image sizes inducing exponential bounds. More generally, the same problem arises for all models relying on polyhedral analysis [6], as the Polyhedral Process Network (PPN) [22], a parameterized extension of it [26], or the OpenStream extension of OpenMP [4]: they are dedicated to loops with affine bounds only. Extensive analyses and graph and code transformations allow to model any kind of loops in PPNs [15] but then do not offer control of the degree of parallelism. Dynamic dataflow languages, such as the one supported by Orcc [23], offer more flexibility on the application representation, however it is not possible to derive static schedules from such languages when their semantics are fully exploited.

6.2 On the Clustering of Dataflow Graphs

Clustering is usually performed on graphs expressing more parallelism than available on the target architecture; clustering simplifies scheduling without increasing the application run time [19]. The standard way to reach a coarse representation is to limit the unfolding of the SDF graph into a precedence task graph. The unfolding is limited by merging different actors, or several executions of the same actor. This operation artificially reduces the repetition vector size, or decreases the values held by the repetition vector. This method has been employed for SDF graphs under real-time constraints [25], and also under data-driven scheduling of Partial Expansion Graphs (PEG) [24]. The StreamIT benchmark has also been successfully transformed into coarse SDF graphs for the RAW architecture [7], by an unfolding technique using actor fusion and fission.

Another method is to completely unfold the SDF graph, and only then, to apply clustering algorithms; however, this significantly increases the scheduling complexity. Clustering algorithms exist for precedence graphs, including compiler intermediate representations [11]. Hierarchical SDF graphs have also been used to model nested loops [18], one per hierarchy, but they require an analysis of the iteration space. Both methods do not offer control on the degree of parallelism.

Finally, all the aforementioned clustering methods rely on algorithms that analyze the graph and create a coarse or hierarchical version of it, while the proposed iterators only require to replace the `for` loop index bounds by the iterator output. Only one iterator per iteration space is needed.

7 Conclusion

This paper has demonstrated that it is possible to model a subclass of nested loops with variable index bounds by an SDF graph, and to control the degree of expressed parallelism. Thus, we can add to the observations of the StreamIt creators that the CSDF model is not only complicated to use, but is also not always compulsory: the SIFT application has been parallelized efficiently thanks to the SDF model and iterators. A future extension of this work is to automatically generate iterator code from a code analysis.

References

1. Bhattacharya, B., Bhattacharyya, S.S.: Parameterized dataflow modeling for dsp-systems. IEEE Trans. Signal Process. **49**, 2408–2421 (2001)
2. Bilsen, G., Engels, M., Lauwereins, R., Peperstraete, J.: Cycle-static dataflow. Trans. Sig. Proc. **44**(2), 397–408 (1996)
3. Boulet, P.: Array-OL Revisited, Multidimensional Intensive Signal Processing Specification. Research Report RR-6113, INRIA (2007)
4. Cohen, A., Darte, A., Feautrier, P.: Static analysis of OpenStream programs. Research Report RR-8764, CNRS; Inria; ENS Lyon (2016)
5. Desnos, K., Pelcat, M., Nezan, J.F., Bhattacharyya, S.S., Aridhi, S.: PiMM: parameterized and interfaced dataflow meta-model for MPSoCs runtime reconfiguration. In: 13th International Conference on Embedded Computer Systems: Architecture, Modeling and Simulation (SAMOS XIII), Samos, Greece (2013)
6. Feautrier, P.: Some efficient solutions to the affine scheduling problem. Part II multidimensional time. Int. J. Parallel Prog. **21**(6), 389–420 (1992)
7. Gordon, M.I., Thies, W., Amarasinghe, S.: Exploiting coarse-grained task, data, and pipeline parallelism in stream programs. SIGPLAN Not. **41**(11), 151–162 (2006)
8. Kahn, G.: The semantics of simple language for parallel programming. In: IFIP Congress (1974)
9. Keinert, J., Deprettere, E.F.: Multidimensional dataflow graphs. In: Bhattacharyya, S., Deprettere, E., Leupers, R., Takala, J. (eds.) Handbook of Signal Processing Systems, pp. 1145–1175. Springer, New York (2013). https://doi.org/10.1007/978-1-4614-6859-2_35

10. Lee, E.A., Messerschmitt, D.G.: Synchronous data flow. Proc. IEEE **75**(9), 1235–1245 (1987)
11. Li, F., Pop, A., Cohen, A.: Automatic extraction of Coarse-Grained Data-FlowThreads from imperative programs. IEEE Micro **32**(4), 19–31 (2012)
12. Liao, S., Du, Z., Wu, G., Lueh, G.Y.: Data and computation transformations for brook streaming applications on multiprocessors. In: International Symposium on Code Generation and Optimization (CGO 2006) (2006)
13. Lowe, D.G.: Distinctive image features from scale-invariant keypoints. Int. J. Comput. Vision **60**(2), 91–110 (2004)
14. Murthy, P.K., Lee, E.A.: Multidimensional synchronous dataflow. IEEE Trans. Signal Process. **50**(8), 2064–2079 (2002)
15. Nadezhkin, D., Nikolov, H., Stefanov, T.: Automated generation of polyhedral process networks from affine nested-loop programs with dynamic loop bounds. ACM Trans. Embed. Comput. Syst. **13**(1s), 28 (2013)
16. Oh, H., Ha, S.: Fractional rate dataflow model and efficient code synthesis for multimedia applications. SIGPLAN Not. **37**(7), 12–17 (2002)
17. Pelcat, M., Desnos, K., Heulot, J., Guy, C., Nezan, J.F., Aridhi, S.: Preesm: a dataflow-based rapid prototyping framework for simplifying multicore DSP programming. In: 6th Embedded Design Education and Research Conference (2014)
18. Piat, J., Bhattacharyya, S.S., Raulet, M.: Loop transformations for interface-based hierarchies IN SDF graphs. In: 21st IEEE International Conference on Application-specific Systems Architectures and Processors (ASAP), Rennes, France (2010)
19. Pino, J.L., Bhattacharyya, S.S., Lee, E.A.: A hierarchical multiprocessor scheduling system for DSP applications. In: Conference Record of The Twenty-Ninth Asilomar Conference on Signals, Systems and Computers, vol. 1 (1995)
20. Thies, W., Amarasinghe, S.: An empirical characterization of stream programs and its implications for language and compiler design. In: Proceedings of the 19th International Conference on Parallel Architectures and Compilation Techniques, PACT 2010. ACM, New York (2010)
21. Thies, W., Karczmarek, M., Amarasinghe, S.: StreamIt: a language for streaming applications. In: Horspool, R.N. (ed.) CC 2002. LNCS, vol. 2304, pp. 179–196. Springer, Heidelberg (2002). https://doi.org/10.1007/3-540-45937-5_14
22. Verdoolaege, S.: Polyhedral process networks. In: Bhattacharyya, S., Deprettere, E., Leupers, R., Takala, J. (eds.) Handbook of Signal Processing Systems, pp. 931–965. Springer, Boston (2010). https://doi.org/10.1007/978-1-4419-6345-1_33
23. Yviquel, H., Lorence, A., Jerbi, K., Cocherel, G., Sanchez, A., Raulet, M.: Orcc: multimedia development made easy. In: Proceedings of the 21st ACM International Conference on Multimedia, MM 2013. ACM (2013)
24. Zaki, G.F., Plishker, W., Bhattacharyya, S.S., Fruth, F.: Implementation, scheduling, and adaptation of partial expansion graphs on multicore platforms. J. Signal Process. Syst. **87**(1), 107–125 (2017)
25. Zhai, J.T., Bamakhrama, M.A., Stefanov, T.: Exploiting just-enough parallelism when mapping streaming applications in hard real-time systems. In: 2013 50th ACM/EDAC/IEEE Design Automation Conference (DAC) (2013)
26. Zhai, J.T., Nikolov, H., Stefanov, T.: Modeling adaptive streaming applications with parameterized polyhedral process networks. In: 2011 48th ACM/EDAC/IEEE Design Automation Conference (DAC) (2011)

System-Level Modeling and Simulation of MPSoC Run-Time Management Using Execution Traces Analysis

S. Yang(✉), S. Le Nours, M. Méndez Real, and S. Pillement

University of Nantes, CNRS, IETR UMR 6164, 44000 Nantes, France
simei.yang@etu.unive-nantes.fr

Abstract. Dynamic management of modern Multi-Processors System on Chip (MPSoC) become mandatory for optimization purpose. Evaluation of these managers is essential early in the design process to guarantee a reduced design cycle. However, most of the existing system-level simulation-based frameworks consider static application mapping and do not consider the run-time management effects. In this work, we present a modeling and simulation approach that allows integration of run-time management strategies in MPSoC system simulation. We have integrated the proposed approach in an industrial modeling and simulation framework. A case-study with seven applications running on a heterogeneous multicore platform is considered and different management strategies are evaluated according to latency and power consumption criteria.

Keywords: System-level simulation · Execution trace · Run-time management strategies · Heterogeneous multicore systems

1 Introduction

Modern multicore platforms contain an increasing number of heterogeneous resources, *i.e.*, processing elements, memories, and communication resources. Such platforms allow more and more functionalities to be supported while satisfying still multiple non-functional requirements such as real-time and power consumption. Due to dynamism between and within applications, the behavior of application workloads can dramatically vary over time. Hybrid application mapping methods [11] have emerged as convenient approaches to cope with applications dynamism and favor the achievement of non-functional requirements such as timing and power constraints in multicore platforms.

Hybrid application mapping methods combine design-time analysis and run-time management of platform resources. In such approaches, the design-time stage performs design space exploration to prepare a set of mappings of the supported applications. The run-time management then maps dynamically the applications on platform resources in such a way that real-time and energy consumption objectives are optimized. In this context, extensive evaluation of the

D. N. Pnevmatikatos et al. (Eds.): SAMOS 2019, LNCS 11733, pp. 281–293, 2019.
https://doi.org/10.1007/978-3-030-27562-4_20

run-time management strategies is essential to guarantee that the non-functional requirements will be respected.

System-level modeling and simulation approaches favor early detection of potential issues and prevent costly design cycles. In existing system-level simulation-based approaches, a system model is formed by a combination of an application model and a platform model. Then these models can be simulated, as executable descriptions, under different situations to estimate system performance and optimize system design. However, in most of the existing frameworks, the allocation of applications on platform resources is statically defined and cannot be modified during the simulation. Extending system-level simulation-based approaches is thus mandatory to allow early evaluation of run-time management strategies.

In this paper, we present a system-level modeling and simulation approach of run-time management for multicore platforms. The proposed model allows modification of applications allocation and scheduling on platform resources during the system simulation. The novelty of the proposed approach lies in the dynamic computation of instants when platform resources are used according to running applications. Using the computed simulation instants, the simulation model of the run-time manager controls both the order of task execution and the advancement of simulation time. We implemented and validated the proposed approach using Intel Cofluent Studio modeling framework [2] and SystemC simulation language [5]. In this paper, the benefits of this approach are demonstrated through a case-study that considers seven applications (85 tasks in total) running on a heterogeneous multicore platform. Different management strategies are evaluated and compared according to application latency and power consumption criteria.

The remainder of this paper is as follows. In Sect. 2, we present relevant related work. The application and platform models are presented in Sect. 3. The principles of the proposed modeling and simulation approach are explained in Sect. 4. We present the implementation of the approach and its application through a case-study in Sect. 5. Finally, Sect. 6 conclude this paper.

2 Background and Related Work

Many run-time management strategies have been proposed [11] to optimize applications running on multicore platforms under real-time and energy consumption constraints. The evaluation of run-time management strategies aims at estimating the achieved resource usage and time properties such as system latency. As illustrated in [12,14], early evaluation of run-time management strategies is mostly done using analytic formal approaches. These approaches are well adapted to predict system properties under worst-case situations but they can lead to pessimistic predictions. To the best of our knowledge only two related works support dynamism in system-level simulation.

In [10], an extension of the Sesame system-level modeling and simulation framework [9] is presented. Especially, a Run-time Resource Scheduler (RRS) is introduced to control mapping of applications for each simulated use-case. Based on trace-driven simulation approach [8], each application model records its action by a set of event traces (*i.e.* computation and communication events). RRS dispatches the event traces to an architecture model during system simulation. Our proposed approach differs in the way system simulation is performed. In our case, at the beginning of each use-case, the design-time prepared database is processed to compute the instants when platform resources are used. With the knowledge of the computed instants, our proposed run-time manager controls when application tasks are run on platform resources during system simulation.

In [7] an extension of Intel CoFluent Studio was proposed to support dynamic application mapping but this proposal is not currently supported in this framework. This proposal was based on some additional SystemC code to control the allocation of tasks on platform resources. In this work, we implement a new simulation approach in Intel CoFluent Studio but it is important to notice that our approach does not need any modification of the used framework, making our proposition portable to other simulation environments.

3 System Models

Application and Use-Case Models: An application, as illustrated in Fig. 1, is characterized by a directed task graph $G_{App_i} = (T_{App_i}, E_{App_i})$, where T_{App_i} is the set of tasks of the application and E_{App_i} is the set of directed edges representing dependencies among the tasks. Tasks and edges in App_i are respectively denoted by $t_{i,j}$ and $e_{i,h}$, where j is the number of the task and h the number of the edge. A task represents an atomic, non-preemptive, code which execution time can vary over time according to the processed data. In this paper, we consider periodic real-time applications and each application App_i shall be executed within its period time $Period_{App_i}$.

In the scope of this work, the synchronous data flow (SDF) semantic [6] is used to capture the applications. In Fig. 1 input tokens define the number of tokens that are read from the edge before executing a task and the output token defines the number of tokens that are written through the edge after the task execution.

The set of simultaneously active applications defines a use-case $uc_i = \{App_1, App_2 \cdots, App_n\}$. Let $UC = \{uc_1, uc_2, \ldots, uc_l\}$ be the set of all possible use-cases. As we consider a dynamic execution scenario, different use-cases are active over time. The set of successive use-cases and their durations are defined in the Use-case Definition in Fig. 1.

Platform Model: This work targets heterogeneous cluster-based platforms, where each cluster consists of a set of homogeneous processing elements associated with a shared memory (Fig. 1). The cores within a cluster have the same voltage and frequency (v/f) settings, and each cluster supports its own ranges of discrete v/f levels. One example of such platform is the Samsung Exynos 5422 [1] with an ARM big.Little multicore architecture.

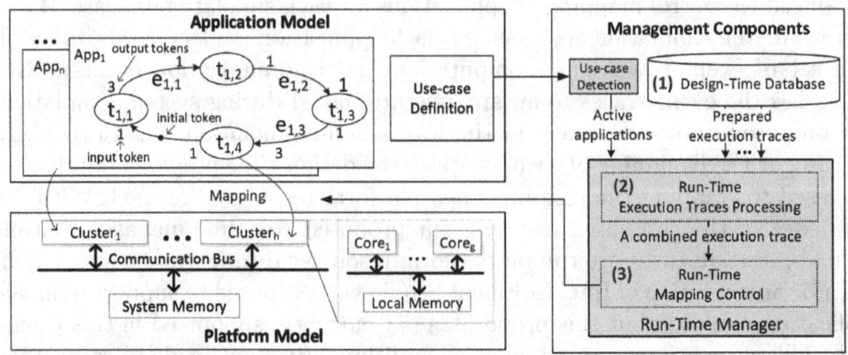

Fig. 1. System models with application, platform and management components descriptions.

According to the platform model, we can define $CommTime_{e_{i,h}}$ as the communication time between dependent tasks via the edge $e_{i,h}$. Similarly, the computation time of a task $t_{i,j}$ executed on a specific cluster C at a given v/f level is defined as $CompTime_{t_{i,j}}(C, v/f)$. Additional power model can also be integrated in this approach (see Sect. 5).

Management Components: Application mapping defines the binding of application tasks to the architecture resources. As illustrated in Fig. 1, we consider run-time management in three steps: **(1)** a design-time preparation, where one or several mappings for each application are prepared and stored in a database. **(2)** A run-time mapping processing is performed when a new use-case is detected (*Use-case Detection*). In this step, a run-time mapping is established based on a particular algorithm (under evaluation) and, on the analysis of design-time execution traces of every active application in the use-case. Finally, **(3)** the run-time mapping control introduces the new simulation approach to control the execution of active tasks during system simulation based on the mapping established in the previous step.

4 Run-Time Mapping Modeling and Simulation Method

4.1 Design-Time Database Preparation

The first step of most of dynamic resource managers is the design-time preparation. This step consists in storing into a database a set of prepared mappings, one or several for each application. The prepared mappings can be obtained by any design-time mapping algorithm. This preparation process is out-of-the-scope of this work.

In our approach, a mapping is characterized by its execution trace, *i.e* a set of instants defining the start (x_s) and end (x_e) times of each task when executed on a specific platform configuration (processing element, v/f, $\cdots$). Only the instants within a period are prepared for a design-time mapping.

Without loss of generality, lets consider that only one mapping is prepared for each application in $A = \{App_1, App_2\}$. According to the mapping strategy presented in [13], each task is mapped into one distinct core. The prepared mappings[1] of App_1 and App_2 are illustrated in Fig. 2.

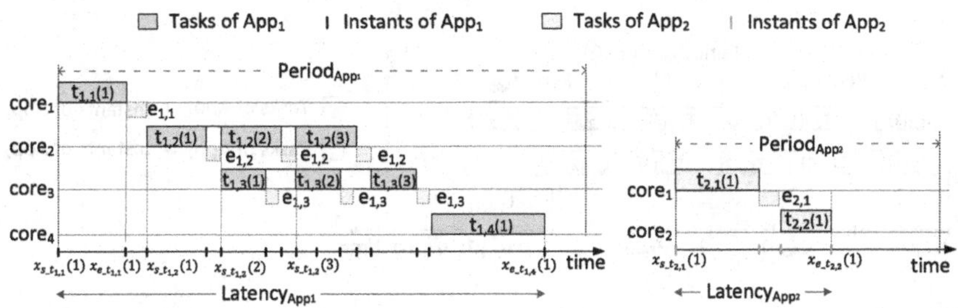

Fig. 2. A design-time prepared execution trace for the mapping of App_1 (a) and App_2 (b), according to [13].

We can define $X_{App_i} = \{x_{s\_t_{i,j}}(1), x_{e\_t_{i,j}}(1), \cdots x_{s\_t_{i,j}}(k), x_{e\_t_{i,j}}(k)\}, j \in \mathbb{N}^+$, $k \in \mathbb{N}^+$ be the execution trace of App_i where k refers to the kth instance of a task. As an example, execution traces for applications App_1 and App_2 in Fig. 2 are respectively defined by $X_{App_1} = \{x_{s\_t_{1,1}}(1), x_{e\_t_{1,1}}(1), \cdots, x_{s\_t_{1,4}}(1), x_{e\_t_{1,4}}(1)\}$, and $X_{App_2} = \{x_{s\_t_{2,1}}(1), x_{e\_t_{2,1}}(1), x_{s\_t_{2,2}}(1), x_{e\_t_{2,2}}(1)\}$.

Instants x_s and x_e are expressed according to dependencies between tasks. In the example of Fig. 2, dependencies of task $t_{2,1}$ for instance, are expressed as follows: $x_{s\_t_{1,2}}(1) = x_{e\_t_{1,1}}(1) + CommTime_{e_{1,1}}(1)$ and $x_{e\_t_{1,2}}(1) = x_{s\_t_{1,2}}(1) + CompTime_{t_{1,2}}(1)$. For sake of clarity, communication time is not illustrated in the next figures. Finally, $Latency_{App_1}$ refers to the execution time of App_1 from the input to the last instant within one period. It has to be noticed that the instants are relative as $CompTime_{t_{i,j}}(k)$ and $CommTime_{e_{i,j}}(k)$ will depend on the real mapping determined at run-time in the next step.

4.2 Run-Time Execution Traces Processing

The processing of run-time execution traces is performed each time a new use-case uc_i is detected. The objective is to obtain at run-time a combined execution trace $X'_{Apps}(uc_i)$ of the n active applications in the use-case uc_i.

For that purpose, the design-time prepared execution traces of each active application (X_{App_i}) are combined according to a given algorithm (different mapping combination strategies can be used). In the following, we denote

[1] As can be seen in Fig. 2, $t_{1,2}$ and $t_{1,3}$ are executed three times for each iteration of App1. App_2 is a 2-task application.

the process of combining execution traces by */processing*. Figure 3 gives an example of one possible combined execution trace of applications of a use-case $uc_1 = \{App_1, App_2\}$ based on the previous example. In this example the *LASP* (Longest Available Slot Packing) strategy presented in [13] has been used. According to this algorithm, $X'_{Apps}(uc_1) = /processing\{X_{App_1}, X_{App_2}\}$, includes all the execution instants, from x_s of the first task to x_e of the last task in the least common multiple LCM of periods, for the active applications in uc_1.

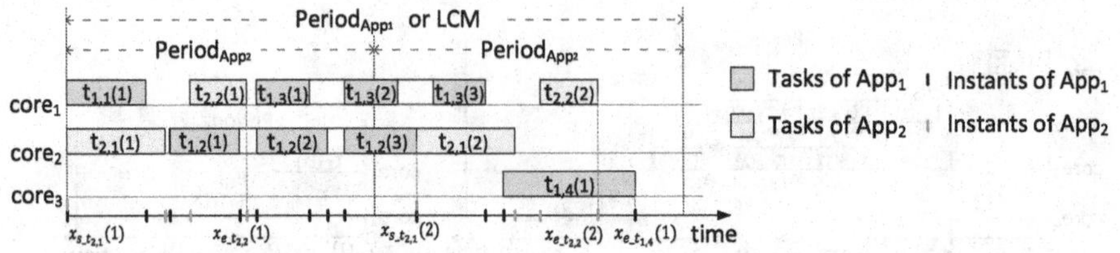

Fig. 3. A run-time combined execution trace $X'_{Apps}(uc_1)$ using strategy in [13].

In LASP, the instances of a task are always mapped into the same core through periods (task instances $t_{2,1}(1)$ and $t_{2,1}(2)$, allocated on $core_2$, are an example). Once the execution traces are combined, the start time of $t_{2,1}(2)$ (i.e. $x_{s\_t_{2,1}}(2)$) is adjusted and delayed in order to start after the previous task allocated into $core_2$ (*i.e.*, starting instant dependency on $x_{e\_t_{1,2}}(3)$). The adjusted instants then increase $Latency_{App_2}$ of the second period. In $X'_{Apps}(uc_1)$ the instants are now absolute and computed according to the active mapping.

4.3 Run-Time Mapping Control

In our approach, the run-time mapping simulation, handled by the *Run-Time Manager* (RTM), aims to control the execution of tasks according to the information provided by the run-time execution traces processing. The proposed simulation approach is depicted in Fig. 4 for $uc_1 = \{App_1, App_2\}$.

As shown, when uc_1 is detected, the */processing* step is performed to determine $X'_{Apps}(uc_1)$. The execution of the */processing* action is done in zero simulation time with no call to the simulation kernel. The RTM then controls the states of each task according to the processed results.

In Fig. 4, at the simulated instant $x_{s\_t_{1,1}}(1)$, $t_{1,1}(1)$ and $t_{1,2}(1)$ are started. The RTM inserts some simulation delays through action */wait*(wt) to wait for the next instant. Simulation time *SimTime* moves forward $SimTime = SimTime + wt$. As the next instant is $x_{e\_t_{1,1}}(1)$, the waiting duration wt is expressed as $wt = x_{e\_t_{1,1}}(1) - x_{s\_t_{1,1}}(1)$. After this time, $t_{1,1}(1)$ is stopped. As for task instances, $x_{s\_t_{1,2}}(1)$, $x_{s\_t_{1,2}}(2)$ and $x_{s\_t_{1,2}}(3)$, the RTM detects that several instances of the same task are executed successively on the same processing core. In this case, only the first instance ($x_{s\_t_{1,2}}(1)$) is started and the last one $x_{s\_t_{1,2}}(3)$ stopped. This further reduces the activity of the simulation effort.

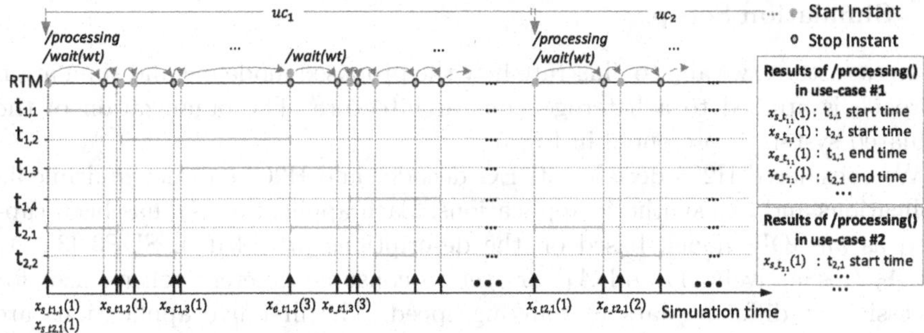

Fig. 4. System-level approach for the simulation of run-time mapping strategies through the dynamic control of the execution of tasks for different use-cases.

This process is repeated for all the task instances in every LCM period. When a new use-case is detected, the RTM performs the dynamic control for the tasks in the new use-case (*e.g.* $X'_{Apps}(uc_2)$).

Heterogeneous platform (different processing cores, different v/f levels, $\cdots$) are handled through the dynamic adaptation of the waiting time wt to the varying values of the computation and the communication time ($CompTime_t$ and $CommTime_e$), according to the heterogeneous resources configuration.

5 Evaluation of the Modeling and Simulation Approach

5.1 Simulation Environment

We used the industrial modeling and simulation framework Intel CoFluent Studio [2] to validate the proposed approach, but our proposal does not need any modification in the used framework and thus can be used in other environments.

In the CoFluent framework, each application is modeled graphically with several functions (*i.e.*, tasks) and communications (*i.e.*, edges). The built system model is then generated as a SystemC description for further execution analysis.

In our implementation, the run-time manager model is captured and can be considered as a specific function of the system. The implementation of the action `processing` corresponds to the call to a C++ code that is developed to manipulate the previously defined data structures X_{App_i} and X'_{Apps}.

During the simulation, the run-time manager controls the states of each function and calls the simulation kernel for the advancement of the simulation time according to the combined execution trace. Elementary procedures available in the used framework (`start`, `stop`, `resume`, `wait`) are used by the run-time manager to control the state of the functions.

5.2 Simulation Setup

In the case study, we aim to illustrate how the proposed modeling and simulation approach is applied to a heterogeneous architecture. The organization of the evaluated system is presented in Fig. 5.

We considered H263 decoder, JPEG decoder and H263 encoder multimedia applications and two synthetic applications. Each application A_i, has been captured as an SDF model, based on the descriptions provided in SDF3 [3]. A_1 and A_3 (respectively A_2 and A_4) are set to consume different tokens sizes for processing at different data exchanging speed. The first five applications are representatives and require different computation time and power. To evaluate the scalability of the proposed simulation approach, A_6 and A_7 are arbitrarily created to significantly increase the number of tasks. They were created by duplicating A_1 5 and 10 times respectively, while the iterations execute successively in one period. Each application is constrained by a predefined period. For further evaluation, in the following, 13 possible use-cases are defined by different active applications (seen on top right part of Fig. 5). The duration of each use-case is not depicted in the figure for the sake of clarity.

Applications	Nb of tasks	Nb of edges	Nb of token for each task	Period (μs)	Latency[2] of X_{A_i} (μs)
A_1: H263-decoder.S	4	3	{1,11,11,1}	60	44
A_2: JPEG-decoder.S	6	5	{1,6,6,6,6,1}	180	118
A_3: H263-decoder.L	4	3	{1,66,66,1}	180	77
A_4: JPEG-decoder.L	6	5	{1,12,12,12,12,1}	270	164
A_5: H263-encoder	5	4	{1,5,5,1,1}	540	451
A_6: 5xA_1	20	19	5x{1,11,11,1}	270	220
A_7: 10xA_1	40	39	10x{1,11,11,1}	540	441

Use-case	Active Apps	Use-case	Active Apps
uc_1	A_1	uc_8	A_6A_7
uc_2	A_3	uc_9	$A_5A_6A_7$
uc_3	A_1A_2	uc_{10}	$A_4A_5A_6A_7$
uc_4	$A_1A_2A_3$	uc_{11}	$A_3A_4A_5A_6A_7$
uc_5	$A_1A_2A_3A_4$	uc_{12}	$A_2A_3A_4A_5A_6A_7$
uc_6	$A_1A_2A_3A_4A_5$	uc_{13}	$A_1A_2A_3A_4A_5A_6A_7$
uc_7	A_7		

Global Manager

Application-to-cluster assignments, cluster frequency settings

Local Manager | Local Manager

Task-to-core allocation and scheduling | Task-to-core allocation and scheduling

Little Cluster (multiple cores) | Big Cluster (multiple cores)

Heterogeneous Cluster-based Multicore Platform

Fig. 5. Evaluated hierarchical run-time management of multiple applications executed on a heterogeneous cluster-based platform. (The latency of X_{A_i} is assumed to be obtained in the little cluster at 1.4 GHz.)

We choose the Samsung Exynos 5422 [1] platform as hardware target. As summarized in [4], the computation time of a task presents a ratio of $1 : 0.5$ when executed on the little (Cortex-A7) or the big (Cortex-A15) cluster. Besides, the ratio of power consumption of a task executed on the little cluster and the big cluster is set to $1 : 4$. This platform allows frequency scaling for each cluster, while the operating voltage is adapted to the frequency setting. The supported frequencies range from 0.2 GHz to 1.4 GHz for the little cluster, and from 0.2 GHz to 2.0 GHz for the big cluster, with a step of 0.1 GHz. We used the Exynos

5422 models defined in [15] to model how computation time and dynamic power consumption of tasks change with frequency.

The hierarchical managers are built to implement a complete run-time management strategies of the system. The two local managers are individually used for each cluster to optimize task-to-core allocation and scheduling. In order to coordinate the local managers, the global manager determines application-to-cluster allocation and sets cluster frequencies. The management strategies are based on design-time prepared execution traces. We established X_{A_i} for each application by using the strategy in [13].

5.3 Validation of the Simulation Approach on Latency Criteria

In this part, the proposed simulation approach is applied for evaluation of a local manager, which considers task-to-core mapping inside a cluster (i.e. on a homogeneous architecture). Once again LASP [13] is applied as the local manager to get a combined mapping of active applications in a use-case and then latency of each application can be obtained.

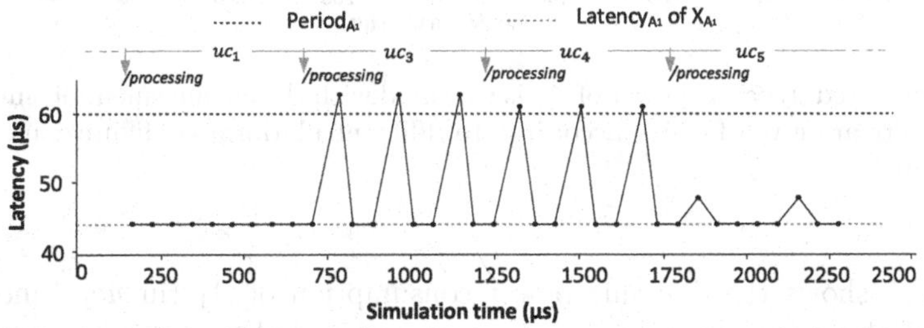

Fig. 6. Evolution of simulated A_1 latency, captured for four different use-cases. Results are given for the LASP strategy [13]. (Color figure online)

Figure 6 shows the latency evolution of A_1 in four different simulated use-cases. The simulations are performed in the little cluster at a fixed cluster frequency of $f = 1.4\,\text{GHz}$. In this figure, the green arrows indicate the instants when a new combined execution trace is computed by */processing* (i.e. A use-case change). For a clear illustration, the latency of A_1 is captured nine times for each use-case. In uc_1 where only A_1 is active, $Latency_{A_1}$ equals to the latency of its design-time prepared mapping. However, $Latency_{A_1}$ can be larger in uc_3, uc_4 and uc_5. In particular, the maximum $Latency_{A_1}$ in uc_3 and uc_4 even violate the timing constraint $Period_{A_1}$. As discussed above, the increase of latency comes from the possible delay of tasks re-allocation using the LASP combination strategy.

The latency of A_1 observed in the simulation is consistent with the latency obtained from the combined execution trace, while the combined execution trace is obtained by a run-time mapping strategy. Therefore, we can see that our simulation approach is able to capture the behavior of an application under a dynamic management.

5.4 Validation of the Simulation Approach on Power Criteria

We then applied the proposed simulation approach to a heterogeneous architecture. In the simulated model, the global manager determines the application-to-cluster allocation and set the cluster frequencies. Different platform configurations lead to different computation time and different dynamic power consumption of a task.

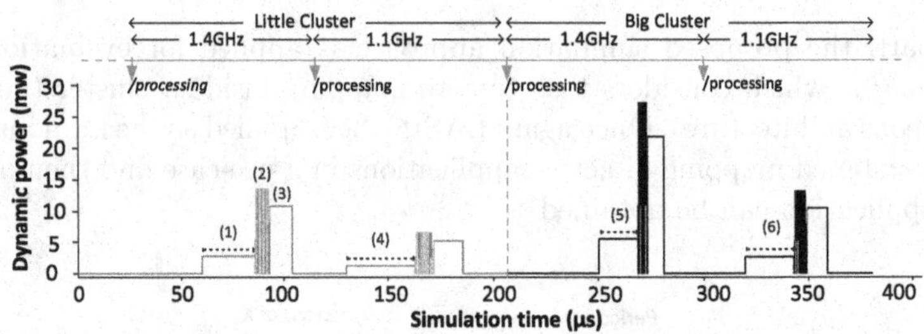

Fig. 7. Simulated dynamic power of A_1 is captured with the advancement of simulation time. Results are given for uc_1 according to different platform configurations. (Color figure online)

Figure 7 shows the dynamic power consumption of A_1 (in uc_1) under the control of the global manager. The green arrows indicate the instants when an execution trace is adapted according to different platform configurations. In the first configuration (little cluster, $f = 1.4$ GHz), index (1) corresponds to the active state of $t_{1,1}$. Index (2) indicates the activities of $t_{1,2}$ and $t_{1,3}$ that are active in parallel. Index (3) shows the activity of task $t_{1,4}$. For task $t_{1,1}$, the power consumption with different platform configurations are represented in indexes (1), (4), (5) and (6), while the task computation time is reflected by the length of the red dotted lines. For indexes (1) and (4), when the operating frequency decreases from $f = 1.4$ GHz to $f = 1.1$ GHz, the dynamic power consumption of $t_{1,1}$ decreases while the task computation time increases. In the case of indexes (1) and (5), $t_{1,1}$ is executed at $f = 1.4$ GHz on the little cluster and the big cluster respectively. The power consumption of the task observed on the big cluster is higher, while the computation time is smaller.

The proposed approach is then able to capture the behavior of an application under different heterogeneous platform configurations (*i.e.* different allocations, various v/f settings) depending on a dynamic mapping.

5.5 Evaluation of the Simulation Approach

Comparison of Run-Time Mapping Strategies: The proposed simulation approach allows to evaluate different run-time management strategies. We compared two Local Management Strategies (LMS). Namely LASP [13] (LMS-1), which allows the task of different applications to be mapped on the same core and a second strategy (LMS-2) introduced in [12], where only the tasks from one application can be mapped on the same core. The simulations are performed for the little cluster with $f = 1.4\,\text{GHz}$. In Table 1, we summarize the estimated application latency for different use-cases. As previously observed, LMS-1 leads to some increase in application latency in some use-cases.

Three Global Management Strategies (GMS) are also compared. They differ in how they allocate applications to the clusters. GMS-1 and GMS-2 denote the strategies that allocate all the active applications to the little cluster or to the big cluster respectively. GMS-3 assigns applications to the two clusters by searching the best power efficiency. Once the application allocation is done, cluster frequency is decreased as much as possible under the timing constraints. Then LMS-2 is used in each local manager to determine task-to-core mapping. From Table 1, we can observe the poor power efficiency of using only one cluster.

Table 1. Evaluation of run-time management strategies based on latency and power

Compared criteria	Strategy	uc_1	uc_2	uc_3	uc_4	uc_5	uc_6
Latency[a]	LMS-1	1	1	1.43	1.39	1.18	1.64
	LMS-2	1	1	1	1	1	1
System Power[b]	GMS-1	1.68	2	1.68	1.89	1.94	2.14
	GMS-2	1	1	1	1.12	1.15	1.07
	GMS-3	1	1	1	1	1	1

[a] Depicts the latency of the application that has the highest variation in a use-case. Each value is normalized by the latency obtained by LMS-2.

[b] Represents the average dynamic power of the system. Each value is normalized by the system power obtained by GMS-3.

Evaluation of Simulation Efficiency: We analyze the scalability of the proposed simulation method by comparing it with the CoFluent default simulation method. The proposed approach simulates the execution of applications under the control of the Run-Time Manager model (RTM), and different mappings can be provided for each application in different use-cases. On the other hand, without the RTM model, the default simulation approach only provides one static mapping of the applications in every use-case. Figure 8 shows the differences in the simulation effort between the two approaches. Simulation effort is characterized by the average time needed to complete one simulation run. The results include the execution traces processing and mapping control overheads.

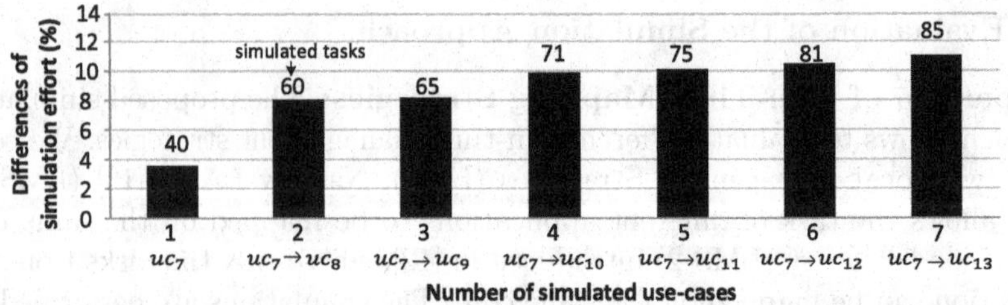

Fig. 8. The differences of simulation effort between the proposed approach and the default approach. Results are given for an increasing number of simulated use-cases and running tasks.

We define an increasing number of running use-cases within a fixed duration of simulation time, allowing each application to execute 100 to 240 periods. When the number of simulated use-cases increases from 1 to 7, the number of considered tasks increases from 40 to 85, while the difference of the simulation effort increases only from 3.8% to 10.8%. Since the proposed approach dynamically starts or stops the execution of tasks during simulation, it is reasonable to use more time to finish a simulation. But this overhead is also due to the fact that our approach takes into account the run-time manager in simulation while the default approach considers a static mapping (requiring eventually more corner-cases study). The improvement of the proposed simulation approach could be considered to reduce the dynamic activity of the run-time manager model.

6 Conclusion

In this paper, we present an approach to allow system-level simulation of run-time management strategies in multicore systems. This approach could be used to consider different numbers of applications executed on heterogeneous architectures at varied v/f configurations. It has been observed that the influence of the proposed approach on the simulation effort is reasonable (less than 10.8% compared to the default Cofluent framework for 85 running tasks). In the future, we plan to extend our approach to fully on-the-fly decision making strategies and to further minimize the simulation cost of the proposed approach.

References

1. Exynos 5 octa (5422). http://www.samsung.com/exynos
2. Intel cofluent studio. http://www.intel.com/
3. Sdf3. http://www.es.ele.tue.nl/sdf3
4. Butko, A., Bruguier, F., Novo, D., Gamatié, A., Sassatelli, G.: Exploration of performance and energy trade-offs for heterogeneous multicore architectures. arXiv preprint arXiv:1902.02343 (2019)
5. IEEE computer society: IEEE standard SystemC language reference manual. IEEE Std. 1666–2011 (9 2011). http://standards.ieee.org/getieee/1666/

6. Lee, E.A., Messerschmitt, D.G.: Static scheduling of synchronous data flow programs for digital signal processing. IEEE Trans. Comput. **100**(1), 24–35 (1987)
7. Lemaitre, J., Le Moigne, R.: Dynamic migration and performance optimization of deterministic applications across platform components using intel cofluent studio. In: DAC Workshop on System-to-Silicon Performance Modeling and Analysis, June 2015
8. Lieverse, P., Van Der Wolf, P., Vissers, K., Deprettere, E.: A methodology for architecture exploration of heterogeneous signal processing systems. J. VLSI Signal Process. Syst. Signal Image Video Technol. **29**(3), 197–207 (2001)
9. Pimentel, A., Erbas, C., Polstra, S.: A systematic approach to exploring embedded system architectures at multiple abstraction levels. IEEE Trans. Comput. **55**(2), 99–112 (2006)
10. Quan, W., Pimentel, A.: A hybrid task mapping algorithm for heterogeneous MPSoCs. ACM Trans. Embed. Comput. Syst. (TECS) **14**(1), 14 (2015)
11. Singh, A., Dziurzanski, P., Mendis, H., Indrusiak, L.: A survey and comparative study of hard and soft real-time dynamic resource allocation strategies for multi-/many-core systems. ACM Comput. Surv. (CSUR) **50**(2), 24 (2017)
12. Singh, A.K., Kumar, A., Srikanthan, T.: A hybrid strategy for mapping multiple throughput-constrained applications on MPSoCs. In: Proceedings of the 14th International Conference on Compilers, Architectures and Synthesis for Embedded Systems, pp. 175–184. ACM (2011)
13. Singh, A.K., Shafique, M., Kumar, A., Henkel, J.: Resource and throughput aware execution trace analysis for efficient run-time mapping on MPSoCs. IEEE Trans. Comput. Aided Des. Integr. Circuits Syst. **35**(1), 72–85 (2016)
14. Weichslgartner, A., Wildermann, S., Gangadharan, D., Glaß, M., Teich, J.: A design-time/run-time application mapping methodology for predictable execution time in MPSoCs. ACM Trans. Embed. Comput. Syst. (TECS) **17**(5), 89 (2018)
15. Zahaf, H., Benyamina, A., Olejnik, R., Lipari, G.: Energy-efficient scheduling for moldable real-time tasks on heterogeneous computing platforms. J. Syst. Architect. **74**, 46–60 (2017)

GEMBench: A Platform for Collaborative Development of GPU Accelerated Embedded Markov Decision Systems

Adrian E. Sapio[1](✉), Rocky L. Tatiefo[1], Shuvra S. Bhattacharyya[1], and Marilyn Wolf[2]

[1] University of Maryland, College Park, MD, USA
{asapio,rtatiefo,ssb}@umd.edu

[2] Georgia Institute of Technology, Georgia, USA
wolf@ece.gatech.edu

Abstract. Markov Decision Processes (MDPs) provide a powerful decision making framework, which is increasingly being used in the design of Embedded Computing Systems (ECSs). This paper presents a detailed accounting of the use of MDPs in this context across research groups, including reference implementations, common datasets, file formats and platforms. Inspired by recent results showing the promising outlook of using embedded GPUs to solve MDPs on ECSs, we detail the many challenges that designers currently face and present GEMBench (the Gpu accelerated Embedded Mdp testBench) in order to facilitate experimental research in this area. GEMBench is targeted to a specific embedded GPU platform, the NVIDIA Jetson platform, and is designed for future retargetability to other platforms. GEMBench is a novel open source software package that is intended to run on the target platform. The package contains libraries of MDP solvers, parsers, datasets and reference solutions, which provide a comprehensive infrastructure for understanding trade-offs among existing embedded MDP techniques, and experimenting with novel techniques.

Keywords: Markov Decision Processes · MDP · GPU · CUDA · Value Iteration · Embedded software · Benchmarking

1 Introduction

In recent years, Markov Decision Processes (MDPs) have become increasingly relevant in the design of Embedded Computing Systems (ECSs) [20]. However, progress in this area currently suffers from a lack of common benchmarking methodologies. The work presented in this paper helps to bridge this gap.

More specifically, this paper presents a summary of challenges associated with MDP-based design for ECSs, a survey of the state-of-the-art in MDP solvers and datasets that are relevant to embedded systems, and a novel open source software package for facilitating experimental research in the implementation

D. N. Pnevmatikatos et al. (Eds.): SAMOS 2019, LNCS 11733, pp. 294–308, 2019.
https://doi.org/10.1007/978-3-030-27562-4_21

and application of embedded MDPs. MDPs have long been used in a multitude of application areas for controlling complex systems in sophisticated ways [2]. However, the incorporation of MDPs into resource constrained systems is greatly hampered by the computational requirements of the MDP *solver*, a critical algorithmic component needed to deploy MDPs in dynamic ways [16]. For this reason, many researchers have studied and proposed techniques to make efficient, compact and optimized MDP solvers.

In recent years, a new class of MDP solver implementations has emerged that uses GPUs for acceleration. Examples of solvers in this class include those presented by Noer [14], Ruiz and Hernandez [17], and Sapio et al. [20]. The results in these works show performance improvements of roughly an order of magnitude beyond what is possible with CPU-only solvers. A variable-dependency analysis has been presented to provide insight into why MDP solvers can benefit significantly from the parallelism available in GPUs [20].

GEMBench is designed to help researchers address significant logistical challenges in incorporating MDPs and their solvers into novel embedded system designs. An important decision point in this context is whether to develop a new MDP solver or to use an existing implementation. This decision point leads naturally to the following questions: Which existing open source MDP solver alternative is the best to use or compare against for a given set of system design constraints? How much processing time, memory and power does a given solver consume in order to solve a given MDP? Can we improve on the MDP solver's performance through optimizations or algorithmic innovations?

GEMBench is targeted to a specific embedded GPU platform, the NVIDIA Jetson platform, and is designed for future retargetability to other platforms. The orientation to a specific platform is important for the objectives of GEMBench, which include promoting quantitative comparison among alternative MDP solvers and implementations.

We additionally contribute an open source software package [1], called the *GEMBench Package*. The GEMBench Package can be downloaded onto the targeted platform to create a development testbench. The testbench contains implementations of published solvers, datasets to run the solvers on, reference solutions to the datasets, documentation on how to measure relevant performance metrics, and guidance on how to contribute future developments to the framework in a consistent manner. The testbench, which encompasses the GEMBench-compatible platform (NVIDIA Jetson) and the GEMBench Package, is what we refer to as *GEMBench*.

A block diagram of the GEMBench Package, illustrating the major components is shown in Fig. 1. The arrows denote the flow of information, where, in a given experiment, a selected solver utilizes a selected MDP format-specification parser to solve a selected MDP. The solver, parser, and MDP are selected from three extensible libraries, respectively. The package is intended to allow new solvers to be written by researchers, who would immediately have datasets to run them on and reference solutions to compare them with in order to validate correctness. Additionally, performance measurements, such as execution time and power consumption, can be obtained and compared to other reference solvers provided by the package. Furthermore, all of this can be automated to efficiently create extensive benchmarking data through the use of execution scripts, which are also included with the package.

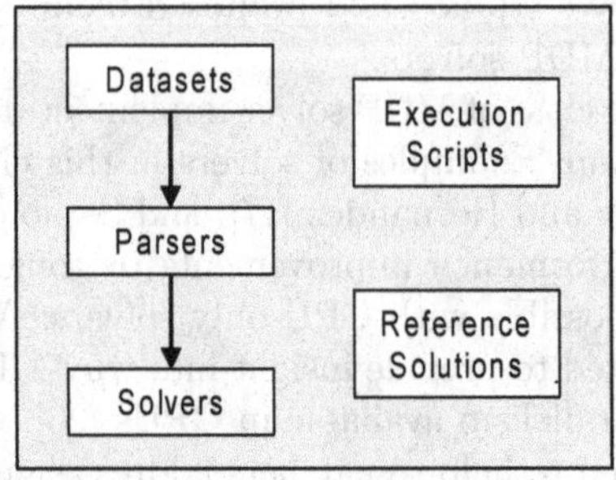

Fig. 1. Block diagram of the GEMBench Package.

2 Background

MDPs provide a generic decision making framework that uses abstract concepts including *states*, *actions*, *transition probabilities* and *rewards*. Once these concepts are defined, they are passed to an MDP solver, which is an algorithm that produces an optimal policy with respect to those definitions. The policy is a mapping from states to actions, such that an ECS using the policy looks up what action to take for any given state.

MDPs are increasingly important in the use of ECSs. Recent examples of MDPs being used to design highly adaptive and dynamic embedded computing systems include a reconfigurable router [26], a reconfigurable digital filter bank [22], [21], a power management module for a microprocessor [5], and a smartphone scheduling program that synchronizes email efficiently [9], among many others.

For computing systems that operate under strict resource constraints, a primary goal is to frame an MDP in a way that produces a well performing solution. Alongside this, there is also the practical issue of whether the solver can be successfully implemented within the processing constraints of the targeted platform, and whether it can complete in an amount of time reasonable for the application. In this spirit, researchers have been working on algorithms to solve MDPs efficiently using limited computing resources for many years. We present a detailed survey of this history in Sect. 3.

2.1 Value Iteration

Value Iteration is a classical algorithm that is used to generate an optimal policy for an MDP. In Value Iteration, a real number (or value) $V(s)$ is associated with each state s. This mapping is known as the Value Function. The value $V(s)$ represents the expected reward that can be obtained from state s. The Value Function V is derived by using an iterative procedure. First, a value of zero is assigned to each state, and then the operations shown in Eq. 1 are used to incrementally converge from that to the optimal Value Function. Once a sufficient number of iterations is performed, the optimal Value Function is known and the optimal MDP policy can be obtained trivially from it.

$$V^n(s_i) = \max_{a \in \mathcal{A}}\{\sum_{s_j \in \mathcal{S}} P(s_j|s_i, a)[R(s_i, a, s_j) + \beta V^{n-1}(s_j)]\} \quad (1)$$

In Eq. 1, $V^n(s_i)$ is the approximation to the Value Function in state s_i at loop iteration n, $\mathcal{S}$ is the discrete state space, $\mathcal{A}$ is the discrete action space, $R(s_i, a, s_j)$ is the reward function for transitioning from state s_i to s_j after selecting action a, β is a scalar discount factor, and $P(s_j|s_i, a)$ is the probability of transitioning from state s_i to state s_j after taking action a. Most of the MDP solvers surveyed employ some variation of the Value Iteration algorithm.

2.2 POMDPs and Approximate Solvers

Another critical issue in deploying MDPs into ECSs is that the runtime system may not have any way to know exactly what state it is in. In this case, the problem statement changes to that of a Partially Observable MDP (POMDP).

In POMDPs, the policy is no longer a mapping from discrete states to actions, but instead a mapping from a continuous space known as the belief vector, to an action [18].

The belief vector represents a probabilistic interpretation of the system's best guess for what state it is likely in. Since the discrete state space is a subset of the continuous belief vector, POMDPs carry with them even more computational burdens for two reasons: (1) the solver is tasked with solving a harder problem, and (2) the system invoking the policy must maintain an evolving time series of the current belief vector, in order to use it as the input to the policy.

The solver survey (Sect. 3) covers both MDP and POMDP solvers, and similarly, GEMBench is developed for use on both solver types.

3 Survey

In this section, we present the results of our survey of existing MDP solvers, reference platforms and benchmarking efforts to date. The results are exhaustive to the best of the authors' knowledge. The survey focuses on aspects of MDP solvers that are important to understand from the viewpoint of experimenting with and deploying them on embedded systems.

We note that this survey is a subset of a much larger body of work. There are dozens of papers in the literature documenting MDP solver algorithms or techniques. Out of those efforts, only a subset contain an attached or referenced software implementation of the technique. It is on those works with a corresponding software implementation that we primarily focus on here.

Table 1. CPU-based MDP solver implementations.

Solver name	Development period	Language
pomdp-solve [4]	1994–2007	C/C++
Symbolic HSVI [23]	1998–Today	Java, Perl
MDP Toolbox for MATLAB [12]	1999–2002	MATLAB
ZMDP [24]	2004–2016	C/C++
SPUDD [8]	2007–2011	C/C++
Symbolic Perseus [15]	2007–2009	MATLAB, Java
APPL [3]	2009–2017	C/C++
C++ MDP Solver [6]	2010–2018	C/C++
MDPSOLVE [7]	2011–2015	MATLAB
libpomdp [10]	2011–2014	MATLAB, Java
AI-Toolbox [25]	2015–Today	C/C++

Table 2. GPU-based MDP solver implementations.

Solver name	Development period	Language
Noer13 [14]	2013	C++/CUDA
VI-Thrust [17]	2015	C++/CUDA
SPVI [20]	2015–2018	C++/CUDA

3.1 Solver Implementations

In Tables 1 and 2, we summarize the CPU-based and GPU-based MDP solver implementations that we have found to date, respectively. From this survey, we conclude first that MDP solvers have been an active area of research and development for the last 25 years. Second, researchers have commonly contributed their own solver implementations to the growing body of work.

We have tried to determine which of these implementations could be labeled as the current state of the art in solvers, but have had little success in doing so. Complications arose of the following types: Some algorithms did not compile on our computing system. We suspect version incompatibilities with dependencies in some cases, and poor documentation of multi-step build sequences in other cases. Some solvers ran successfully, but were not compatible with the same MDP files as other solvers. This is a critical shortcoming that effectively prevented objective comparison (without laborious conversion between different file formats).

3.2 Datasets

Benchmarking a solver requires not only a working solver implementation, but also an MDP for the solver to solve. We surveyed the MDPs used in solver implementations, and summarized the results in Table 3.

Table 3. MDP datasets.

Source	Number of MDPs	Format
SPUDD [8]	70	.spudd
pomdp-solve [4]	55	.pomdp
MDPSOLVE [7]	32	Constants in source code
Symbolic Perseus [15]	21	.spudd
ICAPS-04	20	PPDDL 1.0
ICAPS-16	15	RDDL
libpomdp [10]	15	.spudd and .pomdp
ZMDP [24]	9	.pomdp
AAPL [3]	8	.pomdp and .pomdpx
AIPS-02	8	PDDL 2.1
ICAPS-18	8	RDDL
AIPS-98	6	PDDL 1.0
AIPS-00	5	PDDL 1.0
ICAPS-06	10	PPDDL 1.0
ICAPS-11	11	RDDL
Noer13 [14]	2	.pomdp
AI-Toolbox [25]	4	Constants in source code
MDP Toolbox for MATLAB [12]	2	Constants in source code
C++ MDP Solver [6]	1	Constants in source code

In some cases, researchers simply created one MDP by instantiating the MDP data structures as constants in source code. This approach is perhaps the easiest route to solve a single MDP, but does not scale well to solve many different MDPs. In other cases, researchers stored an MDP's data structures in a file, and then created a means to read in and parse the file in order to provide the MDP to the solver algorithm. Some researchers defined new file formats for representing MDPs, while others adopted formats introduced by previous researchers. Clearly, the use of file-based specification of MDP data structures is more flexible than coding constants into source code, as it allows for one solver to solve many MDPs simply by changing the MDP file. Additionally, this method facilitates sharing of specific MDPs across research groups.

The first standard MDP file format that gained a foothold in this area was the `.pomdp` format [4], sometimes referred to as the Cassandra format (after the last name of the author). This is a human readable text file that describes the MDP components using a custom syntax that seems to have been created precisely for this purpose. The format is well documented, and many example MDPs can be found in this format throughout the literature.

The strength of the `.pomdp` format is that it is easy to read and relatively easy to parse with a few string parsing routines. The downside is that it is inefficient in terms of file size. In one case [24], an 180 MB file was required to specify an MDP, and in our own experiments, we can recall an MDP that went above 750 MB when stored in `.pomdp` format. We believe hundreds of MBs to be too large of a storage size requirement in general for ECSs, at the time of this writing.

In general, we have found that although MDP data structures can be very large, their information content is relatively low compared to their size. As a result, their associated information is highly compressible. See [20] for elaboration on these findings. The findings support the claim that the `.pomdp` format can introduce needlessly high files storage requirements.

The second format that has been re-used across research groups is the `.spudd` format, first created for use by the SPUDD solver [8]. This format is also a human-readable text file, but the MDP format is in the form of tree-shaped data structures known as Algebraic Decision Diagrams (ADDs). ADDs are used in `.spudd` files because the SPUDD solver operates on a specific type of MDP known as a *Factored* MDP.

Factored MDPs can often be stored very compactly using tree-shaped structures, and SPUDD even operates on the MDP using tree-shaped structures for the intermediate solver calculations. Other solvers inspired by or derived from SPUDD also use ADDs and `.spudd` files. The downside to this format is that an unfactored MDP must be factored before being stored in this format, and this factorization process can be very difficult or even impossible if the MDP does not contain a specific underlying conditional dependence property. Another downside to this format is that it is difficult to parse (compared to the `.pomdp` format), due to its use of tree-shaped structures and Lisp syntax.

A third effort at defining MDP file formats arose from a series of MDP solving competitions held as part of the International Conference on AI Planning and Scheduling (AIPS), which later merged with the International Conference on Automated Planning and Scheduling (ICAPS). In these conferences, MDP solver competitions were held on 10 occasions from 1998 through 2018. These competitions defined their own file formats, documented them for use by competitors, and provided the MDP files in those formats.

The file formats steadily evolved over the years, including the Planning Domain Definition Language (PDDL) [11] version 1.0, PDDL version 2.1, the Probabilistic Planning Domain Definition Language (PPDDL) [27] version 1.0, and the Relational Dynamic Influence Diagram Language (RDDL) [19]. These formats are by far the most complex (compared with `.spudd` and `.pomdp`), but also the most powerful and expressive. These file formats are designed to specify many different classes of planning and decision problems, beyond just MDPs and POMDPs.

3.3 Benchmarking Platforms

In the documents associated with each of the solver implementations we have found, there were no common hardware platforms used to conduct performance or benchmarking experiments. One exception to this is in the ICAPS conferences, where the competition organizers ran the candidate solvers on a common computer in order to compare performance objectively.

Aside from the ICAPS competitions, we found that some researchers did not take any runtime performance measurements at all, and of the researchers who did perform such measurements, usually the workstation that was available to that group was used. Commonly, researchers detailed the specifications of their computing systems. This approach seems to be the standard approach to date: each research group runs its algorithm on its own computing system, whatever it may happen to be.

With this approach, it becomes virtually impossible (without large amounts of reimplementation effort) to compare the runtime performance of alternative approaches introduced in two papers describing algorithms that are evaluated on different computing systems. There were no instances we could find where two research groups had the same computing hardware (in terms of processor type, CPU speed, RAM, etc.), even by coincidence.

3.4 Dimensionality of Rewards

An issue that further complicates the landscape is that of the dimensionality of the reward function. In Eq. 1, $R(s_i, a, s_j)$ is the reward function for transitioning from state s_i to s_j after selecting action a. This is an example of a three-dimensional reward function, since the function is a mapping from $\mathcal{S} \times \mathcal{A} \times \mathcal{S}$ to a scalar reward value. However, as noted in [13], some works use a two-dimensional reward function (a mapping from $\mathcal{S} \times \mathcal{A}$) and some use a one-dimensional reward function (a mapping from $\mathcal{S}$ only). This can present logistical challenges when attempting to piece together various works.

For example, if an MDP in `.pomdp` format from [4] is imported into MATLAB using the `.pomdp` parser from [15], the reward function will exist in the MATLAB workspace as a three-dimensional rewards object. That representation is then incompatible with the MATLAB solver MDPSOLVE [7], which only accepts at most a two-dimensional reward function.

Conversion strategies to mitigate this are as follows. Increasing the dimensionality of the rewards is trivial, as the extra function input can simply be ignored. Decreasing the dimensionality (as is required for the `.pomdp`/MDPSOLVE example above) requires some care. To reduce from a three-dimensional reward to a two-dimensional reward, we rewrite Eq. 1 as Eq. 2, and then evaluate the first summation to arrive at the equivalent expression using a two-dimensional reward function in Eq. 3. The resulting conversion formula is then shown in Eq. 4.

$$V^n(s_i) = \max_{a \in \mathcal{A}} \{ \sum_{s_j \in \mathcal{S}} P(s_j|s_i,a) R(s_i,a,s_j) + \beta \sum_{s_j \in \mathcal{S}} P(s_j|s_i,a) V^{n-1}(s_j) \} \tag{2}$$

$$V^n(s_i) = \max_{a \in \mathcal{A}} \{ R(s_i,a) + \beta \sum_{s_j \in \mathcal{S}} P(s_j|s_i,a) V^{n-1}(s_j) \} \tag{3}$$

$$R(s_i,a) = \sum_{s_j \in \mathcal{S}} P(s_j|s_i,a) R(s_i,a,s_j) \tag{4}$$

We note that this reduction can always be done without loss of information, and thus the constraint of at most a two-dimensional reward function is not a limitation for any solver. In spite of this, some solvers and parsers use three-dimensional rewards anyway.

There is no such formula to reduce from two-dimensional to one-dimensional rewards without loss of information. This can only be done in the special case where the content of the two-dimensional reward function is such that it is only a function of one of the arguments to begin with. In such a special case, the dimension can simply be collapsed along the dimension of the unused argument to convert to a one-dimensional reward function, typically $R(s)$.

4 GEMBench

As motivated in Sect. 1, we propose the use of a common benchmarking platform called GEMBench. This section details the components of GEMBench, and justification for the decisions made in its design.

4.1 Selection Criteria

Our selection of the hardware and operating system to target in the first version of GEMBench was made with the following considerations:

- Availability: the platform should be easily accessible to researchers, imposing minimal cost and logistical barriers.
- Repeatability: researchers should be able to reproduce published results from other researchers on their own platform instance, with their own experiments.
- Observability: researchers should be able to easily measure performance metrics that are relevant to ECS design, such as execution time, memory requirements, and power consumption.
- Ease of Use: A file system and robust networking stack is required to move MDP datasets and source code onto the platform with minimal effort.
- Development flexibility: the platform should be compatible with and contain rich support for toolchains of many different programming languages used in technical and scientific programming (e.g., C/C++, Python, Java, MATLAB, Go, Rust, Julia).

- GPU Support: We believe that GPUs will play a big role in the future advancements in MDP solvers, and thus the platform must have a programmable GPU.
- Documentation: The platform must be well documented in order to minimize the amount of initial time researchers need to spend to become productive.
- Long Term Support: The platform must have planned support for many years to come.

4.2 Hardware and Operating System

The common reference hardware of GEMBench, referred to as the GEMBench-compatible platform, is selected as the NVIDIA Tegra TX-1 Development Board. This platform is selected as one that satisfies the requirements summarized in Sect. 4.1. This is a Linux-based platform that contains a Quad ARM A57 CPU and an NVIDIA Maxwell GPU with 256 CUDA cores. The board contains 4 GB of RAM and a 16 GB eMMC storage. The board runs a Linux distribution known as Linux4Tegra (L4T), which is based on Ubuntu Linux. The software development kit provided with the board provides a well documented ecosystem.

The Linux-based OS provides a full-featured set of capabilities for software development and benchmarking, such as TCP/IP networking, USB, Wi-Fi, and HDMI video, to name a few. We favor Linux in this context over smaller embedded operating systems, such as Real-Time Operating Systems (RTOSs), due to its ease of use. Linux enables efficient use of common toolchains, and its file system and networking stack allow datasets to be copied onto the board easily. These two operations can be much more complicated on RTOS-based or smaller embedded OS systems. The lighter-weight OSs generally trade-off productivity in exchange for higher levels of optimization. In the design of GEMBench, we favor ease of use over optimization in this context. This is to provide a lower barrier to researchers getting up and running with the testbench.

4.3 Solvers

As part of the GEMBench Package [1], we have released an open source implementation of one of the GPU-accelerated solvers listed in Table 2: SPVI. This software package is intended to allow researchers who purchase the development board to easily reproduce the performance benchmarks of that solver. Additionally, the package contains guidance for how to contribute additional solvers that can be run on the platform. Specifically, the dependencies (and their versions) should be documented, along with compile and run instructions.

Ideally, researchers will be able to easily run any existing solvers, and then develop and implement new solvers on the platform, and easily produce benchmarking measurements that objectively compare multiple solvers on a robust collection of MDP datasets. The new performance claims can then be easily replicated across other research groups.

4.4 Datasets

A survey of datasets and their file formats used in MDP research was presented in Sect. 3. Due to the existing adoption of the `.pomdp` format across multiple research efforts, along with the large number of MDPs already available in that format, we encourage its continued use, and have selected it for our primary benchmarking dataset. We have included a curated set of `.pomdp` files as a packaged benchmarking dataset. Along with this set, we have provided the corresponding solutions to each of the MDPs, which is something we have not previously found anywhere to date. The reference solutions were obtained using the pomdp-solve [4] and MDPSOLVE [7] solvers, due to their maturity over newer solver packages.

Also included in the GEMBench Package is an open source C/C++ example of how to ingest and parse MDP files in the `.pomdp` format. This example is intended to save researchers time in incorporating this file format into their solvers.

4.5 Measurements

Execution time can be measured on the board using one of two methods. One method is the use of software-based timestamps. Using these involves making calls to the Linux `time` API from user space, and finding the difference between successive calls to compute elapsed time.

Another method to measure time is the use of GPIO combined with an external oscilloscope. A GPIO line can be set from Linux user space at the start of a solver routine, and then cleared at the end. By measuring the resulting square wave voltage on this GPIO pin with an oscilloscope, a very precise timing measurement can be made.

Both CPU and GPU memory use can be measured using the NVIDIA CUDA API. The `cudaMemGetInfo()` function is well-documented and allows for objective measurement of memory consumption.

The power consumption of the entire board can be measured directly from Linux user space. The board contains a Texas Instruments INA3221 Current and Voltage monitor, and instantaneous values can be read directly from the device using a device driver provided by the NVIDIA board support package.

5 Experiments

To demonstrate the use of GEMBench, we have implemented two MDP solvers on the NVIDIA Jetson TX-1 development board. The first implementation is a CPU-only implementation of Value Iteration, which we refer to as VI. This was created directly from the equations detailed in [16].

Our second implementation choice was Sparse Parallel Value Iteration (SPVI), which we developed in our previous work and describe in detail in [20]. SPVI leverages the GPU for execution time acceleration. A key feature of SPVI is that it uses sparse representations and sparse matrix-vector arithmetic operations in the GPU.

In our experiments, we measured the solver execution time on the entire Cassandra dataset using Linux's native timing support. The results for the full dataset are shown in Fig. 2. The curated Cassandra dataset has 55 MDPs on our testbench, and we show the results of solving all of these MDPs in the figure. Each data point represents one invocation of the solver on a specific MDP.

The MDPs in Fig. 2 are sorted by a scalar size metric $N_s^2 N_a$, where N_s and N_a are the number of states and actions in each MDP, respectively. We use $N_s^2 N_a$ to denote the size of the MDP because the largest data structures in an MDP are the state transition matrices, which contain a total of $N_s^2 N_a$ entries.

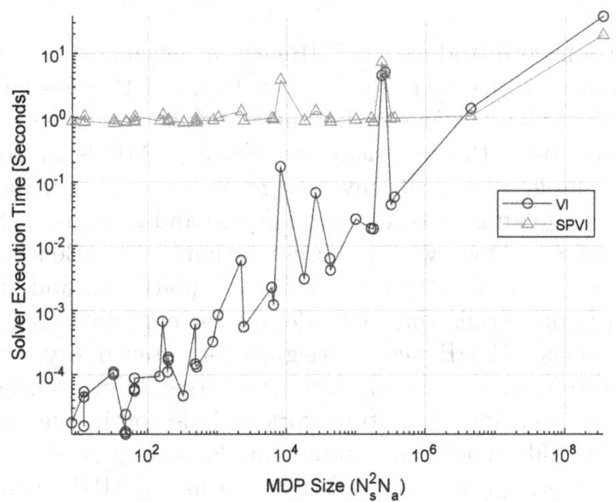

Fig. 2. Solver execution time for Cassandra dataset.

We draw several conclusions from Fig. 2. First, the GPU-based implementation (SPVI) takes at least one second to solve any MDP, regardless of how small it is. This is due to the amount of time it takes to setup the GPU and initialize the CUDA `cuSparse` library used by SPVI. We do not see any such setup time effect in the CPU-based VI algorithm.

Second, there is a crossover point around $N_s^2 N_a \approx 2e6$ beyond which the GPU-based solver is faster. To focus in on this aspect, we list the execution times for solving the four largest MDPs in Table 4. We see that for "baseball.pomdp" (the largest MDP in the dataset), SPVI (the GPU-based solver) is 48.5% faster than VI (the CPU-based solver), a considerable difference.

Third, we conclude that the Cassandra dataset is rich in small MDPs and lacking in large MDPs. Considerably more data is needed to explore GPU-based

Table 4. Solver execution time (seconds).

MDP name	$N_s^2 N_a$	VI	SPVI
cit.pomdp	3.22e5	0.043	0.964
sunysb.pomdp	3.60e5	0.058	0.980
fourth.pomdp	4.42e6	1.390	1.061
baseball.pomdp	3.53e8	37.653	19.373

solver performance on larger MDPs. The GEMBench project aims to spur collaborative research in directions such as this, which support more insightful and comprehensive evaluation of alternative MDP implementation approaches.

6 Conclusion

In this paper, we have introduced GEMBench, a benchmarking tool for evaluating implementations of solvers for Markov Decision Processes (MDPs). The utility of common benchmarking environments has been demonstrated in many application areas. With the increasing relevance of MDPs in embedded systems, and the complex trade-offs involved in MDP solver deployment, GEMBench helps to bridge an important gap in design and implementation of MDP-equipped applications. Along with the presentation of GEMBench, we have surveyed the landscape of MDP solvers, reference platforms and benchmarking with an emphasis on details that are relevant for experimenting with embedded implementations. GEMBench is designed for extensibility with additional file formats, datasets, and solvers, as well as retargetability to other processing platforms. Useful extensions for future work include continuing to add support for additional MDP file types and datasets, implementing more solvers from the literature, and exploring the tradeoffs between using an MDP versus a POMDP model for a given ECS.

Acknowledgments. This research was sponsored in part by the US National Science Foundation (CNS1514425 and CNS151304).

References

1. GEMBench Package (2019). https://ece.umd.edu/DSPCAD/projects/csm/packages/gembench.tar.gz. Accessed 14 Mar 2019
2. Benini, L., Bogliolo, A., Paleologo, G.A., De Micheli, G.: Policy optimization for dynamic power management. IEEE Trans. Comput. Aided Des. Integr. Circuits Syst. **18**(6), 742–760 (1999)
3. Brock, O., Trinkle, J., Ramos, F.: SARSOP: Efficient Point-Based POMDP Planning by Approximating Optimally Reachable Belief Spaces. MIT Press, Cambridge (2009)

4. Cassandra, A.R.: Exact and approximate algorithms for partially observable Markov decision processes. Ph.D. thesis, Brown University (1998)
5. Debizet, Y., Lallement, G., Abouzeid, F., Roche, P., Autran, J.: Q-learning-based adaptive power management for IoT system-on-chips with embedded power states. In: Proceedings of the IEEE International Symposium on Circuits and Systems (ISCAS), pp. 1–5, May 2018
6. Elod, P.: Vision-based quadcopter navigation for following indoor corridors and outdoor railways. Master's thesis, Technical University of Cluj-Napoca (2014)
7. Fackler, P.L.: MDPSOLVE: A MATLAB toolbox for solving Markov decision problems with dynamic programming – user's guide. North Carolina State University. Technical report, January 2011
8. Hoey, J., St-Aubin, R., Hu, A., Boutilier, C.: SPUDD: stochastic planning using decision diagrams. In: Proceedings of the Conference on Uncertainty in Artificial Intelligence, pp. 279–288 (1999)
9. Jung, E., Maker, F., Cheung, T.L., Liu, X., Akella, V.: Markov decision process (MDP) framework for software power optimization using call profiles on mobile phones. J. Des. Autom. Embedded Syst. **14**(2), 131–159 (2010)
10. Maniloff, D.: Libpomdp. https://www.cs.uic.edu/~dmanilof/code.html. Accessed 05 Jan 2019
11. McDermott, D.: PDDL — The Planning Domain Definition Language. Yale University, New Haven (1998)
12. Murphy, K.: Markov decision process toolbox for MATLAB. https://www.cs.ubc.ca/~murphyk/Software/MDP/mdp.html. Accessed 05 Jan 2019
13. Ng, A.Y.: Shaping and Policy Search in Reinforcement Learning. Ph.D. thesis, University of California, Berkeley (2003)
14. Noer, D.: Parallelization of the Value-Iteration algorithm for Partially Observable Markov Decision Processes. Master's thesis, Technical University of Denmark (2013)
15. Poupart, P.: Exploiting Structure to Efficiently Solve Large Scale Partially Observable Markov Decision Processes. Ph.D. thesis, University of Toronto (2005)
16. Puterman, M.L.: Markov Decision Processes: Discrete Stochastic Dynamic Programming, 1st edn. Wiley, New York (2005)
17. Ruiz, S., Hernandez, B.: A parallel solver for Markov decision process in crowd simulations. In: Proceedings of the Fourteenth Mexican International Conference on Artificial Intelligence, pp. 107–116 (2015)
18. Russell, S., Norvig, P.: Artificial Intelligence: A Modern Approach, 3rd edn. Pearson, London (2009)
19. Sanner, S.: Relational dynamic influence diagram language (RDDL): Language description (2010)
20. Sapio, A., Bhattacharyya, S., Wolf, M.: Efficient solving of Markov decision processes on GPUs using parallelized sparse matrices. In: Proceedings of the Conference on Design and Architectures for Signal and Image Processing (DASIP) (2018)
21. Sapio, A., Li, L., Wu, J., Wolf, M., Bhattacharyya, S.S.: Reconfigurable digital channelizer design using factored Markov decision processes. J. Sig. Process. Syst. **90**(10), 1329–1343 (2018)
22. Sapio, A., Wolf, M., Bhattacharyya, S.S.: Compact modeling and management of reconfiguration in digital channelizer implementation. In: Proceedings of the IEEE Global Conference on Signal and Information Processing, pp. 595–599 (2016)

23. Sim, H.S., Kim, K.E., Kim, J.H., Chang, D.S., Koo, M.W.: Symbolic heuristic search value iteration for factored POMDPs. In: Proceedings of the AAAI Conference on Artificial Intelligence (AAAI) (2008)
24. Smith, T.: Probabilistic Planning for Robotic Exploration. Ph.D. thesis, Carnegie Mellon University (2007)
25. Svalorzen, E.: AI-Toolbox. https://github.com/Svalorzen/AI-Toolbox. Accessed 05 Jan 2019
26. Wei, Y., Wang, X., Guo, F., Hogan, G., Collier, M.: Energy saving local control policy for green reconfigurable routers. In: IEEE International Conference on Communications, pp. 221–225 (2015)
27. Younes, H.L.S., Littman, M.L.: PPDDL1.0: the language for the probabilistic part of IPC-4. Technical report

Special Session: Insights from Negative Results

Hardware Deceleration of Kvazaar HEVC Encoder

Joose Sainio(✉), Alexandre Mercat, and Jarno Vanne

Tampere University, Tampere, Finland
{joose.sainio,alexandre.mercat,jarno.vanne}@tuni.fi

Abstract. High Efficiency Video Coding (HEVC) doubles the coding efficiency of the prior Advanced Video Coding (AVC) standard but tackling its huge complexity calls for efficient HEVC codec implementations. The recent advances in Graphics Processing Units (GPUs) have made programmable general-purpose GPUs (GPGPUs) a popular option for accelerating various video coding tools. Massively parallel GPU architectures are particularly well suited for hardware-oriented full search (FS) algorithm in HEVC integer motion estimation (IME). This paper analyzes the feasibility of a GPU-accelerated FS implementation in the practical Kvazaar open-source HEVC encoder. According to our evaluations, implementing FS on AMD Radeon RX 480 GPU makes Kvazaar 12.5 times as fast as the respective anchor implemented entirely on an Intel 8-core i7 processor. However, the obtained speed gain is lost when fast IME algorithms are put into use in the anchor. For example, executing the anchor with hexagon-based search (HEXBS) algorithm is almost two times as fast as our GPU-accelerated proposal and the benefit of GPU offloading is reduced to a slight coding gain of 1.2%. Our results show that accelerating IME on a GPU speeds up non-practical encoders due to their enormous inherent complexity but the price paid with practical encoders tends to be too high. Conditional processing schemes of fast IME algorithms can be efficiently executed on processors without any substantial coding loss over that of FS. Nevertheless, we still believe there might be room for exploiting GPU on IME acceleration but GPU-parallelized fast algorithms are needed to get value for additional implementation cost and power budget.

Keywords: High Efficiency Video Coding (HEVC) · HEVC encoder · Graphics Processing Unit (GPU) · Integer Motion Estimation (IME) · Full-Search (FS)

1 Introduction

High Efficiency Video Coding (*HEVC/H.265*) [1] is currently the state-of-the-art video coding standard. It adopts the conventional *hybrid video coding scheme* (inter/intra prediction, transform coding, and entropy coding) [2] used in the prior video coding standards since H.261. Thanks to its new coding tools and extended block partitioning scheme, HEVC is able to increase coding efficiency by 40% over the preceding *Advanced Video Coding* (*AVC/H.264*) standard [3] for the same objective visual quality. However, these new features also introduce computational overhead of about 40% [2].

D. N. Pnevmatikatos et al. (Eds.): SAMOS 2019, LNCS 11733, pp. 311–324, 2019.
https://doi.org/10.1007/978-3-030-27562-4_22

There are currently three noteworthy open-source HEVC encoders: *HEVC Test Model* (*HM*) [4], x265 [5], and Kvazaar [6]. HM supports all HEVC coding tools and is able to achieve high coding efficiency but it is far too slow for practical use. Kvazaar and x265 are practical solutions, of which academic Kvazaar was chosen for this work.

The complexity of HEVC is particularly leveraged in the inter prediction due to its numerous prediction modes and block partitions that have to be evaluated during the *rate-distortion* (*RD*) optimization. This paper focuses on *integer motion estimation* (*IME*) that is used in HEVC inter prediction to remove temporal redundancy of video scenes by searching the best matching block between the current and reference blocks. IME is only included in the encoder and it is one of the most complex coding tools in practical HEVC encoders [5, 6]. In software encoders, the complexity of IME can be primarily tackled by multithreading and *single instruction multiple data* (*SIMD*) optimizations. Further speedup can be pursued by offloading IME from a *central processing unit* (*CPU*) to external hardware such as *graphics processing units* (*GPUs*) which are considered in this paper.

GPUs have gained a lot of traction over the past decade. Especially, *general purpose GPU* (*GPGPU*) programming has made GPUs a popular option for accelerating various video coding tools. Particularly, several GPU implementations have been proposed for IME [7–13]. The current high-end GPUs are massively parallel platforms with *single instruction multiple threads* (*SIMT*) model and their computational capabilities are much higher than those of CPUs.

The complexity of IME is strongly dependent on the used *block-matching algorithm* (*BMA*). The well-known *full search* (*FS*) is the simplest, but the most computation-intensive BMA, which exhaustively tests all candidate blocks in the search area. In addition, numerous fast BMAs such as *hexagon-based* (*HEXBS*) [14] and *test zone* (*TZ*) [15] algorithms have been developed over the years. They are much faster than FS but they also suffer from somewhat reduced search quality. In addition, their irregular execution flows and arbitrary memory accesses can be executed with CPUs but the nature of GPUs requires regular execution and data flow.

In this paper, we present a GPU implantation of the BMA of the practical Kvazaar HEVC. The FS is chosen as BMA due to the regular data flow and its low control overhead which make it a promising candidate for massively parallel GPU architectures.

The rest of this paper is structured as follows. Section 2 explains the previous work. An overview of the HEVC IME process is given in Sect. 2.1, the concepts behind GPU programming are described in Sect. 2.2, and prior art is surveyed in Sect. 2.3. Section 3 describes our GPU-accelerated FS implementation in Kvazaar. Section 4 presents the performance results of our solution, compares them with those of prior art, and discusses why the results were not as good as one might expect. Finally, Sect. 5 concludes the work.

2 Related Work

In HEVC encoding, each frame is partitioned into *coding tree units* (*CTUs*) of 64 × 64 samples. The coding tree of HEVC utilizes a quadtree structure to partition the CTUs into smaller *coding units* (*CUs*), called nodes in a quadtree, as illustrated in Fig. 1(a). In HEVC, the size of CUs is equal to $2N \times 2N$, where $N \in \{32, 16, 8, 4\}$. The HEVC encoder starts by predicting the blocks from their environment (in time and space).

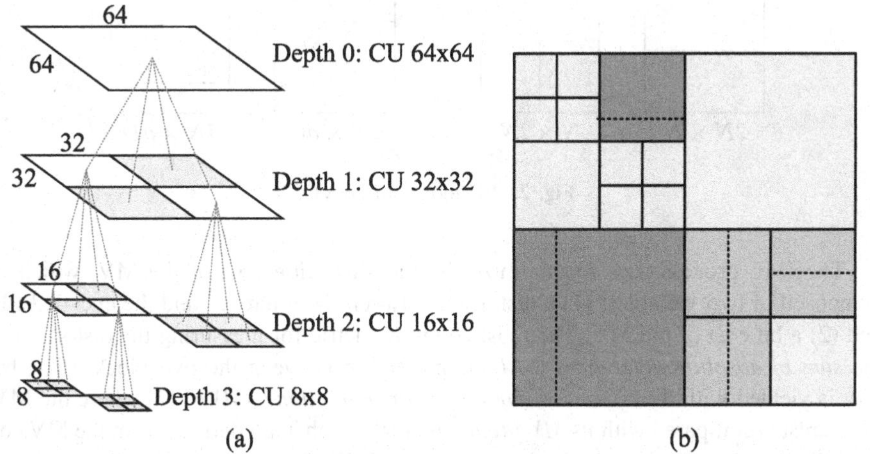

Fig. 1. (a) Partitioning of a CTU structure. (b) Example partitioning of a single CTU. (Color figure online)

2.1 Integer Motion Estimation in HEVC

The IME process determines integer *motion vectors* (*MVs*) in inter prediction. It is one of the most computation-intensive operation in HEVC encoding. In IME, CUs may be split into *prediction units* (*PUs*) of smaller size with the limitation of width and height being at least 4 pixels. A PU represents a picture region that shares the identical prediction information. The horizontal and vertical components of a MV describe the displacement of the PU in the reference frame. CUs can be divided into one, two, or four rectangular-shaped PUs called partition modes.

Figure 2 shows all possible partition modes and associated luma PU shapes specified for the inter-coded CU of size $2N \times 2N$. The supported mode set includes two Square modes ($2N \times 2N$ and $N \times N$), two *symmetric motion partition* (*SMP*) modes ($2N \times N$ and $N \times 2N$), and four *asymmetric motion partition* (*AMP*) modes ($nL \times 2N$, $nR \times 2N$, $2N \times nU$, and $2N \times nD$). Figure 1(b) exposes an example of the final partitioning of a CTU into PUs. The gray, blue, and red blocks represent the Square, SMP, and AMP partition mode, respectively.

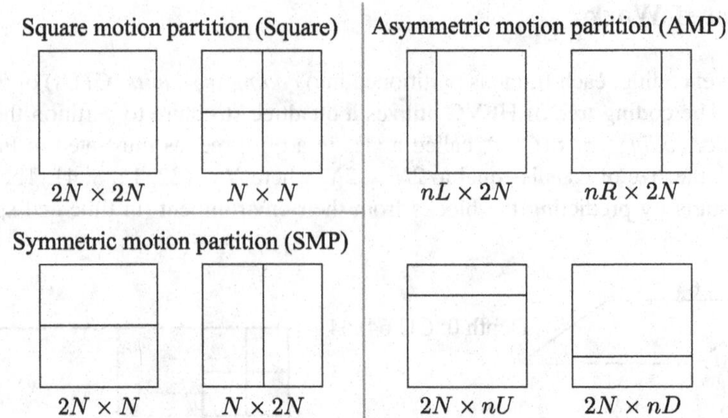

Fig. 2. PU modes in HEVC.

The IME process tries to minimize the rate-distortion cost of the MV, which is composed of two variables: (1) a distortion between the reference and the encoded PU and (2) a bit cost of the MV. The most common metric for measuring the distortion is the *sum of absolute differences* (*SAD*) computation between the two blocks. The bit cost is yielded with the *advanced motion vector prediction* (*AMVP*) [2] where the MV of interest is compared with its *MV predictors* (*MVPs*) that are derived from the MVs of spatially and temporally neighboring PUs. After IME, the result is refined in a quarter pixel domain with *fractional motion estimation* (*FME*).

Three BMAs are considered in this work: *full search* (*FS*), *hexagon-based* (*HEXBS*) and *Test Zone* (*TZ*). FS algorithm, which is the simplest but the most computation-intensive BMA, exhaustively tests all candidate blocks in the search area. HEXBS [14] algorithm selects recursively the best corner of the hexagon until the best location is the center. TZ [15] algorithm combines diamond search and raster search.

2.2 GPU Architecture and Programming

There are two key differences between CPU and GPU programming: the SIMT nature of the GPU and the memory architectural differences. An overview of the GPU memory architecture is depicted in Fig. 3. Unlike CPUs that usually have a few dozen of cores at most, GPUs consist of thousands of less powerful cores. In GPUs, these cores are grouped up to units that are called *Multiprocessors (MP)* in this work. Each GPU vendor has a different number of cores in a single MP, ranging typically from 8 to 64. A single MP has only a single instruction decoder for all cores and all of them execute the same instruction at the same time. When branching takes place, all the cores of a MP execute all branches, including unnecessary branches. To achieve the best performance, GPU programs should avoid branching whenever possible.

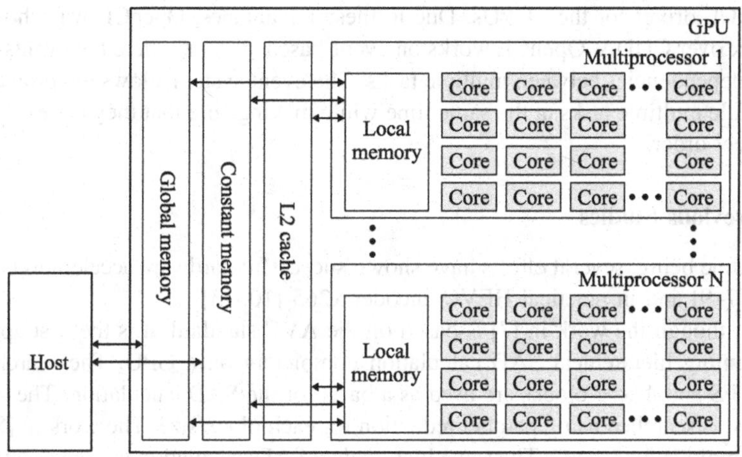

Fig. 3. The memory architecture of a GPU.

CPUs and GPUs have a similar memory structure including a central memory, a couple levels of cache, and registers which are closest to the cores. However, the memory architecture of CPUs is optimized for low latency, whereas the memory architecture of GPUs is optimized for high throughput by extending the width of the global memory. When all the cores in a single MP request a memory access in a single clock cycle, the operation is coalesced into a single access as long as all the cores refer to a single continuous block of memory. Memory access coalescing is an important aspect when designing a GPU-friendly algorithm. Additionally, GPUs can directly access the central memory of CPUs through the PCIe-bus, but the transfer speeds are fairly low. The local memory, which doubles as L1 cache, is shared between the cores of a single MP and can be used for fast data sharing. The programmer has direct control over memory allocation in the local memory, unlike the caches of a CPU. Nevertheless, the local memory size is typically limited to a few dozens of kilobytes per MP.

Work Items are the base elements of GPU programs. A single Work Item runs on a single core of a MP. Work Items are used to form a *Work Group*. A single Work Group is assigned to a single MP and each Work Group keeps this assignation until the end of its execution. A single MP can belong to multiple Work Groups simultaneously, as long as there are enough resources, registers, and local memory for each Work Group. Having multiple Work Groups at the same time allows hiding the latency of the high-throughput global memory. As context switch is a light operation on a GPU, once a Work Group has executed a memory operation, the MP can schedule another Work Group to run. This stresses the importance of reducing the amount of resources used per Work Group.

Currently, there are two notable options for GPGPU programming: CUDA and OpenCL. CUDA is a proprietary language maintained by NVIDIA and it only works for NVIDIA's GPUs. On the other hand, OpenCL is an open standard maintained by the Khronos Group. OpenCL is intended for programming many different platforms, including GPUs. All major desktop GPU vendors (NVIDIA, AMD, and Intel) provide an OpenCL driver for their GPUs. Due to these advantages, OpenCL was chosen for this work over CUDA. OpenCL works on event-based system, where the events can be used as dependencies between multiple tasks. The event system allows the programmer to schedule multiple tasks at the same time while making sure that they are executed in the correct order.

2.3 Previous Studies

For the time being, several efforts have shown successful hardware acceleration of IME in HM [7–9] and in practical HEVC encoder x265 [10–13].

Even though the work in [7] is based on the AVC standard, it is the first approach implementing hierarchical SAD calculation completely on a GPU. The search algorithm is FS and 4 × 4 blocks are used as a basis for the SAD calculation. The optimal SAD cost is searched using parallel reduction for each block size. The work in [8] is an extension of [7] for HEVC. The same hierarchical SAD calculation is used as a base. In addition, FME is performed on the GPU. Both implementations acquire about hundred times speedup when compared with respective CPU-only implementations. Conversely, the solution in [9] implements a nested diamond search that is similar to the TZ search. This solution is GPU friendly, but unlike [8], it cannot use hierarchical SAD calculation. The speedup is comparable to [8] with slightly higher quality.

In [10–12], a refinement search is performed on the CPU, after the GPU search part, to improve quality. The implementation of [10] is similar to that of [8] with the exception of the refinement search. Both IME and FME are refined on the CPU by using pre-calculated SADs transferred from the GPU to the CPU. Because the FME is done before the IME refinement, the FME has to be conducted on a larger area than usually would be necessary. The complexity of the refinement search is reduced in [11] by using a CPU to calculate only the best five search points found by a GPU. Instead of FS, [12] uses a regular search pattern that allows hierarchical SAD calculation. However, the refinement search cannot use the pre-calculated SADs for MVs that have not been calculated on the GPU. The approach of [13] is different since MV refinement is performed on the GPU instead of CPU. This is achieved by performing the IME in three steps where the first step selects an approximate MV for each block by using a sub-sampled picture. In the second step, the approximate MVs are used as the MVPs and updated accordingly. Finally, the updated approximate MVs are used in the FME level search as the MVPs.

3 Proposed GPU Acceleration Scheme for FS in Kvazaar

In this paper, we propose a GPU-accelerated FS IME that is based on [8] and [10]. The core principle of the algorithm is hierarchical SAD calculation with SAD reuse and the refinement search. Unlike in [8] and [10], we use 8 × 8 as a block size for SAD calculation since 4 × 4 blocks are not used in any presets of Kvazaar.

The MVPs in IME make PUs dependent on the previous PUs of the frame, so calculating all PUs at the same time reduces prediction accuracy by default. However, this is also the case with all previous works. Both [10] and our method utilize a pre-calculated table of bit costs and zero MV as the sole MVP. A refinement search is done on the CPU by using the SADs calculated on the GPU. Unlike [10], we use search range (the maximum displacement of the PU) of [−32, 32] instead of [−64, 64], since they do not have significant difference in quality but the latter is four times slower.

Algorithm 1 describes the proposed algorithm at high level. Choosing the granularity of the algorithm is important to gain the maximum benefit of the GPU. Choosing PU as the granularity would be an optimal choice for data dependencies according to AMVP algorithm. Nevertheless, this granularity would be too fine grain and the GPU would not have enough work for each MP. Next logical granularity level would be CTU level since the CTUs from the reference frame have to be fully processed before starting the current CTU. However, it is still too fine grain for efficient GPU implementations. CTU row level is the first level that is able to fully saturate the GPU and is selected for this work. Going to a coarser granularity would increase the waiting time for the GPU and decrease the performances.

Algorithm 1. Overview of the proposed method

```
Send the frame to be compressed to GPU
FOR EACH CTU Row index i:
  Send CTU Row i + 1 of the reference to GPU
  Expand reference
  FOR EACH 8×8 block:
    Assign block to MP
    Load frame to local memory
    Load reference from search area to local memory
    FOR EACH MV in Search Area:
      Calculate SAD
      Save SAD to global memory
FOR EACH PU size:
  FOR EACH PU in CTU row:
    Assign each PU to MP
    FOR EACH MV in Search Area:
      Combine SAD cost from the SADs calculated
      For the 8×8 blocks
      Save SAD to local memory
      Keep track of the smallest SAD cost
    Parallel reduction to find the smallest SAD
    From the search area assigned to the MP
    Save 9×9 SADs around the best MV to global memory
    Refinement search on CPU by calculating accurate
    bit cost using the pre calculated SADs
```

The process can be split into (1) the data transfer between the GPU and CPU and (2) the GPU computation on each MP, as described in Sects. 3.1 and 3.2, respectively.

3.1 CPU Implementation and Data Synchronization

Following Algorithm 1, the current frame is first read by the encoder and fully sent to the global memory of the GPU (line 1). Conversely, the reference frames are moved at a CTU row at a time. Because the MVs may point outside of the CTU, when an encoding of a row starts, the row below the current row of the reference frame is sent to the global memory (lines 2–3). For the first row, both the current row and the row below are sent. For the same reason, the reference rows are then expanded by copying the edge pixels (line 4). A visual overview of the data transfers and computations is depicted in Fig. 4.

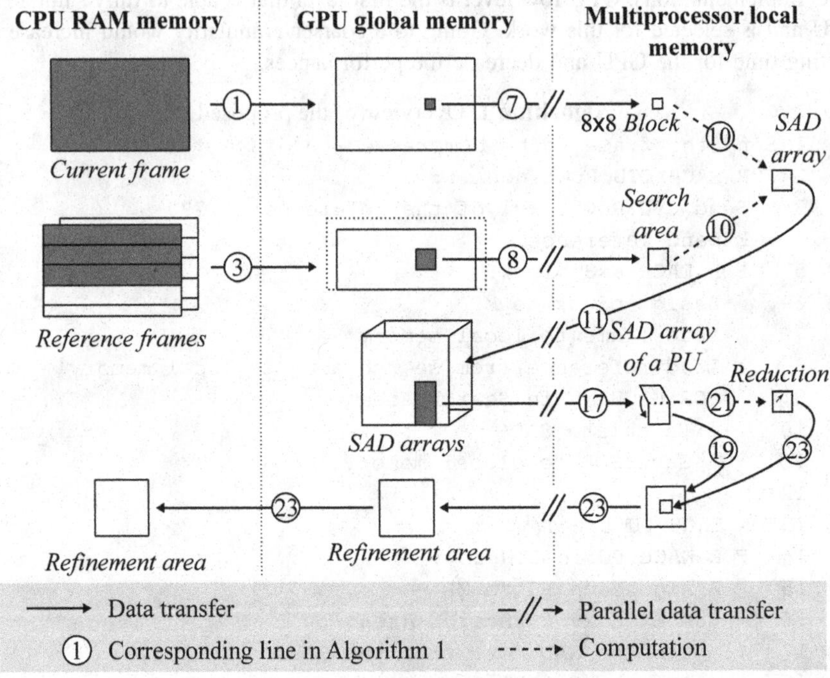

Fig. 4. Overview of the data transfers and computations.

The rest of the execution is split into two halves: the calculation of SAD (lines 9–11) and the reuse part (lines 13–23). For each CTU row, the expansion task, a SAD calculation, and reduction tasks are launched at the same time. The SAD calculation depends on the expansion, whereas the reduction depends on the SAD calculation.

After the GPU has finished the reduction task (line 21), the resulting MVs are transferred back to the central memory of the CPU (line 23). Additionally, some SAD values around the MV are moved to the central memory for refinement search. The refinement search is finally performed like regular FS except that SAD values are read from the memory.

Figure 5 depicts the *Bjøntegaard Delta Bit Rate* (*BD-rate*) of the video according to the refinement area size over the case that omits the refinement search entirely. The more the BD-rate is negative, the more higher coding efficiency. The results show that increasing the range of returned SADs improves the coding efficiency. The experimental set-up and metrics are fully detailed in Sect. 4. The improvement comes from the fact that on CPU, the MVPs can be used to accurately calculate the bit cost of the MV. On the other hand, Fig. 6 depicts the effect of the range of SADs returned to the relative encoding speed in *frames per second* (*fps*). The relative FPS is linearly dependent on the range while the quality changes roughly logarithmically. In order to perform the refinement search with the pre-calculated SADs, some overhead is introduced. The overhead can be seen from the trend line of Fig. 5 at the SAD range 0, which would be 1.00 without overhead. The results of Figs. 5 and 6 show that the quality improvement for larger ranges is low when compared to the increase in encoding time. According to this observation, the range is fixed to four in the rest of this work.

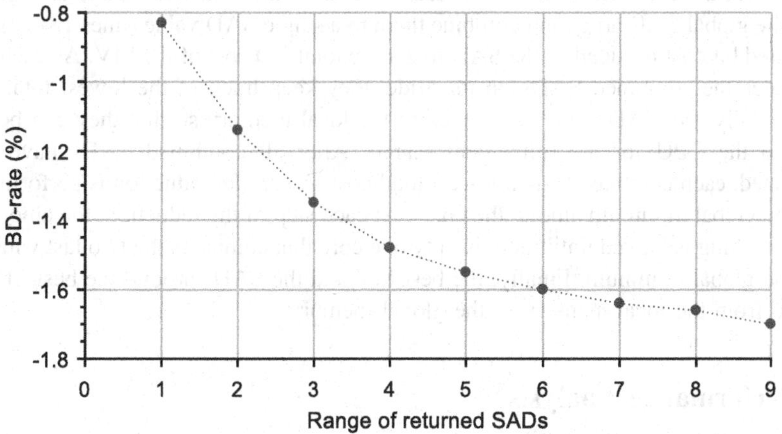

Fig. 5. Coding quality as a function of the search range of SADs.

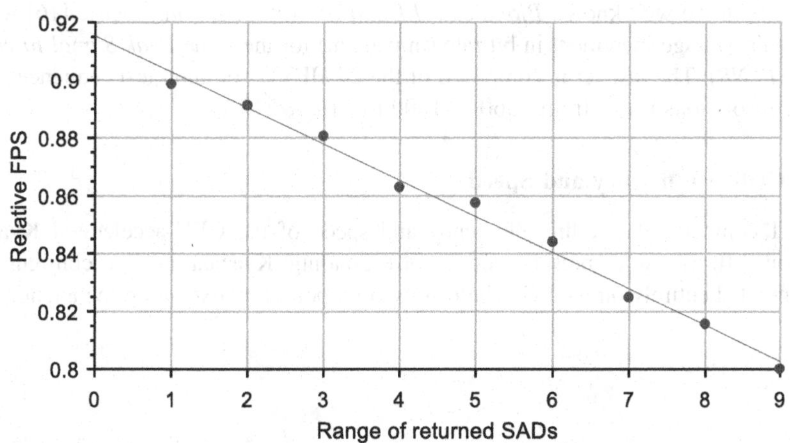

Fig. 6. Relative encoding speed as a function of the search range of SADs.

3.2 GPU Implementation and Computation

As explained in the previous section, the IME implementation on a GPU consist of two distinct steps: calculation of the SADs for each 8 × 8 block (lines 5–11 of Algorithm 1), and combining the SADs to calculate the optimal MV for each PU (lines 12–23). All the Work Groups are run parallel on the GPU. Each 8 × 8 block of the current frame is loaded to the local memory of the MP. The size of the reference area depends on the search range, which is fixed to [−32, 32] in this work, corresponding to a search area of 72 × 72 pixels. In order to reduce the local memory usage, only portion of the referenced area is saved to the local memory at a time. Each core of a MP calculates SADs in a stride of the width of the Work Group and each SAD value is saved into the global memory. The SAD calculation is finished once all SAD costs are saved to the global memory.

The reduction task to find the optimal MV is launched for each PU size. One Work Group is responsible for calculating the optimal MV for one PU. Similarly to the SAD calculation, the cores work in strides. Each core loads the values related to a single PU from the global SAD array and combine them to a single SAD value (lines 18–19). The estimated bit cost is added to the SAD to get the total RD cost of the MV. As each core calculates the combined SADs on its stride, they keep track of the lowest total cost. Additionally, the SAD values are saved to the local memory so that they can be sent back to the CPU for the refinement search. After all combined SADs have been calculated, each core has its own lowest total cost. A parallel reduction is performed to find the global minimum among the cores. At each step of the reduction, the amount of cores working is halved until there is only one core that compares the two last values to find the global minimum. Finally, the best MV and the SADs around the best MV are moved from the local memory to the global memory.

4 Performance Analysis

Our experiments are performed on an Intel i7-5960x 8-core processor with 16 GB of RAM and AMD Radeon RX 480 GPU. Different encoder configurations are benchmarked with the well-known *Bjøntegaard Delta Bit Rate* (*BD-rate*) metric [16] which represents average increment in bit rate (in percent) for the same *Peak Signal-to-Noise Ratio* (*PSNR*). The test set is composed of the 24 HEVC common test sequences [17] whose resolutions range from 2560 × 1600 to 416 × 240.

4.1 Coding Efficiency and Speed

Table 1 compares the coding efficiency and speed of the GPU-accelerated Kvazaar (version 1.0) *veryslow* preset over a corresponding Kvazaar anchor configuration implemented entirely on a CPU. The results are reported by executing the anchor with three different BMAs: FS, TZ, and HEXBS. The negative BD-rate results mean that our solution achieves better coding quality than the anchor (FS, TZ or HEXBS). In Table 1, green and red results correspond to positive and negative results, respectively.

Table 1. Proposed GPU-accelerated Kvazaar vs. original Kvazaar with different IME algorithms.

	Full search		**Test Zone**		**Hexagon based**	
Class	BD-Rate	Speed	BD-Rate	Speed	BD-Rate	Speed
HEVC-A	0.43 %	12.18×	-1.80 %	1.02×	-2.48 %	0.50×
HEVC-B	0.65 %	12.36×	-0.23 %	1.21×	-0.55 %	0.51×
HEVC-C	0.39 %	17.03×	-1.24 %	1.75×	-1.83 %	0.69×
HEVC-D	-0.04 %	16.78×	-1.00 %	1.38×	-1.18 %	0.64×
HEVC-E	0.20 %	6.48×	0.01 %	0.49×	0.00 %	0.36×
HEVC-F	6.04 %	10.61×	1.89 %	1.05×	-1.06 %	0.51×
Average	**1.28 %**	**12.57×**	**-0.39 %**	**1.15×**	**-1.18 %**	**0.53×**

Implementing FS on a GPU makes Kvazaar up to 12.5 times as fast as the anchor with an average BD-rate degradation of 1.28%. The highest quality degradation comes from screen content videos of the test set. The GPU acceleration also performs relatively poorly with sequences having a lot of static content. In these cases, the anchor FS only checks the zero vector most of the time and stops the search because the prediction is good enough whereas the GPU-accelerated FS always checks every possible candidate.

Furthermore, the obtained speed gain is lost when TZ and HEXBS are put into use in the anchor. With TZ, our GPU-accelerated approach is not more than 15% faster anymore. The good news is that our proposal achieves a slight BD-rate gain due to deployment of fast BMA in the anchor. With HEXBS, the gain increases to 1.18% but the anchor is almost two times as fast as our GPU-accelerated solution.

4.2 Comparison with Previous Work

The state-of-the-art techniques, presented in Sect. 2.3, can be split into two categories: techniques implemented on HM and x265. Because there are no previous attempts to accelerate Kvazaar on a GPU, our solution can only be compared with those made for HM and x265. However, comparing the speedup figures of our proposal with those of HM optimization techniques is challenging because HM is not intended for practical or real-time use. Therefore, only coding quality can be compared. Instead, comparing our results with those of x265 is relevant since both Kvazaar and x265 are practical encoders. Though, only the magnitude of speedup can be fairly compared in this case.

Among the existing solutions, the approach presented in [10] is closest to ours. It outperforms our proposal with quality but not with speedup. In [12], the FME was also implemented on a GPU which could explain the existing speedup gap. A quality difference between these two solutions is assumed to be caused by an inherent difference between the internals of x265 and Kvazaar.

The basic idea of [11] is also similar to ours but the speedup is slightly higher than that of [10], with similar effect to quality. However, neither mentioned the anchor version of x265, which makes accurate comparison of the speedups difficult.

The speedup obtained in [12] is really close to ours. Even though the speedup is higher than in [10], again, the anchor versions of x265 were not mentioned. The comparison of coding quality is also a bit difficult since they did not use the standard BD-rate, computed with four *Quantization Parameter* (*QP*) values, but they only reported the difference in bit rate and PSNR with a single QP value. Their solution had only a minimal effect on bit rate, which lets us assume that the coding efficiency of our proposal is at least as high as theirs.

The results of [13] are most interesting since they used a fast BMA as an anchor instead of FS. The main accomplishment of [13] was a real-time 4K 60 fps 10-bit encoder. However, the experiments were conducted using an old version of x265, whose performance is much lower than that of a newer version that would have been available. It is questionable whether the quality stays the same when the algorithm is applied to a more up-to-date version of x265. Moreover, the proposed solution of [13] is proven only on 10-bit video and thus it might not be suitable for general use.

4.3 Lessons Learned

Generally speaking, our results do not seem too poor when compared with typical optimizations introduced in the literature to an HEVC encoder. However, in our case, the overhead of the co-processor has to be counted in. The GPU in our solution has computational power of up to 5.8 TFLOPS and it consumes up to 150 W of power. Considering this overhead, better results than 15% speedup and slightly improved quality can be expected.

In general, FS is not very efficient. As an example, FS checks 4225 different candidates for each PU with a search range of [−32, 32] whereas HEXBS checks a few dozen on average with the same search range. Although GPUs are more powerful than CPUs, the gap is not large enough to compensate for the inefficiency of the FS algorithm. Furthermore, even GPU-friendly fast BMAs might not make GPU acceleration of IME worthwhile. In Kvazaar, IME accounts for only about 15% of the total encoding time in both ultrafast and veryslow presets, so not more than 15-20% speedup is possible even in theory. Moreover, the dependency to MVP makes a perfect offloading difficult to achieve.

The loss in coding efficiency over the anchor FS implementation is as expected. However, it is still somewhat higher than those reported for x265 and HM, which can be explained by the differences in RD optimization processes of Kvazaar, x265, and HM. Nevertheless, our solution outperforms the fast anchor TZ and HEXBS algorithms in coding efficiency.

Overall, quality degradation is not a huge concern for fast IME algorithms compared with the speedup they are able to provide. The BD-rate difference between the anchor FS and HEXBS is about 2.5%, which would be acceptable even for about 1.5 × speedup in most applications. In other words, a faster GPU-based IME implementation could have worse coding efficiency than HEXBS and it could still be considered successful, as long as it has a low overhead.

Though many prior works have included FME as a part of the GPU acceleration, to our best knowledge, nobody has evaluated acceleration of FME on a GPU separately. To conclude, it is in theory possible to accelerate Kvazaar veryslow preset by about 66% since Kvazaar uses about 40% of encoding time on IME and FME. Unfortunately, the feasibility of FME on a GPU is not explored to confirm this hypothesis.

5 Conclusions

In this paper, we presented an attempt to accelerate IME of the practical Kvazaar HEVC encoder on a GPU. The accelerated BMA was FS whose regular data flow and low control overhead make it a promising candidate for massively parallel GPU architectures. Even though our approach was able to accelerate Kvazaar by about 12.5 times at a cost of minor quality degradation, the gain was lost when our solution was compared with fast BMAs such as HEXBS and TZ algorithms. Furthermore, a closer look at previous studies revealed that our results are in line with them.

Despite the fact that our results are discouraging, we still believe HEVC encoder acceleration with GPUs could be a viable option but with more GPU-friendly fast BMAs. Another potential approach is to offload other coding tools such as FME together with IME to a GPU and this way reduce data dependencies and syncing between CPU and GPU. However, the data dependencies might still prove to be too great of a challenge to tackle with the GPU architecture.

Acknowledgements. This work was supported in part by the European Celtic-Plus project VIRTUOSE and the Academy of Finland (decision no. 301820). The authors would also like to thank all contributors of Kvazaar open-source project [6].

References

1. High Efficiency Video Coding, document ITU-T Rec. H.265 and ISO/IEC 23008-2 (HEVC), ITU-T and ISO/IEC, April 2013
2. Sullivan, G.J., Ohm, J.R., Han, W.J., Wiegand, T.: Overview of the High Efficiency Video Coding (HEVC) standard. IEEE Trans. Circuits Syst. Video Technol. **22**(12), 1649–1668 (2012)
3. Advanced Video Coding for Generic Audiovisual Services, document ITU-T Rec. H.264 and ISO/IEC 14496-10 (AVC), ITU-T and ISO/IEC, March 2009
4. Joint Collaborative Team on Video Coding Reference Software, ver. HM 16.0. http://hevc.hhi.fraunhofer.de/
5. x265. http://x265.org/
6. Kvazaar HEVC encoder. https://github.com/ultravideo/kvazaar

7. Lee, D., Oh, S.: Variable block size motion estimation implementation on compute unified device architecture (CUDA). In: Proceedings of the IEEE International Conference Consumer Electron., Las Vegas, NV, USA, January 2013
8. Lee, D., Sim, D., Cho, K., Oh, S.J.: Fast motion estimation for HEVC on graphics processing unit (GPU). J. Real-Time Image Proc. **12**(2), 549–562 (2016)
9. Hojati, E., Franche, J., Coulombe, S., Vázquez, C.: Highly parallel HEVC motion estimation based on multiple temporal predictors and nested diamond search. In: Proceedings of the IEEE International Conference on Image Processing, Beijing, China (2017)
10. Wang, F., Zhou, D., Goto, S.: OpenCL based high-quality HEVC motion estimation on GPU. In: Proceedings of the IEEE International Conference on Image Processing, Paris, France (2014)
11. Wang, X., Song, L., Chen, M., Yang, J.: Paralleling variable block size motion estimation of HEVC on multi-core CPU plus GPU platform. In: Proceedings of the IEEE International Conference on Image Processing, Melbourne, Australia (2013)
12. Kao, H., Wang, I., Lee, C., Lo, C., Kang, H.: Accelerating HEVC motion estimation using GPU. In: Proceedings of the IEEE International Conference on Multimedia Big Data, Taipei, Taiwan (2016)
13. Takano, F., Igarashi, H., Moriyoshi, T.: 4K-UHD real-time HEVC encoder with GPU accelerated motion estimation. In: Proceedings of the IEEE International Conference on Image Processing, Beijing, China (2017)
14. Zhu, C., Lin, X., Chau, L.-P.: Hexagon-based search pattern for fast block motion estimation. IEEE Trans. Circuits Syst. Video Technol. **12**(5), 349–355 (2002)
15. Werda, I., Chaouch, H., Samet, A., Ben Ayed, M.A., Masmoudi, N.: Optimal DSP based integer motion estimation implementation for H.264/AVC baseline encoder. Int. Arab J. Inform. Technol. **7**(1), 96–107 (2010)
16. Bjøntegaard, G.: Calculation of average PSNR differences between RD-curves. Document VCEG-M33, Austin, Texas, USA (2001)
17. Bossen, F.: Common HM test conditions and software reference configurations. Document JCTVC-L1100. Switzerland, Geneva (2013)

On Compact Mappings for Multicore Systems

Andrés Goens(✉), Christian Menard, and Jeronimo Castrillon

TU Dresden, Center for Advancing Electronics Dresden (cfaed),
Chair for Compiler Construction, Dresden, Germany
{andres.goens,christian.menard,jeronimo.castrillon}@tu-dresden.de

Abstract. Application mapping is key for efficient multicore processing, i.e., selecting which resources to allocate to a given application, like computation to cores. Mapping is increasingly difficult in multi-application scenarios, where resource contention might degrade the performance of an application. In order to solve this, a promising avenue is to consider "compact" mappings, those which require a small and (geometrically) compact area within the chip. Compact mappings should decrease contention between applications by providing regional isolation and allowing multiple applications to be mapped simply. Previous work has shown that compact mappings can significantly outperform mappings obtained with a random strategy. In this paper we investigate the promise of compact mappings by running extensive simulations on Noxim, a cycle-accurate network-on-chip simulator. Results show the promises of compact mappings do not hold up in practice. When comparing to mappings selected with a heuristic better than simply choosing cores at random, our experiments do not indicate significant advantages from compact mappings. We outline possible reasons for this.

1 Introduction

As multicores become more ubiquitous, Network-on-Chip (NoC) technologies play a role of continuously increasing importance in modern computing systems. Programming these systems is a difficult task, and a central component of it is that of finding a *mapping*, i.e., an allocation of computation and the flow of data on the system's resources. The mapping problem has been extensively studied [15], in particular in static single-application scenarios [3,5,12,13,18]. For multi-application systems, researchers commonly study so-called hybrid approaches, where (partial) single application mappings are combined dynamically at run-time [2,15]. Besides coordinating execution and communication within a single application, the execution of multiple-applications requires that contention between applications is minimized, which is achieved through a (partial) remapping at run-time in multi-application hybrid approaches [6,14,19] or isolation for security concerns [20].

Systems featuring a NoC are typically arranged in a regular fashion, which falls within only a handful of topology types, e.g. meshes, stars, rings or tori.

D. N. Pnevmatikatos et al. (Eds.): SAMOS 2019, LNCS 11733, pp. 325–335, 2019.
https://doi.org/10.1007/978-3-030-27562-4_23

Out of these, regular $n \times n$ mesh topologies, like the one depicted in Fig. 1 for $n = 4$, are by far the most common in the literature. These topologies allow designers to think in geometrical terms of mappings, which is what makes the idea of finding *compact* mappings for multi-application scenarios an evident one.

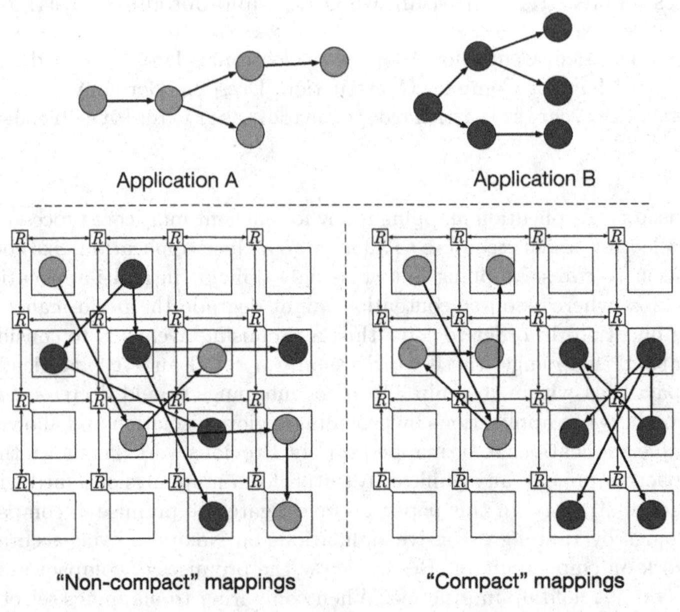

Fig. 1. Comparing compact and non-compact mappings.

Figure 1 illustrates the idea behind compact mappings. It depicts the task graphs of two applications, which are colored in green and blue respectively. The nodes of these task graphs represent computational tasks, and their directed edges the flow of data from one task to another. The figure shows two different multi-application mappings of both applications to a 4×4 mesh network-on-chip topology. Both mappings use exactly the same processing elements (PEs) of the architecture. In fact, if we ignore contention, both mappings should have the exact same behavior: a careful inspection reveals that the distances —in terms of number of hops— between any two communicating tasks in any of the applications are all exactly the same in both mappings. However, it is intuitively obvious that the mapping on the right of the figure is preferable: by being more *compact*, the mapping on the right will isolate communication within both applications. This helps to avoid contention and provides increased security. Additionally, it is intuitively simpler to combine single-application mappings like those on the right, since they are less *fragmented*.

In this paper we explore how the outlined intuition holds up to experimental scrutiny. After a brief formal background (Sect. 2) and discussion of related work (Sect. 3), we explore an experiment designed to assess the strategy of mapping applications to compact regions (Sect. 4). We discuss (Sect. 5) how the results of this experiment do not show significant advantages from compact mappings in practice, and comment on the conclusions (Sect. 6) we can reach from this work.

2 Mapping Tasks to MPSoCs

The problem of mapping can be defined at several levels of granularity. In this paper we focus on the mapping of computational tasks to cores. Let $G = (T, E)$ be the *task graph*, a directed graph representing the application. The nodes $t \in T$ of the task graph represent computational tasks that have to be executed on a core. In this paper we focus on a homogeneous setting, as is the most common setting in multicores featuring regular mesh NoC technologies. For homogeneous cores, we assume all tasks to require a fixed amount of execution time, independent of the core executing them. The focus of a mapping, and what ultimately guides its performance, is the communication between tasks. An edge in the task graph $e = (t_1, t_2) \in E$ represents a (logical) data dependency between tasks. Commonly, tasks graphs are labeled with the computational costs in the nodes and with the communication requirements in the edges. Depending on the status of the communication subsystem and the mapping, an application can incur in different communication costs for the same data. Thus, we do not encode these costs in the problem formulation directly; these have to be estimated, simulated, or better, measured.

A (task) mapping refers to a mathematical mapping $m : T \rightarrow \{\mathrm{PE}_{i,j} \mid i, j = 1 \dots n\}$ from the set of tasks to the set of processing elements (PEs), in this case indexed by two integers representing their position on the mesh. This mapping defines the allocation of tasks to PEs. The mapping problem is that of finding a mapping $m : T \rightarrow \{\mathrm{PE}_{i,j} \mid i, j = 1 \dots n\}$ that fulfills a particular goal, like minimizing execution time, energy consumption or NoC communication. In this paper we will define a mapping as minimizing the execution time, which we will measure by the average latency (network delay) as a proxy for execution time, since the cores are homogeneous. While a mapping m does not need to be injective, i.e., two tasks could be mapped to the same core $m(t_1) = m(t_2)$ for $t_1 \neq t_2$, we will consider mappings where this is not the case. This is common in many NoC-based multicore systems where the cores are smaller and scheduling and computational contention are costly.

3 Related Work

The work focusing on hybrid mapping [6,14,19] usually focuses on transforming single-application mappings or finding mappings at run-time with a particular set of constraints. To the best of our knowledge, none of these approaches directly concern themselves with compact mappings. Other work explicitly investigates the composability of applications in such scenarios, but focuses on explicit hardware support for this, not on leveraging the NoC topology [8,9]. While all of this work proposes sophisticated approaches, far beyond what is presented in this paper, the issue of compact mappings by itself has not been investigated by any of the these approaches. The intention of this paper is not to propose good heuristics for hybrid or composable mapping, but rather, to assess to what extent compactness is useful for this end.

Unlike all the other references focusing on hybrid and composable approaches, authors of [21] do consider compact mappings in multi-application scenarios for NoC architectures explicitly. The rigor of the contribution is unclear, as they compare their strategy to mapping at random. To avoid this, we compare to a non-compact mapping strategy that strives to find good mappings nevertheless. More importantly though, while the work of [21] is focused on proposing a heuristic, we focus punctually on the aspect of compactness in this paper.

4 Evaluation

In this section we evaluate the strategy of defining compact mappings for multi-application scenarios. For this we define an algorithm to find mappings with good communication properties and show how we can use it to generate compact and non-compact mappings.

4.1 Mapping Algorithm

We designed and implemented a mapping heuristic to find mappings with good communication properties. Since we are focusing on homogeneous multicore systems with a NoC in a regular mesh topology, our algorithm is designed for such a regular architecture. However, it would work for any mapping representation which yields a metric space on the architecture and mappings [7].

Our mapping heuristic is described in Algorithm 1. It starts with any node in the application that can be considered a root, i.e., such that there is a path from it to every node in the application. We assume the application graph is (weakly) connected and such a node exists. The algorithm assigns an unused core at random to this node and then iterates through the application graph in a breadth first fashion to assign cores such that the distance from a node to its predecessor is minimized in the mapping. This greedy algorithm does not ensure that the communication is minimized globally for the whole application, but it yields mappings with a total communication close to the minimum. We use it to produce compact mappings as well, by marking every core as occupied, except for an $m \times m'$ rectangle such that $mm' > |V|$, and we choose $\{m, m'\} \subseteq \{\sqrt{|V|}, \sqrt{|V|}+1\}$ minimal with this property. If we leave out the additional rectangle constraint, we get low-communication mappings that are not necessarily compact.

4.2 Experimental Setup

For our evaluation, we use a slightly modified version of the NoC simulator Noxim [4]. Noxim is a SystemC based simulator that is capable of modelling a

Algorithm 1. A greedy heuristic for low-communication mapping

input: A connected application graph $\Gamma = (V, E)$, the size of the mesh n, a set of occupied cores $X \subseteq \{1, \ldots, n\} \times \{1 \ldots, n\} =: M$

output: A mapping $m : V \rightarrow M$

CurNode $\leftarrow$ RandomFrom($M \setminus X$)
$v_0 \leftarrow$ Root(Γ)
mapping $\leftarrow$ ($v_0 \mapsto$ CurNode)
$X \leftarrow X \cup \{\text{CurNode}\}$
for $e = (n_1, n_2) \in$ BreadthFirstEdgeSearch(Γ) **do**
    CurNode $\leftarrow$ mapping(n_1)
    $d \leftarrow \min_{d=1 \ldots n}\{a \in M \setminus X \mid |a - \text{CurNode}| \leq d\} \neq \emptyset$
    $q \leftarrow$ RandomFrom($\{a \in M \setminus X \mid |a - \text{CurNode}| \leq d\}$)
    mapping(n_2) $\leftarrow q$
    $X \leftarrow X \cup \{q\}$
return mapping

wide range of NoC configurations and traffic patterns. We modified Noxim to obtain more detailed statistics that also include the variance of packet delays in order to evaluate the predictability of given mappings. In our configuration, Noxim simulates a mesh topology with xy-routing and worm-hole switching. This basic setup is comparable to current research platforms [1] as well as commercial products like Intel Xeon Phi [16], Intel Xeon Scalable Platform [17] and Mellanox Technologies TILE-Gx series [10,11]. We choose a network size of 10×10 nodes for our experiments.

The execution of dataflow application is simulated by providing a traffic table to Noxim. For each edge in the application task graph we add one entry to the table which specifies source node, target node and the packet injection rate. During the simulation, each node randomly injects packets at the given rate. By varying the packet injection rate of the channels, we can simulate low and high network loads. In the following, we report experiments using a fixed packet size of 32 flits. We did test several packet sizes, up to $2^{12} = 4096$ flits, but found the results to be comparable for all packet sizes tested.

We use 10 applications with 4 to 6 nodes, and generated 100 compact mappings, 100 non-compact mappings and 100 completely random mappings for these 10 applications. Algorithm 1 has some random choices, which results in different mappings for each of the applications. These 100 iterations together with the random choices are intended to account for the variance between mappings and scenarios.

4.3 Results

Figure 2 shows how the average network delay (latency) in the system varied across the different mapping strategies and corresponding mappings for three distinct values of the injection rate. We see how compact mappings are indeed significantly better than a random mapping, in all cases. However, a comparison of the compact and non-compact mappings shows no significant difference between

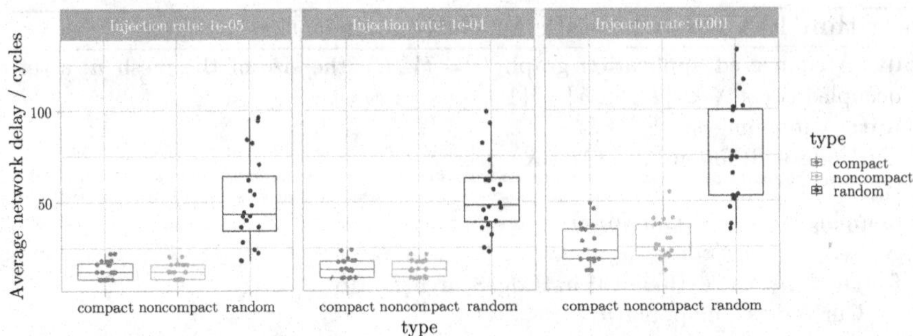

Fig. 2. Comparison of the average network delay of 100 mappings for different strategies and injection rates. Additional to the box and whiskers plot, the actual points are overlayed with random horizontal jitters for visibility.

both strategies, in terms of the average network delay. While non-compact mappings obtained with Algorithm 1 are also designed to reduce the average delay, one would expect more contention between applications to worsen the average delay. This does not seem to be the case in Fig. 2.

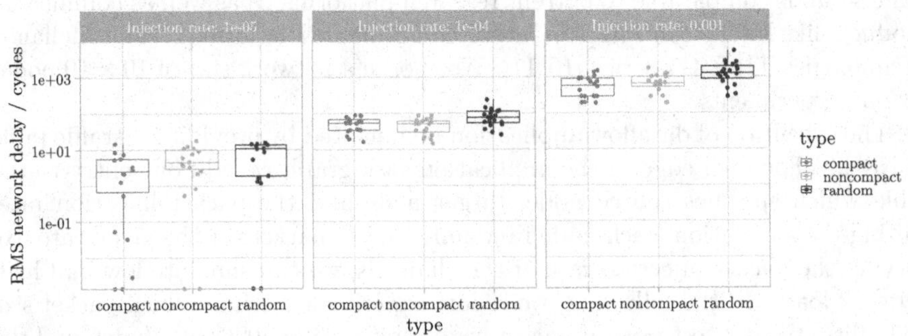

Fig. 3. Comparison of the root mean square network delay (log) of 100 mappings for different strategies and injection rates. Additional to the box and whiskers plot, the actual points are overlayed with random horizontal jitters for visibility.

Predictability is of comparable importance to the average latency in many use cases. To measure how predictable a mapping behaves we used the slightly modified version of Noxim to obtain the root mean square of the network delay. The results for the 100 mappings can be seen in Fig. 3 (note the logarithmic axis). We see how, in a few cases, compact mappings had a significantly higher predictability. However, in general, there does not seem to be statistically significant differences between compact and non-compact mappings.

A better measure of predictability, however, is the comparison between the application running in isolation, i.e. alone in the system with no contention, versus the same application running in a multi-application scenario with possible

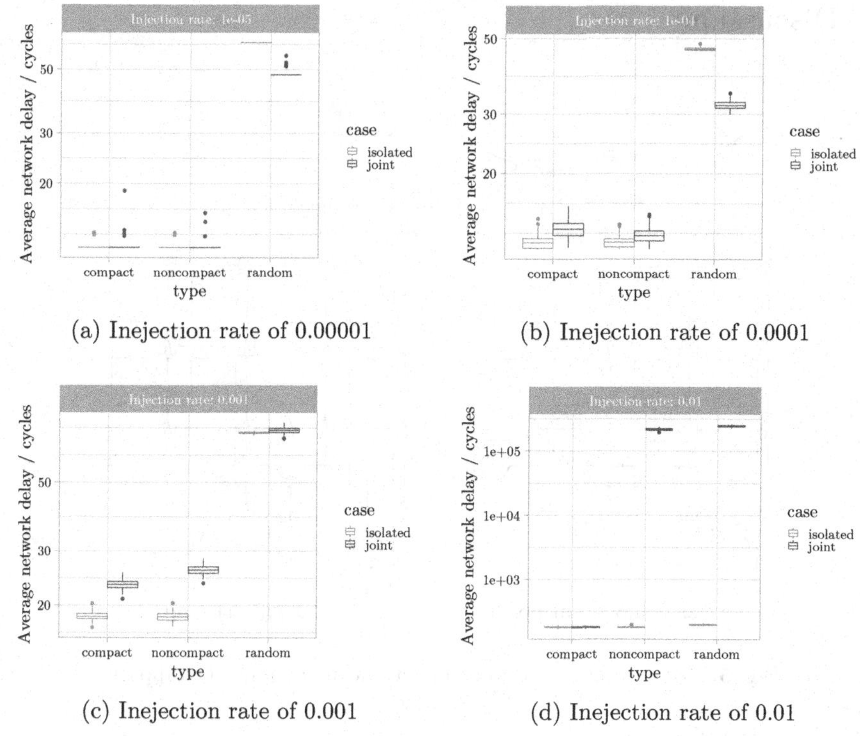

(a) Inejection rate of 0.00001

(b) Inejection rate of 0.0001

(c) Inejection rate of 0.001

(d) Inejection rate of 0.01

Fig. 4. Comparison of average network delay (log) for the first application, running in isolation vs a joint environment with 9 additional applications.

contention. To asses this, we reproduced the previous setup, but instead of all ten applications, we executed only the first one in isolation. We compared it to the values for that same application in the multi-application scenario. In an ideal case, with no contention, these scenarios would result in the same latencies. However, as we can see in Fig. 4, this is not the case. All three mapping types, compact, non-compact and random, suffered significant performance penalties in the multi-application scenario. Moreover, for the lower injection rates (Figs. 4a and b), the results seem to be again very similar between compact and non-compact mappings. However, with an injection rate of 0.001, which means that roughly every 1000 cycles a package is injected, a small albeit significant difference emerges, as seen in Fig. 4c. This injection rate is already extremely fast: it means in a system clocked at 1 GHz, a package is sent every μs. It is unrealistic for many applications to actually fire at these rates. Nevertheless, to investigate it further we repeated the setup with an injection rate of 0.01, shown in Fig. 4d. Here, indeed, compact mappings very significantly outperform non-compact ones when contention is present in a multi-application scenario. Such a high rate is however of no practical relevance.

5 Discussion

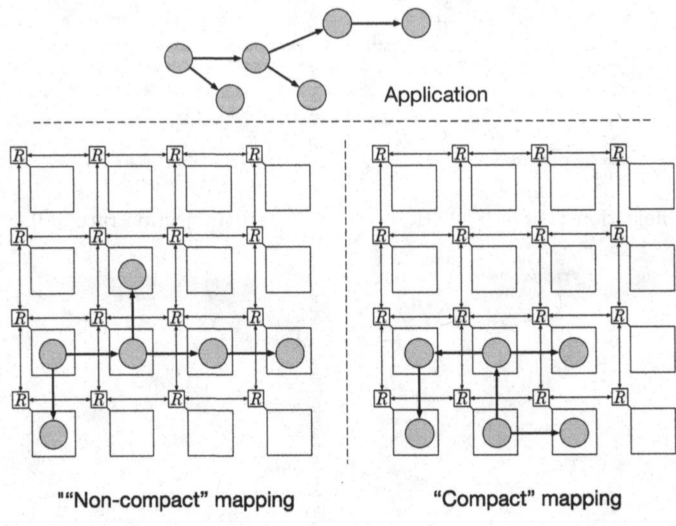

Fig. 5. Comparing a typical compact and non-compact mapping.

The results from Sect. 4 show basically no difference between compact and non-compact mappings for realistic scenarios. The advantages of compact mappings only seem apparent when the network traffic is so high that the average latency becomes hundreds of times higher than the computation time, with computation times between communication instances that would be smaller than a μs in most modern systems. We believe these scenarios are not of practical relevance. Thus, from the results we cannot conclude that compact mappings are better. However, we can neither conclude they are worse from our results. It is evident that ensuring compactness is an additional restriction, which makes algorithms more complex, but also reduces the space of possible mappings. Thus, the engineering investment to find and exploit compact mappings does not seem to be worth the effort.

These results defy intuition. To better understand why this is the case, we can return to the motivating example of Fig. 1. If we simulate both scenarios in a setup like the one used for our evaluation, the non-compact variant turns out to be unequivocally better. If we look at the mappings more carefully, especially the compact ones, they generate a large amount of inter-application contention. In short, they simply are bad mappings. Compare this to the illustration from Fig. 5. The two mappings shown here are typical results of mapping using Algorithm 1. They are significantly better mappings than the mappings shown in Fig. 1 (note that the application graph is slightly different). The two mappings from Fig. 5 are also identical in terms of their topology: the distances, in terms of number of hops, between any two nodes, are identical in both mappings. However, these are also good mappings, since said distances are short (they are all 1 hop). The fact that their geometry is very different becomes irrelevant in practice, as shown from our evaluation. We believe the key takeaway from our evaluations to be that focusing on finding good mappings for an application seems to be more important than finding mappings that can be easily combined, if the latter come at the cost of the performance of the application in isolation. Inter-communication contention is significant for concurrent multi-processor applications.

5.1 Limitations

The evaluation of this paper has some clear limitations, which should be pointed out as part of this discussion.

The setup, including the applications evaluated are, in a sense, very homogeneous. All tasks have identical fire rates and the system is a regular mesh with homogeneous cores. While this type of architecture is indeed very common, it neglects heterogeneous multicores and more exotic topologies. It is possible to define and investigate compactness in these scenarios [7]. However, we do not see a compelling reason to believe these systems would behave differently.

Similarly, most applications have heterogeneity in the amounts of computation and data transfer that occur between tasks. This limitation is exacerbated by the fact that our simulation only considers traffic. This certainly limits the conclusive power of our experiments. However, we believe there is validity in the results even when accounting for these limitations. An application with heterogeneous amounts of data transfer will always have a *critical path* of nodes that effectively bounds the maximal achievable performance. Applications with a homogeneous behavior, like used in this paper, can be seen as an approximation of the behavior of this critical subgraph that neglects the minor effects from the non-critical parts of the application. Similarly, the mappings considered all had no computational scheduling, and thus at most one task per core. This is increasingly common in multi- and manycore systems, but it certainly restricts the generality of the investigation. Additionally, while there was a non-zero probability of cores overlapping, this happened at an average of 0.03 cores per scenario. It means that for a core executing a task in our simulations, chosen uniformly at random, there was a probability of less than 0.0006 that it was a core shared between two different tasks. Even in this case the simulation is not necessarily wrong, if the computational contention is not high enough. This makes the error introduced by this fact negligible.

Finally, we only considered performance as seen by latency in this work. Thus, any conclusions we might draw about compact mappings will only apply to performance-related issues. There might me other reasons for which compact mappings could prove to be a valuable idea, like privacy (see [20]), or when considering thermal effects.

6 Conclusion

In this paper we investigated the concept of compact mappings for multicore systems based on a mesh NoC. Counter-intuitively, our experiments did not show any advantages of compact mappings w.r.t. latency, both in terms of average and deviation, i.e. predictability. For extremely high and unrealistic traffic rates, this ceased to hold and compact mappings performed better than non-compact ones. However, the results seem to suggest that for any practical applications, focusing on finding a good mapping is more important than finding a mapping that can be easily composed in multi-application scenarios.

These conclusions are based on simulations of traffic and with a particular setup of applications. We see reasons to believe this would probably not change even if these limitations were removed. While we cannot rule out the usefulness of compact mappings, especially for goals other than system performance, we believe that there might be more worthwhile avenues of research in the field of multi-application mapping.

Acknowledgments. This work was supported in part by the Center for Advancing Electronics Dresden (cfaed) and the Studienstiftung des deutschen Volkes.

References

1. Balkind, J., et al.: OpenPiton: an open source manycore research framework. In: Proceedings of the Twenty-First International Conference on Architectural Support for Programming Languages and Operating Systems, ASPLOS 2016, pp. 217–232. ACM, New York (2016)
2. Castrillon, J., Leupers, R., Ascheid, G.: MAPS: mapping concurrent dataflow applications to heterogeneous MPSoCs. IEEE Trans. Industr. Inf. **9**(1), 527–545 (2013)
3. Castrillon, J., Tretter, A., Leupers, R., Ascheid, G.: Communication-aware mapping of KPN applications onto heterogeneous MPSoCs. In: DAC 2012: Proceedings of the 49th Annual Conference on Design Automation (2012)
4. Catania, V., Mineo, A., Monteleone, S., Palesi, M., Patti, D.: Cycle-accurate network on chip simulation with noxim. ACM Trans. Model. Comput. Simul. **27**(1), 4:1–4:25 (2016)
5. Eker, J., et al.: Taming heterogeneity-the ptolemy approach. Proc. IEEE **91**(1), 127–144 (2003)
6. Goens, A., Khasanov, R., Hähnel, M., Smejkal, T., Härtig, H., Castrillon, J.: Tetris: a multi-application run-time system for predictable execution of static mappings. In: Proceedings of the 20th International Workshop on Software and Compilers for Embedded Systems (SCOPES 2017), pp. 11–20. ACM, New York (2017)
7. Goens, A., Menard, C., Castrillon, J.: On the representation of mappings to multicores. In: Proceedings of the IEEE 12th International Symposium on Embedded Multicore/Many-core Systems-on-Chip (MCSoC 2018), pp. 184–191. Vietnam National University, Hanoi, September 2018
8. Hansson, A., Goossens, K., Bekooij, M., Huisken, J.: CoMPSoC: a template for composable and predictable multi-processor system on chips. ACM Trans. Des. Autom. Electron. Syst. (TODAES) **14**(1), 2 (2009)

9. Kumar, A., Mesman, B., Theelen, B., Corporaal, H., Ha, Y.: Analyzing composability of applications on mpsoc platforms. J. Syst. Architect. **54**(3), 369–383 (2008)
10. Mellanox Technologies. TILE-Gx36 processor (2015). http://www.mellanox.com/related-docs/prod_multi_core/PB_TILE-Gx36.pdf. Accessed 22 May 2019
11. Mellanox Technologies. TILE-Gx72 processor (2015). http://www.mellanox.com/related-docs/prod_multi_core/PB_TILE-Gx72.pdf. Accessed 22 May 2019
12. Nikolov, H., et al.: Daedalus: toward composable multimedia mp-soc design. In: Proceedings of the 45th Annual Design Automation Conference, pp. 574–579. ACM (2008)
13. Pimentel, A.D., Erbas, C., Polstra, S.: A systematic approach to exploring embedded system architectures at multiple abstraction levels. IEEE Trans. Comput. **55**(2), 99–112 (2006)
14. Quan, W., Pimentel, A.D.: A hybrid task mapping algorithm for heterogeneous MPSoCs. ACM Trans. Embedded Comput. Syst. (TECS) **14**(1), 14 (2015)
15. Singh, A.K., Shafique, M., Kumar, A., Henkel, J.: Mapping on multi/many-core systems: survey of current and emerging trends. In: Proceedings of the 50th Annual Design Automation Conference, p. 1. ACM (2013)
16. Sodani, A., et al.: Knights landing: second-generation intel xeon phi product. IEEE Micro **36**(2), 34–46 (2016)
17. Tam, S.M., et al.: Skylake-sp: a 14nm 28-core xeon® processor. In: 2018 IEEE International Solid - State Circuits Conference - (ISSCC), pp. 34–36, February 2018
18. Thiele, L., Bacivarov, I., Haid, W., Huang, K.: Mapping applications to tiled multiprocessor embedded systems. In: Seventh International Conference on Application of Concurrency to System Design, ACSD 2007, pp. 29–40. IEEE (2007)
19. Weichslgartner, A., Gangadharan, D., Wildermann, S., Glaß, M., Teich, J.: Daarm: design-time application analysis and run-time mapping for predictable execution in many-core systems. In: 2014 International Conference on Hardware/Software Codesign and System Synthesis (CODES+ ISSS), pp. 1–10. IEEE (2014)
20. Weichslgartner, A., Wildermann, S., Götzfried, J., Freiling, F., Glaß, M., Teich, J.: Design-time/run-time mapping of security-critical applications in heterogeneous MPSoCs. In: Proceedings of the 19th International Workshop on Software and Compilers for Embedded Systems, pp. 153–162. ACM (2016)
21. Yang, B., Guang, L., Xu, T.C., Säntti, T., Plosila, J.: Multi-application mapping algorithm for network-on-chip platforms. In: 2010 IEEE 26th Convention of Electrical and Electronics Engineers in Israel, p. 000540. IEEE (2010)

The CAPH Language, Ten Years After

Jocelyn Sérot(✉) and Francois Berry

Institut Pascal, UMR 6602 Université Clermont Auvergne/CNRS/SIGMA, Clermont-Ferrand, France
{jocelyn.serot,francois.berry}@uca.fr

Abstract. This paper is a critical self-assessment of the CAPH dataflow-based programming language. We try to identify some design mistakes which could explain why the language and its associated toolset, despite some very innovative features, never received a wide acceptance.

1 Introduction

CAPH [1–3] is a dataflow-based, domain-specific language for describing, simulating and implementing stream-processing applications. Applications are described as networks of purely dataflow actors exchanging tokens through unidirectional channels. From this description, the CAPH compiler can, as illustrated in Fig. 1:

– simulate the behavior of the application,
– generate a software implementation in SystemC,
– generate an hardware implementation in VHDL, ready to be synthetized on a FPGA circuit.

The development of the CAPH language and associated toolset started in 2008. The initial motivations were very pragmatical[1]. Our research team had started to develop FPGA-based cameras for embedded vision applications and we immediately agreed on the fact that having to use RT-level languages, such as VHDL or Verilog, to program these devices would significantly hinder their usage, esp. by "software" programmers with no specific skills in hardware design. High-Level Synthesis was only emerging at this period and available tools were either too expensive or produced inefficient or platform-specific code. Our target applications, however, shared a particular feature: they had to operate "on the fly" on digital video streams coming directly from sensors and were limited to low level image processing. For this kind of application, the dataflow model of computation offers a very elegant solution to the synthesis problem, because it can be used both as a *programming* and an *implementation* model: actors can be described as finite state automata and channels as FIFOs, which can both be implemented directly and efficiently in hardware, without the need for a global control mechanism. The development of the CAPH language therefore

[1] For a detailed account on the origins of the CAPH project, see [4].

D. N. Pnevmatikatos et al. (Eds.): SAMOS 2019, LNCS 11733, pp. 336–347, 2019.
https://doi.org/10.1007/978-3-030-27562-4_24

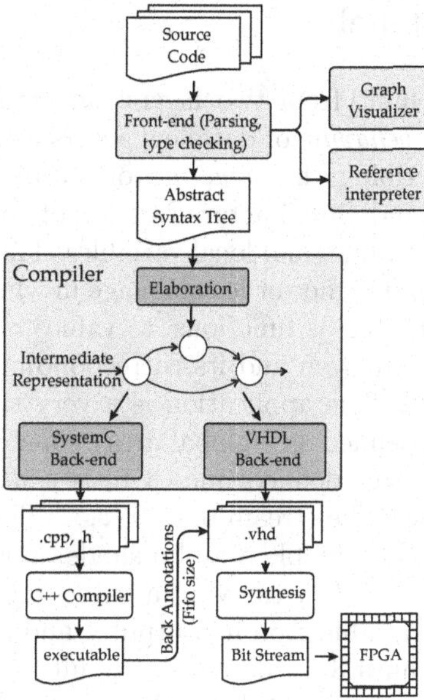

Fig. 1. The CAPH design flow

started with the very simple goal of allowing applications to be described as dataflow graphs in which the behavior of actors could be reduced to some kind of automaton. Compared to other similar projects[2], the two main distinctive characteristics were

- the possibility to systematically derive hardware implementations (by means of RTL transcription of actor behavior),
- the choice of a purely functional formalism for describing the structure of the dataflow networks.

Other features were added to the language latter with the general idea of increasing the *expressivity* of the language[3]. But, and contrary to what we expected, these additions did not help in increasing the audience of the language. In fact, a survey showed that most of users were only relying on the core, "historical", possibilities of the language, ignoring these extra features.

In this paper, we describe, in Sect. 3, two of these features and propose explanations for their non-adoption. In Sect. 4, we try to identify more general reasons why the language did not gain a wide acceptance, with the hope that the drawn conclusions can help language designers in the context of dataflow-based design. In order to be as self-contained as possible, the paper starts by a short presentation of the CAPH language in Sect. 2.

[2] The CAL language, for instance.

[3] Up to very recently. The latest version (2.9.0) was released in November 2018.

2 CAPH in a Nutshell

The CAPH language is built from two layers: an actor description language (ADL) for describing the *behavior* of dataflow actors and a *network description language* (NDL) for describing the *structure* of dataflow networks. The ADL describes the behavior of individual actors as a set of *transition rules* involving pattern matching on input values and local variables. The NDL is a small, purely functional, polymorphic and higher-order language in which graphs are described by applying actors, interpreted as functions, to values representing wires.

A very simple CAPH program and its corresponding dataflow graph representation is given in Fig. 2. The application is a very simple 1×3 FIR filter[4]. The filter coefficients are defined as a global array constant line 1. The program uses two actors. The `d` actor, defined lines 3–6, is a *delay*. Given a stream of token $x_0, x_1, \ldots$, it produces the stream $0, x_0, x_1, \ldots$. The behavior of this actor is described using a internal variable `z` and a single activation rule, saying that whenever the actor reads a token carrying a value x on its input `a`, it writes the value of the internal variable `z` on its output `c` and replaces this value by x. The `madd` actor, defined lines 8–12 describes a multiply-accumulate operation. Given a pair of tokens x and s, it produces the token $s + x \times c$, where c is given here as a (static) parameter. Lines 14–16 describes the global inputs and outputs of the program. In this version of the program, used for simulation, both input and output streams are read (resp. written) to files[5]. The input port `z` produces a stream of 0's. The dataflow graph (DFG) describing the filter itself is defined lines 18–22. The `d` actor is instanciated twice, producing respectively the one and two sample(s) delayed streams `x1` and `x2`. The `madd` actor is instanciated three times, implementing the classical "cascade" describing the filter. Each instance specifies a distinct value both for the parameter `c` and the actual IOs. The corresponding DFG is also given in Fig. 2.

3 Extra Features

The program in Fig. 2 only uses the so-called "core" features of the language. In particular

- the involved actors are very simple and operate on basic types (signed, 8-bit integers),
- the application DFG is described in a low level, explicit manner, by simply naming intermediate wires.

[4] This program is given only to illustrate some features of the language. It should not be viewed, in particular, as representative of the complexity of typical CAPH programs.

[5] A version intended for hardware synthesis will bind these inputs to process performing the physical IOs.

```
const coeff = [1,2,1] : signed<8> array[3];

actor d in (a:signed<8>) out (c:signed<8>)
  var z : signed<8> = 0
rules
| a:x -> (c:z, z:x);

actor madd (c:signed<8>)
   in (x:signed<8>, s:signed<8>)
 out (y:signed<8>)
rules
| (x:x, s:s) -> y:s+x*c ;

stream x:signed<8> from "sample.txt";
port z:signed<8> init 0;
stream y:signed<8> to "result.txt";

net x1 = d x;
net x2 = d x1;
net y1 = madd (coeff[0]) (x,z);
net y2 = madd (coeff[1]) (x1,y1);
net y = madd (coeff[2]) (x2,y2);
```

Fig. 2. A simple FIR filter described in CAPH

In the sequel, we describe several reformulations of this program, each introducing a new feature of the CAPH language. In each case, we first try to demonstrate the benefits of the feature and then speculate on the reasons why, despite this, it has not been adopted.

The reader must keep in mind that most of the explanations are very speculative because they were drawn from feedback from a very small set of users (less than a dozen) and from indirect observations[6].

3.1 Higher-Order Functions

A *higher-order* function (HOF) is a function accepting other functions as argument. A classical example is the `map` HOF, which takes a function f, a list of values $(x_1, \ldots, x_n)$ and returns the list obtained by applying f to each value x_i:

$$\text{map } f \ (x_1, \ldots, x_n) = (f \ x_1, \ldots, f \ x_n)$$

In functional programming languages, HOFs play a key role by allowing the encapsulation of common, recurring patterns of computation. In the context of network description languages, HOFs naturally map to the concept of *higher-order wiring function* (HOWF). For example the program in Fig. 2 can

[6] For example, if there's an obvious bug in the implementation of a feature which is not reported, we know that this feature has not been exercized....

be rewritten as in Listing 1.1 (in which all unchanged parts have been denoted as ...). The `fir` HOWF is defined lines 2–7 as taking an array of coefficients `c`, a wiring function[7] `tap`, an input wire `x` and instanciated as specified line 9 to generates the "cascading" graph pattern shown in Fig. 2. In Listing 1.1, the `tap` argument passed to the `fir` function is a single actor (`madd`). But – and this is where higher-orderness really shows its power – nothing prevents from passing a *function*. Listing 1.2, for example, gives another reformulation of the program in Fig. 2 in which the single actor `madd` is replaced by a *wiring function* `madd`, describing a subgraph composed of two distinct actors, `mult` and `add`. The corresponding DFG is given in Fig. 3.

Listing 1.1. A reformulation of the program in Fig. 2 using a higher-order wiring function

```
1  ...
2  net fir c tap x =
3    let x1 = d x in
4    let x2 = d x1 in
5    let y1 = tap (c[0]) (z,x) in
6    let y2 = tap (c[1]) (y1,x1) in
7    tap (c[2]) (y2,x2);
8
9  net o = fir coeff madd i;
```

Listing 1.2. Another reformulation of the program in Fig. 2 using the `fir` higher-order wiring function defined in Listing 1.1

```
...
actor mult (c: signed<8>)
  in (i:signed<8>) out (o:signed<8>)
rules
| i:x -> o:c*x;

actor add in (i1:signed<8>, i2:signed<8>)
          out (o:signed<8>)
rules
| (i1:x,i2:y) -> o:x+y;

net madd c (x,s) = add (s, mult c x);
...
net o = fir coeff madd i;
```

Discussion. Despite the fact that they significantly increase the abstraction level and reusability of programs, HOWFs do not seem to have been widely used by CAPH programmers, at least as a means of *defining* their own abstractions[8]. Here is a list of potential reasons:

[7] The reason for using this term is given below.

[8] The CAPH standard library provides several pre-defined HOWF.

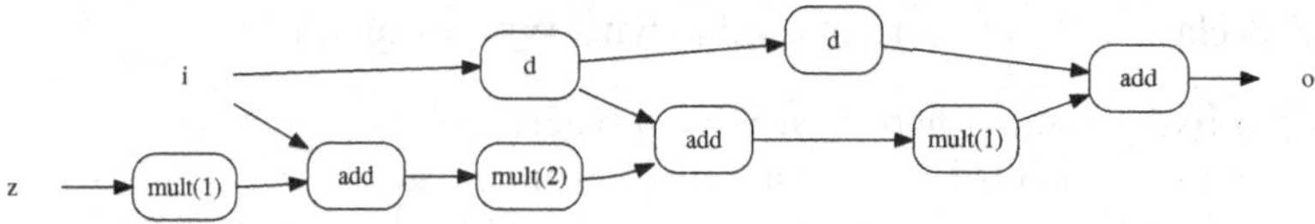

Fig. 3. The DFG corresponding to the program described in Listing 1.2

▷ The main usage of higher-order wiring functions is for encapsulating *graph patterns* and such patterns are only present in DFGs exhibiting some kind of *regularity*. Such regularity simply does not exist or is not worth to be encapsulated for "small" DFGs, containing only a few actors. This might be the case for the applications which have been developed with the tools.
▷ Large DFGs, describing applications at a finer grain level, essentially come from explicitely data-parallel formulations, for which specific solutions have already proposed to the "node explosion" problem. For example, in PREESM [5], replication is generally handled at the actor level. The LABVIEW dataflow-oriented IDE has a builtin factorisation mechanism to replicate actors.
▷ Higher-order functions ultimately requires a fully polymorphic type system, which can be disruptive for programmers not familiar with the subtleties of Hindley-Millner type inference and checking[9].
▷ The CAPH compiler systematically flattens the graph resulting from the instanciation of HOWFs. This is because all functions, including higher-order ones, are viewed as *specification*-level entities, not *implementation*-level ones. As a result, HOWF cannot be used to describe hierarchical graphs, in the sense used in the PiMM meta-model for example [6]. Having a direct interpretation of the former in terms of the latter would probably help for their adoption.

3.2 Algebraic Data Types

Algebraic data types (ADTs), also called *tagged unions*, allow values of different types to be mixed together by tagging them with a distinct label. Taking again our FIR example, consider the situation in which the data tokens could carry either real or complex values and that decision of how to process these values can only be made at runtime. A type for this kind of tokens could be defined with the following type declaration:

```
type sample =
    Real of signed<8>
  | Complex of signed<8> * signed<8>
```

[9] As a illustration, here's the type of the `fir` function given in Listing 1.2: $\forall \alpha, \beta.\ \alpha\ \text{array}[\beta] \rightarrow (\alpha \rightarrow \text{signed}\langle 8\rangle \times \text{signed}\langle 8\rangle \rightarrow \text{signed}\langle 8\rangle) \rightarrow \text{signed}\langle 8\rangle \rightarrow \text{signed}\langle 8\rangle$.

This declaration says is that a value with type `sample` is

- either a real, encoded here as a 8-bit integer,
- or a complex, encoded here as a pair of 8-bit integers.

The associated tag (`Real` or `Complex`) is used to distinguish between these two cases. More generally speaking, the declaration of a variant type lists all possible "shapes" for values of that type. Each case is identified by a specific tag, called a *value constructor*, which serves both for constructing values of the variant type and inspecting them by pattern-matching. This is illustrated in Listing 1.3, which is a reformulation of the program in Fig. 2 in which the type `signed<8>` has been replaced by the type `sample` defined above (again, all unchanged parts are denoted as ...). The filter coefficients are here defined (line 1) as an array of values with type `sample`[10]. Both the `d` and `madd` actors now consume and produce values with type `sample`. The behavior of the `madd` actor is now described using four activation rules (lines 10–15). These rules respectively handle the situation in which both inputs are real, both inputs are complex and one input is real and the other complex. The actual computation is here supposed to be carried out by a function `madd_f`, taking the real and imaginary parts of the arguments and returning either a real or a complex value[11].

Listing 1.3. A reformulation of the program in Fig. 2 using algebraic data types

```
1  const coeff = [Complex(1,0), Complex(2,1), Complex (1,1)]
2    : sample array[3];
3
4  actor d in (a:sample) out (c:sample) ...;
5
6  actor madd (c:sample)
7    in (x:sample, s:sample)
8    out (y:sample)
9  rules
10 | (x:Real x, s:Real s) -> y:Real (madd_f(s,0,x,0,c))
11 | (x:Complex (xr,xi), s:Complex (sr,si))
12                       -> y:Complex(madd_f(s_r,s_i,x_r,x_i,c))
13 | (x:Complex (xr,xi), s:Real s)
14                       -> y:Complex(madd_f(s,0,x_r,x_i,c))
15 | (x:Real x, s:Complex (sr,si))
16                       -> y:Complex(madd_f(s_r,s_i,x,0,c);
17
18 stream x:sample from "sample.txt";
19 port z:sample init (Real 0);
20 stream y:sample to "result.txt";
21 ...
```

[10] With the convention, for simplicity, that the real coefficients are stored in the real parts.

[11] The code of this function has not been reproduced in Listing 1.3 for simplicity.

Algebraic data types can be polymorphic, *i.e.* they can be parameterized over (an)other type(s), called the *argument types(s)*. For example, we could have defined the type `sample` as follows

```
type $t sample =
    Real of $t
  | Complex of $t * $t
```

where `$t` can be any type suitable for encoding the real and imaginary parts, so that

- the program of Listing 1.3 can be rewritten by replacing all instances of type `sample` by `signed<8> sample`,
- another version of the program, in which the real and imaginary parts are encoded, let say, as 32-bit float values, can be readily obtained by replacing, in the same program, the type `sample` by `float32 sample`.

Algebraic data types were originally introduced in CAPH to support the "data is control" concept. The idea that all the information required to interpret data streams must be embedded in the transported tokens. For example, images are encoded in CAPH using the following type:

```
type $t img = SoI | EoI | SoL | EoL | Pixel of $t
```

Tokens with values `SoI` and `EoI` (resp. `SoL` and `EoL`) are control tokens indicating the start and end of images (resp. lines) and pixels are carried by tokens having values `Pixel v`, so that, for example, the 4×4 image of Fig. 4 may be represented by the following stream of tokens:

```
SoI, SoL, Pixel(10), Pixel(30), Pixel(55), Pixel(90), EoL,
     SoL, Pixel(33), Pixel(53), Pixel(60), Pixel(12), EoL,
     SoL, Pixel(99), Pixel(56), Pixel(23), Pixel(11), EoL,
     SoL, Pixel(11), Pixel(82), Pixel(46), Pixel(11), EoL,  EoI
```

10	30	55	90
33	53	60	12
99	56	23	11
11	82	45	11

Fig. 4. A 4×4 image

With this representation, the dimensions of the images are explicitly contained in the token stream and hence no global control and/or synchronization is needed, which both allows the definition of size-generic actors and significantly eases the generation of RTL code. Moreover, it can be used to encode not only images but arbitrarily structured data.

Discussion. Except for the `img` type described above[12], the use of ADTs seems to have been limited in programs. Again, there are several possible explanations.

▷ Historically, most of dataflow-based programming languages have only supported "flat", unstructured data, essentially viewing tokens as "black boxes", the interpretation of which was left to the actors themselves. As a result, programmers in the related fields are not familiar with the typing concepts and mechanisms used by functional programming languages – from which CAPH borrowed the notion of polymorphic ADT[13].
▷ The idea of encoding the size of the manipulated data structures *within* the token stream is in strong contrast with other incarnations of the dataflow MoC, such as PSDF [7] and PiSDF [6], in which these dimensions are explicitely and separately specified as *parameters* passed to the concerned actors during a specific configuration step. Our experience shows that for programmers used to model applications with the latter kind of MoC, the former idea is often disruptive.
▷ Moreover, this idea seems to imply that the CAPH MoC is a purely dynamic one and this may have taken away programmers requiring a more static MoC. Even if CAPH *allows* specification of DDF applications, it can also be used to describe application obeying to the SDF (Synchronous Dataflow) or CSDF (Cyclo Static Dataflow) MoCs.
▷ The initial choice of representing images using ADTs was maybe a bad idea since it actually forces the programmer to delve into the syntax and semantics of ADTs even for trivial image processing applications. Having a pre-defined, dedicated type for images with ad-hoc syntax elements to access the individual pixels might have been preferable[14].

4 Lessons Learned

Several reasons can be invoked to explain why CAPH did not gain a wide acceptance as a programming language. We believe that these reasons can be related to three key questions that we probably have overlooked.

The first question concerns the **problems** the language is supposed to tackle.

The features discussed in Sects. 3.1 and 3.2[15] are undoubtedly powerful features confering to CAPH a distinctive position on the landscape of dataflow-based programming languages. They can also be viewed as a good example of the benefit of cross-fertilization between scientific domains (hardware design and

---

[12] Which is predefined in the standard library.

[13] A similar concept exists in C++-11, under the name "variant" but it was introduced recently and does not seem to be widely used.

[14] Moreover, representing images as lists of lists, as described above, has a very "lisp-ish" flavor which seems to induce strong repulsive reactions on certain kinds of programmers.

[15] And a few others not presented here, such as higher-order actors and dependent types for example.

programming language theory here). The problem is just that they were introduced not because there was a need for them expressed by the users, but because we, the designers of the language, thought there was.

Innovative and disruptive concepts may have an interest if the goal is to foster scientific or engineering understanding – which may perhaps later catalyze development of future languages – but, as long as the primary goal is to gain wide acceptance, these concepts should be introduced only if they solve a clearly identified problem or bottleneck in the existing design flow.

In this light, if we had the opportunity to restart the project from the beginning, we would probably devote more time to "low level" and pragmatic issues such as:

1. FIFO size minimisation whenever possible (the actor classification and static computation of these sizes for SDF DFGs only appear in version 2.9),
2. automatic retiming/pipelining for actors with long critical paths,
3. support for "soft" actors, written in C or C++ (and implemented as either as soft cores or on the HPS on the target FPGA),
4. support for common, cheap target platforms.

(1+2) would have helped breaking the "adoption barrier" among the hardware designers. Within a community which is much more concerned with resource usage and performance than the software one, a 50% overhead is often not acceptable, whatever the associated gain in productivity [8], as it is in sofware, by contrast.

(3) would have allowed to use CAPH as a high-level dataflow modeling tool within which the behavior of actors could be specified using a sequential imperative language such as C or C++. Of course, the scalability of the derived implementations remains low in this case because it is ultimately limited by the number of cores that can be instanciated on the target FPGA. But, with this approach, users can start by writing simple programs using their favorite programming language to specify actor behavior and then, if required, gradually switch to more hardware-friendy descriptions, such as those currently used in CAPH (a kind of Trojan horse, in a sense).

(4) Because such a support is, by essence, platform-specific, we did not provide one in the CAPH distribution (we had one, of course, but for our own needs, targeting a custom board designed in our laboratory). The idea was that CAPH was essentially platform-agnostic and that the so-called *board support packages* (BSPs) should be provided by the user. This makes sense of course when the target board is a specialized board (using for example specialized hardware drivers for image acquisition). But for the casual user, who simply wants to experiment with the language, the required effort is simply too high.

The second question concerns the **audience** of the language.

There clearly was an ambiguity, right from the start, concerning this audience. Was CAPH targeting in priority hardware of software designers? In the first case, the language should have been presented as a way of increasing the productivity by, for instance, removing the hassle of explicit synchronisation between computation units and extending the data abstraction levels compared to classical HDLs such as VHDL or Verilog. In the second case, it should preferably have been presented as an introductory path to FPGA design, making HDL coding unnecessary whenever dataflow is an appropriate MoC. This question is of great practical importance because hardware and software designers, as far as our experience has shown us, do not seem to put focus on the same concerns. Many of the former view expressivity as a secondary concern and are reluctant to the adoption of any tool increasing productivity as long as the price to pay is a decrease in performances. Many of the latter are not ready to give up the "good old sequential imperative" way of thinking and are simply waiting for C++ HLS because they view efficiency and resource optimisation as a secondary concern.

The third and last question is not specific to CAPH and probably concerns all dataflow-based programming languages and frameworks. It has to do with the **invasive** nature of the proposed language and toolset.

In many cases, the dataflow model is only used to give a very coarse grain formulation of an application, in which the actors implement complex functions, even algorithms, and the edge essentially carry "opaque" packets of data (full images for example). This interpretation limits the shift in programming paradigm imposed to the programmer, who essentially continues to think in a imperative way[16]. Going to lower granularity requires that the semantics of the underlying MoC is exposed. Many (most) programmers are reluctant to this: unless they have no other choice, they frequently think that the price to pay is too high[17].

The situation is even worse if using a dataflow model requires a *complete* reformulation of the algorithm. Unfortunately, this is exactly what CAPH does.

In this light, we'd better have provided, right from the start, a way to use actors written in C or C++. This would have made possible to introduce the language in a less invasive and hence more attractive way, as follows:

1. describe how CAPH can produce a software implementation from a set of actors written in C or C++,
2. exhibit some typical, performance critical, applications for which a few actors are acting as bottlenecks,
3. show how these actors – which are likely to be associated to low level compute-intensive operations – can be rewritten using CAPH actor description language,
4. demonstrate that the resulting effort/gain ratio is significative (compared to direct re-coding in VHDL or Verilog).

On a technical side, for this approach to be effective, some work should have been devoted in developing a general mechanism/framework allowing a dataflow application, composed both of software actors, running on a soft core for example, and hardware actors, implemented on a reconfigurable part of an FPGA, to seamlessly exchange tokens. This task has been in the "TODO" list of the CAPH project for years. Not giving it a high priority is likely to be one the worst mistake we made.

[16] The DFG is in this case nothing more than a call-graph in disguise.

[17] To be fair, the subtleties in the taxonomy of dataflow-based MoCs does not help.

Acknowledgements. Some ideas developed in this paper stem from numerous and fruitful discussions held during visits at the IETR laboratory in Rennes, in particular with M. Pelcat, K. Desnos and J.F. Nezan.

References

1. The CAPH software and reference manual. http://dream.ispr-ip.fr/CAPH
2. Sérot, J., Berry, F.: High-level dataflow programming for reconfigurable computing. In: 2014 International Symposium on Computer Architecture and High Performance Computing Workshop, Paris, pp. 72–77 (2014)
3. Sérot, J.: The CAPH Reference Manuel. http://dream.ispr-ip.fr/CAPH/dist/caph-lrm.pdf
4. Sérot, J.: CAPH - A bit of history. http://dream.ispr-ip.fr/CAPH/papers/misc/caph-history.pdf
5. Pelcat, M., Desnos, K., Heulot, J., Guy, C., Nezan, J.-F., Aridhi, S.: Preesm: a dataflow-based rapid prototyping framework for simplifying multicore DSP programming. In: 6th European Embedded Design in Conference on Education and Research, Milan, pp. 36–40 (2014)
6. Desnos, K., Pelcat, M., Nezan, J.-F., Bhattacharyya, S.; Aridhi, S.: PiMM: parameterized and interfaced dataflow meta-model for MPSoCs runtime reconfiguration. In: SAMOS XIII, Samos (2013)
7. Bhattacharya, B., Bhattacharyya, S.: Parameterized dataflow modeling for DSP systems. IEEE Trans. Signal Process. **49**(10), 2408–2421 (2001)
8. Pelcat, M.: Models, Methods and Tools for Bridging the Design Productivity Gap of Embedded Signal Processing Systems. Habilitation à Diriger des Recherches. U. Clermont (2016)

Comparison of Exponentially Decreasing Vs. Polynomially Decreasing Objective Functions for Making Quantum Circuits Nearest Neighbour Compliant

Leo Rogers[(✉)] and John McAllister

Queen's University Belfast, Belfast, UK
{lrogers08,jp.mcallister}@qub.ac.uk

Abstract. Many proposed architectures for quantum computing involve arranging qubits in a lattice, and then using swap gates to move the quantum states between qubits to enable any pair of qubits to interact with each other. Since swap gates perform no useful computation, they can be viewed as an overhead whose number should be minimised in efficient quantum programs. The location of the swap gates in a quantum circuit are chosen by minimising an objective function characterising the structure of the quantum circuit. Those which currently offer the lowest swap cost reduce the significance of each gate to the objective function relative to its position in the circuit. The criterion that describes how quickly the significance must decrease. In this paper, we show that to satisfy this criterion, it is necessary and sufficient for the decay to be exponential. However, when applying this new objective function, there is no significant improvement over the old function, with most of the benchmark circuits having less than 5% improvement. Only three circuits had more than 10% improvement in swap cost, and these circuits were all less than 100 gates long. The three longest circuits in the benchmark suite had less than 1% change in swap cost. There is also a significant penalty in run time, in one case reaching 265.48%.

1 Introduction

For Quantum Computers (QCs), there are certain problems that can be solved efficiently which would be intractable in classical computers, such as Shor's algorithm for factoring numbers [11], and algorithms for simulating quantum systems [4]. Current QCs have too few qubits and error rates which are too high to be able to solve these problems, but it is expected that we will soon be able to perform useful experiments with these Noisy Intermediate-Scale Quantum (NISQ) devices [1,3,9].

However, the error rates in NISQ devices will limit the maximum circuit depth possible before the result is dominated by noise. It is therefore necessary to minimise the length of quantum circuits and hence minimise the number of any operations required to move quantum information around a quantum processor

D. N. Pnevmatikatos et al. (Eds.): SAMOS 2019, LNCS 11733, pp. 348–357, 2019.
https://doi.org/10.1007/978-3-030-27562-4_25

due to the limitations of its architecture. In many proposals for QCs, qubits have fixed spatial locations, such as in ion traps [8], and can only intereact with other qubits that are near them. When non-local interactions (interactions between physically distant qubits) are required, some other mechanism must be used to mediate them. These mechanisms include using a quantum continuous variable as a quantum bus [12], or they could be mediated through swapping the quantum states of neighbouring qubits until the quantum states of the qubits that needed to interact are located in neighbouring qubits [6]. These architectures are called Nearest-Neighbour (NN) architectures, and the resultant quantum circuit after inserting these swap gates is said to be Nearest-Neighbour Compliant (NNC).

There is an algorithm that will make a circuit NNC using the minimal number of swaps, however it is intractable for anything other than very small circuits [7]. For larger circuits, several sub-optimal heuristics which reduce this complexity have been proposed. These use an objective function [2,5,14] to determine the best location for swap operations. The best results so far are in [5], which uses an objective function that takes the location of each gate into account, and reduces the contribution of that gate to the objective cost according to a 'priority' criterion. They propose an objective function that weakly satisfies this criterion.

The contribution of this paper is to show that for an objective function to strongly satisfy this criterion, it is both necessary and sufficient that the objective function contribution of each gate must decay exponentially with respect to it's distance from the earliest gate yet to be processed. However, when this objective function is applied, no significant benefit in swap cost is observed. This calls into question whether the ideal objective function needs to satisfy the priority criterion at all.

2 Background

A quantum algorithm is often presented as an idealised quantum circuit. One of the ways these circuits are idealised is that it is assumed that any qubit can be part of a 2-qubit gate with any other qubit. In reality, the architecture of the quantum computer limits which qubits can interact directly with each other, and the cost associated with indirect interactions will depend on the pair of physical qubits. In a swap-based architecture, the physical qubits are arranged in a lattice, and each qubit can only directly interact with its nearest neighbours. To facilitate indirect interactions between qubits that are not neighbours, swap gates are inserted prior to the relevant gate to exchange the quantum information between qubits until the quantum states associated with the idealised qubits in the circuit (logical qubits) are located in neighbouring physical qubits which can interact directly.

Automatically minimising the number of swap gates has been tackled as an objective function minimisation problem. The placement of the qubits (i.e. a 1 to 1 mapping of logical to physical qubits) at the beginning of the circuit, and just prior to each subsequent gate in the circuit, is determined by calculating the objective function cost of the remainder of the circuit for a number of placements, and the one with the lowest cost is chosen.

This technique was introduced in [10], in which the authors used the optimisation package Gurobi to minimise the objective function in (1), in order to find the initial placement, and then used an algorithm independent of the cost of the placement to insert the swap gates for the rest of the circuit.

$$Cost(P) = \sum_{i,j \in L} W(i,j)D(P(i),P(j)) \tag{1}$$

$$W(i,j) = \sum_{1 \leq m \leq N_g}^{N_g} 1 \tag{2}$$

$W(i,j)$ is the number of gates shared by logical qubits i and j, m is the time-step of all the gates using qubits i and j and N_g is the total number of gates. P is the placement, mapping logical qubit i to it's physical position $P(i)$, and $D(k,l)$ is the shortest distance between two physical qubits (which, on a rectangular lattice is equivalent to the Manhattan Distance), L is the set of all logical qubits.

However, [10] did not consider the objective function in choosing the swap gates to insert. Instead, they always swapped the control qubit towards the target qubit, first along the x-axis and then along the y-axis.

In [2], this objective function was used to choose the swap gates inserted in the circuit, after optimising the initial placement using Harmony Search (a special case of the Evolutionary Strategies algorithm [13]). This led to an average improvement in swap cost of 31%, over a shared benchmark suite, compared to [10].

The objective function was updated in [5] to not only take into account the number of gates shared by a pair of logical qubits, but also where in the circuit each gate is located. The rationale is that since the swap gates being inserted are non-optimal, after swap gates have been inserted for the gates near the beginning of the circuit, the placement of the qubits will no longer be strongly correlated to the placement at the beginning. Therefore gates located further into the circuit should have less of an impact on the initial placement than gates located nearer the beginning. They argue that each gate should be assigned a priority, P, subject to (3).

$$P_i > \sum_{j=1}^{n_i} P_{i+j} \tag{3}$$

P_i is the priority of the ith gate in the circuit, and n_i is the number of subsequent gates. The modified objective function takes the same form as (1), but with an altered weight function, W', defined in (4). However this weight function only loosely satisfies (3), i.e. it is satisfied only for specific pairs of N_g and k.

$$W'(i,j) = \sum_{1 \leq m \leq N_g}^{N_g} \frac{1}{T_m^k} \tag{4}$$

T_m time step of the mth gate that uses logical qubits i and j, and k is an integer larger than 1.

In this paper, we attempt to formulate an objective function that strongly satisfies (3), and prove that to do this it is necessary and sufficient that the contribution of each gate must decrease at least exponentially with its position in the circuit.

3 Theory

3.1 Sufficiency Proof

It is simple to prove that there is an exponentially decreasing function which is sufficient to satisfy (3). It is well-known that the sum of the reciprocals of the powers of 2 converges:

$$\sum_{i=1}^{\infty} \frac{1}{2^i} = 1 \tag{5}$$

And from this, it is clear that by dividing through both sides by 2^j, we have

$$\frac{1}{2^j} = \sum_{i=1}^{\infty} \frac{1}{2^{j+i}} \tag{6}$$

If we then rewrite i as j (and vice versa), and truncate the sum at N_i, the number of remaining gates, then we have

$$\frac{1}{2^i} > \sum_{j=1}^{N_i} \frac{1}{2^{i+j}} \tag{7}$$

This satisfies (3).

3.2 Necessity Proof

By rewriting (3) as

$$P_i = \sum_{j=1}^{N_i} P_{i+j} + \epsilon \tag{8}$$

Here, ϵ is defined as the difference between P_i and $\sum_{j=1}^{N_i} P_{i+j}$. It is assumed that ϵ need not depend on i.

$$P_{i-1} = P_i + \sum_{j=1}^{N_i} P_{i+j} + \epsilon \tag{9}$$

Substituting in (8)

$$P_{i-1} = P_i + P_i - \epsilon + \epsilon \tag{10}$$

$$P_{i-1} = 2P_i \tag{11}$$

Then, rewriting $i-1$ as i, it follows that:

$$P_i = 2P_{i+1} = 2(2P_{i+2}) = 2(2(2P_{i+3})... \tag{12}$$

This can be more simply expressed as:

$$P_i = 2^j P_{i+j} \tag{13}$$

which rearranges to:

$$\frac{P_i}{2^j} = P_{i+j} \tag{14}$$

Define $P_0 = c$, as some arbitrary scaling constant.

$$\frac{c}{2^j} = P_j \tag{15}$$

Since c is arbitary, we can define $c = 1$ to make it equivalent to the result from the sufficiency proof.

$$P_i = \frac{1}{2^i} \tag{16}$$

Which satisfies the priority criterion 3.

$$P_i = \frac{1}{2^i} = \sum_{j=1}^{N_i} \frac{1}{2^{i+j}} + \epsilon > \sum_{j=1}^{N_i} \frac{1}{2^{i+j}} \tag{17}$$

$$\epsilon = \sum_{j=N_{i+1}}^{\infty} \frac{1}{2^j} \tag{18}$$

Leaving ϵ equal to what was truncated from the infinite sum in Sect. 3.1.

4 Swap Insertion and Placement Algorithms

As the number of qubits increases, the size of the search space for the initial placement grows factorially. So while it is feasible to perform an exhaustive search for small numbers of qubits, this quickly becomes impractical due to both memory and time constraints. We use an exhaustive search method for circuits of 8 or fewer physical qubits. This entails generating a list of all permutations of 8 objects, calculating the objective cost for the placement corresponding to each, and selecting the placement with the lowest objective cost.

When the number of physical qubits exceeds 8, we use Harmony Search [2]. This works by generating an initial population (of size nP) of random placements, choosing a selection of them at random, mutating them with some probability of a small mutation (swapping a logical qubit with its neighbour), and another probability of a large mutation (swapping a logical qubit with another random qubit), and then the best nP placements out of the union of the initial population and the mutated population are carried over into the next generation. This is repeated either until the difference between the best and worst

```
   input : C, nPhys, p1, p2, nGen, nP, nChildren
   output: bestP
 1 for i ← 1, nP do
 2     randP ← RandomPlacement
 3     population[i] ← randP
 4 end
 5 for i ← 1, nGen do
 6     children ← random_sample(population, nChildren)
 7     for j ← 1, nChildren do
 8         child ← children[j]
 9         for k ← 1, nPhys do
10             if rand(0, 1) ≤ p1 then
11                 if rand(0, 1) ≤ p2 then
12                     Swap(child(k), rand_neighbour(child(k)))
13                 end
14             else
15                 Swap(child(k), child(rand(0, nPhys)))
16             end
17         end
18     end
19     population ← population||children
20     sort(population, key = cost(P, C))
21     population ← population[: nP]
22     if cost(population(best), C) − cost(population(worst), C) ≤ 1 then
23         break
24     end
25 end
26 bestP ← population(best)
27 return bestP
```

Algorithm 1: Harmony Search for finding initial placement

placements in the population is less than or equal to 1, or until a certain number of generations has been reached. This process is illustrated in Algorithm 1.

The circuit to be synthesized, C, is input along with the number of physical qubits $nPhys$; p_1 and p_2 are the probabilities of either a small or large mutation; $nGen$ is the maximum number of generations to go through before stopping, nP is the population size and $nChildren$ is the number of placements to mutate in each generation. Lines 1 to 3 fill the initial population with random placements. Then the loop starting on line 5 cycles through the generations, stopping at $nGen$ unless the costs of the placements converges before then. In each generation, a random selection of placements is selected, line 6, which are then mutated. The placements are mutated by going through all of the physical qubits, in the loop starting on line 9, and generating two random numbers between 0 and 1 and comparing them with the probabilities p_1 and p_2 to either swap it with a neighbouring qubit (line 12), a random qubit (15) or not at all. Once all the child placements are mutated, in lines 19 to 21 they are concatenated with the original population, which is then sorted by the objective cost 1, and only the best nP placements are kept. If, at the end of any generation, the costs of the population converge to the point that the best and worst differ by less than 1, then it will leave the loop at line 23. After the loop, the placement with the lowest cost is selected.

In [5], the exhaustive approach was also used for circuits with 8 or fewer qubits, however they used a Genetic Algorithm (GA) for larger circuits. The primary difference in implementation is that the GA uses 'crossover' as a mutation operator, meaning a mutated placement can be produced from 2 'parent' placements, whereas Harmony Search only uses single placement mutations. We do not expect that this accounts for a significant amount of the improvement of [5] over [2], compared to the updated objective function and swap insertion algorithm. For this reason, we chose to implement the placement algorithm from [2], as the specific mutation operators in this paper were more clearly described. As such, we will be comparing the results of our objective function to our own implementation of the previous objective function, as well as to the published results in [5].

We use the same swap insertion algorithm as in [5]; when a gate between two non-neighbouring qubits is processed, all the paths of length equal to the Manhattan distance (the shortest distance between two points on a rectangular lattice) are identified, and then for each point it is possible to swap the two qubits to, on each path, the objective function is calculated for the remainder of the circuit, and the placement with the lowest objective cost is chosen. Since the number of paths grows very quickly, for most of the benchmark circuits [5] chose one path at random instead of comparing all possible paths. In order to eliminate the effects of randomness as much as possible, we will considering all paths, and we will be comparing our results for the circuits for which they did the same.

5 Experimental Results

The experiments were implemented in Python 3, using iGraph to represent the circuit and physical qubit array, and perform the relevant graph operations. Where Harmony Search was used (on circuits with 8 or fewer physical qubits), the parameters were set the same as in [2]: $p_1 = 0.9$, $p_2 = 0.3$, $nP = 20$, $nChildren = 1$, and $nGen = 100{,}000$. In our implementation of the old objective function, using the weight function 4, we set $k = 2$, which is how it was set in [5].

In the implementation of the new objective function, the scaling factor from (15) was defined as 2^{N_g}. This has the effect of scaling the contribution of the final gate to 1, and the first gate to 2^{N_g-1}, otherwise 2^{-N_g} will be represented as 0 when stored as a float for a large enough N_g.

Table 1 shows the swap costs S found for a range of benchmark circuits, as well as the run-time T of the placement and swap insertion, the percentage improvement in using the new objective function, and the results published in [5].

Table 1. The swap costs and run times for a range of benchmark circuits

			Old Obj. Fn.		New Obj. Fn.		Improvements (%)		
Circuit	N_g	Dim	S	T (s)	S	T (s)	S	T	[5]
3_17_13	14	2 × 2	4	0.01	4	0.01	0	−95.08	4
4gt10-v1_81	36	3 × 2	12	0.36	11	0.35	8.33	1.95	12
aj-e11_165	60	2 × 3	18	0.38	18	0.37	0	0.53	19
cycle10_2_110	1212	3 × 4	481	331.63	490	387.32	−1.87	−16.80	457
ham15_108	458	3 × 5	206	6974.58	212	7007.40	−2.92	−0.47	201
ham7_104	87	4 × 2	39	90.15	27	91.85	30.77	−1.88	34
hwb5_55	109	3 × 2	42	0.45	40	0.44	4.76	0.89	33
hwb6_58	146	3 × 2	53	0.51	53	0.50	0	3.00	52
hwb7_62	2663	3 × 3	1029	183.87	974	225.06	5.35	−22.40	934
hwb8_118	16610	3 × 3	6349	37137.34	6403	37615.74	−0.85	−1.29	5838
hwb9_123	20421	4 × 3	8815	82244.63	8754	82530.76	0.69	−0.35	7914
mod5adder_128	87	3 × 2	28	0.41	26	0.41	7.14	1.74	30
QFT7	21	4 × 2	10	95.98	10	93.97	0	2.10	10
QFT8	28	4 × 2	18	98.26	18	97.65	0	0.63	15
QFT9	36	3 × 3	24	51.87	20	58.56	16.67	−12.91	20
QFT10	45	5 × 2	30	131.77	32	80.42	−6.67	38.97	32
rd53_135	78	4 × 2	39	93.78	32	94.61	17.95	−0.87	29
Shor3	2076	4 × 3	1123	143.12	1110	523.08	1.16	−265.48	999
Shor4	5002	3 × 4	2900	1745.26	2853	2630.67	1.62	−50.73	2717
Shor5	10265	3 × 5	6487	16341.35	6479	27879.03	0.12	−70.60	5895

For most of the benchmark circuits, there is little difference between the two objective functions. There are three circuits which show a significant improvement in swap cost with the new objective function, however, it should be noted that these circuits are quite short, with the biggest improvement coming from *ham7_104*, which has an improvement of 30%, which corresponds to an absolute improvement of 12 swap gates. The difference in runtime varies quite drastically, from almost no difference at all up to 265% worse. Since there is no significant difference in swap cost, particularly for large circuits, and there is a potential to incur a very large run-time penalty.

In conclusion, there is no value in pursuing an objective function that strictly satisfies the priority criterion set out in [5], at least so far as improving the speed of the circuit placement and swap insertion algorithm, and the swap cost of the final result, are concerned.

6 Conclusion

Error rates will limit the maximum circuit depth possible in near-term QCs, therefore it is necessary to reduce the swap overhead as much as possible, ideally without incurring a large overhead in the runtime of the compilation of these circuits. Therefore, in order to accept these overheads in runtime, the improvement in swap cost needs to be large and consistent enough that it cannot be attributed to the randomness inherent in the search algorithm for the initial placement, or to the fact that it might be better for a specific circuit by coincidence. In this paper, we have demonstrated that this is not true for an exponentially decaying objective function vs a polynomially decaying one. And therefore, the ideal objective function should not strongly satisfy the priority criterion from [5], and might not even need to weakly satisfy it.

Further work on this topic could be to investigate the correlation between the objective function cost and the swap cost over a number of random circuits, using various objective functions, in order to improve the initial placement. Also, it could be valuable to investigate objective functions that decrease more slowly than polynomial. For instance, there is no reason the second gate of a circuit should have a lower objective contribution than the first, since for any given pair of gates, it is always possible to find a placement that can implement both without any swaps. Therefore a step-wise, but still monotonically decreasing, function might yield the best results.

References

1. A Preview of Bristlecone, Google's New Quantum Processor. https://bit.ly/2KweJSF. Accessed 11 Oct 2018
2. Alfailakawi, M.G., Ahmad, I., Hamdan, S.: Harmony-search algorithm for 2D nearest neighbor quantum circuits realization. Expert Syst. Appl. **61**, 16–27 (2016). https://doi.org/10.1016/j.eswa.2016.04.038. http://www.sciencedirect.com/science/article/pii/S0957417416302172
3. Boixo, S., et al.: Characterizing quantum supremacy in near-term devices. Nature Phys. **14**(6), 595–600 (2018). https://doi.org/10.1038/s41567-018-0124-x
4. Kassal, I., Jordan, S.P., Love, P.J., Mohseni, M., Aspuru-Guzik, A.: Polynomial-time quantum algorithm for the simulation of chemical dynamics. Proc. Natl. Acad. Sci. USA **105**(48), 18681–18686 (2008). https://doi.org/10.1073/pnas.0808245105. http://www.ncbi.nlm.nih.gov/pmc/articles/PMC2596249/, 5752[PII]
5. Kole, A., Datta, K., Sengupta, I.: A new heuristic for n -dimensional nearest neighbor realization of a quantum circuit. IEEE Trans. Comput. Aided Des. Integr. Circuits Syst. **37**(1), 182–192 (2018). https://doi.org/10.1109/TCAD.2017.2693284
6. Kumph, M., Brownnutt, M., Blatt, R.: Two-dimensional arrays of radio-frequency ion traps with addressable interactions. New J. Phys. **13**(7), 073043 (2011). http://stacks.iop.org/1367-2630/13/i=7/a=073043
7. Lye, A., Wille, R., Drechsler, R.: Determining the minimal number of swap gates for multi-dimensional nearest neighbor quantum circuits. In: The 20th Asia and South Pacific Design Automation Conference, pp. 178–183, January 2015. https://doi.org/10.1109/ASPDAC.2015.7059001
8. Monroe, C., Kim, J.: Scaling the ion trap quantum processor. Science **339**(6124), 1164–1169 (2013). https://doi.org/10.1126/science.1231298. http://science.sciencemag.org/content/339/6124/1164
9. Preskill, J.: Quantum Computing in the NISQ era and beyond. Quantum **2**, 79 (2018). https://doi.org/10.22331/q-2018-08-06-79
10. Shafaei, A., Saeedi, M., Pedram, M.: Qubit placement to minimize communication overhead in 2D quantum architectures. In: 2014 19th Asia and South Pacific Design Automation Conference (ASP-DAC), January 2014
11. Shor, P.: Algorithms for quantum computation: discrete logarithms and factoring. In: Proceedings 35th Annual Symposium on Foundations of Computer Science, p. 124

12. Spiller, T.P., Nemoto, K., Braunstein, S.L., Munro, W.J., van Loock, P., Milburn, G.J.: Quantum computation by communication. New J. Phys. **8**(2), 30 (2006). http://stacks.iop.org/1367-2630/8/i=2/a=030
13. Weyland, D.: A critical analysis of the harmony search algorithm-how not to solve sudoku. Oper. Res. Perspect. **2**, 97–105 (2015). https://doi.org/10.1016/j.orp.2015.04.001. http://www.sciencedirect.com/science/article/pii/S221471601500010X
14. Wille, R., Keszocze, O., Walter, M., Rohrs, P., Chattopadhyay, A., Drechsler, R.: Look-ahead schemes for nearest neighbor optimization of 1D and 2D quantum circuits. In: 2016 21st Asia and South Pacific Design Automation Conference (ASP-DAC). pp. 292–297, January 2016. https://doi.org/10.1109/ASPDAC.2016.7428026

Special Session: Machine Learning Implementations

Transport Triggered Array Processor for Vision Applications

Mehdi Safarpour(✉), Ilkka Hautala, Miguel Bordallo López, and Olli Silvén

Center for Machine Vision and Signal Analysis, University of Oulu, Oulu, Finland
mehdi.safarpour@oulu.fi

Abstract. Low-level sensory data processing in many Internet-of-Things (IoT) devices pursue energy efficiency by utilizing sleep modes or slowing the clocking to the minimum. To curb the share of stand-by power dissipation in those designs, ultra-low-leakage processes are employed in fabrication. Those limit the clocking rates significantly, reducing the computing throughputs of individual cores. In this contribution we explore compensating for the substantial computing power needs of a vision application using massive parallelism. The Processing Elements (PE) of the design are based on Transport Triggered Architecture. The fine grained programmable parallel solution allows for fast and efficient computation of learnable low-level features (e.g. local binary descriptors and convolutions). Other operations, including Max-pooling have also been implemented. The programmable design achieves excellent energy efficiency for Local Binary Patterns computations.

Keywords: Massive processing arrays · Internet-of-Things · Embedded systems · Computer vision · Binary Patterns

1 Introduction

With the decreasing costs of cameras and wireless communications, an unprecedented growth in the number of imaging sensors deployed in our environment is taking place. This is coupled to the growth of Internet of Things (IoT) and cloud computing that transforms the little-data from distributed sensors to centralized big-data. Examples of rapidly growing applications include Advanced Driver Assistance Systems (ADAS), data gathering using drones, surveillance systems and service robotics. These applications try to interact with the environment or to extract information from the scene, necessitating high performance computing, while demanding extreme energy efficiency if they depend on energy harvesting or battery power.

Considering the volume of image and video data, and the bandwidth and energy needs of wireless communications, it is often difficult to justify transmission to cloud or edge processing. Therefore, some sensor level or near sensor

The support of Academy of Finland for project ICONICAL (grant 313467) and 6Genesis Flagship (grant 318927) is gratefully acknowledged.

D. N. Pnevmatikatos et al. (Eds.): SAMOS 2019, LNCS 11733, pp. 361–372, 2019.
https://doi.org/10.1007/978-3-030-27562-4_26

(memory) processing [16] is inevitable. Furthermore, in some applications real-time reactivity is required and even few millisecond delays are not tolerable (e.g. ADAS, drones). In other words, lots of computing power are needed during a short instance of time.

If a large number of cameras is used, the data transmission may locally clog even in case of the 5G network, unless the image information can be sent in a substantially condensed form. This can also result in significant energy savings as the wireless transmission of a single bit is often more costly than, say, 1000 arithmetic operations. For example, Walsh [22] showed that a significant portion of energy can be saved by employing simple parallel operations, such as convolutions, before transmission to the cloud.

In conventional embedded processors, up to 70% of the power dissipation is due to the instruction and data supply [2] making those the prime targets for architectural optimization. In low level computer vision most of the operations deal with neighbourhoods of pixels, providing opportunities to avoid memory round trips in local processing. This calls for application-specific architectures [13], and has lead to array processor proposals, mostly in a 2-D mesh configuration [7]. Unfortunately, they seldom provide for flexible programmability, and as such mostly serve as energy efficiency and raw throughput benchmarks.

Previous studies have demonstrated the usefulness of GPUs and 1-D SIMD processors for low-level vision operations [12]. Although these architectures tend to suffer from memory and I/O bottlenecks due to frequent data transfer to and out of the PEs [25], several studies [3,7,22,25] have demonstrated their attractiveness.

The sizes of the processing arrays have varied, e.g., from 170×120 [7] to 256×256 PEs [5], while both digital and mixed mode technologies have been employed. All of these works are very similar in implementation. It has been shown that analog/mixed signal based massive arrays possess superior area-energy efficiency, but the analog computation is susceptible to noise in deep sub-micron technology. This issue is almost non-existent for the digital counterpart [4,22].

In previous works single core and coarse-grained high performance TTA based solutions were already developed and demonstrated. Ijzerman et al. [12] proposed programmable SIMD TTA-based accelerator for convolutional neural networks. The solution exploits the data locality of dense networks and it is able to operate with a performance of 143 GOPS at 400 MHz of clock frequency and with power consumption of 11.3 mW when implemented on 28 nm ASIC technology. In [11] a coarse-grained multi-core TTA was designed for video coding applications.

In the current contribution, we address the design of a massive array processor using the TTA architecture template. To the best knowledge of the authors, this is the first such study. For the design, we used the available advanced TTA co-design environment [8]. The motivation for the study stems from the observation of potential energy efficiency benefits attainable from ultra-low-leakage silicon technologies. The massive parallelism offsets the speed penalty from the low clock frequency, consequently, we decided to realize the design using a near-threshold technology [6].

The clocking frequency is not a constraint in this type of massive arrays, so one extreme design approach is to operate in sub-threshold regime with optimum sub-threshold voltage that minimizes the energy per instruction. We notice the energy efficiency of sub-threshold voltage designs (e.g. sub-threshold voltage FFT processor [23] with $155\,nJ$ per 16-b 1024-point FFT, clocked at only 10 kHz in $180\,nm$ technology). Unfortunately our tool chain didn't allow comparable experiments.

In addition, to show the advantages of the programmability of our architecture, we evaluate it with relevant low-level image processing operations, including learnable local descriptors, variable convolutions and Max-pooling operation. The operations are components in the inference stage of the current state-of-the-art computer vision algorithms. In all the operations our architecture shows its advantages in memory bound algorithms since it does not need to flush data back and forth between memories [19].

2 System Architecture

2.1 The Array Processor Architecture

In our proposed architecture, all PEs are directly connected to neighbouring PEs. The instruction memories are shared between groups of processors. Vertical and horizontal indices are assigned to each PE to make it feasible to selectively run instructions or to form PE groups, where each group executes its own instruction stream. As an example, an 8×8 example architecture is shown in Fig. 1. As depicted in the figure, each PE is connected to the neighborhood register bank that contains its immediate neighbours in eight directions.

Some image processing operations require activating only a small set of PEs, while the rest could function as memory. For example, in some forms of max-pooling non-overlapping windows must be selected. For the purpose of grouping a bundle of PEs to certain operations, each PE is aware of its horizontal and vertical index. This enables instructing a PE to remain idle depending on its indices.

The PEs where chosen to be based on the TTA architecture due to their relative architectural simplicity, ease of design and the exposed bypass network of the processors. In this architecture, similar to a general approach in massive array processors, all processing elements receive a single instruction stream and simultaneously execute the same instruction on their local data [4]. However, in our scheme multiple instruction memories can feed different groups of PEs and each PE can multiplex between different instruction memories.

Vision applications usually require a large number of computations, especially for pixel level operations. Generally, the frame rate for the cameras integrated to current embedded systems do not exceed 120 frames per second, while the rates typically range from 30 to 60 Hz. Even applications, such as visual odometry that usually require high frame rate, rarely exceed rates higher than a few hundred frames per second.

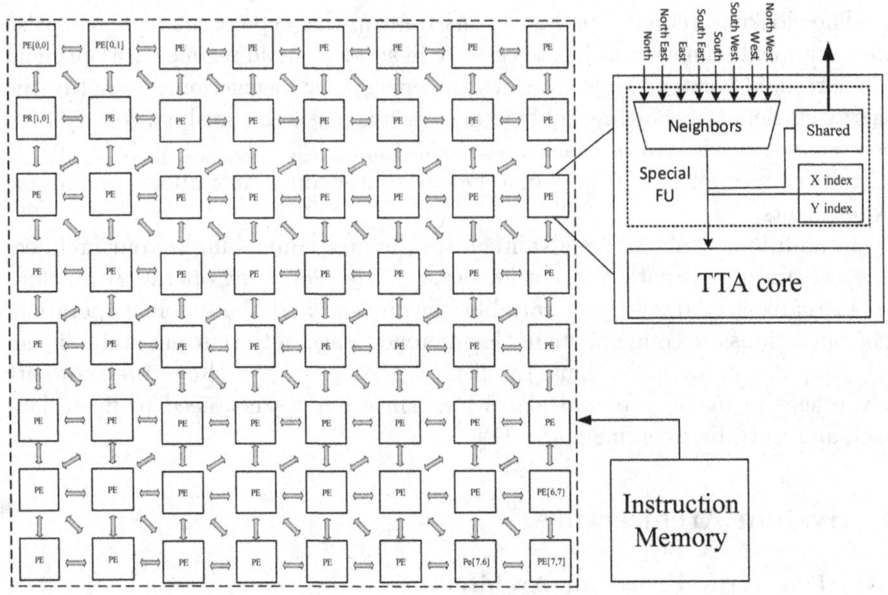

Fig. 1. General view of the massive array architecture

In this context, we aimed at an architecture that could flexibly employ varying numbers of processors (e.g., PE arrays from 3×3 to 128×128), while we could operate them at a very low frequency and voltage, using ultra-low power strategies. Moreover, the array can be put in sleep mode during frame intervals, essentially functioning in a race-to-sleep mode, which significantly reduces the average power consumption [1].

2.2 Sensor Processor Arrangement

Generally, two forms of arrangement can be considered for 2-Dimensional sensor and digital processing arrays [25]. In the first one, each pixel is coupled to a pixel level Analog-to-Digital Converter (ADC) [15] and a PE and the ADC directly writes into the corresponding PE. This approach mostly is used in applications where the number of sensors is limited. In the second approach, sensor plane and processing array are separated.

Two examples of this approach are shown in Figs. 2 and 3. In Fig. 2, row parallel ADCs quantize image pixels column by column and fed the output into first column of the processing array (alternatively a single ADC can be coupled to a 1-D column buffer and the buffer is flushed into the array) [15]. Subsequently, data is propagated in the array in a wave manner. This way the maximum number of cycles to load a totally new image onto the array is equal to the number of columns. In case that the processing array is not large enough to accommodate the whole image, a moving window called *Fovea arrangement* (Fig. 3) [25], swept throughout the image plane, is read and fed into the array. Benefiting from the exposed bypass networks of TTA, our design provides means to pass data from PE to PE efficiently without any extra hardware.

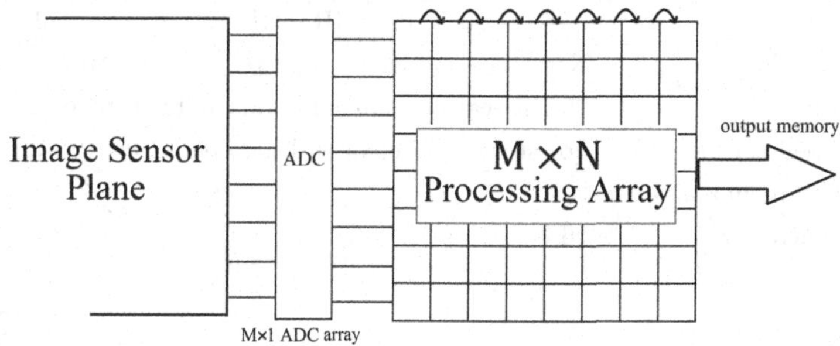

Fig. 2. Sensor readout in column by column fashion

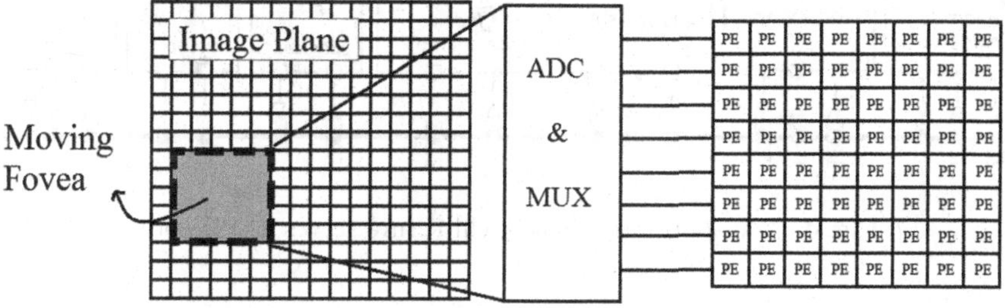

Fig. 3. Fovea arrangement where number of processor is less than number of sensors

3 System Implementation

The proposed architecture was implemented and simulated using SystemC, since the TCE toolchain provides means to integrate its cycle accurate simulator with custom designs that are implemented this way. At first, after experimenting with basic image processing operations, the TTA core was pruned to consume minimum energy and logic gates. The detail of the TTA core employed as the architecture PE is presented in Table 1, while a scheme depicting the core itself is shown in Fig. 4.

3.1 Neighbor Communication Functional Unit

A special functional unit (FU) to communicate with the eight adjacent neighbors of each PE was designed using behavioral models written in SystemC and VHDL. This unit contains both the vertical and horizontal indices of the PE. It consists of two internal ports (one input and one output) that are connected to the main bus of the TTA core and nine external ports (eight inputs and one output) that communicate with the neighbouring PEs.

Table 1. Detail of general TTA core

Component	Details	Quantity
ALU	ADD, EQ, GTU	1
Logic	AND, OR, XOR, SHR, SHL	1
Special custom FU	Neighborhood shared register, inputs ports	1
Register file	16-Bit registers for temporary data storage	4
Boolean register file	For storage outcome of logic operations	2
Instruction memory width	23 b	
Short immediate	16 b	

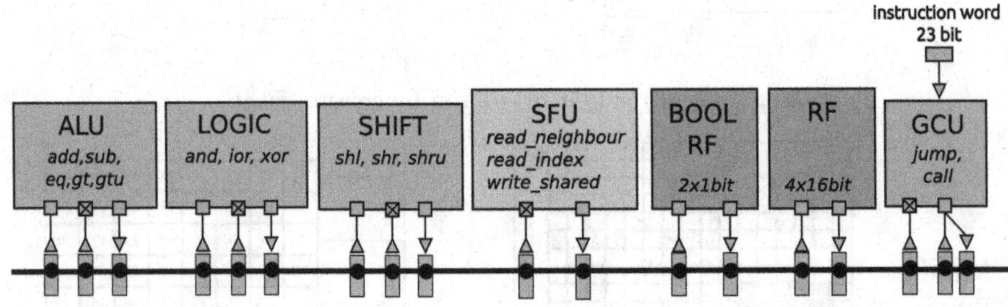

Fig. 4. Transport Triggered Architecture serves as PE core

Each PE can store its output on a register named *Shared register* which can be read only by the neighbouring PEs. One of the external ports of the custom functional units is devoted to this register. The other eight external input ports named *North, North_East, East, South_East, South, South_West, West, North_West*, are connected to corresponded Shared register of neighbouring PEs. The custom functional units provides three instructions *read_neighbour*, *read_index* and *write_Shared*. Example transports to read and write from the custom FU are shown in Table 2. The SystemC model of the FU was integrated to the TTA based PE core. A small scale version of the architecture was implemented on FPGA and as ASIC in 28 nm deep sub-micron CMOS technology.

Table 2. Code examples of the custom FU transports

Reading neighbours	1. 0 → CustomFU.Inp1.read_neighbour 2. CustomFU.output → RF.0;	0 for North,...
Reading index	1. 0 → CustomFU.Inp1.read_index 2. CustomFU.output → RF.0	0,1 for X,Y
Writing output	1. RF.0 → Custom_FU.Inp1.write_Shared	–
Data passing	1. CustomFU.output → CustomFU.Inp1.write_Shared	–

4 Results and Discussion

4.1 Application Example: Descriptive Features

To evaluate the usefulness of our architecture, we have implemented several low-level image processing operations, including local descriptors such as the Local Binary Patterns, 3 × 3 convolutions using integer coefficients and max-pooling. All the operations were tested on the processor. We provide cycle accurate simulations.

Local Descriptors represent features in small local image patches. Handcrafted local descriptors include binary operators such as Local Binary Patterns (LBP), symmetric operators, e.g., Local Phase Quantization (LPQ), and Binarized Statistical Image Features (BSIF) that are learned from image statistics. They are used in applications that range from face analysis to texture classification [10].

As opposed to handcrafted descriptors, there is a recent surge of learnable local descriptors. This generation of compact and efficient operators is emerging due to schemes that allow individual filters to be learned for different applications and image regions. Examples include regressing Local Binary Features (rLBF) that are utilized in state of the art shape and facial landmark detection [20], or local binary kernels used in neural networks [26] demonstrated in several image classification applications.

The local descriptors share a common computational structure, as they can be expressed in a way that allows for pipelined implementations. The exposed bypass networks of TTA processors enables building these pipelines by software controlled transports.

We decided to evaluate the performance of our processor with the simple, yet useful local descriptors, including LBP [18]. LBP is considered to be computationally cheap, but it needs to be computed for every pixel and is therefore a memory-bound algorithm. In its simplest form, for each pixel value, a binary vector is constructed by comparing the pixel value with values of its immediate surrounding neighbours. Several hardware implementations for efficient LBP extraction have been proposed and thoroughly evaluated [17].

The LBP descriptor can be computed with the proposed processor in a few cycles and using few resources. The number of cycles consumed is 74, while two 16-bit registers and one 1-bit Boolean register suffice. Table 3 contains an excerpt from an LBP TTA transport program. Table 4 summarizes the results of SystemC cycle accurate model simulations for each operation.

Convolution is a fundamental image processing operation in which the input is spatially convolved with arbitrary kernels.

We implemented and evaluated a 3 × 3 convolution on our proposed TTA system utilizing integer and fixed-point calculations. In our implementation, the precise number of consumed cycles depends on the actual kernel weights. Sobel edge detector and Box blur [9] have minimum arithmetic needs and their implementations were evaluated in our experiments. In addition, we implemented

Table 3. Code excerpt from LBP program (3 × 3 window)

```
mainloop :
    0 → RF.0;
    0 → RF.3;
    0 → FU.P1.read_neighnour;
    FU.P2 → RF.5;
    RF.5 → FU.P1.write_Shared;
    RF.6 → alu_comp.in2 ;
    5 → FU.P1.read_neighnour ;
    FU.P2 → alu_comp.in1t.gtu ;
    alu_comp.out1 → bool.0 ;
    1→ RF.1;
    ?bool.0 RF.0 → RF.1;
    RF.1 → alu_comp.in2;
    RF.3 → alu_comp.in1t.add;
    alu_comp.out1 → RF.3;
    6 → FU.P1.read_neighnour ;
    FU.P2 → alu_comp.in1t.gtu ;
    alu_comp.out1 → bool.0 ;
    2 → RF.1;
    ?bool.0 RF.0 → RF.1;
    RF.1 → alu_comp.in2;
    RF.3 → alu_comp.in1t.add;
    alu_comp.out1 → RF.3;
    ...
```

Table 4. Summary of results of SystemC cycle accurate model simulations

Operations	Window size	Number of clock cycles
LBP	3 × 3	74
Conv. (binary weights)	3 × 3	56
Conv. (integer weights)	3 × 3	1553
Max-pooling	3 × 3	271

kernels with random weights. The number of cycles required is reported in the simulation results is presented in Table 4.

Pooling layers are important in Convolutional Neural Networks [14]. Pooling is a down-sampling operation implemented using a custom stride (down-sampling factor). Typical CNN architectures commonly use Max-pooling in which the maximum value in a window region is selected.

Pooling operations can be applied on non-overlapping windows. Hence, a method to divide PEs into independent slices is required. Our implementation can achieve this through selecting the PEs with indices that are multiple of our desired stride (e.g in case the stride is equal to two, PEs with indices of multiples of two are activated). To find if an index is multiple of a number, we do not need to compute the remainders since, for example, multiples of 2, 3 and 5 can be computed through simple iterative methods [21]. The pooling operation with stride of 2 is depicted in Fig. 5. The results for Max-pooling also are presented in Table 4.

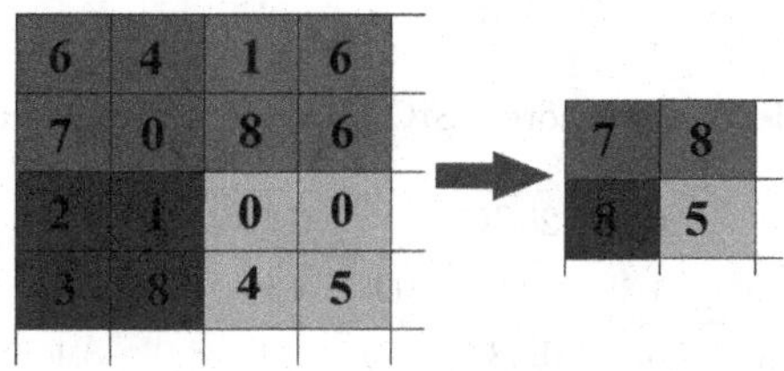

Fig. 5. Max pooling example with a stride of 2

4.2 FPGA and ASIC Implementation

To show the implementation feasibility of our processor, and for verification purposes, we have carried out a small-scale design into both FPGA and ASIC. In both implementations we measure and extrapolate estimations of power consumption, occupied area and number of gates.

FPGA Results: We carried out our FPGA implementation starting from our SystemC and HDL modelling, and employed an Altera Cyclone IV EP4CE115-F29C7 FPGA. Our small scale implementation is comprised of 110 cores (10×11). The number of used logic elements and the measured power consumption results are presented in Table 5. The static power is constant for this FPGA regardless of the design and clock frequency. The dynamic power for this 10×11 array is similar to the static power, and is relatively low for a FPGA implementation.

Table 5. Implementation of a 10×11 TTA array on Cyclone IV FPGA

	10×11 Array	Single TTA core
Static power	104.30 mW	-
Dynamic power	113.79 mW	1 mW
Total power	234.30 mW	-
Logic cells	69,983/81,264 (86%)	630
Clock	50 MHz	

ASIC Results. In addition to the FPGA implementation, we have synthesized our design to an ASIC using 28 nm low power libraries. In addition, we have performed post-layout simulations. We obtained the results of the power estimations per PE (TTA core) based on a small scale implementation. Based on the measurements and simulations, we expect the total power consumption to be roughly proportional to the number of PEs with almost negligible overheads. The following table summarizes the ASIC implementation results for three different settings (Table 6).

Table 6. TTA core ASIC implementation results

	0.8 V 25 °C			0.6 V 125 °C			0.8 V 125 °C		
Clock (MHz)	1	10	100	1	10	100	1	10	100
Static power (μW)	0.7	0.68	0.55	8.2	8.0	8.1	15.1	15.5	15.2
Dynamic power (μW)	1.76	17.51	184	0.96	10.4	101	1.8	19.1	186
Total power (μW)	2.4	18.1	185	9.2	18.4	109	16	34	202
Static/total power	0.29	0.04	0.003	0.89	0.44	0.07	0.89	0.45	0.07
Area	55 μm × 55 μm								

Each PE occupies an area of 55 μm × 55 μm while the array size growth is almost linear with the number of PEs. Extrapolating, we can expect that a array of 128 × 128 processors, would occupy around 6.5 mm × 6.5 mm. We expect the leakage current to be substantially lower in typical settings, for the near-threshold results.

The available technology libraries allowed us to only carry out simulation in extremes corners for 0.6 V (i.e. 125 °C and −40 °C). Therefore, simulation results for both 0.8 V typical (25 °C) and 0.8 V worst case (125 °C) are added to help understanding the impact of leakage to total power consumption.

Based on the simulation results, the array consumes 18 uW per core at 10 MHz operation. Considering the results in Table 4, the processor is fast enough to complete multiple image operations and to be turned off (clock gated) before the next frame comes available.

5 Discussion and Future Work

In our design, we explored implementing massive array processors with TTA processing elements for low level image analysis algorithms. Our results appear promising, in particular, when considering the programmable flexibility of the solution, a feature that is not present in similarly power efficient solutions for the same purpose. The energy consumed per pixel is just 1.4 nJ per pixel in the FPGA case for each LBP operation. In case of the ASIC implementation at 10 MHz clock frequency (0.6 V worst case 125 °C), the energy dissipation is around 0.17 nJ per pixel. Our results are very close to the best ones achieved for hardwired LBP implementations [17].

Future work includes investigation of race-to-sleep schemes [24], which could reduce the average power consumption. Depending on the required image operations and the input frame rate, the array could be turned off for relatively long periods, permitting to tolerate wake-up overheads.

References

1. Carey, S.J., Barr, D.R., Dudek, P.: Demonstration of a low power image processing system using a SCAMP3 vision chip. In: 2011 Fifth ACM/IEEE International Conference on Distributed Smart Cameras, pp. 1–2. IEEE (2011)
2. Dally, W.J., et al.: Efficient embedded computing. Computer **41**(7), 27–32 (2008)
3. Debrunner, T., Saeedi, S., Bose, L., Davison, A.J., Kelly, P.H.: Camera tracking on focal-plane sensor-processor arrays
4. Debrunner, T., Saeedi, S., Kelly, P.H.: AUKE: automatic kernel code generation for an analogue SIMD focal-plane sensor-processor array. ACM Trans. Archit. Code Optim. (TACO) **15**(4), 59 (2019)
5. Di Federico, M., Julián, P., Mandolesi, P.S.: SCDVP: a simplicial CNN digital visual processor. IEEE Trans. Circuits Syst. I: Regul. Pap. **61**(7), 1962–1969 (2014)
6. Dreslinski, R.G., Wieckowski, M., Blaauw, D., Sylvester, D., Mudge, T.: Near-threshold computing: reclaiming moore's law through energy efficient integrated circuits. Proc. IEEE **98**(2), 253–266 (2010)
7. Dudek, P., Hicks, P.J.: A general-purpose processor-per-pixel analog SIMD vision chip. IEEE Trans. Circuits Syst. I: Regul. Pap. **52**(1), 13–20 (2005)
8. Esko, O., Jaaskelainen, P., Huerta, P., Carlos, S., Takala, J., Martinez, J.I.: Customized exposed datapath soft-core design flow with compiler support. In: 2010 International Conference on Field Programmable Logic and Applications, pp. 217–222. IEEE (2010)
9. Gonzalez, R.C., Woods, R.E.: Digital Image Processing. Interscience, New York (2001)
10. Hadid, A., Ylioinas, J., López, M.B.: Face and texture analysis using local descriptors: a comparative analysis. In: 2014 4th International Conference on Image Processing Theory, Tools and Applications (IPTA), pp. 1–4. IEEE (2014)
11. Hautala, I., Boutellier, J., Silven, O.: Programmable 28 nm coprocessor for HEVC/H.265 in-loop filters. In: 2016 IEEE International Symposium on Circuits and Systems (ISCAS), pp. 1570–1573. IEEE (2016)
12. IJzerman, J., et al.: Aivotta: an energy efficient programmable accelerator for CNN-based object recognition. In: Proceedings of the 18th International Conference on Embedded Computer Systems: Architectures, Modeling, and Simulation, pp. 28–37. ACM (2018)
13. Jacobs, M.: Visual processing sparks a new class of processors. In: 2015 International Conference on Embedded Computer Systems: Architectures, Modeling, and Simulation (SAMOS), pp. ii–ii. IEEE (2015)
14. Krizhevsky, A., Sutskever, I., Hinton, G.E.: Imagenet classification with deep convolutional neural networks. In: Advances in Neural Information Processing Systems, pp. 1097–1105 (2012)
15. Leñero-Bardallo, J.A., Fernández-Berni, J., Rodríguez-Vázquez, Á.: Review of ADCs for imaging. In: Image Sensors and Imaging Systems 2014, vol. 9022, p. 90220I. International Society for Optics and Photonics (2014)

16. Liu, Z., Calciu, I., Herlihy, M., Mutlu, O.: Concurrent data structures for near-memory computing. In: Proceedings of the 29th ACM Symposium on Parallelism in Algorithms and Architectures, pp. 235–245. ACM (2017)
17. López, M.B., Nieto, A., Boutellier, J., Hannuksela, J., Silvén, O.: Evaluation of real-time LBP computing in multiple architectures. J. Real-Time Image Proc. **13**(2), 375–396 (2017)
18. Ojala, T., Pietikäinen, M., Mäenpää, T.: Gray scale and rotation invariant texture classification with local binary patterns. In: Vernon, D. (ed.) ECCV 2000. LNCS, vol. 1842, pp. 404–420. Springer, Heidelberg (2000). https://doi.org/10.1007/3-540-45054-8_27
19. Ranjan, R., Patel, V.M., Chellappa, R.: Hyperface: a deep multi-task learning framework for face detection, landmark localization, pose estimation, and gender recognition. IEEE Trans. Pattern Anal. Mach. Intell. **41**(1), 121–135 (2019)
20. Ren, S., Cao, X., Wei, Y., Sun, J.: Face alignment at 3000 fps via regressing local binary features. In: Proceedings of the IEEE Conference on Computer Vision and Pattern Recognition, pp. 1685–1692 (2014)
21. E.S.: General rule to determine if a binary number is divisible by a generic number. Mathematics Stack Exchange. https://math.stackexchange.com/users/424075/evanseverson, https://math.stackexchange.com/q/2228305. (version: 2018-04-05)
22. Walsh, D.: Design and implementation of massively parallel fine-grained processor arrays. Ph.D. thesis, University of Manchester, Manchester, UK (2015)
23. Wang, A., Chandrakasan, A.: A 180-mv subthreshold FFT processor using a minimum energy design methodology. IEEE J. Solid-State Circuits **40**(1), 310–319 (2005)
24. Wolf, M.: CPUs. In: Wolf, M. (ed.) Computers as Components. The Morgan Kaufmann Series in Computer Architecture and Design, 4th edn, pp. 99–159. Morgan Kaufmann, Burlington (2017)
25. Zarándy, Á. (ed.): Focal-Plane Sensor-processor Chips, 1st edn. Springer Science & Business Media, New York (2011). https://doi.org/10.1007/978-1-4419-6475-5
26. Zhang, X., Liu, L., Xie, Y., Chen, J., Wu, L., Pietikainen, M.: Rotation invariant local binary convolution neural networks. In: Proceedings of the IEEE International Conference on Computer Vision, pp. 1210–1219 (2017)

Approximate Similarity Search with FAISS Framework Using FPGAs on the Cloud

Dimitrios Danopoulos[1(✉)], Christoforos Kachris[2], and Dimitrios Soudris[1]

[1] Department of Electrical and Computer Engineering, NTUA, Athens, Greece
{dimdano,dsoudris}@microlab.ntua.gr

[2] Democritus University of Thrace & ICCS-NTUA, Athens, Greece
kachris@microlab.ntua.gr

Abstract. Machine Learning algorithms, such as classification and clustering techniques, have gained significant traction over the last years because they are vital to many real-world problems. K-Nearest Neighbor algorithm (KNN) is widely used in text categorization, predictive analysis, data mining etc. but comes at the cost of high computation. In the era of big data, modern data centers adopt this specific algorithm with approximate techniques to compute demanding workloads every day. However, high dimensional nearest neighbor queries on billion-scale datasets still produce a significant computational and energy overhead. In this paper, we describe and implement a novel design to address this problem based on a hardware accelerated approximate KNN algorithm built upon FAISS framework (Facebook Artificial Intelligence Similarity Search) using FPGA-OpenCL platforms on the cloud. This is an original deployment of FPGA architecture on this framework that also shows how the persistent index build times on big scale inputs for similarity search can be handled in hardware and even outperform other high performance systems. The experiments were done on AWS cloud F1 instance achieving 98× FPGA accelerator speed-up over single-core CPU and 2.1× end-to-end system speed-up over a 36-thread Xeon CPU. Also, the performance/watt of the design was 3.5× from the same CPU and 1.2× from a Kepler-class GPU.

Keywords: Big-data · Similarity search · Approximate KNN · Cloud · FPGA · Reconfigurable computing

1 Introduction

The new age of big data requires trillion or even quintillion bytes of data to be processed every day. Emerging applications on the cloud are constantly learning

This project has received funding from the Xilinx University program and the Hellenic Foundation for Research and Innovation (HFRI) and the Genal Secretariat for Research and Technology (GSRT), under grant agreement No 2212- Hardware Acceleration of Machine Learning Applications in the Cloud.

D. N. Pnevmatikatos et al. (Eds.): SAMOS 2019, LNCS 11733, pp. 373–386, 2019.
https://doi.org/10.1007/978-3-030-27562-4_27

from large scale data in all kinds of real world problems, such as data analytics and internet media. This large computational complexity motivates efforts to accelerate these tasks using hardware-specific optimizations by leveraging different architectures such as CPUs, GPUs, FPGAs. The increasingly growing demands for efficient and fast processing in the recent years can be addressed by heterogeneous computing systems such as Field Programmable Gate Arrays (FPGAs). This architecture is highly parallelizable and re-configurable and can be mapped well to classification or clustering problems, which are usually repetitive, such as KNN. Specifically, data centers tend to search for efficient ways for high performance and low energy cost solutions, and FPGAs play a major role in this evolution [1,2].

Similarity search in data centers is characterized by large scale datasets and many times high dimensional inputs. Even very modern high performance computers cannot handle these requests resulting in a computer phenomenon known as the *curse of dimensionality* [3]. Approximate nearest neighbor algorithm (ANN) overcomes the high-dimensional problem that usually comes with arithmetic complexity and/or high data bandwidth demands [4]. In that way, the extremely intensive exhaustive distance calculation of the basic KNN algorithm become a less time and energy consuming task by implementing a partial query search. Exact results are impractical on billion-sized databases on the cloud so new techniques that index or compress the vectors with quantization methods have been introduced [5]. FAISS, an optimized library for efficient similarity search produced by Facebook [6], contains algorithms that can search in sets of vectors of any size using approximate methods. Nevertheless, the index building algorithms used for implementing KNN graphs are time consuming and therefore energy inefficient and often cannot readily scale to the billion-sized databases on the cloud especially when frequent retraining is needed due to statistically different data.

Asides from the software approaches, an underlying hardware solution is necessary to boost the performance on these kind of tasks. With the increasing popularity of data classification recently, FPGAs as parallel implementation platforms are very suitable as they can be programmed in such a way in order to reduce the total computational overhead. They provide fine grain programmable hardware resources with high performance and much lower power compared to multi-core systems. Moreover, as the energy footprint in big data centers that operate today on large-scale KNN tasks is crucial, the problem becomes challenging. In this paper, we present a novel implementation of FAISS framework using FPGAs and achieve a significant speed-up compared with other multi-core solutions. More specifically, in this work we make the following contributions:

- We implement a partition-based FPGA accelerator on Xilinx VU9P in order to speed-up the index building time for approximate KNN search used on FAISS.
- We make several dataflow and memory optimizations on FAISS framework in order to match and benefit from the FPGA hardware that we integrated.
- We ported and ran the full hardware accelerated framework on AWS cloud, achieving superior performance and power efficiency to other high performance systems.

2 Previous Work

A lot of research interest has been shown on the KNN algorithm especially for the acceleration and optimization both in software and hardware. Moreover, energy efficiency, the crucial criterion nowadays which concerns the big companies has not shown the equivalent importance. And as the big-scale data is processed on the cloud, developers need to find clever heterogenous architectures to port these applications.

Pu et al. [7] presented a bubble sort enhanced KNN algorithm using the FPGA based computing system. This implementation focuses on the query search, however the algorithm is based on the exhaustive naive KNN implementation that lacks performance when compared with an approximate solution. Even the proposed FPGA accelerated solution of that work cannot surpass the performance of FAISS running in a traditional CPU. This is because FAISS is an already CPU/GPU optimized library for approximated similarity search which achieves fast query results while maintaining generally negligible reduction in accuracy.

Zhang et al. [8] presented a method for PQ (Product Quantization) based approximated nearest neighbor search using OpenCL FPGAs. They focus on the codebook size reduction in order to limit the memory overhead over the dataset when doing query search. However, the cost of the training/clustering, which is a crucial part of the approximate KNN graph construction, is not reflected in the measurements. Secondly, they do not describe specifically the hardware implementation/architecture of the accelerator and they only show a part of the algorithm in pseudocode. Last but not least, their proposed solution does not proceed to an implementation of FPGAs on the cloud.

Hussain et al. [9] present a K-means clustering method in FPGAs for processing large scale datasets. However, their implementation is inferior to this work's partition-based accelerator in terms of performance. They state that they achieve 0.0042 $s/iteration$ for $N = 65500$ dataset with $K = 4$ clusters and $D = 9$ dimension. K-means, in the world of algorithm complexity has an $O(n \cdot d \cdot i \cdot k)$ complexity so this translates in ~0.56 GFLOPs which is proportionately (of our FPGA resources) smaller than the performance we achieve in this work as we will see in the next chapters.

3 Background

In this section we describe how classic KNN search and ANN search on FAISS work. Different approximation techniques are used in the framework based on IVF (inverted indexing) methods in order to cluster dense vectors but in this work we chose to focus on the *IVFFlat* optimization because it is generally the fastest and more accurate technique used in the framework. Furthermore, we introduce the FPGA architecture and the environment used to develop the application dataflow and kernels.

3.1 KNN Search

KNN algorithm is one of the most popular machine learning algorithms used in pattern recognition scenarios, recommender systems and even financial research [9,10]. The function returns the K nearest neighbor points to a specified object among a dataset. The "weights" of each object are defined by D attributes which is the data dimension. The plurality vote of this algorithm is often characterized by the distance between the query points. A commonly used distance is the *Euclidean distance* because very often it has intuitive meaning [11] and the computation scales. For discrete variables the overlap metric is used which is also known as *Hamming distance*. In Cartesian coordinates the Euclidean *n-space* is the following:

$$dist(x_i, y_i) = \sqrt{\sum_{i=1}^{n}(x_i - y_i)^2}$$

The exhaustive query search using the above algorithm, especially for large-scale datasets, becomes quite high in terms of number of operations as we need to compute each distance between every point in the samples. So approximate solutions need to take place in order to find effectively the K most possible nearest neighbors.

3.2 ANN Search

The idea behind this approach is that, in many cases, an approximate nearest neighbor is almost as good as the exact one because small differences in the distance should not matter. This makes KNN computationally tractable even for large datasets as they reduce the number of distance evaluations performed in total. There are mainly two types of methods in ANN search that focus either on data and dimension reduction (or both) for the query search. One type is spatial clustering based method, such as K-means clustering [12] or hierarchical KD-trees [13]. These methods employ a partition algorithm technique by constructing a k-nearest neighbor graph via splitting-clustering the samples into regions. Another method for ANN search is hashing based methods such as Locality Sensitive Hashing (LSH) [14] which groups the points into "buckets" based on the distance metric. Near vectors are mapped into the same bucket and thus the algorithm retrieves the closest neighbors of the target vector.

3.3 FAISS Framework Operation

Faiss contains several methods for similarity search on dense vectors of real or integer number values and can be compared with L2 distances or dot products. Vectors that are similar-close to a query vector are those that have the lowest L2 distance or equivalently the highest dot product with the target-query vector. The framework is built upon different indexing schemes for storing vectors and the distance function is calculated using several metrics such as the previously mentioned. The indexing structures differ from each other, ranging from exact search to product quantization techniques which are shown to be more effective than binary codes. This, of course, comes at a cost of accuracy but also determines the trade-off between other important measurements such as speed of search time, training time, memory, etc. In this subsection we will analyze some basic indexing techniques in FAISS so as to have an overall understanding of the framework architecture before proceeding to choose which one to accelerate via the FPGA hardware. Our implementation, described on the next section, chooses IVFFlat indexing as a use case for demonstration (best for high-accuracy regimes) but the design can be easily applied to other indexes such as IndexIVFPQ. Both methods, especially the latter, have a little less precision than exhaustive search but are proven to scale to billions of vectors in sufficient a memory on a single server.

IVFFlat Indexing. Several studies have exploited the properties of *Voronoi* diagrams to improve variations of the nearest neighbor search [15]. Voronoi diagram is a partitioning of a plane into regions based on distance to points in a specific subset of the plane [16]. FAISS constructs the *IndexIVFFlat* index by defining Voronoi cells from a codebook C_{coarse} in the d-dimensional space, and each database vector falls in one of the cells. At search time, only the database vectors y contained in the cell that the query x is mapped to along with a few neighboring ones are compared against the query vector. So, two parameters are essential to the query process method: *ncells*, the number of cells, and *nprobe*, the number of cells (out of *ncells*) that are visited to perform a search. The number of cells stands for the number of inverted lists which might be denoted also as *nlist*. This probing process is a partition-based method based on Multi-probing (a reminiscent variant of best-bin KD-tree [17]). The database vectors are assigned to the cells thanks to a hashing function, specifically K-means (closest query to centroid) and stored in an inverted file structure. As a result, IVFFlat effectively reduces the search space, and achieves a substantial speed-up over the exhaustive search. By all means, in order the results to be accurate, they must fall into the visiting Voronoi cells.

IVFPQ Indexing. This generalizes the inverted index idea by combining inverted indices with product quantization so as to avoid exhaustive search. The natural product quantization method is denoted as PQ and its non-exhaustive version is denoted as IVFPQ [18]. The vectors are still stored in Voronoi cells, but their size is reduced to a configurable number of bytes m (dimension must be a multiple of m). The compression is an additional level of quantization, that is applied on sub-vectors of the vectors to encode. In this case, since the vectors are not stored exactly, the distances that are returned by the search method are also approximations and often have less accuracy than IVFFlat for example. Also, if this indexing has to handle uniform data, it is very hard because there is no regularity that can be exploited to cluster or reduce dimensionality. Nevertheless, IndexIVFPQ is a very useful indexing structure for large-scale search which can also be deployed into our FPGA design.

LSH Method. Another very popular cell-probe method is probably the original Locality Sensitive Hashing method (LSH). It reduces the dimensionality of high-dimensional data by hashing input items into similar buckets. Points that are close to each other under a specific distance metric (i.e. Euclidean) are mapped to the same bucket with high probability. Faiss implements this algorithm, however, it lacks some characteristics that are found in the other algorithms such as memory optimizations. The large number of hash functions leads to extra memory, something which is prohibitive for big-scale datasets on the cloud and thus not ideal for this work.

3.4 FPGA OpenCL Framework

The OpenCL specification in FPGAs consists of host code and kernels where host lies on a x86-64 CPU which handles the application's dataflow. Our FAISS application which runs on the host leverages the hardware kernels that translate the OpenCL hardware abstraction to an FPGA implementation on the device fabric. For this task we utilized the SDAccel environment [19] which offers software and hardware emulation capabilities to verify and debug the application before synthesizing and running on the FPGA device. Then, by analyzing the system reports and checking the device data tracing and application timeline for potential bottlenecks in our design up to the precision of clock cycles we could finalize the optimized application with the hardware integrated into FAISS framework. Cloud service providers, such as Amazon AWS, who specialize in heterogeneous accelerator clouds for big data and machine learning offer FPGA-based boards and with this way we deployed our application on the cloud.

4 Implementation

In this section we first describe the framework analysis in order to profile FAISS and specify which parts of the algorithm are going to be implemented on hardware, selecting IVFFlat as a use-case for profiling. Next, we represent the new framework which uses an in-memory FPGA format for minimum latency overhead over the memory transactions. Last, we specify the hardware accelerator and all the optimizations done on the host and kernel side so as to achieve maximum throughput and reduce the overall latency of the design.

4.1 Framework Profiling

We first had to select an efficient ANN implementation, so we identified from previous work and ours that the IVF indices, especially IVFFlat, perform the best among the other indexing techniques used in FAISS. In this algorithm, using several profiling tools (i.e. valgrind/callgrind, gprof), we determined the memory and compute bottlenecks with the use of call-graph techniques. The functions that consume the most execution time are good candidates to be offloaded and accelerated into FPGAs (see Fig. 1). Our work shows that index creation for the dataset consumes a lot of time, even orders of magnitude from a modest query search of thousands of vectors. This comes from the fact that ANN search is very agile but comes with a cost of long training-clustering times. Particularly, the training algorithm contains a lot of Multiply-Accumulate operations (MAC) which are implemented with optimized BLAS routines on the default FAISS CPU implementation. These algorithms are good candidates for hardware parallelization because they have a high number of $\frac{total\ operations}{bytes\ transferred}$.

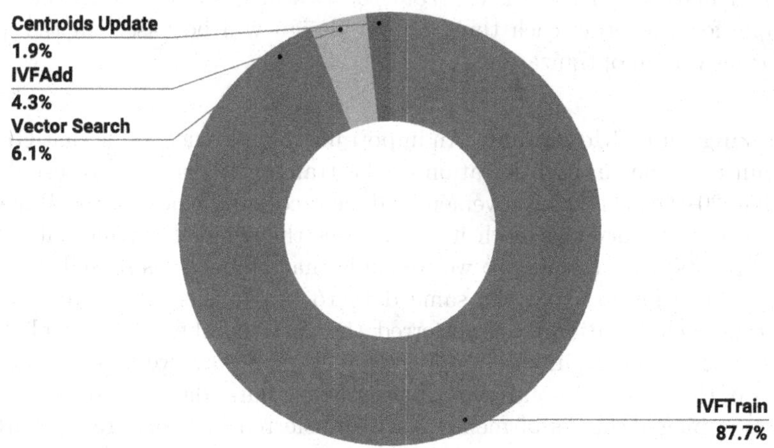

Fig. 1. FAISS profiling with IVFFlat indexing

4.2 Optimization Schemes

For an efficient hardware implementation we had to take into account specific principles that comprise the design methodology for FPGAs. These include as a first step to design the host and kernel side of the accelerator function so as to map well to the FAISS framework and at the same time keep the correctness of the application. Furthermore, concerning the memory, optimizing data movement is crucial between the host from/to global memory and global memory from/to kernels [20,21]. Last, we created an optimized custom logic for the FPGA kernels to achieve a low latency design.

Defining the Accelerator. The key transformations for high level synthesis start from the host code. In order to define a scalable function for acceleration we implemented a custom column-major GEMM (General Matrix Multiplication) routine where the first matrix is transposed:

$$C = alpha * T(A) * B + beta * C \tag{1}$$

In this way, more efficient hardware is implemented accessing both arrays with consecutive elements in the 2nd dimension as the data is stored. Also, it is essential to know before-hand if possible, how large the dimensions of the matrices are going to be. In our case, FAISS defines the first input of GEMM as an $nlist \times vector\_dim$ matrix while the second one as a $vector\_dim \times centroid\_points$. The integer $nlist$ is usually small (compared with the database) and depicts the number of inverted lists as stated previously. As a rule of thumb this number is usually multiples of $\sqrt{dataset}$ (i.e. IVFFlat4096, etc). Furthermore, the $vector\_dim$ which is the dimension of the vectors, is not a large number as well (below one thousand) because compressing is used for higher data dimensions. The larger matrix dimension is $centroid\_points$ which are defined as the points to sample for clustering each time. So our design will be based on the above facts for maximum optimization.

Optimizing Data Movement. An important thing we noticed is that GEMM runs multiple times in each iteration of the training (iterations are usually no more than 20–25 as little improvement is done) accessing blocks of the B matrix. We know from theory that each iteration uses the same clustering data (total centroid points) over training so we conclude that B matrix is reused over each iteration. In order to avoid the same data to be transferred to global memory during each iteration we transferred the total number of centroid points to DDR one time only in the first iteration. In this way, we avoided memory requests of the same data and also achieved faster burst data transfers to global memory as bigger chunks of memory are transferred in higher rates. Furthermore, to maximize data throughput we implemented a 512-bit user interface on each kernel side which is the maximum memory bandwidth supported in our FPGA using OpenCL vector datatypes. Particularly, we used *float16* datatype in order to maintain maximum accuracy for the dataset and not append another layer of approximation into ANN search. Along with the use of all four DDRs of the device for read-write operations we achieved optimal memory transfer rates between host-DDRs and DDRs-kernels. It is worth mentioning that careful selection of SLR assignment to kernels was took into account. Our design was placed in a way that did not exceed SLR resources and kernels were put in the same SLR as the memory banks with which they had the most connections. This avoids SLR crossing and limits critical paths, something that leads to inefficient synthesis and more power consumption. Last, we allocated matrix blocks in physically contiguous memory using on-chip BRAMs, which are physically located near the computation of kernels. Hence, we guaranteed a fast communication allowing one-cycle read-writes of 512 bit data with the most efficient data movers.

Optimizing Kernel. In order to achieve large throughput we had to enable a high degree of fine-grained parallelism in application execution within the PL fabric. We avoided data dependencies and increased the level of parallelism in the algorithm of the hardware kernels. Using appropriate OpenCL directives such as pipeline or unroll, we constructed a highly parallel and pipelined architecture with minimum latency that performed the MAC operations very efficiently.

We achieved initiation interval II = 1 in every loop and by using the dataflow directive the kernel consumed all the data as soon as they arrived at memory interfaces and wrote back to DDRs as soon as they were ready. Also, it was more efficient to create larger and fewer compute units (CU) to access chunks of global memory than creating multiple smaller CUs because this results in absurdly heavier usage of FPGA resources and area due to which design fails timing. The design for a single kernel fully parallelizes up to 192 output data (MAC), thus in every cycle it produces 192 output elements. This translates to:

$$2 \cdot 192 \cdot kernel\_freq \, \text{FLOPs}$$

4.3 Final System Design

In order to integrate the hardware accelerator with FAISS and port it into the FPGA on the cloud we had to export it as a shared library and then link it with the rest of the FAISS framework. Through the SDAccel Development Environment we were able not only to create the dynamic library but also the final FPGA binary that the device would load from. We made specific modifications on the Makefile of FAISS so as to direct the SDAccel compiler to successfully compile the whole framework using our in-memory FPGA OpenCL model.

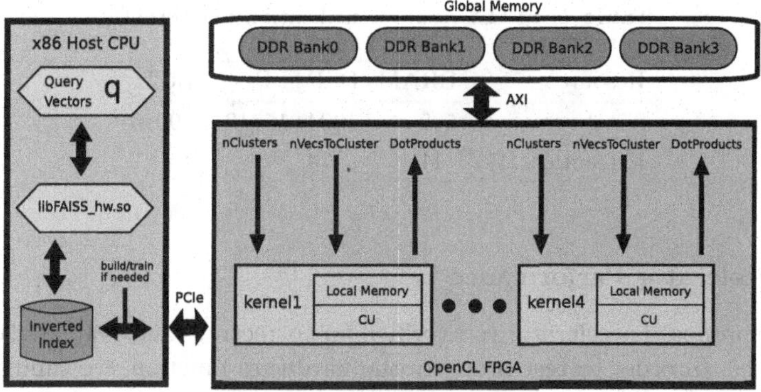

Fig. 2. Software and hardware dataflow

As a result, all cluster points resided in FPGA global memory the whole time and our hardware function accessed part of the global memory when needed.

The already optimized CPU BLAS function called "sgemm" was replaced by our custom function which manipulates carefully all the input data with OpenCL task synchronization via command queues on the host side. The general application dataflow of FAISS can be observed on Fig. 2. To conclude, host code optimization (concurrency from OpenCL Command Queue), buffer management regarding data exchange between the host and kernels, general pipelining on the FPGA, and synchronization between host and kernels were all precisely constructed according to FPGA design principles for high performance.

5 Experiments

In order to evaluate the design we confirmed the correctness of the accelerator and measured its performance. Then after the integration with FAISS we tested the final system's accuracy and performance on real-world data and measured the power efficiency compared with other systems such as CPU, GPU.

5.1 System Setup

The mapping of the final system was done on cloud FPGAs based on the Amazon AWS F1 platform. This consists of a Xilinx Virtex Ultrascale+ VU9P Acceleration development board with four DDR4 channels along with a host system of 8 vCPUs and 122GiB RAM. For a fair end-to-end comparison with a high performance CPU we chose a c4.8xlarge instance which comes with 36-vCPU Xeon and 60 GiB of RAM, and has the same price tag (per hour) as an f1.2xlarge ($\sim 1.6/h$). Also, for the final system evaluation we compare the performance/watt of the same CPU and a Kepler-class K40 GPU. Our FPGA hardware design uses all DDRs and makes good use of each SLR's resources with routing across the three SLRs being the primary bottleneck preventing further scaling. Table 1 shows the resource utilization of a single kernel on the FPGA device.

Table 1. FPGA resource utilization per kernel

Resource	BRAM	DSP	FF	LUT
Total	502	1004	157131	89096
Percentage (%)	11	14	6	7

5.2 Accelerator Performance

First, the proposed accelerator was verified for correctness and evaluated on AWS F1 instance. In order to test properly the hardware function, we simulated the FAISS inputs for different dataset scenarios, generating random cluster data for a number of Voronoi cells. On Fig. 3 we observe the FPGA accelerator efficiency measured in percentage of GFLOPs for a number of Voronoi cells.

The arrow shows the maximum speed-up achieved when compared with a single-core CPU. This comes from the fact that for more cells the impact of data transfer is less evident. It's worth mentioning here that the lower efficiency value which happens to be from ~500 cells and below does not impact the overall performance of the algorithm. Usually in real-world datasets, especially in larger ones used in data centers, the Voronoi cells are multiples of thousands for satisfactory clustering, even for a modest 1-million dataset.

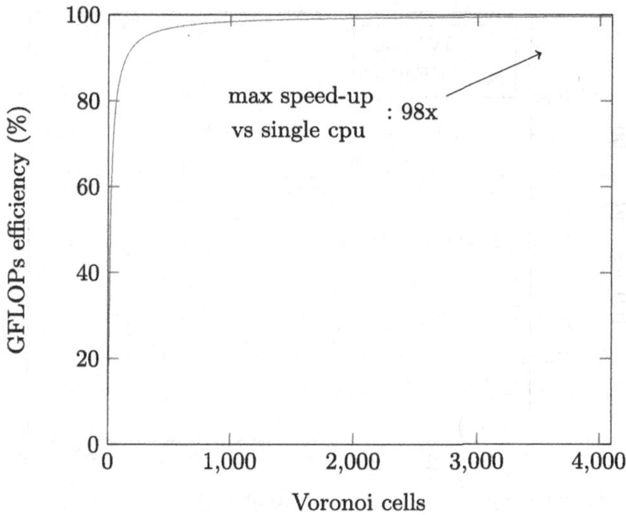

Fig. 3. Hardware accelerator efficiency

5.3 Final System and Evaluation

For the final system performance evaluation we first compared the end-to-end execution with the 36-thread Xeon CPU mentioned previously achieving $\sim$2.1$\times$ speed-up. Next, for the purposes of demonstration we used a million-scale dataset, specifically the SIFT 1M which is a well-known dataset and can fit easily in any RAM. In Fig. 4 we make an accuracy evaluation on this dataset with our FPGA design in order to make an assessment of the quality of our algorithm on actual real-world data. KNN models are usually evaluated using the *recall* measure which is the ratio of correctly predicted positive observations to all observations in the actual class. However, for the quality of our custom Inverted Index method we use the more appropriate "R – *recall at* R" also known as *intersection*, which the fraction of the R found nearest neighbors that are within the ground-truth R nearest neighbors (we use R = 100).

In the above figure, we evaluate the accuracy of two Inverted Index (Flat) methods using different probe values. The construction of the IVF4096 index takes much longer as we have a larger number of cells to train (4096 vs 256). However, for the same accuracy values (y axis) between each method, the query search is much faster on the IVF4096. This is because a smaller fraction of the database is compared to the query ($nprobe/ncells$). For example in order to maintain 0.6 accuracy we have to probe $\frac{2}{256}$ cells of the dataset on IVF256 whilst we select $\frac{8}{4096}$ cells of the dataset on IVF256 as seen from Fig. 4. So we conclude that for more thorough index building-training times we have more efficient query results. Thus, someone that invests computational time in a proper index can have fast results of similarity search. Consequently, as more efficient search can be performed this way, the index build algorithm which our FPGA design targeted and improved, is inevitably crucial.

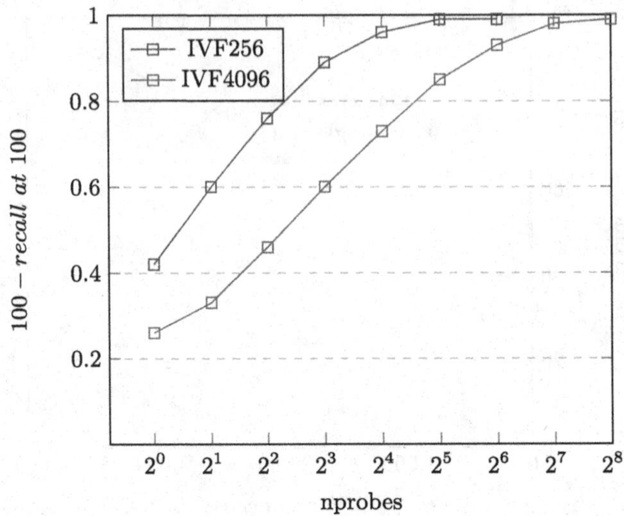

Fig. 4. Inverted index accuracy for different probe values on SIFT 1M

Next, we proceeded to make an actual live real-world measurement of our FPGA board on the cloud (including data transfers) using AWS metric tools. We then compared the measured performance/watt of our hardware design with the maximum theoretical performance/watt of the Xeon CPU and a K40 GPU. The results are illustrated in Fig. 5 with a clear advantage over our FPGA architecture. We used the following Eq. (2) for the other devices in order to make a comparison of the maximum power efficiency they can achieve compared with our FPGA design.

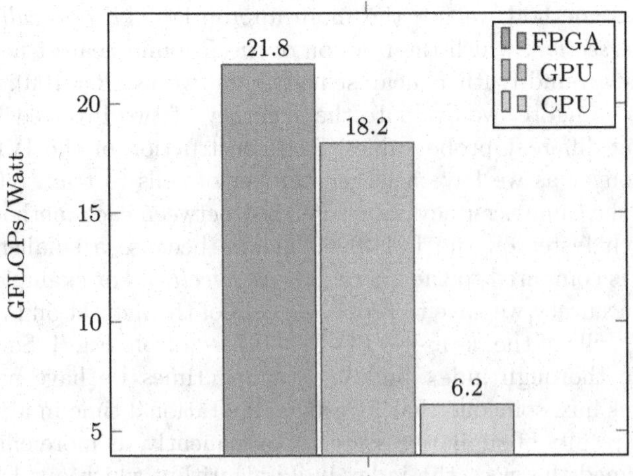

Fig. 5. Power efficiency comparison

$$power\ efficiency = \frac{device\ FLOPS}{device\ TDP} \tag{2}$$

6 Conclusion

Hardware accelerators can improve significantly the performance of machine learning applications. However, many frameworks such as FAISS do not support the transparent utilization of such acceleration modules. In this study, we implemented a novel scheme for the seamless utilization of FPGA hardware in FAISS framework for big-data similarity search used on the cloud.

Our results showed than our hardware accelerator outperforms a 36-thread Xeon CPU and has better performance/watt when compared with the same CPU and also with a Kepler-class GPU. Thus, SW/HW codesign is in fact a valid solution for the cloud computing workloads, in this case for the persistent indexing times of approximated KNN algorithms. The superior performance and performance/watt of our design can leverage the use of FPGA hardware on the cloud and in big data-centers as power efficiency plays a very important role today with the constantly increasing workload demands.

As Future Work, in order to solve the memory issue of billion-scale datasets which was our only restriction, the distributing of the application to a number of FPGAs is needed. Our algorithm was designed in such a way that the host application can easily distribute the dataset and thus the workload on a number of FPGAs on the cloud which due to limited infrastructure at that time we could not accomplish.

Acknowledgment. This project has received funding from the Xilinx University program and the Hellenic Foundation for Research and Innovation (HFRI) and the General Secretariat for Research and Technology (GSRT), under grant agreement No 2212-Hardware Acceleration of Machine Learning Applications in the Cloud.

References

1. Kachris, C., Soudris, D.: A survey on reconfigurable accelerators for cloud computing. In: 2016 26th International Conference on Field Programmable Logic and Applications (FPL), pp. 1–10, August 2016
2. Mavridis, S., et al.: Vinetalk: simplifying software access and sharing of FPGAs in datacenters. In: 2017 27th International Conference on Field Programmable Logic and Applications (FPL), pp. 1–4, September 2017
3. Kouiroukidis, N., Evangelidis, G.: The effects of dimensionality curse in high dimensional KNN search. In: 2011 15th Panhellenic Conference on Informatics, p. 42 (2011)
4. Andoni, A., Indyk, P., Razenshteyn, I.P.: Approximate nearest neighbor search in high dimensions. CoRR, vol. abs/1806.09823 (2018)
5. Norouzi, M., Fleet, D.J.: Cartesian k-means. In: Proceedings of the 2013 IEEE Conference on Computer Vision and Pattern Recognition, CVPR 2013, Washington, DC, USA, pp. 3017–3024. IEEE Computer Society (2013)

6. Johnson, J., Douze, M., Jégou, H.: Billion-scale similarity search with GPUs. arXiv preprint arXiv:1702.08734 (2017)
7. Pu, Y., Peng, J., Huang, L., Chen, J.: An efficient KNN algorithm implemented on FPGA based heterogeneous computing system using OpenCL. In: 2015 IEEE 23rd Annual International Symposium on Field-Programmable Custom Computing Machines, pp. 167–170, May 2015
8. Zhang, J., Li, J., Khoram, S.: Efficient large-scale approximate nearest neighbor search on OpenCL FPGA, pp. 4924–4932, June 2018
9. Hussain, H.M., Benkrid, K., Erdogan, A.T., Seker, H.: Highly parameterized k-means clustering on FPGAs: comparative results with GPPs and GPUs. In: 2011 International Conference on Reconfigurable Computing and FPGAs, pp. 475–480 (2011)
10. Chen, Q., Li, D., Tang, C.: KNN matting. In: 2012 IEEE Conference on Computer Vision and Pattern Recognition, pp. 869–876, June 2012
11. Liu, S., et al.: Matching-CNN meets KNN: quasi-parametric human parsing. In: 2015 IEEE Conference on Computer Vision and Pattern Recognition (CVPR), pp. 1419–1427, June 2015
12. Fukunage, K., Narendra, P.M.: A branch and bound algorithm for computing k-nearest neighbors. IEEE Trans. Comput. **24**, 750–753 (1975)
13. Bentley, J.L.: Multidimensional binary search trees used for associative searching. Commun. ACM **18**, 509–517 (1975)
14. Gionis, A., Indyk, P., Motwani, R.: Similarity search in high dimensions via hashing. In: Proceedings of the 25th International Conference on Very Large Data Bases, VLDB 1999, San Francisco, pp. 518–529. Morgan Kaufmann Publishers Inc. (1999)
15. Sharifzadehand, M., Shahabi, C.: Approximate voronoi cell computation on geometric data streams, March 2019
16. Li, K., Li, W., Chen, Z., Liu, Y. (eds.): ISICA 2017. CCIS, vol. 874. Springer, Singapore (2018). https://doi.org/10.1007/978-981-13-1651-7
17. Kybic, J., Vnučko, I.: Approximate best bin first kd tree all nearest neighbor search with incremental updates, vol. 10, pp. 420–422, August 2010
18. Chen, Y., Guan, T., Wang, C.: Approximate nearest neighbor search by residual vector quantization. Sensors **10**, 11259–11273 (2010)
19. Xilinx Inc.: SDAccel development environment
20. Danopoulos, D., Kachris, C., Soudris, D.: Acceleration of image classification with caffe framework using FPGA. In: 2018 7th International Conference on Modern Circuits and Systems Technologies (MOCAST), pp. 1–4, May 2018
21. Yinger, J., et al.: Customizable FPGA OpenCL matrix multiply design template for deep neural networks. In: 2017 International Conference on Field Programmable Technology (ICFPT), pp. 259–262, December 2017

Automatic Memory-Efficient Scheduling of CNNs

Luc Waeijen(✉), Savvas Sioutas, Yifan He, Maurice Peemen, and Henk Corporaal

Eindhoven University of Technology, 5612 AZ Eindhoven, The Netherlands
{l.j.w.waeijen,s.sioutas,y.he,m.peemen,h.corporaal}@tue.nl

Abstract. Accessing large external DRAM is costly, and poses a challenge to efficiently evaluate data-intensive convolutional neural networks (CNNs) on embedded devices. These external memory accesses can be minimized by exploiting data reuse in on-chip memory. Selecting the combination of code transformations that minimize the external DRAM accesses is however an extremely complex task. In this work a mathematical model is presented to quickly and very precisely evaluate combinations of code transformations on CNNs. An accompanying open source tool is developed which leverages this model to perform automated design space exploration and code generation for CNNs. The correctness of the developed model is demonstrated by measurement of seven neural networks. Results show the transformations selected by the tool can reduce external memory accesses by over an order of magnitude.

Keywords: Memory efficient · Reuse · Scheduling · CNN

1 Introduction

Energy efficient evaluation of convolutional neural networks (CNNs) [1] is essential to enable state-of-the-art machine learning applications, such as computer vision, speech synthesis, and natural language processing, on embedded devices. CNNs are however highly data-intensive, as network evaluation requires many pre-trained weights (>100 MB for some networks [16]), and generates large amounts of intermediate data. Accessing external DRAMs requires orders of magnitude more energy than computation [3,12], hence it is imperative for an efficient CNN implementation to minimize external memory accesses.

The key to achieve this is maximizing data-reuse in on-chip buffers by altering the temporal memory behaviour of the network. In general this is a well studied problem, and many scheduling techniques such as loop tiling and interchange are available [6,11,19]. The complexity however lies in the size of the scheduling space, which is particularly large for CNNs due to their many independent convolutions. An analytic method is required to derive the optimal point in this space, as exhaustive search by implementation is far too time consuming.

D. N. Pnevmatikatos et al. (Eds.): SAMOS 2019, LNCS 11733, pp. 387–400, 2019.
https://doi.org/10.1007/978-3-030-27562-4_28

To enable fast design space exploration (DSE) this work presents a generic mathematical model for CNNs which, given a set of code transformations, closely approximates the external accesses, and required internal memory. Moreover the model is integrated into an open source tool [17] which automates the DSE and code generation. The correctness of the model is experimentally verified for seven state-of-the-art networks. Compared to a straightforward schedule external accesses are reduced by 1–2 orders of magnitude, or all reuse can be captured with 2–3 orders of magnitude smaller on-chip memory.

2 CNN Background, Coding, and Notation

Conceptually CNNs are loosely modelled after neurons in the human brain. These neurons are organized in successive layers, where each layer provides input to the next (See Fig. 1). In general the neurons in the earlier layers learn to detect simple features, e.g. horizontal or vertical lines for the traffic sign detection network in Fig. 1. Neurons that detect the same feature in different positions are grouped in feature maps (FMs). The neurons in FMs in later layers are typically connected to multiple input FMs of the preceding layer, combining simple features into complex, higher order features. To detect various features, neurons have weighted inputs. Since neurons in one FM detect the same feature at different locations, they reuse the same weights. For a more complete introduction the reader may refer to the deep learning book by Goodfellow et al. [1]. Note that although the described example concerns two dimensional FMs, the model presented in Sect. 4 can trivially be applied to networks used for problems of lower dimensionality by setting any unused dimensions to one.

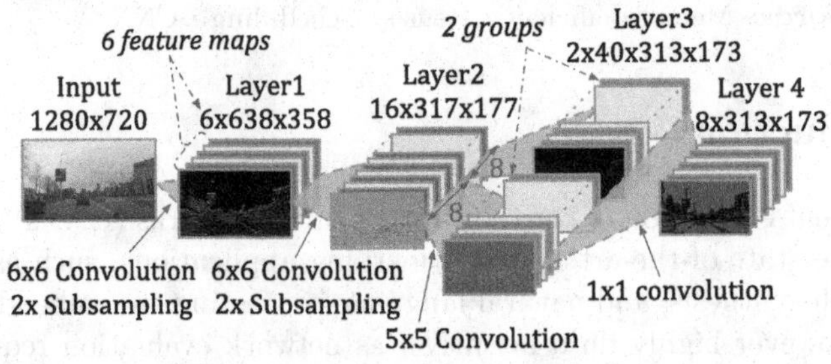

Fig. 1. A four layer CNN for speed sign detection [10].

In code a single convolutional layer can be represented as a set of six nested loops (Code 1.1). The notation of network dimensions and loop bounds used in the code is visualized in Fig. 2. After initialization with a bias (line 5), a neuron reads its inputs from a typically small (e.g. 3 × 3) 2D kernel within a preceding FM in lines 6–7. The loops on lines 3–4 apply the same neuron to all x and y positions, possibly subsampling with factors S_x and S_y. This process is repeated for all preceding FMs on line 2. Finally different feature detecting neurons generate multiple output FMs on line 1. Inputs X are scaled with learned weights from array W, and summed to form output Y on lines 8–10.

```
1  for(int z=0; z<Dz; z++)
2   for(int i=0; i<Di; i++)
3    for(int y=0; y<Dy; y++)  //SL
4     for(int x=0; x<Dx; x++){//CL
5      Y[z][y][x]=bias[z];
6      for(int k=0; k<Ky; k++)
7       for(int l=0; l<Kx; l++)
8        Y[z][y][x]+= \
9         X[i][y*Sy+k][x*Sx+l] \
10         * W[i][z][k][l];
11     }
```

Code 1.1. Loopnest for a single convolution layer

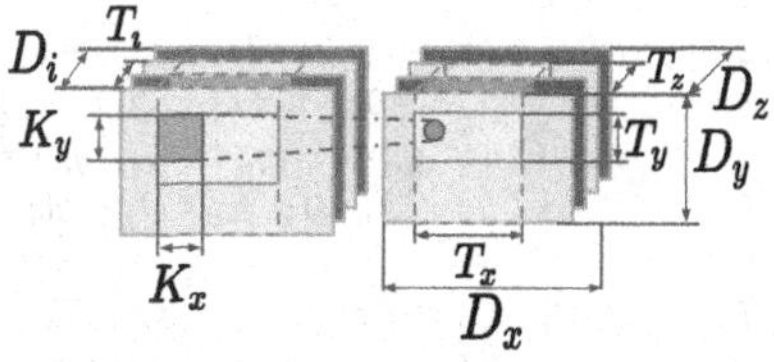

Fig. 2. Notations D_n, T_n and K_n respectively represent the size, tiling, and kernel size in dimension n.

3 Scheduling Space

The objective is to efficiently evaluate CNNs using a typical accelerator setup. The accelerator is assumed to have access to some large off-chip memory for storage of the complete CNN models. Furthermore the accelerator is equipped with smaller, on-chip, software controlled, memories, i.e., scratchpads. To achieve high energy efficiency and performance, data-reuse is to be captured as much as possible in the available on-chip memory by reordering operations and deciding when to store what data on-chip. Since convolution layers are the main part of CNNs, this work exclusively focuses on such layers. *All* operations within a convolution layer as represented in Code 1.1 can be reordered freely on the merit of the associative property of the accumulation on line 8, yielding $(D_z D_i D_y D_x K_y K_x)!$ valid operation orders. Almost all of these orders result in irregular data accesses, complex address calculations, and large code size. To avoid impractical schedules strictly conventional *loop tiling and interchange* are considered. Furthermore for each array X, Y, and W, it needs to be determined when to store what data in on-chip buffers, which is captured by *compute and store levels*. The remainder of this section details these concepts, and defines the considered scheduling space.

3.1 Tiling

Tiling is the process of partitioning the iteration space of nested loops into n-dimensional hypercubes, with n the number of loop dimensions. The iterations within a cubes are executed atomically, i.e., all the iterations within a cube have to be completed before the iterations of a different block may start [19]. An example is shown for loops x and y in Fig. 4b, where the x dimension is tiled with $T_x = 2$. In particular for a convolution window of 2×2, i.e. $K_x = K_y = 2$, input element $X[0][1][1]$ is used in the four numbered iterations. In the original schedule uses 2 and 3 are scheduled five iterations apart, while in the tiled schedule all uses are consecutive. A downside is that the uses of $X[0][2][2]$ now are scheduled further apart than in the original schedule. Therefore it depends on the dimensions and kernel sizes of the network what tile size best suits a particular on-chip buffer.

```
//outer tile loops
for(int z_o=0; z_o<D_z; z_o+=T_z)
  for(int i_o=0; i_o<D_i; i_i+=T_i)
    for(int y_o=0; y_o<D_y; y_o+=T_y)
      for(int x_o=0; x_o<D_x; x_o+=T_x){
        //inner tile loops
        for(int z_i=z_o; z_i<z_o+T_z; z_i++)
          for(int i_i=i_o; i_i<i_o+T_i; i_i++)
            for(int y_i=y_o; y_i<y_o+T_y; y_i++)
              for(int x_i=x_o; x_i<x_o+T_x; x_i++){
                Y[z_i][y_i][x_i]=bias[z_i];
                for(int k=0; k<K_y; k++)
                  for(int l=0; l<K_x; l++)
                    Y[z_i][y_i][x_i]+= \
                      X[i_i][y_i*S_y+k][x_i*S_x+l] \
                      * W[i_i][z_i][k][l];}}
```

Code 1.2. Tiled loopnest for a single convolution layer

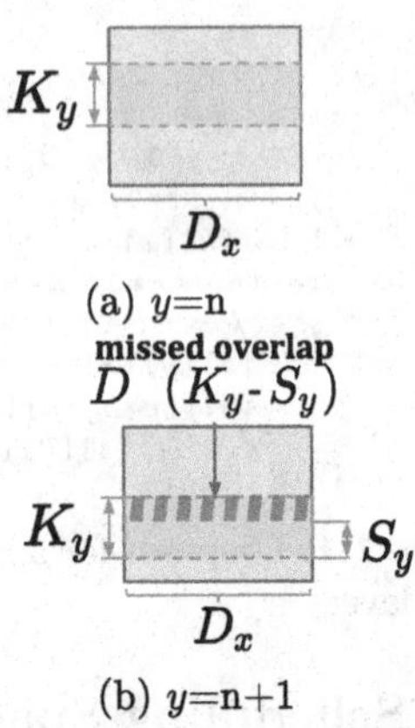

Fig. 3. Data volume required for one iteration of y, and the missed overlap for consecutive iterations when $\mathrm{SL}_X = y$.

All six loops in Code 1.1 can be tiled, but the dimensions of the kernel loops (lines 6–7) are typically very small making tiling unprofitable for these loops. Instead the focus is on tiling the loops in dimensions x, y, i and z, resulting in layer Code 1.2. A schedule thus specifies tile sizes $\{T_x, T_y, T_i, T_z\}$.

3.2 Loop Interchange

Another well known loop transformation is loop interchange, which reorders the loops in a loop nest. An example is given in Fig. 4c where loops x and y are interchanged, showing that the uses of $X[0][1][1]$ in iterations 2 and 3 are scheduled closer together than in the original schedule in Fig. 4c. Since each assigning statement in Code 1.2 accumulates into the same array, an associative operation, the loop order can be changed arbitrarily. When interchange is combined with tiling, the interchanges can be limited to within the set of outer tile loops, and within the set of inner loops in order.

To denote the loop order, a loop is referred to by the name of the loop variable in Code 1.2, such that the complete set of loops $L = \{zo, io, yo, xo, zi, ii, yi, xi, k, l\}$. A schedule defines a complete order LO on L. Additionally the binary relation a≺b is defined to be true when loop a is outer to loop b for a given LO.

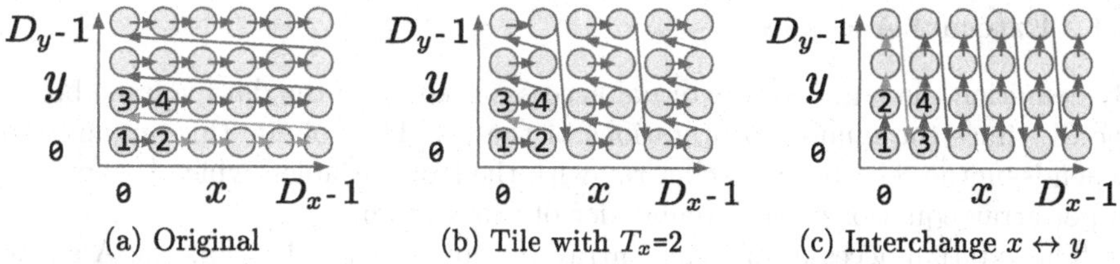

(a) Original (b) Tile with T_x=2 (c) Interchange $x \leftrightarrow y$

Fig. 4. Iteration space of loops x and y before and after tiling and loop interchange.

3.3 Store and Compute Levels

Apart from the order of the computations, also the memory transfers need to be scheduled. To express a schedule for data movement, a Store Level (SL) and Compute Level (CL) are used, which are concepts taken from the Halide language [12]. The SL and CL respectively specify *what* data are moved *when*.

These concepts are best explained using an example using Code 1.1. The SL for array X is set at loop y, which means all data from X that is required to complete one iteration of y is to be loaded only one time from the main memory. This implies that any reuse of elements of X inside one iteration of Y *must* be covered by storing in internal memory. The volume of required elements for iteration $y = \mathrm{n}$ is visualized in Fig. 3a, and amounts to $K_y D_x$ elements.

To capture all reuse however, the actual buffer size can be much smaller than $K_y D_x$ depending on *when* the data are loaded. Since in the loop order of Code 1.1 the kernel moves from left to right through the strip, at any given iteration of x only $K_y K_x$ elements of X are alive. Setting the CL to loop x to load the data at each iteration of x allows to capture all reuse with a rotating buffer sized $K_y K_x$.

Note that at the start of iteration $y = \mathrm{n}+1$ the $K_y D_x$ volume is conceptually cleared from internal memory. Consequently the reuse in the overlap between these iterations is not captured in internal memory, as highlighted in the Fig. 3b. To capture this reuse, the SL should be moved to a higher loop, which as a result would increase the required buffer size. Setting the SL and appropriate CL therefore express different points in the scheduling space. The SL and CL have to be defined for each array. Therefore a schedule defines SL_X, SL_Y, SL_W, CL_X, CL_Y, $CL_W \in L$.

4 Model

With the scheduling space defined, this section presents a mathematical model which given a schedule estimates the number of external memory accesses (Sect. 4.1), and the required internal memory size (Sect. 4.2) for a single layer. Finally it is detailed how this model can be used to perform efficient DSE for complete CNNs (Sect. 4.3).

4.1 External Accesses

By definition the number of external accesses is equal to the data volume below the SL times the number of iterations of the SL. The volume this amounts to depends on the relations of each array with the loop variables, which is captured in per-array equations in the remainder of this section.

The external accesses of weight array W can be derived as follows. A single neuron requires $K_x K_y$ weights for all D_i input FMs, which are reused for all x and y positions. In the simplest case the store level of the weights, i.e. SL_W, is below both x_i and y_i, and the reuse of the weights is not captured in on-chip memory. This means $K_x K_y D_i$ weights are to be transferred $D_x D_y D_z$ times to produce all D_z output FMs, yielding $K_x K_y D_x D_y D_i D_z$ transfers from external memory.

A more complex case is when SL_W *precedes* x_i in the loop order, i.e. $SL_W \prec x_i$ as defined in Sect. 3.2, forcing reuse of weights in the x-dimension. The weight transfers for the x-dimension reduce from D_x (for every x) to the number of tiles in x ($\lceil \frac{D_x}{T_x} \rceil$, where the ceiling operator is used to obtain a conservative upper bound), yielding $K_x K_y \lceil \frac{D_x}{T_x} \rceil D_y D_i D_z$ weight transfers in total. Similar reasoning can be applied to the y-dimension when $SL_W \prec y_i$. Since x and y are orthogonal from the perspective of W, the transfers reduce even further when both $SL_W \prec x_i$ and $SL_W \prec y_i$, in which case the number of transfers can be expressed as $K_x K_y \lceil \frac{D_x}{T_x} \rceil \lceil \frac{D_y}{T_y} \rceil D_i D_z$. These relations are generically formalized into Eq. 1. Notice that all weight reuse is captured in on-chip memory when $T_x = D_x$ and $T_y = D_y$, reducing the accesses to the minimum $K_x K_y D_i D_z$.

$$W_{acc}(SL_W, LO) \leq K_x K_y D_i D_z \times \prod_{d \in \{x,y\} \wedge SL_W \prec d_i} \left\lceil \frac{D_d}{T_d} \right\rceil \times \prod_{d \in \{x,y\} \wedge SL_W \not\prec d_i} D_d \tag{1}$$

Here the set in the first product term, i.e. $d \in \{x, y\} \wedge SL_W \prec d_i$, captures dimensions x_i and y_i if they precede SL_W, and otherwise they are captured in the second product term. Note that the product of an empty set is defined as the multiplicative identity 1.

The external accesses of array X are derived similarly and captured in Eq. 2. The first and second product terms of Eq. 2 account for the number of iterations of loop SL_X. The last two terms of the equation represent the volume of the transfer in the x and y dimensions. When x_i and/or y_i precede SL_X, still the kernel in those dimensions is part of the required volume (fourth term). When x_i and/or y_i do not precede SL_X, the tile plus an extra border of $K_d - 1$ is required with $d \in \{x, y\}$. Here subsampling is accounted for by the stride amount S_d, which is equal to one if no subsampling is performed (fifth term). Finally for each output FM all input FMs are required regardless of tiling, which is captured by the fixed D_i (first term).

$$\begin{aligned}X_{acc}(SL_X, LO) \leq & D_i \times \\ & \prod_{d\in\{x,y,z\}\wedge SL_X \not\prec d_i} D_d \times \prod_{d\in\{x,y,z\}\wedge SL_X \prec d_i} \left\lceil \frac{D_d}{T_d} \right\rceil \times \\ & \prod_{d\in\{x,y\}\wedge SL_X \not\prec d_i} K_d \times \prod_{d\in\{x,y\}\wedge SL_X \prec d_i} (T_d-1)\,S_d+K_d\end{aligned} \tag{2}$$

Also output array Y can induce external transfers when partial results are evicted from on-chip memory. These transfers are modelled in Eq. 3. Notably a factor two is present in this equation, because partial results need to be both stored to external memory, and reloaded later to be completed. Y only has reuse in i, hence this is the only dimension where can be saved on transfers. Finally a correction with -1 is performed, because at the first use no partial results need to be loaded.

$$Y_{acc}(SL_Y, LO) \leq 2D_xD_yD_z \times \prod_{d\in\{i\}\wedge SL_Y \not\prec d_i} D_d \times \prod_{d\in\{i\}\wedge SL_Y \prec d_i} \left\lceil \frac{D_d}{T_d} \right\rceil -1 \tag{3}$$

4.2 Internal Buffer Space

The models for the required internal buffer space are highly similar to the volume terms of their access counterparts, with the notable exception that the buffers be can folded into significantly smaller, software managed, circular buffers in one or more dimensions depending on the CL (Sect. 3.3). To express these fold dimensions (FDs), a predecessor function *pred*(d) is defined which yields the first loop level preceding loop d according to the loop order (LO). E.g., in Code 1.2 $pred(i_i) = z_i$.

Using this *pred* function, the FDs for weight array W can be expressed. W can potentially fold in dimensions i and/or z if they immediately precede SL_W, but not x or y since W is independent of these dimensions. When i and z consecutively precede SL_W, *both* dimensions can be folded. F_W, the set of FDs of W, is expressed in Eq. 4.

$$\begin{aligned}F_W(SL_W, LO) = \{\, & pred(SL_W) \mid pred(SL_W) \in \{i_i, z_i\}\,\} \quad \cup \\ \{ & pred(pred(SL_W)) \mid pred(SL_W) \in \{i_i, z_i\} \wedge pred(pred(SL_W)) \in \{i_i, z_i\}\}\end{aligned} \tag{4}$$

Without folding the required buffer size for the weights equals the first term of the access Eq. 1 ($K_xK_yD_iD_z$). When the i and/or z dimensions are folded according to Eq. 4, their contributions, i.e. D_i and/or D_z, are reduced to one, yielding:

$$W_{buf}(SL_W, LO) = K_xK_y \times \prod_{d\in\{i,z\}\setminus F_W(SL_W, LO)} D_d \tag{5}$$

Where $S\setminus S'$ represents the set difference, i.e, all elements which are in S, but not S'.

The fold dimensions of data array X are complexer, since X depends on the i, x, and y dimensions which can all fold. Furthermore, when the first predecessor of SL_X is i_i, then a directly preceding x or y can also be folded. This does not hold the other way around, e.g., when $pred(SL_X) = x_i$ and $pred(x_i) = i_i$, a fold in i would prohibit reuse in x. The fold dimensions of X are captured in Eq. 6.

$$\begin{aligned} F_X(SL_X, LO) = \{pred(SL_X) \mid pred(SL_X) \in \{i_i, x_i, y_i\}\} \quad \cup \\ \{pred(pred(SL_X)) \mid pred(SL_X) = i_i \wedge pred(pred(SL_X)) \in \{x_i, y_i\}\} \end{aligned} \tag{6}$$

The buffer size for array X is expressed in Eq. 7. The terms accounting for x and y are copied from their counterparts in Eq. 2. Dimension i is a bit more complicated, since if it precedes SL_X or is in F_X, its contribution folds to one. Otherwise a tile T_i needs to be stored.

$$\begin{aligned} X_{buf}(SL_X, LO) = \prod_{d \in \{l \mid l \in \{i\} \wedge SL_X \prec l_i\} \setminus F_X} T_d \quad \times \\ \prod_{d \in \{l \mid l \in \{x,y\} \wedge SL_X \not\prec l_i\} \cap F_X} K_d \quad \times \\ \prod_{d \in \{l \mid l \in \{x,y\} \wedge SL_X \prec l_i\} \setminus F_X} (T_d - 1)\, S_d + K_d \end{aligned} \tag{7}$$

The buffer calculation for output array Y is simple. F_Y is equal to Eq. 4 after substituting SL_W with SL_Y, and $\{i_i, z_i\}$ with $\{x_i, y_i\}$. When dimension d is folded, only T_d elements need to be accounted for versus D_d otherwise, leading to Eq. 8.

$$Y_{buf}(SL_Y, LO) = \prod_{d \in \{x,y,z\} \setminus F_Y \wedge SL_Y \preceq d_o} D_d \times \prod_{d \in \{x,y,z\} \setminus F_Y \wedge SL_Y \npreceq d_o \wedge SL \prec d_i} T_d \tag{8}$$

4.3 Multi Layer Design Space Exploration

The model introduced so far is only applicable to single layers. To model complete networks, the design spaces of individual layers have to be merged. When design points $p_1 \in L_1$ and $p_2 \in L_2$ of layer design spaces L_1 and L_2 are combined, the external accesses must be summed, while the maximum of the buffer sizes is taken. The maximum is taken as the buffer space can be reused each sequential layer execution. To get all network design points each combination of points p_1 and p_2 has to be merged, which rapidly expands the overall design space. However, it can be easily proven that since the combining functions, i.e. sum and max, are strictly monotonic, it is sufficient to consider only the combinations of the Pareto optimal points [8]. More formally, the combination of *any* point $p_1 \in L_1$ with a non-pareto-optimal point $p_2 \in L_2$ will always be dominated by the combination of p_1 and a Pareto optimal point $p_3 \in pareto(L_2)$. The same holds for the reverse, thus it is sufficient to only consider the combinations of points in $pareto(L_1)$ and $pareto(L_2)$. Note that the resulting space is a *superset* of the overall set of Pareto points, and should be pruned to obtain the pareto points of the combination of L_1 and L_2. Further layers in the network can be recursively merged with the resulting pareto set until the pareto front for the complete network is obtained. This way the design space growth caused by merging multiple layers is minimized.

5 Automated DSE and Code Generation

To automate schedule design space exploration and code generation, the mathematical model presented in the previous section is integrated into an open source CNN implementation tool [17]. This tool searches the space of valid schedules, and after selection of the desired schedule generates a statically scheduled network implementation. The tool has a modular design as depicted in Fig. 5.

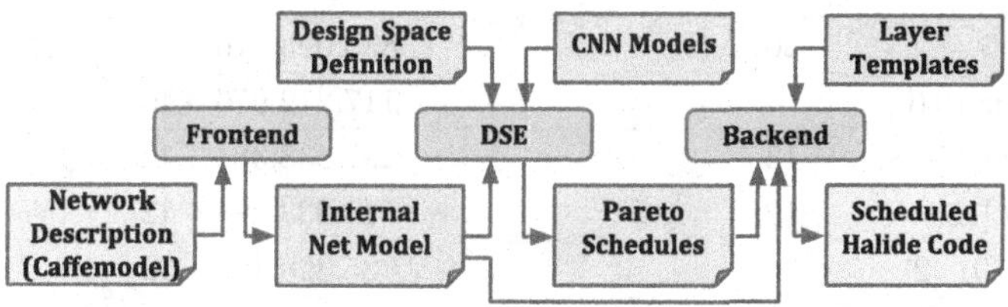

Fig. 5. Toolflow; from (caffe) network description to scheduled Halide implementation.

A frontend module translates a network specification into an internal representation. At the time of writing a frontend for caffe models [4] is implemented, which supports state-of-the-art networks. Next the DSE module reads the internal network representation, and searches the schedule space using the cost models presented Sect. 4. Due to the simplicity of the models an Intel i5-4460 can evaluate about 4×10^4 schedules per second, despite the tool being implemented in pure python. The design space per layer is checked using a complete brute force search to ensure the best point is found. Future work may include adding smarter search strategies, which could quickly eliminate whole parts of the design space if a target on-chip buffer size is specified.

After the DSE the designer is presented with a JSON file containing the discovered Pareto points. One or more points may be selected from this file for implementation by a backend. To facilitate the verification of the model presented in this work a template based Halide [12] backend is provided, which can emit regular and instrumented code. The instrumented code allows tracing of accesses to special buffers which emulate on-chip scratchpad memory.

Halide is particularly suited as a target language for this tool, as it explicitly splits specification of functionality and schedule. Functionality is specified once in a generic way without order. Scheduling of this functional part is done with dedicated statements that allow automatic loop tiling, reordering, and selection of store and compute levels. For portability of the code, Halide's `compile_to_c` feature can be used to convert the generated Halide code to C/C++ for platforms without native Halide support.

6 Validation and Evaluation

To validate the correctness of the model seven CNNs are selected: a network to enhance low resolution images (VDSR [5]), a network for speed sign detection [10] (Fig. 1), and five state-of-the-art networks trained for the ImageNet Large Visual Recognition Challenge [13]; VGG16/19 [15], ResNet101/152 [2], and MobileNetV2 [14]. More details are available in Table 1.

Table 1. Benchmark networks

Network name	Convolution layers (#)	Schedules (#)	Pareto points [8]
VDSR [5]	20	836.093.016	37
Speed sign [10]	4	117.212.976	49
VGG16 [15]	13	497.838.384	42
VGG19 [15]	16	613.833.264	42
ResNet101 [2]	104	2.835.398.124	62
ResNet152 [2]	155	4.252.104.864	62
MobileNetV2 [14]	54	1.377.686.448	22

The model is validated by performing a full design space search using the tool presented in Sect. 5, with the limitation that for tile sizes only powers of two are considered. This is not a limitation of the model, but rather a measure to keep the schedule space manageable. All Pareto optimal schedules discovered during the DSE are automatically implemented in Halide. The generated Halide code is instrumented using the tool such that external accesses are emulated and traceable. This is achieved by prefixing dummy layers in front of each convolution layer, which pass data onwards by a copy. Using Halide's built-in `trace_stores()` primitive on these dummy layers, traces are generated which represent external memory accesses. Furthermore Halide's profiling options report the dynamically allocated memory sizes per dummy layer, which reflects the used internal buffer space. A limitation of this method is that the output buffers Y can not be emulated accurately in Halide, as there is no concept in the language to transfer partial results to a different buffer, only to read them back later for completion. Therefore the contributions of the output buffers, both in size and accesses, have been disabled in the tool using a dedicated experimentation flag.

The modelled and measured external accesses and required internal buffer sizes for VGG19 are shown in Fig. 6. As the model is very accurate, the modelled and measured lines largely overlap in these images. There are some differences between the measurements and the estimations, as can be seen more clearly seen in the zoomed in section in Fig. 6b. These small deviations are caused by the ceiling operators in the model, used to give a conservative bound. When the tile size is not a multiple of the respective dimension, Halide will process the remainder in a compact manner, while the model accounts for a complete extra tile. That this conservative bound is maintained is verified in the experiments, as the modelled line always remains above the measured line in Fig. 6b.

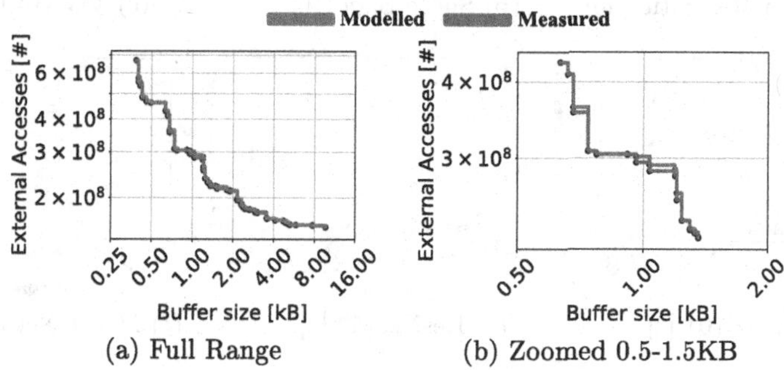

Fig. 6. Modelled and measured curves for VGG19 [15]

Similar model accuracies are observed for the other networks as shown in Fig. 7, verifying the correctness of the presented model which is the main goal of the instrumented experiments. Additionally, to obtain insight into the gains of being able to find the pareto schedules, the pareto curve of the other networks is compared to a baseline implementation. In the baseline, the loop order of the straightforward schedule of Code 1.1 is used for each layer. No tiling is applied, but the store level and compute level are varied per layer to find different trade-off points. The results demonstrate the Pareto schedules reduce the number of external accesses by 1–2 orders of magnitude for smaller buffer sizes compared to the baseline. Furthermore to capture all reuse the internal buffer size required is between 2–3 orders of magnitude smaller. This clearly indicates the need for smart scheduling of CNNs, and how high the penalty might be when a straightforward schedule is used.

Note that the modelled *number* of accesses is independent of the hardware. Platform parameters such as the memory bus width and spatial locality of the accesses may however affect the achieved performance. When targeting a hardware platform, schedules with properties that do not suit the available hardware are to be excluded from the DSE. The tiling dimensions, e.g., can be restricted to an integer multiple of the bus width to allow accesses to occupy the complete bus. Spatial locality can also be considered, in case of a row-major layout of FM data for example loop x can be selected as the SL to ensure accesses are to sequential addresses. The presented models are generic, in the sense that the predicted number of elements that needs to be loaded is accurate for any schedule. When targeting a specific platform it is up to the designer to exclude schedules with bad characteristics from the overall design space.

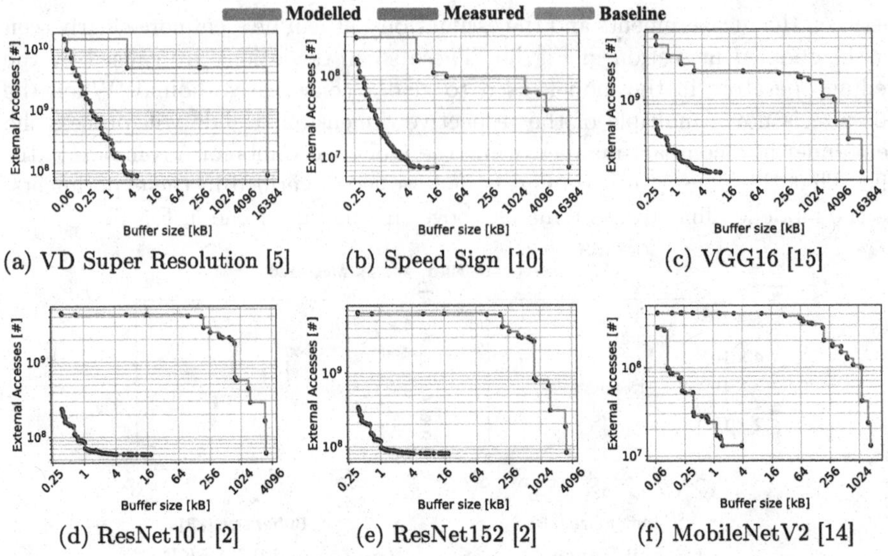

(a) VD Super Resolution [5] (b) Speed Sign [10] (c) VGG16 [15]

(d) ResNet101 [2] (e) ResNet152 [2] (f) MobileNetV2 [14]

Fig. 7. Modelled, measured, and baseline curves for various networks

7 Related Work

With the popularity of CNNs, a lot of effort has been put into the coding of these networks. Traditional frameworks, e.g. caffe [4] and pytorch [9], transform the convolution operation into matrix multiplication (GEMM), which duplicates data and therefore increases data complexity. Although this enables the use of optimized GEMM libraries, our model constructs schedules for pure convolutions which inherently require fewer external memory accesses making it much more suited for the embedded domain.

Low et al. show that for linear algebra programs analytical modelling can be used to automatically optimize code for different platforms [6]. Furthermore Pradelle et al. obtain performance on par with hand-optimized code by using the polyhedral model to select code transformations for neural networks specifically [11]. Much in line with these works our model can be used to select code transformations for CNNs. In contrast the focus of our work is not on throughput, but rather on reducing data movement which is more important for energy efficiency as accesses off-chip memory is about 200× more expensive than computation [3,12].

The work of M. Peemen also explores tiling for CNNs with a focus on data movement [10], but does not define a generic model hindering automatic application to arbitrary schedules. Similarly Sze et al. [16] classify different scheduling options for CNNs, but lack formalization and abstraction. Another work focused on FPGA acceleration by Motamedi et al. [7] suffers the same. In their search for good schedules for FPGA implementation, scheduling options are discarded early on, and only tiling in the i and z dimension is considered.

Yang et al. also use the expressive power of Halide to model the design space of schedules for their CNNs accelerator [20]. In particular the compute level, tiling and reordering are considered. Inclusion of the store level, enabling buffer folding, is missing however. Analogous to the framework presented in this work a model is used to quickly evaluate the design space. No details about this model are available in the paper, prohibiting detailed comparison. It is stated however that the access model *is a function of the loop orders, tiled loop sizes, and loop unroll factors* [20], suggesting the store and compute levels are not taken into account in this model in contrast to our work.

To the best of our knowledge the presented work is the first to introduce both store and compute levels as part of the schedule, facilitating the introduction of a generalized formal model that does not require any manual interaction and can be applied to any schedule with arbitrary tiling and loop order, enabling a true fully automated design space exploration.

8 Conclusions and Future Work

In this work a generic mathematical model is presented which can be used to quickly, i.e. $\sim 4 \times 10^4$ schedules per second on an i5-4460, and accurately estimate external memory accesses and required internal buffer space for CNNs. A tool is released which leverages this model, and features automated code generation [17]. Experimental results verify the correctness of the model, and show moreover that compared to a straightforward schedule external accesses are reduced by 1–2 orders of magnitude, while all reuse can be captured with 2–3 orders of magnitude smaller on-chip memory. To enhance reproducibility of this work, not only the constructed CNN tool is released, but also a repository with the experimental setup is made publicly available [18].

Future work includes accounting for spatial locality and vectorization, which shrinks the design space. This is expected to increase the data movement in favour of higher parallelism and thus performance. Furthermore loop fusion and recomputation in CNNs will be investigated to further reduce the external accesses, and provide a larger trade-off space. Finally research is ongoing into a backend to automatically generate CNN accelerators for FPGA and ASIC.

Acknowledgements. This work is supported by NWO project CPS-P3 (12695).

References

1. Goodfellow, I., Bengio, Y., Courville, A.: Deep Learning. MIT Press, Cambridge (2016). http://www.deeplearningbook.org
2. He, K., Zhang, X., Ren, S., Sun, J.: Deep residual learning for image recognition. CoRR abs/1512.03385 (2015)
3. Horowitz, M.: Computing's energy problem (and what we can do about it). In: 2014 IEEE International Solid-State Circuits Conference Digest of Technical Papers (ISSCC), pp. 10–14, February 2014

4. Jia, Y., et al.: Caffe: convolutional architecture for fast feature embedding. arXiv preprint arXiv:1408.5093 (2014)
5. Kim, J., Lee, J.K., Lee, K.M.: Accurate image super-resolution using very deep convolutional networks. In: The IEEE Conference on Computer Vision and Pattern Recognition (CVPR Oral), June 2016
6. Low, T.M., Igual, F.D., Smith, T.M., Quintana-Orti, E.S.: Analytical modeling is enough for high-performance BLIS. ACM Trans. Math. Softw. **43**(2), 12:1–12:18 (2016)
7. Motamedi, M., Gysel, P., Ghiasi, S.: Placid: a platform for FPGA-based accelerator creation for DCNNs. ACM Trans. Multimedia Comput. Commun. Appl. **13**(4), 62:1–62:21 (2017)
8. Pareto, V.: Manual of Political Economy. Scholars Book Shelf, Cranbury (1971). https://books.google.nl/books?id=qAC8AAAAIAAJ
9. Paszke, A., et al.: Automatic differentiation in pytorch (2017)
10. Peemen, M.: Improving the efficiency of deep convolutional networks. Eindhoven University of Technology (2017). https://pure.tue.nl/ws/portalfiles/portal/77700147/20171012_Peemen.pdf
11. Pradelle, B., Meister, B., Baskaran, M., Springer, J., Lethin, R.: Polyhedral optimization of tensorflow computation graphs. In: 6th Workshop on Extreme-Scale Programming Tools (ESPT, Associated with SC 2017) (2017)
12. Ragan-Kelley, J.: Decoupling algorithms from the organization of computation for high performance image processing. Ph.D. thesis, Massachusetts Institute of Technology, Cambridge, MA, June 2014. http://groups.csail.mit.edu/commit/papers/2014/jrkthesis.pdf
13. Russakovsky, O., et al.: ImageNet large scale visual recognition challenge. Int. J. Comput. Vis. (IJCV) **115**(3), 211–252 (2015)
14. Sandler, M., Howard, A.G., Zhu, M., Zhmoginov, A., Chen, L.: Inverted residuals and linear bottlenecks: mobile networks for classification, detection and segmentation. CoRR (2018)
15. Simonyan, K., Zisserman, A.: Very deep convolutional networks for large-scale image recognition. CoRR abs/1409.1556 (2014)
16. Sze, V., Chen, Y., Yang, T., Emer, J.S.: Efficient processing of deep neural networks: a tutorial and survey. Proc. IEEE **105**(12), 2295–2329 (2017)
17. Waeijen, L.: https://github.com/lwaeijen/cnn-demo
18. Waeijen, L.: https://github.com/lwaeijen/cnn-mapping-tool
19. Wolf, M.E., Lam, M.S.: A loop transformation theory and an algorithm to maximize parallelism. IEEE Trans. Parallel Distrib. Syst. **2**, 452–471 (1991)
20. Yang, X., et al.: DNN dataflow choice is overrated. CoRR abs/1809.04070 (2018). http://arxiv.org/abs/1809.04070

Special Session: European Projects

Low Precision Processing for High Order Stencil Computations

Gagandeep Singh[1,2(✉)], Dionysios Diamantopoulos[2(✉)], Sander Stuijk[1], Christoph Hagleitner[2], and Henk Corporaal[1]

[1] Eindhoven University of Technology, Eindhoven, Netherlands
{g.singh,s.stuijk,h.corporaal}@tue.nl
[2] IBM Research-Zurich, Rüschlikon, Switzerland
{sin,did,hle}@zurich.ibm.com

Abstract. Modern scientific workloads have demonstrated the inefficiency of using high precision formats. Moving to a lower bit format or even to a different number system can provide tremendous gains in terms of performance and energy efficiency. In this article, we explore the applicability of different number formats and exhaustively search for the appropriate bit width for 3D complex stencil kernels, which are one of the most widely used scientific kernels. Further, we demonstrate the achievable performance of these kernels on state-of-the-art hardware that includes CPU and FPGA, which is the only hardware supporting arbitrary fixed-point precision. Thus, this work fills the gap between current hardware capabilities and future systems for stencil-based scientific applications.

1 Introduction

Stencils are essential for numerical simulations of finite difference methods (FDM) and are applied in iterative solvers of linear equation systems. Stencils are used in a wide range of applications [6], including computational fluid dynamics, image processing, atmospheric modelling, etc. A stencil operation [10] defines a computation pattern where elements in a multidimensional grid are updated using contributions from a subset of its neighbors based on a fixed pattern.

Stencil computations perform on data structures that are generally much larger than the capacity of the available system cache [4]. Besides, the amount of data reuse within a sweep is limited to the number of points in a stencil. Due to the cache unfriendly, complex data access patterns and low operational intensity [20], stencil compute kernels do not perform very well on traditional CPU or even GPU systems.

High-performance implementations of stencils on modern processors operate using the single precision or the double precision floating-point data type, which are the most widely supported datatypes by our current hardware devices. Using these datatypes in the context of real-world applications that make use of large grid sizes, puts huge stress on the memory subsystem. Therefore, storing the data

D. N. Pnevmatikatos et al. (Eds.): SAMOS 2019, LNCS 11733, pp. 403–415, 2019.
https://doi.org/10.1007/978-3-030-27562-4_29

in memory using a smaller number of bits reduces the pressure on the memory when retrieving the requested data. Where possible [8], industry trends show a clear shift away from using floating-point datatypes, e.g., applications like neural network workloads are using 8 bits fixed-point format or lower precisions [11]. Hence, in this paper, we look into the precision tolerance of 3D stencil kernels, which are one of the most widely used kernels in real-world applications.

To summarize, the major contributions of this paper are:

- We perform a systematic precision exploration of 3D stencil kernels for future mixed-precision systems using a wide range of number systems including fixed-point, floating-point, and posit.
- Based on an exhaustive exploration of a broad range of number systems – fixed-point, floating-point, and posit, we provide optimum precision and the corresponding accuracy deviation.
- We tune these kernels on current state-of-the-art IBM® POWER9[1] CPU and further evaluate them on an FPGA supporting arbitrary precision, which is coherently attached to the host memory. Thus, this work fills the gap between the current hardware capabilities and future hardware design.

The remainder of this article is structured as follows. Section 2 provides details on the various 3D stencil kernels and the benefits of lower precision. In Sect. 3 we describe the methodology and different number systems explored. Section 4 mentions the system setup and provides the results of our experiments, including a case study of implementing and optimizing these kernels on current state-of-the-art hardware devices. We list the related work in Sect. 5 and Sect. 6 concludes our paper with future directions.

2 Background

In this section, we provide details on the 3D stencil kernels used and discuss the relevance of the precision analysis.

2.1 Stencil Benchmark

A stencil computation has several different patterns across various applications. Performance of a stencil kernel on the current multicore system depends heavily on the neighborhood elements of the grid. For instance, suppose a 3D grid in (*row*, *column*, *depth*). When the grid is stored by *row*, reading elements in the other dimensions typically results in cache eviction because for real-world applications the problem size is too large to fit in the processor cache. In this paper, we focus on both a 7-point and 25-point 3D elementary stencil, and a compound horizontal diffusion stencil, shown in Fig. 1. The 3D 7-point and 25-point (ref.

[1] IBM and POWER9 are registered trademarks or common law marks of International Business Machines Corp., registered in many jurisdictions world-wide. Other product and service names might be trademarks of IBM or other companies.

Fig. 1a) stencils commonly arise from the finite difference method for solving PDEs [20]. The 7-point stencil performs eight FLOPS per grid point, while the 25-point stencil performs twenty-seven FLOPS per point (without any common subexpression elimination). Thus, the arithmetic intensity, the ratio of FLOPS performed for each byte of memory traffic, is much higher for the 25-point stencil than the 7-point stencil.

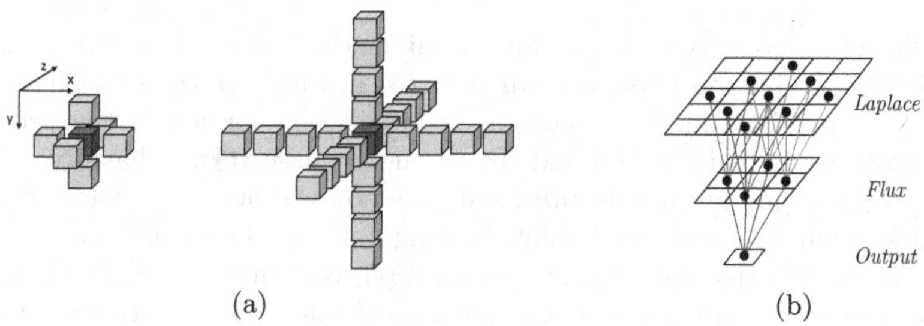

Fig. 1. (a) 7-point stencil and 25-point elementary stencil (b) Compound horizontal diffusion stencil that is used in weather forecasting

Unlike stencils found in the literature [3,7,16,19], real-world atmospheric stencils consist of a collection of stencils that performs a sequence of element-wise computations. Horizontal diffusion (hdiff) kernel is an example of one such kernel that executes each stencil using a separate loop nest. It iterates over a 3D grid that performs *laplacian* and *flux*, as depicted in Fig. 1b, as well as calculations for different grid points. Such compound kernels have complex memory access patterns because they apply a series of elementary stencil operations. Although such implementations may be straightforward to write, they are not efficient in terms of data locality, memory usage, or parallelism.

2.2 Precision

IEEE-754 floating point representation has become the universal standard in modern computing systems. Floating-point numbers have a mantissa and exponent with an additional bit to represent the sign of a number. This floating-point arithmetic, in terms of computing resources, requires complex circuitry leading to high latency and power consumption.

The use of low-precision arithmetic with a minimal loss in accuracy, has been proposed as a promising alternative to the commonly used floating point arithmetic. This is valid for emerging workloads, e.g., machine learning workloads, in terms of performance and energy efficiency. From the system perspective, there are two main benefits of moving to a lower precision. Firstly, the hardware resources for a given silicon area may enable higher operations per second (OPS) at lower precision as these operations require less space and power. Note, this also necessitates efficient memory traffic management. Secondly, many operations are memory bandwidth bound [17,18] and reducing precision would allow for better usage of cache and reduction of bandwidth bottlenecks. Thus, data can be moved faster through the memory hierarchy to maximize compute resource utilization.

3 Methodology

The following section provides detail on our methodology to explore precision for different number systems, which is depicted in Fig. 2. In the first phase (❶), we analyze and instrument a part of an application for which the precision exploration needs to be performed. In the next phase (❷), exhaustive search is done to find the appropriate precision based on the number system used. In this work, we make use of fixed-point, floating-point, and posit number systems. During the exhaustive design space exploration, continuous error tracking (❸) is performed to measure the extent of accuracy deviation compared to the IEEE floating-point arithmetic format.

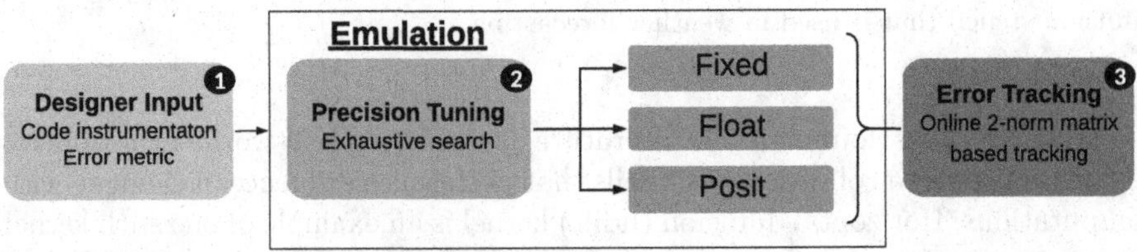

Fig. 2. Overview of application precision exploration. The designer inputs the code with an appropriate precision template. Exhaustive precision exploration is performed for different number systems that include fixed-point arithmetic, floating-point arithmetic, and posit arithmetic. While exploring, error tracking is performed using the 2-norm matrix approach.

Accuracy: In our experiments, for precision tuning we have considered the induced 2-norm of a matrix [1] as our measure of the accuracy. The induced 2-norm of an $m \times n$ matrix A is the supermum of the ratio between the 2-norm of a vector Ax and the 2-norm of x, where x is an n-dimensional vector. We calculate the relative norm or mean relative error (MRE) ϵ_i to indicate how close the predicted value A_i' is to the actual value A_i. MRE provides an unbiased estimate of the error variance between two matrices.

$$\epsilon_i = \frac{||A_i' - A_i||_2}{||A_i||_2} \tag{1}$$

3.1 Evaluated Arbitrary Precision

As an alternative to the currently used IEEE single and double precision floating point number, we explore the precision of 3D stencil kernels using the following arbitrary number formats that are also shown in Fig. 3:

(1) Fixed-Point Arithmetic: A fixed-point consists of an integer and a fraction part where total width could be any multiple of 2, which is based on the bit width of the data path. Compared to the floating-point format, fixed-point numbers simplify the logic by fixing the radix point.

In an FPGA, the fixed-point format offers a more resource efficient alternative to the floating-point implementation. This efficiency is because floating-point support often uses more than 100× as many gates compared to fixed-point support.

(2) Floating-Point Arithmetic: By lowering the precision of a floating-point format, we could retain the advantages of floating point arithmetic (e.g., higher dynamic range) with a lower bit-width. Dynamic floating-point arithmetic uses an arbitrary number of bits for the exponent and significand (or mantissa) parts of a floating-point number. We determine the precision bit-width through bit accurate simulations for different bit-width configurations. While changing mantissa and exponent bits, we analyze the trend of the relative error.

(3) Posit Arithmetic: Posit [9] borrows most of the components from the IEEE 754 floating-point scheme, such as the exponent and fraction (or mantissa) fields. However, posit has an additional *regime* bit that is introduced to create a tapered accuracy, which lets small exponents have more accuracy. One could choose to either represent a large number by assigning more bits to the exponent field or opt for more decimal precision by having more fraction bits.

Figure 3 shows the different datatypes explored in this paper. While analyzing these types, there are several things to take into account. Firstly, compared to the other number systems, posit can provide the highest dynamic range, and fixed-point offers the lowest [2]. Additionally, floating-point numbers are susceptible to round errors and could lead to an overflow or underflow [9].

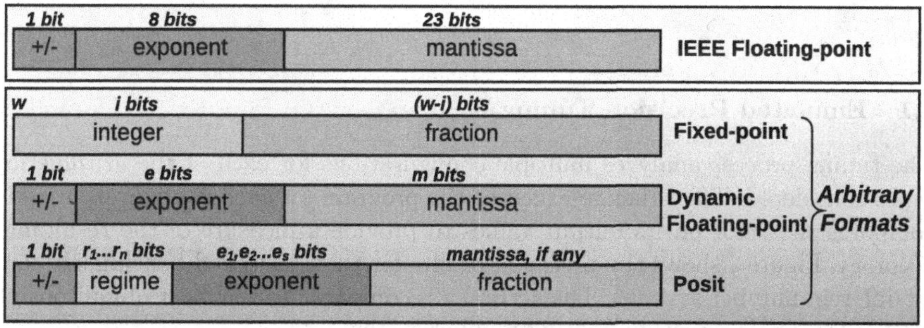

Fig. 3. Arithmetic types used with field widths indicated above each field. IEEE single precision floating-point number is 32 bits where a positive sign bit is represented by a 0 and a negative by 1. Fixed-point has fixed integer and fraction bits where w (total bits) could be any multiple of 2, based on the bit-width of the data path. Dynamic floating-point arithmetic uses arbitrary exponent and mantissa bits. A posit number [9] is similar to floating-point with additional bits for the regime part. It has e_s exponent bits, but depending upon the data this could be omitted (same is valid for mantissa bits).

4 Evaluation

We used IBM® POWER9 as the host system comprising of 16 cores, each of which supports four-thread simultaneous multi-threading. Table 1 provides complete details of our system parameters. To provide a full-scale analysis of stencil optimization techniques, we set the grid size of all stencil kernels as $1280 \times 1080 \times 960$, which is much larger than the on-chip cache capacity of POWER9, with input data distribution as a Gaussian function. The problem size dictates which input dataset would reside in the cache, hence is an important parameter while measuring the system performance.

For precision tuning of the fixed-point number system, we made use of Xilinx fixed-point library from the Vivado 2018.2 tool. We used the C++ template based floatx library[2] to explore arbitrary precision for floating-point arithmetic. Software-based posit implementation is available as part of the ongoing efforts to emulate the universal number system[3]. All three libraries are provided in C++ header format, which allows us to replace the datatypes in the source code of the application and study the effect of low precision using the same software toolchain as that of the application itself. To make a performance comparison between floating-point and fixed-point number systems, we developed a highly optimized FPGA accelerator for all the kernels. The accelerator was implemented on an Alpha-Data ADM-PCIE-9V3 card featuring the Xilinx Virtex Ultrascale+ XCVU3P-FFVC1517-2-i device.

Table 1. System configuration for IBM POWER9

Architecture	Physical Cores	Frequency	On-chip Memory (Per Core)	Off-chip Memory
IBM Power 9 (ppc64le)	16-cores/socket; (SMT4)	Min: 2.3GHz Max: 3.8GHz	L1-cache: 32KiB L2-cache: 256KiB L3-cache: 10MiB	DDR4: 32GiB RDIMM 2666MHz

4.1 Emulated Precision Tuning

The tuning process analyzes multiple configurations for each of the arithmetic types considered. The tuner re-executes the program for each configuration and computes the error on its output values to provide a measure of the resultant accuracy. Figure 4 shows the precision results for the considered benchmarks for all different number systems. The accuracy is compared to the most ubiquitously used IEEE single precision floating number system.

For all the kernels we were able to achieve full accuracy with much lower bits. Moreover, as the error tolerance increases, we could make use of a lower number of total bits. Based on this, we made several observations. First, in the

[2] https://github.com/oprecomp/FloatX.
[3] https://github.com/stillwater-sc/universal.

case of a 7 and 25-point stencil, we could reduce bits by more than 50% for all the datatypes, with a precision loss of 1%. Second, elementary 3D stencil kernels (7 and 25-points) were not able to exploit the high dynamic range offered by posit, and thus with lower bit width floating-point arithmetic, we could achieve better results. Third, the atmospheric compound kernel comparatively needs a higher dynamic range; therefore with 0.1% tolerance in the accuracy we could cut the number of bits to half compared to the IEEE floating point and move to a posit of (16,2).

4.2 Case Study for Current Multi-core Systems and Arbitrary Precision Supported Hardware

We performed a case study for the 3D stencil kernels to measure the capabilities of current hardware systems. We tuned these kernels for POWER9 CPU and further evaluated these benchmarks on FPGA supporting arbitrary precisions, which is coherently attached to our host CPU. For the FPGA and the POWER9 node, we used the AMESTER[4] tool to measure the active power.[5]

Current FPGA systems only support floating-point and arbitrary fixed-point arithmetic. Therefore, we compared hardware implementations across the stencil benchmarks for floating-point single and half precision with fixed-point datatype for the bit width that gave similar accuracy to the floating-point. Note, as current state-of-the-art hardware devices do not support posit datatype, we did not include it in our hardware comparison because the emulation of posit datatype

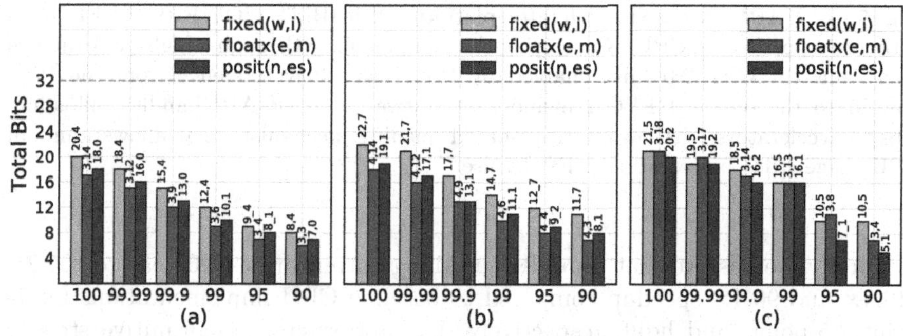

Fig. 4. Totals bits vs accuracy (percentage) for (a) 7-point, (b) 25-point, and (c) horizontal diffusion compared to single precision IEEE floating-point. Notation fixed (w,i) defines a fixed number with total w bits including i integer bits. With floatx, e refers to the exponent bits and m defines the mantissa. In the case of the posit number system, n is the total number of bits with es bits for the exponent part.

[4] https://github.com/open-power/amester.

[5] Active power denotes the difference between the total power of a complete node (including CPU, memory, fans, I/O, etc.) when an application is running compared to when it is idle.

would be expensive in FPGA and thus would lead to unfair comparisons with other datatypes.

Figure 5a shows a high-level overview of our integrated system. The FPGA is connected to a server system, based on the IBM® POWER9 processor, using IBM® coherent accelerator processor interface 2.0 (CAPI 2.0). The FPGA implementation consists of accelerator function units (AFU) that interact with the power service layer (PSL), which is the CAPI endpoint on the FPGA. The co-designed execution flow is shown in Fig. 5b. We provide the experimental results of tuning stencil kernels for current CPU and FPGA based systems. Figure 6 shows the roofline of all the kernels used in this study. By mapping both, arithmetic intensity of all examined stencils (7-point, 25-point and hdiff) and peak attainable GFLOPs/sec (GOP/sec for fixed-point), on the roofline of our heterogeneous system (CPU + CAPI based FPGA), we can come to several conclusions.

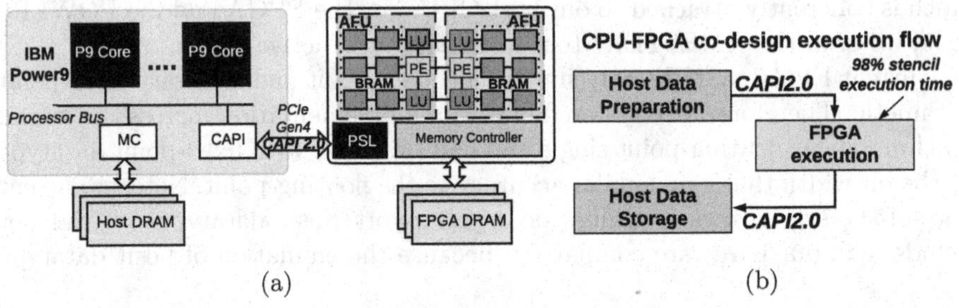

Fig. 5. (a) CAPI 2.0 based accelerator platform with IBM® POWER9 (b) FPGA is acting as a peer to the CPU by accessing the main memory through a high-performance cache-coherent CAPI2.0 link, enabled by PSL. Data flow sequence from the Host DRAM to the onboard FPGA memory. A software-defined API handles offloading jobs to accelerators with an interrupt-based queuing mechanism that allows minimal CPU usage (thus power) during FPGA use.

Firstly, we observe that compiler and tiling optimizations [20] lead to 125.2× 119.4× and 90.4× speedup compared to baseline CPU implementations for 7-point, 25-point, and hdiff, respectively. The performance of primitive stencils (7-point, 25-point) is constrained by the memory bandwidth, since the stencil points can be located far away in the memory, leading to limited cache locality. We note that although hdiff has higher arithmetic intensity, its access patterns are more complex because it applies a series of elementary stencil operations. Secondly, we observe that the floating-point FPGA implementations increase the additional speedup to 2.5×, 3.3× and 4.1× compared to the CPU-optimized implementation, for 7-point, 25-point and hdiff, respectively. By allowing the accelerators to use the FPGA on-chip memory, the implementations are not constrained by the DRAM memory bandwidth. However, the CAPI2/PCIe4 link is offering an order of magnitude less bandwidth to that of DRAM. Since our

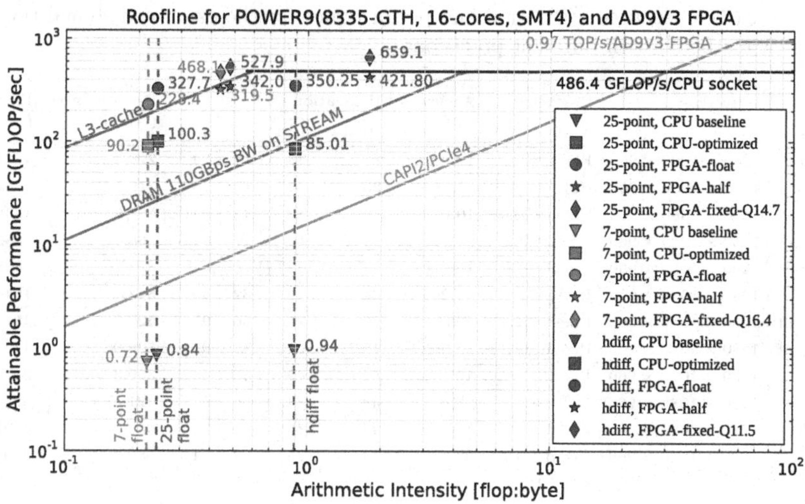

Fig. 6. Attainable performance for the examined stencils, in CPU and FPGA testbeds, with different precision.

platform offers memory-coherent access of FPGA to the system memory, we build a pipelined execution, where communication time for transferring data from host to FPGA memory is masked with the actual FPGA processing [5]. This technique allows us to exploit FPGA processing capabilities completely.

Thirdly, by replacing floating-point data-types with lower precision data-types, we have measured additional gains. Specifically, in the roofline of Fig. 6, we plot the performance of three stencils using half and fixed-point data-types. The specific bit-width for the integer and fractional part of the fixed point was selected at 99% of accuracy, i.e., Q14.7 for 25-point, Q16.4 for 7-point and Q11.5 for hdiff. Arithmetic intensity is improved for both half and fixed data-types since the bytes fetched from memory are half that of the single precision floating point (i.e., 2B instead of 4B). Since fixed-point implementations use fewer resources on the FPGA, compared to float and half, we were able to add more accelerators on the same FPGA device, allowing us to measure 468.1, 527.9 and 659.1 GOPs/sec for 7-point, 25-point, and hdiff, respectively. These numbers are very close to the theoretical peak performance of the FPGA device of 0.97 TOPs/s, when the device is configured with the stencil micro-architecture of 7-point, 25-point and hdiff[6].

Table 2 shows the resource utilization for our examined stencil kernels on FPGA using different precisions. In all the scenarios, going from single to half

[6] While the three stencils comprise different access patterns and acceleration kernels, the primary operations, i.e., vectorized multiply-accumulate products, which define the FPGA micro-architecture, remains the same. Using this approach and [15], we have calculated 0.97 TOPs/s theoretical top performance for stencils, for our AD9V3 FPGA.

Table 2. FPGA resource utilization and performance for the examined stencil kernels on FPGA testbeds, with different precisions

Kernel	Data size	Precision	Accuracy (%)	Utilization (%)				Performance (GLOP/s)	Energy (mJ)
				BRAM	DSP	FF	LUT		
7-point	1280 × 1080 × 960	Float	100	38	35	18	29	228.4	4617.2
7-point	1280 × 1080 × 960	Half	99.95	25	24	15	28	319.5	2887.6
7-point	1280 × 1080 × 960	Fixed (20,4)	100	16	12	49	95	467.6	1832.3
7-point	1280 × 1080 × 960	Fixed (16,4)	99.96	12	12	47	92.5	468.1	1689.4
25-point	1280 × 1080 × 960	Float	100	42	62	36	44	327.7	1608.7
25-point	1280 × 1080 × 960	Half	99.06	32	43	32	43	342.1	1541.5
25-point	1280 × 1080 × 960	Fixed (22,7)	100	29	21	56	95	527.9	1510.3
25-point	1280 × 1080 × 960	Fixed (14,7)	99.05	19	21	55	91	528.9	1497.9
Hdiff	1280 × 1080 × 960	Float	100	52	89	65	61	350.3	3010.5
Hdiff	1280 × 1080 × 960	Half	98.02	44	84	35	57	421.8	2031.1
Hdiff	1280 × 1080 × 960	Fixed (21,5)	100	24	45	77	76	653.9	1007.9
Hdiff	1280 × 1080 × 960	Fixed (11,5)	97.92	14	35	69	71	659.1	997.9

precision increases the performance with a corresponding reduction in the number of resources. Further, moving to fixed-point arithmetic increases the performance due to a decrease in the number of bytes loaded, at the cost of LUT utilization. However, the utilization of other FPGA resources is reduced. Figure 7 shows the achieved energy efficiency with different precisions. For all considered kernels, as the number of bits reduces, we see an increase in energy efficiency. Designs implemented in fixed-point will always be more efficient than their equivalent in floating-point because fixed-point implementations consume fewer resources and less power (ref Table 2). As our stencil kernels do not require the high dynamic range achievable with floating-point, moving to fixed-point implementations could provide better energy efficiency. In the case of hdiff, on moving to a lower precision, we see a huge increase in energy efficiency. This increase is because hdiff is a compound kernel; therefore, each elementary stencil's energy improvement with lower precision leads to much higher cumulative gains.

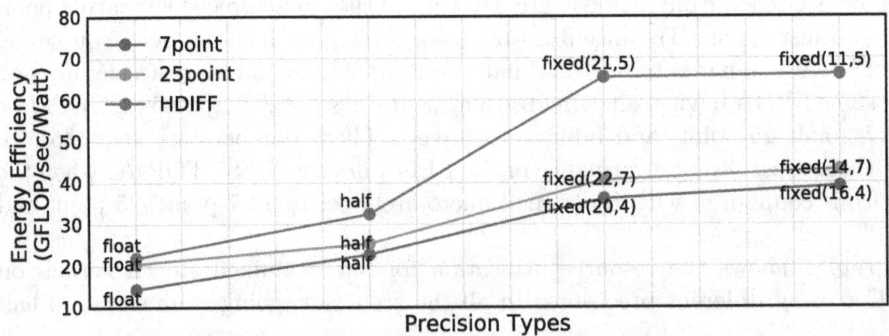

Fig. 7. Evaluated design points for different stencil kernels. The plot shows energy efficiency (GFLOPS/Watt) with varying types of precision implemented on an Alpha-Data ADM-PCIE-9V3 card featuring the Xilinx Virtex Ultrascale+ XCVU3P-FFVC1517

5 Related Work

Recently, in various domains, there has been a significant amount of research to explore error resilience across the complete stack of computer architecture from application to device physics. At the application level, research on lower-precision using fixed-point and floating-point has been widely studied [11]. With the emergence of the posit [9] number system, research into lower precision with these alternate number systems is regaining attention. In the field of neural-networks, Langroudi *et al.* [13] showed minimum accuracy degradation by using 7-bit posits. In another study, Klöwer *et al.* [12] studied the applicability of posit in weather modelling.

High-performance implementations of stencils on modern processors usually make use of the IEEE single precision or double precision floating-point data types, which are the most widely supported datatypes by current hardware devices. There have been various efforts to improve these kernels for various architectures using different techniques. Datta *et al.* [4] optimized the 2D and 3D stencil for multicore architectures using several hardware adherent optimizations. Similarly, Nguyen *et al.* [14] worked on algorithm optimization for CPU and GPU based systems. Gysi *et al.* [10] provided guidelines for optimizing complex kernels for CPU–GPU systems using analytic models. However, to the best of our knowledge, this work is the first to study the precision tolerance for scientific 3D stencil kernels for a wide range of number systems which includes fixed-point arithmetic, floating-point arithmetic, and the most recently developed posit arithmetic.

6 Conclusion

Stencils are one of the most widely used kernel types in various real-world applications. In this work, we analysed the precision tolerance for different 3D stencil kernels using fixed-point, floating-point, and posit number system. We demonstrated by exhaustive precision exploration that these kernels have a margin to move to a lower bit width with minimal loss of accuracy.

Further, in a case study, we measured the performance of these kernels on a state-of-the-art multi-core platform and designed lower bit-width based accelerators for all considered 3D stencil kernels on an FPGA device. FPGA is the only device which gives us the capability to implement arbitrary fixed-point precision datatype. Hence, we leveraged this capability to show the advantages of accelerating these kernels with lower precision compared to the ubiquitous IEEE floating-point format. In future, we will use this analysis technique in an integrated design-flow to build efficient systems for stencil-based applications. In addition, we aim to study the effects of low precision processing not only for streaming applications, e.g. stencil and convolution, where computation is done locally, but also for iterative applications where errors accumulate.

Acknowledgement. This work was performed in the framework of the Horizon 2020 program for the project "Near-Memory Computing (NeMeCo)". It is funded by the

European Commission under Marie Sklodowska-Curie Innovative Training Networks European Industrial Doctorate (Project ID: 676240). We would also like to thank Martino Dazzi for his valuable remarks. This work was partially supported by the H2020 research and innovation programme under grant agreement No 732631, project OPRECOMP.

References

1. Anderson, E., et al.: LAPACK Users' guide, vol. 9. Siam (1999)
2. Carmichael, Z., et al.: Deep positron: a deep neural network using the posit number system. arXiv preprint arXiv:1812.01762 (2018)
3. Chi, Y., Cong, J., Wei, P., Zhou, P.: SODA: stencil with optimized dataflow architecture. In: 2018 IEEE/ACM International Conference on Computer-Aided Design (ICCAD), pp. 1–8. IEEE (2018)
4. Datta, K., et al.: Stencil computation optimization and auto-tuning on state-of-the-art multicore architectures. In: Proceedings of the 2008 ACM/IEEE Conference on Supercomputing, p. 4. IEEE Press (2008)
5. Diamantopoulos, D., Giefers, H., Hagleitner, C.: ecTALK: energy efficient coherent transprecision accelerators–the bidirectional long short-term memory neural network case. In: 2018 IEEE Symposium in Low-Power and High-Speed Chips (COOL CHIPS), pp. 1–3. IEEE (2018)
6. Doms, G., Schättler, U.: The nonhydrostatic limited-area model LM (lokal-model) of the DWD. Part I. Scientific documentation. DWD, GB Forschung und Entwicklung (1999)
7. de Fine Licht, J., Blott, M., Hoefler, T.: Designing scalable FPGA architectures using high-level synthesis. ACM SIGPLAN Not. **53**(1), 403–404 (2018)
8. Finnerty, A., Ratigner, H.: Reduce power and cost by converting from floating point to fixed point. In: WP491 (v1. 0) (2017)
9. Gustafson, J.L., Yonemoto, I.T.: Beating floating point at its own game: posit arithmetic. Supercomput. Front. Innovations **4**(2), 71–86 (2017)
10. Gysi, T., Grosser, T., Hoefler, T.: Modesto: data-centric analytic optimization of complex stencil programs on heterogeneous architectures. In: Proceedings of the 29th ACM on International Conference on Supercomputing, pp. 177–186. ACM (2015)
11. Iwata, A., et al.: An artificial neural network accelerator using general purpose 24 bits floating point digital signal processors. In: IJCNN-89, vol. 2, pp. 171–175 (1989)
12. Klöwer, M., Düben, P.D., Palmer, T.N.: Posits as an alternative to floats for weather and climate models (2019)
13. Langroudi, S.H.F., Pandit, T., Kudithipudi, D.: Deep learning inference on embedded devices: fixed-point vs posit. In: 2018 1st Workshop on Energy Efficient Machine Learning and Cognitive Computing for Embedded Applications (EMC2), pp. 19–23. IEEE (2018)
14. Nguyen, A., et al.: 3.5-D blocking optimization for stencil computations on modern CPUs and GPUs. In: Proceedings of the 2010 ACM/IEEE International Conference for High Performance Computing, Networking, Storage and Analysis, pp. 1–13. IEEE Computer Society (2010)
15. Parker, M.: Understanding peak floating-point performance claims. Technical White Paper WP-012220-1.0 (2014)

16. Sano, K., Hatsuda, Y., Yamamoto, S.: Multi-FPGA accelerator for scalable stencil computation with constant memory bandwidth. IEEE Trans. Parallel Distrib. Syst. **25**(3), 695–705 (2014)
17. Singh, G., et al.: A review of near-memory computing architectures: opportunities and challenges. In: 2018 21st Euromicro Conference on Digital System Design (DSD), pp. 608–617. IEEE (2018)
18. Singh, G., et al.: NAPEL: near-memory computing application performance prediction via ensemble learning. In: Proceedings of the 56th Annual Design Automation Conference 2019, DAC 2019, pp. 27:1–27:6. ACM, New York (2019)
19. Waidyasooriya, H.M., et al.: OpenCL-based FPGA-platform for stencil computation and its optimization methodology. IEEE Trans. Parallel Distrib. Syst. **28**(5), 1390–1402 (2017)
20. Xu, J., et al.: Performance tuning and analysis for stencil-based applications on POWER8 processor. ACM Trans. Archit. Code Optim. (TACO) **15**(4), 41 (2018)

Hardware/Software Self-adaptation in CPS: The CERBERO Project Approach

Francesca Palumbo[1], Tiziana Fanni[2(✉)], Carlo Sau[2], Alfonso Rodríguez[3], Daniel Madroñal[3], Karol Desnos[4], Antoine Morvan[4], Maxime Pelcat[4,5], Claudio Rubattu[1,4], Raquel Lazcano[3], Luigi Raffo[2], Eduardo de la Torre[3], Eduardo Juárez[3], César Sanz[3], and Pablo Sánchez de Rojas[6]

[1] Università degli Studi di Sassari, Sassari, Italy
fpalumbo@uniss.it
[2] Università degli Studi di Cagliari, Cagliari, Italy
tiziana.fanni@diee.unica.it
[3] Universidad Politécnica de Madrid, Madrid, Spain
[4] IETR, UMR CNRS 6164/INSA Rennes, Rennes, France
[5] Institut Pascal UMR CNRS 6602, Aubière, France
[6] Thales Alenia Space España, Madrid, Spain

Abstract. Cyber-Physical Systems (CPS) are interconnected devices, reactive and dynamic to sensed external and internal triggers. The H2020 CERBERO EU Project is developing a design environment composed by modelling, deployment and verification tools for adaptive CPS. This paper focuses on its efficient support for run-time self-adaptivity.

Keywords: Cyber-Physical Systems · Self-adaptivity · HW reconfiguration · HW monitoring · Run-time management

1 CERBERO Context and Challenges

Cyber-Physical Systems (CPS) operate in complex compute-intensive scenarios, which are usually characterized by a strong interaction with environment and users [10]. Often deployed in hard-to-reach environments, CPS are meant to be dynamic, providing efficient ways to adapt to mutable and evolvable requirements. The H2020 CERBERO[1] European Project [16,19] is developing a continuous design environment for CPS, relying on a set of tools developed by project partners, it combines modelling, deployment and verification tools, interconnected to provide complementary features. The efficient support for run-time adaptation presented in this paper is among the CERBERO outcomes.

CERBERO technological propositions are motivated by technical specifications from the project industrial partners. This paper puts the focus on the requirements and technological proposition of the *Planetary Exploration* (*PE*)

[1] *Cross-layer modEl-based fRamework for multi-oBjective dEsign of Reconfigurable systems in unceRtain hybRid envirOnments* - (http://www.cerbero-h2020.eu/).

D. N. Pnevmatikatos et al. (Eds.): SAMOS 2019, LNCS 11733, pp. 416–428, 2019.
https://doi.org/10.1007/978-3-030-27562-4_30

use-case of the CERBERO project [2]. The *PE* use-case aims at assessing a new technology for computing purposes in space applications, where robustness to faults has to be guaranteed. The final demonstrator is the controller of a robotic arm implemented over a Field Programmable Gate Array (FPGA) device, with advanced self-monitoring and self-adaptive processing capabilities to ruggedize the systems under stringent survival conditions (radiation and harsh environment) and meet the reliability constraints of a robotic exploration mission.

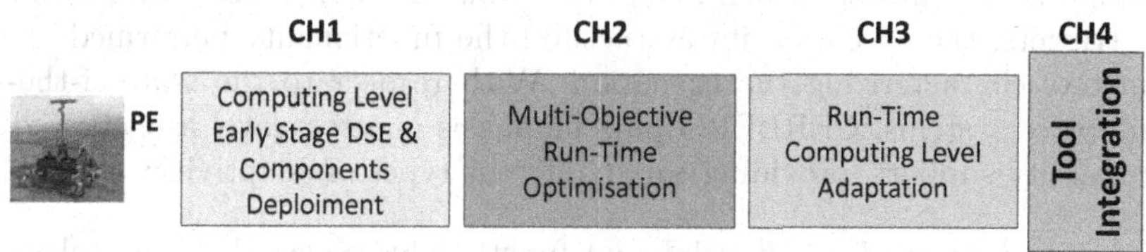

Fig. 1. CERBERO challenges for the *Planetary Exploration* use-case.

The goals, needs and targets of the *PE* use-case present different challenges in terms of analysis, optimization and management of the system. The challenges, summarized in Fig. 1, are described as follows:

- **CH1** - To provide developers with assistance and automation from design-time analysis to run-time optimization, in order to master the numerous trade-offs in building complex and heterogeneous computing platforms - e.g., optimal system payload characterization and hardware/software co-design.
- **CH2** - To define strategies for assessing the system status at run-time through efficient sensing and monitoring - e.g., faulty accelerators have to be detected to be either refreshed or excluded from computation.
- **CH3** - To ensure that the system is always as close as possible to the requirements and/or its optimum by putting in place self-adaptive behaviours - e.g., the *PE* embedded computing platform has to decide upon strengthening its robustness to faults, at the cost of being less energy efficient.
- **CH4** - Challenges 1 to 3 address issues and limitations of run-time adaptability, self-awareness and design-time automation of CPS. Challenge 4 sums up to the design of a common semantic to integrate the project proposed tools, while guaranteeing a valid solution and minimizing the integration side-effects.

This paper focuses on CH2 and CH3 adaptation strategies, defining the adaptation loop and the Multi-Level Self-Adaptation Infrastructure that implement CERBERO compliant systems (see Sect. 2) and presenting the achieved mid-term results (see Sect. 3). Specifically, this paper presents the infrastructure of a self-adaptation loop for CPS and, additionally, a set of tools that, working together, aims at implementing the loop in a real use-case.

2 CERBERO Self-Adaptation Infrastructure

Self-adaptation aims at changing structure, functionality or parameters of the systems according to different pieces of information coming from the environment, the user or the system itself. In literature self-adaptation is mainly software (SW), while hardware (HW) is rarely addressed [13]. In CERBERO, self-adaptation is intended to be the combination of system self-awareness and reconfiguration. System reconfiguration is decided within the system itself by a self-adaptation manager, which makes decisions to change, according to adaptivity triggers, the execution infrastructure, the functionality performed or the parameters characterizing the execution. With respect to the state-of-the-art self-adaptive systems, CERBERO puts emphasis on cross-level aspects and on heterogeneity support, providing three different types of adaptivity:

- *Functional oriented*: to offer different functionalities over the same substrate or to maintain the correct functionality. It may be parametric (e.g., working-point changes) or fully functional (e.g., algorithm changes) - e.g., the type of a data filtering can be modified according to the nature of the filtered noise.
- *Non-functional oriented*: functionality is fixed, but system requires adaptation caused by non-functional requirements, such as performance or available energy - e.g., the precision of a filter could be reduced in case of low battery.
- *Repair oriented*: Adaptation may also be used for safety and reliability purposes by providing self-healing or self-repair mechanisms - e.g., HW task migration for permanent faults, or repair using memory scrubbing.

Considering these three types of adaptation, the adaptation strategy can be considered to perform well when the Key Performance Indicators (KPIs) of the produced system are higher than without using the strategy, either on average or in the worst case.

2.1 CERBERO Adaptation Loop

Self-adaptation involves a feedback loop from sensors to a decision entity. Many works decompose the loop structure of self-adaptive systems into phases such as Collect-Analyze-Decide-Act [5] or Monitoring-Analyzing-Planning-Executing [24]. These cycles are at the heart of self-adaptivity, making systems react to sensor information as an individual or as a group. Figure 2 illustrates the decomposition of self-adaptation activities into CERBERO project:

1. *Run-time sensing/monitoring capabilities* - To capture environment, human-commanded and system status changes with proper interfaces. For instance, the *PE* use-case requires high efficiency and low power consumption to ensure the autonomy of the robot. Monitoring of the controller is enabled by instrumenting the computing fabric with Performance API (PAPI) [3] compliant monitors, while proximity sensors on the arm enable adaptation to the physical environment.

2. *Run-time estimation capabilities* - To estimate, during the system execution, the KPIs representing the system status [1]. These estimations can be performed leveraging on lightweight run-time system models, parametric with respect to the actual sensed and monitored data, suitable to be embedded in the cyber part of the system. In the *PE* example, power consumption on the actuator joints will be estimated from a model.
3. *Decision making capabilities* - To define, given the evaluated KPIs and a set of predefined criteria, if adaptation is required to meet the expected goals or to maintain the execution as close as possible to its current status. Run-time optimization problems are meant to be solved by this block leveraging on different state-of-the-art techniques, such as non-linear programming or genetic algorithms. In the *PE* use-case, if the estimated KPIs reveal a faulty execution, the system should opt for repair-oriented adaptation. The actions to be put in place then depend on the target infrastructure and are defined for each engine with low-level mastering capabilities.
4. *Mastering capabilities* - To select the adaptation type on the available computing infrastructure. The adaptation engine executes the decision made by the adaptation manager in a target-dependent manner, e.g., dynamic task migration or HW accelerator reconfiguration. In the *PE* use-case, to implement repair-oriented adaptation in case of faults, the reconfiguration engine should switch off the configurable logic on the FPGA and move all the tasks back to the available rad-hard cores (cores hardened for radiation effects).
5. *Reconfiguration capabilities* - Execution of the changes on the available adaptable fabric. In the *PE* use-case with faults, the fabric is physically configured to continue the execution of all the tasks over the rad-hard core.

This loop does not refer to any specific level of abstraction and thus, the self-adaptive infrastructure should be implemented in all the CPS levels, involving (as in the CERBERO case) a hierarchy of decision-making and mastering elements.

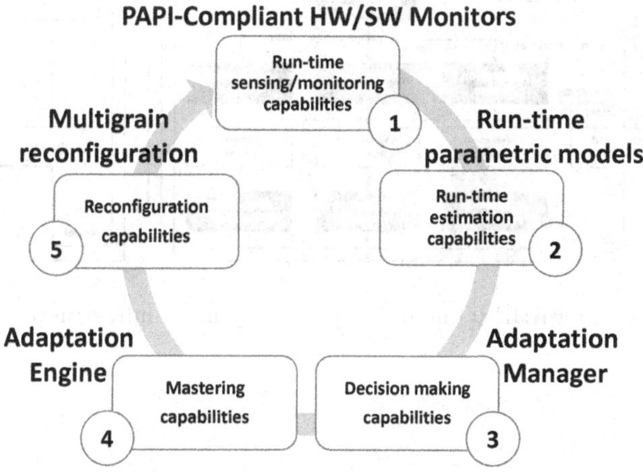

Fig. 2. Generic, level-agnostic, self-adaptation loop.

2.2 CERBERO Self-adaptation Infrastructure

The loop has been translated into the multi-level self-adaptation infrastructure depicted in Fig. 3, where different levels and layers are combined through a hierarchy of monitors, managers and engines. The cyber part interacts with the physical part, and direct triggers come from the environment, the humans in the loop or the components of the system. At the system level, tasks are executed on heterogeneous platforms, and are continuously monitored over time. Monitored data are used to determine current KPIs, which provide the adaptation manager with sufficient information to decide whether the system needs adaptation. Proper engines are used to restructure the computation activating or deactivating resources, re-mapping tasks, and/or re-programming the configurable logic.

The hierarchy of monitors/managers contributes to the realization of the loop also at the system of systems level, as shown in the upper part of Fig. 3. Higher-level monitors retrieve information from system-level managers (which have the knowledge of the execution at system level) and use them to decide upon higher-level adaptation strategies, where the different sub-systems may influence each other. Such hierarchy is meant to allow a high-level adaptation manager to coordinate adaptation between several lower-level subsystems.

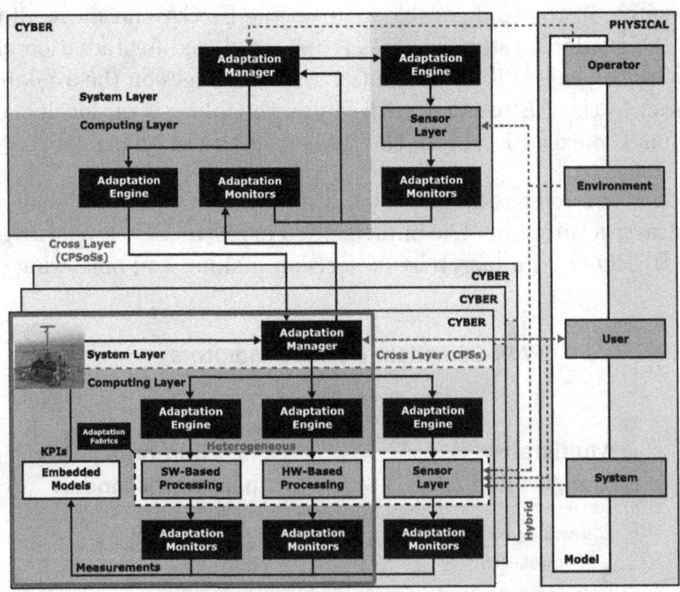

Fig. 3. CERBERO multi-level self-adaptation infrastructure.

3 Heterogeneous Self-adaptation

CERBERO offers an integrated toolset to support the analysis, implementation and management of CPS, from the computation to the system level, delivering also user-level features (i.e., requirements/model verification).

- Model/Requirements verification features are provided by SAGE that automatically checks consistency of a set of requirements provided by the user [17].
- At the system level, different tools are available. AOW [26] solves large scale hybrid optimization problems to return frontier of Pareto optimal solutions. DynAA [11] finds optimal solutions by means of model simulations. MECA [4] provides system, environmental and human monitoring and diagnosis, and high level decision support in cases of unforeseen conditions and events.
- At the computational level (i.e., algorithmic description), CERBERO environment leverages on tools that can directly communicate to each other. Figure 4 illustrates the current composition of the CERBERO design-time and run-time environment, at the computational level. Related tools are illustrated in detail in Sect. 3.1 (design-time support) and Sect. 3.2 (run-time support).

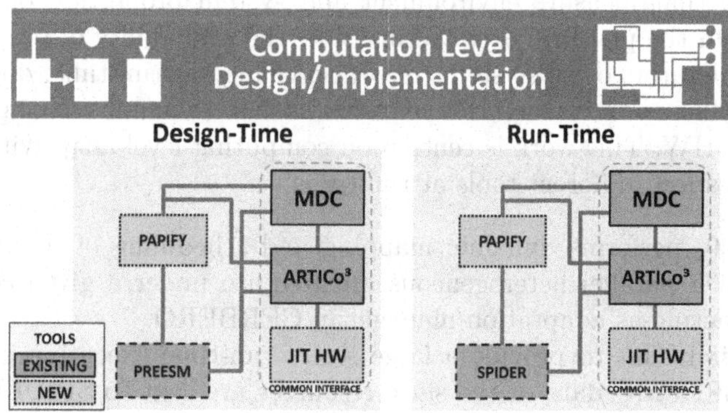

Fig. 4. Design-time and run-time support at the computational level.

3.1 Design-Time Support

At the computational level, the CERBERO design environment leverages on PREESM [20], PAPIFY [15], MDC [18] and ARTICo^3 [23].

- PREESM enables parallel-application development with design-time prediction, as well as code generation and re-use capabilities. Using application, architecture and scenario models as input, PREESM simulates the execution and provides early performance predictions in terms of latency, workload and memory footprint. Moreover, it can generate an optimized code to execute the application on the given parallel and heterogeneous architecture.

- PAPIFY generalizes PAPI to provide monitoring capabilities for heterogeneous architectures, extending this approach to HW accelerators with custom Performance Monitoring Counters (PMCs) [14,25]. PAPIFY instruments dataflow applications according to user-defined monitoring configurations.
- MDC and ARTICo^3 offer support for Coarse Grain Reconfiguration (CGR) and Dynamic and Partial Reconfiguration (DPR). CGR performs register-based virtual reconfiguration to switch between different datapaths that are physically present in the computing substrate [8], whereas DPR relies on low-level technology dependencies to completely change the implemented circuit [12]. MDC takes as input the dataflow descriptions of the desired functionalities and generates a Xilinx-compliant CGR accelerator. ARTICo^3 exploits a DPR-enabled multi-accelerator scheme, going from user-defined application directly to application execution on a DPR-capable substrate.

3.2 Run-Time Support

Most algorithms composing CERBERO use-case applications are, because of their adaptive nature, data dependent. Their resource requirements, parallelism and internal data streams depend on constantly changing parameters received from sensors, that measure environment and system properties, or from user commands. On the platform architecture side, the availability of resources such as cores, accelerators or subsystems may also change at run-time, due to either subsystem failures or advanced HW features, such as dynamic reconfiguration or self-repairing HW. This work is centred on computing-level adaptivity support, which involves four different tools at run-time.

- SPIDER [9] performs dynamic mapping and scheduling of dataflow applications on a parallel heterogeneous architecture under a given constrained scenario, acting as adaptation manager in CERBERO.
- PAPIFY is meant to provide a large set of run-time execution information to SPIDER. PMC data of the slave resources are sent to SPIDER to make decisions more effective, enhancing execution efficiency.
- MDC and ARTICo^3 deploy and configure proper engines over the physical substrate at design-time. These engines are used at run-time to execute all the actions needed to support run-time reconfiguration of the HW.

In the following more technical details on resource re-allocation, run-time monitoring and trade-off oriented HW reconfiguration are provided.

Resource Re-allocation: The SPIDER Tool. SPIDER is a system run-time manager that takes on-the-fly resource re-allocation decisions based on sensing, monitoring and KPI constraints. SPIDER is tailored for stream-processing applications and rely on the Parameterized and Interfaced Synchronous Dataflow (PiSDF) Model of Computation [6] and on a Model of Architecture (MoA) [21]. These models, which are constantly updated to match the current state of the system, balance expressiveness and system predictability.

SPIDER is a library for scheduling and mapping applications at run-time on heterogeneous multi-processing elements systems. As illustrated in Fig. 5, SPIDER is composed of a Global Run-time (GRT) that makes resource allocation decisions and issues job execution requests to a set of Local Run-times (LRTs) managing the execution of self-contained tasks, called actors. LRTs report to GRT the modifications of parameters, which affect application properties, KPI monitoring informations. The main KPI observed in SPIDER is the latency of the system and the run-time overhead of the manager has been strongly optimized for supporting large applications and architectures. Table 1 shows the experimental energy consumption measured per frame for an adaptive image filtering running on an 8-core ARM big.LITTLE architecture[2]. For two configurations of the adaptive filter, two SPIDER scenarios are considered: with or without platform heterogeneity knowledge. With the heterogeneity knowledge available, between 16% and 40% of processing energy energy is saved by SPIDER.

SPIDER LRTs are planned to support MDC and ARTICo^3 execution within the CERBERO project (see dashed arrows in Fig. 5), which offers new opportunities in terms of multi-modal self-awareness and HW/SW run-time coordination. As explained in the next sections, this aggregation of tools enables constantly updating knowledge of the system and advanced reconfiguration capabilities, preparing for the future of heterogeneity and parallelism in CPS.

Table 1. Energy consumption of an image filter with SPIDER on an 8 heterogeneous cores.

Algorithm	Energy with platform heterogeneity information	Energy w/o platform heterogeneity information
Full filter	2.35 J/frame	>4 J/frame
Reduced filter	1.92 J/frame	2.3 J/frame

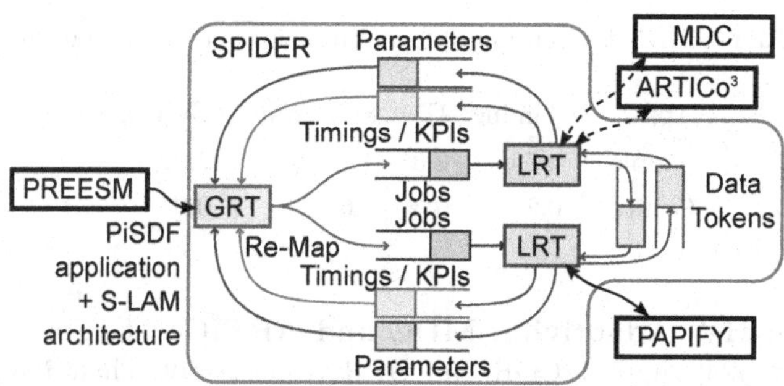

Fig. 5. SPIDER structure with Global Run-time (GRT) and Local Run-times (LRTs)

[2] Experiments available at: http://youtu.be/a9WIucWfjkU.

Monitoring: PAPIFY Run-Time Tool. PAPIFY [15] tool aims at monitoring the system by accessing PMCs to provide the adaptation manager with detailed performance information. After its integration with PREESM and SPIDER, developers are now able to configure and manage PMC-based monitoring.

At design-time, the user can load the available PMC data of the target platform when defining the PREESM scenario constraints. Once this information is loaded, the user interface allows to define, for each actor within the application, the set of performance events that needs to be monitored. Finally, PREESM automatically generates the corresponding instrumented code that will be used in both static and dynamic (SPIDER) mapping and scheduling. This instrumentation is based on a set of function calls to a library built on top of PAPI to increase the level of abstraction and support heterogeneity. At run-time, the monitoring is transparently managed, as each LRT is dynamically configured to monitor the specific set of events associated with each actor. By doing so, performance data are obtained for each actor being executed on each resource of the architecture. This information can be used by the developer to refine its implementation or by the adaptation manager to make decisions. It should be highlighted that previous research works have proven the possibility of estimating KPIs, such as energy consumption, based on PMC information [22].

Table 2 gathers the overhead in terms of execution time related to the use of PAPIFY. Specifically, results for a simple application (around 10000 actor executions per second) and a complex one (around 300 actor executions per second) are displayed. Additionally, for each application, four different scenarios with different monitoring complexity are evaluated: (1) timing monitoring, (2) monitoring the same event for every actor (1Ev), (3) monitoring the same 8 events for every actor and (8Ev-Same) (4) monitoring 8 different events for every actor. As can be seen, the overhead remains below 5% for every experiment except for case (8Ev-Diff) (4) using the simple application, which performs more than 10000 kernel requests per second. This last experiment is considered a corner case as this type of non-uniform monitoring is not usually required.

Table 2. PAPIFY-SPIDER execution time monitoring overhead (%) using 4 SW cores.

App	Timing	1Ev	8Ev-Same	8Ev-Diff
Simple	2.79	2.01	4.32	17.02
Complex	0.2	0.3	0.6	0.95

Multi-Grain HW Adaptivity: MDC and ARTICo^3 Engines. MDC [18] and ARTICo^3 [23] support CGR and DPR respectively. Their integration [7] offers a unique environment (see Fig. 6) capable of automatically implementing and managing multi-grain reconfigurable systems, while offering, at the same time, support for advanced adaptivity.

At design-time, high-level dataflow descriptions of the tasks to be accelerated are used as entry point. Then, the automated toolchain generates the

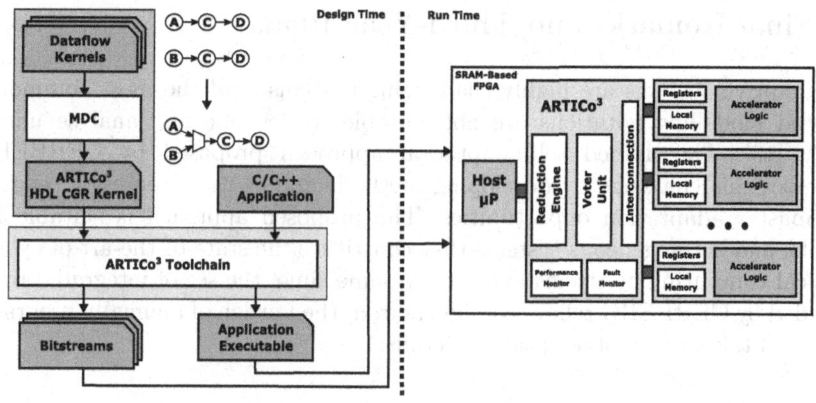

Fig. 6. MDC + ARTICo^3 at both design- and run-time.

corresponding HDL-based computational kernel with virtual reconfiguration capabilities. To enable also DPR, this logic is automatically instantiated, together with the required glue logic, in an ARTICo^3 kernel wrapper. Finally, the toolchain builds the multi-grain reconfigurable system and produces the configuration binaries (bitstreams and application executable). At run-time, both reconfiguration mechanisms are transparently managed by a set of user-friendly APIs, to be placed by the user in the code running on the host processor. A reduced set of function calls allows developers to decide the type of reconfiguration to use, or the number of data-parallel accelerators to load as well as their configuration.

Table 3. Reconfiguration overhead, for 4 accelerators in parallel. *Real on-board power measurements.

Design	Size [B]	Time [ms]	Energy* [mJ]
DPR	3430k	106.14	94.11
CGR	2	0.09	0.11

Table 3 shows the quantitative evaluation of both DPR and CGR (i.e., virtual reconfiguration) in a setup with 4 HW accelerators. With a negligible memory footprint and roughly 1000 times less reconfiguration time and energy consumption, CGR proves to be faster than DPR. However, DPR renders SW-like functional flexibility and resource utilization efficiency, two features that cannot be provided by virtual reconfiguration. The combination of MDC and ARTICo^3 leads to solutions that are inherently prepared to deal with the changing requirements present in CPS operational contexts.

4 Final Remarks and Third-Year Plans

Self-adaptive systems are highly-challenging systems, and the most commonly adopted modelling notations are not suitable to describe and analyse uncertainty [13]. The unified self-adaptation approach proposed by CERBERO addresses this challenge by developing methods and tools to represent, exploit and master adaptation opportunities. The proposed approach is suitable for parallel and heterogeneous systems that constitute the state-of-the-art of cyber-physical computing platforms and, at the same time, the set of integrated tools provided by CERBERO relieves designers from the burden of manually programming and taking care of adaptation details.

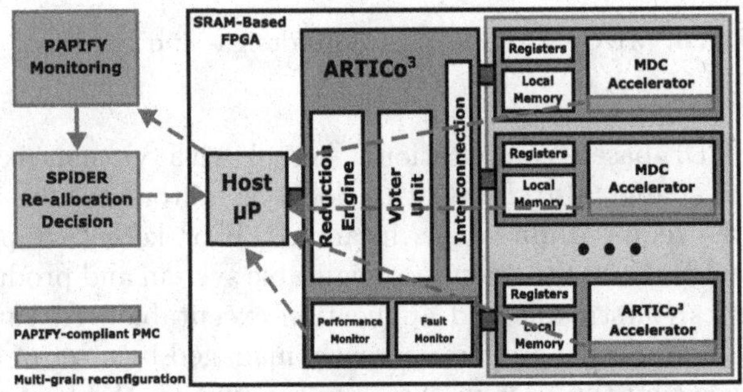

Fig. 7. Third-year integration plan.

Figure 7 provides a summary of the current status: integration of MDC and ARTICo^3 provides multi-grain adaptivity support [7]; PAPIFY is already passing information to SPIDER allowing it to master resource re-allocation in a multi-core infrastructure [15]. Figure 7 depicts also the next step of our integration agenda. Ongoing activities include the automatic insertion of HW-PMCs in the reconfigurable HW substrate [14,25]. We are providing a common PAPIFY interface for both HW and SW PMCs and defining the proper events to be monitored to enable efficient run-time trade-off management. Furthermore, we are working on defining proper MoAs of the HW accelerators and porting SPIDER on board to use it as manager for the proposed heterogeneous infrastructure.

In this last year of the CERBERO project we intend to use the described self-adaptive infrastructure in three industry relevant use-cases of significant size. In particular, what we described in this paper is meant to be assessed in the *Planetary Exploration* case for monitoring faults, energy and execution performance to be able to guarantee dynamic trade-off management.

Figure 8 depicts a schematic overview of the *PE* demonstrator. At the beginning of the design stage, the requirements of the robotic arm SW controller are formally checked for consistency by means of the ReqV tool comprised in SAGE, as shown in [17]. Then PREESM partitions the application among the available

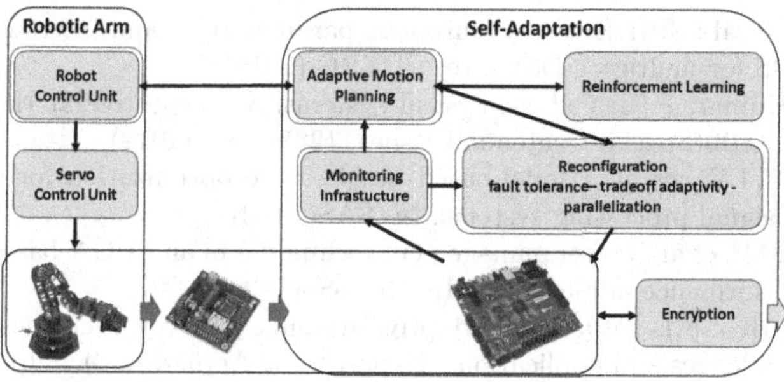

Fig. 8. Planetary exploration demonstrator.

cores and the HW fabric. The HW computing fabric leverages on the multi-grain reconfiguration [7]. The proper instrumentation of the architecture with ad-hoc PAPI-compliant HW monitor, allows PAPIFY and PAPIFY VIEWER to pass relevant information to SPIDER [15]. SPIDER triggers the self-adaptation depending on the measured KPIs, user needs and the system constraints. Therefore, motion planning adaptation can be managed by using these tools to dynamically select the optimal trajectory, both physical environment and self-awareness adaptivity through Reinforcement Learning techniques.

Acknowledgments. This work has received funding from the European Union's Horizon 2020 research and innovation programme under grant agreement No 732105. The authors would like to thank the Spanish Ministry of Education, Culture and Sport for its support under the FPU grant program.

References

1. CERBERO Deliverable D3.4 - CERBERO Modelling of KPI. https://www.cerbero-h2020.eu/wp-content/uploads/2018/12/D3.4.pdf
2. CERBERO Deliverable D6.8 - Planetary Exploration Demonstrator. https://www.cerbero-h2020.eu/wp-content/uploads/2018/12/D6.8.pdf
3. Performance API (2019). http://icl.utk.edu/papi/
4. Bosse, T., et al.: Developing ePartners for human-robot teams in space based on ontologies and formal abstraction hierarchies. J. Agent-Orient. Softw. Eng. **5**(4), 366–398 (2017)
5. Brun, Y., et al.: Engineering self-adaptive systems through feedback loops. In: Cheng, B.H.C., de Lemos, R., Giese, H., Inverardi, P., Magee, J. (eds.) Software Engineering for Self-Adaptive Systems. LNCS, vol. 5525, pp. 48–70. Springer, Heidelberg (2009). https://doi.org/10.1007/978-3-642-02161-9_3
6. Desnos, K., et al.: PiMM: parameterized and interfaced dataflow meta-model for MPSoCs runtime reconfiguration. In: SAMOS (2013)
7. Fanni, T., et al.: Multi-grain reconfiguration for advanced adaptivity in cyber-physical systems. In: ReConFig 2018, December 2018
8. Hartenstein, R.: Coarse grain reconfigurable architecture (embedded tutorial). In: Conference of the Asia and South Pacific Design Automation (2001)

9. Heulot, J., et al.: SPIDER: a synchronous parameterized and interfaced dataflow-based RTOS for multicore DSPs. In: EDERC (2014)
10. Kim, K., Kumar, P.R.: Cyber-physical systems: a perspective at the centennial. Proc. IEEE **100**(Special Centennial Issue), 1287–1308 (2012)
11. Leeuwen, C.J.V., et al.: Model-based architecture optimization for self-adaptive networked signal processing systems. In: SASO (2014)
12. Lombardo, M., et al.: Power management techniques in an FPGA-based WSN node for high performance applications. In: ReCoSoC (2012)
13. Macías-Escrivá, F.D., et al.: Self-adaptive systems: a survey of current approaches, research challenges and applications. Expert Syst. Appl. **40**(18), 7267–7279 (2013)
14. Madroñal, D., Fanni, T.: Run-time performance monitoring of hardware accelerators: POSTER. In: CF (2019)
15. Madroñal, D., et al.: Automatic instrumentation of dataflow applications using PAPI. In: CF (2018)
16. Masin, M., et al.: Cross-layer design of reconfigurable cyber-physical systems. In: DATE, March 2017
17. Narizzano, M., Pulina, L., Tacchella, A., Vuotto, S.: Consistency of property specification patterns with boolean and constrained numerical signals. In: Dutle, A., Muñoz, C., Narkawicz, A. (eds.) NFM 2018. LNCS, vol. 10811, pp. 383–398. Springer, Cham (2018). https://doi.org/10.1007/978-3-319-77935-5_26
18. Palumbo, F., et al.: Power-awarness in coarse-grained reconfigurable multi-functional architectures: a dataflow based strategy. J. Signal Process. Syst. **87**(1), 81–106 (2017). https://doi.org/10.1007/s11265-016-1106-9
19. Palumbo, F., et al.: CERBERO: cross-layer model-based framework for multi-objective design of reconfigurable systems in uncertain hybrid environments. In: CF (2019)
20. Pelcat, M., et al.: PREESM: a dataflow-based rapid prototyping framework for simplifying multicore DSP programming. In: EDERC (2014)
21. Pelcat, M., et al.: Reproducible evaluation of system efficiency with a model of architecture: from theory to practice. IEEE Trans. Comput. Aided Design Integr. Circ. Syst. **37**, 2050–2063 (2017)
22. Ren, R., et al.: Energy estimation models for video decoders: reconfigurable video coding-CAL case-study. IET Comput. Digit. Tech. **9**(1), 3–15 (2014)
23. Rodríguez, A., et al.: FPGA-based high-performance embedded systems for adaptive edge computing in cyber-physical systems: the ARTICo^3 framework. Sensors **18**(6), 1877 (2018). https://doi.org/10.3390/s18061877
24. Salehie, M., Tahvildari, L.: Towards a goal-driven approach to action selection in self-adaptive software. Softw. Pract. Exper. **42**(2), 211–233 (2012)
25. Suriano, L., et al.: A unified hardware/software monitoring method for reconfigurable computing architectures using PAPI. In: ReCoSoC (2018)
26. Zadorojniy, A., et al.: Algorithms for finding maximum diversity of design variables in multi-objective optimization. In: CSER (2012)

A Lean, Low Power, Low Latency DRAM Memory Controller for Transprecision Computing

Chirag Sudarshan[1], Jan Lappas[1(✉)], Christian Weis[1], Deepak M. Mathew[1], Matthias Jung[2], and Norbert Wehn[1]

[1] Technische Universität Kaiserslautern, Kaiserslautern, Germany
{sudarshan,lappas,weis,deepak,wehn}@eit.uni-kl.de

[2] Fraunhofer Institute for Experimental Software Engineering (IESE), Kaiserslautern, Germany
matthias.jung@iese.fraunhofer.de

Abstract. Energy consumption is one of the major challenges for the advanced System on Chips (SoC). This is addressed by adopting heterogeneous and approximate computing techniques. One of the recent evolution in this context is transprecision computing paradigm. The idea of the transprecision computing is to consume adequate amount of energy for each operation by performing dynamic precision reduction. The impact of the memory subsystem plays a crucial role in such systems. Hence, the energy efficiency of a transprecision system can be further optimized by tailoring the memory subsystem to the transprecision computing. In this work, we present a lean, low power, low latency memory controller that is appropriate for transprecision methodology. The memory controller consumes an average power of 129.33 mW at a frequency of 500 MHz and has a total area of 4.71 mm^2 for UMC 65 nm process.

Keywords: DRAM · DDR3 · Memory controller · Transprecision · PHY

1 Introduction

Approximate computing has been recognized as an effective technique to overcome the energy scaling barrier of computing systems by compromising the accuracy of results. Inspired by approximate computing, *transprecision computing* [1] has emerged as a new computing paradigm that offers a dynamic precision reduction to the intermediate computation stages in order to achieve higher energy efficiency without inheriting any errors in the final output. In other words, the accuracy of the final result is same as that of a traditional full-precision computing. The dynamic precision reduction is achieved by spanning all the layers of the computing system (i.e. from algorithm to the specifically tuned hardware that supports a variety of precision settings) and offering multiple control loops

D. N. Pnevmatikatos et al. (Eds.): SAMOS 2019, LNCS 11733, pp. 429–441, 2019.
https://doi.org/10.1007/978-3-030-27562-4_31

across these layers. The objective of H2020 European project OPRECOMP is to implement transprecision computing platforms for applications ranging from *Internet-of-Things* (mW Platforms - ASIC) to *High Performance Computing* (KW platforms - FPGA).

OPRECOMP project uses the PULP (An Open Parallel Ultra-Low-Power Processing) platform [2] that is implemented using RISC-V cores for energy efficient computing. RISC-V is an open Instruction Set Architecture (ISA) that has acquired a lot of recognition across industry and academia. The high degree of customization offered in RISC-V architecture enables the design of energy efficient transprecision computation units. However, the ASIC implementation of the PULP is bound to low memory density devices like Static Random Access Memories (SRAMs). But, many applications demand larger memory footprints i.e external memories. The most prominent external memories are the Dynamic Random Access Memories (DRAMs). DRAM require a specialized circuitry called memory controller to manage the complex protocol. These memory controllers are designed for general purpose and are not available as an open hardware architecture. Additionally, DRAMs consume a major portion of the overall system power and deteriorate the system performance due to its long latency. This is partially due the DRAM operations such as refresh, activation and precharge (refer Sect. 2) that contribute high energy [3] and results long latency for the data accesses [4]. The impact of the refresh further increases for the next generation high density DRAM devices (64 Gb devices) [5,6].

In this work we focus on the mW platform that has a memory channel consisting of a single DDR3 DRAM device (×8 device). We present a DDR3 memory controller that includes several advanced features and optimizes the memory subsystem for transprecision computing.

One of the fundamental feature is to adapt the idea of approximate computing to the DRAM (i.e *Approximate DRAM*) [7–9]. The key knobs of approximating the DRAM is to vary the refresh rate in order to enable the trade-off between energy efficiency, performance and reliability. This technique allows the processing units to store the application data in an appropriate refresh/reliability zone (ranging from no refresh to high refresh rate) without incurring any computation errors. For example, the data are stored in no refresh zone if the lifetime of the application is less than the required refresh period of the DRAM [10]. A typical approximate DRAM employs a fine granular refreshing technique in order to refresh different zones of reliability at varied rates. The most favourable approach to realize a fine granular refresh is using *Optimized Row Granular Refresh (ORGR)* methodology [11]. The authors of [11] present a reverse engineering method to determine the user unknown minimum DRAM timings to realize the fine granular refresh that is as effective but more flexible than the conventional DRAM *Auto-Refresh.*

The second important feature is to exploit the application knowledge. General purpose memory controllers are confined to online scheduling techniques that only have a local view on the executed application. However, numerous applications feature deterministic memory access patterns, which can be exploited to improve bandwidth and energy. The authors of [4] present the methodology to generate an *Application-Specific Address Mapping* (ASAM), which has a global view on the application and exploits the application knowledge to optimally map the data to a DRAM location that decreases the number of row misses, i.e. the number of precharge and activate operations. The authors of [4] showed upto 9x and 8.6X improvements in bandwidth utilization and energy efficiency by employing this technique.

However, all the discussed previous works (i.e. Approximate DRAM, ORGR, ASAM) presented the proof of concepts mainly by simulations. To the best of our knowledge for the first time our memory controller (i.e. frontend + physical layer or PHY) combines all the previously discussed advanced techniques. The designed DDR3 memory controller will be integrated with the PULP cluster to demonstrate the advantage of transprecision computing for IoT/embedded applications (mW platform). The key features of our memory controller are as follows:

- Lean, low latency and low power, optimized for embedded systems that apply the transprecision computing methodology.
- Enables fine granular refresh control using ORGR.
- Supports the exploitation of application knowledge using ASAM.
- Scalable and robust PHY design with an All-Digital-DLL (AD-DLL) that uses glitch-free delay-lines without special filters.

The paper is structured as follows: Sect. 2 gives a brief overview on DRAM and its operation. We present our implementation of the transprecision memory controller and PHY in Sect. 3 and Sect. 4 respectively. Section 5 discusses the post layout results and power estimation. Finally the paper is concluded in Sect. 6.

2 DRAM Background

In this section we first introduce the basic terminology and the operation of a DRAM device. DRAM devices are organized as a set of memory banks (e.g. eight) that include memory arrays. The banks operate concurrently (bank parallelism) with some constraints on data access due to the shared data and command/address bus. Accessing data from the DRAM is a two step process. First, the *activate* command (ACT) must be issued to the row of a certain bank. Then, the column access (CAS) i.e. *read* (RD) or *write* command (WR) are executed to read or write data from/to the specific column. The ACT command opens an entire row of the memory array and buffers in the *Primary Sense Amplifiers* that mimics a small cache, often called as row buffer. If a memory access targets the same row as the currently cached row (called row hit), it results in a low latency and low energy memory access. Whereas, if a memory access targets a different row as the currently activated row (called row miss), it results in higher latency and energy consumption. If a certain row in a bank is active it must be *precharged* (PRE) before activating another row in the same bank. Additionally, to the normal RD and WR commands, there exist CAS commands with an

Table 1. Key timings for a DDR3-800D device

Name	Explanation	Value
tRCD	*Row to Column Delay:* The time interval between ACT and RD on the same bank	5 clk
tRAS	*Row Active:* The minimum active time for a row	15 clk
tRTP	*Read-to-Precharge Delay:*The time interval between RD and PRE command on the same bank	4 clk
tWR	*Write Recovery:* The minimum time interval between the end of a WR burst and a PRE command	6 clk
tRP	*Row Precharge:* The time interval between PRE and ACT on the same bank	5 clk
tRRD	*Row-to-Row Delay:* The minimum time interval between 2 consecutive ACT command to different bank	4 clk
tCCD	*Column-to-column Delay:* The minimum time interval between 2 consecutive WR or RD command	4 clk
tWTR	*Write-to-Read:* The minimum time interval between the end of a WR burst and a RD command	4 clk
RL	*Read Latency:* Delay between the RD command and the availability of the first RD data bursts on the DRAM data interface	5 clk
WL	*Write Latency:* Delay between the WR command and the availability of the first WR data bursts on the DRAM data interface	5 clk
tRTW	*Read-to-Write:* The minimum time interval between the end of a WR burst and a RD command $tRTW = RL + tCCD + 2clk - WL$	6 clk
tRFC	*Refresh cycle time:* The minimum time interval between the refresh command and any valid command	110 ns
tREFI	*Refresh Interval:* The minimum time interval between the consecutive refresh commands	7.8 us

integrated auto-precharge (RDA, WRA). If auto-precharge is selected, the row being accessed will be precharged at the end of the read or write access. Further, the DRAM device is issued an *Auto-Refresh* (AREF) command at every tREFI duration that internally performs refresh operation. Table 1 shows the key timings of DDR3 DRAM device and its values as defined in [12].

3 Memory Controller Architecture

Figure 1 shows the architecture of the transprecision memory controller. In this section, we describe on the architecture of the frontend. It is designed to satisfy the mW platform requirements i.e. low power, low area and low latency. The frequency ratio between the PHY and the frontend is 1:4, similar to state of the art memory controllers, such as [13,14]. This allows the frontend to be operated at a lower clock frequency, satisfying the timing constraints and consuming lower power. In order to compensate the frequency difference and avoid stalling of the PHY, the frontend issues 4× DRAM commands/addresses (i.e. commands/addresses corresponding to next 4 PHY cycles) to the PHY.

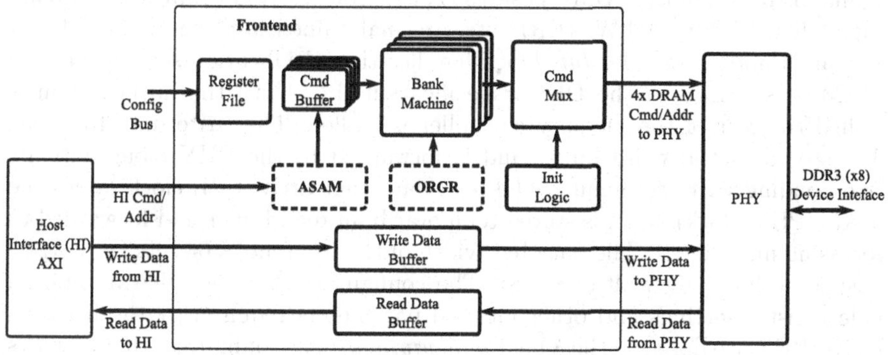

Fig. 1. Transprecision memory controller architecture

As mentioned in Sect. 1, the ASAM technique presents better energy and bandwidth results as compared to an online scheduler for the applications with deterministic memory access pattern. Additionally, the online scheduler block requires large buffers for reordering the incoming requests and introduces a very high area overhead and latency penalty. Hence, this architecture does not integrate any online scheduler but rather employ ASAM block. The ASAM block is a dedicated address decoder that translates the incoming address bits from the *Host Interface* (HI) like AXI interface to an equivalent DRAM row, column and bank addresses as per the configured custom address map. The ASAM block incorporates a configurable address scrambling hardware as shown in Fig. 2. The incoming logical address from the HI is typically 32 bit, out of which only 30 bits are valid since the maximum density of a DDR3 device is 8 Gb. Note that the addresses from HI are byte addressable and the requests are in the granularity of a cache line (i.e. 8 bytes). The lower 3 bits of HI address are directly mapped to the lower 3 bits of the DRAM column address (C2-C0). The remaining 27 bits of the HI address are scrambled by the 27 × 27 bit multiplexers to determine the DRAM addresses i.e. bank (B2-B0), row (R15-R0) and column (C10-C3). A typical general purpose memory controller also supports multiple HIs and has an *N-Port Arbiter* to prioritize the incoming request and delivers it to the scheduler. However, this arbiter would further add a lot of resources and latency to command processing. Thus, our controller is integrated with only one HI interface, which is sufficient for a typical embedded processors like mW platform.

The translated addresses and the corresponding HI command (i.e. read or write) are forwarded to one of the eight command buffers (FIFO) depending on the bank address. The *Bank Machines* (BM) consecutively process the incoming traffic associated with its respective DRAM bank. A BM keeps track of the current active row of its respective bank and translate the incoming transactions to a sequence of DRAM commands. The command sequence depends on the current state of the bank and the target row of the incoming transaction. The BM also guarantees all bank specific timings such as tRCD, tRTP, tWR, tRAS and tRP. The *Command Multiplexer* (Cmd Mux) prioritizes the DRAM commands from multiple BMs, ensures that the bus related timings (inter-bank timing) like tWTR, tRTW, tRRD etc. are maintained, and packs 4× DRAM commands/addresses. The *Init* block handles the initialization sequence of the DRAM as specified in the DDR3 specification [12]. Until the initialization is finished the rest of the memory controller is stalled. The write data from the HI is stored in the write buffer and is forwarded to the PHY along with its corresponding write command. The read data that arrives RL clock cycles (i.e DRAM/PHY clock) later, is stored temporarily in read buffer and forwarded to processing unit via HI. The data bus width of the frontend is 64 bits i.e. DRAM Burst Length × DQ width (8 × 8). The configuration of the DRAM timings, mode register settings and other internal parameters required by the frontend and the PHY are done via the 8 bit *Configuration Bus* (Config Bus) that employs a custom protocol.

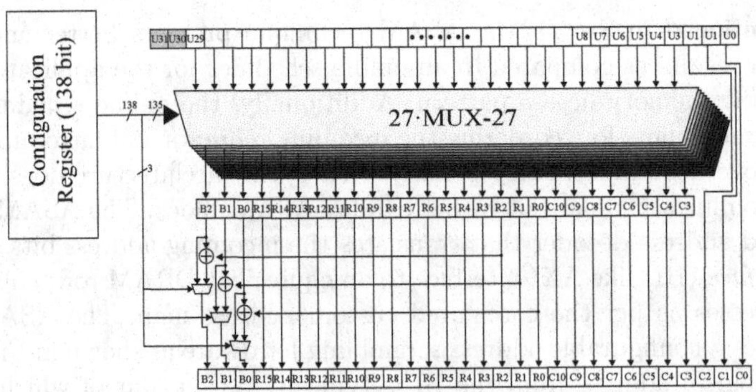

Fig. 2. ASAM architecture

The *ORGR* block manages the DRAM refresh operation using optimized fine granular refresh technique. The ORGR block consists a set of counters to track the refresh interval of different DRAM zones of reliability. As the counter expires, the ORGR sends the corresponding BMs the row addresses to be refreshed. That appropriate BMs will stall its further transactions and services the ORGR request with the sequence of ACT and PRE commands (i.e. fine granular refresh) with reduced DRAM timings. These ACT and PRE commands are given the highest priority by the cmd mux. The reverse engineering methodology presented in [11] to identify the user unknown minimum timings is executed during the initialization. However, it is not triggered at every initialization due to the fact that the identified minimum timings in most cases remain unmodified for the entire course of operation of that device. Hence, it is triggered occasionally and for the rest of the initialization, the last known minimum timing values are configured via the config bus from the software. The config bus is also used to define the DRAM reliability zones and their respective refresh intervals.

4 DDR3 Physical Layer (PHY) Architecture

This new PHY is designed with the focus on simplicity and robustness. All full-custom atomic components are designed to be massively reused in the total design, to decrease design time, implementation time and time to test. The architecture of our DDR3 PHY is shown in Fig. 3. The PHY consists of two major blocks:

- Data Bus (see Fig. 3 ①)
- Address/Command (ADDR/CMD) Bus (see Fig. 3 ②)

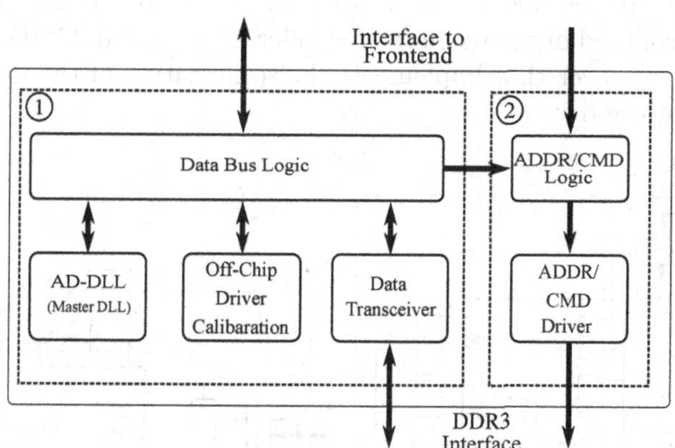

Fig. 3. DDR3-PHY architecture

The bidirectional Data Bus consists of nine Data Transceivers, eight for data (DQ[7:0]) and one differential data strobe (DQS, nDQS). Each transceiver is implemented by seven parallel push-pull drivers where each of them has the pull-up (PMOS) and the pull-down (NMOS) path calibrated by the Off-Chip Driver Calibration Unit to $R_{dri} = 240\,\Omega$. The push-pull driver transistors are build with thick-oxide transistors (60 Å gate oxide thickness). This allows a simple and robust ESD protection of the driver transistors and avoids complicated and fragile stacked transistor design with thin-oxide transistors as presented in [15]. This seven parallel push-pull drivers can be individual selected to set the required on-chip-termination value and to implement different driving strengths depending on write or read operations. The on-chip-termination impedance is then $(R_{dri}/N_{dri-sel})/2$ and off-chip-driver impedance $R_{dri}/N_{dri-sel}$. Where $N_{dri-sel}$ is the number of selected drivers. The overall driver architecture is based on [16].

The receivers for the data transceivers are single-ended receivers with their reference pin connected to the voltage V_{ref} (for DDR3 $V_{ref} = VDD/2 = 0.75\,\text{V}$). The data strobe receiver is implemented as a fully differential amplifier with a common-mode-voltage equal to V_{ref}. All receivers are biased locally to simplify the analog signal global routing. To reduce the power consumption bias circuits are shared between two receivers. This PHY architecture implements also the 90° phase shift delay needed in DDR interfaces to center align the data strobe signals (DQS, nDQS) to the data signals (DQ) with a master-slave DLL configuration. After power up the Master DLL does a 360° lock to the internal clock. After locking the Data Bus Logic broadcasts the new configuration values from the Master DLL to the Slave DLLs. The Slave DLLs are built using a replica delay line from the Master DLL that represents a quarter of the Master DLLs delay. The Slave DLLs are placed inside the read and write path of the Data Bus (see Fig. 4). The ADDR/CMD Bus consists of 26 single data rate drivers (ADDR, nCS, nWE...) and two clock drivers (CLK, nCLK). These drivers are using the same driver topology architecture as the Data Bus drivers but in a single data rate configuration. This allows to reuse the same impedance control values that are broadcasted by the Data Bus. The ADDR/CMD Bus is direct controlled by frontend of the memory controller. The ADDR/CMD Logic is only a thin abstraction layer that implements the serialization of the inputs and the configuration of the drivers.

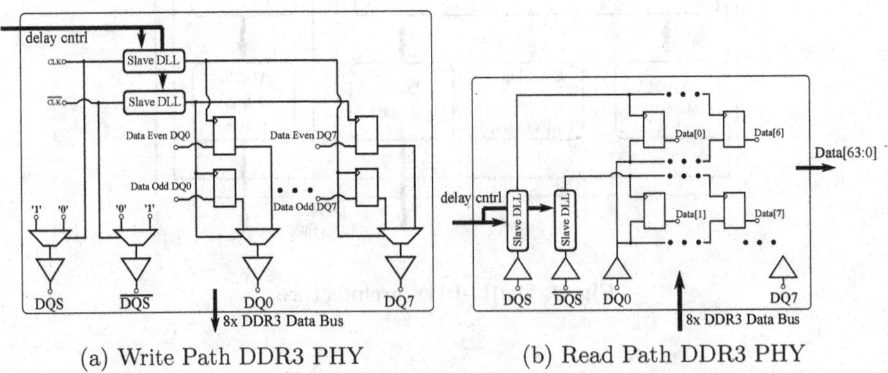

(a) Write Path DDR3 PHY (b) Read Path DDR3 PHY

Fig. 4. DDR3-PHY data bus

4.1 All Digital Delay Locked Loop (AD-DLL)

An AD-DLL is selected for this DDR3 PHY due to its robustness and good scaling in deep-sub-micrometer CMOS processes., This enable fast design time and lower complexity compare to the analog counterparts [17]. The AD-DLL is composed of the following main components (see Fig. 5):

- Phase Frequency Detector (PFD),
- DLL-Controller,
- four digital controlled delay lines (DCDL) with fine and coarse delay control.

An abstracted version of the Phase Frequency Detector used in this DLL is shown in Fig. 7. The Phase Frequency Detector (PFD) compares the leading edges of the reference clock (clk_in) with the delayed clock (clock coming from the digital controlled delay lines). Depending if clk_in or the delay_clk is leading a small pulse on the internal up_int or down_int port will be generated. To enable the digital DLL Controller to detect these ports a RS-NAND latch is used to hold the last status. This kind of PFDs are common for All-Digital DLLs, but they have a major drawback to be very susceptible to glitches at their input. Missing clock edges due to glitches cause fault detection. This AD-DLL solves this problem by using digital controlled delay lines (DCDL) that suppress to generate glitches when switched to a different delay values. The coarse delay of the DCDL is constructed by using 32 glitch-free NAND-based delay element (DE) structure in a special three step switching scheme proposed by [18] (see Fig. 6a). The fine delay is implemented by two standard invertes and a RC-Delay where the capacitor is trimmable with a 4bit resolution. The trimmable capacitor is build out of MOSFETS were drain and source are connected to the signal. By switching the gate to VDD or to VSS the capacitor changes its value.

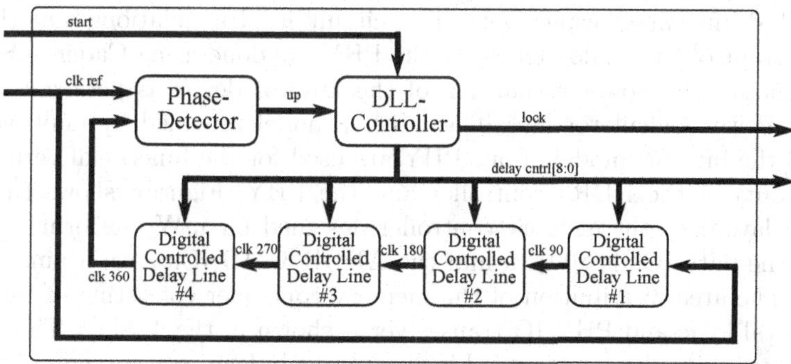

Fig. 5. All digital delay locked loop architecture

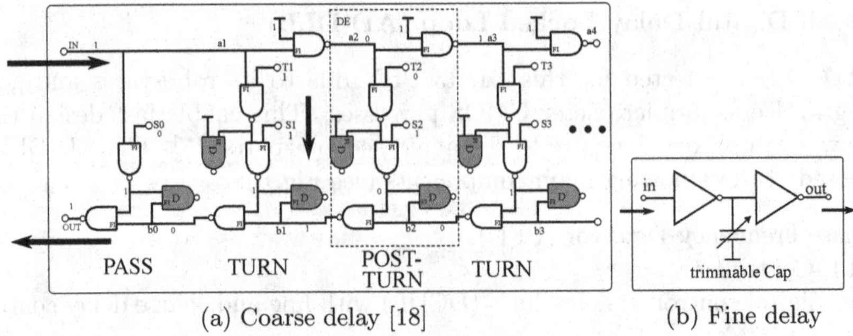

(a) Coarse delay [18] (b) Fine delay

Fig. 6. Coarse and fine delay elements

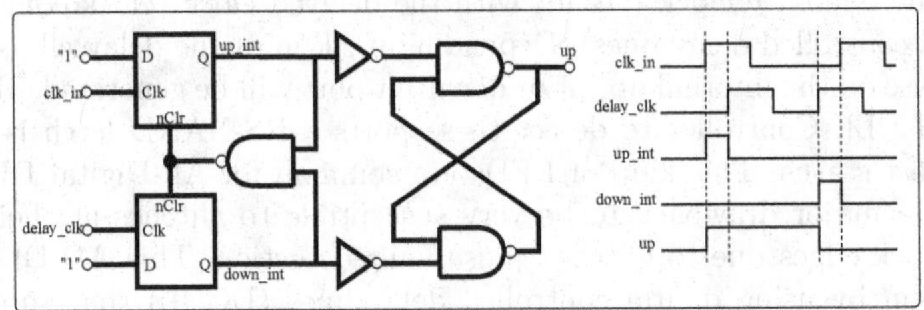

Fig. 7. Phase Frequency Detector (PFD) with latch output

5 Results

The memory controller is implemented using the UMC 65 nm Low-Leakage CMOS bulk technology. The synthesis, place and route, and timing/power analysis of the digital logic are carried out using Synopsis' DesignCompiler, IC Compiler and PrimeTime, respectively. The circuit level simulations and the full custom layout of the analog blocks of the PHY are done using Cadence Spectre and Virtuoso. The power estimation of the DRAM device is performed using Micron's Power Calculator [19]. The DRAM model provided by multiple vendors and the bit true model of our PHY are used for the functional verification (post-layout) of the DDR3 controller and the PHY. Figure 8 shows the floor plan and layout of our memory controller designed for mW platform. The pin pitch of the data IOs is 200 µm and the ADDR/CMD IOs have a pin pitch of 100 µm. The area distribution of the memory controller consisting of frontend, PHY digital logic and PHY IO transceiver is shown in the Table 2. The core of the memory controller i.e. frontend is is extensively lean, consuming only 2% of the total chip area.

The post-layout results show that the DDR3 controller achieves a performance of 533 MHz (PHY clock) leading to a data rate of 1066 Mbit/pin/s under worst case condition (i.e slow process, low VDD and high temperature). The peak frequency of the design is limited due to the package (QFN64) used for the mW demonstrator. The controller has a very low latency of 3 frontend cycles

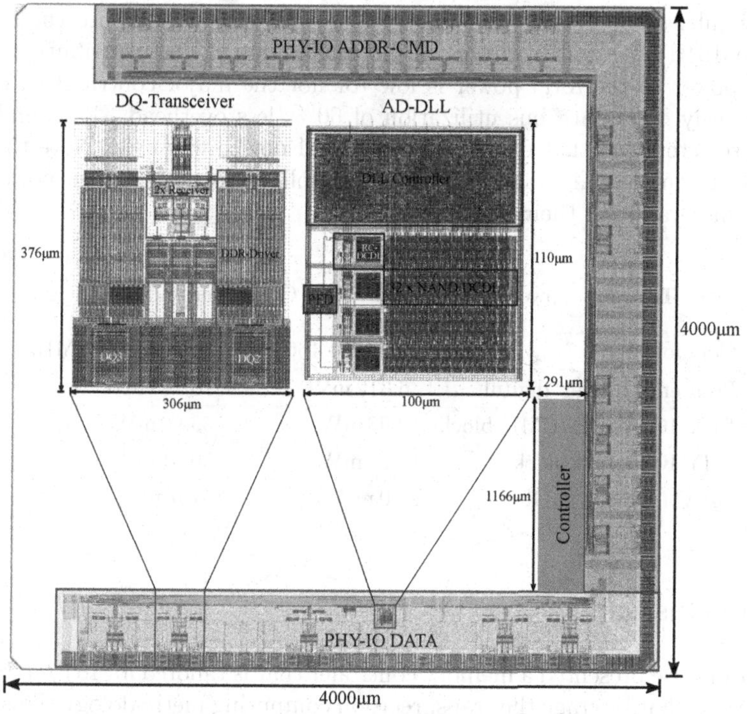

Fig. 8. Floor plan

Table 2. Area distribution of the controller and PHY

Component	Area
PHY-IO transceiver	$3.820\,\text{mm}^2$
PHY-digital	$0.551\,\text{mm}^2$
Frontend	$0.339\,\text{mm}^2$

plus 1 PHY clock for processing the host interface (AXI4) requests and delivering the associated commands to the DRAM.

The power consumption of a single I/O driver when subjected to 100% toggling rate for the frequencies 166 MHz and 500 MHz are 6.0 mW and 18.0 mW, respectively. Similarly, a single data receiver consumes 3.75 mW and 5.5 mW power for the aforementioned frequencies. The power estimation of the memory controller is done using a random trace (for worst case estimation) with equal number of reads and writes as an input to the controller that resulted in a data bus utilization of 60%. Table 3 shows the distribution of the estimated power for the frequencies 166 MHz and 500 MHz. The power consumed by the ADDR/CMD block has no substantial difference with the DATA block power and the DRAM device power. This is true only for a single DRAM device memory subsystem. However, in a typical SO-DIMM architecture the DRAM power and PHY-IO DATA power will be predominant. The contribution of the DRAM power to the total power is low (or not the major contributor) due to the relatively good data bus utilization of 60% (less overhead - low number of row misses etc.) and that only a single DRAM device was used. Note that the vendors of commercial available DDR3 controllers do not disclose power and performance values of their IPs.

Table 3. Power Distribution of the Controller and PHY

Component	Power at 166 MHz	Power at 500 MHz
Frontend + PHY digital	6.312 mW	18.764 mW
PHY-IO ADDR/CMD block	19.98 mW	59.96 mW
PHY-IO DATA block	15.96 mW	50.61 mW
DRAM Device (2 Gb)	24.0 mW	67.0 mW

6 Conclusion

In this work, we presented a memory controller that is tailored for IoT/embedded applications that leverage the transprecision computing methodology. This memory controller adapted several advanced techniques, such as approximate DRAM, sophisticated refresh policy, and optimal address mapping and data placement by exploiting application knowledge. These techniques allow the energy and performance optimization of DRAM subsystems. Experimental results show that the memory controller's design is lean, low latency and low power. Furthermore the presented design of the DDR3 PHY is scalable, low-complexity and robust even under worst case corner conditions (i.e slow process, low VDD and high temperature). Finally, with this memory controller design we enable open hardware platforms, such as RISC-V, to integrate external DRAM devices.

Acknowledgment. The project OPRECOMP acknowledges the financial support of the Future and Emerging Technologies (FET) programme within the European Unions Horizon 2020 research and innovation programme, under grant agreement No. 732631 (http://www.oprecomp.eu). This work was also supported by the Fraunhofer High Performance Center for Simulation- and Software-based Innovation.

References

1. Malossi, A.C.I., et al.: The transprecision computing paradigm: concept, design, and applications. In: 2018 Design, Automation Test in Europe Conference Exhibition (DATE), pp. 1105–1110, March 2018
2. Rossi, D., et al.: Energy-efficient near-threshold parallel computing: the PULPv2 cluster. IEEE Micro **37**(5), 20–31 (2017)

3. Weis, C., et al.: DRAMSpec: a high-level DRAM timing, power and area exploration tool. Int. J. Parallel Program. **45**(6), 1566–1591 (2017)
4. Jung, M., et al.: ConGen: an application specific dram memory controller generator. In: Proceedings of the Second International Symposium on Memory Systems, MEMSYS 2016, pp. 257–267. ACM, New York (2016)
5. Bhati, I., et al.: Flexible auto-refresh: enabling scalable and energy-efficient DRAM refresh reductions. In: Proceedings of the 42nd Annual International Symposium on Computer Architecture, pp. 235–246. ACM (2015)
6. Liu, J., et al.: RAIDR: retention-aware intelligent dram refresh. In: Proceedings of the 39th Annual International Symposium on Computer Architecture, ISCA 2012, pp. 1–12. IEEE Computer Society, Washington (2012)
7. Jung, M., et al.: Approximate computing with partially unreliable dynamic random access memory - approximate DRAM. In: Proceedings of the 53rd Annual Design Automation Conference, DAC 2016, pp. 100:1–100:4. ACM, New York (2016)
8. Lucas, J., et al.: Sparkk: quality-scalable approximate storage in DRAM. In: The Memory Forum, June 2014
9. Liu, S., et al.: Flikker: saving DRAM refresh-power through critical data partitioning. SIGPLAN Not. **46**(3), 213–224 (2011)
10. Jung, M.., et al.: Omitting refresh - a case study for commodity and wide I/O DRAMs. In: 1st International Symposium on Memory Systems, MEMSYS 2015, Washington, DC, USA, October 2015
11. Mathew, D.M., et al.: Using run-time reverse-engineering to optimize DRAM refresh. In: International Symposium on Memory Systems (MEMSYS17) (2017)
12. Jedec Solid State Technology Association. DDR3 SDRAM (JESD 79–3) (2012)
13. Cadence Inc.: Cadence® Denali® DDR Memory IP, October 2014. http://ip.cadence.com/ipportfolio/ip-portfolio-overview/memory-ip/ddr-lpddr. Accessed 18 Feb 2015
14. Synopsys, Inc.: DesignWare DDR IP (2015). http://www.synopsys.com/IP/InterfaceIP/DDRn/Pages/. Accessed 18 Feb 2015
15. Fan, X., et al.: ESD protection circuit schemes for DDR3 DQ drivers. In: Electrical Overstress/Electrostatic Discharge Symposium Proceedings, pp. 1–6 (2010)
16. Yoo, C., et al.: A 1.8 V 700 Mb/s/pin 512 Mb DDR-II SDRAM with on-die termination and off-chip driver calibration. In: 2003 IEEE International Solid-State Circuits Conference, ISSCC 2003. Digest of Technical Papers, vol. 1, pp. 312–496, February 2003
17. Chen, S., et al.: An all-digital delay-locked loop for high-speed memory interface applications. In: Technical Papers of 2014 International Symposium on VLSI Design, Automation and Test, pp. 1–4, April 2014
18. De Caro, D.: Glitch-free NAND-based digitally controlled delay-lines. IEEE Trans. Very Large Scale Integr. (VLSI) Syst. **21**(1), 55–66 (2013)
19. Micron: DDR3 SDRAM System Power Calculator, July 2011. Accessed 03 July 2014

Optimized FPGA Implementation of a Compute-Intensive Oil Reservoir Simulation Algorithm

Aggelos D. Ioannou[1(✉)], Pavlos Malakonakis[1,2], Konstantinos Georgopoulos[2], Ioannis Papaefstathiou[3,4], Apostolos Dollas[1], and Iakovos Mavroidis[2]

[1] School of Electrical and Computer Engineering, Technical University of Crete, Chania, Greece
{aioannou1,pmalakonakis,adollas}@isc.tuc.gr

[2] Telecommunication Systems Institute, Campus Kounoupidiana, Chania, Greece
kgeorgopoulos@mhl.tuc.gr, iakovosmavro@gmail.com

[3] School of Electrical and Computer Engineering, Aristotle University of Thessaloniki, Thessaloniki, Greece
ygp@ece.auth.gr

[4] Synelixis Solutions Ltd., 10 Farmakidou Street, 34100 Chalkida, Greece
ygp@synelixis.com

Abstract. Modern-day High Performance Computing (HPC) trends are shifting towards exascale performance figures in order to satisfy the needs of many compute-intensive and power-hungry applications. Hence, the European-funded ECOSCALE project introduces a highly innovative architecture, which spreads the workload among a number of independent and concurrently-operating conventional (CPU) as well as reconfigurable (FPGA) processing elements that execute OpenCL cores whilst significantly minimizing the need for data transfers. The accelerator cores implemented on the ECOSCALE platform correspond to the project use cases and have been the source of a meticulous exploration process for optimal performance results such as execution time. This paper focuses on performance and power optimizations of the Michelsen algorithm. This algorithm is an efficient calculator of the Rachford-Rice equation, which is extensively used in the field of oil Reservoir Simulation (RS). The algorithm was first optimized manually through Vivado HLS and, subsequently, using a Design Space Exploration (DSE) tool we developed in [1]. Here we present up-to-date optimization results based on the latest FPGA ECOSCALE platform in order to reveal bottlenecks, saturation points and design alternatives. The measurements are performed on real data and the evaluation results register significant gains in calculation times over conventional CPU platforms; an achievement that carries added value considering the significantly reduced power consumption costs commonly associated with reconfigurable hardware.

This work is supported by the European Commission under the H2020 Programme and the ECOSCALE project (grant agreement 671632).

D. N. Pnevmatikatos et al. (Eds.): SAMOS 2019, LNCS 11733, pp. 442–454, 2019.
https://doi.org/10.1007/978-3-030-27562-4_32

Keywords: High-Level Synthesis · Accelerator architectures · OpenCL · Exascale

1 Introduction

In order to sustain the ever-increasing demand for storing, transferring and processing data, HPC servers need to improve their capabilities. Scaling in number of cores alone is not a feasible solution any more due to the increasing utility costs and power consumption limitations. Also, while current HPC systems can offer petaflop performance, their architectures limit their capabilities in terms of scalability and energy consumption. To that end, the ECOSCALE [2,3] approach puts forward a scalable programming environment combined with a hardware architecture tailored to the current and future trends of HPC applications. Such an approach can facilitate significant reduction in network traffic as well as energy consumption and execution time. This is due to data processing addressed by reconfigurable technologies, which are economical in energy consumption, memory units spread out across the system as well as the UNILOGIC architecture [2], which allows for efficient sharing of reconfigurable resources in a multi-FPGA system.

At the core of the ECOSCALE system, which consists of multiple interconnected FPGAs, lie the processing elements which can accelerate tasks of the application in hardware. This functionality takes place in the reconfigurable part of the architecture. Hence, those elements, also referred to as accelerator cores, are re-programmable and can be reconfigured in order to implement different types of functionality since the corresponding hardware fabric allows it. These cores are generated using a High-Level Synthesis (HLS) [4] tool and can be deployed as building blocks in a design that has an acceleration oriented purpose. It is imperative, therefore, to ensure that a core's characteristics are best suited to and take maximum advantage of the hosting hardware platform. Only such an accelerator core can yield the best possible performance figures.

This paper documents this process for an ECOSCALE use case algorithm, i.e. Michelsen. The algorithm facilitates the calculation of the Rachford-Rice [5] equation which provides insight as to the flow of liquids in the depths of an oil reservoir. It is a variation on the Newton-Raphson [6] method that provides results at less iterations and, therefore, in less time. The algorithm has gone through a specialized optimization flow, already described in [1]. Here we report up-to-date results that are the product of implementing the Michelsen accelerators on the final ECOSCALE prototype. Hence, further optimization exploration steps have taken place by fine tuning the accelerator core in various aspects.

The various alternatives have been executed on the ECOSCALE platform and real measurements have been obtained allowing for key observations to be extracted, which reveal bottlenecks and saturation points that eventually lead to improved design alternatives on important evaluation criteria such as execution time, power consumption and resource utilization.

The paper is organized as follows. Section 2 presents related work. Section 3 provides a brief but concise introduction to the ECOSCALE architecture. Section 4 presents the design space exploration activities performed on the algorithm and Sect. 5 unfolds a thorough evaluation analysis on the system's performance depending on various design alternatives. Finally, Sect. 6 concludes the paper.

2 Related Work

In the last decade, there has been an increasing interest in employing FPGAs in the HPC domain. In [7] Escobar et al. present a thorough survey on implementing algorithms in heterogeneous HPC infrastructures that integrate diverse resources including CPUs, GPUs and FPGAs, and provide guidelines for employing FPGAs in HPC. In this survey, it has been estimated that half the lifetime cost of HPC platforms is devoted to power consumption. Moreover, another important observation of this survey is that in order to overcome the low-programmability issues of older FPGA-based architectures, High Level Synthesis (HLS) tools such as Vivado HLS (Xilinx) and Catapult C (Mentor Graphics) have been improved supporting languages like C/C++, OpenCL and SystemC. It is also noted that a basic part of the success of CPUs and GPUs is the widespread adoption of libraries, in contrast to custom FPGA based solutions. Finally, this survey notes that the hardware implementation on FPGAs is less efficient than on ASICs due to routing overheads, while the maximum performance included in the FPGA datasheets can be significantly higher than the sustained performance. While this may be true, our performance per watt results are still encouraging.

Several other publications [8–10] present encouraging performance results for FPGAs especially when comparing the performance per watt of FPGAs to their CPU and GPU counterparts. Moreover, these publications also emphasize the fact of low programmability when designers build FPGA accelerators using common design tools, such as the Xilinx tool flow.

Many cases show that FPGAs provide an energy efficient platform and the flexibility required by high-performance applications. Microsoft is using FPGAs in its Bing search engine [11] under the Catapult project to achieve 95% higher performance at a cost of 10% higher power consumption. Cray is using FPGAs as co-processors in the XD1 [12], while delivering a CS500 cluster system with Stratix FPGAs for the Noctua project [13]. Baidu is using low cost FPGAs to accelerate Deep Neural Networks [14], while IBM deploys FPGAs for large NoSQL data stores [15].

With respect to Oil Reservoir Simulation, oil and gas majors were among the enthusiastic early users of GPU acceleration, which led to significant work on improving the performance of related applications [16–21]. While there was some research on accelerating such algorithms on FPGAs [22,23], to the best of our knowledge there is no recent work on FPGA-accelerated Oil Reservoir Simulation algorithms. However, based on our performance and power results in this work, we highly believe that the new powerful FPGAs, including a growing number of LUTs and deploying a wealth of DSPs, can provide a high performance accelerator for oil-related algorithms, while retaining power efficiency which is a major issue for these algorithms due to the huge amounts of data processed.

Our work is part of the ECOSCALE project which collaborates closely with the ExaNeSt [24] and ExaNoDe [25] EU projects, as successor projects of the Euroserver project [26]. ExaNeSt focuses on interconnect while ExaNoDe focuses on improving the on-chip packaging technologies. ExaNeSt has designed and implemented the quad FPGA compute node that we deployed in our prototype.

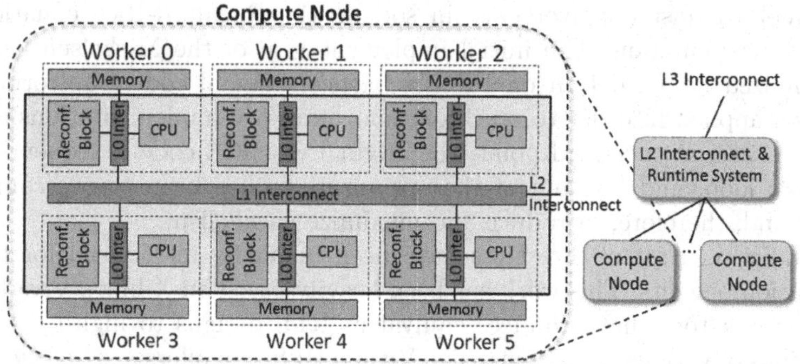

Fig. 1. The Compute Node & its use within the ECOSCALE tree-like structure

3 The ECOSCALE System

ECOSCALE provides a methodology and the corresponding architecture that automatically executes HPC applications on a platform, which, can potentially support millions of accelerators cores, included in the reconfigurable blocks shown in Fig. 1, while taking into account the projected trends and characteristics of HPC applications. Within this context, ECOSCALE aims at introducing FPGA-based acceleration as an integral part of the processing nodes within the system architecture and adapting them to work in an HPC environment.

As explained in [2], at the heart of the ECOSCALE system lie several *Workers* communicating through a multi-layer interconnection, Fig. 1. The actual number of Workers inside a single Compute Node depends on the integration capabilities of future technologies. Each Worker is an independent computing node, which runs an Operating System (OS) that can execute, fork, and join tasks or threads of an HPC application in-parallel with other Workers. It includes a CPU, a reconfigurable block and an off-chip DRAM memory. Such a worker constitutes a perfect match to a single System On Chip (SoC) that combines a processing system along with configurable logic (FPGA), as will be presented in Sect. 5. The communication and synchronization between Workers is performed through a multi-layer interconnection, which allows load and store commands, DMA operations, interrupts, and synchronization between Workers within a

Compute Node. Compute Nodes are interconnected in a tree-like structure to form larger Partitioned Global Address Space (PGAS) regions also hierarchically interconnected.

4 Reconfigurable Cores

In this work we describe the implementation of a kernel that is a variation of the Newton-Raphson method, specifically tuned for the Reservoir Simulation (RS) problem. The respective OpenCL kernel used in this work is "Michelsen" and provides a faster convergence in solving the Rachford-Rice equation for oil reservoir simulation. The initial implementation of the Michelsen kernel is not optimized for execution on FPGAs. Hence, manual code transformations have been applied in order to reach efficient hardware implementations. In the Michelsen case, at each grid point, the original OpenCL code is sequential due to a *while* loop, and the aim of the optimizations has been to overcome this obstacle and, therefore, introduce and maximize parallelism.

In addition, a set of directives have been manually introduced for further optimization benefits. This work has been heavily based on Xilinx's Vivado HLS [27]. This is a tool that produces equivalent RTL designs to high-level model descriptions of various algorithms. The Vivado HLS tool offers a set of *Directives* in order to make the respective codes more efficient for FPGA implementation.

4.1 Code Optimization

The manual analysis consisted of carefully investigating the Michelsen OpenCL kernel. The main characteristic of the algorithm to take advantage of, is that of multiple small *optimization* problems, which are independent of one another. A suitable way for doing this is by pipelining the process.

Listing 1.1. Initial RS pseudocode

```
int a, b
for (all grid points)
    /*initialization*/
    a=amin
    b=bmin
    operation 3
    ...
    while (optimization target)
        b=b+1
        a=a+1
        operation 3
        operation 4
        ...
    end while
    operation 1
    ...
    write result
end for
```

The original OpenCL pseudocode of the target application looks like the one shown in Listing 1.1. The problem here is that this form of the code description does not allow for the use of a pipeline directive due to the *while* loop, otherwise called *optimization* loop since the coefficient it produces approximates, to an acceptable level of deviation, a real-life value. This loop is burdened with dependencies as well as being non-statically bounded, thereby making it a sequential process that cannot be pipelined. This would make the FPGA implementation of such algorithms inefficient due to the inherently slow FPGA clock frequency, which results in significant slow downs compared to the equivalent software running on a conventional processor.

Hence, we propose a method for making such cases efficient for implementation on FPGAs. The HLS tools cannot pipeline non-statically bounded *while* loops but they can pipeline statically bounded loops very efficiently. A restriction is that the small optimization problems have to be independent from one another. Therefore, we had to move the *while* loop to the top of the code and the *for* loop inside it. As such the tool can pipeline the latter which results in significant speedups. Consequently, the pseudocode that represents the modified architecture is shown in Listing 1.2. The two architectures, i.e. *initial* and *optimized* are also graphically depicted in Figs. 2 and 3.

The improvement of such an approach is that the hardware that would remain unused while each loop is executing is now utilized by another optimization problem. Each independent problem will have exactly the same amount of iterations inside the *while* loop as it had with the previous code.

Listing 1.2. Optimized RS pseudocode

```
Buffer data
/*All variables become arrays*/
int a[pipeline_size]
int b[pipeline_size]
while (all problems solved)
    for (n : all grid points)
        if (initialization)
            /*initialization*/
            a[n]=amin
            b[n]=bmin
            operation 3
            ...
        end if
        else /*while loop code*/
            b[n]=b[n]+1
            a[n]=a[n]+1
            operation 3
            operation 4
            ...
            If (optimization reached)
                operation 1
                ...
                write result[n]
                    solved++
            end if
        end else
    end for
end while
```

Finally, an automated tool-based analysis (DSE tool), has been used to enable automated design space exploration and micro-architecture definition in order to acquire the optimal set of directives for each kernel. For a more detailed analysis of the DSE tool usage in this work we refer the reader to [1].

A significant optimization on the kernel compared to the ones presented in [1] was the usage of vector types (float4) for the I/O in order to support 128bit, a feature already supported by the ECOSCALE platform. This, along with the modification of the code segments that perform the I/O in order to invoke 256 word bursts provide significant reduction of the I/O overhead, as will be presented in the following section.

For the initial kernel, a manual set of directives was chosen as the appropriate directives were obvious. The main calculations are done inside the unbounded *while* loop body which cannot take any performance oriented directive. The only meaningful performance improvement was achieved by partitioning the temporary input tables which allowed pipelining the smaller *for* loops over the components in the code, including those inside the *while* loop.

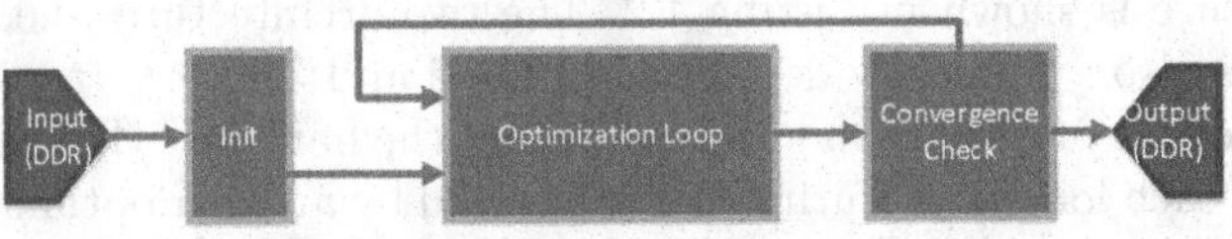

Fig. 2. Block diagram of initial architecture

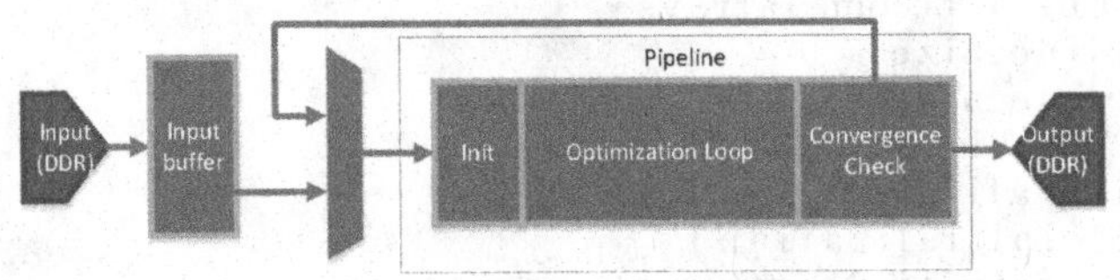

Fig. 3. Block diagram of optimized architecture

5 Evaluation

The generated accelerator cores have been evaluated on the ECOSCALE architecture, using the final prototype that is comprised of a set of Workers. The cores have been mapped to the reconfigurable fabric of one of the Workers and measurements have been obtained with respect to the execution time of the algorithm on two data sets of different size, i.e. data for 100 K and 200K oil Reservoir Simulation grid points. Subsequently, the measured times have been compared against those for the identical procedure but on a different execution platform, i.e. i5 Quad-core CPU at 3.1 GHz.

5.1 Implementation Platform

The hardware platform used is the custom Quad-FPGA Daughter Board (QFDB), which has been designed and manufactured within the context of an ECOSCALE sister-project, i.e. ExaNeSt [24]. It features four Xilinx Zynq Ultra-Scale+ (US+) MPSoC devices, which include a 64-bit quad-core ARM Cortex-A53 platform running up to 1.33 GHz with a dual-core Cortex-R5 real-time processor up to 533 MHz. The board also provides 16 GB of DDR4 SDRAM per US+ device. Subsequently, either a single QFDB is placed on a hosting board called the "Mini-Feeder", or up to eight QFDBs can be placed on a custom motherboard, which is called the "Base-Board" within the ECOSCALE project. Both hosting boards enhance the utilization potential of the QFDB by providing a range of different I/O, and inter-board communication links.

Table 1. Execution time (ms) for a single semi-optimized (pipeline 2) Michelsen core in various configurations.

Time (ms)	Optimization version	Frequency (MHz)
300	No optimization	125
100	32-bit with bursts	125
25.0	128-bit with bursts	125
17.4	-//-	200
15.3	-//-	250
13.8	-//-	300
13.3	-//-	333

5.2 Results

The first evaluation results, that mainly proved the feasibility of our approach, were based on a single-FPGA board and they are presented in [1]. In this work, we mainly reported execution metrics for two accelerators implementing the Michelsen and Hyperbolic algorithms, which are utilized in Oil Reservoir Simulation. The main outcome was that the UNILOGIC/UNIMEM architecture can be implemented; even this simple implementation on a single FPGA triggered a 30% speedup of a multi-core CPU and a 12x less energy consumption.

By analyzing the performance of the accelerator in our QFDB platform, we realized that the problem was mainly I/O bound since the bottleneck was on the AXI interconnect (which is connected to the memory controller) since its standard version does not support more than a mere of two pending transactions. In order to overcome this bottleneck we first implemented burst-enabled transactions. By adding bursts to the original 32-bit configuration the execution time for a 200 MHz design dropped down to one third (1/3). Then we observed, that the AXI interconnection is still the bottleneck since it supports only two burst transactions outstanding, and thus cannot saturate the path to the memory;

in particular we measured the interconnection latency to be 300 ns. This is the latency from e.g. a read request from an accelerator until the corresponding data arrive from memory, through the MPSoC's DDR controller. This remains almost unchanged no matter what the programmable logic's (configurable logic) clock speed; this is due to the fact that most of the latency comes from the MPSoC path to the DDR. In particular, when the accelerator was clocked at 200 MHz we measured a 60 clock cycles (cc) delay, while at 125 MHz we got 37cc, which both give $(60cc \times \frac{1}{200}) \simeq (37cc \times \frac{1}{125}) \simeq 300$ ns. And these measurements were executed with the MPSoC set at its highest possible clock frequency (1.33 GHz for our -2 speed grade FPGA).

The next step was to upgrade the accelerators and all the design blocks in its datapath to match the maximum bus-width supported by the AXI implementation on the new FPGAs, i.e. 128-bits while still supporting bursts. Looking in Table 1 we can see the considerable performance improvement. This new version not only allows four times more data to be sent to the accelerator, but it also offers a reduced latency path, which triggers faster completion of the issued requests, and thus newer request issuing, keeping in mind the AXI's two pending transactions limitation. We now measured a latency of 50 cc at 200 MHz and 76 clock cycle ate 300 MHz which give a latency of $(50cc \times \frac{1}{200}) \simeq (76cc \times \frac{1}{300}) \simeq 250$ ns. This is due to the now removed width converter that has been issued inside the interconnect.

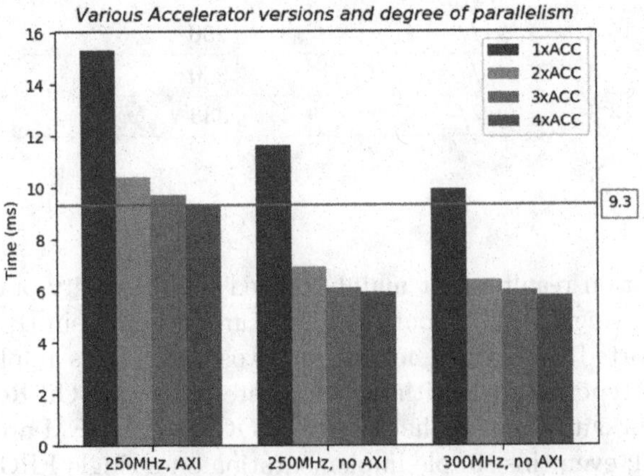

Fig. 4. Results for multiple accelerator cores, running in paraller, in a single FPGA, either with an interveining AXI interconnect or directly connected to the MPSoC ports.

In the remaining rows of Table 1, we can see how the execution time drops as we improved the design's clock frequency, until reaching the 333 MHz frequency barrier allowed for the MPSoC ports by Xilinx tools.

Moving on with the performance quest, we added more accelerators to run in-parallel. The results can be seen in Fig. 4. Two different versions were considered. One has an AXI interconnect between the accelerators and the MPSoC (and hence the DRAM memory). Instead, in the other version the accelerators are connected directly to the MPSoC ports. We have implemented and executed the second version, which offers better performance. As this design deploys many accelerator cores, it results in higher FPGA resource utilization, and thus the maximum frequency could now reach up to 300 MHz, a bit lower than the maximum of 333 MHz.

Observing the results, we should note that the intervening AXI interconnect hinders performance. Even with wide 128 bit buses and bursts, the latency of the path to the memory, although quite low, again does not allow the path to be saturated and fully utilized. This is the reason we get these differences in execution times. To make sure it was this case, we again reverted to observing the hardware execution. Indeed, the latency of the non AXI version, drops from 250 ms down to 180 ms. Chipscope assisted measurement showed 36cc @200 MHz ($36cc \times \frac{1}{200} \simeq 180$ ns). Also, the 5.8 ms execution time with 4xACC (Fig. 4), is the lowest execution time and quite lower that the 9.3 ms achieved at the quad-accelerator version of the Trenz platform. This corresponds to a 60% improvement from our previous reported results, which translates to a 2 times faster execution than the 4-threaded CPU run. Another information worth noticing on this Figure, is that execution speed reaches a boundary somewhere around the 5.8 ms to 6 ms mark, and the improvement in frequency cannot offer much once we come near this. This actually reveals a point where the DDR path throughput gets saturated. We thus succeeded in parallelizing the originally compute bound algorithm until it became memory bound on the current platform. Of course, depending on the platform used, this could probably be further improved (Table 2).

Table 2. Software execution times (ms)

Software				
Platform	CPU		CPU OpenMP (4 thread)	
Data size	100K	200K	100K	200K
Michelsen	29	56	11.7	22.3

It is clear that the execution of the optimized accelerator cores on reconfigurable hardware yields the best performance and this is better displayed in Table 3. First, the optimized cores offer a speedup of 5 over single-thread CPU execution and a speedup of 2 over a 4-thread execution.

Moreover, considering that the CPU consumes significantly more power, the advantages of using reconfigurable hardware becomes even more apparent since the CPU comes at a typical cost of 77 W of power consumption whereas an

Table 3. Execution times (ms) on different hardware platforms

Hardware			
Data size	100K	200K	SpeedUp vs. SW
Initial 8-core	117	235	0.1
Opt. 4-core AXI	9.3	18	1.2
Opt. 4-core no AXI	5.8	11.2	2

average US+ FPGA's programmable logic power consumption reaches 5.9 W. The FPGA implementation is 26x more energy efficient vs. the i5 CPU. This is the number corresponding to the 4x Michelsen cores 300 MHz design, and is measured with the help of the many power sensors featured by the QFDB. This design flavor reaches about 50 GFLOPs, and thus we get a power efficiency of 8.5 GFLOPs per Watt.

What is more, although this is a number comparable to the Green500's GFLOPs/watt CPU measurements, and also real measurements on GPUs, this can be much improved on such an FPGA platform. Our implemented and primarily used Michelsen accelerator actually has a data transfer to calculation rate that does not favor consumption metrics. Accelerator cores that execute more calculation per data moved, will benefit greatly by the FPGA's low power consumption.

6 Conclusion

The ECOSCALE project is a collective effort of European academic and industrial institutions to bring closer the utilization of reconfigurable technology so as to execute HPC applications at exascale speed. This is achieved through the introduction of a novel architecture, real-time reconfiguration and programming model all integrated into one framework.

This paper demonstrates that by using a combination of design optimizations, we can execute on the ECOSCALE platform mathematical cores very efficiently. The ECOSCALE prototype, i.e. QFDB, is a powerful hardware platform that hosts four state-of-the-art FPGAs. These FPGAs are an ideal platform for implementing compute-intensive processing algorithms such as the one used in the RS use case of ECOSCALE.

Specifically, in this publication we outline the incremental process with which this algorithm was first transformed into a parallel process, so that we take advantage of the parallel nature of the FPGA. Subsequently, it was subjected to a number of design modifications that led to significant performance improvements that were measured during the evaluation phase of the project. These have been very notable and they are almost two times faster than a state-of-the-art multicore CPU while consuming an order of magnitude less power.

These results, therefore, substantiate the belief that using reconfigurable hardware could help in achieving the performance as well as power efficiency targets for future generation HPC systems.

References

1. Malakonakis, P., Georgopoulos, K., Ioannou, A., Lavagno, L., Papaefstathiou, I., Mavroidis, I.: HLS algorithmic explorations for HPC execution on reconfigurable hardware - ECOSCALE. In: Voros, N., Huebner, M., Keramidas, G., Goehringer, D., Antonopoulos, C., Diniz, P.C. (eds.) ARC 2018. LNCS, vol. 10824, pp. 724–736. Springer, Cham (2018). https://doi.org/10.1007/978-3-319-78890-6_58
2. Mavroidis, I., et al.: ECOSCALE: reconfigurable computing and runtime system for future exascale systems. In: 2016 Design, Automation and Test in Europe Conference and Exhibition, Dresden, Germany, 14–18 March 2016, pp. 696–701 (2016)
3. ECOSCALE Web-Site. http://www.ecoscale.eu/
4. Coussy, P., Morawiec, A.: High-Level Synthesis: From Algorithm to Digital Circuit, 1st edn. Springer, Heidelberg (2008). https://doi.org/10.1007/978-1-4020-8588-8. ISBN 1402085877, 9781402085871
5. Whitson, C., Michelsen, M.: The negative flash. J. Fluid Phase Equilib. **35**, 51–71 (1989)
6. Abramowitz, M.: Handbook of Mathematical Functions, With Formulas, Graphs, and Mathematical Tables. Dover Publications (1974). ISBN 0486612724
7. Escobar, F.A., et al.: Suitability analysis of FPGAs for heterogeneous platforms in HPC. IEEE Trans. Parallel Distrib. Syst. J. **27**(2), 600–612 (2016)
8. Blott, M.: Reconfigurable future for HPC. In: International Conference on High Performance Computing Simulation (HPCS), pp. 130–131, July 2016
9. Cilardo, A.: HtComp: bringing reconfigurable hardware to future high-performance applications. IJHPCN J. **12**(1), 74–83 (2018)
10. Kobayashi, R., et al.: OpenCL-ready high speed FPGA network for reconfigurable high performance computing. In: International Conference on High Performance Computing in Asia-Pacific Region, HPC Asia 2018, Tokyo, pp. 192–201, 28–31 January 2018
11. Putnam, A., et al.: A reconfigurable fabric for accelerating large-scale datacenter services. Commun. ACM **59**(11), 114–122 (2016)
12. El-Araby, E., et al.: Virtualizing and sharing reconfigurable resources in high-performance reconfigurable computing systems. In: Second International Workshop on High-Performance Reconfigurable Computing Technology and Applications, Austin, TX, pp. 1–8 (2008)
13. Plessl, C.: Bringing FPGAs to HPC production systems and codes. In: Fourth International Workshop on Heterogeneous High-performance Reconfigurable Computing, workshop at Supercomputing (2018)
14. Ouyang, J., et al.: SDA: software-defined accelerator for large-scale DNN systems. In: IEEE Hot Chips 26 Symposium (HCS), Cupertino, CA, pp. 1–23 (2014)
15. Brech, B., et al.: Data engine for NoSQL - IBM power systems edition. White Paper, 2015
16. Chen, Z., Liu, H., Yu, S., Hsieh, B., Shao, L.: GPU-based parallel reservoir simulators. In: Erhel, J., Gander, M.J., Halpern, L., Pichot, G., Sassi, T., Widlund, O. (eds.) Domain Decomposition Methods in Science and Engineering XXI. LNCSE, vol. 98, pp. 199–206. Springer, Cham (2014). https://doi.org/10.1007/978-3-319-05789-7_16

17. Zaza, A., et al.: A CUDA based parallel multi-phase oil reservoir simulator. Comput. Phys. Commun. **206**, 2–16 (2016)
18. Klie, H.M., Sudan, H.H., Li, R., Saad, Y.: Exploiting capabilities of many core platforms in reservoir simulation. In: SPE Reservoir Simulation Symposium. Society of Petroleum Engineers, January 2011
19. Esler, K., et al.: Realizing the potential of GPUs for reservoir simulation. In: ECMOR XIV-14th European Conference on the Mathematics of Oil Recovery, September 2014
20. Yu, S., et al.: GPU-based parallel reservoir simulation for large-scale simulation problems. In: SPE Europec/EAGE Annual Conference. Society of Petroleum Engineers, January 2012
21. Bayat, M., Killough, J.E.: An experimental study of GPU acceleration for reservoir simulation. In: SPE Reservoir Simulation Symposium. Society of Petroleum Engineers, February 2013
22. Barros, A., et al.: Performance evaluation model based on precision reduction and FPGAs applied to seismic modeling. In: Simpósio em Sistemas Computacionais, October 2011
23. Medeiros, V., Barros, A., Silva-Filho, A., de Lima, M.E.: High performance implementation of RTM seismic modeling on FPGAs: architecture, arithmetic and power issues. In: Vanderbauwhede, W., Benkrid, K. (eds.) High-Performance Computing Using FPGAs, pp. 305–334. Springer, New York (2013). https://doi.org/10.1007/978-1-4614-1791-0_10
24. Katevenis, M., et al.: The ExaNeSt project: interconnects, storage, and packaging for exascale systems. In: Euromicro Conference on Digital System Design (DSD), Limassol, pp. 60–67 (2016)
25. Rigo, A., et al.: Paving the way towards a highly energy-efficient and highly integrated compute node for the exascale revolution: the ExaNoDe approach. In: Euromicro Conference on Digital System Design, Vienna, pp. 486–493 (2017)
26. Durand, Y., et al.: EUROSERVER: energy efficient node for European micro-servers. In: 17th Euromicro Conference on Digital System Design, Verona (2014)
27. Vivado Design Suite User Guide v2017.4, Xilinx Inc. http://www.xilinx.com/

Accelerating Automotive Analytics: The M2DC Appliance Approach

Giovanni Agosta[1], Carlo Brandolese[1], William Fornaciari[1(✉)], Nicholas Mainardi[1], Gerardo Pelosi[1], Federico Reghenzani[1], Michele Zanella[1], Gaetan Des Courchamps[2], Vincent Ducrot[2], Kevin Juilly[2], Sébastien Monot[2], and Luca Ceva[3]

[1] DEIB – Politecnico di Milano, Milan, Italy
{giovanni.agosta,carlo.brandolese,william.fornaciari,nicholas.mainardi, gerardo.pelosi,federico.reghenzani,michele.zanella}@polimi.it

[2] AS+ Groupe Eolen, Malakoff, France
{gaetan.descourchamps,vincent.ducrot,kevin.juilly, sebastien.monot}@eolen.com

[3] Vodafone Automotive Telematics, Zurich, Switzerland
luca.ceva@vodafone.com

Abstract. The Modular Microserver DataCenter (M2DC) project provides low-energy, configurable, heterogeneous servers for applications that focus on the elaboration of large data sets, but can take advantage of performance enhancement provided by transparent acceleration techniques. In this paper, we exemplify the M2DC approach through one of the project's use cases, namely automotive Internet of Things analytics. We present the main goals of the use case and we show how an appropriate M2DC microserver can be used to accelerate the application without significant modifications to its code.

Keywords: Data analytics · Embedded systems · Compilers · Applied cryptography · Automotive

1 Introduction

Analytics applications extracting valuable knowledge from the large amount of data collected by Internet of Things connected devices are already becoming a killer application for data centres. In particular, the automotive application domain is expected to expand vastly in the next few years. The 20% of the circulating cars will be connected vehicles by 2020 and this number will double by 2024. This makes the market of automotive telematics viable, paving the way for a large number of different applications. Consequently, the market space for fleet management and added value services will skyrocket, with a compound annual growth rate of 65%[1].

[1] http://analysismason.com.

D. N. Pnevmatikatos et al. (Eds.): SAMOS 2019, LNCS 11733, pp. 455–469, 2019.
https://doi.org/10.1007/978-3-030-27562-4_33

To cope with the requirements of value-added applications leveraging automotive telematics data, data-centres need to update their technologies. The Modular Microserver for Data Centers (M2DC) project aims at prototyping a highly efficient and customizable cost-optimized server architecture [8,21]. These servers are composed of microserver computing resources, which can be tailored to a specific application domain. In the M2DC approach, an application developer can select from a range of turnkey appliances that are easily configured, deployed, and maintained. The appliance is composed of a collection of hardware resources and of a software stack needed to exploit them in a transparent way.

In this work, we present an example of the M2DC customised microserver, tailored for an automotive data analytics scenario provided by Vodafone Automotive Telematics, and leveraging specific accelerators – called System Efficiency Enhancements (SEE) in the M2DC parlance – developed by Politecnico di Milano and AS+ Groupe EOLEN. The SEEs focus on accelerating key portions of the data analytics application, namely the decryption of source data and the computational kernels of the analysis. The complete appliance provides a key demonstrator for the M2DC microservers.

Organization of the Paper. The rest of the paper is organized as follows. Section 2 introduces the M2DC approach to provide turnkey appliances for data centres. Section 3 describes the automotive use case and its requirements, while in Sect. 4 we describe the main System Efficiency Enhancements which will be embedded in the IoT Analytics appliance, obtaining an high-performance, low-energy solution for the automotive use case. Finally, Sects. 5 and 6 present the roadmap towards higher technology readiness levels for the use cases and the conclusions that can be drawn from this work.

2 The M2DC Approach

The M2DC project [13] aims at developing turnkey appliances for specific application domains, leveraging a novel modular server architecture featuring heterogeneous processing elements, including GPGPU and custom-developed reconfigurable accelerators. Such appliances are going to achieve a lower Total Cost of Ownership (TCO), thanks to improved energy-efficiency, dependability, customisation, scalability, and integration. The M2DC servers are composed of a baseboard which connects up to 16 microservers with a dedicated high-speed, low-latency communication network, which instead supports also connection to storage and I/O extensions. Microservers can feature Intel x86_64 or ARM Aarch64 server processors, as well as low-power solutions (e.g., based on NVIDIA Jetson), GPGPUs, or FPGAs, allowing individual appliances to tailor the architectures to their specific energy/performance trade-offs. The M2DC appliances can hinge upon a set of so called System Efficiency Enhancements (SEE), which are low-power accelerators for common tasks in the data-centres scenario, such as bulk data encryption or pattern matching. Given the requirements of M2DC microservers, in particular achieving a low TCO for appliances and allowing the flexible allocation of a task among different nodes, ASIC implementations are not considered in the M2DC project. Full details of the server architecture and its possible configurations can be found in [21].

3 The Automotive IoT Scenario: Driver Identification

Willing to assess the effectiveness of M2DC infrastructure in providing high throughput and energy efficiency to applications addressing real world data analytics scenarios, we focused on a common task in the automotive area: the processing and the analysis of data gathered by on-vehicle monitoring devices.

3.1 The Driver Identification Scenario

The adoption of embedded devices in vehicles, equipped with a variety of sensors, has recently been observed as an emerging trend, especially among insurance companies. The data collected are often used to: (a) develop more complex and adaptive Driver Assistance System (DAS) or (b) profile drivers, in particular for anti-fraud purposes. In this context, there are mainly two similar problems in literature: Driving Style Classification and Driver Identification. In the first case, the goal is to classify a driver according to predefined driving styles (e.g. calm/aggressive, lawful/unlawful) [20] in order to provide feedback to the driver with the extent of optimizing the energy usage of the car or improving the ride comfort. In the second case, the goal is to uniquely identify the driver for a given trip, which is useful for insurance purposes and anti-theft methods [1,14]. In particular, the IoT application, presented in this work, addresses the problem of identifying the number of people usually driving a vehicle, a problem closer to the latter case. To deal with this type of problem, three main approaches have been identified in a comprehensive survey of the literature [20]: rule-based, model-based and learning-based.

In particular, data-driven machine learning algorithms became one of the promising solutions due to the increasing volume of data gathered by sensors. Nevertheless, there are two relevant limitations in most of the previous works: they rely on *input data* mainly retrieved with invasive methodologies [9,11,18] and they leverage supervised techniques [9,18,24] (e.g., SVM, Random Forest Classifier, Neural Network). The former requires the reading from the vehicle Electronic Computed Board or the CAN bus, leading to compatibility issues between different car manufactures and safety-related concerns. The latter approaches require a labelled training data, which is generally harder to be obtained in real world application scenarios.

Our proposed approach overcomes the aforementioned issues through a data analytic workflow specifically designed to tackle the identification of number of drivers problem by using *unsupervised* technique on data collected with *non-invasive* methodologies. In this section, we present this workflow, which will be accelerated on the M2DC infrastructure. Further details of this workflow can be found in [19].

Driver Identification Workflow. In the context of the M2DC project, Vodafone automotive provided some data collected on real vehicles. This dataset contains motion data (speed of the vehicle and accelerations on the three axis), geolocalization data (position and altitude) and some additional information, such as the type of road run across by the vehicle (highway, urban etc.) and its speed limit. These data are sampled at 1 Hz rate. A set of such measurements from engine switch-on to engine switch-off is denoted as *trip*. To devise our workflow, we hinge upon a reasonable assumption: there is only one driver for each trip, hence we can perform driver identification trip-wise instead of sample-wise.

The idea of our workflow is to represent a trip with a set of features characterizing the driving style; we expect that trips of the same driver are quite similar, hence by clustering all the trips of the same vehicle, the trips of the same driver form a cluster. Therefore, the workflow estimates the number of usual drivers as the number of clusters found in the set of trips of the same vehicle. The first challenge of this approach resides in the design of a set of features able to characterize the driving style. To this extent, we discard the geolocalization data from the trips, since these information are not related to the driving style. Then, we devise a set of features computed from the remaining data of a trip. These features are either statistical measures (mean, variance, skewness, kurtosis) of motion data or specific values representing a particular aspect of the driving style (number of speed infringements, number of acceleration peaks to denote a nervous driving style).

A second challenge of our workflow is the need to reduce the number of features characterizing each trip. This avoids the well-known *curse of dimensionality* issue: points in high dimensional spaces are generally too far from each other to get any cluster. In our case, a trip characterized by m features is considered as a point in m dimensional space by the clustering algorithm, hence we want to keep this number m low. This requirement is not satisfied by the set of features of our application scenario, whose size is $m = 40$. Therefore, the well-known Principal Component Analysis (PCA) is used to shrink the dimensionality of the data and fulfill this requirement for the clustering algorithm. Indeed, PCA is able to represent the dataset in new components, such that the first few ones are sufficient to retain an high percentage of statistical significance of the original data. In our case, by retaining 75% of statistical significance, we are able to shrink the dimensionality of the data from 40 to 5–7 components, depending on the specific dataset of a vehicle.

After dimensionality reduction given by PCA, the trips are ready to be clustered. Among the variety of clustering approaches, given that specifying the number of clusters to be formed in advance would make the results of our workflow meaningless, we choose to employ density-based clustering. In particular, we employ the *dbscan* [10] algorithm, whose input parameters are estimated according to heuristics proposed in [10, Section 4].

Data Confidentiality Issues. Data processed by the IoT application concern the driver's personal behavior, such as speed infringements and GPS locations. Therefore, if these data are stored on a remote server, their confidentiality against possible security breaches needs to be guaranteed. To address this relevant issue, we are going to add a decryption layer to the application, allowing the storage of encrypted data. The addition of this layer should be straightforward, since there already exists an R wrapper for the well-known OpenSSL cryptographic library. Furthermore, among the System Efficiency Enhancements (SEE) developed in the context of M2DC project, there is an FPGA accelerator for bulk data encryption. Thus, we are planning to employ this Cryptographic SEE available in the project (see Sect. 4.1) to speed-up data decryption needed by the IoT application.

3.2 Implementation Details and Preliminary Experimental Results

A baseline implementation of the proposed workflow is a single core application, employing the R programming language. This choice is motivated by two factors: (a) R is widely employed for data analytics tasks, since it provides several packages and functionalities commonly required in these applications; (b) R is supported by the heterogeneous compilation toolchain developed by AS+, which enables the possible heterogeneous platform exploitation running the algorithm both on CPU and on GPU, improving both the performances and the energy consumption of the application (see Sect. 4.2). Hinging upon this baseline implementation, we evaluate the application workflow focusing on two aspects: (a) the estimation of the algorithm accuracy; (b) the analysis of the computational complexity and scalability of the data analytics portion of the application, i.e. PCA and clustering. Conversely, since feature extraction is mainly I/O bound, we will not mention its performance evaluation.

Accuracy Analysis. At this step we aim to evaluate if the proposed approach produces realistic results. Unfortunately, the dataset provided by Vodafone Automotive is unlabelled: we do not know the actual number of drivers for each vehicle. This hardens the validation of our workflow, since we do not know if the number of drivers identified is correct. To overcome the aforementioned limitations and maintain consistency with the geosocial conditions of the dataset, we derive the average number of drivers per vehicle for UK, the country where Vodafone Automotive actually gathered these data. From the publicly available government data [12] we get the average number of adult people per vehicle and the number of drivers per adult people, thus obtaining an average value of drivers per vehicle of 1.095. Our workflow identifies more than one driver in around 10% of the vehicles, which is in line with the aforementioned deduced geosocial data.

Scalability Analysis. The goal of this step is providing a scalability evaluation in terms of execution time with respect to the number of trips n of the same vehicle. First of all, we expect that the DBSCAN algorithm, which has a complexity of $O(n \log n)$, dominates the average-case complexity of the overall workflow, given the linear execution time of PCA. Then, in order to measure the actual execution times, we setup a server machine, equipped with AMD Opteron-8435 cores and 128 GB of RAM, running the single-core R implementation of the application. The experimental results, shown in Fig. 1, highlight

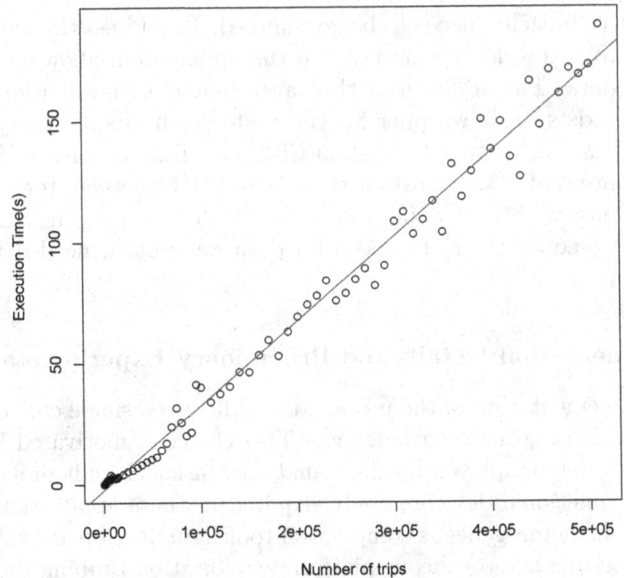

Fig. 1. Execution time of PCA and clustering w.r.t. the number of trips. The red line represents the linear regression model: $Time \approx 3.490 \cdot 10^{-4} \cdot n$. (Color figure online)

that the value of execution time can be approximated by a linear trend, due to the minimal impact of the $\log n$ term. Regarding the absolute execution times, we observe that the current application is able to perform PCA and clustering for a vehicle with $500k$ trips in approximately 3 minutes. We remark that this analysis is expected to be performed for thousands of customers, in turn requiring several days of computation. Therefore, in order to improve the scalability of the application with the number of vehicles, we will hinge upon the R compilation toolchain developed by AS+ (described in Sect. 4.2), which provides the following benefits and capabilities: (a) the application could be run on a single GPU instead of several high-end CPUs, in turn allowing the decrease of both TCO and energy consumption; (b) the R application is compiled instead of being interpreted, thus it is executed directly from machine code; (c) the compilation toolchain is able to perform several optimizations which are generally hard to be directly applied on R code (e.g., exploiting data parallelism and the vectorized operations available in recent CPUs).

4 The IoT Analytics Appliance

The M2DC appliance employed for the IoT application will be tailored to the performance and energy requirements of the application. As the IoT application focuses on the processing of large quantities of data, with a computational effort mostly devoted to small set of kernels, the plan is to use x86_64 servers attached to accelerators suitable for two types of kernels: encryption primitives employed to access the securely stored data and acceleration of R primitives. Specifically, for the encryption acceleration, the appliance will include an FPGA module based on the Altera Stratix 10 SX[2] series. The FPGA will be exploited via a dedicated OpenSSL engine. For the acceleration of R primitives, the appliance will enclose a parallel R optimized implementation, obtained with the R compilation toolchain, which performs data analytics computation of our workflow.

In the rest of this section, we provide an overview of these two acceleration techniques, including initial experiments carried out in isolation. During the final phase of the project, we will integrate the application on the final testbed.

The resulting appliance will be highly reusable, thanks to the seamless integration of the accelerators in standard components: the cryptographic SEE employs OpenSSL as its interface, whereas the data analytics accelerating toolchain is installed as part of the R compiler. Thus, the application can be run with or without the accelerators with minimal modifications – essentially, it is sufficient to specify if the application employs default OpenSSL implementations or the ones provided by our SEE to perform the cryptographic operations.

4.1 Accelerating Cryptography

One of the fundamental application domains for datacenters is represented by bulk data encryption and decryption, as it has to be performed on the data being stored as well as on data being transmitted or received. For this purpose, fast disk encryption software support has been explored using GPGPUs [2].

Cryptography SEE proposed in M2DC [7] exploits the OpenCL programming model to realize high-performance FPGA accelerators. This way provides a viable and more versatile alternative to the use of ad-hoc cryptographic accelerators, currently available in high-end server CPUs only. OpenCL provides functional portability across a wide range of platforms, which have recently been extended to support FPGAs. However, it is well known that performance portability is much harder to achieve. A domain-specific analysis for symmetric encryption highlighted that even within the architectural class of GPGPUs there are major differences, requiring an almost entire rewriting of the encryption code to achieve optimal performance [3]. We therefore analyzed the programming practices to exploit the High Level Synthesis (HLS) toolchains available to deploy OpenCL programs onto FPGA based accelerators, identifying a set of best-practices to design OpenCL kernels for FPGA. In particular, we found out that single work-item, single work-group implementations are more suitable for FPGAs. We also identified other best-practices related to loop optimization, caching techniques, memory coalescing, I/O latency hiding and host-side synchronization, whose details can be found in [7].

By exploiting the best-practices identified, we were able to obtain high throughput and energy efficient implementations for all the nine ISO standard ciphers implemented by the Cryptographic SEE. The comparison between our

[2] The accelerator was developed on an Arria 10 GX board, but Stratix 10 is the expected target for the deployment of the accelerator in the M2DC context.

Table 1. Comparison of the energy efficiency of the OpenCL implementations for FPGA accelerator of the nine ISO standard block ciphers, on a Intel Xeon E5-1505M v6 CPU based host with DDR4-2133 DRAM. The CPU AES implementation employs the dedicated `AES-NI` instructions

Block Cipher	Platform	Throughput (MB/s)	Power (W)	Energy Efficiency (GB/J)
AES	FPGA	1020.8	15.02	67.96
	`AES-NI`	1678.4	25.79	65.09
HIGHT	FPGA	824.0	21.87	37.68
	CPU	20.0	26.01	0.77
DES	FPGA	764.8	12.62	60.61
	CPU	85.0	22.24	3.82
CAST5	FPGA	814.2	13.63	59.75
	CPU	132.0	23.14	5.70
SEED	FPGA	930.8	14.49	64.23
	CPU	102.3	22.46	4.54
Camellia	FPGA	957.6	15.06	63.59
	CPU	198.0	22.68	8.73
MISTY1	FPGA	1006.0	25.59	39.31
	CPU	22.0	26.07	0.84
CLEFIA	FPGA	1202.0	22.60	53.19
	CPU	3.0	26.38	0.11
Present	FPGA	979.0	25.57	38.29
	CPU	11.2	23.87	0.46

FPGA implementations and CPU ones in terms of throughput and energy efficiency is reported in Table 1. We observe that the throughput achieved on the FPGA by all ciphers is between 750 MB/s and 1200 MB/s, with a speed-up over software implementations ranging from 5× to 400×. It is worth noting that the throughput of the FPGA implementations is currently limited by the PCI-Express channel employed in our host. At the moment this limits the communication to be half-duplex, introducing significant idle time in FPGA kernels due to the time spent on waiting data transfer completion. In particular, we believe throughput could even been doubled in case a full-duplex communication channel is available. From the point of view of energy efficiency, our FPGA implementations achieve an average improvement of 22.78× (geometric mean) and 79× (arithmetic mean) in terms of GB encrypted per Joule spent. Finally, we remark that our AES implementation is more energy efficient than Intel `AES-NI`, which is an hardware AES implementation included in Intel CPUs usable via a specific assembly instruction added to the ISA. Indeed, our implementation exhibits a comparable throughput and lower power consumption.

Currently, the cryptographic SEE is embodied in an ad-hoc OpenSSL engine, making its usage quite transparent to the application. Indeed, OpenSSL library exhibits a standard interface for each cryptographic operation; OpenSSL engines provide different implementations of these interfaces. Therefore, an application simply needs to specify which engine must be employed to implement interfaces for several cryptographic operations, requiring a minimal modification to the application code. Therefore, shipping the SEE in an OpenSSL engine enables an easy integration at application level, which is a desirable feature to boost the usage of the cryptographic SEE.

As discussed in Sect. 3, we will introduce an encryption layer on the IoT application to ensure data confidentiality and we will hinge upon this SEE to accelerate the cryptographic operations required by the IoT application. In this scenario, where an R wrapper exists for OpenSSL, the availability of the SEE as an OpenSSL engine greatly aids its integration. Nevertheless, the interface exposed by this wrapper appears insufficient for the integration of the SEE. Indeed, the wrapper provides only AES algorithm as a symmetric cipher and there are no functions to manage OpenSSL engines. Nevertheless, we analyzed the wrapper and we identified the modifications required in order to handle OpenSSL engines and other symmetric encryption algorithms directly from the R application; thus, we will obtain such an enriched wrapper without a significant effort through these simple modifications (Fig. 2).

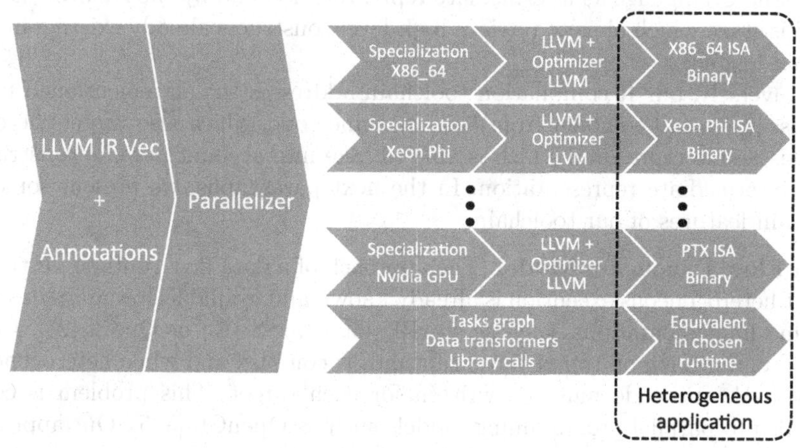

Fig. 2. Back-end architecture for the compiler

4.2 Accelerating Data Analytics R Application

R is a publicly available implementation of the high-level S language for statistical computing. The R language is now widely used for statistical calculations in various application fields such as biology, medicine, financial applications.

R language is not widely regarded as a platform for developing scalable, high-performance codes: indeed, it is an interpreted language and the execution of programs typically involves dynamic allocation of large data structures, particularly arrays. However, several approaches have emerged to address both performance and scalability of R programs, which have however showed some relevant limitations. In particular, distributed approaches rely on process-based distribution framework such as MPI and Map Reduce. These approaches imply that each process is a separate instance of the R interpreter without any shared memory. These approaches include RMPI[3], an implementation of MPI bindings in R which enables master-slave like scheduling, and Snow Extension (Simple Network Of Workstations))[4], which provides a further level of abstraction above existing communication frameworks, masking communications details and enabling the creation of different kinds of *clusters*. Although they partially address the scalability issues of R, these approaches do not solve the overhead introduced by the interpretation layer and hardly target heterogeneous systems. Just In Time (JIT) compilers minimize performance degradation of interpreted languages by caching the code once it is translated. There are two R packages providing JIT compilation[5,6], which have been deprecated since 2011. Lastly, full blown compilers, such as RCC [22], are advanced optimizing compiler for R or S programs. RCC is based on three successive stages: static analysis of R program to extract call graphs and dataflows, translation of R programs to C and eventually optimization of translated C code. This approach suffers from the complexity brought by using tshe C language as intermediate representation and by the resulting static analysis stage which aims to retrieve high-level constructs already existing in the original language.

Conversely, our R compilation toolchain addresses the aforementioned limitations: it is a full compiler from R to machine code, which also targets heterogeneous architectures and which is able to take into account parallel constructs in its intermediate representation. In the next paragraphs, we present some of the main features of our toolchain.

Data Flow Execution Model. The approach of a data flow runtime for transparent heterogeneous execution is already known and available nowadays in some runtime implementations, such as starPU [6], StarSS [15] or Quark [25]. However, programming on top of those runtimes is complex and when heterogeneity is involved, one code must be written for each target. This problem is common also to parallel programming models such as OpenCL [3–5]. Our approach aims to provide transparent compilation for heterogeneous targets, with direct support of data flow runtime, for an high-level DSL like R. To ease the achievement of these goals, we define our own programming model, which relies on the following concepts:

---

[3] https://cran.r-project.org/web/packages/Rmpi/index.html.
[4] https://cran.r-project.org/web/packages/snow/index.html.
[5] http://stat.ethz.ch/R-manual/R-devel/library/compiler/html/compile.html.
[6] http://www.milbo.users.sonic.net/ra/jit.html.

- all data are either managed by the runtime or used for control flow and simple parameter of a function;
- a program is a bunch of actions on numerous data, where the control of ordering the actions is done by evaluating data dependency;
- a task is a function with two kind of parameters: managed data references and control parameter which are copied argument and cannot be reaccessed outside of the task.

Therefore, we need a runtime compatible with these concepts and that handles multiple implementation of a task. It also requires an efficient heuristic to choose the place of execution and the best implementation of a task on this place. StarPU fits in those constraints, so we chose it as our effective execution runtime.

A Modular Design. The full toolchain and runtime support is designed as a modular framework by leveraging the modular property of LLVM [16] based compilers. Following the design principles of LLVM framework, the compilation workflow is split into two main stages: the input program is first translated by the front-end into an Intermediate Representation (IR), which is further translated and optimized for the target architecture by the back-end. Therefore, the front-end is programming language specific, while the back-end is related to a specific architecture. Our toolchain strongly decouples these stages, allowing to independently choose the front-end and back-end to be employed. In order to support multiple architectures from one representation, we did extend the LLVM IR at some points. These IR extensions are then handled by specialized LLVM passes in order to generate a complete program on top of starPU. For instance, vectorization is easier to be performed in the front-end, thus we need a way to express vectors operation without the knowledge of vector unit size. To this extent, we introduce an unknown sized vector type to handle manipulation of data in an abstract way.

Code Parallelization. Despite R programming model is sequential, our toolchain aims at building parallel program from a standard R program. In particular, we can induce parallelism if the functions are using non overlapping data at some point; the analysis of these data dependencies is easy since each task announces both the data it uses and the intent on them.

Task Based Runtime Support. Our toolchain, when compiling the task code itself, generates multiple implementations for each possible target as well as an initialization function which creates the runtime multi-implementation structure binding each implementation to the runtime. For instance, we generate multiple versions of one task to handle different vector unit sizes on an x86 processor (128, 256 and 512 bits wide). We also generate the test functions to execute the best possible implementation depending on runtime parameters. The calls for an extracted task are then transformed into a runtime call for further submission to the runtime. The runtime itself is built on top of starPU, with some wrapping function to ease code generation and support function for managed data manipulation. Another interesting feature of our toolchain is the availability of a runtime interface to prepare plugin development for supporting other runtimes without any modification of the compiler itself, provided that this new runtime is able to implement the interface to our toolchain. In conclusion, by hinging upon our toolchain, it is possible to obtain a parallel heterogeneous (CPU/GPU) application from a sequential single-core R one without significant modifications to the application code.

5 Towards Advanced Applications

In this section, we highlight some open issues in the IoT automotive data collection and analysis scenario; these problems will not be investigated in the context of M2DC project, but their solution provide some interesting research and innovation directions that are planned for the next future.

Data Privacy. The collection and usage of data from private car and fleets managers can open new business avenues, including insurance price customisation based on driver profiling. Inertial and geo-located data can be collected from a vehicle through aftermarket telematic boxes, endowed with GPRS communication capabilities as well as sensing capabilities. However, such data, which are sufficient for basic applications such as crash detection, are insufficient for more complex ones such as the driver profiling performed in the M2DC scenario. In this case, an integration with third party information, such as meteorological or speed limit data, acquired commercially or from (reliable) open data sources, is needed. Furthermore, in a real-world scenario, different telematic boxes may collect different data, or use different format, becoming a further source of heterogeneity for the assembled data.

Given the nature of the data, privacy is particularly important: simple anonymization by removing the contract holder name and replacing it with a unique identifier can be easily proved insufficient. As an enlightening example, let us consider the scenario of a malicious employer willing to acquire personal information on his commuting employees. By selecting contracts that consistently show trips ending at or near the company premises during the work start times, the employer can identify a set of employees. Then, by identifying the most common destination of the last trips for each day of the identified employees, the employer can identify an approximate location of their residence, which can be easily compared with data legitimately held by the employer to associate the contract ID with the employee identity, thus foiling the anonymization. Needless to say, the employer can now easily check if one of the employees has, e.g., regular visits to a local hospital, and thereby infer information about the employee's health status he has no right to be privy to.

It is important to understand, however, that the personal information items cannot be easily separated from the non-personal, but useful, elements of the information. For instance, the data could be more strongly anonymized by removing georeferences, but then they would become much less useful to insurance companies willing to customize prices based on the locations usually traveled and the frequency of accidents on those routes.

Scalability. Another key challenge is scalability. Whereas for small fleets trip information can be stored at a fine grain in data centers, scaling up would easily produce a veritable data deluge. In this case, it is necessary to rethink the data collection phase, the processing, and the storage. A viable solution would be to move part of the computation, namely the feature extraction, from the cloud server nearer to the sensor [17]. Since the sensor itself has limited computation capabilities, this implies adding an edge node to the system. The edge node may be endowed with reasonably powerful processing elements at a limited cost, thus enabling complex feature extraction to take place before the data transmission. However, although such an edge node would not require a significant amount of energy to affect the overall vehicle system, key-off operation would be much less viable, unless the edge node is turned off. As a result, the best scenario would be to enable a flexible runtime configuration of the IoT system (sensor–edge node–cloud) such that the edge node can be excluded when operating off the vehicle battery and turned back into operation when the vehicle is running, as potentially discussed in [26].

6 Conclusions

In this article, we presented the automotive IoT scenario employed in the M2DC project to demonstrate the effectiveness of the microserver approach, combined with some of the SEEs developed. We showed how we plan to achieve significant speedups against our preliminary implementation, without significant impact on the cost of development of the application, thanks to the transparent embedding of the SEEs in the existing software stack.

During the next months, we will finalize the integration of CryptSEEs to fully expose their cryptographic capabilities to the R OpenSSL wrapper and we will address the scalability issues by hinging upon the R compilation toolchain. In the longer term, the application will be enriched with additional components aiming at providing increased data privacy so that third party applications can leverage the data set, as well as improving scalability to larger vehicle fleets through a flexible allocation of feature extraction (currently performed on the data centre servers) to edge and Fog nodes and integration of the driver identification in a more complex, multi-application scenario [23].

Acknowledgements. Work supported by the EU's H2020 programme (grant n.688201), Modular Microserver DataCentre (M2DC).

References

1. Agosta, G., Barenghi, A., Brandolese, C., Fornaciari, W., Pelosi, G., et al.: V2i cooperation for traffic management with SafeCOP. In: 2016 Euromicro Conference on Digital System Design (DSD), pp. 621–627, August 2016. https://doi.org/10.1109/DSD.2016.18
2. Agosta, G., Barenghi, A., De Santis, F., Di Biagio, A., Pelosi, G.: Fast disk encryption through GPGPU acceleration. In: 2009 International Conference on Parallel and Distributed Computing, Applications and Technologies, pp. 102–109, December 2009. https://doi.org/10.1109/PDCAT.2009.72

3. Agosta, G., Barenghi, A., Di Federico, A., Pelosi, G.: OpenCL performance portability for general-purpose computation on graphics processor units: an exploration on cryptographic primitives. Concurrency Comput. Pract. Experience **27**(14), 3633–3660 (2014). https://doi.org/10.1002/cpe.3358
4. Agosta, G., Barenghi, A., Pelosi, G., Scandale, M.: Towards transparently tackling functionality and performance issues across different OpenCL platforms. In: 2nd International Symposium on Computing and Networking (CANDAR), pp. 130–136, December 2014. https://doi.org/10.1109/CANDAR.2014.53
5. Agosta, G., Fornaciari, W., Massari, G., Pupykina, A., Reghenzani, F., Zanella, M.: Managing heterogeneous resources in HPC systems. In: Proceedings of PARMA-DITAM 2018, pp. 7–12. ACM (2018). https://doi.org/10.1145/3183767.3183769
6. Augonnet, C., Thibault, S., Namyst, R., Wacrenier, P.A.: StarPU: a unified platform for task scheduling on heterogeneous multicore architectures. Concurrency Comput. Pract. Experience **23**(2), 187–198 (2011)
7. Barenghi, A., Madaschi, M., Mainardi, N., Pelosi, G.: OpenCL HLS based design of FPGA accelerators for cryptographic primitives. In: Proceedings of the 13th International Workshop on Security and High Performance Computing Systems (SHPCS 2018), pp. 3:1–3:8. IEEE Computer Society, July 2018
8. Cecowski, M., Agosta, G., Oleksiak, A., Kierzynka, M., et al.: The M2DC Project: Modular Microserver DataCentre. In: 2016 Euromicro Conference on Digital System Design (DSD), pp. 68–74, August 2016. https://doi.org/10.1109/DSD.2016.76
9. Enev, M., Takakuwa, A., Koscher, K., Kohno, T.: Automobile driver fingerprinting. In: Proceedings on Privacy Enhancing Technologies, vol. 2016, no. 1, pp. 34–50 (2016). https://doi.org/10.1515/popets-2015-0029
10. Ester, M., Kriegel, H., Sander, J., Xu, X.: A density-based algorithm for discovering clusters in large spatial databases with noise. In: Proceedings of the 2nd International Conference on Knowledge Discovery and Data Mining (KDD-96), Portland, Oregon, USA, pp. 226–231 (1996). http://www.aaai.org/Library/KDD/1996/kdd96-037.php
11. Fugiglando, U., et al.: Driving behavior analysis through CAN bus data in an uncontrolled environment. CoRR abs/1710.04133 (2017). http://arxiv.org/abs/1710.04133
12. UK Government: Driving licence holding and vehicle availability (nts02), National Travel Survey (2016)
13. Kierzynka, M., et al.: Data centres for IoT applications: the M2DC approach (invited paper). In: 2016 International Conference on Embedded Computer Systems: Architectures, Modeling and Simulation (SAMOS), pp. 293–299, July 2016. https://doi.org/10.1109/SAMOS.2016.7818361
14. Kwak, B.I., Woo, J., Kim, H.K.: Know your master: driver profiling-based anti-theft method. CoRR abs/1704.05223 (2017). http://arxiv.org/abs/1704.05223
15. Labarta, J.: StarSs: a programming model for the multicore era. In: PRACE Workshop 'New Languages and Future Technology Prototypes' at the Leibniz Supercomputing Centre in Garching (Germany) (2010)
16. Lattner, C., Adve, V.: LLVM: a compilation framework for lifelong program analysis & transformation. In: International Symposium on Code Generation and Optimization, CGO 2004, pp. 75–86. IEEE (2004)
17. Li, C., Xue, Y., Wang, J., Zhang, W., Li, T.: Edge-oriented computing paradigms: a survey on architecture design and system management. ACM Comput. Surv. **51**(2), 39:1–39:34 (2018). https://doi.org/10.1145/3154815

18. Ly, M.V., Martin, S., Trivedi, M.M.: Driver classification and driving style recognition using inertial sensors. In: 2013 IEEE Intelligent Vehicles Symposium (IV), pp. 1040–1045, June 2013. https://doi.org/10.1109/IVS.2013.6629603
19. Mainardi, N., Zanella, M., Reghenzani, F., et al.: An unsupervised approach for automotive driver identification. In: Proceedings of the 1st ACM International Workshop on Intelligent Embedded Systems Architectures and Applications. ACM (2018). https://doi.org/10.1145/3285017.3285023
20. Martinez, C.M., Heucke, M., Wang, F.Y., Gao, B., Cao, D.: Driving style recognition for intelligent vehicle control and advanced driver assistance: a survey. IEEE Trans. Intell. Transp. Syst. **19**(3), 666–676 (2018). https://doi.org/10.1109/TITS.2017.2706978
21. Oleksiak, A., Kierzynka, M., Piatek, W., Agosta, G., et al.: M2DC - modular microserver datacentre with heterogeneous hardware. Microprocess. Microsyst. **52**, 117–130 (2017). https://doi.org/10.1016/j.micpro.2017.05.019
22. Qi, F., Zhang, X., Wang, S., Mao, X.: RCC: a new programming language for reconfigurable computing. In: 2009 11th IEEE International Conference on High Performance Computing and Communications, pp. 688–693, June 2009. https://doi.org/10.1109/HPCC.2009.74
23. Sansottera, A., Zoni, D., Cremonesi, P., Fornaciari, W.: Consolidation of multi-tier workloads with performance and reliability constraints. In: 2012 International Conference on High Performance Computing Simulation (HPCS), pp. 74–83, July 2012. https://doi.org/10.1109/HPCSim.2012.6266893
24. Vaitkus, V., Lengvenis, P., Žylius, G.: Driving style classification using long-term accelerometer information. In: 2014 19th International Conference on Methods and Models in Automation and Robotics (MMAR), pp. 641–644, September 2014. https://doi.org/10.1109/MMAR.2014.6957429
25. Yarkhan, A., Kurzak, J., Dongarra, J.: Quark Users' Guide. Electrical Engineering and Computer Science, Innovative Computing Laboratory, University of Tennessee (2011)
26. Zanella, M., Massari, G., Galimberti, A., Fornaciari, W.: Back to the future: resource management in post-cloud solutions. In: Proceedings of the Workshop on INTelligent Embedded Systems Architectures and Applications, INTESA 2018, pp. 33–38. ACM, New York (2018). https://doi.org/10.1145/3285017.3285028. http://doi.acm.org/10.1145/3285017.3285028

Predictive Resource Management for Next-Generation High-Performance Computing Heterogeneous Platforms

Giuseppe Massari, Anna Pupykina, Giovanni Agosta, and William Fornaciari(✉)

Politecnico di Milano – DEIB, via Ponzio 34/5, Milano, Italy
{giuseppe.massari,anna.pupykina,giovanni.agosta, william.fornaciari}@polimi.it

Abstract. High-Performance Computing (HPC) is rapidly moving towards the adoption of nodes characterized by an heterogeneous set of processing resources. This has already shown benefits in terms of both performance and energy efficiency. On the other side, heterogeneous systems are challenging from the application development and the resource management perspective. In this work, we discuss some outcomes of the MANGO project, showing the results of the execution of real applications on a emulated deeply heterogeneous systems for HPC. Moreover, we assessed the achievements of a proposed resource allocation policy, aiming at identifying a priori the best resource allocation options for a starting application.

Keywords: HPC · Heterogeneous systems · Resource management

1 Introduction

Thanks to the major efforts brought on by the industrialised countries, in the upgrade of their High-Performance Computing (HPC) infrastructures, *Exascale computing* is becoming a closer reality. For example, the Summit supercomputer, for which a theoretical peak performance of 200 Petaflops has been declared, on November 2018 scored 143 Petaflops on the High Performance Linpack benchmark[1]. Although Exascale computing promises a major increase of available computational capabilities, to solve scientific and industrial challenges, the management of HPC infrastructures is growing in complexity. This is due to both the sheer size, the massive energy requirements (Summit nears the 10 MW power envelope) and the architectural complexity introduced by the presence of heterogeneous computing elements (such as CPUs, GPUs, or HW accelerators).

New access methods, such as Cloud HPC [29], are pushing for achieving a high utilisation level of such infrastructures, while hosting the execution of diverse applications, under the constraint of a limited power envelope. To meet

[1] www.top500.org.

D. N. Pnevmatikatos et al. (Eds.): SAMOS 2019, LNCS 11733, pp. 470–483, 2019.
https://doi.org/10.1007/978-3-030-27562-4_34

such requirements, while managing to the growing complexity previously discussed, is a challenging task for which new resource management approaches are required. Several efforts are ongoing in Europe to address these issue, developing appropriate tools to combine programming models and resource management [8,24].

Main Contribution. In this paper, we explored the definition of multi-level policies to manage the computing resources (cores and memory). Since the policy identification can be quite time consuming, we propose a faster but simpler management policy at fine (temporal) grain, as well as a slower management policy [23] at a coarser grain. We show how the proposed approach allows a resource manager to identify a priori the best resource mapping solutions, given the application description and the topology of the target hardware node. We demonstrate the effectiveness of the proposed approach, by using a Low-Density Parity Check (LDPC) coding application, and an *Image Processing Filter*, executed on a deeply heterogeneous emulated HPC node.

Organization of the Paper. The rest of this paper is organised as follows. In Sect. 2 we briefly introduce the target heterogeneous architecture and the resource management support developed and exploited for the application execution. In Sect. 3 we describe the proposed multi-level policy, while in Sect. 4 we assess its effectiveness through an experimental campaign on an emulated HPC prototype. Finally, in Sect. 5 we review related approaches in the state of the art, and in Sect. 6 we draw some conclusions and highlight future research directions.

2 Background: HPC and the MANGO Project

2.1 Deeply Heterogeneous Architectures

To achieve the necessary performance/watt figures in future Exascale HPC systems, architectural heterogeneity has been widely proposed. Its effectiveness is already demonstrated by the large number of heterogeneous systems listed in the Top500[2] and Green500[3] lists. In particular, the Green500, which focuses on performance/watt rather than pure performance, is dominated by heterogeneous systems, typically coupling general purpose multi-core CPUs with accelerators such as GPGPUs. Reconfigurable accelerators then, have been proposed as a further step for improving the capabilities and introduce flexibility in HPC infrastructures [14,15].

The MANGO project [10] aimed at exploring future architectures exhibiting even more heterogeneity. In MANGO, the general-purpose cores associated to a node (GN) are supported by an heterogeneous set of processing units (including multi/many-core and accelerators), forming an *Heterogeneous Node (HN)*. Considering that (1) the HN can include multiple memory nodes, and (2) the

[2] www.top500.org.
[3] www.green500.org.

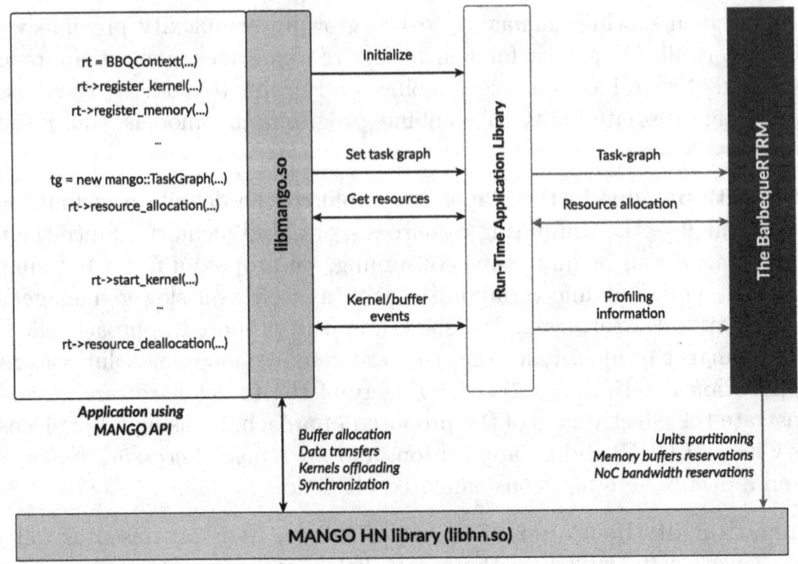

Fig. 1. MANGO Programming Model and the BarbequeRTRM integration.

processing units are interconnected through a Network-on-Chip (NoC) [9,31,32], it follows that performing resource allocation is a critical task. On architectures like this in fact, we may experience significant differences among resource allocation solutions, in terms of performance and, of course, power consumption.

2.2 Resource Management

The resource management infrastructure developed for supporting heterogeneous platforms explored in MANGO, is characterized by a tight integration between the programming model and the resource manager daemon. Through the programming model, the developer can build a task-graph based description of the application, along with per-task performance requirements. This description is then made available to the resource manager, which can lift the developer from the burden of implementing a logic for mapping the application's tasks (or kernels) and offloading them to the specific processing unit. As well as, mapping the memory buffers, needed to exchange data between tasks, onto the suitable HN-side memory nodes [2]. The resource manager is therefore aware of the system requirements and constraints, as well as of all the applications requirements. Accordingly, it can allocate resources taking into account both the system status, from the hardware perspective, and the application requirements and priorities.

In Fig. 1, we sketched the integration between programming model and resource manager (the *BarbequeRTRM*) [3,25,26]. The application uses the API provided by the programming library (*libmango*) to build the task-graph based description. This is sent to the resource manager by using a specific function call.

An intermediate *Run-Time Application Library* is then responsible of managing the communication flow between application and resource manager. Once the task-graph is available on the resource manager side, the mapping policy is invoked. After the policy execution, the task-graph encloses the resource mapping information, that will be exploited by the programming library to transparently perform task offloading and buffer allocation, by using the API provided by the underlying *HN library (libhn)* [7].

3 Hierarchical Policy Definition and Update

3.1 Design-Time Driven Resource Mapping

Problem Statement. We are given a HN topology, $H = \{U_f, U_b, M_f, M_b\}$, where U_f and U_b indicates the set of free and busy units, respectively, M_f and M_b indicates the set of free and busy memory units and task-graph $Tg = <B, K>$ where B is a set of requested memory buffers and K is a set of kernels. For each buffer $b \in B$ of size $S(b)$, there is a kernel or set of kernels $K(b)$ which uses b (e.g. kernel read buffer $k \xrightarrow{r} b$ and/or write to buffer $k \xrightarrow{w} b$). For each kernel $k \in K$ there is a set of preferred target processing architectures $Arch_{prefs}(k) = <Arch^0, ..., Arch^l>$ that is noted by developer. Each application has a specific priority level $appl = \{appl_h, appl_n\}$, where the high priority application $appl_h$ needed to be allocated with the requested QoS on the current HN, and the normal priority application $appl_n$ could be rescheduled on the another HN.

We aim to find all possible partitions $P = \{<M, U>_0, ..., <M, U>_m\}$ appropriate to allocate b on HN, where M is a memory unit of size $S(M)$, $M \in M_f$, $U \in U_f$ and $\forall k_i \in K\ \exists u_j \in U$ that able to execute $k_i(Arch(u_j) \in Arch_{prefs}(k_i))$, and range them by the criteria $C = \{C^m, C^{prefs}\}$. The criterion C^m defines the memory-kernel characteristics in order to select the best memory modules and includes the following specifications:

- bandwidth between the allocated processing units and the memory module;
- distance between the allocated processing units and the memory module(in hops);
- direction of data transfer (in/out);
- available space on the memory module.

More criteria could be added depending on the application requirements. The criterion C^{prefs} defines the level of the processing unit l_{arch} in $Arch_{prefs}$.

In this paper, we focused on the design-time exploration of the best units and memory nodes mapping solutions. Given the size of the solution space in fact, the time needed to find good solutions, can be often too long for considering the execution of the policy at run-time. The BarbequeRTRM allows us to perform this exploration and insert the set of mapping solutions found into a specific file, called *recipe* [20]. This file is used to specify both the per-task requirements and, optionally, a set of resource mapping solutions that the resource manager should consider at run-time.

ALGORITHM 1: Simulation based heuristic units mapping

```
Data: Task-graph Tg =< B, K >, a set of preferred accelerators architectures
      Arch_prefs(K) =< Arch^0, ..., Arch^l >, a topology H = {U_f, U_b, M_f, M_b}
Result: an ordered set of partitions P = {< M, U >_0, ..., < M, U >_m}
1 Buffers ⇐ BruteForce(H, B_f);
2 Archs ⇐ BruteForce(Tg, Arch_prefs) ;
3 foreach a_i ∈ Archs do
4     Units ⇐ FindAvailableUnits(U_f, a_i) ;
5     foreach u_i ∈ Units do
6         if u_i ∉ P then
7             b_i ⇐ Select(Buffers);
8             P ⇐ newPartition(u_i, b_j) ;
9 P ⇐ RangePartitions(P, Scores(P)) ;
```

All combinations of the preferred processing architectures can be found by following a brute-force exploration. As well as all the possible mappings of the kernel to the specific unit. However, since this approach can be time consuming, other than leading to find a redundant set of mapping solutions, we propose a heuristic policy, based on the exploitation of historical data about the previous application executions. The heuristic goal is to limit the number of the resource partitions to consider for the allocation, on the basis of the minimal mean distance to the memory unit. The pseudo-code is reported in Algorithm 1. The first line looks over all possible buffers allocations on memory units. Line 2 creates a set of all task mappings to preferred architectures. At lines 3 and 4, for each possible combination of architectures, the sets of free units U_f of a particular HN topology are searched. Next, at lines 5–8 for each unit set that is not already included, a new partition is created with the memory mapping selected as a best of possible mappings. At the end, all partitions are sorted. Buffer mapping and partition ranging are based on the fuzzy multi-criteria analysis, with pairwise comparison of the memory-unit specifications along with the memory usage prediction in the simulation based approach. In general, simulation based approaches update a *partition score* on the basis of continuously updated information about the state of the system resources. By predicting the future state of resources we can improve the quality of the resource allocation decisions [1]. The overview of partition evaluation algorithm is presented in Algorithm 2. The Algorithm 2 first evaluates each buffer across all mappings (lines 2 and 3) by accumulating kernel-memory characteristics for each kernel what reads and/or writes to this buffer (lines 4–8). Some of these characteristics change during simulation (e.g., available bandwidth) or are constant (e.g., distance in hops). At line 9 all kernel-memory characteristics are sent to a fuzzy multi-criteria analysis [23] supplemented by the calculation of the resources utilization prediction. Lines 10–11 multiplies the scores of the current buffer with the scores of the previously evaluated buffers. In the next step, Algorithm 2 for each partition (line 12) calculates the score of the allocation according to the unit architecture in the

ALGORITHM 2: Partitions evaluation

Data: Task-graph $Tg =< B, K >$, a set of partitions $P = \{< M, U >_0, ..., < M, U >_m\}$, a set of preferred processing architectures $Arch_{prefs}(K) =< Arch^0, ..., Arch^l >$

Result: Scores $s = \{s_0, ..., s_m\}$

1 $s[] \Leftarrow 1.0$;
2 **foreach** $b_i \in B$ **do**
3   **foreach** $p_j \in P$ **do**
4         $m_i \Leftarrow p_j(b_i)$;
5   **foreach** k *such that* $\exists k \xrightarrow{r} b_i$ **do**
6             $prop_r(p_j) \Leftarrow GetProperties(m_i, p_j(k))$;
7   **foreach** k *such that* $\exists k \xrightarrow{w} b_i$ **do**
8             $prop_w(p_j) \Leftarrow GetProperties(m_i, p_j(k))$;
9     $eval(b_i)[] \Leftarrow BufferAnalysis(m_i, prop_r, prop_w)$;
10   **foreach** $e \in eval(b_i)$ **do**
11         $s[i] \Leftarrow s[i] \times e$;
        /* with keeping negative scores to indicate the predicted usage of m_i by $appl_h$ */
12 **foreach** $p_i \in P$ **do**
13     $score_{prefs} \Leftarrow 1$;
14   **foreach** $u \in p_i$ **do**
15         $score_{prefs} \Leftarrow score_{prefs} \times n_k^{level(Arch_{prefs})}$;
16     $err \Leftarrow Allocate(p_i)$;
17     $Deallocate(p_i)$;
18   **if** $err! = Success$ **then**
19         $s[i] \Leftarrow OutOfMemory$;
20   **else**
21         $s[i] \Leftarrow Normalise(s[i])$;
22     $s[i] \Leftarrow s[i] \times 100 \div score_{prefs}$;

list of preferred architectures (lines 13–15). After that, at line 16–17 the algorithm attempts to allocate and deallocate buffers (without changing statistics and calculating prediction). On allocation failure, at line 19 the score changes to indicate the memory segmentation. On the allocation success, score is normalized (line 21). Finally, at line 22 the overall score is calculated.

4 Experimental Evaluation

4.1 Hardware Setup

The experimental hardware platform consists of a FPGA-based prototype, on which we deployed an heterogeneous set of custom processors, distributed in tiles interconnected through a 2D-mesh Network-on-Chip (NoC). The system

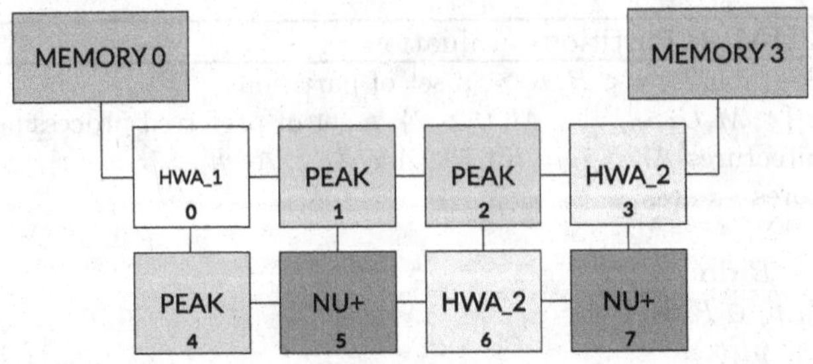

Fig. 2. Topology of the MANGO platform (single Heterogeneous Node) used for the experimental evaluations.

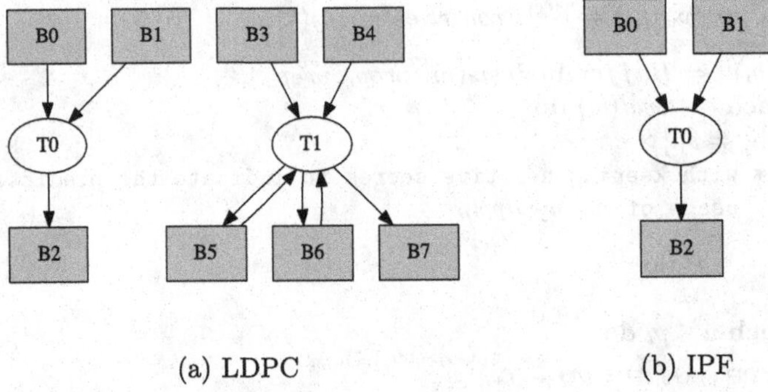

Fig. 3. Task-graph based description of the test applications.

also includes multiple memory nodes, each attached to a different tile. In the MANGO project, we explored several possible hardware configurations. For our experimental evaluations, we considered the one shown in Fig. 2. This includes 8 processing units: 3 dual-core PEAK processors (MIPS), 2 GPU-like units for SIMD executions (NU+) and 3 HW accelerators for vectors and image processing. This configuration includes two memory nodes, attached to tiles 0 and 1.

4.2 Test Applications

In this work, we used a *Low-Density Parity Check (LDPC)* application and an *Image Processing Filter*. In particular, LDPC is a type of linear error correction algorithm, devised in the 1960s [12], that have become practical to implement only since the 1990s [19], due to its high computational requirements.

In Fig. 3 we observe the task-graph based description of the two applications. For LDPC, the resource allocation policy must find good mapping solutions for the 8 buffers and the offload of 2 kernels. The kernel binaries are available only for architecture PEAK. The Image Processing Filter instead, uses 2 input buffer to store frames coming from two streams, plus 1 output buffer to store the result. The processing is performed by a single kernel, for which two mapping options are available: PEAK and HW accelerators (HWA_2).

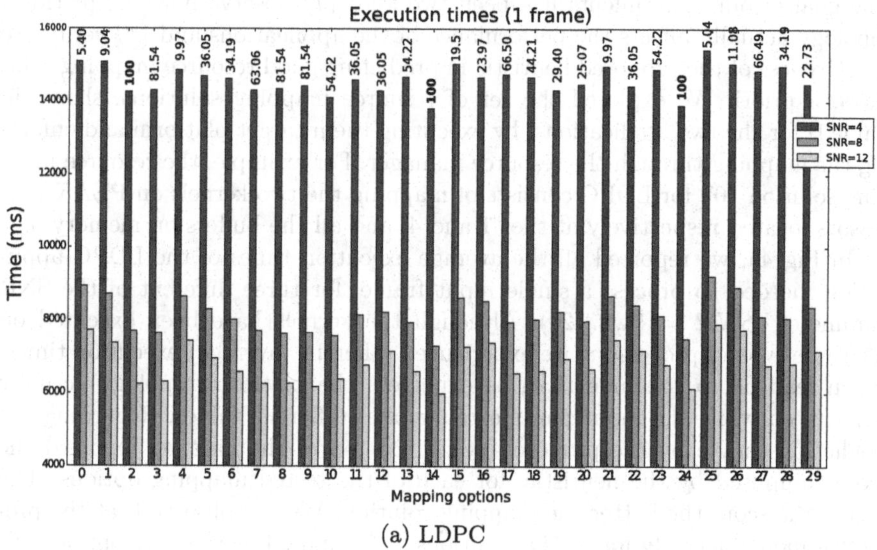

(a) LDPC

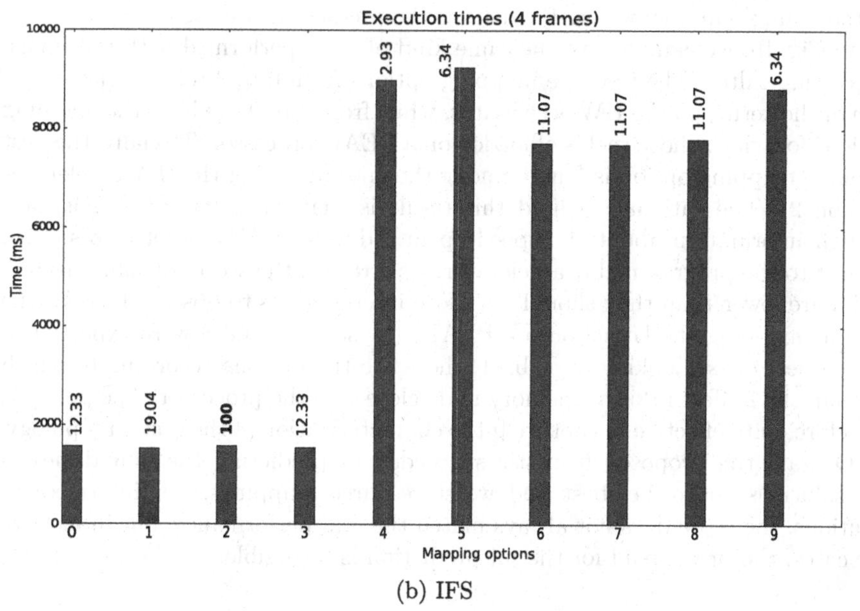

(b) IFS

Fig. 4. Execution times for each explored mapping solution. The LDPC SNR input parameter has been set to 4, 8 and 12 (no noise). The Image Processing Filter has been executed for processing streams of 4 frames.

4.3 Experimental Results

The goal of our experiments has been two-fold: *(1)* observe how the platform topology actually affects the performance of the applications and *(2)* verify the effectiveness of the proposed heuristic in predicting good resource mapping solutions, a priori. We explored the set of resource mapping solutions, shown in Table 1, for the two applications, by executing them target platform and enforcing the mapping through the resource manager. For example, the resource mapping solution "0" for LDPC consists of mapping the two kernels on PEAK processors located respectively at tiles 1 and 4, and all the buffers on memory 3.

In Fig. 4a, we reported all the average execution times of the LDPC application, needed to process a single input frame, for three different of the SNR parameter ($SNR = \{4, 8, 12\}$). Although the kernels have been executed on the same type of processors, we experienced different (average) execution times, which lead us to conclude that, as expected, the platform topology actually impacts on while the input parameter assumes different values. Regarding the predictions made by the proposed policy, on top of the bars we reported the score computed by the heuristic, for each of the tested mapping options. The higher the score the better the mapping solution. We can observe that the predictive model actually found the solutions 2, 14 and 24 as the best options. To the contrary, solutions 0, 1, 4 and 25 were expected to be the worst performing. In the real executions, we verify whether the prediction was valid.

In Fig. 4b, we can observe the same kind of tests performed with the Image Processing Filter. The resource mapping options from 0 to 3 refer to the execution of the kernel on the HW accelerator, while from 4 to 9, we have the mapping options for which the kernel is offloaded on a PEAK processor. Trivially, the best resource mapping option is found among the ones including the HW accelerator (option 2). The rationale behind this result is that the policy does not have enough information about the speed-up introduced by HW accelerators, with respect to the programmable accelerator. As a result, the scores of solutions 0, 1 and 3 are lower than they should be. More interesting is to observe how for the options mapping the kernel onto a PEAK, the set 6, 7 and 8 were expected to be the best ones. Looking at Table 1, these are the options according to which we map the buffers into the memory node closest to the processor. The policy is therefore quite effective in capturing the characterization of the system topology.

Overall, the proposed heuristic succeeded in predicting the boundaries of the solutions space, i.e, best and worst resource mappings. For intermediate solutions, the score does not always match the real performance, but in most of the cases, the prices paid for the misprediction is negligible.

5 Related Works

Traditionally, resource management in HPC is limited by assigning to each application a set of physical nodes at the job scheduler level taking into account different aspects of the cluster architecture, such as the topology of the machine

Table 1. Explored resource mapping solutions for LDPC application running on the target MANGO platform.

LDPC			IFS		
Solution ID	Processors	Memories	Solution ID	Processors	Memories
0	1 4	3 3 3 3 3 3 3 3	0	3	0 0 0
1	4 1	3 3 3 3 3 3 3 3	1	6	3 3 3
2	1 4	0 0 0 0 0 0 0 0	2	3	3 3 3
3	4 1	0 0 0 0 0 0 0 0	3	6	0 0 0
4	1 4	0 0 0 3 3 3 3 3	4	4	3 3 3
5	4 1	0 0 0 3 3 3 3 3	5	1	3 3 3
6	1 4	3 3 3 3 0 0 0 0	6	2	3 3 3
7	4 1	0 0 3 0 0 0 0 0	7	4	0 0 0
8	4 1	0 0 0 0 3 0 0 0	8	1	0 0 0
9	1 4	0 0 3 0 0 0 0 0	9	2	0 0 0
10	1 2	3 3 3 3 3 3 3 3			
11	2 1	3 3 3 3 3 3 3 3			
12	1 2	0 0 0 0 0 0 0 0			
13	2 1	0 0 0 0 0 0 0 0			
14	1 2	0 0 0 3 3 3 3 3			
15	2 1	0 0 0 3 3 3 3 3			
16	1 2	3 3 3 3 0 0 0 0			
17	2 1	0 0 3 0 0 0 0 0			
18	2 1	0 0 0 0 3 0 0 0			
19	1 2	0 0 3 0 0 0 0 0			
20	4 2	3 3 3 3 3 3 3 3			
21	2 4	3 3 3 3 3 3 3 3			
22	4 2	0 0 0 0 0 0 0 0			
23	2 4	0 0 0 0 0 0 0 0			
24	4 2	0 0 0 3 3 3 3 3			
25	2 4	0 0 0 3 3 3 3 3			
26	4 2	3 3 3 3 0 0 0 0			
27	2 4	0 0 3 0 0 0 0 0			
28	2 4	0 0 0 0 3 0 0 0			
29	4 2	0 0 3 0 0 0 0 0			

to determine the best choice among the available nodes based upon their position within the network [13], or emphasizing various targets, such as power-awareness [22] or resilience-awareness [5]. More recently, resource management has focused on the specific type of applications, such as MapReduce-based applications. A widely used cluster resource managers in the Hadoop system, e.g. YARN [27] or Mesos [16], allow allocating resources, such as CPU and memory, to multiple big data applications. However, none of them can directly support the management of the deeply heterogeneous resources, out-of-box. Based on the YARN framework, the resource management strategy and scheduling mechanism to suit for the heterogeneous CPU-FPGA cluster was proposed in [17]. This approach modifies the resource representation scheme that manages logical FPGA accelerator functionality for better scheduling and provides development interfaces for easily usage of FPGAs. An heterogeneous ARM/FPGA SoC was considered as the target architecture for the power capping technique proposed in [28]. This approach combines power capping with coordinated dynamic voltage and frequency scaling (DVFS), data partitioning and core allocations for efficient use of both ARM processor and streaming accelerators on FPGA concurrently. A similar approach, leveraging a hardware implementation for the power capping, was proposed in [30,33], based on the modeling of DVFS and power gating actuators provided in [34]. A run-time task allocator for heterogeneous many-core platforms, SPARTA, was presented in [6]. It uses the variability in workload memory and computational requirements in order to provide energy efficient task-to-core allocations. SPARTA is proposed for a generic Linux environment and single-ISA shared memory heterogeneous multi-processing. Three resource allocation algorithms suitable for heterogeneous HPC systems focused on the efficient management of critical, accelerator-like resources were presented in [21]. In the context of heterogeneous high-end embedded systems, co-scheduling of multiple application has also been studied. A recent survey of such approaches, and a technique that leverages Linux Control Groups can be found in [18].

6 Conclusions

In this work, we briefly introduced the MANGO Project, in which we explored the architectural possibilities of next-generation HPC systems, based on a deeply heterogeneous set of processing units and multiple memory nodes. We developed a programming model integrated with a resource management framework. We proposed a heuristic-based policy to predict the best resource mapping solutions for each application, such that the resource manager can quickly pick them at run-time, without introducing additional overhead. We validated the policy by executing two real applications on a emulated heterogeneous platform prototype, enforcing different resource mapping options. We observed how the policy succeeded in the identification of the best and the worst options.

Future works will go in the direction of collecting more information about the behaviour of the applications and response of the hardware resources, especially in scenarios of resource contention. With this knowledge, we will be able to improve the policy and therefore the capabilities of the resource manager in taking decisions at run-time. Furthermore, we plan to extend the capabilities of the programming model to include dynamic recompilation of the kernels, through a partial dynamic compilation library supporting arbitrary C++ code [4].

Acknowledgments. This research was partially funded by the H2020 EU projects "MANGO" (grant no. 671668) and "RECIPE" (grant no. 801137 [11]).

References

1. Ababei, C., Ghorbani Moghaddam, M.: A survey of prediction and classification techniques in multicore processor systems. IEEE Trans. Parallel Distrib. Syst. **PP**(99), 1 (2018). https://doi.org/10.1109/TPDS.2018.2878699
2. Agosta, G., Fornaciari, W., Massari, G., Pupykina, A., Reghenzani, F., Zanella, M.: Managing heterogeneous resources in HPC systems. In: Proceedings of PARMA-DITAM 2018, pp. 7–12. ACM (2018). https://doi.org/10.1145/3183767.3183769
3. Bellasi, P., Massari, G., Fornaciari, W.: Effective runtime resource management using Linux control groups with the BarbequeRTRM framework. ACM Trans. Embed. Comput. Syst. **14**(2), 39:1–39:17 (2015). https://doi.org/10.1145/2658990
4. Cherubin, S., Agosta, G.: libVersioningCompiler: an easy-to-use library for dynamic generation and invocation of multiple code versions. SoftwareX **7**, 95–100 (2018). https://doi.org/10.1016/j.softx.2018.03.006
5. Dauwe, D., Pasricha, S., Maciejewski, A.A., Siegel, H.J.: Resilience-aware resource management for exascale computing systems. IEEE Trans. Sustain. Comput. **3**(4), 332–345 (2018). https://doi.org/10.1109/TSUSC.2018.2797890
6. Donyanavard, B., Mück, T., Sarma, S., Dutt, N.: SPARTA: runtime task allocation for energy efficient heterogeneous manycores. In: 2016 International Conference on Hardware/Software Codesign and System Synthesis (CODES+ISSS), pp. 1–10, October 2016
7. Flich, J., et al.: Enabling HPC for QoS-sensitive applications: the MANGO approach. In: 2016 Design, Automation Test in Europe Conference Exhibition (DATE), pp. 702–707, March 2016
8. Flich, J., Agosta, G., et al.: MANGO: exploring manycore architectures for next-generation HPC systems. In: 2017 Euromicro Conference on Digital System Design (DSD), pp. 478–485, August 2017. https://doi.org/10.1109/DSD.2017.51
9. Flich, J., Alessandro, C., Kovač, M., Tornero, R., Martínez, J.M., Picornell, T.: Deeply heterogeneous many-accelerator infrastructure for HPC architecture exploration. In: Parallel Computing Conference (ParCo) (2017)
10. Flich, J., et al.: Exploring manycore architectures for next-generation HPC systems through the MANGO approach. Microprocess. Microsyst. **61**, 154–170 (2018). https://doi.org/10.1016/j.micpro.2018.05.011
11. Fornaciari, W., et al.: Reliable power and time-constraints-aware predictive management of heterogeneous exascale systems. In: Proceedings of the 18th International Conference on Embedded Computer Systems: Architectures, Modeling, and Simulation, SAMOS 2018, pp. 187–194. ACM, New York (2018). https://doi.org/10.1145/3229631.3239368
12. Gallager, R.: Low-density parity-check codes. IRE Trans. Inf. Theory **8**(1), 21–28 (1962)

13. Georgiou, Y., Jeannot, E., Mercier, G., Villiermet, A.: Topology-aware resource management for HPC applications. In: Proceedings of the 18th International Conference on Distributed Computing and Networking, ICDCN 2017, pp. 17:1–17:10. ACM, New York (2017). https://doi.org/10.1145/3007748.3007768
14. Georgopoulos, K., Mavroidis, I., Lavagno, L., Papaefstathiou, I., Bakanov, K.: Energy-efficient heterogeneous computing at exaSCALE—ECOSCALE. In: Kachris, C., Falsafi, B., Soudris, D. (eds.) Hardware Accelerators in Data Centers, pp. 199–213. Springer, Cham (2019). https://doi.org/10.1007/978-3-319-92792-3_11
15. Herbordt, M.C., et al.: Achieving high performance with FPGA-based computing. Computer **40**(3), 50–57 (2007)
16. Hindman, B., et al.: Mesos: a platform for fine-grained resource sharing in the data center. In: Proceedings of the 8th USENIX Conference on Networked Systems Design and Implementation, NSDI 2011, pp. 295–308. USENIX Association, Berkeley (2011). http://dl.acm.org/citation.cfm?id=1972457.1972488
17. Li, R., Yang, Q., Li, Y., Gu, X., Xiao, W., Li, K.: HeteroYARN: a heterogeneous FPGA-accelerated architecture based on YARN. IEEE Trans. Parallel Distrib. Syst. **PP**, 1 (2019). https://doi.org/10.1109/TPDS.2019.2905201
18. Libutti, S., Massari, G., Fornaciari, W.: Co-scheduling tasks on multi-core heterogeneous systems: an energy-aware perspective. IET Comput. Digit. Tech. **10**(2), 77–84 (2016). https://doi.org/10.1049/iet-cdt.2015.0053
19. MacKay, D.J., Neal, R.M.: Near Shannon limit performance of low density parity check codes. Electron. Lett. **32**(18), 1645 (1996)
20. Massari, G., et al.: Combining application adaptivity and system-wide resource management on multi-core platforms. In: 2014 International Conference on Embedded Computer Systems: Architectures, Modeling, and Simulation (SAMOS XIV), pp. 26–33, July 2014. https://doi.org/10.1109/SAMOS.2014.6893191
21. Netti, A., Galleguillos, C., Kiziltan, Z., Sîrbu, A., Babaoglu, O.: Heterogeneity-aware resource allocation in HPC systems. In: Yokota, R., Weiland, M., Keyes, D., Trinitis, C. (eds.) ISC High Performance 2018. LNCS, vol. 10876, pp. 3–21. Springer, Cham (2018). https://doi.org/10.1007/978-3-319-92040-5_1
22. Patki, T., et al.: Practical resource management in power-constrained, high performance computing. In: Proceedings of the 24th International Symposium on High-Performance Parallel and Distributed Computing, HPDC 2015, pp. 121–132. ACM, New York (2015). https://doi.org/10.1145/2749246.2749262
23. Pupykina, A., Agosta, G.: Optimizing memory management in deeply heterogeneous HPC accelerators. In: 2017 46th International Conference on Parallel Processing Workshops (ICPPW), pp. 291–300, August 2017. https://doi.org/10.1109/ICPPW.2017.49
24. Silvano, C., Agosta, G., et al.: The ANTAREX tool flow for monitoring and autotuning energy efficient HPC systems. In: 2017 International Conference on Embedded Computer Systems: Architectures, Modeling, and Simulation (SAMOS), pp. 308–316, July 2017. https://doi.org/10.1109/SAMOS.2017.8344645
25. Silvano, C., Fornaciari, W., Crespi Reghizzi, S., Agosta, G., et al.: 2PARMA: parallel paradigms and run-time management techniques for many-core architectures. In: 2010 IEEE Computer Society Annual Symposium on VLSI, pp. 494–499, July 2010. https://doi.org/10.1109/ISVLSI.2010.93
26. Silvano, C., Fornaciari, W., Crespi Reghizzi, S., Agosta, G., et al.: Parallel paradigms and run-time management techniques for many-core architectures: the 2PARMA approach. In: 2011 9th IEEE International Conference on Industrial Informatics, pp. 835–840, July 2011. https://doi.org/10.1109/INDIN.2011.6035001

27. Vavilapalli, V.K., et al.: Apache Hadoop YARN: yet another resource negotiator. In: Proceedings of the 4th Annual Symposium on Cloud Computing, SOCC 2013, pp. 5:1–5:16. ACM, New York (2013). https://doi.org/10.1145/2523616.2523633
28. Wu, Y., Nikolopoulos, D.S., Woods, R.: Runtime support for adaptive power capping on heterogeneous SoCs. In: 2016 International Conference on Embedded Computer Systems: Architectures, Modeling and Simulation (SAMOS), pp. 71–78, July 2016. https://doi.org/10.1109/SAMOS.2016.7818333
29. Ziegler, W., D'ippolito, R., D'Auria, M., Berends, J., Nelissen, M., Diaz, R.: Implementing a "one-stop-shop" providing SMEs with integrated HPC simulation resources using Fortissimo resources. In: eChallenges e-2014 Conference, pp. 1–11. IEEE (2014)
30. Zoni, D., Cremona, L., Fornaciari, W.: All-digital energy-constrained controller for general-purpose accelerators and CPUs. IEEE Embed. Syst. Lett. **PP**(99), 1 (2019). https://doi.org/10.1109/LES.2019.2914136
31. Zoni, D., Flich, J., Fornaciari, W.: CUTBUF: buffer management and router design for traffic mixing in VNET-based NoCs. IEEE Trans. Parallel Distrib. Syst. **27**(6), 1603–1616 (2016). https://doi.org/10.1109/TPDS.2015.2468716
32. Zoni, D., Canidio, A., Fornaciari, W., Englezakis, P., Nicopoulos, C., Sazeides, Y.: BlackOut: enabling fine-grained power gating of buffers in Network-on-Chip routers. J. Parallel Distrib. Comput. **104**, 130–145 (2017). https://doi.org/10.1016/j.jpdc.2017.01.016
33. Zoni, D., Cremona, L., Cilardo, A., Gagliardi, M., Fornaciari, W.: Powertap: all-digital power meter modeling for run-time power monitoring. Microprocess. Microsyst. Embed. Hardw. Des. **63**, 128–139 (2018). https://doi.org/10.1016/j.micpro.2018.07.007
34. Zoni, D., Fornaciari, W.: Modeling DVFS and power-gating actuators for cycle-accurate NoC-based simulators. J. Emerg. Technol. Comput. Syst. **12**(3), 27:1–27:24 (2015). https://doi.org/10.1145/2751561

Author Index

Printed in the United States
By Bookmasters